THIRD IN LINE

THIRD IN LINE

THE 3RD AIR DIVISION OVER EUROPE IN WORLD WAR II

Ron Mackay

Schiffer Military History
Atglen, PA

Photograph Credits

Mike Bailey
Stan Bishop
James V Crow
Cliff Hall
Ian Hawkins
Harry Holmes
Ernest Osborn
Peter Pallett
Jerry Scutts
Eric Swain
Thorpe Abbotts (100th Bomb Group Memorial Museum)
Geoff Ward

Air Force Museum, Dayton
USAF Academy, Colorado Springs

Book Design by Stephanie Daugherty.

Library of Congress Control Number: 2009935137

Printed in China
ISBN: 978-0-7643-3346-0
We are interested in hearing from authors with book ideas on related topics.

Published by Schiffer Publishing Ltd.
4880 Lower Valley Road
Atglen, PA 19310
Phone: (610) 593-1777
FAX: (610) 593-2002
E-mail: Info@schifferbooks.com.
Visit our web site at: www.schifferbooks.com
Please write for a free catalog.
This book may be purchased from the publisher.
Please include $5.00 postage.
Try your bookstore first.

In Europe, Schiffer books are distributed by:
Bushwood Books
6 Marksbury Avenue
Kew Gardens
Surrey TW9 4JF, England
Phone: 44 (0) 20 8392-8585
FAX: 44 (0) 20 8392-9876
E-mail: Info@bushwoodbooks.co.uk.
Visit our website at: www.bushwoodbooks.co.uk

Contents

1

Small Beginnings

The Stage is Set...

The date is 13 May 1943, and the VIII Bomber Command is gearing up for the latest foray from its bases in southern England into the increasingly bitter-contested skies of Western Europe. Over the past nine months the American combat crews have "tested the waters" in pursuit of their Air Force's hopes for a successful strategic bombing campaign. After an initial spell of four months operating over France and the Low Countries, the B-17s and B-24s have expanded their activities in a manner that, although still reflecting a staccato pattern of missions primarily due to weather disruption, is about to become more and more centered on the Third Reich's industrial base within Germany itself. However, today's mission will witness yet another shallow penetration run to an airfield at Meaulte, in northern France...

The main force is assembled from the ranks of the four veteran Bomb Groups based at Bassingbourn (91st BG), Molesworth (303rd BG), Chelveston (305th BG), and Thurleigh (306th BG). These 1st Bomb Wing (BW) Groups are now supplemented by the first of what will soon be a flood of units that will increase the Wing's strength almost threefold by mid-autumn. The Polebrook-based 351st BG has been assigned an even shorter-distanced run into northern France to bomb St. Omer/Ft. Rouge airfield...

A second force of three Groups is also being readied for its mission to St. Omer/Longuenesse airfield, another location

A sizeable group of airmen from the 96th BG are marching down the flight-line at Pyote, Texas. The Censor has blocked out fuselage details on the left-hand B-17; the bomber had previously served with the 43rd BG in the Pacific Theater before reassignment to its current training status.

The arid and mountainous regions of America's Middle West provided plenty of opportunity for practice; conversely, there was ever the risk of crashing into high ground in the event of bad weather or while aloft during nocturnal flights. This B-17F, although in use by the 100th BG, did not go overseas, but was on hand during the group's time at Sioux City, Idaho.

for the fighters of JG26 *Schlageter*, whose skilled pilots in their Bf109s and Fw190s constitute a major stumbling block to the secure progress of the American bombers. Unlike their veteran fellow-units, the 94th, 95th, and 96th BGs are currently "orphans" in terms of operating from permanent bases. The first-named unit has two Sqdns each operating out of Bassingbourn and Thurleigh; the 95th BG shares Alconbury with the reactivated 92nd BG – not due to resume combat missions until 24 hours later; while the 96th BG is in temporary residence at Grafton Underwood. In all three cases it is only the Air Echelon that is on hand here. The Ground Support elements, following an uncomfortable but safe passage across the North Atlantic in the face of the still-threatening U-Boat offensive, are in the process of setting up facilities at airfields located further east and within the East Anglia region; in fact, the 96th BG teams are moving into Andrews Field, Essex, this same day, while the 94th BG and 95th ground personnel had made the same move the day before. The birth pangs of the 4th BW are about to be given their initial, albeit fruitless expression...

The main force strikes Meaulte in the later afternoon with 88 of the 97 assigned B-17s and loses three bombers. The 351st BG abandons its run to St. Omer/Ft. Rouge while over the English Channel. As for the other three "freshman" Groups, only the 94th and 95th BGs get through to their target, with 31 of the 38 crews dispatched releasing a hail of 300-lb bombs upon the airfield. The 96th BG not only does not gain mission "credit," but loses one bomber due to a tragic error. B-17F/42-29752/BX, flown by Lt. D Rogers, has most of the right stabilizer literally sawn off by a waist gun that has been accidentally discharged by its gunner. The formation is still close to Grafton Underwood, to which Rogers returns to bail out the Enlisted Men, after which he heads back towards the Wash, a large stretch of water where he has decided to abandon the B-17, thus allowing it to crash harmlessly. All four officers clear their charge, but Rogers and Lt. Gorse (CP) land in the sea; the latter airman is later fished out alive, but not Rogers—a sad postscript to an all-round day of frustration for the Group's airmen. Over the intervening 24 months there will be many days of positive and negative experiences for the "*Snetterton Falcons*,' as the 96th BG will become known, as well as its 94th and 95th BG fellow groups. However, the stage is now set for what will evolve from the current and embryonic 4th BW into a full Division that will serve its proud nation in the best possible manner...

Parades were a regular and, to most of the airmen, a time-wasting distraction from the business of gearing up for combat. A 100th BG parade is bypassing an as yet anonymous B-17F. On 25 June 1943, by then named **Angel's Tit**, 42-3260/XR: would be shot down into the North Sea, killing all but one of Lt. A Adams III's crew during what was the group's first mission.

Many of the training bases were at locations well away from townships of any size. This is believed to be Wendover, Utah, whose positioning adjacent to the high ridges in the background would have made for uncomfortable safety margins in taking off and landing during poor weather conditions.

In the Beginning...

Even before the onset of WWII the American military had initiated and developed a policy for its long-range bombers that foresaw no viable alternative to striking an adversary during the hours of daylight. Prior to the onset of that ultimately global conflict, this attitude was paralleled by the RAF authorities as an article of faith; the *Luftwaffe's* concentration on the bomber as primarily a tactical weapon placed it on a different level to its future principal adversaries' strategic thinking. Consequently, the German bomber crews' severe rebuff over southern England in the summer of 1940 that saw their being switched to the nocturnally-directed *Blitz* was only coincidental in comparison to RAF Bomber Command's prior experience. During the *Phoney War* period up to April 1940 the British airmen had been dispatched on what were called "reconnaissance in force" sorties that did not even close in over the German mainland, but concentrated on stalking *Kriegsmarine* warships at sea, or at best when moored in Naval ports, but at berths away from civilian areas. Several formations of Hampdens and Wellingtons—the even more pedestrian Whitley being basically employed on propaganda leaflet sorties—were intercepted and seriously mauled by *Luftwaffe* fighters. By the onset of the Nazi advance into Western Europe in May 1940 Bomber Command had also virtually been switched over to night operations, a situation that would be maintained up to D-Day.

These rather regressive, if seemingly enforced stances by two of the major European military powers did not

A tragic postscript to the 96th BG's totally "abortive" combat inauguration was the loss to "friendly fire" of 42-29752/338BS. One stabilizer was totally excised after a waist gunner's weapon went off as he was un-stowing it. The crew were bailed out, and Capt. D Rogers and Lt. J Gorse headed for the Wash, where they also jumped. Unfortunately the pilot died of exposure after both airmen landed in the water.

Personnel from the 95th BG survey the cratered dispersal at Alconbury that held 42-29685/QW: prior to a bomb loading explosion in which the B-17F was destroyed and eighteen airmen killed instantly, with one more who died later. Three other group bombers were salvaged following the tragic incident that occurred on 27 May 1943.

detract the United States Army Air Corps (USAAC) from continuing to pursue its avowed goal of daylight strategic bombing. After all, a combination of the high-flying and high-performance B-17 and the precision Norden bombsight was expected to bring about the right results. As for enemy fighter opposition, by 1941 the heavy armament borne by the B-17E and subsequent F and G variants, as well as its emerging strategic bombing "partner" the B-24D (up to ten .3 and .5 caliber machine guns), was regarded as more than adequate to fend off attackers and, by extension, dispense with the need for long-range fighter escorts. The stage was seemingly set for a future enemy's resources—with Germany as the likely source steadily moving into the frame between the 1939 invasion of Poland and Pearl Harbor—to be effectively eliminated in this implacable manner.

1st BW's "Kid Brother" Takes Shape

On 1 June 1942 the bones of the 4th BW were created when the 100th Bomb Group (H) was activated. Fourteen days later three more Bombardment Groups were officially activated. Two of these were the 94th and 95th BGs, whose Florida bases were McDill and Barksdale, with the 96th BG being "born" much further west at Salt Lake City. As it was, this was a "paper" creation only in respect of these locations since the personnel never arrived there.

In the case of the 94th BG, its original cadre of Senior and Support officer personnel was gathered together far to the north-west at Pendleton Field, Oregon. The Group had been established by a War Department (WD) Letter dated 28 January 1942, and on 15 June it was re-designated HQ 94th BG (H). The senior staff nucleus of ten was commanded by Col. "Dinty" Moore, but it was 24 October at Davis Monthan Field, AZ, before a basic structure of four Sqdns involving 39 more officers in total was established, although no flying was yet indulged in; this would await further expansion under Special Order 297, which was fulfilled by the month's end. (Col. Moore was 40 years old and well beyond the age for regular combat flying; this physical limitation, coupled with a suggested over-identification with his combat personnel, would lead to his still-controversial substitution after the Group's arrival in England.)

On 1 November the Group transferred to Biggs Field at El Paso, TX, from where flying training was begun on an initially extremely small scale—one B-17E to each Sqdn! Col. Moore

This is a view of the other three B-17s involved in the Alconbury explosion. The overall damage to 42-29706 appears to be the least in scale, but was sufficient for her to join the other two on the scrapheap.

was a taskmaster when it came to formation flying and rightly so—he had been in Europe as an observer during 1939-40 and was aware of the need to "tuck in close" in order to avoid becoming an MIA statistic.

As the flow of both combat crew and ground support personnel steadily grew, the schedule of training with the still limited number of B-17s included bombing practice at Muroc Dry Lake, CA, and air to ground gunnery practice during the four-hour flights. By the end of December the Group was deemed ready for transfer to Pueblo, CO, for what would be the third training phase. The movement was initiated on 2 and 3 January respectively for the Air Echelon and ground support parties. The new location had a more permanent feel about it compared to the "old frontier" atmosphere of El Paso.

Formations comprising up to three Sqdns in strength were flown, and long-range navigation became another regular aspect of training. A specific formation flight on 14 January entailed flying to Wilcox Dry Lake, near Phoenix, AZ, where a remote-controlled unit was the target. The result must have been negative, since, in the words of one line from the Group song, "but the bombardiers tore their hair out – when the Wilcox ship reversed!" A similar flight to El Paso to bomb a simulated Axis seaport met with partial success, apart from one load of incendiaries that descended perilously close to a party of cavalrymen before setting the scrub brush alight.

The raw material with which to transform a still nascent force into a massive and efficient fighting entity was still basically lacking as America completed its first full year of hostilities. This key factor applied as much in respect of human as materiel resources. Tens of thousands of personnel would be required both to fly and to service the USAAF's aircraft. This in turn meant taking civilians with no previous military experience and turning them as quickly as possible into fully functioning service personnel.

In the case of combat crews, particularly the pilots, navigators, and bombardiers, a great percentage had been channelled at maximum pace through Flying Schools; now their basic skills capability would have to be polished in a similarly paced manner. The same pace of development applied to the ground support personnel. Individuals, many of whom possessed marginal mechanically trained backgrounds prior to WWII, would find themselves assigned to train-up with a view to carrying out servicing of the bombers. The enforced pace of training-up would be reflected in the following manner; the average period a Bombardment Group would spend between practical activation and being assigned to a combat theatre would extend over no more than four months on average.

In the case of the 94th BG, its personnel, having either arrived at Pueblo from El Paso or assigned during the phase three training spell, were given barely six weeks to carry out flight practice sorties or hone their skills at Ground School or out on the Flight Line. All the time, the sense of belonging to a huge team whose successful function depended upon everyone, from Colonel to cook, pilot to crew chief, and gunner to postman was being consciously emphasized and honed.

On 1 March 1943 the first step in the Group's overseas deployment commenced when four officers reported to Salinas, KS. Seven days later the party was on its way to Atlantic City ready to fly to Europe, the Group's destiny having already been linked with the planned assault on Hitler's *Festung Europa*. As it was, their arrival in England would not occur for a further seven weeks.

On 22 February, the ground personnel had returned from leave and now prepared to pack up and leave the field to the incoming 351st BG, whose ranks included the actor Clark Gable. Actual shipping-out orders were not received until 12 April, however; in the meantime, the men had been kept "busy" with parades, drill sessions, and route marches—military discipline had to be seen to be seen! A protracted rail journey lasting fully eight days culminated in the weary airmen de-training close to Camp Kilmer, NJ, on 20 April.

The 95th BG holds a steady course during the bomb run of what is an early mission judging by the absence of aircraft code letters or Division insignia. B-17F at left center (42-3267) was assigned on 28 May 1943 when the Group was still based at Framlingham; as BG:A it was successfully "ditched" in the Channel on 28 June when all ten of Lt. Thomas' crew survived.

Here further kit inspections, immunization sessions, and more packing gave little time for savoring the pleasures of New York, the city lights literally being an eye opener to many whose upbringing had been in isolated rural communities. Finally, on 4 May the men boarded the British ocean liner *Queen Elizabeth*, which departed the next day on its swift, unescorted crossing of the North Atlantic to Scotland.

By the time the *Queen* had berthed on 11 May the Group's combat crews were already settled in their temporary airfields. Their passage across the "Big Pond" had not been quite as uneventful, however. The spell spent at Salina had been physically unpleasant due to the tarpaper barracks proving totally inadequate to counter the Kansas winter conditions. Having been assigned a B-17, each crew settled down to prepare its charge for the coming trans-Atlantic flight. The original flight plan involved a protracted arc pattern via Mississippi, Florida, South America, Ascension Island, Africa, and finally England—a flight of several thousands of miles and a daunting test of a navigator's skills.

The initial departure from Salinas to Gulfport, MS, proved abortive, however, this being due to an alarming series of engine failures; Lt. Hendershot's crew suffered the worst experience when all four Cyclones failed and the crew had to bail out, while other crews landed en route or at their primary destination. The problem was traced to defective metal in the piston rings fitted to the Studebaker-produced motors, whose failure resulted in unacceptable levels of engine oil loss; this deficiency threatened an attendant risk of engines seizing, or wind-milling propellers becoming incapable of being controlled, since their feathering mechanisms were dependent upon the flow of oil. A further three weeks elapsed before complete engine changes were carried out at Mobile, AL.

During the enforced delay the Northern Deployment route across the Atlantic had been opened up, and it was decided to dispatch the Group in this direction. Presque Isle, Maine, was the initial point on the route, but adverse weather after arrival pinned the crews down for a week. Movement overseas via Gandar finally commenced around the second half of April, and all arrived safely in Prestwick, Scotland, albeit not without potential failure for one crew; solid cloud cover on the way over was only broken through—not on approach to Prestwick, but several hundred miles south over the neutral soil of Eire! The situation was duly and gratefully rectified by steering a northeasterly course to the briefed Scottish destination.

Once safely assembled at Prestwick, the crews of the 331st and 332nd Sqdns were then "led" to their temporary home at Bassingbourn, while the 333rd and 410th Sqdns headed for Thurleigh. The need for aerial "guides" had first seemed an unnecessary service to the newly-arrived pilots, but when confronted with the checkerboard landscape below

Ellis Scripture arrived at Horham as a member of the original cadre, and functioned as the 95th's Group Navigator during 1943. His qualities in discharging this vital duty were latterly recognized by promotion to Division Navigator at 3rd BD HQ.

Early days for 4th BW operations also demonstrate the relative lack of markings on VIII BC B-17s. The Square insignia on the vertical fin and right-upper wing denoting assignment to the 4th BW is absent, as are the squadron codes, in this case denoting one belonging to the 96th BG. The national markings lack their bar surrounds that were only introduced in July 1943.

they swiftly changed their minds—successful navigation over Britain would be an acquired art, as well as a sound if somewhat ominous indicator of what awaited the novice navigators over Europe!

The three other Groups that were destined to form the nucleus of the 4th BW were the 95th BG, 96th BG, and 100th BG. Of the first two named Groups, the 96th commenced its active life at Gowen Field, Idaho, on 6 August 1942, to be followed towards the month's end by the 95th. The 100th BG's induction into practical existence also occurred at Gowen Field, but not until the end of October. The pace of training was generally stepped up in line with the 94th BG's experience, although there were to be diversions from this basic pattern for both the 96th and 100th BGs that would in turn result in a delayed arrival "over there" to participate in what was already established as the "Big League of Sky Fighting" for the USAAF.

Training Experiences Stateside

All the training in the world could not fully prepare any crewmember for the harsh realities of combat operations. However, the initial elements of what would develop into the 4th BW would enjoy at least a marginal advantage over their contemporaries within the 1st BW. The latter group of airmen had had to learn this grim art in the most direct and often painful manner when up against their *Luftwaffe* adversaries. In contrast, those combat-tested personnel who had survived their combat tour and been returned Stateside could now be on hand to pass on their experience to the "greenhorns." (Not that there were too many veterans currently being dispatched back home during the winter of 1942/43, since the situation within the 1st BW regarding available combat crewmembers would remain somewhat critical up to the April/May period of 1943.)

96th BG

The 96th BG was created, albeit on paper, only on 28 January 1942, and it was General Order 113/10 July before official activation was ordered at Salt Lake by HQ, 2nd AF.

As with several other fledgling groups, the initial cadre of personnel would be provided by the 29th BG, but the 96th's time at Salt Lake was treated as temporary, with Walla Walla, WA, the permanently assigned base; this Order was almost immediately rescinded in favor of Gowen and Pocatello, both in Idaho. By early August a small group of officers and senior Sgts headed by Col. Archie J Old as Group CO had been formed and transferred out of the 29th BG, with further personnel infusions made during the month. On the 14th and 30th came the order for the ground and the air echelons (of which there were 36 crews) to transfer—not to Pocatello, but Walla Walla! The small numbers of ground personnel on hand at Boise meant that what was "First Phase" training was largely limited to the combat crews.

Inflating the currently ground echelon strength within days of encampment at Walla Walla was the majority of the ground crew and other support personnel totalling 500 and provided by the Personnel Replacement Center, Salt Lake City. M/Sgt. Hilton recalled the month-long sojourn at Walla Walla, "We started with a full teaching schedule – training new personnel, working with the four sqdn ops, reports, etc." Lt. S Hand (413BS CO) said:

> "To ensure maximum utilization of men and equipment, the 2nd AF created the '24 hour Work Schedule.' This entailed the individual splitting the 24 hours equally between work, recreation, and sleep – if a crew landed at midnight it was expected to play for eight hours before going to bed. The mess halls served breakfast twice round the clock and everyone worked their butts off. No leave, no true recreation, no nothing – just work, shakedown, and continue to get organized."

A second officer noted:

> "Bombardiers were scheduled on the bomb trainers at 0200 hours, while pilots had to be in the Link Trainers at 1600 hours or at suppertime; gunners were also scheduled round the clock. In these early days it was not unusual for specialists to be appointed to a supposedly incorrect function. Sgt C Powell was told to report to the 337th BS Line Chief, M/Sgt. E Gould. When informed by Powell that his trade was in the sheet metal business, the M/Sgt erupted 'What the Hell am I supposed to do with you – what I need is an engine mechanic!' This was hardly gratifying for a guy who had spent four months intensive study on aircraft skin and structure repair. Eventually Powell was assigned as a mechanic's helper whose first duty was basic to say the least; this was washing out a B-17's wheel wells with pure octane gas, an act that nearly asphyxiated him!" (The value of Powell's and other specialists' skills would come to be appreciated when overseas and battle damage of all shapes, sizes, and degree soon began to accrue.)

The group's time at Walla Walla was somewhat marred by three B-17 crashes, one of them fatal, but under the fiery, hard-driving, but honestly-pitched leadership of Col. Old, the spirit of the men in general did not flag, but rather gained positive momentum. During this "Second Phase" period combat crews further developed their skills, with the pilots flying in formations up to sqdn level and bombardiers and navigators honing their specific functions.

The next of three further transfers before the year's end occurred at the end of September to Rapid City, SD, where "Third Phase" activities involved the crews engaged in the necessary art of long-range flights that also tested the navigators' skills; these were generally conducted via Texas to Florida. While here the first of two sessions of involvement with Hollywood occurred, when three crews were "detached" to Albaquerque, NM, to provide flying sequences for the film "Bombardier" that had Pat O'Brian and Randolph Scott as lead actors. However, the month ended with a mood of depression settling upon the personnel, who had been informed that their latest transfer to Pocatello, Idaho, would see them serving as

Hard Luck was an early assignee to the 388th BG on 15 June 1943. The airframe bears the initial lack of Division insignia and bar surrounds to the star marking found on VIIIBC bombers until July 1943. This bomber belied its name through the bitter summer and autumn period of combat before Fate struck; on 14 October it crashed on take-off, but Lt. Swift's crew came through intact.

an Operational Training Unit—a definite step down for any immediate prospect of getting into combat, and a status that could continue indefinitely. Nor was the mood improved by the sub-zero weather conditions encountered on arrival in late October. Fortunately, a further change of mind by the authorities returning the group to combat potential status was made just one month later.

So it was that as 1943 commenced the airmen exchanged Pocatello's ice and snow for Pyote, TX, blazing sunshine, dust, brushwood—and rattlesnakes. At least the total lack of social amenities in the shanty town bearing the base's name permitted a near full concentration upon training, if only to get the Hell out of the place as quickly as possible! While there a second involvement with the film "Bombardier" also occurred. The 96th BG's time at Pyote alongside the equally fledgling 381st BG resulted in a degree of logistical piracy practiced by the latter unit. Practice bombs were never on hand in more than adequate numbers. Consequently, when the future Ridgewell-based airmen felt a shortage was looming they had a simple solution. They would monitor the area occupied by the 96th BG's bomb storage; when that Group's trailers were laden, but its personnel were not around, they would dispatch a towing vehicle, hitch it up to one or more trailers, and smartly depart!

The terrible twins. John Egan (left) and Gale Cleven both bore the nick-name "Bucky" and were "original" Sqdn COs at Thorpe Abbotts. They were also noted for their flamboyant conduct and raunchy image, as exemplified by Cleven's "crush" hat. Both were also destined for a Stalag; Cleven on the Bremen mission (8 October 1943) and Egan barely 48 hours later.

At long last the initial orders for transfer overseas arrived as April opened. By then the combat crews had moved to two airfields in Kansas, where they collected their assigned establishment of new B-17s. By 4 April the initial moves to fly the extended northern route to England via Maine and Labrador had commenced by the 38 participating crews. Meanwhile, the ground support personnel were still cooling their heels at "sunny" Pyote, and it was not until mid-April, with all equipment securely packed, that the troop trains started out on their much more extended journey to New York. Here the men were loaded on board the British Liner *Queen Elizabeth*, along with upwards of 17,000 G.I.s. for an uncomfortable if fast passage across the North Atlantic. On arrival in Scotland the men were transported by train, not to Grafton Underwood, but further east to Great Saling, arriving there on 11 May.

95th BG

A similar protracted training-up process faced the third unit destined to form the nucleus of the 4th BW. The actual formation of the 95th BG commenced at Geiger Field, WA, in late August. Further transfers to Ephrata, WA, on 31 Oct., hen back to Geiger Field, WA, on 24 Nov. culminated with the final training spell at Rapid City, SD, between 14 Dec. and 11 March '43.

Lt. Ellis Scripture, who was to finish as a senior navigational officer within the hierarchy of the ultimately titled 3rd Air Division, recalled that within the 95th BG the

The day Maj. Egan was shot down witnessed another and more positive legend's beginning within the 100th BG. Robert Rosenthal brought the sole B-17 to survive from the group formation otherwise lost over Muenster (10 October 1943). His quiet but firm demeanour was in stark contrast to that of either Egan or Cleven; he also went on to complete over 50 missions and earned the Distinguished Service Cross and Silver Star in the process.

A line of P-47s assigned to the 56th FG are seen on a bomber base, in this case Shipdham, home for the B-24s of the 44th BG. **Sugar Baby** bears the original Red surround to the stat and bar insignia, which was introduced around July 1943; in September the order was issued to change this color to Blue.

average flight time logged by navigators and bombardiers was around 35 hours when they were assigned to the Group, while gunners had even less flight experience; pilot experience was somewhat better at around 100 hours, even if it seemed barely adequate for assuming quick and sure control of the four-engine and multi-instrumented B-17.

Being located in the northwestern states of Washington and South Dakota did nothing for the personnel's ability to learn their trades in sound weather conditions. Indeed, the regular pattern of snow, rain, and fog experienced during that winter tended to badly inhibit aircraft maintenance and flight scheduling. (Ellis remembered how icicles formed on thermometers at Rapid City, SD.) Of course, these conditions were the very kind that would be encountered in "sunny" England and over Europe, and surely provided the combat and ground staff with a future advantage over those Groups training in more weather-friendly areas within the USA.

A steadying influence in bringing the 95th BG fliers on was the presence of experienced senior officers. In the Group's case their first Group CO (Col. Kessler) and Air Executive (Col. Jack Gibson) provided this vital backing. Gibson, for example, had been flying since 1934, and among other duties had flown the U.S. Mail in light aircraft, a truly "hairy" experience. He had accumulated 10,000 hours flight time, within which was time spent with American Airlines. (In March '44 this officer would assume command of the 44th BG at Shipdham.) Several other senior staff provided similar long term experience following service with the USAAC or Royal Canadian Air Force (RCAF). Their firm guidance would help to bring on the individual's transition from raw aviation recruit to one capable of handling his specific duty with his assigned crew. A similar pattern of equally vital assistance would be passed down by Capt. Fields (Chief Engineering Officer) and his team to the ground crew and other support personnel.

Having received the "Fit for combat duty" signal from the Inspector General's Office, the Air Echelon moved to Kearney Field, NE, in mid-March; here the crews learned that they would be heading for the "Big League of Sky Fighting" as part of the VIII BC. A range of problems with the newly-assigned B-17s resulted in a full third being replaced before the group headed for England via Florida and Natal, Brazil, before crossing the Atlantic to land at Dakar, West Africa; from here a northerly course to Marrakesh, Morocco, was followed by the last leg to the British Isles. As for the Ground Echelon, it left mid-April and arrived at Greenock 11 May, having travelled along with the 96th BG on the *Queen Elizabeth*.

100th BG

The final first-stage group was the 100th BG, whose subsequent combat career would see them foisted with an unenviable reputation as a "jinx outfit." However deserved this notoriety might have been, a parallel degree of controversy attended their time stateside. Whereas the other three groups had progressed through their training schedule with little delay, matters for the 100th BG went awry during its final phase. Prior to this the personnel, having assembled initially at Walla Walla, WA, on 1 Nov, were on their way to Wendover, UT, by the month's end. This temporary posting was followed by a move to Sioux City, Iowa, on 28 December.

The final transfer was to Kearney, NE, at the end of January 1943. It was here that a major change in command occurred when Col. Alkire was relieved as group CO. In mid-April a planned long-distance transfer to Hamilton Field, California, ended in numerous cases of crews aborting for various and not always justified reasons. The fact that this was the first foray in the air for the group over several months did not persuade the authorities that the blame should be spread wider, hence Alkire's fate. As it was, he would soon be re-instated as CO of the 449th BG, whose B-24s he would lead over to Italy and with whom he would fly twelve missions before ending up as a POW.

May saw the Air Echelon commence overseas movement on the 1st, a process that was finally completed by arrival at their permanent base of Thorpe Abbotts on 8 June. The Ground echelon made the same wearying train journey to Camp Kilmer during the month that culminated with embarkment on the *Queen Elizabeth* on 26 May and arrival at Greenock on 3 June. Unlike their flight brethren, the ground personnel wound up not at Thorpe Abbots, but in 1st BW territory at Podington. The unsatisfactory state of the airfield's runways, perimeter track, and dispersals was swiftly noted, hence the swift decision to switch to Thorpe Abbotts prior to the Air Echelon's arrival.

Col. Archie J Old brought the 96th BG over from America, but his tenure of office in this function was relatively brief. On 6 September he handed over to Col. James L Travis and transferred as a Brig/General to 45th CBW HQ, where he assumed the post of Commanding General (CG) until VE-Day. He was known for his peppery language, but was well respected at Snetterton Heath.

False Optimism?

There is little doubt that the weather conditions generally existing within the USA could encourage a natural but ultimately false sense of ability, and therefore security for the acolyte combat crewmen. Formation flying, although demanding physically, was made without any opposition to quicken one's nerve ends, as well as in weather conditions that basically permitted sound to good visual observation. As regards bombing, the absence of enemy opposition coupled with good visibility naturally permitted an enhanced degree of success on the bombing ranges. Navigation was similarly granted a much superior set of weather conditions compared to the daunting weather front variations experienced over Britain and the European continent. It was true that poor weather conditions did exist within the USA, especially during the winter months in the form of high winds, snowstorms, etc., while dust storms were a common occurrence out on the arid, open landscape of the mid- and far western interior. On the other hand, unless their aircraft were already aloft, the combat crews could have their training sessions held back until more suitable conditions prevailed. This was a luxury that could not often be indulged in when the Groups were subsequently on full operational status in an actual combat theatre. Still, the airmen could only train within their present geographic conditions—the sober truths about combat flying conditions would have to be held back until these were confronted "over there!"

May 1943 Missions

No MIA losses were incurred for the Wing during its inaugural mission on the 13th; however, as previously mentioned, the 96th BG's "blood debt" commenced even before the Group had departed British soil. The 4th BW's debut was the start of a three-day sequence of missions, although the 14th involved another short-range lunge at an aircraft plant in Antwerp for the 94th and 95th BGs, while the 96th BG joined with the 351st BG in bombing one of JG26's airfields at Courtrai.

The 95th BG's 42-3115/OE and single crews from the Antwerp-assigned units failed to return, as did two of the

The 550BS' Slo-Jo artwork is liberally spread across the aircraft's lower nose. Note the flash-eliminator on the machine gun and the colored forward section of the D/F loop fairing. The 385th BG B-17F lasted from 26 June until the Emden run (11 December 1943), when seven on Lt. T Jenning's crew, including the pilot, failed to survive the "ditching" attempt.

351st BG, which was flying its inaugural strike. The combat blood debt in terms of bombers and personnel for the 4th BW was applied literally when none from Lt. McKinley's crew survived after fighter attacks caused their B-17 to enter a fatal spinning motion that saw it impact on the island of Noord Beveland, on the Dutch coastline's southern fringe. Next day witnessed a potentially greater test of endurance when all three Groups fielded 80 crews in all and struck at the naval port of Emden, again with the 351st BG on hand. Fifty-nine crews completed the mission and returned without loss.

A more staccato mission pattern transpired for the remainder of May. On the 17th U-Boat facilities at Lorient absorbed the bomb loads of 118 bombers from both B-17 Bomb Wings, although the 500-lb and 1,000-lb bombs used could only have caused damage to other than the massively constructed pens. Once again, two of the 4th BW force of 38 attacking aircraft, one each from the 94th and 96th BGs, were declared MIA.

Lt Spevak (P) not only managed to bail out from 42-29627/GL: **Midnight**, but joined three from among the other nine surviving personnel in evading capture. An even greater number of evaders (six), including Capt. Garnham (P), emerged from 42-29767/BX **Boot Hill** before it fell to destruction near Spizet shortly after bombing; two of the remaining five were killed. A combination of flak and fighters had sealed both bombers' fate.

One 95th BG crew ended up diverting into RAF Exeter, in the West Country. Lt. R Bender bore the nickname "Spook," and 42-29704/ET: J was accordingly named. With two engines knocked out by flak the bomber's landing approach was erratic; after touching down it careened the full length of the runway, down a slope, and halted astride a bridge bearing the town's main road link with London. A gang of British workers laboring in direct line with the B-17's path fortunately scrambled away to safety; one of them then was seen digging furiously under the ball turret. When asked why by Lt. Merten (CP) the airman was tersely informed that the man's jacket was buried thereabouts! This bomber was declared *Category E*, but was destined to be succeeded by three fellow aircraft bearing the "Spook" title with Roman numerals added in sequence.

Two days later the accent on anti-submarine operations was resumed, and indeed would be continued throughout the month. This time, construction yards at Kiel and Flensburg were briefed for assault, with the 4th BW heading for the latter location. Both attacks went in almost simultaneously, with *Luftwaffe* activity seemingly concentrated upon the 1st BW, which lost six B-17s in contrast to the 4th BW, whose ranks remained unscathed other than for four injured personnel.

The first of the two remaining missions for May went out on the 21st against U-Boat production yards at Wilhelmshaven and Emden; the latter target was given to the 4th BW along with the 92nd BG, but the small six-aircraft force from the 1st BW's participant did not reach the target, unlike 46 of the other 63 crews. However, the first of many and increasingly severe rebuffs to be handed out by the *Luftwaffe* and flak gunners during the ensuing months of 1943 occurred today, since the Wing suffered five bomber losses, including three from the 94th BG that made a Group total of five and half of all losses to date.

Lt. Wetzel's 42-29727/QE: M **In der Fuehrer's Face** caught fire from a flak strike that set No. 3 engine and the radio room on fire. One officer was already dead when the bomber exploded, killing the pilot and five others, and coming to earth at Stobben, in northeast Holland. Amazingly the other three were ejected into mid-air, although S/Sgt. Hendricks died after reportedly being shot at as he neared the ground; his more fortunate crewmembers ended up as POWs. **Boomerang** (42-29682/ GL:) was battered by, and finally succumbed north of the target to fighter attacks, but not before Lt. Ecklund gave the bail out order from the fast disintegrating B-17; sadly, only one of the enlisted men was still alive and able to join all four officers in a safe exit into German custody. The worst loss scale reportedly occurred on Lt. Wieand's 42-29834 **Easy Aces**, with all ten airmen failing to survive their bomber's terminal "ditching" in the North Sea. (A lack of MACR records for all three Group losses has led to speculation regarding the latter-named B-17 and crew's fate, however.)

The sole 96th BG loss involved a similar fatal conclusion for all on Capt. G Stephenson's crew when 42-29734/ET:

This 94th BG group of B-17Fs display the evolving pattern of USAAF National markings. Aircraft in the lead has the original star on the fuselage as opposed to the bars applied to the bomber above. All four carry the "square A" on fin and right wing to denote the group's presence within either the 4th BW or 3rd BD, depending when the picture was taken.

found its last resting place under the North Sea far to the north of Texel. As the formations cleared the target area to the south 42-3110/QW: D finally succumbed to a fighter/flak combination of damage. Lts D Schnebly (P) and G Miller (CP) were among the four fatalities as the bomber crashed near Drieborg, just inside Dutch territory south of Groningen.

A full eight days elapsed before the VIII BC again took to the air. The U-Boat pens at St. Nazaire and La Pallice were taken on by the 1st and 2nd BWs, although the latter force aborted its attack. The 4th BW headed for Rennes, where a naval storage depot was focused upon. The defenders made it a costly mission by taking out 14 crews in all during what was the latest foray to deal with the U-Boat threat to the Atlantic lifeline.

Four Groups, one of which was a BW Composite unit assembled from all three Groups, were involved in today's assault, and ended up with a 10% loss factor among the 57 bombers whose crews gained mission credit. Once again the 94th BG came home short of three B-17s (all from the 410th BS), with two and one MIA casualties borne by the 95th and 96th BGs.

The bulk of losses were concentrated around a small geographic area whose primary reference was the port of St. Malo. Lt. M Brown (KIA), flying 42-29692/GL:, went down near Dinard with all but one of the crew either killed or failing to bail out when their bomber was dispatched by fighters. Then, 42-29476/GL: flown by Lt L Hecox, one of nine out of the ten on board to be killed, came down south of the port. Lt Workman ended up as a POW along with seven crewmembers after his B-17F/ 42-29710/GL: **Hell Below** was dispatched east of St. Malo.

Both the 95th BG losses involved aerial collisions. The first was 42-5858/ET: L (Lt. L Clark). This group Lead bomber, with Maj. Cole in the right seat, having suffered damage, then arced upwards to make contact with 42-29709/OE: C **Yo Brother**. At least one of the three airmen killed probably died through bailing out over the Channel waters abutting the Cherbourg Peninsula's western edge. **Yo Brother** returned to Alconbury, unlike 42-29689/OE: H (Lt. C Watson), which was run into by a fighter, with the impact tearing off a sizeable section of one outer wing panel and the No. 4 engine. The bomber was kept aloft long enough to be headed back over French soil where all ten airmen bailed out safely, half of whom then avoided landing up in a *stalag*.

The single B-17 loss to occur anywhere near the target area involved 42-3042/AW:, which had its right wing set on fire before veering off to the left of the homeward-bound formation. The MACR stated Lt. McMath's aircraft was last seen north of Cherbourg, but the report states the actual crash site for the 96th BG machine was fully 100 miles further south in the vicinity of Rennes. The pilot's body, along with two of the other officers and the Engineer, was never recovered, while only half of the remaining six crewmembers survived to become POWs.

General "Fred"

B/Gen. Frederick Anderson had been assigned to command the 4th BW in April. The normal policy was for senior staff to desist from flying combat missions, which made sense from two angles. First, the individual's command experience would be lost should his bomber be shot down. Second, his undoubted knowledge of current and future tactical and strategic planning could be forced out of him by his captors. The RAF largely adhered to this policy, but the USAAF tended to be more lenient, as exemplified by Anderson's actions. While in charge of the 4th BW he made it his "policy" to fly with each of the Groups on hand. As an example, on the 15th he was on board a 332nd BS bomber for the run to Emden, along with the 94th BG's CO, Col "Dinty" Moore. Other senior figures, such as Generals LeMay and Doolittle, would also fly combat missions in the ETO. However, Doolittle and Anderson did so not only with their Air Force, but also with the RAF. Anderson was destined to fly to Essen and Hamburg with No. 83 Sqdn at the end of July, doing so in both cases in R5868/OL: S, which survived 137 operations (missions) and now resides in deserved splendor within the RAF Museum in London! The morale factor for the airmen in knowing their commanders were willing to share the risks of combat flying had to be set against the aforementioned knowledge loss and security risks.

27 May 1943

The loading of bombers with extremely volatile munitions and fuel was a constant hazard for not only the ground crew, but sometimes for other personnel in the near vicinity of, and even farther distant from the aircraft dispersals. On the late evening of 27 May the 95th BG was preparing the aircraft on its current airfield at Alconbury. Suddenly a loud explosion intruded violently upon the sunny and almost somnolent early summer atmosphere. B-17F/42-29685/BG completely disintegrated, and in the process summarily took the lives of most of the final fatal casualty figure of 19 with a further 29 seriously injured. The blast waves reached out to strike home in unpredictable and lightning-like fashion. Lt. Metzger (N), on one crew lounging on the ground alongside their bomber, was the sole member sitting up, and paid for this physical variation when he was killed by the concussion that left his fellow crewmembers totally unscathed. Further away, an engineering officer standing scant feet away from other personnel fell down in what appeared to be a fainting action, but in fact he was another fatality, although his body was totally unmarked; nobody else in his vicinity was even slightly injured. Apparently only part of the bomb load had detonated, but the overall effect was to bring about Category E treatment for four B-17Fs in all, while several further bombers suffered varying but reparable scales of damage. (Twenty-seven days later the 381st BG would suffer a similar disaster during loading that expunged the lives of 23 airmen.)

Postscript to a Disaster

The exact cause of the tragedy was never to be fully established, but two linked issues were regarded as major contributors to the Alconbury incident. The 412BS armorer cadre had been severely depleted during training, and only five raw recruits, three of whom were classified as Ordnance Armorers but who had trained only in handling 20-mm shells, were assigned prior to departure overseas. During the crossing they were briefed on how to handle bombs, but only theoretically, via the Ordnance Munitions manual. Further dilution of even the trained squadron personnel occurred after reaching Framlingham when those in near contact with a spinal meningitis case also had to be quarantined. Thus, when more armorers were requested at Alconbury it was the group of raw Ordnance Armorers who were dispatched; the fact of their "rookie" status was passed on via Lt. Erwin, who tragically was the engineering officer lost in the incident.

At this time bombs were being fitted with fuses *prior* to hoisting into the bomb-bay. Also fitted was a cotter-pin that went through the arming vane blade and a designated hole in the fuse before being flared out to prevent the vane spinning and activating the weapon. Also in place at this point was the arming wire that was positioned between the bomb-bay shackle and the arming vane, but remained in the aircraft at "bombs away." The hoisting procedure involved placing the single lifting sling at each bomb's C of G as indicated by a painted yellow strip; armorers were firmly briefed to ensure that the bomb remained in a horizontal position while being raised; otherwise it could very easily slip out.

It was surmised in postscript analyses that on 27 May the two personnel loading 42-29685 were from the original trio of inexperienced airmen, and had failed to ensure the detonating bomb did not drop out of the sling. A safety feature of the fuse involved a set of disks located under the flange of the striker head, which was encased in a 3-inch diameter cup. As the bomb dropped the detaching of the arming wire from the vane permitted it to spin in the slipstream, which in turn caused the nose cup to unscrew itself from the fuse and thereby permit the ejection spring to force out the safety disks. Upon impact with the ground the now fully-armed weapon would explode under the unimpeded action of the firing pin....

As a result of recommendations submitted by Lt. Meek (Ordnance Section) to the Division's Chief Ordnance Officer—after dummy tests of bombs at Aberdeen Proving Ground, MD, had confirmed the safety cups could be wrenched off if an accidentally-released bomb fell in a sharp enough arc—orders were issued that: 1) not only should bombs remain on the trailer from where they would be hoisted, as opposed to the current procedure of unloading onto individual cradles, but; 2) fusing and attaching of arming wires would only be made after bombs were in position within the bomb-bay, albeit that this was a time consuming matter for the Ordnance personnel concerned. The most important recommendation was 3), that all Ordnance personnel be fully qualified in the task of loading as confirmed by Armament Officers.

Ultimate Sanction

There was no way in which the stark facts of combat operations could be inculcated into the trainee airmen back in the States. It was only when actual missions were flown that the reality of facing injury, or the "ultimate sanction"—death—could begin to be brought home; imprisonment rarely came up as a possible fate. (Some airmen returning from the 381st BG's first mission were clearly dazed by the experience and accosted the Padre, saying "Capt. Brown, they were trying to kill us!") The initial shock reaction of being shot at in earnest soon gave way in most cases to mood swings varying between quiet resignation at the odds against surviving a combat tour and resurgent optimism that all would work out well.

A Major serving with one Group noted the following:

> "I think some of the fellows who meet Death so often do a lot more thinking than they once did. The Catholics have just completed a 'mission' and they have excellent attendance every night. Even .... says he catches himself praying when he gets into a tight spot though I don't suppose he does much praying any other time! In the several months we have been here it is very striking that some of the young officers have aged ten years or so. When they first came they stayed out as late as possible and as often as possible. I went to a movie in a local town recently and was amazed to see a sizeable number of the most notorious playboys catching the 2215 bus back to the airfield."

Somebody else made a telling comment when studying the faces of crews at debriefing: "That clock in the sky must go round at a frightening rate, because these airmen seemed to have aged overnight." It was true that airmen of any nation, the majority of whom were mere adolescents, who entered the field of aerial combat generally matured very quickly once the odds against surviving injury, imprisonment, or the ultimate sanction became grimly apparent. The days of their youth were in essence long gone.

Gen. LeMay, during his time as 305th BG CO, recalled:

> "Reading the last letters written by my crews who did not return, I was struck by the calm and logical manner in which they faced up to their possible, and sadly often realized, fate."

2

THE 4TH BOMB WING TAKES SHAPE

(JUNE/JULY 1943)

As June 1943 was entered the VIII BC authorities took stock of the Campaign to date. The stated intention to strike at and eliminate the Nazi industrial base as a prime source of its ability to sustain the conflict was gaining positive if rather hesitant strength. Since January targets in the German hinterland had come under intermittent attention of the Command's bombers, in concert with RAF Bomber Command's greater if somewhat more generally directed thrusts at its adversary's prime production source in the Ruhr. The logical, if somewhat emotively expressed principle of "bombing the Devils round the clock" declared at Casablanca by Gen. Eaker still had a way to go towards its total and irreversible conclusion. As it was, the American airmen were quietly but firmly determined to play their part in achieving this very desirable intention.

Such an intention was basically subverted for the first ten days in June, almost certainly due to the adverse weather conditions existing over Western Europe, which in turn subverted any guarantee of achieving accurate visual sighting of selected targets. At last, on 11 June the 4th BW, along with seven 1st BW groups, got aloft and headed for the combined targets of Wilhelmshaven's U-Boat yards and port facilities. However, and perhaps due to an effective smoke screen raised over the Primary, no less than 20 of the seventy-nine 4th BW crews granted mission credit ended up bombing targets of opportunity. The cost to the Wing was light at one 95th BG bomber, but not for the crew concerned. As the enemy coastline was receding Lt. M McKinnon's 42-29693 /QW: O **Lonesome Polecat** was seen to fall away from the formation under fighter attack before exploding and depositing its remains and the crews' bodies into the North Sea.

By now the recently-arrived Americans must have been aware that any hopes of swiftly besting their *Luftwaffe* adversary were at best to be postponed indefinitely. By this stage of WWII the *Luftwaffe's* Fighter Command (*Jagdwaffe*) was becoming ever more versed in the art of issuing painful challenges to the Allied aviators. Not only did it possess two of the most effective fighter designs in the form of the Bf109 and the arguably even more daunting Fw190, but the continuing expansion of flak battery strength provided a secondary but equally severe challenge to the future course of the Allied Bombing Offensive. Two days following the Wilhelmshaven mission, this stark fact with all its dreadful implications would impinge upon the fortunes of the 4th BW in particular…

Structural Adjustments

What had initially been titled the 4th BW, 401st Provisional Combat Bombardment Wing (PCBW), which encompassed the three groups on hand, received its first change in nomenclature on 6 June when the 95th BG was transformed into the 402nd PCBW. The 96th BG would retain the abovementioned status until 23 June, when it became the 403rd PCBW, and the 94th BG would become part of the 4th CBW on 13 September. All three groups would form the nucleus for Combat Bombardment Wings (CBW) from the latter-stated date, with each of these sub-forces ultimately comprising three groups as the VIII BC's strength continued to build up.

Calamity at Kiel

Kiel, on the western extreme of the Baltic coast, was an important naval base, as well as possessing sizeable surface vessel and U-Boat construction yards. On 14 May the 44th BG in particular had experienced a serious rebuff from the defenders. Now a full month later, on 13 June two of the three groups within the 4th BW would absorb an even greater degree of punishment. The structure of the Wing formation was to have the 95th BG in the lead and the 94th BG as High group, while a Composite group within whose ranks the 96th BG was rather unwillingly included constituted the third element.

The British Foreign Secretary Anthony Eden toured a number of VIIIBC airfields during 1943. Here he is accompanied by Gen. Jacob Devers with Col. Old (96th BG CO) on the right during Eden's visit to Snetterton Heath.

The crews lounging in studied casualness in the 4th BW Briefing rooms were by now well aware of the odds facing them in their endeavors to complete a combat tour. To date, the seven missions flown had cost a total of sixteen B-17s declared MIA with their crews, while a number of airmen on returning aircraft had been killed or seriously injured. But today's mission was destined to add an even more frightening dimension in terms of survival odds…

The intention was to bomb the U-Boat yards at Kiel in concert with similar assaults by the 1st BW upon parallel facilities at Bremen. Although the targets were some 100 miles apart, there was always the possibility that the enemy controllers would opt to split up their fighter force and thereby dilute its overall effort against the incoming formations…

At Framlingham the proceedings were graced by the presence of B/Gen. Bedford Forrest, who had recently arrived to take command of one of the three planned CBWs. However, the crews were probably not enamored by the suggestion he had raised regarding formation patterns. From the beginning of 1943 and up to date the basic group formation had been arranged so that the three squadrons and the elements within each of these sub-units flew in stepped up angles from right to left as viewed from ahead. The General had previously decreed that the 95th BG was to fly a much flatter vertical and lateral pattern on this occasion. (However, a chart recorded in a book on the Group that has been written by a well-respected author indicates a pattern that was not materially different from the normal one flown, regardless of the criticism that might still be raised against Bedford Forrest in the light of events this day.) Whatever the facts, the group had apparently been following the General's suggestion in practice formations for up to two weeks prior to the Kiel mission. The thirty crews due to fly the mission were split between eighteen in the High and twelve in the Composite group; this total would be diluted by four B-17s either failing to take off or, in one instance, aborting after take off.

The bulk of the Bremen force gained its target and bombed the Primary or targets of opportunity with the loss of just four B-17s out of the 122 crews releasing their loads. Fighter opposition seems to have been sparse judging by both the low loss factor and conversely the handful of claims made by the

The Vibrant Virgin was assigned to the 385th BG on 17 June and is seen following the addition of the Division "square" applied during July. The nose bears more than twenty mission symbols, but the national marking with a dulled-down star still lacks its bars. Bomber was MIA on 8 October 1943, although Lt. R Jenson and crew bailed out.

gunners. Could the same relatively good fortune attend the efforts of its companion Wing? Only time would tell, although the omens were not good in the light of the *Luftwaffe's* absence over Bremen…

In the case of the 4th BW take-off and assembly of both the main and composite formations was achieved, and the total of 76 assigned crews from the Wing headed across the ever-forbidding stretches of the North Sea. The General was riding in the right-hand seat of Capt. Stirwalt's 42-30164/BG: E. It was many minutes prior to even approaching the enemy coast when there arose the first indication that matters were likely to deteriorate for the Wing, as the first fighter assaults swept in. In addition, a continual undercast from the crossing-in point onwards promised to hinder if not totally subvert all efforts at achieving a positive bombing result. However, this stage of the mission as well as the bulk of the fifty or sixty miles that had to be traversed from the coast to Kiel appeared to have passed without any significant attrition occurring among the ranks of the Wing; that unfortunate development would only unfold on final target approach.

Lt. Cozens, flying No. 4 in the Lead squadron, soon realized the folly of the "flat" formation, since his B-17 was flying almost level with Stirwalt's aircraft; his gunners could not accordingly focus on the fighters without risking striking the Lead bomber! Capt. Miller, on Stirwalt's right wing, then noted that, with the bomb run completed and the Lead B-17 still in position, he was so concentrating on their flight attitude that he almost collided with Cozen's bomber before veering off to the right! (Miller lost his oxygen flow around this time but recovered by turning onto "Emergency.") No sooner had the run been completed than the latest fighter assaults ended with the Lead B-17 being thoroughly shot up and dropping away to the right.

Ed Charles (N) recalled looking over to Capt. Stirwalt's bomber and witnessing his head sagging, upon which act he uttered a silent but tragically relevant "farewell." The tragedy then evolving lay not in the fact that the crew forfeited their lives within the bomber, but that all thirteen successfully bailed out—only for the wind to unerringly direct their parachutes out over the frigid Baltic waters. With two exceptions, Lts. W Brown (N) and Gannon (Observer), who wisely free-fell through thousands of feet before pulling their ripcords, death by drowning or exposure in the sea became the common fate of Bedford Forrest, Stirwalt, and the remaining nine crewmembers. Even then, Brown was still very fortunate, in that although he also landed in the sea, he was close by a fishing boat that promptly picked him up.

What transpired with Stirwalt's aircraft was but a small element of the overall disaster visited upon the group, since no less than nine other 95th BG crews would never return. One crew led by Lt.L Morissette was perhaps more unfortunate, in that their problems commenced with a technical matter, namely oxygen. Their 42-29737/QW: N Louise remained intact in the face of the fighter attacks, but then lost the bulk of its oxygen facility as the formation was withdrawing. The pilots had no recourse other than dropping out of formation to normal breathing levels, but by doing so lost all gunnery support while still under persistent fighter assault most of the route back to the North Sea coast. Then, with one engine on fire and a second smoking the decision was made to "ditch," and the landing gear was lowered in an act of surrender. However, the looming presence of a sandbar persuaded the pilots to attempt a landing, which succeeded in quick and successful time due to the extremely retarding effect of the sand! The crew hastily evacuated the burning bomber, whose ammunition was freely "cooking off," and were soon apprehended by the German military, who later shipped the airmen out on a fishing boat that transported them to the port of Husum.

The swathe of destruction among the ranks of the Horham group as well as the overall Wing formation was largely concentrated over the rectangle of enemy territory extending east from Kiel and out over the Baltic. Lt. C Rubin's team in 42-29763/OE: X was flying No. 2 in the Low squadron. The risks ever attendant when fighters attacked, especially from head-on, reportedly occurred here when one made contact. The mal-action had the tragic knock-on effect of causing the stricken B-17 to veer into the path of 42-30118/OE: N (Capt. Cornett), heading the second element. Neither crew survived after the Rubin-piloted bomber fell into the Baltic near Heiligenhafen and the other equally crippled B-17 also descended into the sea at an unidentified location.

The area round the Danish Island of Langerland was also where the High squadron lost 42-29702/BG: H **Rat Killer** (Lt. W Renaud, flying No. 6); the location was well to the north of Kiel and on the direct route to Sweden, so the pilots may well have been attempting a bid for salvation in that neural country. The Low squadron forfeited 42-29675/OE: S flown by Lt. W Adams. The bomber came down in between the German and Danish islands of Fehmarn and Lollard, a direction that paralleled the heading of the Renaud B-17 with the same possible but sadly unfulfilled intention in mind. The fifth main group bomber to be lost was 42-29680/ET: R with Lt. J Nunes' crew, whose last resting place was in the Baltic off Oldenburg/Holstein. The continuing grisly toll of bombers was equalled by the reported deaths of all thirty airmen. From the Composite group was culled 42-29827/OE: V, which was shot out of the sky to crash at Silzen, west of Neumuenster. Lt. K Mason (P) was one of the six fatalities, with the other four airmen being captured.

The remaining two Group losses occurred away from the target area, one from each sub-formation. Lt. J Perry was

Capt. Robert Brown, second from right, stands with four of his 390th BG crew in front of **Cabin in the Sky** (42-30338/FC: P). This team survived their combat tour, as did the bomber; assigned on 11 July 1943 it finally returned home almost exactly two years later. The "kill" tally on the nose of three rose dramatically to fourteen after the 10 October 1943 Muenster mission when the gunners were officially credited with eleven fighters.

All USAAF groups indulged in regular social events on base, with parties top of the list, to which local and British Service women as well as WACs were guests. This example is taking place at Snetterton Heath.

piloting 42-3206/OE: T in the main group—Low squadron's extremely exposed No. 6 slot—when his bomber was mortally damaged, but at least all but one of the crew bailed out, leaving the B-17 to crash into the Barkuersee, a lake northwest of Luebeck. This was in grim contrast to all ten of Lt. V Stone's crew flying in 42-3286/ET: E, none of whom survived the loss of their aircraft after it dropped inexorably out of its position within the Composite group and finally disappeared into the Baltic.

Briefed Anomaly

According to 94th BG records, the withdrawal route from the target initially followed a protracted course of 60 degrees right before looping 270 degrees to the left and taking up the homeward heading; this in turn explains why several B-17s crashed well to the east of Kiel and were recorded inside an 8-minute time span (0928 - 0936), at least according to III/JG26 records.

94th BG Fortunes

It was not only the 95th BG that was to be crucified almost wholly over enemy territory, because it seems that the equal measure of punishment of the 94th BG was handed out to the Group during this stage of the mission. At least three out of the final total of ten MIA bombers did come down on enemy soil. The first of these was 42-30113/TS:, flown by Lt. W Dauth. The B-17 was one of only three aircraft in the Low squadron and suffered ultimately terminal damage crossing in from the Danish coast that included two engines "out" and a third on fire. Easing down and away from the already truncated sub-formation, the pilots made a successful if heavy crash landing at Rendsburg, west of Kiel, with all either still on board or having previously acted upon orders to bail out ending up alive. Lt. R Tower (POW) realized an almost perfect survival rate of nine from his aircraft, 42-29949/XM: **Sick Call**. The bomber was culled from the formation and reportedly tumbled to destruction at Gross Koenigsforde, west of Kiel.

Once again, the cruel vagaries of combat struck at 42-29715/GL: **KLO Kay** and Capt. J Hebert's crew, who were leading the group's Composite formation. Also on board was Capt. Rawlinson (410th BS CO). At some point over the target the bomber, which was last seen descending with an engine on fire following prolonged *Luftwaffe* attention, exploded, and only Rawlinson was thrown clear and alive to deploy his parachute before floating down into captivity. The crash site for the B-17 was at Pohnsdorf, just southeast of Kiel.

Everett Blakely, a 100th BG "original" pilot, was noted for his calm, measured control of an aircraft, with one crewmember describing him as "a dream of a pilot who just sat hunched in his seat." On 8 October 1943, along with Maj. John Kidd, he brought the severely damaged **Just A' Snappin'** back to a crash landing. He went on to survive the war.

The *Luftwaffe* defenders were far from finished with the 94th at this point.

As the formation reduced height out over the sea the latest fighter assault set one wing of 42-29822/QE: **Visiting Fireman** (Lt. Hendershot) on fire. Shortly afterwards the wing separated to throw the aircraft into an uncontrollable spin and take its hapless human load into the watery depths. In the same series of attacks, 42-29708/XM: **Shackaroo!** carrying Maj. Thorup had one stabilizer blown off and was also set on fire. The severely damaged B-17 was kept aloft as long as possible before "ditching" action became necessary. This proved successful for the entire crew, but signalled the start of an undoubtedly worrying spell of eleven hours before an RAF ASR launch turned up, having responded to the SOS and crash location coordinates dispatched by another B-17's ROG.

Just over 90 Group airmen would not return from this mission to land at their new permanent airfield at Rougham, and so far the death rate among the five listed crews was 21 out of the 50 involved. However, the mortality statistic worsened within the ranks of the other four teams who were lost. Lt. Roemke (P) died, along with five of his crew on board 42-29957/GL: **Helno Gal II**, which was downed close to the target. There were sole listed survivors from the remaining three aircraft, none of whom were pilots. The exact site of 42-3187/GL: **Buckshot's** (Lt. Weldon) final demise would never be determined, since it was another bomber that found a Baltic Sea grave. However, two crewmembers were subsequently washed ashore, one near Kiel and one on a Danish shore, and one enlisted man became a POW. Lt. Johnson's 42-3063/GL: **Ole Tobe** impacted with the sea south of a Danish island to leave Lt. Hale (B) as the sole survivor; he reportedly floated in his Mae West for two hours before being picked up by a German vessel. Finally, 42-29940/XM: (Lt. Loog) is believed to have succumbed on the return route to crash at Marienhof/Padenstedt, west of Neumuenster, along with nine of the crew. (There was an almost exact arithmetic progression in Group losses, being 331st BS (one), 332nd BS (two), 333rd BS (two), and 410th BS (four).)

96th BG

During the nine missions flown to date, the lowest casualty rate in aircraft (three) had been borne by the 96th BG, although it had suffered the first Wing loss during the inaugural mission on 13 May. Now that statistic was destined to be trebled today, commencing with 42-29748/BX: **Paradise Lost**. Lt. Rossman's B-17 was brought down in the target area, and the pilot was one of eight crewmembers killed. Dorphof, near Kappeln, bounding the Baltic coastline some 30 miles north of the target, was where 42-3107/AW: **Miss Carriage** came down with the same death rate as on Rossman's crew, although Lt. Webster (P) was one of the two survivors; at least seven of the other crewmembers suffered the same dreadful fate as the Stirwalt crew when the stiff wind blew their parachutes out over the Baltic. Lt. Decaro (N) was a very lucky exception, because although he also landed in the sea a German naval vessel was nearby to fish him out. Lt. Webster, having landed, then managed to evade capture for several days, during which time he trudged northwards towards Denmark. Sadly, any prospect of gaining friendly assistance in that occupied land was snuffed out when he was apprehended in the vicinity of Flensburg, located on the Danish /German border.

Much more fortunate in surviving their watery immersion was Lt. McKell's officer complement and T/Sgt. M Smithson (ROG) in 42-29756/QJ: **Big Chief II**. A combination of fighters and flak finished off the bomber on the way back, and the parachuting airmen must have reacted with growing apprehension as they floated down towards and finally into the sea. Very fortunately all landed close to the shoreline of Island of Pellworm, west of Husum, and gratefully waded ashore with one exception; Lt. Anderegg (B) had to be rescued by a rowboat manned by an old man and two young boys.

The final tally of bomber and personnel casualties was increased as the Wing returned to its airfields. Two groups

The thin fuselage skin on a B-17 provided no material protection from flak or fighter strikes, as this anonymous crewmember's solidly bandaged head attests to; hopefully his eyesight has not been affected. Two other crewmembers are assisting him out of the door while two Medics stand by to take him off to the base hospital.

suffered a single Category E statistic with a further pair borne by the 95th BG in terms of aircraft, along with two wounded and one deceased crewmember, the latter unfortunate airman serving with the 96th BG. S/Sgt. Pauboinsly (RWG) had been killed during the initial stage of the air battle, and Lt. Attaway's 42-29766/QJ: Black Heart was deemed too badly shot up to be capable of restoration to combat status.

Blow for Blow

Among the attacking fighter force were 32 Bf109Gs belonging to III/JG26 operating out of Nordholz and led by Hptm. Ruppert. During an assault from the rear on the Lead group Ruppert's fighter was squarely struck by return fire and he was forced to jump. The current *Luftwaffe* parachute harness was manufactured from hemp and had already shown an alarming tendency to detach itself from its human carrier should the ripcord be pulled precipitately before the airman's fall rate had decelerated to a tolerable level. This was to be the fate of the III/JG26 leader, who accordingly fell to his death. (It was some months later before nylon replaced hemp as a more reliable manufacturing material for the harnesses.) The *Gruppe's* pilots made up for Ruppert's demise by taking out four or five bombers from the 95th BG's ranks.

Comments

The Kiel mission became the latest to be placed in the "defeat" category for VIII BC. All positive comments on the scale of destruction visited upon either the Primary, or targets of opportunity for a proportion of the attackers, could not conceal the reverse punishment inflicted upon the Command's strength in bombers and crews.

The German's equivalent of the Allied Fighter Commands had flexed its muscles efficiently in a manner that was all the more potent for two reasons.

The first concerned the current inability of either the Spitfire or P-47 units to provide cover when the bombers operated other than very close to the western European coastal stretches. This limitation had to be put in context, however. The USAAF authorities had commenced their Campaign on the basis of the "self-defending" bomber. The heavy armament on board both "heavies," coupled with the intention to fly a tight defensive formation, had been expected to see the crews achieving good results over their targets, and what was of equal importance, regaining friendly territory with a minimum loss scale.

The second was centered round the bombers' defensive provision. The results arising from a study of captured B-17Fs and B-24Ds had highlighted a totally inadequate forward-angled weight of firepower on both bombers. This primary weakness had quickly been fastened upon by the *Luftwaffe* pilots, whose assaults were being evermore directed from the head-on angle. The hand-held .5 machine guns up front on both four-engine designs were providing a very inferior response to the fixed firing platform of the enemy fighters, which usually supported between three and five cannon and machine-gun calibre weapons. The top turret possessed a more powerful deterrent effect with its twin .5 guns, but the swift approach of the fighters, along with their tendency to "split-S' and dive under the bomber formation, tended to limit the timespan in which its striking power could be deployed.

Officially filed and confirmed claims by the bomber gunners on the Kiel mission were an example of gross exaggeration regarding the perceived punishment being handed out to the *Luftwaffe*. The rosy statistics of 39-5-14 (Kills-probable-damaged) were miles wide of the true figures, although the accurate details were only unearthed after WWII. Of course, the VIII BC authorities had to consider the morale factor in making, or rather "confirming" the foregoing figures; in addition, many claims were made in good faith as opposed to being created by an individual's over-excited imagination, especially when operating under the dreadful pressures of combat flying.

Transit Risk

There now ensued a period of eight days during which no materiel VIII BC incursions over enemy territory were made. There were twin losses of bombers along with their crews

An armorer has found a solid, if potentially lethal, perch on what is probably an M-44 1,000-lb explosive bomb (but could equally be an incendiary cluster bomb to judge by the close-spaced vertical lines directly behind the airman), which is strapped in place on the trailer. The almost cloudless sky was a far from regular weather condition in British skies, much as it was desired by the bomber crews when taking off, assembling, and landing back.

that occurred outside England, however. In both cases the incidents involved the transfer of groups assigned to the Command. On 21 June Lt. H Powley (385th BG) lifted off from Gandar in 42-30254 and disappeared into the lowering evening light. This was the final visual sighting of the B-17, and although two radio contacts were subsequently effected the aircraft disappeared somewhere over the North Atlantic. Also departing Gandar the same day was the 388th BG's 42-30229 with Lt. M Kamholz in charge, but a further ten airmen's names were sadly destined to be entered upon a *Wall of the Missing* memorial in concert with the Powley team. Placing the piloting and precise navigation of an aircraft across the lengthy and trackless wastes of the Atlantic in the hands of still relatively novice crews was an unavoidable measure that inevitably led to the aforementioned events during the entire course of the bombing campaign. As it was the great majority of the flights passed off in order.

End of a Nomadic Existence

In most instances USAAF units, particularly those bomber and fighter examples assigned to a strategic function in England, arrived and remained at their specific airfield during the course of WWII. The experiences of the founding groups for what would be transformed into the 3rd Bomb Division on 13 September 1943 was very different.

The 94th BG's air echelon was sent in mid-April to Bassingbourn, home of the veteran 91st BG, from where it had conducted operations until 27 May. In contrast, the ground echelons shipped-in from the USA and moved directly to the Essex location of Earls Colne on 12 May; fifteen days later the combat crews joined their ground support colleagues. However, the Group's tenure of occupation only lasted another seventeen days before the final move to Rougham, close to Bury St. Edmunds, was effected. (The date would not be soon forgotten, since it involved the traumatic events of the Kiel mission!)

A similar nomadic pattern applied to the other two Groups. The 95th BG had flown into Alconbury and remained there until early June. In contrast, the ground echelons were shipped straight from the USA to Framlingham, in Suffolk (12 May), where they were joined by the air echelon on 11 June. A mere four days later came the second upheaval, when the short distance to the Group's permanent airfield at Horham was carried out.

Finally, the Grafton Underwood original site for the 96th BG, assumed on 16 April, witnessed the same pattern of ground and air echelon movements, with the former going directly to Andrews Field (13 May) to be joined by the combat crews two weeks later. As with the other two Groups, the final transfer to Snetterton Heath was made within a further short time period on 12 June.

Huels

German scientists had proved to be masters at the art of producing synthetic variations for key strategic materials, with oil and rubber being two primary examples. This was absolutely vital to Nazi Germany's military progress, given that she did not possess geological or arboreal resources in these respective instances and was almost totally cut off from regular and wholesale imports, with the exception of the massive oil complex at Ploesti, Rumania.

The town of Huels, just north of Recklinghausen on the northwest fringe of the Ruehr, was home to a large synthetic rubber factory that was selected for attack by both B-17 Wings on 22 June. In a bid to deflect the full weight of the *Luftwaffe* away from the main force, two acolyte Groups (381st and 384th BGs) would be dispatched under strong escort cover to attack a target in Antwerp around the time that the Huels formations were heading in further to the north over Holland. In the event the plan would only partially succeed, with both the main and diversionary forces absorbing punishment...

Weather conditions were good for visual bombing, but equally sound for counterstrikes by the German fighters. The intended arrival over Antwerp of the 42-strong diversionary

Donald Duck's lugubrious expression as he is surrounded by bursting flak shells appears on the nose of 42-30367/AW:Y. **Flak Happy** turned up at the 96th BG's airfield on 1 July and lasted until the costly Bremen mission that commenced Black Week on 8 October; three out of the ten in Lt. Bolstad's (KIA) crew survived their bomber's loss near the target..

This 561BS B-17F was in at the very start of combat operations from Knettishall. Unlike so many of her contemporaries, she was not claimed in combat or even salvaged; instead, she returned home in July 1944. The **Sweetheart** title is inscribed in huge letters ahead of a mission total exceeding twenty. Note the combination of a dark group letter on a dull square surface.

formation under escort cover did not occur; instead, missed rendezvous times with the P-47s and Typhoons and late take-offs by the "heavies" left the latter on their own until they had turned for home. By then between four and six B-17s were either heading for destruction over the area of the Schelde Estuary or were destined to be "written off" following their return to friendly shores.

The depredations wrought upon the Antwerp attackers by elements of JG26 would be mirrored to a similar degree among the ranks of the main force. A figure of 235 B-17s took off, including eleven "shotgun guard" YB-40s. The latter were to prove a palliative, and a pretty ineffective one at that, to the current absence of proper long-range escorts for the bomber crews.

Sixty-three 4th BW crews, of which thirty were contributed by the 95th BG, took off to join up with seven full and one composite group from the 1st BW. The formations crossed the North Sea and tracked in over northern Holland before angling southeastwards to initiate what was the first USAAF attack on a Ruehr target. The first *Luftwaffe* thrusts occurred over Dutch soil. Several bombers were dispatched or left in a terminal state by the time the I.P. was looming up, with the 1st BW bearing the brunt, and destined to lose ten MIA and one "ditched" crew in the course of the mission.

It would appear that four of the five 4th BW crews followed the same terminal route during approach to the target. Lt. Sabella's 42-5880/TS: was set on fire by flak northeast of Nijmegen, but all ten airmen bailed out safely. A second 94th BG crew, having lagged behind the formation, had their B-17/42-30240/GL: brought down near Goch by fighters; Lt. McFarland and six of his crew managed to escape. A few miles further into German territory 42-30211/OE: T, piloted by Capt. J Bunch, was brought down near Wesel, having finally dropped out under seeming control after being thoroughly shot up. This time round just two crewmembers failed to survive, with one—Lt. King (N)—cruelly denied the right to life when he impacted with the bomb bay doors while bailing out. Around the same time the first of two 96th BG casualties blew up and its remnants crashed to earth north of Wesel. This was 42-3284/MZ: **Guess Who?**, whose crew, led by Lt. Morrison, had fortunately evacuated their posts prior to the bomber's disintegration.

The bombers found the factory to be in the clear; some of the staff had emerged to gaze at what they took to be an over-flying *Luftwaffe* formation and many paid with their lives for such curiosity. As it was, only a small proportion of the bomb loads actually descended directly on the plant, and although production loss was later estimated at three months, normal service was resumed in less than a third of this time.

The final 4th BW "payment" for this mission occurred as the formations headed home. A flak-damaged 42-5877/AW: (96th BG) was steadily expiring as it was crossing central Holland, and finally gave up near Gorinchem, directly east of Dordrecht, after Lt. Russell gave the bailout order and followed the others out into mid-air.

There may well have been a third 94th BG loss that, had it occurred, would have been initiated by "friendly fire." During the inward leg a .5 bullet from another B-17 lodged in the oil cooler of one engine, which then overheated and had to be shut down. Since 42-3190/XM: **Mr Five by Five** was flying Lead, with Maj. Steele and Capt. Kee Harrison in charge, the pilots had little option but to hand over to the Deputy B-17 and turn back even though deep in enemy territory. Fighters soon intervened, whereupon the bomber dropped down to skim the ground and make a perilously protracted but finally successful run for home.

The sweet innocence of Youth in the midst of destruction is exemplified in this picture of a little girl sitting on the end of a scrapped stabilizer that in turn is part of a collection of shattered B-17 segments.

Three days after Huels the crews were briefed for their latest German targets that would prove to be two of the most feared in the minds of VIII BC personnel. Hamburg was Germany's second major industrial city, with numerous important production plants that included ship and U-Boat yards scattered within its boundaries.

The flak battery strength allotted the city was on a par with its strategic importance and assured any attacking force of a protracted and potentially severe reception. Bremen, further south on the river Weser, was another major seaport and industrial source, and its defenders had already shown their mettle on 17 April by downing fifteen out of the total force of 115.

To date, all recently arrived groups had been assigned to the 1st BW, but today would see the operational debut of the first unit addition to the 4th BW since the latter's inception. The 100th BG had enjoyed a mixed fortune during its training period prior to arrival in England. In late April the group CO, Col. Alkire, had apparently been deemed inadequate to carry out his function following a very poor performance by the 100th while flying a long-range practice flight and was displaced by Col. H Turner. (However, he must have quickly regained his superiors' confidence because he soon assumed command of the B-24 equipped 449th BG that was assigned to the Italian Theatre of Operations.)

The future combat fortunes of the Group during its time at Thorpe Abbotts would land it with an unenviable reputation as a "jinx outfit" among its contemporaries; indeed, the term *The Bloody 100th* was and still is a sobriquet worn with defiantly perverse pride by its surviving personnel. (Several other Groups would receive sustained punishment, including the 96th, which lost around 100 crews in the first half of 1944—but none were ever similarly labelled.)

Nineteen crews took off as part of a 78-strong 4th BW force heading for Bremen's U-Boat yards with the 1st BW assigned to Hamburg. However, as the North Sea was being crossed a steady build-up in cloud allied to persistent and heavy contrails finally forced a search for a target of opportunity as the 4th BW formation was skirting the Frisian island chain, although the 1st BW did get through to Hamburg. A convoy steaming off Juist was sighted and duly attacked with indeterminate results by just 18 bombers, all but two from the 95th BG. The weather conditions, however poor, did not prevent the *Luftwaffe* intervening to cull eighteen crews in all, three of whom were from the 4th BW.

Worse still for the 100th BG was that all came from its ranks, who in turn were deemed to be spread out to the extent that any form of a group structure was never assumed, as reported by some returning airmen. The initial assaults took out Capt. Petrich's 42-29986; XR: Q, which simply faded away into the clouds and finally disappeared into the sea with all on board. Just one officer survived the destruction of 42-3260/XR: K Angels Tit, flown by Lt. A Adams III, the pilot's body being the only one to be recovered. Lt. Demchak (N) recalled that the bail out order had been given, but his next memory was of regaining consciousness on the German vessel that had rescued him; it is likely that he was the lucky exception who survived his aircraft's disintegration while he was still on board. Finally, 42-30038/XR: D Bar Fly exploded under a hail of gunfire north of Wangerooge, but although the bomber found a watery grave its fate was not shared by four of its crew, although S/Sgt. Goodwin (BT) later had one leg amputated thanks to his wounds. The spectacularly gory record of the 100th BG had been established during its first combat "outing," although the *Bloody 100th* sobriquet had its origin in events still two months ahead. Next day's run proved totally wasteful thanks to the same pattern of adverse weather. Consequently, the 81 crews sent out turned back before attaining their airfield target at Le Mans, France.

Hard Choices

The change of command at any of the VIII BC units normally caused feelings of regret when the original incumbent was being transferred on grounds of inefficiency. A reverse swell of resentment was likely to be directed against the replacement CO, particularly in instances where no perceived reason for the switch seemed justified. Col. Moore and Col. Kessler had led the 94th and 95th BGs since their inception. Nevertheless, on 22 June both were officially relieved of their commands and replaced by Cols. John Gerhart and Fred Castle. There was reportedly a feeling at Command HQ—akin to that portrayed in the film *Twelve O'Clock High*—that morale on both units had slumped by an alarming degree and that both COs had not enforced discipline, but had over-concentrated on their men's well being at the expense of re-establishing a sense of getting on with the task at hand—"over-identification with the personnel" was the phrase reputedly being bandied about.

Col. Fred Castle's appointment was probably the source for increased resentment since he had been one of Gen. Eaker's seven subordinates arriving in England in early 1942, with the attendant hint of favoritism dictating such a negative atmosphere. The fact that he was also a Godson of Gen. "Hap" Arnold did little or nothing to allay the suspicions of those Group members aware of this fact! However, the reputed "Desk jockey," unbeknownst to the group, was far from deserving this sardonic sobriquet, since he had already flown several missions, and promptly added to his tally on the 22nd. However, it was over a month before his quiet but firm rebuttal of the personnel's complaints regarding his demands on them began to pay off, after which he was to be held in ever higher regard until relinquishing his stewardship in April 1944 upon promotion to Brigadier/Gen.

Sack Time arrived at Great Ashfield on 16 June, but graced her dispersal for exactly two months. Then, on 17 August she became one of three MIA casualties, coming down between Worms and Darmstadt en route to Regensburg; happily all ten on Lt. L Reichardt's crew bailed out.

Kiplings Error III does not yet display her 413BS codes MZ. The 96th BG B-17F came from a Vega-production batch where the cheek gun window positions were reversed. Almost ten months after assignment in June 1943 (11 April 1944) the bomber disappeared into the Baltic along with all of Lt. Johnson's crew.

28 June

VIII BC Mission No. 69 signalled an end to the Command's regular involvement with bombing U-Boat facilities on the French western coast. *Flak City* was briefed for attack by seventy-one 4th BW crews from among the 191 dispatched. Today witnessed the debut of a technical advance for the Wing. This was the presence of some B-17s delivered to the 100th BG whose outer wing panels bore additional fuel cells that would be christened "Tokyo tanks," the total fuel capacity enhanced by this addition being deemed sufficient for a strike at the Japanese capital—but one-way only!

Overall losses among the total force unloading on St. Nazaire's lock gates and other support units (eight) was around 5% of the158 effective sorties. Ditching any aircraft, let alone a multi-engine bomber such as the B-17, was ever an unpredictable action that all too often resulted in the partial or total loss of all on board. On this day the three latest such incidents within the VIII BC all involved the 95th BG. First, 42-3267/BG: A, flown by Lt. W Thomas, was eased into the sea with all ten crewmembers surviving the ordeal, although one received unspecified injuries. Then, Lt. R Smith's 42-30284/BG: B delivered its occupants alive for later pick-up by ASR launch before sliding under the waves. Lt. R "Spook" Bender had loaned his nickname to the latest B-17 to bear this title, 42-30286/ET: M Spook IV. The ten-man crew was added to by Capt. Berryman's (Observer) presence; once again, the pilots succeeded in bringing off a successful ditching. It was simply amazing that a 100% survival rate had been achieved, although the following 6 September an even more astounding success rate for the overall VIII BC force would occur when no less than thirteen bombers came down in the English Channel with fatalities limited to three out of 130.

There was an ironic slant to the ditching action forced upon Lts. Thomas and Smith, in that these would probably not have been necessary had the relevant "topping-up" of the fuel tanks been made prior to take-off thanks to the extreme duration of the mission. Although one of Lt. Thomas' crew confirmed this current omission to an individual who had driven up in a Jeep while the airmen were standing by the bomber and had raised the matter, the order was then given that take-off could not be delayed, and that sufficient fuel was on hand anyway! Furthermore, it was as well that the Thomas crew were able to wrench one of the dinghies free from its hatch in the bare minute or so between ditching and the B-17 sinking, while the Channel waters proved to be relatively warm, otherwise a needless tragedy might well have ensued.

Mixed Fortunes for July

The second half of 1943 commenced with VIII BC authorities in a mood of quiet optimism regarding the prospects for its Bombing Campaign in striking at German industry at a bearable cost in bombers and crews. After an initial depressing five-month spell involving shallow penetration missions with poor bombing returns, the Command had then begun to reach into the Nazis' heartland, albeit with a staccato pace of operations that still threw up a majority of targets outside Germany. Now, the accelerated build-up of strength commenced around April/May had resulted in no less than thirteen Groups being currently on hand, of which four were assigned to the 4th BW. However, the majority of the month's operations would be recorded during the final eight days along with its ledger of positive and negative statistics.

Further structural changes within the 4th BW had occurred during June. The 385th, 100th, and 388th BGs had been assigned to the 401st, 402nd, and 403rd PCBWs, thereby linking up with the 94th, 95th, and 96th BGs respectively. Three months later (13 September) the creation of the CBW concept of three Groups would see the 401st, 402nd, and 403rd transformed into the 4th, 13th, and 45th CBWs.

Independence Day was the apt inauguration date for July's run of ten completed missions, with three assigned Primaries on French soil, of which lock-gates at La Pallice, on the Biscay coast north of Bordeaux, went to the 4th BW. The bulk of the 83 crews dispatched completed their bomb runs at the minimal cost of one B-17; unfortunately, it was the 100th BG who paid this cost. With two engines out during the bomb-run, Lt. Pearson elected to jettison his load and head southwards, probably with a view to making a run into neutral Spain. However, fighters promptly latched onto the isolated 42-30051/EP: J and inflicted further terminal damage to a third engine. With an inability to even maintain flight the pilot rang the bail out; bell, whereupon all ten jumped clear; nine ended up as POWs, but Lt. J Dunbar (B) received civilian assistance and eventually made it back via Spain.

A further six days elapsed before a mission was briefed and launched, with widely dispersed airfields at Caen, Abbeville, and Le Bourget, spread across northern France, the focus for assault. The latter, situated at Paris, was scheduled to receive the full attention of the 4th BW, but none of the 101 crews reached there thanks to adverse weather conditions, which at this stage in the offensive at least forbade the bombing of visually obscured targets in Occupied Europe. The bad luck of the 100th BG continued, however; Lt. Duncan's 42-30052/LN: X **Judy D** was taken out by Fw190s near Dieppe, but the crew all bailed out before the aircraft crashed at St. Valery-en-Caux. Sgt. P. Reynolds (WG) managed to gain local support after several months in captivity; where he was held and how he escaped have never been divulged. However, he was destined to continue remaining in "captivity"—albeit in a positive sense—for nearly one year in the villages of Fontaine-le-Dun and Lonqueville before the area was liberated by British Army units. Reynold's natural frustration at being physically confined over this prolonged period often led to almost violent mood swings, and on one occasion almost compelled him to clear out and surrender rather than continue in physical and verbal isolation!

On return to Rougham, S/Sgt. J Jones, having been discovered unconscious during the mission, was hastily placed into an ambulance and taken to a hospital, but he died shortly after admission. He had become the latest victim of that insidious killer anoxia, thanks to his oxygen mask having become disconnected, and was a sadly regular example of this particular fate destined to affect a number of combat crewmembers during the course of the bombing campaign. The B-17 in question, 42-3287/GL: O **Sugar Puss**, was being flown by Lt. F Colby, who at 42 years was way over the maximum age for combat flying, but who completed his combat tour late in 1943!

Another national celebration date, in this instance Bastille Day (14 July), which commemorated the beginning of the French Revolution, appropriately involved VIII BC in operations over that country. Three airfields were again selected, with Le Bourget assigned to the 4th BW. On this occasion the disappointment of the previous mission was balanced by a successful thrust from three of the four Groups, albeit an expensive one for the 94th BG, who bore all four losses.

Lt. Kee Harrison had brought his B-17 back on a solo run from Huels on 22 June, but today his luck was partially but not totally about to run out. A fighter assault on 42-3190/QE: W **Nip N' Tuck** that caused damage to two engines and set the area behind the pilots on fire from punctured oxygen bottles caused it to lag and fall behind. When the inevitable "unfriendly escort" then closed in behind, Harrison dived for a still-distant cloud layer. This effort proved in vain, but when the pilot called for a bale out the Engineer was unable to respond thanks to his parachute pack having been consumed in the fire, so a crash landing was elected. The ailing bomber was finally brought down successfully in a small tree lined field near Evreux, and Harrison had the subsequent luck along with two others of evading capture and regaining British shores.

Lt. Watts and five of his crew on 42-3071/QE: enjoyed the same benevolent fate when the eight surviving personnel also bailed out of 42-3071/QE: near Evreux. Yet another 331st BS machine to be brought down around the same area was 42-30243/QE: Z2 **Good Time Cholley II** in the hands of Capt.W. Frank. For the third time an entire crew that included Maj. Saltsman (331st BS CO, POW) parachuted safely, of which two joined their colleagues in evading capture. The particular martyrdom of the 331st BS was completed by the cruel demise of 42-3331/QE: Z, piloted by Capt. E Purdy; this time round the reported mid-air collision with an Fw190 left just two of the eleven airmen alive, the extra man being Capt. Jefferson (Photographer).

17 July

It was back to "Big League" operations on the 17th with Hamburg and Hannover on the Briefing maps, the former location going to the 4th BW. By now the Wing's strength had been doubled to six Groups with the addition of the 385th and 388th BGS stationed at Great Ashfield and Knettishall, respectively. These "freshman" outfits were to head for Amsterdam and its Fokker aircraft plant for their operational "blooding"; the relatively short-range thrust would be under sound escort cover and act as a diversion for the two main forces. In the event barely half of the 42 crews taking off gained mission credit, of which only five came from the 385th BG. Worse still was the fact that bomb loads landed on surrounding housing and caused some 150 deaths—a propaganda coup for the Nazis.

An even smaller percentage of the main force was restricted to seeking out targets of opportunity. This was due to adverse weather conditions en route that forced a "recall" to be issued. Single crews were culled from both Wings, with the 94th BG losing 42-3219/TS: N **Dear Mom** as the group was heading back near Helgoland. Two engines were smoking as the B-17 commenced a gliding action before being immersed in the clouds. The names of Lt. R Powledge and nine of his crew ended up on a U.S. military cemetery "Wall of the Missing" in Holland, all having been claimed by the ever remorseless North Sea.

A 96th BG crew were very fortunate to return after a life raft was blown out of its compartment by gunfire and tangled with a stabilizer on 42-3275/MZ: Q **Sack Time**. Lt. Shelton's B-17 nosed upwards before falling into a steep descent that was only arrested fully 15,000 ft below. The navigator was seen by the co-pilot to appear and disappear from view in the astrodome; the latter's observation on this was "It was like a funny movie – first you saw him, then you didn't." In fact, Lt. Hocklin (N) was only just prevented from exiting the nose hatch by Sgt. Christen (Eng.) after normal flight was resumed. The centrifugal forces applied as the precipitate plunge was arrested were such that the bomb shackles with their load tore loose, along with the bomb-bay doors; several crewmembers had been badly bruised amid the welter of equipment being hurled around. Sgt. Miles attempted to shoot the offending dinghy off without success as the bomber staggered homewards. Then, as the airfield loomed up the pilot informed the crew that the landing would be at a hazardously high speed since to reduce power to a normal approach pace could easily stall out the aircraft. His offer for all to bail out was rejected with the words "Hell no, Lieutenant, you pulled us this far, we'll go in with you!" Fortunately the bomber landed safely, although a final potential crisis arose as the wheels made contact with the runway. No. 2 engine's propeller flew off and slashed into the nose compartment. Lt. Hocklin's good fortune continued, since he had moved up into the cockpit. As he later stated "Boy, I would have hated to have come through the flight, only to be conked by a prop!" (The incident was included in *Target Germany*, the official account of the VIII BC's first year of operations, although the B-17 was credited with the name **Short Stride** rather than **Sack Time**.)

A B-17 needed every foot of runway to get safely aloft when fully laden. It is likely this group of 385th BG bombers are on the main runway that extends 6,000 ft., compared to the 4500/4680 ft of the subsidiary runways, since the aircraft in the foreground has already advanced several hundred precious feet along its length.

Norma J (42-30223/FC: S) has its star-and-bar marking "dulled down," as do the two B-17s in the right background. Exactly five months after assignment to the 390th BG, on 11 July the B17F fought its last battle on the Emden mission when only two on Lt. G Ryon's (KIA) crew survived their bomber's loss as POWs.

"Blitz Week" Beckons

The weather patterns over Western Europe had so far proved to be a major stumbling block in either achieving access to targets or finding them visually open to assault. What was required as a partial solution, at least, was a prolonged spell of clear weather that usually occurred with the advent of a high pressure system. This very desirable condition was accurately forecast as the 24th loomed up; from then until the month's end a series of five missions would be dispatched deep into western Germany, along with an inaugural example that would be directed at Norway.

Adverse weather over England created a prime problem in attempting a safe and prompt Group and Wing assembly. The RAF possessed *Splasher* beacons whose use was made available to VIII BC in May. These medium frequency units had three (later expanded to four) transmitters operating on different frequencies but pulsing the same call-sign; this was a deceptive measure to ensure the Germans never confirmed which beacons were in current operation, and therefore could not attempt to jam or otherwise divert the signals. The value of these electronic guides was amply demonstrated at the onset of "Blitz Week." Individual units were instructed to make assembly on an assigned *Splasher* after breaking out of the persistent but rather shallow overcast. Wing Assembly was then effected by groups utilizing a line of three *Splashers*, and the entire force came together perfectly.

The twin targets selected in Norway were the newly-constructed aluminum plant at Heroya in the extreme south of the country and the ports of Bergen and Trondheim. By now all B-17s in the 4th BW bore "Tokyo tanks" that provided the necessary extended range to reach their more northerly situated targets. The former source was devastated by the 1st BW, but only the 95th and 100th BGs struck their Primary, since Bergen proved to be cloud-covered and forced all four assigned Groups to haul their loads back home. Lt. C. Biddick, in 42-30184/XR: Z **Muggs**, diverted towards Scotland and finally brought off a safe crash landing at RAF Fraserburgh, on the Moray coast. Sadly, the pilot's lease on life was to run out just 24 days later.

One of the two danger-filled stages in operating an aircraft is deemed to be during take-off and the other when landing. Capt. R Knox was returning to Thorpe Abbotts from the Strategic Air Depot (SAD) at Burtonwood when he lost control of B17E/41-9132. The engines were cut, and the bomber described a 270 degree arc that ended with the left main landing gear being torn off. None of the nine airmen was injured, but Knox was censured for the incident. Twenty-four days later Knox would be killed during the same Regensburg mission that would claim Lt. Biddick. He and his crew's mal-action on that occasion would (wrongly, as it transpired) be held responsible for creating the still enduring myth that the 100th BG was then singled out for particular annihilation by the *Luftwaffe* right up to VE-Day.

This easy-paced and inexpensive start to what became known as Blitz Week was not sustained the next day by the 1st BW, at least as the crews battled through the heavy defenses guarding Hamburg. Elsewhere the full strength of the 4th BW assumed a more northerly course to Warnemuende, on the Baltic coast, with a simultaneous ETA over the target compared to the other sub-force.

However, heavy clouds at either Primary ensured that targets of opportunity, which included Kiel's shipyards, featured prominently in debriefing reports. Adding to this sense of frustration was the absence of single crews from four bases. The third mission for the 388th BG threw up its first MIA statistic. After bombing Rerik-West airfield the Group was out over the North Sea when 42-5907/M **Wing and a Prayer**, with Lt. Fuller in charge, dropped away to what transpired as a failed ditching for all on board.

A more successful ditching involved 42-30206/GL: **Happy Daze**; Lt. J Keelan managed to get his B-17 into the sea some 30 miles distant from the Danish coast. The nine survivors spent the next 18 to 24 hours floating in their dinghies, and the pilot later recalled:

> "The wing swelled up like a balloon and burst into flames after the fighters hit us. We went into a dive but I didn't give the bail out order because I thought I could pull out. I regained control very low down in time to ditch. The landing was not much worse than on a runway, but the ball turret was knocked up to break the ship in two; two men escaped via the radio room hatch, the others walked out through the split but had barely time to inflate the rafts before the B-17 sunk.

We tied the dinghies together and started worrying that we were well away from home and close to German soil with the danger of being captured. That night we had a grandstand view of Kiel burning, as well as watching the RAF "Blockbusters" striking along the German coast and the flak coming up.

Next day we were spotted by an RAF plane that dropped three dinghies and hovered in a protective role against a distant Ju88. He was joined by two more RAF closely followed by three B-17s—it looked like the combined Allied air force above us. One RAF plane parachuted down a boat that was a sight to see as it settled down right beside us. On opening it up we found sleeping bags, food, water, gasoline, and operating directions. I had an idea I might get the boys to head for New York...."

Another 24 hours elapsed before the westward-bound vessel made contact first with some fishing boats, and then with an ASR launch. This crew had enjoyed an enhanced degree of luck with the ditching itself, since the ball-turret's dislodgement had not created a more violent separation of the fuselage sections; otherwise, some or all of the surviving crew might not have gotten clear. The comment on the RAF bombing effort raises the issue of the actual target. Hamburg was receiving its second massive battering from RAF Bomber Command that was destined to culminate in a horrific firestorm on the 27/28th. Although certainly further distant from the dinghies' location than Kiel, Germany's second city would already have been casting up a fearful scenario of fires on the 25/26th that could be seen at a greater than normal distance thanks to the clear conditions.

Also ditched was 42-5862/LN: T **Duration plus Six**; this time round only Capt R Carey (P) and Lt. W Styles (CP) and two gunners ended up as POWs after initially being picked up by a Danish fishing boat. Finally, a 90% casualty rate affected the Horham crew of Lt. L Mauldin after flak struck home to throw 42-3277/ET: G into a lethal spinning motion that ended at Kiel-Gaarden.

Harder Times for the 4th BW

So far Blitz Week's casualty rate had been focused more upon the 1st BW units, but the Grim Reaper's scythe swung decisively in the opposite direction on the 26th. This time round parts of the 1st BW (the three Groups comprising the 102nd PCBW) were to combine with the 4th BW over a single target whose location was one of the furthest to date inside Germany's hinterland. Two rubber production plants—Nordhafen and Continental Gummiwerke —were respectively assigned. The other six 1st BW Groups were bound for Hamburg, and once again the geographically well-separated attacks were to go in simultaneously as a defense splitting measure.

Hannover lay around 100 miles east of the Rhine and was "deep in there" in terms of sustained counter-assault from fighters and flak. Although the overall force comprised nine Groups, only two-thirds arrived over Hannover. The 94th and 385th BG crews ended up bombing targets of opportunity at Wilhelmshaven and Wesermuende, while the Thorpe Abbotts airmen did not even progress this far, having attacked a convoy.

Marginally over 300 B-17s took off, of which two-thirds gained their crews mission credit. Hamburg's fearsome reputation was surprisingly allayed on this occasion, with only two crews MIA, although less than half of the 121 dispatched did gain the Primary. Elsewhere the picture was far less rosy, beginning with the thrust at Hannover.

The German defenses soon made their presence felt, cutting ever deeper into the bomber formations. In the case of the 4th BW the 403rd PCBW was fully present, but the 402nd was only represented by the 95th BG; the 100th BG had been designated the Wing Lead slot, but had failed to make the necessary rendezvous. (A Group history asserts that final PCBW Assembly was not to be made until the units were approaching the Frisian Islands. Weather conditions intervened with this strange variation in forming up the

The photographer has caught the moment of impending tragedy for some or all on board two B-17s that have just collided. The indistinct shape directly below the tail of the intact aircraft appears to be the severed rear section of the other bomber; the remainder of the airframe drooped into a dive that took all to their deaths.

overall force—normal procedure was to achieve this when still over England—and the 100th finally headed back.)

It is not clear what overall formation was adopted by the other groups, but whatever measure was adopted did not prevent two of them from being adversely affected. In the case of the 95th BG all four of the MIA B-17s appeared to have survived the inward leg intact until target approach. The first to go down was 42-3264/OE: N, which lost all power in Nos. 1 and 2 engines thanks to flak. Lt. S Foutz's aircraft fell away under seeming control and did sustain a homeward course until it came down off the mouth of the river Weser to leave no survivors. Around the same time 42-3298/QW: Q dropped out with two engines ablaze; the bomber remained airborne over a much shorter distance with Dehsen, less than 20 miles southwest of Hannover, as the reported crash site; Lt. L Massey (P), who was shot while attempting to avoid capture, was one of two fatalities. This region was also where 42-30304/BG: B descended to leave Lts. Quirk (P) and Cisar (CP) dead along with four others. The last Group casualty involved 42-5893/ET: F, whose further progress following heavy damage from flak and fighters was also relatively brief. Dorrieloh, between Hannover and Diepholz, was where it crashed after being abandoned; nine of Lt. Robichuad's crew ended up as POWs, but T/Sgt. H Smith (ROG) later died from his wounds.

The spectre of regular or severe bomber and crew losses had so far not affected the 388th BG, which was flying its fourth mission, but Hannover brought about the first brutal awakening regarding this operational issue. Five B-17s and 16 airmen killed out of the fifty remaining absent from Knettishall was to be the final count. Two of the incidents occurred on approach to or over the target. First, Lt. Denton's 42-30225/J **Mister Yank** absorbed two serious flak strikes and crashed on Vechta airfield, killing Denton and five other crewmembers. Lt. Horn (POW) appeared to have steered his 42-30224/G off the bomb run despite a burning engine, but the bomber was then assailed by fighters and, after exploding, found its last resting place at Deckbergen, west of Hameln; three crewmembers died.

The formations rallied before assuming a northwest course with the intention of linking up with the Hamburg force to present a united front to their attackers. The 388th BG had skirted Bremen and Oldenburg before one more bomber was culled by the fighters, this being Lt. A Bobbitt's 42-30198/R. Half the crew were killed before their bomber impacted near Holtland, in Ostfriedland. The North Sea claimed one of the two other MIA bombers; 42-30208/U was clear of the coast by Lts. Porter and E Thompson before ditching and being picked up by ASR launch, a happy outcome for all ten. There were mixed results for Lt. B Gunn's crew in 42-30189/U **La Chiquita** after the bomber finally succumbed to fighter attacks to come down at Kleinheide, north of Emden. Three airmen descended into the sea with two being plucked out alive, and one of the remaining seven died several weeks later from his head injury.

The 96th BG element of the 403 PCBW contributed a single MIA B-17. As the formations were heading inward near Oldenburg 42-3281/AW: **Mary R** lost half its power due to fighter-inflicted damage, but still managed to hold position to complete the bomb run. Lts. F Spino and Middaugh then kept their charge on a homeward course for several minutes before the situation deteriorated enough for a bail out; to be ordered. All ten drifted down into captivity while the B-17 finally piled into the ground near Eindorf, roughly midway between Hannover and Bremen. To the ten 4th BW losses over Hannover was added six from the 1st BW.

The 401st PCBW did not escape the defenders' lethal intentions either, with both groups losing three crews apiece while seeking targets of opportunity. Ten of the thirty airmen from the 94th BG did not survive, nine of whom came from Lt. W Alsop's 42-3280/TS: M **Cherokee Maid**. The bomber went down into the sea north of the target area to leave just Lt. Kreischer (CP) alive, and that after several hours immersed in the water or afloat in a dinghy. In direct contrast, nine on board 42-30174/GL: successfully abandoned their battered bomber, leaving it to come down near Aurich, west of the target. The second group ditching in 24 hours proved successful. This involved 42-30450 (Lt. T Smith), which had sustained flak damage to a degree that forced it to lag behind. Fighter attacks ensued as the coast was being left behind, but the decision to ditch not only came off, but ended up far enough distant from enemy territory for the crew to be fished out within an hour or so by a British ASR launch.

The furrowed brows and grim attention of these airmen is evident as a briefing session gets under way.All personal thoughts are subordinated to the need for cooperating with one's fellow-crewmembers and so balance up the odds of survival that during 1943 and into 1944 were set at 3 to 1 against completing a combat tour.

A far higher death rate—22 out of 31—was suffered by the 385th BG as it assaulted a separate target of opportunity (described as Wesermuende in the MACR but a nonexistent location on current German maps!). Nobody survived from F/O G Duncan's crew on 42-30281/E, which was reported to have exploded as it was settling down to be ditched. The other two bombers, 42-5895 (Lt. R Harris) and 42-30279 (Lt. W Daniel), succumbed well out over the North Sea. The former-named pilot called for a bail out;, and six of the eleven on board seem to have ridden their luck in being picked up by fortuitously-positioned German vessels—especially Lt. Mills (B), who was not located until the next day! Only three from the Daniels team enjoyed similar good fortune following their aircraft's violent disintegration in mid-air between Helgoland and the coast. (It was as well these incidents occurred in mid-summer, although immersion in the North Sea at any time of the year is a potentially lethal business.)

Oschersleben's Bloody Toll

The average number of bombers dispatched on the first three Blitz Week missions had been in excess of 300, and this figure was adhered to on the 28th. However, the number of effective sorties proved to be barely one-third of this total, and arose from the intervention of Mother Nature; just over half the overall force aborted due to adverse weather conditions. The 4th BW amassed 120 B-17s for its briefed target at Oschersleben, while the 1st BW headed for a strike at Kassel, due south of Hannover and possessing the Fiesler aircraft production plant. Oschersleben's FW fighter production plant was the Wing's assigned target, and this location was undoubtedly the farthest to date that the VIII BC had sent its bombers. An equally hot reception to the day before could be anticipated, and indeed would come to pass for the surely apprehensive bomber crews...

All six Groups were dispatched, but once again ill fortune or operational failure attended the efforts of the 100th BG, with none of the 21 crews attacking. On the other hand, the results attained by the remaining groups were to prove very patchy, since just under one quarter of the 99 bombers involved gained the target. Not only was this a poor return for the Wing, but a further 15 crews would be absent from the debriefing sessions, nearly half of which (seven) came from the 96th BG, while the 385th BG mourned the loss of four more B-17s.

The planned route for the Wing assumed an initial heading that took the formations north of the Frisian Islands before angling sharply southeastwards near Emden, on the mouth of the Weser. However, the build-up of cloud layers as the formations approached Northwest Germany's coastline soon began to have a deleterious effect, in that it forced further splits in the already badly dispersed bomber stream. This naturally caused a dangerous dilution of overall defensive firepower, although the prolonged distance to Oschersleben and absence of Allied escorts was in itself a promise

The 95th BG's **Patsy Ann III**, with the red surround to the fuselage insignia making it stand out, is divesting itself of its load of incendiary bombs. The B-17F was assigned to the 334BS in mid-June, but finally went down at Lingen along with half of Lt. W Buckley's (KIA) crew on 10 October 1943.

of the odds against a bearable casualty rate being raised. As it was, these odds were further lengthened when a good proportion of the crews aborted the mission even before crossing-in.

The *Luftwaffe* assaults upon the 403rd PCBW in general and the 96th BG in particular appear to have borne deadly fruit out over the North Sea, thereby increasing the risk to life and limb for the USAAF airmen even more than when operating over land. Lt. C Covert's 42-30394/QJ caught fire in the bomb-bay on the way in and, although the pilots ended up ditching, all on board were forced to float in their Mae Wests until picked up, due to the life rafts either failing to inflate, or more likely having been destroyed by fire; only six were still alive when a launch arrived.

Also seriously damaged on the way over was 42-30351/QJ **Alcohol Annie**, which was also set on fire, forcing Lt. E Wilcox to dive in a bid to douse the flames. Although successful in this endeavor, it availed the crew none as the bomber was headed back; further fighter attacks fatally crippled the straggler and a bail out; was made near Helgoland. (Five, all from the forward fuselage area, enjoyed the best fate in later being picked up by ASR launch; three had mixed blessings, in that after being cast adrift for six days in a dinghy dropped by another B-17 they too were picked up—but by the enemy—while the other two perished.)

A particularly cruel twist of events cost the lives of four of Lt. W Nance's crew on 42-30355/AW: **Dallas Rebel**. Once again, a fighter attack set the bomb-bay area alight and knocked out the intercom. The five airmen in the rear had no definite knowledge of whether the bomber was under control, and four promptly bailed out to die from drowning or exposure after the pilots had levelled out from their attempt to blow out the fire. Had they remained on board they would have probably survived the ditching that left the other six able to scramble out into the dinghies, from which they were "rescued" by a *Luftwaffe* seaplane. (Lts. N Gorse (CP) and J Hudson (N) had already survived the loss of Lt. Rogers' B-17 during the Group's inaugural mission on 13 May.)

The region around the island of Helgoland also proved lethal for all but two on 42-3326/MZ: **Moore Fidite** (Lt H Moore, KIA), as was the case for 42-30141/AW: **Liberty Bell** (Capt. M Fulton, KIA); in the latter instance an eight-hour immersion for Lt. L Wolford (B) before a *Luftwaffe* seaplane landed and got him out left him as the severely physically exposed sole survivor out of eleven on board the group's Lead B-17. Fortune favored all on 42-3345/QJ: **Paper Doll** (Lt. E Deshotels) when a ditching near Ijmuiden went off smoothly. The final loss occurred almost simultaneously with the Lt. Deshotels incident affecting 42-30401/BX: (Lt. Hettrick), which was abandoned over the sea, a last desperate bid for life that failed for the entire crew.

The inward route appears to have been the costly leg for the Snetterton Heath Group, a supposition strengthened by the fact that only five crews out of 21 were to be credited with bombing Oschersleben. The other PCBW unit fared much better in not only gaining the target with nine out of 14, but returning to Knettishall just one B17 light. The third mission for Lt. R Swanson and crew concluded with their taking to their parachutes between Osnabrueck and Hannover as 42-30216/S **Johnnie** headed inexorably towards German soil.

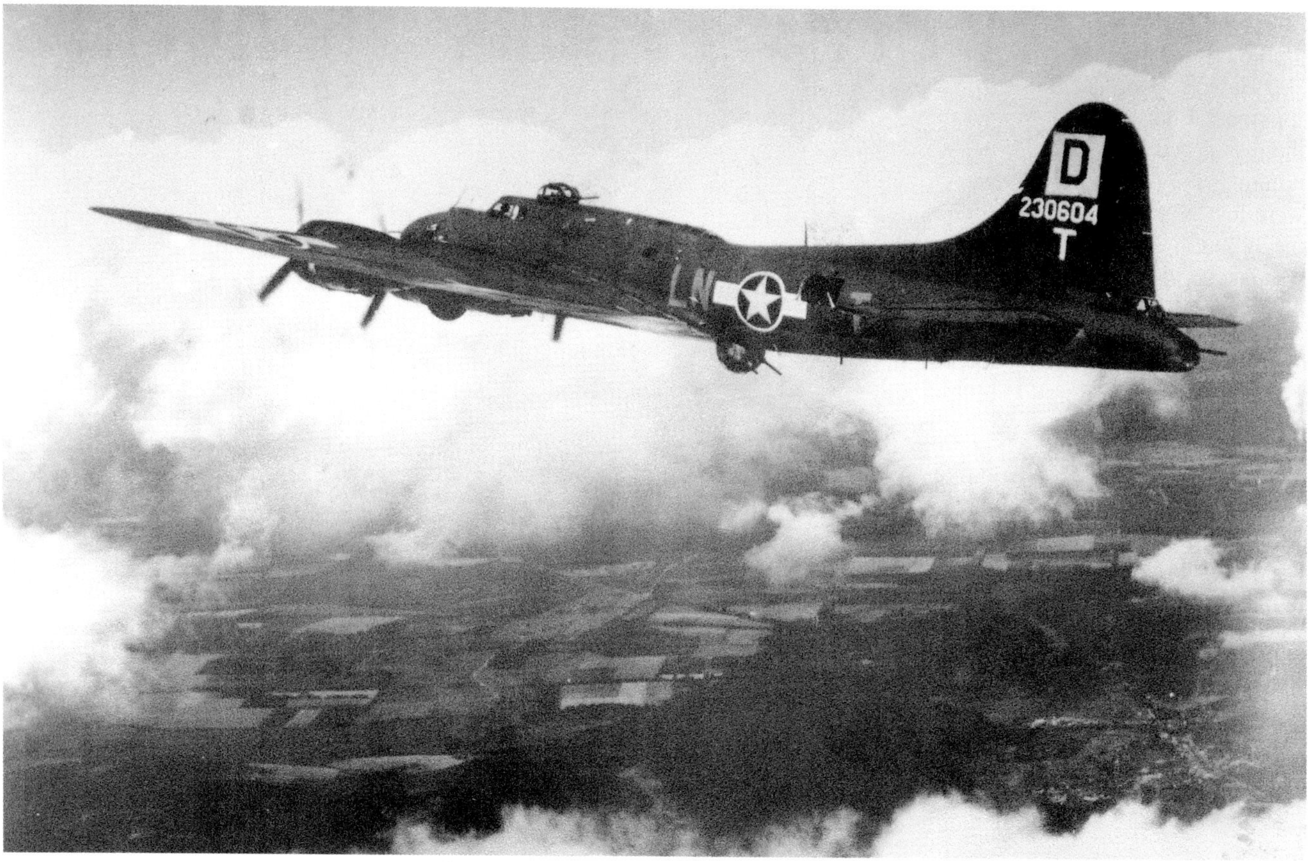

The dulled-down codes on **Badger Beauty V** are rather compromised by the glaring white segments on the fuselage and wing insignia. Just six weeks after joining the 100th BG the B-17F was crash landed near Caen, in France, after flak landed fatally crippling strikes; no less than four on Lt. Helstrom's crew did evade capture, however.

An even greater disparity in losses within the 401PCBW (four to nil) occurred, with the 385th BG adding to its Blitz Week woes in a manner that was largely self inflicted. Tight formation flying was the prime requirement for defense, but therein lay the reverse danger of collision. In this instance 42-30192/J (Lt. W Robbins, KIA) was reportedly struck by flak when close to Helgoland. The bomber careened out of control and impacted with 42-3316/F **Betty Boom** flown by Lt. W Storr. A third bomber, 42-30285/R **Roundtrip Ticket** (Lt. J Noel), became embroiled with one or both of the other two stricken B-17s and all three tumbled away to find graves in the sea. Out of thirty airmen just the two pilots on **Roundtrip Ticket** and two Enlisted men on the Robbins bomber managed to parachute to safety. (A barometric-fused bomb dropped by a fighter with the deliberate intention of bringing about such an occurrence has been quoted in several books as an alternate explanation for this disaster.) The fourth loss was on the way back; 42-30179/C **Murder Incorporated** was yet another victim of the fighters and exploded, its disintegrated airframe coming down northeast of Bielefeld. Lt. H Gurgel (P) died along with three others.

The 95th BG was the sole 402nd unit on hand and shed three of the twenty crews dispatched. Two crews succumbed on the inward route, being in 42-3282/BG: (Lt. J Rivers) and 42-5882/ET: D **Spook III** (Lt. F Regan). Not one of the latter crew survived their aircraft's demise over the sea, unlike all on the other machine, who bailed out, leaving their charge to crash near Hohenhausen. As the group was clearing the enemy coast on the way back 42-30150/QW: S **Exterminator** tragically lived up to its name in respect of Lt. F Hodges' team. It descended into the sea, which swallowed it up along with its hapless occupants.

The mission had been a double disaster. Not only had heavy losses been inflicted upon the 4th BW for the second successive day, but a meagre total of 28 crews, within which figure the 96th and 385th BGs had contributed only seven between them, landed their bomb loads upon the Primary, while eight 95th BG aircraft out of a further nine mistakenly bombed an alternate location at Alsleben, over 30 miles to the southeast—a very poor return indeed. The "Big League of Sky Fighting" was demanding an ever higher entrance fee for intruding upon and striking at Nazi Germany, and the immediate future for VIII BC was looking ominously negative...

Running down the Clock...

To the weary survivors, the briefings for yet another deep penetration target must have seen their spirits sink almost to zero. This time round the 4th BW, having been forced to abort on 25 July, would again endeavor to plaster the Heinkel factory located at Warnemuende, close to Rostock and at least

100 miles east of Kiel, which itself was to be targeted by the 1st BW. Both attacks were to go in at the same time.

Having been dealt heavy blows on the previous two missions, it must have been with great relief that over 80% of the dispatched force made a very solid strike and did so at a minimal cost of single crews from three groups. Two of these were lost in a similar but even more self inflicted manner to the 385th BG experience 24 hours previous. The 402nd PCBW was fast approaching the English coast on the way home when 42-30370/BX: **Little Ceasar** (Lt. C Walters) was reported to have split in two after being struck from below by Knettishall's 42-5908/X, piloted by Lt. W Curling. With less than 3,000 ft altitude below there was not much time for anybody to jump clear before the doomed B-17s fell into the sea; a total of 21 airmen were lost, of which the bodies of only two were subsequently recovered. (Lt. Quigley (B) on the Walters crew had been hospitalized with wounds suffered on the previous day's mission and did not learn the fate of his fellow airmen until reassigned in November.) Back in Denmark, Lt. N Palmer's 94th BG crew were already in custody after the pilots had crash landed 42-30146/TS: A **Down and Go** near Copenhagen.

The 403rd PCBW's ill luck continued next day when the final Blitz Week strike was launched. Kassel lay 100 miles east of the Ruehr and possessed a massive armor vehicle production plant, as well as today's Primary target, the Waldau Fiesler factory. The strain upon the VIII BC's technical and human resources was by now revealed, since only 186 B-17s, of which 67 were from the 4th BW, were deemed available for combat. Both Wings were dispatched to Kassel and each lost six bombers, three of which ditched.

Two of these were from the 95th and 96th BGs. The first was flown by Lt. R Jutzi, and had staggered back after suffering flak damage on the way in, at which stage six crewmembers had jumped from 42-30192/OE: Y over the Schelde estuary. A few miles short of the Channel coast the pilots laid their charge into the water and were then picked up by an RAF "Walrus" floatplane. One of Snetterton's two casualties was 42-30183/BX: **Dry Run II** (Lt. A Miracle), who also landed his flak and fighter-crippled charge onto the English coastal waters, from where all ten airmen were taken onto an ASR launch. A fellow squadron crew had come down near Antwerp thanks to the same lethal combination, but with fatal consequences for Lt. P Pelusi and four others on 42-30290 **Lucky Lady II**. Lt. Falk (CP) later recalled that Pelusi and Hurwitz (N) were already dead when he gave the order to abandon the blazing B-17; a huge explosion then occurred, and Falk came to in mid-air with his parachute already deployed.

Two of the 388th BG casualties did not even bomb. Lt. C Penn's 42-30210/W fell out to crash at Nettersheim, southwest of Koeln, the pilot being one of seven survivors. Then, as Kassel was looming up flak dealt a lethal blow to 42-30238/V **Classy Chassis**, although Lt. F Kelley got all his crew clear. The flak defenses around the eastern fringe of Antwerp handed out their latest deadly blow to 42-30208/R; Lier, southeast of the Belgian Capital was where the B-17 descended, thankfully without any of Lt. E Pickard's complement.

Comments

Blitz Week was over, and this was perhaps none too soon for the Command. No less than 82 MIA bombers, along with a further sixteen declared Category E had been permanently deleted from its strength, along with a good proportion of their crews. The bald statistics for each day's effort reveals the following. *(See chart below).*

It was a seeming irony that as the total of available bombers decreased on the last two days the percentage of effective sorties increased. The total of bombs and incendiaries released came to marginally over 2,500 tons for the 998 effective sorties dispatched during Blitz Week, indicating that most aircraft were loaded to their maximum capacity, which was a credit to the hard working armorers in particular.

Where the VIII BC authorities unconsciously diluted the overall effect of their attacks could be perceived in the number of targets selected and the weaponry in current use. On all six missions, the Command had struck at separate targets as opposed to combining its strength against a single source. This in turn reduced the total of the bomb loads involved, and therefore the degree of destruction visited upon each target. In addition, the ability of the manufacturing machinery to withstand even telling damage, let alone destruction from the American high explosive missiles—the largest of which to be mounted internally by the B-17 or B-24 was the M34 2,000-lb weapon—often resulted in their neither being permanently knocked out nor being held back from re-use for more than a matter of weeks at most. (The RAF bombs were much larger by comparison, but they were being dropped at night with a consequent huge loss in accurate targeting of industrial plants.)

Date	Crews Dispatched			Effective Sorties		Remarks
	Total	1st BW	4th BW	1st BW	4th BW	
24	309	167	109	167	41	84 x 4BW a/c 'aborted' Trondheim - weather
25	323	182	141	100	118	59 x 1BW a/c abandoned the mission.
26	303	121	182	96	54	49 x 4BW a/c attacked Targets of opportunity
28	302	182	120	58	37	155 x a/c 'aborted' or hit Targets of opportunity
29	249	168	81	139	54	48 x 1BW a/c hit Targets of opportunity
30	186	119	67	94	40	

3

Enter the Maestro

Curtis LeMay stands on the right as he addresses a gathering of Senior staff from various 3rd BD groups. By the time this picture was taken on the very Eve of D-Day he was a Brig. General heading the 3rd BD. Shortly afterwards he returned home prior to reassignment to the Pacific Theater of Operations.

The heavy damage to **Duchess'** left-inner wing-root and flap as well as a shorn-off stabilizer-end did not prevent the B-17F being restored to combat duty. Assigned on 15 May just after the 96th BG's operational debut, the B-17F finally met its end the following 11 April in the Baltic, along with all but one from Lt. W Young's (KIA) crew.

Col. LeMay (then 305th BG CO) is seen with Brig/Gen. "Possum" Hansell (third from right) and Lt. A Martini's crew following a mission in the late spring of 1943. Ironically, LeMay later replaced his former superior officer as CG of the 21st Bomber Command in the Pacific during January 1945.

Curtis Emerson LeMay was an airman who presented a taciturn, forbidding image to many of his subordinates. He was in fact an individual who commanded in the best manner possible by expecting no more of those under his charge than from himself. His heavy jawed facial appearance was further highlighted by a downward twist of his lips to one side. The anecdote going the rounds during WWII as to how this latter feature arose was as follows. During one mission the aircraft windshield was punctured by gunfire, and although the freezing slipstream then played upon LeMay's upper torso, he resolutely held his position and ended up with a permanently warped mouth. In fact, the truth was much more prosaic; LeMay discovered one day that he had contracted the medical condition known as Bell's palsy, whose outward effect was to pull down the mouth of the victim in this manner, although leaving him otherwise physically intact!

Although LeMay graduated from Ohio State University as a civil engineer at age 22, he elected to enter the military by applying for and being accepted as a flying cadet in 1928. One year later he won his wings from Kelly AFB, Texas, and commenced a career, which thirty-two years on would witness his assuming the highest post in the postwar USAF as its Chief of Staff.

From there he was assigned to the 27th Pursuit Sqdn based at Selfridge Field, Michigan, this being the start of seven years involvement with fighter aircraft. However, the young officer's field of expertise would prove to be not so much in piloting as navigation. This particular skill was not easy to attain at this stage in aviation development, since facilities such as radar, as well as meteorological equipment providing accurate weather pattern forecasting, were still many years in the future; even in the field of radio the facilities were relatively basic. Deduced reckoning using a combination of airspeed and wind speed, along with astro-navigation when clear weather conditions permitted was the name of the game, and a rather tricky game at that.

In 1937 he made the transition to multi-engine designs when his latest assignment was as Operations Officer for the 49th BS of the 2nd BG at Langley, VA. This was a unit that was pioneering the use of the first thirteen YB-17s to enter USAC service. At this time an agreement between the U.S. Army and Navy authorities was in force that restricted flights by their respective air components to 100 miles seaward and inland respectively. In the YB-17's case this limitation flew in the face of its potential as a strategic bomber, although there were also deeper and seemingly more valid financial and moral queries over proceeding on this course.

As regards the financial angle, the existence of the twin (and less expensive to produce) Douglas B-18 held back further materiel production of the Boeing bomber. An added objection to further long-range bomber development was the moral revulsion expressed in the USA amongst other western

A B-17F from Thorpe Abbotts is photographed "away from home" at Ridgewell (381st BG) alongside one of the group "hack" machines, a P-47. LN:W/42-30380 was far luckier than most of her contemporaries since she survived prolonged combat during the worst spell of VIIIBC operations and went home in June 1944.

A line of ambulances skirt the end of Great Ashfield's runway as a B-17F flares out for landing. The thin smoke trail directly above the vertical fin relates to a flare fired from this aircraft to indicate wounded personnel on board.

The co-pilot on 42-30246/DI: H **Spot Remover** waves from his window as the B-17F taxis in past the control tower. Both inboard engines are switched off in accordance with standard practice after landing off a flight. Aircraft arrived at Framlingham on 14 July 1943.

The atmospheric conditions at altitude played variable tricks as seen here. The 94th BG formation in the foreground is partially pulling condensation trails, whereas the higher-flying bombers in the background are free from such visual guides to the enemy. B-17F in foreground is believed to be 42-30427 **Lil' Operator** from the 410BS, which was finally lost in a midair collision while aborting the 3 March 1944 run to Berlin.

Democracies following the aerial assaults against civilian populations in China, Ethiopia, and Spain. Such actions only strengthened the isolationist stance the nation had retreated into following the holocaust of the 1914-1918 war, and the need to have long-range bombers appeared totally unnecessary.

The covert moves by those at the head of the USAAC to free itself completely from the grasp of their Army "controllers" and ultimately forge an independent U.S. Air Force was primarily dependent upon proving the bomber as a strategic as opposed to a tactical weapon, hence the concentration on expanding YB-17 operations. With this in mind Col. Olds (2nd BG CO) ensured that his crews were the best available for current and, in a number of instances, future command functions; LeMay fell firmly into this bracket, with an emphasis placed upon long-range navigation in his case.

In May 1938 the 100 mile seaward restriction was even more vigorously applied in light of a "stunt flight" made by the 2nd BG—at least in U.S. Navy circles. The Italian liner *Rex* was making its westward voyage to New York when, in what was a pre-planned action, it was intercepted by three Group bombers when still over 700 miles distant. Not only was LeMay the Lead navigator that day, but he had also made a bet regarding the actual time when the interception would be effected; his ETA was only out by one minute!

His clear expertise as a navigator was to be further tested in the following three years prior to the entry of the USA into WWII. Two flights down to South American locations were made by the YB-17 aviators that established new records in time and distance flown; a third flight of nearly 3,000 miles over the Galapagos Islands by the prototype (and sole example) of the XB-15 was also made during mid-1940 with LeMay again navigating. Such acts were usually a sure-fire method of attracting positive publicity, whether within or without military circles.

At first sight this is just an indistinct, normal picture of a B-17 formation. Closer inspection of the single aircraft at the top right reveals a tragic outcome, however; the tail unit has just been excised by fighter gunfire or flak, and unless the crew promptly bail out they are likely to be entrapped by centrifugal forces and borne to their deaths.

A "Toonerville Trolley" goods locomotive belonging to the London and North Eastern Railway (LNER) hauls its goods wagon load along the London to Norwich line. Although much smaller compared to the American equivalent, these hardy engines could pull a very respectable weight of wagons or passenger coaches.

Two airmen are attending to the twin .5 machine guns mounted in the ball turret. The weapons were normally retained in position as regards the top, ball, and tail turrets, but were removed from the waist positions on the B-17 E and F variants that were not equipped with enclosed hatch frames in the air.

His initial venture into full command occurred in January 1941, when he organized the 7th BS that subsequently expanded into the 34th BG. Six months later he was seconded from Langley to what was somewhat of a covert duty, considering that the USA was still officially neutral. This involved the flying of B-24s into Africa by Ferrying Command, for whom he acted as command navigator; presumably these were for use by the RAF under Lend/Lease terms.

This latest duty concluded in October, and LeMay returned to the 34th BG to serve as Group Operations Officer. At this point in his career his rank for the time he had served (13 years) was no more than average for any serving officer in between the World Wars. Better times were beckoning, however, especially after Pearl Harbor. Four months after that cataclysmic event he became Air Executive of the recently formed 306th BG, and in July assumed full command of the 305th BG. Both Groups would link up in England to become components of what finally evolved into the 40th CBW.

Harsh Realities

With several months of training completed the "Can Do" ground personnel shipped out on the *Queen Mary* on 5 September and arrived at Grafton Underwood seven days later. The Air Echelon's arrival was several weeks later, the crews having undergone unspecified "advanced flight training" and received new B-17F models before heading out over the North Atlantic and assembling at their temporary English airfield of Grafton Underwood—soon to be dubbed "Grafton Undermud"—by around 27 October.

The late 1942 spell of operations in England must have been faced with a mood of frustration bordering on despair for the airmen who comprised VIII BC's initial cadre. The logistical trail, both in human and technical terms, was simply not on hand at this time, and much in the latter category had to be borrowed from the RAF. The pace of operations was extremely staccato, with the unpredictable European weather patterns playing as important a part in this undesirable scenario as the foregoing shortages.

In the air formation patterns were none too sound, especially from a defensive point of view. Then, even when the bombers gained their targets, there was sometimes a very poor bombing return for the effort expended.

Ever the thinker and therefore a sound innovator, LeMay soon decided to address these problems that were prime sticking points in carrying out effective missions on a regular scale. In one meeting with the then Col. Armstrong (future CO of the reportedly "hard luck" 306th BG) LeMay was advised never to have his crews fly in a straight course during the bomb run, otherwise the flak gunners would reap a rich reward. The undesirable corollary in taking this course of action was that bombing accuracy would be badly compromised, since the precise aiming procedure required from each Norden bombsight would also be compromised.

As regards formation flying, the crews were currently flying in compact six-aircraft Sqdn. formations consisting of two "Vee" flights; moreover, each sub-formation was greatly separated in lateral and longitudinal terms from the others. Worse still was the practice for each sub-flight to commence its bomb run from a different angle. While this arrangement

Right: Three combat crewmembers pose beneath the nose of **Old Puss** (42-30073/MZ: U), whose nose bears sixteen visible mission "bombs" and an equally impressive row of fighter "kills." The chances of this 96th BG B-17F or the three airmen surviving a combat tour around the autumn of 1943 were 3 to 1 against; the bomber survived until April 1944, when it was "written off" in a crash at East Wretham.

Below: The indistinct white strip on the nose indicates that this B-17F has already completed a run of missions. Lt. McCarter (2nd from left, standing) and crew would end up POWs from the Muenster run of 10 October 1943. By contrast, 42-30170/XR: G, variously named **Oh Nausea**, **Miss Carriage**, **Torchy II**, and **Pride of the Century** soldiered on until claimed in combat off the first full Berlin strike; Lt. C Montgomery (P) was the sole fatality.

Just Ag arrived at Knettishall on 3 July 1943 just ahead of some of the roughest missions flown by VIII BC, culminating in the disaster of Black Week in mid-October. Having come through unscathed, the B-17F was then "written off" thanks to a crash landing on 30 November. This early view shows the simple National marking and absence of Division insignia on the airframe.

Sequatchiee rolls along the runway at Framlingham, probably during a landing run, since the crewmember's head peering above the radio-room hatch bears no helmet. As DI: K the B-17F enjoyed just over one year's service. Then it was MIA over Dreux airfield in France on 22 June 1944 along with a single fatality among Lt. J Bonner's (POW) team.

The chalking of slogans, ranging from the patriotic to the frankly obscene, was regularly indulged in within the Command. Two officers have carried out the duty on several heavy-caliber bombs in Snetterton Heath's bomb dump.

permitted freedom of movement for manoeuvring as an anti-flak measure, it conversely laid the bombers wide open to serious attention from the *Luftwaffe*.

It was not long before LeMay advanced the proposal that would create the principle of *Group Integrity*. The need was to bring a formation close enough together to present a strong degree of defensive firepower against enemy fighters in a manner that still permitted an equally sound bomb pattern to be released over the target. However, the limitations on accurate bombing provided by individual sighting while also engaging in last-minute evasive action tended to militate against maintaining a consistently tight formation, as well as seriously affecting the degree of bombing accuracy.

The initial "flat" alignment of bombers within each "Vee" and Sqdn formation had to be altered, if only to permit the gunners better access to fighters approaching at level angles. Therefore, the sub-formations began to be "staggered" both in elevation and azimuth, which provided enhanced sighting and firing opportunities for the gunners. The "stagger" principle was further applied to each Sqdn in relation to the others within the Group formation, thus permitting a much tighter overall formation compared to what had been flown during the initial run of missions.

LeMay's solution to the indifferent bombing results was twofold. First, he suggested dispensing with individual sighting of a target. Instead, he advised that the best bombardiers be selected to fly in the Lead and Deputy Lead bombers. Their duty would be to sight for the remaining bombers; all loads were to be released simultaneously on either seeing the Lead B-17 drop its load or acting on the flares released simultaneously by the Lead bomber. (A close friend of the author, Lt. DeBolt, acknowledged that the art of Lead Bombardier was to many of his contemporaries a matter that could be easily achieved by most bombardiers. This was far from the truth, as only time would tell. In fact, Darrell suggested that his skill was due to his sitting by his bombsight "fat, dumb, and happy"—a world

An early view of the 385th BG shows the transition from a plain star insignia on 42-30263 to added bars on the B-17F at top right, while the group letter is enclosed in a dulled-down square. The nearest bomber, which was finally "written off" after a crash landing on 30 October, seems to bear flame dampers on the outer engines.

away from his true ability to direct his group's bomb loads directly onto the target, as a specific event on 11 January 1944 would confirm.)

The other prime problem with achieving better bombing accuracy—weaving on the bomb run—was to be countered by the groups flying a straight course from the IP to the target. The inevitable complaint was raised that this undeviating action would provide the flak gunners with an enhanced chance to wreak havoc among the formations. In his methodical way, LeMay calculated the odds against surviving a bomb run while flying in this revised manner as being little worse than was likely to occur when operating the current wayward style. He further reasoned that the flak gunners would be able to fire off less rounds since the formations would be out of range that much quicker. There was really no option in truth to adopting LeMay's scheme if targets were to be struck in the best possible manner.

In late 1942 the war was in a dangerous state of flux for both major adversaries. The Axis powers were relying on a combination of dividing the unnatural alliance between Soviet Russia and the West and also attempting, with a frightening degree of success, to sever the vital North Atlantic convoy

Two mechanics from the 388th BG are snapped while working on the No. 1 engine of a B-17F that bears more than twenty mission "bombs." The bomber is believed to bear the name **Quarterback**, which as 42-30212 flew with the 562BS before being retired from normal combat operations for inclusion in the Aphrodite Project. On 6 August 1944 she was dispatched against a V-weapon site at Watten, in northern France.

lifeline; should the latter battle fail then any hopes for an invasion of Western Europe would disappear, and with it any prospect of final success for the Allied cause.

LeMay addressed every possible avenue with a view to improving the efficiency of, and with it the survival prospects for his crews. A simple issue concerned the readiness of the flexible gunners in particular to have their machine guns unlimbered and ready for use as early as take-off. His valid point was that there was no guarantee of immunity from counter-assault at any stage of a mission since the *Luftwaffe* was as capable of carrying out intruder operations over Britain as the Allied Air Forces did over the Continent. Any airman found disobeying the stricture was accordingly liable to face a court martial. During his time at Chelveston he also found he had to disabuse some gunners from a natural tendency to smother their guns in oil; although a fine protective on the ground, the natural propensity for this substance to freeze up at altitude would render the weapon useless.

An article of faith to be challenged at a pilot's peril was to break out of formation over enemy territory when the bomber was not actually damaged, regardless of the circumstances dictating such an act. During the Regensburg mission's progress in the region of Sardinia, the then General noticed one B-17 easing away to the right and steadily gaining distance on the main formation. This was Lt. H Nagorka's **Iza Angel** from the 388th BG, on board which Lt. Tierney (N) had suffered a bullet wound that had almost severed one wrist. His pilot had radioed ahead regarding Tierney's condition in the hope that medical attention that might prevent amputation could be immediately on hand when he landed. In LeMay's view, however, Nagorka had violated "group integrity," and therefore reduced the formation's overall defensive firepower. A crippled bomber—or in this case the parlous medical state of a crewmember—was an expendable issue; what was *never* expendable was a pilot's obligation to his group. LeMay's terse response to the incident was simple, "If I had found out who he was he would no longer have been an airplane commander!" (Unfortunately, all of his pilot's accelerated efforts were of no avail, since Tierney lost his hand).

In July 1943, following promotion to Brig./General, LeMay transferred from Chelveston to assume command of the 4th BW with his HQ at Elveden Hall, Suffolk. Here he held the post for a full calendar year before handing over to Earle Partridge and heading back to the United States. As it was, his overseas service in WWII was far from over, because a further rank increase to Maj./General saw him posted to India to take over the 20th Bomber Command, where the initial missions with the B-29 were casting up serious operational problems.

The 21st Bomber Command had commenced operations from the Mariana Island chain in late 1944, but the bombing results continued to yield a marginal degree of success when flying at the normal briefed altitudes. LeMay had been reassigned to the Command in January 1945, and soon began to work upon a more viable form of assault, one that was not even guaranteed to receive approval from "Hap" Arnold in Washington, and was destined to be met by a mix of anger and horror from his crews.

The principal change related to the switch from daylight attacks to one delivered by night. He had assessed the AA and night fighter defensive chain covering Japan's major cities as far less organized in numbers and tactics compared to their German ally. Therefore, the bombers were to be stripped of armament and the bomb loads increased; moreover, the use of high explosives was to give way to incendiaries. But the crucial factor lay in the bombing altitude, which was reduced to less than 10,000 ft compared to the current average of around 30,000 ft—surely a recipe for wholesale losses, when revealed to the crews briefed for the inaugural strike upon Tokyo on 9/10 March...

As matters transpired, the mission proceeded in sound order with PFF aircraft laying a huge cruxiform flare pattern

Lt. Rodney Snow was an "original" pilot at Horham whose regular B-17 was **Herky Jerk II**. On the Muenster mission of 10 October 1943 Snow was forced to drop out over western Holland; his luck in evading Luftwaffe attention was reinforced over England; while penetrating the minimal visibility then present, he narrowly missed a church steeple while on his landing approach. Snow successfully came through his combat tour.

Curtis LeMay, by now a Brig/Gen, is seen third from the right with Lt/Gen. Doolittle (far left) during an inspection tour of Thorpe Abbotts. Set out in front of LeMay is his pipe that was his social indulgence and an object that he was rarely seen without.

Lt. Owen "Cowboy" Roane suffered a collapsed left landing gear while landing off a practice mission on 2 August 1943. The Vega-production B-17F (42-5861/XR: J **Laden Maiden**) was restored to combat status and lasted until 30 December; then, Lt. Leininger and seven of his crew died when the bomber was downed by fighters at Liry, in France.

over the city upon which the main force of nearly 300 deposited its mass of incendiaries for the loss of fourteen bombers. The main danger came not from the defenders, but from the tremendous thermal effect cast up by the blazing target that threw aircraft almost (or perhaps in some instances) out of control. Here was the future pattern for Command operations that persisted up to VJ-Day. (Ever the realist, LeMay was reputed postwar to have commented upon his plan, "If we had lost the War, then I would probably have been put on trial as a War criminal.") In truth, the loss of life among the Japanese population that in some instances exceeded that borne by the Germans was a regrettable but almost inevitable aspect of the Total War scenario that dominated this 20th century conflict.)

4

Double-Strike Fortunes – Regensburg (17 August 1943)

The exhausted VIII BC survivors from Blitz Week could not have anticipated the prolonged pause from combat operations, however welcome, that set in during the first eleven days in August. There was no doubt that this time was necessary, and therefore well spent, in building up the Command's strength, although sufficient reserves appeared to be on hand to at least conduct some degree of active operations.

It was only on the 12th that the CQ's ever unwelcome call to wake up and get dressed for breakfast and briefing aroused the combat crews in the early hours. The VIII BC was ready to resume full-scale operations with a total force equal to that on hand before Blitz Week. All fifteen available groups were to be dispatched, and between them would field 310 B-17s. The strike was to be directed against targets in the extensive Ruehr industrial zone that had so far only been attacked on one occasion (22 June). However, the assigned locations remained free of the bombers' lethal intentions; an added damper lay in the fact that no less than 25 crews were added

This 390th BG crew rode their luck during the Regensburg mission. The shell strike on the right wing-tip not only left the aileron intact but also failed to set the "Tokyo tank" occupying the outer wing area on fire.

One of the B-17s that never made it through to Regensburg on 17 August 1943 was 42-30315/CC: S – **Battle Queen, Peg O' my Heart**, after Lt. Rapport diverted into Switzerland and landed at Utzendorf. The fuselage, bereft of wings, stabilizers, rudder, and center-fin, is being carefully hauled along a Swiss street for likely disposal at a smelting plant. Top turret guns still appear to be in position.

to the MIA total. It was the 1st BW that bore the bulk of these losses (23).

Targets of opportunity became the order of the day. In the case of the 4th BW its assigned target, an oil refinery at Wesseling, remained unscathed, and the university city of Bonn nearby was picked upon. In the case of the 100th BG, Lt. Crosby (N) recalled, "I realized where we were heading and yelled out 'Hey, we can't drop here – this is where Beethoven was born!'" Alas, in spite of this historically-based admonition the bombardiers went about their business, probably since the city was listed as an (undefined) secondary target!

The unfortunate 4th BW duo failing to return home belonged to the 95th BG. Capt. Hamilton's (KIA) 42-30194/OE: O **We Ain't Scared** turned back just before the IP, but was soon latched onto by fighters, whose fire shattered the cockpit area. Four further crewmembers were killed, and south of Lommel, Belgium, was where their bomber impacted. Two middle ranking officers had displaced the RWG and TG personnel, being Col. Jenkins (Wing HQ) and Lt/Col. Scott. The latter was on detachment from the States on a fact finding visit regarding aerial gunnery—he certainly gained immediate experience, but in the most unfortunate manner, since he was killed. (Maj. Cole (Group Operations), flying as co-pilot, would begin his eventually successful bid to get back to England.) **Piccadilly Commando** (42-30418/BG: L) had previously suffered fatal battle damage that saw its final demise near Monschau, south of Aachen; this time round all of Lt. Lemke's crew escaped unscathed but at the price of their freedom.

Unbeknownst to the majority of the airmen was a plan for a daring double-strike at German industry. The scheme had been hatched some several weeks previous, and in its final form would involve both BWs carrying out almost simultaneous assaults.

In the meantime, two missions were flown to French and Belgian targets. On the 15th, in an evening assault the 4th BW deployed its full strength against three airfields in northern France at a minimal cost of two aircraft. The 385th BG surrendered 42-30598/L to flak batteries around Dunkirk with none of Lt. E Stone's crew surviving their bomber's crash in the Channel. The other loss emphasized the inherent risks in flying tight formation. Near St. Omer, 42-30320 of the fledgling 390th BG pulled up and excised the entire tail section of its fellow-569BS aircraft 42-3306/CC: L **Phoenix**. The stricken

Lt. D Oakes' **High Life** (42-30080/EP: F) was another bomber forced to divert into Switzerland off the Regensburg mission. The 100th BG B-17F lies in the pasture where it was finally "bellied-in," leaving the crew to face a relatively relaxed future as internees.

B-17 fell into a vertical plunge; somehow Lt. W Lawrence and the four occupants up front not only survived, but it was only the pilot who ended up in captivity. The remaining five airmen went to their deaths in the truncated remains.

Next day three Groups dispatched 66 crews, all of whom bombed their Primaries at no cost in bombers or crewmembers. As the airmen landed back at their airfields off this "milk run" they had little or no inkling of the marathon flight awaiting them within the next 24 hours, nor the traumatic circumstances under which it would be conducted...

The "Anniversary" Plan

When the Casablanca Conference was held in January 1943, agreement was reached on the target priorities for the RAF and VIII Bomber Commands. Included in this grouping were the Nazis' aircraft and oil-production facilities, as well as their transportation network. As it was, a fair measure of attention was paid to combating the U-Boat threat to the Atlantic convoys by assaulting U-Boat pens up to the end of June. By the early summer it was quite clear that concentration on fighter production had to be accorded the top position on this list; otherwise there was a grave risk of the Daylight Bombing Offensive and its nocturnal partner being permanently placed on the back foot.

However, an immeasurably more humble item whose loss to the German

The first wave of the Regensburg force provided by the 45th CBW has laid a partially concentrated pattern of bombs on the Messerschmitt factory; the over-shoots have impacted with one end of the airfield surface and wiped out a number of completed Bf 109 airframes.

A post-mission reconnaissance picture of Regensburg provides outlines for the buildings, with evidence of strikes on most of the structures. Smoke arising from the initial bomb pattern obscured the target area for the succeeding CBWs, while many bombs have hit between the buildings. The factory, although suffering serious disruption to its overall production, was back to normal output levels within a month or so.

War effort could have an equally swinging effect was the ball bearing. Most machinery was dependent upon these for their efficient function. The Allied planners reasoned that if the major complex of factories located at Schweinfurt and manufacturing ball bearings could be eliminated there was a sound chance of much of the enemy's production potential—including that element involving fighters—literally "grinding to a halt." The presence of similar factories in Stuttgart, France, and Italy, as well as the Germans' ability to call upon supplies from Sweden and Switzerland, were counter aspects of the discussion that seem to have been discounted at this time. Nevertheless, a "double strike" scenario involving the VIII BC's B-17- equipped Wings was finally adopted and set in motion.

Schweinfurt's ball bearing plants would receive the attention of the 1st BW; shortly before this attack the 4th BW would be scheduled to bomb the Messerschmitt factory at Regenburg, lying to the southeast of the 1st BW's target. A key variant in this double strike lay in the route to be flown. Up to now, the entire VIII BC force had flown out of, and back to, its English bases. Now the 4th BW would not reverse course in common with its fellow Wing, but would head much further south to airfields in North Africa. In this way, coupled with the simultaneous nature of the attacks, there was a sound chance of creating a big irreconcilable split in the *Luftwaffe's* overall defensive effort...

This was the final variation of three sub-plans that had also involved the North African-based 9th USAAF, albeit only in the first and final example. Its B-24s were to have attacked the Messerschmitt plant at Wiener Neustadt, Austria, while the 4th BW assaulted the same Company's facility at Regensburg, Germany, before heading south to Africa; ironically, the 1st BW's participation was somewhat secondary, in that it would fly a diversionary mission to the Ruehr. Then it was mooted that both England-based BWs would fly a combined mission to Schweinfurt, supported by a small scale diversion to attack airfields at Lille, France, before heading back to their airfields. In the final plan, the B-17 Groups flying out of North Africa would strike at Istres, in southern France.

Mother Nature intervenes...

The fact that this daring and novel form of assault was now to go ahead on 17 August, exactly one year following the VIII BC's inception of its Campaign, was a pure coincidence in

This group of B-17Fs are only identified as 3rd BD aircraft by the white Division squares on the two aircraft at the top left of the picture. Although no group letter is shown, these bombers are reportedly from the 96th BG, which is traversing the formidable barrier of the Alps after attacking Regensburg. The right wing surface on the nearest aircraft has a "quilted" appearance.

timing. This day, over thirty-fold the minute figure dispatched to Rouen on 17 August 1942 (Twelve B-17s) would contest the skies over central Europe in a bid to land telling blows against twin industrial pillars sustaining the Nazis' war economy. The compression of time in carrying out the attacks to limit the effect of counter-assault was wholly dependent upon both Wings' ability to get airborne and head out in a single bomber stream. Adverse weather had regularly thrown a "spanner in the works" to cause delay or cancellation to a mission, and the early hours of 17 August proved no exception to this frustrating issue.

In place of clear visibility there descended overnight a fog pattern over the entire East Anglian region that still persisted after the personnel had attended briefing and gone out to their B-17s. The weathermen were confident that the fog would clear as the morning wore on. The operational limitation in awaiting this development before sending the bombers aloft affected the 4th BW, whose Groups would then arrive over North Africa after nightfall; there was a real risk of the crews, who had no definite knowledge of the Theater's geography, going astray and running out of fuel before getting safely down.

The Plan Unfolds...

After much pondering on what positive action to take, Gen. Anderson elected to allow the 4th BW to depart alone in order to reach its foreign airfields before nightfall. Gen. LeMay (CG, 4th BW) had reportedly been training his crews in the art of minimal visibility take-offs, and had probably expressed enough confidence in his personnel's ability to convince Anderson that he could give the go-ahead. In doing so, he must have been well aware that the Plan's intention to swamp the German defensive system was now seriously eroded.

The reactions of the crews when the target was announced ranged from stunned, apprehensive silence to pandemonium that lasted several minutes on one airfield. The novelty aspect of ranging over hundreds of miles to another Continent caught the imagination of some, but a more normal expressed reaction was the fear that fuel reserves would be dissipated before reaching their desert destination.

At Snetterton Heath (96th BG) the CO, Col. Old, was intent on participating, even though he must have been aware that his place was already allotted to Gen. LeMay. However, he professed ignorance of the fact and indeed remonstrated

The 94th BG element of the Regensburg force is closing in on the North African coastline. With steadily diminishing fuel reserves, the priority is to seek out the briefed airfields that are located in relatively featureless geographic terrain before the tanks run dry.

heatedly with his superior over the matter after the General's staff car arrived at the dispersal. The latter unsurprisingly won the argument; still furious but also undaunted, Col. Old joined another crew, only for the B-17 to abort the mission after losing an engine as the enemy coastline was looming up!

Visibility as the Cyclone motors coughed fitfully into life was still extremely minimal; at Snetterton Heath flashlights were used by ground crew to even get the lumbering bombers out of their dispersals and onto the perimeter track—a far from encouraging start for the pilots and their crews. The first aircraft lifted off from Framlingham (390th BG) at 0621 hours to be the first of 147 to roll along a runway and tentatively ascend at around 300 ft a minute up through the enveloping gloom. Amazingly, although one or two near misses were reported, there were no actual collisions; Group and Wing assembly duly progressed above the fog's upper base as the bombers emerged into blinding sunlight. It was nevertheless well over 2 ½ hours from mission start that the three PCBWs were in line, at the briefed altitude, and ready to cross out over the Norfolk coast.

Across the North Sea, the "signatures" of the B-17 formations would have long registered on German radar screens even if their ultimate course was still undetermined. Although the *Jagdwaffe's* current strength in fighters was sound, there were not enough on hand to cover the entire western approaches into central Europe. Diversionary tactics utilized by VIII BC had sometimes thrown the enemy pilots off the scent completely or succeeded on a scale sufficient to blunt their effect. Today's mission was destined to prove a disappointment for the Americans in this respect, although the absence of diversionary forces provided the Germans with a swifter than usual indication of the attacking body's approach route. III/ JG26, based at Schipol, were alerted, as was I/JG1 stationed at Deelen. The first to take off were the Fw190s of II/JG1 in concert with III/JG26's Bf109s; then I/JG1 would follow with the intention of being fed into the bomber stream further inland along with I/JG3 flying out of Moenchen Gladbach. In the meantime, III/JG1 at Leeuwarden would redeploy to Deelen, and III/JG3 would similarly do so from Muenster to Woensdrecht, the intention behind this being for these units to await the homeward flight of the bombers…

Battle Commences…

Landfall was made over Schowen Island, in southern Holland, by the 139 crews still in position and maintaining a southeasterly course to the target. The P-47s of the 353rd FG made the initial but hurried contact with the enemy when its pilots dispersed a group of Fw190s in a swiftly executed "bounce." Further to the south of the bomber stream, the two Woensdrecht-based *Gruppen* were biding their time as well as observing the spacing between the three PCBWs, which had widened noticeably between the second and third sub-force.

Lt. R Wolff's **Wolf Pack** (42-30061/LD: Q) sustained heavy damage, including a large gash in the vertical fin that made control difficult. In spite of this, the pilots successfully traversed the Alps as seen in the first picture. The second picture shows Wolff's charge on its sparse North African dispersal in a still unrepaired state. However, repairs were carried out that allowed the aircraft to return to Thorpe Abbotts to continue operations and ultimate return Stateside in June 1944.

Flying in the very rear were the 95th and 100th BGs, and it was to be their misfortune to suffer more than half of the final Wing loss figure.

As matters unfolded, it was the 94th BG that suffered the first MIA casualty as it flew High group in the 401st PCBW. The I/JG26 swoop was made through this unit and on into the ranks of the 95th BG, flying the same slot within its PCBW and now down to sixteen of the 21 briefed crews. Lt. B Nayowitz was positioned in the left rear of the High sqdn. When Ltn. Borris landed his gunfire squarely on the forward section of the B-17 all four officers and two Enlisted men were almost certainly killed by the fusillade, and the other four airmen were fortunate to get out after the tail section broke away and the truncated remains landed east of Diest, in Belgium; T/Sgt. McDonnell received permanently crippling injuries thanks to a bad landing in a tree.

Four further B-17s spread between the 385th BG and the trailing groups of the 402nd PCBW received degrees of damage during the ensuing battle over Belgium territory that in three cases was inflicted by flak, and finally impelled their pilots to turn back for England. **The Jolly Roger** (42-5886/D) had suffered severe strikes during the initial fighter lunge. The 385th BG bomber was banked out of formation southeast of Antwerp, but all too soon it was picked up and dispatched close to Woensdrecht airfield, Lt. P Sommers (P) being one of six fatalities. Around the same time Lt. J Sundberg's 42-30176/OE: P **Assassin**, which had departed its Horham formation soon after the Sommers-piloted aircraft had managed to get as far as a point northeast of Antwerp, it too was homed in upon by fighters from I/JG26, at which point all nine surviving crewmembers "hit the silk" from the burning airframe, of which four evaded capture.

To these two losses was added a 100th BG victim. This was **Alice from Dallas** (42-5867/LN: O) leading the High sqdn's second Element, which received a devastating burst, setting the right wing ablaze. The stricken B-17 veered right and described a full circle before attempting to regain the formation, but shortly after it dropped down and crashed east of Hasselt; of the eight survivors five, including Lt. Claytor (P), commenced the high road to ultimate freedom thanks to gaining access to the Belgian Resistance. The third flak victim further reduced the 95th BG's already diminished force. Lt. W Baker, in charge of 42-30274/BG: Q **Bay-Be**, reversed course on the Liege/Aachen stretch of the inward route, but any hope of landing back at Horham soon disappeared under a hail of cannon shells and bullets. All ten airmen safely evacuated before their aircraft smashed into the ground close to Turnhout.

False Lull

Although the 4th BW's travails were far from over at this point, the final tally of 24 MIA bombers would occur in a rather staccato manner, thanks partly in turn to a similar pattern of *Luftwaffe* intervention. Despite the presence of a goodly number of fighters, only one B-17 had been directly dispatched out of the force's ranks, with two others finished off as they straggled homewards alone. The USAAF fighter pilots had also played their part in inhibiting the full extent of *Jagdwaffe* attacks by interception and dispersal of their adversaries on several occasions. As the Belgian/German border was traversed near Eupen, a location that marked the maximum range for the P-47 escorts, there began a period of around 30 minutes extending over roughly 100 miles during which relatively few fighters intervened. The dispatch of I/JG1

The extended and wearying Regenburg mission is over for this 94th BG crew who are gathered round a truck. The sparse geographic conditions of North Africa form a backcloth to the airmen and 42-30453/TS: K – **Thunderbird**, as well as several other B-17s from the 4th BW. This bomber was subsequently MIA on 14 October with Lt. Davidson's (POW) crew.

Shack Bunny also occupies a temporary and barren airfield patch hundreds of miles distant from Great Ashfield; among the mix of Division airmen and local spectators is one of "Africa's own" - a camel. Almost two months later (20 October) the 531BS B-17F would lie wrecked near Namur, in Belgium, after mechanical failure caused Lt. Fryer to bail out his crew.

from Deelen had been initiated too late, while I/JG3 seemed to have made little effective contact despite their airfield at Moenchen Gladbach being quite close to the bombers' course and their having plenty of fuel reserves after intercepting the American force.

This welcome respite was abruptly ended as the Rhine loomed up south of Koblenz. Such a downturn occurred thanks to the unfortunate recent arrival in the region not of a standard, but rather an irregular unit, *Jagdgruppe* 50. The constant threat posed by the RAF's aerial "gadfly"—the Mosquito twin-engine multi-purpose design—had led to the recent creation of two *Jagdgruppen* (25 and 50), with a view to challenging its opponent's depredations over central Germany in general and Berlin in particular. The pilots were a mix of new and combat-experienced personnel led by Majors Ihlefeld and Graf based respectively outside Berlin and Erbenheim, near Wiesbaden. *Jagdgruppe* 50 occupied the latter airfield that was almost directly below the Regensburg force's approach route, and it was accordingly called into action. Also dispatched to this airfield were all other available single-engine fighters, such as those assigned to training or Factory Defense Flights, while two night-fighter units (I/NJG6 and NJG101) were also ordered to participate. What at first sight was a somewhat motley force with which to issue the latest challenge to the 4th BW's advance was nevertheless destined to hand out a stiff measure of punishment before finally falling behind. (Quite why the *Luftwaffe* had not made direct provision for combating USAAF incursions this deep into central/southern Germany is somewhat of a mystery. After all, the Germans had already been made aware of the B-17's ability to strike targets at Warnemuende and Kassel, both of which were of a distance from England that almost measured up to today's planned targets; in addition, this sector of the Nazi Empire possessed sufficient industrial output to place it in the same category as any other national zone vulnerable to attack.)

The Cull Intensifies

The 100th BG had so far lost one from its 21 participating B-17s, but matters took a distinct turn for the worse as the *Jagdgruppe* 50-led group of attackers, having gone aloft and reached the bombers' altitude, then swept into the attack. The *Luftwaffe*

B-17s from the 385th BG (left hand column) and 94th BG (right hand column) are parked in the straggling grass flanking a dirt taxiway that forms the bombers' temporary "home" in North Africa. Nearest Rougham aircraft is 42-3135/XM: K – **Larrupin' Lou**, which still lacks its Group letter A or individual letter on the fin.

A closer view of the 385th BG line-up picks out **Miss Nonalee II** with dulled-down bar-and-star insignia that also bears a red border. On 9 October, with Lt. Bell's crew on board, she suffered mechanical failure that culminated in a forced landing in Denmark.

pilots were fully aware of the absence of escorts, a factor that permitted them complete indulgence in making regular passes, especially from head-on, or "twelve o'clock high," as the bomber crews labelled the tactic. All too soon gaps began to appear in the ranks of the 402nd PCBW in particular.

Lt. D Hummel's 42-30311/LN: T was in the dreaded "tail-end Charley slot"—that is, No.6 in the Low squadron. A burst of fire caused the No. 2 propeller to go out of control and the bomber fell back. A second onslaught set the left wing Tokyo tank ablaze to seal the B-17's fate. The bail out; order was issued and, while Hummel and five others appeared to have jumped out, S/Sgt. Williams (BT), along with three other Enlisted men gathered in the rear fuselage, was ejected into mid-air when the bomber blew up, but with two of the four failing to survive. The Hummel aircraft's crash site near Mainz was none too distant from where 42-30002/XR: F **The WAAC Hunter** descended just north of Mannheim. Lt H Shotland managed to get all but one of his crew clear following fatal damage to his B-17 incurred during the course of at least three fighter passes.

Bare minutes later a third Group aircraft burst into flames around the cockpit section. F/O R Synder, co-pilot to Lt C Biddick, was observed to scramble out of the side window in a desperate but initially successful bid for salvation. He amazingly retained position on the wing-root in spite of the fierce slipstream effect while apparently reaching back inside for his chute pack. Having clipped the pack to his harness he let go, at which point fortune deserted him, as he struck the stabilizer while his opened canopy snagged the tail surface. It is unclear whether he was immediately killed or died after the canopy later became detached as 42-5860/LD: P **Escape Kit** headed down to crash at Schweinberg, south of Wuerzburg. Three others, including the pilot, also died, with Biddick's body never subsequently found.

One more 100th BG crew tasted the bitter seeds of failure, that being Lt. R Braley's team. Their B-17 42-30070/LN: S **Tweedle-O-Twill** was the other wingman in the Low sqdn's second Element and was fatally assaulted around the same time as the Biddick B-17 to judge by the final crash site of Pulferingen, which was barely two miles distant from where the other bomber came down. One gunner was killed during the air battle and the other nine parachuted into captivity.

Enduring Controversy

Belgium had been the focus for all five of the initial wave of B-17s lost, as was the case with 42-30063/LD: S **Picklepuss**. Capt. R Knox was No. 5 in the 100th BG's Lead squadron, but he was still holding position prior to *Jagdgruppe* 50's

The 385th BG's **Pregnant Portia** (42-5892) never reached North Africa, after fuel shortage caused Lt. J Keeley to ease her into the Mediterranean. All ten crewmembers got out and were picked up next day; sadly, the pilot and some of the others were killed in a midair collision over England on 26 September.

intervention. At this point damage first to one and then a second engine that saw all bids to keep up rendered hopeless led to the pilots following the example of Lt. Hummel and attempting a solo run for England. As with the other would-be returnees, the B-17 remained unmolested all the way back to a point south of Aachen, near the Belgium/German border. Here it was reportedly homed in upon by three Bf110 night fighters. Two were claimed as "kills" by the gunners, while the survivor brought about the end of Picklepuss with a frontal assault that tore off one wing. The spinning wreckage that finally impacted at Schmalgraf, north of Eupen, was the probable reason why only four airmen emerged alive; Knox was one of the six killed. (Confusing the issue is that all Bf110 losses this day were ascribed either to P-47s or, in three instances, to a foolhardy rear approach on a returning 1st BW formation!) Whoever was involved in this incident, the fact remains that the B-17 crew were reputed to have violated the "Airman's Code" by firing on the fighters who had closed in without opening fire because the bomber had been observed with its wheels down—the sign of surrender. So began the myth of the Luftwaffe's continual bid to focus on the 100th BG thanks to this perceived blatant breaking of the Rules of War. It is all the more ironic that another B-17 crew from the 390th BG have since been "credited" with initiating this "Code breaking" incident.

403rd PCBW Fortunes

So far the Lead PCBW had remained surprisingly almost unscathed, and indeed, the 96th BG would come through the day intact, while the 388th BG, flying Low group, was equally blessed at this stage in the mission. This was not to be the case for the 390th BG, who had already suffered the first of six final casualties. As the formations were approaching Mainz, fire took hold of the forward fuselage on Lt. A Tyson's 42-30017/BI: G All Shot to Hell, which was ironically living up to its title. This was another crew that Fate treated relatively well, since all bailed out safely, albeit at the cost of their continued freedom; their bomber exploded in the region of Bingen on the Rhine.

Lt. R Regan was piloting 42-30016/BI: J Madie that suffered damage to two engines, one of which continued to partially function. Drifting inexorably back through the succeeding PCBWs, the point was reached when the isolated B-17 was headed south for Switzerland. Fighters continued to peck at the B-17 as it traced a route along the Rhine, but Regan ultimately realized that with power fading in the second damaged engine he would have to give up. He accordingly lowered the wheels in a surrender action, but the gunners in the rear were not informed of this action. Consequently, when a Rotte of Bf109s appeared and took up a parallel position, Sgt Kahler (LW) opened up, followed by the two power-turret operators; one of the fighters caught fire, whereupon his companion roared in upon the B-17 and delivered a devastating fusillade. The bomber headed downward with two crewmembers bailing out at minimum altitude; the wheels were eliminated by a row of trees, and the aircraft settled down for a heavy but successful crash landing in a field north of Karlsruehe. And so was created the true "Code violation" incident ascribed to Lt. Knox's 100th BG crew, but only subsequently uncovered in the 1980s by a prominent British military author!

The 401st PCBW had been equally blessed up to now with single losses from each Group. Lt. L Reichardt was flying No. 3 in the 385th BG's Low squadron, which had already surrendered Lt. Sommers back over Belgium. Now the incessant head-on assaults again bore fruit as Mannheim was being skirted. The pilot realized that his charge was doomed and lowered the landing gear, an act of surrender that this time brought no retribution; all ten on board 42-5914/Q Sack Time jumped clear, leaving their B-17 to find its eternal resting place close to Darmstadt.

As the Rhine was left behind the force was short of fourteen of the 139 crews that had crossed in over enemy territory, but the number of effective sorties would be further reduced by three after one bomber jettisoned its load and two others headed south for neutral Switzerland. The total tonnage of explosives and incendiaries still on hand was nevertheless sufficient to inflict a telling blow provided the target was clear and the Lead bombardier's aim were true.

One of the pair of bombers heading for Switzerland contained the combat experienced crew of Lt. Oakes (100th BG), all of whom had flown ten or more missions. Good fortune was on the side of them and their fighter-damaged B-17, 42-30080/EP: F High Life; despite having to make their solo run over a distance of between 100 and 150 miles of hostile skies, they finally won through the enemy defenses to "belly in" on Dubendorf airfield. Paralleling this experience was the 390th BG's 42-30315/CC: S Peg O' My Heart flown by Lt. Rapport. Flak and fighter-inflicted damage was on a scale sufficient to force this desperate

While in North Africa, an anonymous 4th BW airman took this picture of an aircraft "graveyard," littered with Allied and Axis airframes. In the background can be seen the outline of a Ju88 with the main cockpit removed and swastika marking cut out of the tail. Rearing up on the left is the distinctive fin and rudder of an RAF Wellington medium bomber.

act upon the crew, but all ten airmen finally ended up as internees after the bomber was force landed at Utzensdorf, near Berne.

Target Fortunes

The mayhem spread among the 402nd PCBW in particular had scarcely been repeated among the Lead Wing as Regensburg appeared. The 42 bombers split equally between the 96th BG and 388th BGs were still on hand, as were seventeen of the 20 dispatched from Framlingham. The perfect visibility allied to barely any interference from the handful of fighters sent up from the Messerschmitt plant's Defense Flight augured well for a good bombing performance. Capt. Latham, the 96th BG Lead Bombardier, who acknowledged that he "enjoyed dropping bombs," took over from Capt. Kenny (P) on the Automatic Flight Control Equipment (AFCE). The ensuing three or four minutes would determine whether the manifold hours of preparation would pay off.

The flak barrage being put up was surprisingly ineffective, although the fact that the formations were running in at a reduced altitude probably threw off the gunners' calculations in the field of shell fuse setting. However, at least two B-17s absorbed damage that adversely affected their subsequent ability to hold formation. The "bombs away" signal denoted by the string of 500-lb weapons streaming from Latham's B-17 was acted upon by his group. Less than 30 seconds later a burgeoning mass of mushroom clouds shot up among the left-hand complex of buildings—a first-class testimony to the principle of precision bombardment as envisaged by the USAAF hierarchy, even allowing for some "creep back" onto

Genesis of a myth. Capt. Robert Knox (front, second from left) and crew are credited with being the reason why the 100th BG was allegedly singled out for punishment by the Luftwaffe. On 17 August 1943, while "aborting" the Regensburg mission, they reportedly violated the Code of the Air by firing on several fighters who, on seeing the landing gear extended, assumed the pilots were surrendering. In fact the incident did occur – not to the Knox B-17, but to an aircraft and crew from the 390th BG.

"Lady Moe" gains her first and undoubtedly confusing impression of her new home at Snetterton Heath, while Sgts. Louis Klimchak (left) and Coots Matthews act as her guardians. The donkey was brought back from North Africa on board Lt. Miracle's B-17 aptly named **The Miracle Tribe**.

the landing ground that nevertheless inflicted a measure of destruction among finished airframes parked in this area.

Within a further seven minutes the 388th and 390th BGs had added their weight of bombs to the still visible target area. The 390th BG was still a combat "fledgling" in terms of missions flown (two), but the seventeen crews completing the bomb run were destined to put up a sterling bombing performance, although also bearing the second-highest cost in bombers downed (six) between the seven participating groups. (Although this figure constituted six-sevenths of the total losses for the Lead PCBW, only one of the sixty-one airmen was killed with a second lost in a returning B-17.)

The down side to achieving sound precision bombardment now made its presence felt as the second and third Wings made their bombing runs. In place of a clearly defined aiming point appeared an almost complete smoke shroud cast up by the preceding Wing's bombing effort. Maintaining Wing integrity was as equally vital as within each group, and it was here that matters could have gone badly wrong for the 401st PCBW. The Lead group's (94th BG) leader, having decided that his Aiming Point was currently obscured, took up the logical but extremely unpopular option (at least among his crews) of making an orbit in order to hopefully have a clearer view of the target the second time around. This action unconsciously extended the "integrity" problem for its companion group (385th BG), whose Lead Bombardier had managed to find his Aiming Point and duly unloaded. To continue onwards would leave the Group isolated during the extended flight to North Africa, and Maj. Piper accordingly decided to retain contact with the 94th BG. However, by doing so he added pressure to the other critical matter of fuel reserves, since the time taken to orbit would consume fuel that was already badly needed to ensure a safe landing. Before the Wing had completed its action it found itself trailing as opposed to preceding the 95th and 100th BGs, whose bombardiers released their loads of incendiaries into the smoke pall with undetermined results. The entire action had spanned twenty minutes, and now the somewhat battered force took up course for far-distant North Africa.

Harsh Aftermath

Behind them they left a stunned if not shell-shocked atmosphere among the survivors at the Messerschmitt plant. Despite the series of mandatory air raid alerts issued prior to

An enterprising crewmember on this 94th BG B-17 has snapped all or part of two fellow-group bombers through the navigator's window; the almost silhouetted outline contrasts dramatically with the layered clouds whose tops are partially illuminated by the sun. The mission on 2 September 1943 to bomb French airfields was recalled thanks to the persistent undercast seen here.

the bombers' arrival, the prospects of such an assault had not been envisaged since Regensburg was so far into Germany. In addition, there was a palpable sense of individual and corporate confidence that the German fighter and flak resources would either badly blunt or even repulse any attempt to penetrate so far. Indeed, that confidence extended in some individuals' minds to treating the approaching formations as belonging to the *Luftwaffe*! Now, the shocked workforce gazed upon the seeming ruination of their source of employment.

However, the scale of permanent destruction was far smaller, while the anticipated pace of recovery would also prove to be disappointingly swifter than estimated at *Pinetree* following photographic reconnaissance evaluation. As in a number of previous and future instances, the ability of USAAF bombs to effect heavy damage, let alone permanent destruction, among German heavy machinery would prove open to question. The explosive content of even the largest weapon in the USAAF's inventory was too small to achieve this basic aim. Equally sound if not sometimes better results could be, and were, obtained by a heavier use of incendiaries. Their inflammable contents set alight the lubricants required to make the machinery function and often led to irreparable distortion of frames and mechanisms; by contrast, blast damage from explosives was largely inclined to leave the equipment still capable of being brought back into service.

Heading for "Home"

The American crewmembers had discharged their duty, and in one anonymous airman's heart-felt words "Up to now we have flown for the U.S, but now we fly for US!" There lay ahead a protracted and still threatening run lasting upwards of five hours before arriving over the North African shores, with the constant worry of fuel supplies running out adding to the possibility of further aerial interceptions that might be even harder to fend off, given the often extremely low levels of ammunition existing on many B-17s. The initial route took the bombers over the peaks of the Alps, whose undoubtedly relaxing beauty in some airmen's recollection was balanced by the minimal chances of surviving a crash landing therein. Two bombers were in fact damaged by a solo fighter attack during this time, one of which suffered damage to a second engine, but both held course for an ultimately safe arrival.

Several crews would not parallel this positive outcome to the mission, as battle damage and fuel shortage made their presence felt. The unfortunate 402nd PCBW surrendered two more crews before leaving the European mainland. First, yet another 100th BG crew were forced to evacuate their terminally crippled bomber close to Ghedi, in Italy, although all ten on Lt. Hollenbeck's crew bailed out safely from 42-3232/LN: V **Flak Happy**. Four members on Lt. Hayden's eleven-man team were less fortunate, as their bomber (42-3194/BG: A **Little Hell**) finally failed and fell to earth northwest of Parma. A third bomber in the former category involved Lt. Shaver's 390th BG crew on 42-3305/BI: E **Princess Pat**, which pulled out of position as the enemy coastline was left behind and headed west in a bid to reach neutral Spanish territory. Their efforts ended in vain near Toulon, in southern France, where the B-17 was crash landed and the crew ended up as POWs.

The fourth crew that also ended up in captivity contained a senior member flying as a waist gunner. Col. Kennedy was making a visit to Britain in his capacity as a gunnery expert based in America. During the mission that he had undertaken his waist gun had refused to discharge more than one shot each time. Then, the B-17 (42-30042/XR: L **Oh Nausea**) with Lt.G Van Noy's crew, which had a reputation of being a jinxed aircraft—displaying a series of operational failures and having lost two engines earlier in the mission—finally lived up to its reputation by suffering a third and terminal power failure less than 100 miles from North Africa that saw it flopping into the sea in a successful ditching action. All ten airmen got into

The 388th BG lost no less than eleven B-17s off the failed Stuttgart mission on 6 September 1943. Lt. Beecham's crew were more fortunate, since their 560BS B-17F **Impatient Virgin II** limped into Dubendorf, in Switzerland, where aircraft and the ten airmen were interned.

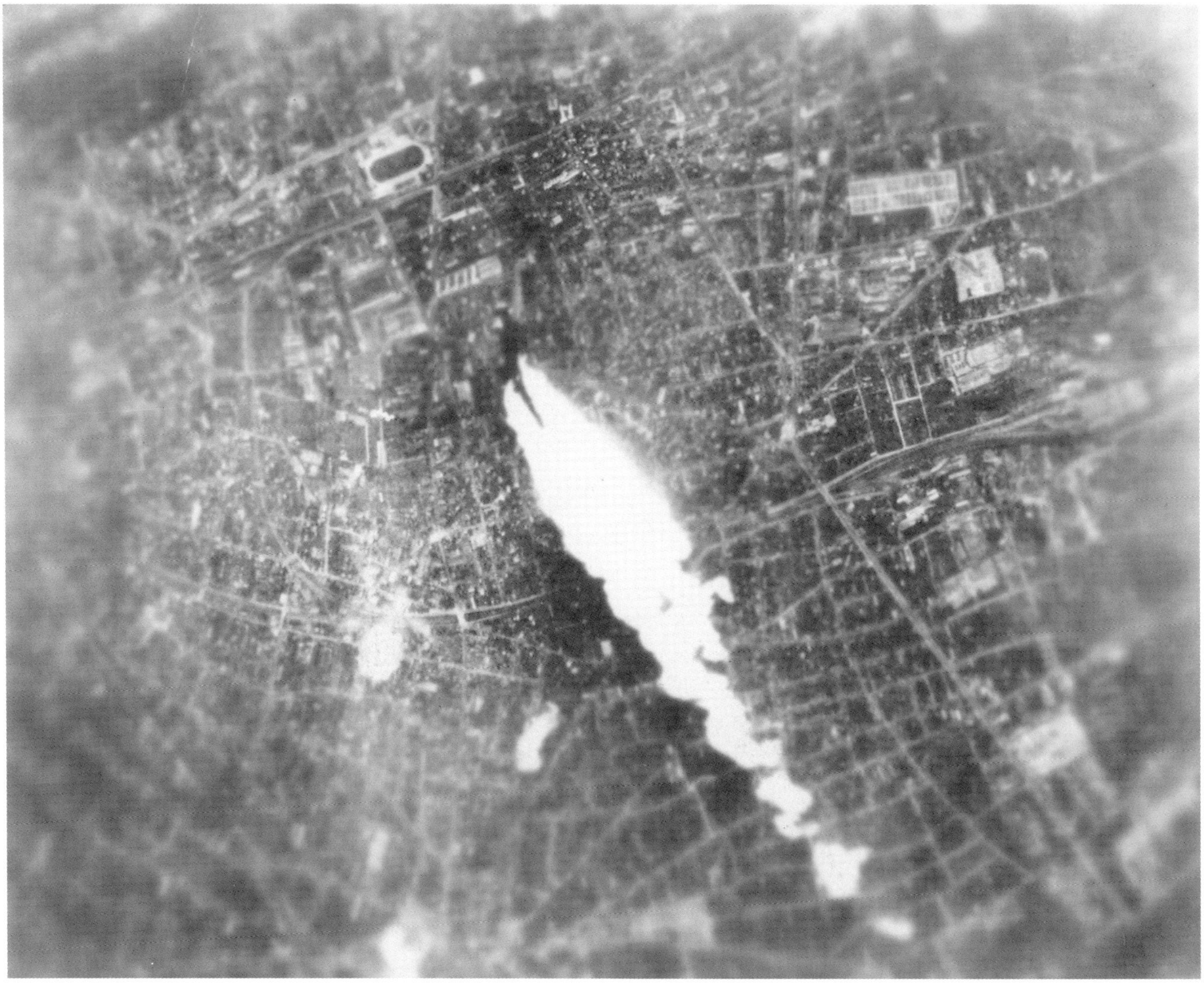

"We live in Fame, go down in flame" – the penultimate line of the Air Corps Song – is dreadfully fulfilled over Paris on 15 Sept. 1943. A flak strike on 42-30607/AW: **Pat Hand** has ignited a fuel tank and ten of Lt. Ken Murphy's crew are fighting in vain to escape their flaming tomb....

their dinghies, but after an overnight sojourn afloat it was their relative misfortune that a German floatplane arrived overhead and plucked them out of the thankfully calm Mediterranean waters.

Pregnant Portia (42-5892/B) was one of four bombers that got out over the Mediterranean but fell short of a safe landing in North Africa. The 385th BG aircraft suffered a potentially lethal failure when one life raft emerged from its hatch and became entangled in the vertical stabilizer. To the potentially lethal destabilizing effect of the "foreign" appendage was the drain on fuel reserves, as more power had to be applied to keep up with the formation. An attempt to detach the raft by shooting it off (and even a reported, albeit apocryphal, bid by a gunner from Texas to lasso it!) came to naught. The B-17 was nevertheless held successfully on course, but when still over 100 miles distant from their goal the swift illumination of the red warning lights revealed that the final dregs of fuel were now expended. The smooth sea surface provided a good ditching base, but now the single available dinghy could not accommodate all ten crewmembers as it drifted in the near presence of the bomber, which floated for upwards of 45 minutes before keeling over and sinking.

The following remarks on what was an even more potentially lethal situation for him and his companions as darkness enfolded their isolated dinghy were made by a crewmember in *Target Germany*:

> "I never want to spend another night like that. Five of us sat in the dinghy and five hung on outside. Don't let anyone tell you about the warm Mediterranean – it ain't so. The night got blacker and we got gloomier. When trails of daylight finally came up we were all half dead. With the sun, though, our spirits rose again and we took stock of ourselves. During the night everything we had – even the stuff in our pockets – had floated away. Then, at 1100

The second picture shows the shattered remains of **Pat Hand** within the confines of a railroad station or yard being examined by a mixed group of German military and French civilians. Only S/Sgt. S Ferrucci (LWG) managed to survive from among the eleven airmen on board; the extra man had flown as an observer.

On 21 September 1943 42-30246/DI: H - **Spot Remover** suffered battle damage that ended in a crash landing on its base at Framlingham. Several crewmembers are among the personnel clustered in front of the stranded B-17F. It was restored to combat duty, but finally went down over Tirstrup, Denmark, on 20 February 1944, although all of Lt. Gallard's crew bailed out safely.

hours the little automatic radio transmitter went out, and that is when we started praying in earnest. (Incidentally, the following Sunday we attended church en masse!). Anyway, as the afternoon wore on a B-26 sighted and stayed right over us until one of those British ASR launches came out and picked us up. We thought we were as hard as nails; after all, we were a combat crew. But right now we felt like ninety-year-old men...." (In truth Keeley's crew, especially those immersed in the sea, had been very fortunate not to succumb to hypothermia during the 21-hour experience, while the chances of anyone aloft sighting what was a mere dot in the vast watery expanse were normally extremely poor. Having come through this fraught experience, it is sad to report that Lt. Keeley and some if not all of his regular team would be lost in a banal mid-air collision over Essex on 26 September.)

The second fuel-starved B-17 was 42-3414/F **Paddlefoot** (388th BG), in Lt. J Parker's charge, which ditched at a point roughly 30 minutes flying time short of friendly territory. Having taken off early due to misinterpretation of mission orders, it was not surprising that the remaining two out of this group of B-17s to ditch came from Framlingham. Lt. W Sneed's 42-3310/BI: **Blood, Guts and Rust** and 42-3333/CC: O **Purgatory Pete**, flown by Lt. A Becker, were the unfortunate aircraft in question; however, all twenty airmen clambered out of their sinking mounts—one of whose last resting place was almost within sight of North Africa—to be later picked up by Allied vessels, as was the case with Parker's crew. A 100% survival rate in these circumstances was one that was to be rarely achieved during WWII.

Frustrated Expectations

As the red fuel warning lights blinked on the cockpit instrument panels, the 4th BW pilots and their crews arriving at the various North African airfields could relax in the confident assumption that proper facilities on a level with that enjoyed back in England would be on hand. The initial jolt to such expectations must have come as those bombers now circling the airfields gazed upon perimeter zones that were largely devoid of hangars, barrack blocks, and other support structures. As it was, the immediate concern was to get down as quickly as possible. This necessary act was badly compromised by a combination of dust and thunderstorm conditions linked with confusion in the advice being handed out by the control tower staff. A number of emergency landings were made at Bone, an RAF airfield with very short runways, as well as on dry lake beds or similar non-airfield surfaces. One 385th BG bomber did run into the tail of its predecessor, although thankfully without lethal results for either crew, but this was the sole recorded incident of serious damage.

Unlike the invasion-free situation back in England, the conflict in the Mediterranean had been fought in a manner that placed most airfields squarely in the path of the contesting ground forces; many of them had been hastily created with little or no time to set up solid support units, and "tent cities" were consequently the norm for work and accommodation purposes. In the case of the few permanent airfields, these had been bombed in an effective manner, especially by the Allied Air Forces, and the few short weeks between the Axis surrender in late May and the arrival of LeMay's force had granted little time in which to bring the facilities back up to full functioning levels. In addition, Tunisia was no longer a direct front-line region; the island of Sicily, off to the east, "enjoyed" that current honor, and within three weeks the conflict would

The name **Spot Remover** was a reference to the British use of the expression "Spots of enemy resistance were encountered and removed" when discussing military actions – hence the adaptation applied to this USAAF bomber whose duty was viewed in the same manner.

move even further away with the initial invasion of the Italian mainland. The 4th BW force had in effect found its way to an operational "back-water!"

Gen. LeMay was to assert during his pre-mission visit to North Africa he had been assured by Gen. Norstad, Chief of Staff to Gen. Spaatz, that everything would be up to scratch for the proper handling of his force. The designated airfield was Telergma, whose function as an Air Depot was of particular relevance to refurbishing and reloading the B-17s. What the General found on 17 August was that Telergma's Depot stocks had been transported elsewhere since his reconnaissance visit. It was hardly surprising that he later expressed his strong displeasure at the overall lack of facilities for his bombers and crews, who now faced upwards of one week before the return flight home. Sleeping out under the wings of their B-17s was to literally prove "cold comfort" for many of the airmen that first night, and pup tent or even slit-trench provision was the subsequent basis for living accommodation, with cooking facilities being on an equally basic level.

Any feeling of having been officially "deserted" technically and personally had to be put aside and attention turned to making the best of what was on hand to carry out necessary repair work. As it was, no more than 85 airframes would finally be deemed worthy of restoration to combat status. Bombing-up and refuelling activity was carried out in basic fashion, the latter duty regularly involving the manual cartage and discharge into the tanks of 5-gallon containers.

Whenever the opportunity arose the airmen roamed the local terrain to make contact with a variety of nationalities and social groups ranging from Tunisian villagers to British and Commonwealth troops, as well as French personnel and their womenfolk, who currently controlled their nation's North African colonies. Fez hatwear was freely adopted and retained, while at least two enterprising crews from the 96th and 100th BGs added to their crew complement in the form of one donkey each.

In the former instance *Lady Moe* would grace Snetterton Heath and the surrounding countryside for around two years before succumbing to the inexorable force of a railroad train after she strayed onto the tracks.

Homeward Bound

On 24 August those crews whose bombers were serviceable attended Briefing for the mission that would end with their landing back in England. Their target was Bordeaux/ Merignac airfield, on France's southwest coast, and the protracted course to be flown assumed an elliptical clockwise pattern. The flying time, extending up to eleven hours, would be as great as on the 17th, but *Luftwaffe* opposition was expected to be much more desultory.

By the time the force was on its bomb run it was short nine aircraft that had turned back with various mechanical failures, in addition to which a total of eighteen crews, including twelve from the 385th BG, did not bomb the Primary. (The latter unit was already on the MIA list, after 42-30364 flown by Lt. Grodi came down thanks to unknown causes near Toulouse; the pilot and five others were the latest Americam airmen to benefit from landing in an Occupied country, since they were spirited away out of the Germans' reach.)

Further misfortune attended the 385th BG as the formations were skirting the Brest Peninsula. Maj. Piper's 42-30187/K **Lulu Belle** was still well short of the southwest coast of England when it had to be ditched. The No. 4 replacement engine had been disabled, followed by the loss of No. 3 and precious fuel thanks to punctured tanks. The aerodynamic imbalance due to the loss of power on one wing did not prevent Piper and Lt. V Masters from bringing off a successful entry into the choppy Atlantic surface. It was now that the problems multiplied. It was bad enough that the single dinghy on hand was released in an inverted position and had to be hastily retrieved as it floated clear of the wing before being inflated—worse still was the total absence of the radio equipment permitting access to the "international distress" channels! Two crewmembers were washed away, while only five of the nine others on board could get into the raft. Of the four clinging to the raft rat-lines, only Piper and Lt. Schultz (N) were left to clamber into their precarious refuge after Capt. Dewey (Lead navigator) and Lt. Jones (B) lost their battle to hold on in the frigid and by then night-shrouded seas. (An RAF aircraft had previously dropped a raft that sadly could not be reached.) It was around mid-day before another RAF "Hudson" chanced upon the final flare of three fired to attract the crew's attention as they carried out a "square search" pattern; the two other flares had been used during the night, but had either not been seen or in the second instance malfunctioned. The RAF ASR Launch that finally loomed up in response to the circling aircraft's directions signalled the end of almost 24 hours exposure to the full and daunting forces of wind and water for the seven survivors.

A 390th BG crew in 42-30308/BI: A **Hot Rocks** also landed in the English Channel off Selsey Bill; all but one of Lt. Dougherty's crew was picked up by an ASR Launch based at Newhaven. A final aircraft loss occurred over the Knettishall circuit. B-17/42-30230/L **Homesick Angel** suffered two fuel-starved engines in quick succession and had to be crash landed by Lt. Lt. P Humphries in a field at Stanton, near the base; Category E status was conferred on the bomber seven days later.

Although this latest 388th BG aircraft was only the second Group loss suffered off the Regensburg "shuttle" run, it was actually the third borne in six days. The B-17 and crew concerned had been part of a reduced force of seven that in turn had joined with 38 other 4th BW bombers on 19 August. The intended target was Woensdrecht airfield, in Holland, but none

Lt. John G Winant Jr. stands fourth from left among his 390th BG crew in front of their B-17 named **Tech Supply**. This officer was the son of the wartime United States Ambassador to the Court of St. James.

of the bomb loads struck the Primary due to adverse weather conditions. Lt. B Howe, piloting 42-30068, had had his No. 4 engine set alight by flak; he was one of eight crewmembers killed during the incident as the doomed machine staggered westward before coming down near Haamstede, on the Dutch coastal fringe. A second 4th BW bomber crash landed in Norfolk after it caught fire during Assembly, being 42-30172/ QJ: F **Black Heart II** from the 96th BG.

The VIII BC elements of its B-17 strength had now been reunited in England, but their ability to strike out in strength had again been badly blunted by the events of the Anniversary missions. To the 24 MIA losses and unserviceable aircraft left behind in North Africa had been added a further 36 crews lost from the 1st BW, along with a number of returning bombers declared Category E. Of particular disappointment to those at *Pinetree* were the very poor results arising from the attack on Schweinfurt's ball-bearing plants, while the degree of destruction at Regensburg was to be nothing as extensive or long lasting as the reconnaissance pictures seemed to promise.

Comment

No further month's missions were in fact flown by the 4th BW, although the 1st BW did go out to French targets on 27 and 31 August. And so the bright hopes for a major, if not decisive thrust at the very heart of the Nazi war machine faded away as far as this stage of the Bombing Offensive was concerned. As it was, a major contradiction in the planning of the Anniversary thrusts would appear to have been the splitting of the VIII BC's strength. After all, the Washington based planners had regarded the assaults upon Schweinfurt as central to the Allied prospects for a fore-shortened conflict in Europe at least. The "drying up" of ball bearing supplies from this perceived "bottleneck" source that in turn was expected to grind German industrial output to a literal halt was a paramount feature in the issue. Why then was almost a third of the Command's strength devoted to attacking a separate industrial base, however important that it was currently deemed to be? After all, if ball bearing supplies could have been so vitally disrupted following a well directed strike, then

Three officers and a single airman are attending to the primary stage of bomb loading at Knettishall.The pair on the left is fitting the support-frame with which the weapon will be hoisted into the bomb-bay and secured.The bombs appear to be of British origin to judge by the circular shape of the tailfins compared to the USAAF square-pattern units.

At first sight this is a standard picture of the center section of a B-17F. Closer inspection of the top turret reveals it has been blasted away, however. The photograph's 17 September date witnessed no combat for the VIII BC bombers, and there is no record of what happened to the turret's occupant. BX:A **Fertile Myrtle III** led the 96th BG on Black Thursday and was salvaged following a crash at Taverham the following 16 December.

the Bf109s being turned out from the Regensburg plant would soon never have taken to the air in the first place. Surely, it would have been more logical to send all available bombers to Schweinfurt in the first place—something that was only addressed nearly two months later (and it might be added at no greater cost to the Command's overall strength as well as with more positive effect) than had been the case on 17 August.

September 1943

Ten missions would be flown by VIIIBC's two B-17-equipped Bomb Wings during September, with only two of the targets located in Germany and with very variable results in these two instances. The first went out on the 2nd to airfields in northwest France and saw a full-strength effort launched that was almost totally frustrated by heavy cloud; two Groups did bomb airfields reported at debriefing as targets of opportunity. A more effective strike was made 24 hours later when six Groups were dispatched. The majority of the 65 401PCBW crews struck their briefed target of Mureaux airfield, whereas the 94th BG unknowingly released their loads over a target of opportunity that was actually a "dummy" airfield close to Dieppe—not something to mention to Gen. "Hap" Arnold, who was visiting Rougham that very day!

A "Solo" Disaster

The "Bloody Hundredth" bore all five 4BW losses on 3 September, and all for nothing. The intended target at Paris, the Renault factory, was cloud-covered and the mission aborted. During the diversion to assault the Secondary at Beaumont Le Roger Lt. Henington's 42-30611/XR: suffered an engine fire due to flak and steadily lost altitude; the Channel was reached, but the pilots were finally forced to "ditch." The crew's luck was in because no less than three RAF "Walrus" amphibians under Spitfire escort ultimately arrived to pluck all ten out of the sea.

This situation contrasted forcefully with forty of their colleagues, sixteen of them dead, left behind under confusing circumstances in France. A midair collision was the focal point for the confusion with any two of the four B-17s reported as involved. Flak struck home on 42-30089/EP: J **Sunny** (Lt. R King) during the bomb run, and the bomber was thought to have veered up to impact with Lt. C Floyd's 42-30059/EP **Barker's Burden**. King was one of five fatalities and Floyd one of eight. A separate source suggests that King's B-17 impacted with **Torchy** (42-30035/XR), killing Sgt. Bankhead (TG), although Lt. Winkleman and eight others managed to bail out. Further spreading the confusion was a subsequent report by Floyd's navigator, Lt. Rosenberg. Lt. Fienup's 42-5865/EP: **Janie** was already on fire as the latest batch of enemy fighters began attacking; Rosenberg asserted that his aircraft swung into the path of, and struck, **Janie**, from which all but two gunners parachuted safely! (The descent into what was friendly territory paid off for eleven of the 24 survivors, who evaded capture.)

Ball bearings were back on the assault menu three days later, with the location of the plants at Stuttgart, laying deep in Southwest Germany, promising a lengthy and hotly contested run for the crews. B/Gen. Travis was the overall Task Commander whose decisions would raise insuperable problems for many of his subordinates. The anticipated good weather conditions did not materialize, with ever-increasing cloud formations being encountered as the force bored solidly southeastwards across France and into Germany. When finally reached, a mere handful of crews managed to unload onto the actual target area. It was now that the General's ordering the force to make a 360 degree turn for a new bomb run unconsciously opened the way for chaos to reign. Sighting of the Primary was no more successful this time round, and units spent even more precious time and fuel seeking out targets of opportunity.

By the day's end 45 bombers from the overall Command strength would be gone, eighteen of which belonged to the 4th BW. These in turn were shared out between three Groups, two of them belonging to the relatively unfortunate 402nd PCBW. The 100th BG had already laid the (spurious) grounds for its "Jinx outfit" reputation on the Regensburg mission, and today witnessed the excision from its ranks of three B-17s, although only one descended over enemy territory. These losses appear to have been initiated as the Group was searching out "last resort" targets. Fighter gunfire knocked out two engines on 42-30335/LN: U **Sans Finis** (Lt. W Grenier), and the final crash landing site at Villingen saw the nine survivors swiftly rounded up. (Another more minor Group myth surrounded the pilot, who was later identified as "the man who came to dinner"; this was an allusion to the alleged mere matter of hours between his arrival at Thorpe Abbotts and his being shot down. However, he and his crew were on hand for nearly two weeks before going down!)

Lt. S Turner's 42-30057/EP: D **Raunchy** was quickly forced out of formation, whereupon the pilots decided on a heading for Switzerland. However, the final forced landing was not on Swiss soil, but rather the more unyielding waters of Lake Constance. The battering the B-17 received from this encounter saw it soon sink, taking with it the body of S/Sgt. Maloney (BT); the other nine airmen survived despite being unable to release either dinghy. Joining them as an internee was a single member of Capt. F Woodwards' crew on 42-30402/LD: W **The Poontang**. This bomber had also been re-directed towards neutral territory and abandoned when adjudged to be well away from German soil. The parachute descent of nine crewmembers must have been much closer to the Swiss/German border, since their final landing point ended up inside the latter country. The very lucky exception was none other than Woodward, who was the last to evacuate.

The other 402nd unit to suffer gave up four crews, albeit at minimum human cost. One of the three bombers lost over enemy territory was 42-30161/ET: B **Cuddle Cat**. The No. 1 engine was seen to be smoking as the aircraft eased out of formation in a southerly direction. If the intention was to reach Switzerland this bid failed, since all ten airmen on Lt. J Cabeen's team ended up as POWs. The second B-17 to be lost was probably 42-30300/BG: C **Hell N' Back**, which also fell out and headed in the same direction. Once again all ten crewmembers, led by Lt. G Tyler, cleared their mount before it blew up south of Stuttgart. The third Group loss involved Lt. G Ransom's crew flying in 42-30271/OE: R **Bomboogie**; the aircraft fell behind the formation despite jettisoning its bomb load and inevitably invited fighter attacks. Terminal damage concluded with the crew bailing out near Soissons, France, with half of them getting into Resistance hands. (One out this ultimately fortunate group, T/Sgt. Peacock (ROG) suffered the dreadful fate of dying from exposure while attempting the crossing of the Pyrenees mountain chain into Spain at the end of 1943.) The fourth crew were more fortunate; their B-17/42-3321/ET: K **Kathy Jane II** (Lt. N Rothschild) was one of the sizeable number managing to stagger back as far as the English Channel, where a successful ditching ended with all ten airmen being rescued.

Knettishall Woes

To date the 388th BG had suffered eleven crews MIA in the course of seventeen missions, which was a tolerable loss rate, but today's mission would bring about a savage 100% increase in this basic statistic. Twenty-three crews had lifted off Knettishall prior to 0600 hours and arrived back at their airfield short eleven crews. Fully 110 airmen were missing from the debriefing sessions, although 75 were still alive, from which latter figure ten enjoyed the arguably better fate of becoming internees.

This crew, led by Lt. P Beecham, had dropped out near the I.P. and made the relatively short although still deadly stretch from the target into Switzerland in 42-30478/L **Impatient Virgin II**. The subsequent debate about this action being necessary, given the apparent lack of damage and the presence of around 800 gals. fuel, should be set against the fact that this fuel reserve was barely ¼ of even a "Tokyo tank"-equipped B-17 and provided a bare minimum of capacity to guarantee a safe return to England.

Only three crews went down over German territory, one of which was 42-3289/A **Wolfpack**. Once again fighter assault between the IP and the target brought about engine and flight control damage that impelled Lt. A Wick to attempt a run towards Switzerland. The right wing caught fire as the bomber struggled southwards over the region near Reutlingen, and all but two Enlisted men killed during the air battle jumped clear, although Sgt. Allard (TG) also forfeited his life. Also claimed over Germany was 42-3378/Q **Silver Dollar** in Lt. A Roe's hands that came down through unknown circumstances at an equally anonymous location along with nine survivors. Flak knocked out two engines on 42-5942/R **Sky Shy**, flown by Lt. M Bowen. One crewmember was already dead of wounds and

Heavenly Daze (42-5918/ET: J) was an early arrival at Horham. This picture is taken over the inhospitable Norwegian terrain. The B-17F survived nearly six months before being claimed in battle on 11 January 1944, when all but one of Lt. Foley's crew ended up as POWs.

a second died next day from a fractured skull; their eight more fortunate colleagues ended up in a Stalag.

The remaining seven losses occurred over France, a circumstance that permitted almost 20% of the airmen involved to evade capture. Much of the action appears to have occurred in the vicinity of Troyes, well to the southeast of Paris. It was the 563 BS that suffered over half the losses on the mission, one of which was 42-42-3425/X **In God We Trust**. The Deity's faith in this crew was sorely tried since they failed him, although all ten on Lt. R Cunningham's crew did reach the ground safely, with the pilot and one other evading capture. An even more fortunate crew, other than the single fatality, was led by Lt. Lt. A Kramer in 42-30222//T **Lone Wolf**; their parachute descent northeast of Troyes ended with seven also evading capture.

Much less fortunate at this stage of the mission was 42-20234/P (Lt. L Miller) and 42-30349/W (Lt. R Wilken). Both pilots were among the fifteen personnel killed, although two on the latter crew joined their colleagues who had evaded capture.

The 560 BS surrendered a further trio of bombers, beginning with two crews downed as the Group skirted south of Paris. The Melun area was where 42-30203/G **Shack Up**, now flying on one effective engine during the return leg arbitrarily parted company with Lt. H Mohr's (KIA) six surviving crewmembers. Chartres, further to the west of the French capital, was the last resting place for 42-30201/F **Shedonwanna?**; Lt. S Melville was yet another airplane commander to lose his life, along with three Enlisted men. The final squadron loss involved 42-3293/A **Slightly Dangerous**, which made its terminal descent near the village of La Chapelle-Champigny, further to the southeast of Paris, along with half Lt. D Karnezis' crew; the pilot was one of the two survivors to escape capture.

Retrenchment Again

The Stuttgart mission had proved to be a disaster that was almost on a scale with the first Schweinfurt mission in terms of losses suffered for a very poor return in strike effect. The *Luftwaffe* was at peak efficiency in numbers and counter-assault, and the prospects for the Daylight Bombing Offensive continued to promise a dark outcome for VIII BC. The Command's claws were again pulled in to some degree since targets in France and the Low Countries were briefed 24 hours later, with the 4th BW heading across the English Channel to bomb what ultimately turned out to be V-1 launch sites at Watten. No losses were suffered by the 58 crews credited with a mission, although this figure was barely one-third of the 147 bombers dispatched. Two days later French airfields and an industrial plant in Paris were assaulted at the cost of two 4th BW B-17s. Both were from the 403rd PCBW, beginning with 42-3353/AW: L **Tar Fly**, which was fatally crippled by flak over the target; the bomber returned as far as the vicinity of Evreux where it crashed, to leave Lt. E Nordewier to face captivity along with seven other crewmembers. Downed during the bomb run was 42-30209/U **Wee Bonnie** II from Knettishall. Fire caught hold between Nos. 1 and 2 engines and, having jettisoned the bomb load, all eleven from Lt. D Porter's crew successfully "took to the silk," of which five evaded capture.

Paris, as with most major metropoli, possessed a sizeable degree of industrial plants that naturally contributed to the Nazi war effort. Three of these sites—Caudron-Renault, Billancourt-Renault, and Hispano-Suiza—were targeted by LeMay's crews on the 15th. The bald statistics on the mission's conclusion were 152-139-5 (dispatched-bombed-MIA), but the marginal nature of the latter figure was cold comfort for the 96th BG, who contributed three crews over the latter named target, of whom only three survived out of the 31 airmen. Flak struck home twice, first of all against 42-3437/QJ:, piloted by Lt. V Richardson, and the resultant explosion expunged the lives of all but one of the ten on board. Then, as the group was clearing the area after bombing, another flak strike created a fire on the right wing of Lt. E Murphy's 42-30607/AW: **Pat Hand** that rapidly enveloped much of the airframe in a torching banner of flame. Once again, just one crewmember out of eleven bailed out as the flaming B-17 spun down into the city center, with the ghastly image captured for eternity on another bomber's camera. The third group loss also occurred at this stage, but this time to fighters. Lt. C Reed was flying No. 5 in the Low Sqdn's second Element when 42-30493/QJ: came under attack during the bomb run. The same tithe of a single survivor was the grim fate of this ten-man crew.

Single losses from the 95th and 100th BGs completed the 3rd Bombardment Division's loss tally, the new nomenclature having displaced the former 4th Bomb Wing title two days previous. The former unit's 42-3266/BG: T **Sitting Bull** was still in formation as the English Channel was being re-crossed, but then dropped out and down under seeming control; whatever happened then would never be confirmed, other than that all ten on F/O. J Noyes' crew were lost, with only the pilot's body later recovered from a French beach. By contrast, 42-3452/LN: Z remained on French soil near Clermont-Oise. Flak had crippled one engine, and the B-17 was last seen being swallowed up in cloud as the Rally Point was being attained. However, all but one of Lt. A Vetter's crew got out safely, of which total only one was captured. A particularly tragic fate awaited one of the evaders in December, when Lt. McConnahan (N) died of exposure while attempting the mountainous Pyrenean route into Spain.

As with the previous day's mission, both B-17 Bomb Divisions were dispatched to well-separated French targets, with the 3rd BD facing the longer run down to Cognac/Chateaubernard airfield, which had already felt the weight of assault from the Division on 24 August. Some 231 tons of explosives were dropped by the 93 crews gaining mission credit, but the bulk of this fell upon locations further north at La Pallice/La Rochelle. The newly re-titled 402nd PCBW—this nomenclature having also been changed to Combat Bomb Wing (CBW) with the numerical prefix 13 in this instance—surrendered two crews over France. First, 42-30276/ET: F **Terry and the Pirates** (Lt. R Jutzi) came down after bombing La Pallice, but all ten airmen bailed out safely, with all but one being captured. Also downed in this target

Lt. McGuire and his acolyte crew are pictured on 5 October 1943; they are posed with their B-17G that they will bring over to Rattlesden as part of the group's "original" cadre. This team would survive their combat tour that included a "ditching" on 29 April 1944. Second from left is Lt. Ken Anderson (CP).

Stingy was among the initial batch of B-17Gs that were rushed into service without "cheek" gun windows and assigned to the VIIIBC. The bomber successfully flew combat operations for over thirteen months. She was finally lost, not on operations, but thanks to a midair collision during a practice flight on 11 October 1944; Lt. N Jorgenson and six other crewmembers were killed in the banal incident.

zone was 42-30064/LD: T **Wild Cargo**, which descended into the sea, but not before all of Lt. R Wolff's crew not only jumped, but did so in time to float down onto solid ground. (This crew had flown much of the Regensburg mission with a large gash in the upper fin where an inadvertently released life raft had smacked into the surface.)

The extended distance back to England now left the crews not only facing a scenario of rapidly fading daylight, but also a solid weather front that led to some Groups straying up over western England and Wales, whose rather mountainous terrain boded ill for any aircraft wending its way thereabouts. The 388th BG still possessed all 21 bombers as the Channel was left behind, but the decision was taken to disperse the formation in order for the pilots to seek out available airfields; not all would make it safely down...

Lt. Jarrendt, flying 42-5904/ **Gremlin Gus**, was descending cautiously over the county of Devon when the B-17 made an initially marginal contact with high ground. S/Sgt. Jones (TG) had an amazing escape from death or even serious injury when he was ejected through his exit hatch, but his injuries proved to be slight. Ironically, two other crewmembers were badly injured and one killed when the B-17 made a final crash landing several miles further on. Another Group crew were much less fortunate when 42-5906/E **Sondra Kay** crashed near Shobdon airfield further to the northeast, killing all ten on Lt. H Cox's crew.

Lt. Henry Nagorka had suffered the loss through a hand amputation of his navigator Lt. Tierney during the Regensburg run. On this occasion seven of the crewmembers' luck was fully in following 42-30030/A **Old Ironsides'** ditching—off the Farne Islands in northeast England and around 250 miles distant from Knettishall! All eight surviving this action scrambled into the dinghies as their mount rapidly filled up and sank. (The eighth airman, S/Sgt. J Harris (TG), was relatively lucky, in that he escaped with his life, but at the cost of a leg injury that later necessitated the limb's amputation.) Fate still had something in store for the Nagorka team in the weeks ahead...

Mother Nature had conspired against the three aforementioned crews and probably added a fourth thanks to her malign activities. The Welsh town of Abergavenny lies on the eastern edge of the Brecon Beacon mountain chain, and it was there that the 390th BG's 42-5903/FC: R **Ascend Charlie** impacted to kill all of Lt. H Turner's crew in the process. The single Great Ashfield crew lost had got back to the vicinity of their Base, but then were operationally compromised thanks to a mid-air collision with a 95th BG bomber. The latter crew managed to land safely, whereas Lt. A Schley and his nine colleagues were consumed in the violent crash of 42-30601 /K **Mary Ellen II** at Rickinghall just a few miles short of a safe landing at their airfield.

Heading Towards Disaster Again

French targets continued to dominate the target schedule for the remainder of the month, starting on the 23rd when two airfields in Brittany were struck by 108 out of 130 B-17s dispatched at a cost of one crew from the 96th BG. Next day an intended mission to Stuttgart was "scrubbed" after take off, but barely had the bombers landed back when a practice mission was ordered. One of Gen. LeMay's tenets was that, regardless of whether a mission or non-operational flight was involved, any crew proceeding aloft without having all their guns unlimbered and ready for use were ripe for a court martial. This vital requirement was apparently not fully applied at Thorpe Abbotts and was to result in a grimly unnecessary outcome for one crew led by Lt. J Gossage. The formation droned up and out over the Wash, where an escort of P-47s was scheduled to appear. Sure enough, a group of "bogies" were picked up behind, but in place of the blunt snouts of the Republic fighters there loomed the shark-like outlines of *Luftwaffe* fighters.

Lt. Gossage's B-17/42-30259/XR: N **Damfino II** was No. 2 in the High squadron, and received a battering that thoroughly sieved the rear fuselage and set No. 3 engine ablaze. Some of the forward flexible weapons, such as the one assigned to Lt. Don (B), were still in the stowed position when the assaults began; worse still was the absolute absence of guns from the radio room back, so very little could be done to ward off the passes made by the attackers. The burning bomber dropped out and down for an intended ditching, but the pilot changed his mind and called for a bail out, even though the coast was out of sight; as it was he did remain on board and managed to scramble out through a cockpit window. Fortunately for the final tally of five survivors a flotilla of Royal Navy MTBs heading out for an active patrol were on hand to fish them out. However, there was no question of their being returned to dry land until the patrol was completed, and it was only the following morning that they disembarked at an undisclosed RN base. (This was the first of three incidents involving the pilot that culminated with his falling inadvertently into German hands along with his crew on 3 March 1944.)

Three days later a planned assault on Reims/Champagne airfield in France was abandoned thanks to adverse weather conditions. As the 3rd BD came back in over the Thames Estuary the grim spectre of collision arose for the second time in ten days as regards the 385th BG. This time around 42-3290/R **Raunchy Wolf** and 42-30264/S **Dorsal Queen** made lethal contact. The latter B-17, flying in No. 3 position, had dropped below and right of the Element leader before apparently attempting to occupy the No. 2 slot vacated by Lt. Morgan in 42-3422. The prop wash that had thrown the errant bomber out of position probably re-asserted its malign nature by bringing its vertical fin in contact with the Lead bomber's right wing, causing the rear fuselage to break off. A farm near West Horndon, in Essex County, received the remains of both B-17s, along with all of Lt. T Keeley's crew and ten from Lt. M Yarnello's team respectively; S/Sgt. J Adams from **Dorsal Queen** was the very fortunate survivor. (There is a picture of **Dorsal Queen** as it begins its terminal dive; the picture appeared in the wartime book *Target Germany* with the caption perhaps naturally indicating the loss had occurred over enemy territory. The visibility in the picture appears to be perfect; hence, there is no clear reason for the incident to have arisen. On the other hand there was little margin for error when flying formation, as confirmed here.)

The impending return to regular *Big League* activities over Germany came next day with a thrust at industry in Emden. Six 3rd BD groups got the bulk of their crews through to the target, whereas only six out of nineteen from Rougham gained mission credit, in addition to which three of the four MIA bombers belonged to this unit. **Elusive Elsie** (42-5888/QE: X) was last observed falling into a spiral with heavy smoke exuding from both outboard engines. Eyewitnesses claimed seeing two parachutes blossoming out, but in fact only S/Sgt. R Scott (TG) reached the ground alive. Lt. Thalmann's 42-30454/TS: B **Reluctant Dragon** developed a fire in one engine and descended in a controlled manner over the target area. This bomber's progress home ended several minutes later on the east bank of the Ems estuary at Greetsiel with the pilot the sole fatality. The North Sea stretch just north of Greetsiel claimed 42-5989/QE: S **Marge H** after it was fatally crippled by fighter attacks; none of the ten-man team led by Lt. M Haskins survived the final impact close to the target area. The day's MIA tally was completed by 42-30792/QJ: E flown by F/O Drabnis. The 96th BG bomber had both inboard engines set on fire with the pilot and Lt. Leonard (N) killed. Although the other eight crewmembers managed to bail out, three of them suffered injuries that subsequently led to their repatriation in late 1944; Lts. Fisher (CP) and Cooper (B) had each lost a leg during the action, while Sgt. Miller's (TG) injury was unknown.

The Stage Door Canteen in London was a key social establishment. Its staff gave out information for U.S. Service personnel visiting the capital on Leave passes. Whether the glass emblazoned with a "Coca Cola" motif held that product or something more volatile remains a matter of conjecture!

Another period of regeneration for VIII BC was now over, and with its conclusion was signalled the onset of a further period of sustained operations as September slipped over into October. The quest to permanently disrupt the Nazis' capacity to produce ball bearings in viable quantities had only been temporarily withheld despite the setbacks at Schweinfurt and Stuttgart. The lure of Schweinfurt's major facilities in particular was not to be resisted before the onset of deteriorating weather conditions and shortening hours of daylight might render the venture extremely doubtful over the winter months. Gen. Eaker's crews were ready as ever to go, but in doing so would have their physical and spiritual endurance tested as never before....

5

"Black Week's" Unbearable Cost

Full Stride Again

The total establishment of heavy bomber Groups within VIIIBC on 1 October 1943 now stood at twenty, split between the 1st BD (nine), 2nd BD (four), and 3rd BD (seven), although two of the B-24 units from the middle listed sub-force were still on detachment in North Africa. The average number of bombers currently being dispatched from each airfield was twenty-one, which in turn indicated an ability to strike the enemy with around 400 in total on any given day. The bomb and incendiary concentration deriving from this assault force's focus on a single target could theoretically at least transform the selected location into an irredeemable state of chaos. Prior to 27 September the onset of cloud conditions blanketing the Primary target had largely led to the mission being abandoned, but the American adaptation of the British blind-bombing and navigation aid *H2S* had been utilized for the first time that day over Emden's weather shrouded boundaries. The results of bombing were naturally undetermined, but at least a general pattern of strikes, however dispersed, had been achieved. No longer would the time and effort in loading bombers be rendered partially or totally useless because of the weather, and the expression "bombing round the clock" was henceforth to become even more relevant in the months ahead.

The Gathering Storm

Emden was briefed for the second time in six days (2nd), and of the 349 VIII BC crews sent out, 186 came from the 3rd BD; the overall step-up from the aforementioned 21 aircraft per group was explained by the 96th BG contributing 42 crews, with only the 388th BG holding to this minimum figure. Once again the presence of Pathfinder aircraft from the 482nd BG

Lt. W Winnisheik's crew had to fight for their lives on 4 October 1943 after falling behind the group and being set upon by fighters. The B-17F (42-3082/TS: E **Double Trouble**) lived up to her title, but stayed aloft as far as the Kent coast, where it was force-landed, skidding for several hundred yards before slewing to a halt; one seriously wounded gunner was then swiftly removed to a hospital.

Two views of the 100th BG's 42-3393/LD:Y **Just A Snappin'** seen after landing off the Bremen mission of 8 October 1943. The B-17F, flown by its regular crew under Capt. Everett Blakely, had veered off course after landing at Ludham airfield and rammed into a large oak tree. None of the crew was seriously injured in the incident, but S/Sgt. L Saunders later died from his combat wounds.

"The Bombing of the Year," as stated by Gen Eaker (CG, VIIIBC), has just been accomplished over the Focke-Wulf plant at Marienburg, in East Prussia. The highly concentrated bomb patterns ensured the newly-commissioned factory's production capability was totally if not permanently disrupted. Photograph was taken from a 390th BG aircraft. Date was 9 October 1943.

proved to be necessary, and nearly 960 tons of explosives fell in a deluge upon this major seaport's facilities. Single losses were recorded by both participating Divisions. The 388th BG came back short of Lt. J Felece's crew on board 42-30421/. The 361 BS B-17 sustained flak strikes over the target; one propeller was feathered and a second engine caught fire after the coast was re-crossed. The final crash site near Helgoland Island proved fatal for all ten airmen.

By this stage of the Daylight Offensive the technical assistance to the bomber navigators was of a standard that would appear to provide relatively accurate means of gaining access to a target, no matter how distant from the British Isles, and—arguably just as important—of regaining that island's shores. Frankfurt-am-Main was located in central Germany and was regarded as a key source of Nazi industrial output. Two days after Emden featured on the VIII BC Briefing maps for both B-17 Divisions, and a force almost equalling that dispatched on the 2nd was launched.

In the event barely 30% of the crews (all from the 1st BD) gaining mission credit even struck their Primaries. Even worse for the 3rd BD was the fact that none of its crews got through to the Secondaries; Saarlautern's industry and marshalling yards received the bulk of the bomb loads.

Postwar records stated the following "Leaders of the mission ended up 100 miles off course." It is not clear at what stage of the mission this cardinal error occurred, but the fact that Saarlautern is far to the southwest of Frankfurt gives a degree of credence to the suspicion that the remark points to the 3rd BD having been the culprit. Whatever the facts, the mission was not one that added greatly to the laurels of the Command. Sixteen crews were absent from the debriefing sessions that day, with single bomber losses recorded by four 3rd BD Groups. One of these bombers at least delivered its crew safely on friendly soil before expiring. This was 42-3308/M (385th BG); Lt. C Duwarske's crew jumped clear of their battle-damaged charge, which had previously been directed towards, and obligingly descended into, the North Sea. An almost similar degree of fortune affected all on board the other MIA aircraft. Lt. D Carlson's 42-3538/TS: W **Ten Knights in a Bar Room** was successfully abandoned near Rheims, France; 42-30045/BG: M **Fight'n-n-Bitin'** was ditched off the Seine Estuary by Lts. M Crowder and Taylor; and Capt. H Helstrom brought 42-30604/LN: T **Badger's Beauty V** in a for a crash landing near Caen, in Normandy, following power loss in two engines as well as rapidly diminishing fuel reserves. No less than eleven airmen on board the 94th and 100th BG machines concerned evaded capture, with the remaining nineteen also surviving, but only as POWs. (Two more B-17s were declared Category E, one of which (95th BG) had aborted during Assembly and was crash landed and the other (94th BG) after crash landing in Kent on return.)

Black Week Beckons...

Bremen is a city located on the river Weser and none too distant from the northern Dutch border. The defenses covering this large industrial complex had already displayed their ferocity way back in April when the then 1st BW had lost 15% of its attacking force. The ship and U-Boat construction yards at Bremen and Vegesack were of primary importance, and therefore very worthy of assault. It was therefore somewhat strange that the city center itself was briefed for the 3rd BD (although this might have been a precursor to a similar unconditional and arguably emotionally-based briefing laid on just 48 hours later.)

The 100th BG was part of a 170-strong 3rd BD force that headed out across the North Sea in the early afternoon. Approach to the target was made from the northwest, with the 1st BD flying a split route directly across Holland. The 100th BG was leading the 13th CBW and Maj. J Kidd was Wing Leader in 42-3393/LD: Y **Just A' Snappin'**, along with Lt. E Blakely. Also participating in the mission was Maj. G. Cleven (350 BS CO); normal procedure was for no more than one middle or senior ranking officer to fly a mission, since doing otherwise was risking the unnecessary loss of more than a single key member of staff. Be that as it may Cleven was there, but sadly his presence was to end up contravening the foregoing stricture...

Chaos

The formations were coursing in towards the target with fighter opposition building up ominously, along with a flak barrage, when the first blows were struck, with the 100th BG in the forefront of the punishment. A combination of flak and fighter damage inflicted upon 42-30818/LN: S **Salvo Sal** ended with Lt. W McDonald (POW) finally carrying off a crash landing between Lippenhuizen and Beetsterzwaag in northern Holland.

According to official records the first bombs were released by the 3rd BD at 1505 hours, and 22 minutes later the last bomb-bays were relieved of their loads. (The 100th BG Lead Bombardier released at 1525.) Two Thorpe Abbotts bombers were mortally affected shortly after coursing over the target. Maj. Cleven was on board 42-3233/LN: R **Our Baby** piloted by Capt. B DeMarco (POW). Confusion among the High squadron formation had led to its break-up, and DeMarco found his B-17 isolated from the others, to become rich prey for three fighters that homed in from a left frontal angle. Control surfaces and their connecting cables were thoroughly shot up and fuel streamed freely from one tank. Gunners were hampered by the state of the shot-up fuselage. Quakenbrueck, SW of Bremen, was where the unequal battle was given up by the crew, all of whom parachuted into captivity. A second High squadron bomber taken out just after bombing was 42-30154/XR: H **War Eagle** flown by Lt. A Becktoft (POW). Only S/Sgt. Lowe (ROG), who had been killed by a cannon shell, failed to join the other nine in a Stalag after they drifted down into the eastern suburbs of Bremen. Also downed at Ottersberg after "bombs away" was Lt. F Meadows' (KIA) 42-30358/LN: X **Phartzac**. Part of the bomb load was still on board and may well have been the reason why flak strikes caused the B-17 to blow up, with Lt. Hubbard (B) and Sgt. Ward (RWG) the only survivors.

The litany of destruction continued as the target was left behind. First, 42-30840/LN: O with Lt. H Nash (KIA) in charge was another flak victim and came down near Damme, west of Hoya, along with half its crew. Flak was also credited with the fatal crippling of 42-5864/EP: A **Piccadilly Lily** in Capt. A Barker's (KIA) charge. The final crash site near Bremerhaven, well north of Bremen, indicates that the bomber was attempting a solo homeward run, since the briefed homeward route had described a right-hand curve that had taken the formation south of the city. Whatever the circumstances, the bald fact was that only five of the eleven on board got out alive.

An Fw190 flown by an Oblt. Hondt added the final and most cruel twist to the Group's sufferings. As the formation was passing over the Dutch/German border zone the *Luftwaffe* pilot, making a head-on lunge, failed to avoid impacting with Lt. R Gormley's 42-3386/EP: H **Marie Helena**; the disintegrated remnants of the B-17 were scattered around Bellingwolde, east of Groningen, and not surprisingly all ten USAAF airmen forfeited their lives, while their adversary's fate was not stated.

The expressions on this group of Great Ashfield airmen following the wearying run to Marienburg on 9 October range from easing tension to grateful relief at surviving yet another hurdle on the road to salvation. Sadly, the odds against completing a combat tour at this stage of the Offensive were akin to a sufferer of deep-seated cancer enjoying complete remission from his condition.

The Culling Continues...

Further misery was put upon the 13th CBW this day when three 390th BG crews went down. First down was 42-30330/BI: A **Blood Guts & Rust II**. Flak disabled both in-board engines and all the gunners in the rear fuselage were killed, either then or after the bomber descended a few miles east of Bremen. Also recorded as coming down in the same area was Lt. M Sheppard's team flying in 42-30292/CC: Q **Pulsatin' Poly**. A volley of cannon shells across the forward fuselage probably killed both pilots, and the other four fatalities occurred when the B-17 subsequently exploded. Then, as the Group was swinging right off the target flak landed strikes on **Devil's Daughter** (42-30318/DI: G) that set an engine on fire; this proved to be uncontrollable, and several minutes later near Vechta the bomber exploded. Lt. A Rennels nevertheless managed to get himself and eight of the crew safely out, but Lt. Wetzel (CP), who had been wounded, proved to be the sole fatality.

...with even more culling

A similar loss scale to the 390th BG was borne by the 96th BG, with one each from three of its squadrons. Even more distressing was that this cost was not balanced by any form of successful bombing, since a bomb rack failure in the Lead B-17 over the IP caused all eighteen loads to land harmlessly short. A mass assault by fighters had ensued around this time, and among the bombers mortally affected was 42-37752/QJ: A. The B-17G was seen with an engine on fire after which it eased out, with the landing gear lowered, to an eventual and unstated crash site, but not before Lt. P Flashive's crew had jumped clear. (The landing gear action could have been a "surrender" signal to the fighters, or alternatively could have been done with a view to slowing the bomber to a safe speed for bailing out.) The other two Group losses occurred as the formation was withdrawing. Verden, southeast of Bremen, was the final resting place for 42-30373/BX: T **Lucky Lady III**, who belied her title's implied good fortune. Rocket and conventional fighter gunfire brought about her demise, leaving Lt. W Jones and five others alive out of the eleven on board. Around the same time 42-30367/AW: Y **Flak Happy** smashed into the ground southwest of Bad Zwischenahn. A determined Bf109 pilot swept in from above to land lethal blows upon the bomber that threw her out of control. One of the three survivors from Lt. E Bolstad's crew, S/Sgt. W McFadden (TG), recalled being thrust backwards and held down by centrifugal forces until the bomber temporarily levelled off. He then exited through his exit hatch with his parachute pack still detached, but with one arm through the carrying loop, before it was snapped in place and the ripcord pulled. His final sight of the B-17 was of a wingless fuselage tumbling end-over-end. A single 385th BG loss completed the sorry MIA figure for the Division's crews but the final tally in aircraft was not yet completed...

The Saga of "Just A' Snappin"

The once-proud 100th BG formation cleared the Dutch coast with eleven of the B-17s that went over Bremen still huddled together. Now far behind was a twelfth, namely Lt. Blakely and Maj. Kidd's Lead B-17, **Just A' Snappin'**. Flak had struck home as the bomb run was about to be completed, but Lt. Douglass (B), although wounded by shell fragments, stuck to his task and made a good release for the other bombardiers to land their bombs around the MPI. Then No. 4 engine was disabled and control cables damaged or destroyed, thus throwing the B-17 into a spiralling dive. Somehow or other the pilots brought their seemingly expiring charge back into level flight, but by then they were out on their own, with several more crewmembers badly—or in one still unknown case mortally—wounded. For whatever reason the fighter assaults that had occasioned some of these injuries ceased, but the likelihood of the bomber, which was staggering westwards at a pace not far short of stalling speed, regaining friendly soil appeared very doubtful.

The dreaded renewed onslaught from a second group of three enemy fighters did not immediately materialize, at least not until they had disposed of two other stragglers up ahead of the 100th BG aircraft in swift and depressing succession. However, the anticipated easy third *Abschuss* (Kill) for the three Bf109s was never to occur. Instead, two of them were either severely damaged or even downed during the short, sharp exchange of fire and the third finally peeled away. (The final count of confirmed claims by the crew accruing from the overall air battle would reach double figures.)

No. 4 engine was still on fire, but a slewing motion by the pilots fed enough air-blast over the engine mass to extinguish the flames. The Dutch coast was finally reached, but the crew were still in deep trouble; any prospect of ditching had to be abandoned, since even a success would leave the survivors without either life raft, these having suffered irreparable damage along with a number of Mae Wests. All available equipment was jettisoned, and this action enabled the bomber to regain a margin of altitude around 4,000 ft.

After an interminable sluggish passage over the sea the English coast loomed up. Bare minutes after crossing-in an airfield was sighted and a landing approach carried out successfully. However, on touching the ground firmly **Just A' Snappin's** brake cables did just that. Since the main control cables were also inoperable there was no way for the pilots to prevent the B-17 veering inexorably in the direction of a massive oak tree. Forward momentum was far from spent when B-17 and tree impacted in between the fuselage and No. 2 engine. It was therefore all the more amazing that not one of the ten-man crew was either injured or further affected, in the case of the wounded airmen. Sadly, the 20mm shell that had penetrated Sgt. Saunder's body early in the battle was to prove fatal. He lingered for some time, but died while being taken to a Norwich hospital in an RAF ambulance. (The airfield landed upon was Ludham, which was currently unoccupied, and the medical assistance had actually attended from nearby RAF Coltishall).

The Continuing Escort "Gap"

The ever-mounting cost of the Daylight Offensive had been apparent for some time even before the latest setback over Bremen. Matters were clearly unlikely to stabilize, let alone improve, for VIII BC until an adequate number of escort fighters were on hand to at least take some of the pressure off the bomber gunners by in turn warding off the *Luftwaffe* thrusts. The current strength of VIII Fighter Command rested wholly with the P-47 that currently equipped six Groups. Total numbers of the Republic fighter on hand now reached towards 300, as evidenced by the 274 dispatched 8 October. Although a very sound aircraft in tackling the Bf109 and Fw190, it suffered from a frustrating lack of range thanks to the very

Two Swedish guards stand by 42-3543/BX:W – **Sack Time Suzy**, one of the first B-17G variants to serve with the 96th BG. Lt. Greene headed north for Bulltofta on 9 October 1943 in the course of the planned mission to attack port facilities at Gydnia. The initial batch of G Model airframes lacked "cheek gun" window frames.

thirsty fuel consumption demanded of its 2,800 hp Pratt & Whitney engine. Targets located just inside the German borders with Holland and Belgium were barely attainable, with the final run-up to Bremen being a point in case.

The validity of the "self-defending bomber" theory had been steadily gnawed at over the past six months and was virtually cut to shreds by now. Nevertheless, the Strategic Planners felt the need to hammer German industry still had to be pressed home in spite of the cost in bombers and crews. And so it was that on 8 October, far from signalling a retrenchment in deep-penetration missions, was to lead to a further trio of assaults, two of which fell into this category...

"Strategic Bombing at its Best"

The target selection on 9 October was daring, if not potentially suicidal, at least as viewed by the crews assembled at briefing. All four were situated up on or near the Baltic coast, and at least 200 miles beyond Denmark's eastern regions. Anklam's industry was assigned wholly to the 1st BD, but a mix of Groups from all three Divisions, which included the 96th and 388th BGs, was also briefed for the port facilities at Gdynia and Danzig. The remaining five Groups from the 3rd BD were granted a specialist target of prime importance not only for the *Luftwaffe*, but by extension for the future survival prospects for the bomber crews.

A newly-constructed factory for Focke-Wulf fighter production had been created at Marienburg, just south of Gdynia and Danzig, but no work had yet been commenced—and it was VIII BC's intention to maintain that very desirable status.

One hundred B-17s lifted off for Marienburg with a further 54 heading for Gdynia. The very long flight across the North Sea and even more extended stretch across Denmark and the Baltic were naturally viewed with even greater apprehension than usual. Surely the time over enemy soil would invite an overwhelming reaction by the *Luftwaffe*? As it transpired, the degree of challenge was surprisingly light over the inward leg, but so not from then onward. However, it was the 1st BD whose ranks were to be most sorely mauled, with eighteen out of the overall total of 28 MIA crews.

The wearying passage to Marienburg finally came to a welcome end that had thankfully involved no discernable resistance from the defenders and the bombardiers were

Lt. John Pettenger (kneeling second from left) is seen with his crew alongside a 385th BG B-17F. This particular group bomber was MIA on 8 October 1943; two days later Lt. Pettenger's team bailed out of 42-6155 to become POWs during the Muenster*mission.

Treading the Valley of Death. An Fw190 appears to be angling in for a beam assault on the 95th BG; by the end of the Muenster mission five crews had succumbed to the defenders, although the group had the highest number of bombers (19) dropping their bomb loads out of the seven Division units.

A second shot taken from a 95th BG B-17 picks out the swooping pass made by two Luftwaffe fighters. The much steeper descent of the lower fighter might be related to his having picked out a straggling bomber ripe for dispatch at its adversary's leisure.

greeted by perfect visibility during the bomb-run. An additional boost to prospects of achieving a good strike was the fact that bombing altitude had been reduced to around 12,000 ft. Sure enough, 96 loads of explosives and incendiaries totalling 218 tons in all cascaded unerringly into the factory complex. The thick pall of smoke cloaking the plant even as the last elements banked for a far-distant England must have boosted the spirits of all, with the bombardiers heading the list!

One of the two crews missing from the Marienburg debriefing sessions largely ended up as "guests" of the Germans, albeit in unfortunate circumstances. One engine on 42-30336 **Miss Nana Lee II** (Lt. G Bell) had failed as the formations were crossing in, but the remaining power still enabled the pilots to press on for Marienburg, complete the bomb run, and head for home. Then, a report by Lt. Bachman (N) to Lt. Bell that his calculations placed the B-17 over Sweden impelled the pilot to call for a bail out;, after which he settled the bomber down for a landing on a flat stretch of grass. Any sense of relief at being in that neutral country was peremptorily cut short for the ten parachutists when they were greeted by very un-neutral German military personnel and civilians! Meanwhile Lt. Bell, having established—surely with the same initial sense of shock—that his charge now rested in a Danish field at Varde, would ironically end up in Sweden after managing to gain access to Danish Resistance sources.

The wearying grind to and from Marienberg had attained an apparent stage of salvation from *Luftwaffe* attention out over the North Sea when a final tragedy struck the 95th BG. The night before Lt. Jim Goff (N) had been conversing with his navigator friend Bob Wing, who was assigned to Lt. Ehert's crew. The latter had spoken of a premonition that the impending mission was to prove fatal for him, a mood that all of Jim's gentle dismissal of Bob's assertion could not dispel. Now, **Roger the Lodger II** (42-30377 /

Roger the Lodger II/ 42-30377 has lost its No. 2 engine, from which a burst of flame crests the wing trailing edge. Scant seconds later the B-17F suffered further fighter strikes that caused it to come apart. Incident occurred over the North Sea on 9 October 1943, and none of Lt. R Ehert's crew survived the experience.

QW: R) was one of the formation coming under particular fire as a number of rocket firing fighters—probably twin-engine Bf110s and/or Me410s—made a mass lunge. The No. 2 engine was set on fire, followed by a near or direct strike of a missile on No. 3 that initiated a huge blaze, according to Jim's observations. Up to seven parachutes emerged, but although the coordinates of the descending airmen's location was radioed to the ASR Service it was cruelly certain that their fate was already sealed.

45th CBW Fortunes

The 96th and 388th BGs had joined with the 1st BD's 40th CBW and two B-24 Groups to strike at Gdynia. The results here were nothing like as spectacular as at Marienburg, while both 3rd BD Groups lost two each out of the overall figure of six. Once again the loss factor arose on the return leg. One of the 96th BG's bombers suffered so much from fighter gunfire that F/O. R Greene felt compelled to divert northward towards Sweden, where 42-3543/BX: W **Sack Time Suzy** and her crew were duly interned after landing at Bulltofta.

The remaining three MIA bombers survived as far as the western coastline of Denmark. First, Lt. C Kinney's 42-30802 from Knettishall went down over the coastal zone south of Esjberg and all ten personnel were fortunate to survive; after bailing out they drifted down onto a tidal basin from where they could gain more solid ground. Even greater fortune was enjoyed by the survivors from Lt. H Nagorka's (POW) crew. The nose and right wing were set on fire by cannon shells as the Danish coast was receding and the 388th BG B-17 (42-30371/H) hastily abandoned to fall to its watery grave. Although the crew were immersed for upwards of an hour, supported only by their Mae Wests, six were finally hauled from the sea by a German vessel.

No such luck attended any of Lt. W Hunt's crew on board 42-30781/MZ: M. Fighters dispatched the B-17 into the sea and the simple, sad epitaph for all ten 96th BG airmen was their names inscribed on a "Wall of the Missing" at two U.S. military cemeteries....

Lts Frank Murphy (left) and C Cruikshank (to Murphy's left) were navigator and pilot respectively on **Aw-R-Go!** Photograph was taken at Thorpe Abbotts in much happier circumstances compared to what awaited them and their fellow crewmembers on 10 October 1943.

Summary

Marienburg's demise was proof, however intermittently achieved, of the value of precision daylight bombing. The relative absence of counterattack against the assigned Force prior to bombing, allied to the lower-than-normal altitude and clear weather conditions all played their part in the success. Not unnaturally, Gen. Eaker and his Staff at *Pinetree* ensured that maximum publicity would be accorded the event. Elsewhere, however, the returns for the other three sub-forces arguably did not match the cost. Champions of the Daylight Offensive would have their convictions that this was the path to ultimate success against Axis industry firmly challenged for many months ahead. The events occurring over Muenster just 24 hours after Marienburg surely only served to strengthen the sceptics' views.

Massacre at Muenster

Up to now, the clear separation between industrial and military facilities and civilian housing as potential targets had been adhered to by the VIII BC suthorities.

The severed tail section of **Aw-R-Go!** with the fabric surface of its rudder burnt off lies several miles north of Muenster. Only eight of Capt. C Cruikshank's 100th BG crew that was flying its 21st mission ended up alive from the 10 October 1943 assault upon the city center.

This crushed fuselage is all that remains of 42-30262/BI: **Tech Supply** following its downing on 10 October 1943 by rocket-firing Bf 110s of ZG26. Lt. John G Winant (P) was one of six survivors who jumped clear before the bomber plummeted to earth near Ladbergen, north of the target, Muenster.

Area bombing, as indulged in by RAF Bomber Command, was regarded by its American contemporary as completely unnecessary, if not also morally repugnant. Where civilian property had been struck during the day it was seen as an accidental, rather than deliberate, feature of combat operations. But WWII was steadily but inexorably being transformed into a Total War, with civilian workers perceived as a necessary element in War production and therefore open to military assault, whether or not at their place of work. This revised policy was now initiated on 10 October 1943 for the USAAF bomber crews.

Muenster possessed a vital complex of railroad facilities, including marshalling yards. Transport was a key element in the efficient movement of equipment and personnel. Following the Casablanca Conference it was accorded a third-place priority for assault after the U-Boat and aircraft construction industries. Indeed, by 1944 the Nazi transportation system, along with the synthetic oil industry, would become the perceived twin keys to successfully bringing about a swift end to the Conflict in some Allied circles.

However, when Munester was briefed on 10 October with the city center as the Primary and the MPI the city's cathedral, the fact that it was a Sunday, along with several of the Briefing officers' references to "messing up the housing of the German railway staff" did not sit well with many combat crewmembers. After all, the avowed intention of the VIII BC Campaign had been created and pitched on the basis of striking at purely military and industrial targets. Indeed, Gen. Eaker was to be credited with making the following specific statement, "We will never be accused of throwing the bomber at the man in the street." One highly respected officer at Horham made his scruples and inability to participate known to Col. Gerhart (Group CO). The latter tersely reminded his subordinate as follows in what is recorded here as a condensed version, "Lieutenant, this is war, spelled W-A-R; I'm leading, and you are my navigator – any further questions?," and the issue was thus resolved! (On the other hand, at Thorpe Abbotts Maj. Egan recalled leaping to his feet and cheering along with many others when such remarks were made during the briefing.)

The pressures, both physical and mental, of gearing up for a third mission in barely 48 hours must have left the combat crewmen concerned in a lethargic state. In spite of this the prospect of completing one more leg in the longed-for completion of their operational tours when allied to the natural optimism of youth came to the fore. The crews clambered aboard their B-17s and were aloft and heading out over the English coast by 1400 hours.

The need to assemble the various Groups and Wings into their stream before departing England naturally provided the *Luftwaffe* with more than ample time to anticipate an incursion of their territory. Although the ultimate destination of the attacking force was not yet known, the *Freya* long-range radar sets could detect aerial activity up to 100 miles away. The existence of the 2nd BD "decoy" force heading towards the Danish/German border could have acted as a lure for the Germans; unfortunately, the premature withdrawal of this force due to technical failures did not, therefore, divert the enemy's attention from what was perceived to be the major threat. On the other hand, the probability of the B-24s constituting a "decoy" force could be discounted thanks to the radar "signature" that would be on a smaller scale to that of the main attacking force.

The 3rd BD was the lead attacking force, and was therefore the one likely to catch the major if not the full attention of the defenders. The course in over southern Holland progressed in deceptively good order, with flak the prominent countermeasure at this stage. The P-47 escorts linked up and commenced to fly a cross-over pattern around and above the bombers in order to relate their greater minimum speed to that of the much more pedestrian-paced *Big Friends*. Approaching Dorsten, which was barely 15 minutes flying distance from the Primary, the fighter pilots from the current Groups on hand began to reluctantly bank for home, having reached the prudent limits of their fuel endurance. Unbeknownst at this time to the bomber crews was the fact that the 36 P-47s of the 352nd FG that should have taken up covering duties in the target area were still languishing on their Bodney airfield, the helpless victims of the fog blanket. The scene was thus unknowingly set for an aerial battle between the bombers and an unimpeded *Luftwaffe* of an intensity that had hardly ever been exceeded to date...

Although 133 bombers had taken off during the assembly process, the inevitable human and technical failures accruing from sustained operations reduced the launched force by a noticeable number of aircraft that in

Col. Old (96th BG CO) stands on the left. Next to him is Capt. T Kenny with most of his crew. This team enjoyed Lead status at Snetterton Heath and headed the 4th BW over Regensburg (17 August.) and the 3rd BD over Schweinfurt (14 October).

Lt. Robert Bolick (P) is photographed with his 96th BG crew during training in the States. His co-pilot, Lt. Ed Downs (1), is the baby-faced officer on the left who was badly injured on 14 October 1943. Lt. Miles McFann (N), who flew the B-17 back home after Bolick was fatally injured, is not included in the picture.

turn weakened the overall defensive firepower. The 100th BG was destined to cross into Europe with fourteen B-17s, of which one actually belonged to the 390th BG (ironically the smallest sub-force among the seven Groups, although one respected 8th USAAF author noted that six more B-17s, including one detached from the 390th BG, had aborted the mission before or as this point was reached.) Further attrition in this manner was experienced within the 95th BG and 390th BG ranks. The Thorpe Abbotts Group was again assigned the Low position in the CBW, and as with Regensburg was destined to absorb the worst attentions of the *Luftwaffe*, this time in the worst possible manner, although the other two Groups were also to feel the sting of that still redoubtable entity.

Disappearing Act

The enemy fighter force had assembled in sufficient time and numbers to launch yet another sustained and bloody assault upon their already sorely-tried adversaries. The B-17 flown by Maj. Egan, along with Capt. J Brady, was among the first to feel the lethal effect of fighter gunfire. The welter of strikes impacting with the airframe of 42-30830/LD: U **Mlle Zig Zag** all too soon convinced both pilots that their charge was fatally damaged. One airman was killed, but the other nine bailed out near to Nottuln, where their B-17 crashed.

The loss of the Lead bomber was symptomatic of the fate of the entire formation, which would soon reach epidemic proportions. The descent of the Lead B-17 unfortunately led to several other pilots following on in an action that split the already heavily-assailed formation asunder. Xanten lies to the northwest of the Ruehr, and it was here that 42-30087/EP: M **Shackrat** came to earth; Lt. M Beatty (P) was not one of the two survivors.

A few miles north of Dorsten 42-3433/LN: W **Lena** smashed into the ground. Flak had previously set the bomber on fire and Lt. Kramer had called for a bail out; that sadly did not succeed for him or two gunners. More fortunate was the entire crew led by Lt. W McCarter. A rocket strike ignited one main fuel tank and the crew rightly deserted 42-30090/XR: B **El P'issofo**, whose airframe was shattered into fragments near Haltern. Although the fighters were by now swarming in upon the Group, it was flak that took out another B-17 as the bomb run was in progress. Lt. E Stork had ultimately brought his ailing B-17 back on a single engine two days previous, but today saw no similar reprieve. He and seven other surviving crewmembers took to their parachutes before the inverted bomber 42-30023/ XR: M **Forever Yours** came to ground at Amelsburen. The bomb run stage also cost the group 42-3237/LD: R **Stymie**, which had already sustained fighter-inflicted damage and was now further crippled by flak. Lt. Stephens dropped out in a desperate bid to make a solo run home, but his efforts soon came to naught after further fighter attacks. A crash landing at Holthausen, west of Coesfeld, left all ten airmen facing a POW fate.

Marginally further back from the target, Lt. D Walts suffered five fatalities on board 42-30823/LN: Y after the gunfire of Hptm. Hoeckner (2/JG1) landed fatal strikes, with the final crash site at Hohenholte. Another B-17 finally downed by fighters at this point that had also been previously flak-damaged was 42-30734/EP: G **Slightly Dangerous**; Uffz Rubbau (4/JG1) was the executioner, with his victim spiralling down less one wing to impact at Havistock, along with three on Lt. C Thompson's crew.

Spreading the Destruction Further

The 390th BG, flying High group, was the second element of the 13th CBW to come under similar deadly scrutiny to a degree that would ultimately chop eight crews from its ranks, two in a particularly gruesome manner. Strikes on the left wing of 42-5915/DI: J **Cash & Carrie** after the IP had been traversed knocked out No. 1 engine, followed soon after by No. 2 "running away." The bomber fell behind, and as the assaults by the fighters upon the straggler intensified, the order to salvo the bomb load was given, followed almost immediately by a second command to bail out. This was acted upon by half the crew, but the other five were still on board when a crash landing near Ahaus was successfully performed.

Capt. Short's 42-30826/FC: R **Short Stuff** appears to have been next on the execution list prior to bombing, although the crash site NE of Muenster seems to contradict the MACR time of its demise (1500 hours), since bombing only commenced three minutes later. Fire rapidly took hold of the strike-afflicted right wing and the mortally crippled B-17 swung down into a spiral; reports of up to nine parachutes among the eleven-man crew proved basically correct, although Lt. Hughes (N) subsequently died after being severely injured on landing.

Horham's Grim Contribution

Lt. Riggs was flying the particularly vulnerable No. 6 slot in Horham's Low squadron and was latched onto by Fw. Wiegand (JG26). The initial burst of gunfire blew shards of metal away from around the No. 3 engine, and Wiegand then observed the shape of a body hurtling past and barely missing his canopy. The stricken bomber, trailing smoke, eased away out of formation, and Wiegand duly made a second pass that inflicted further damage and initiated a prolonged series of erratic swoop

The single USAAF escort fighter regularly on hand until October 1943 was the P-47, whose operational effectiveness was primarily restricted by the heavy fuel consumption of its 2,800 hp Pratt and Witney engine. **Little Demon** was the 353rd FG mount of Capt. W Beckham, who ran up a healthy list of "kills" before becoming a POW. Note the minimal ground clearance on the drop tank.

and zoom maneuvers as some of the crew commenced to bail out of 42-5986/BG: J **Brown's Mule**. The *Luftwaffe* airman, along with his wingman, now kept track of the dying B-17 as it wandered northwards before finally falling to earth near Saerbeck, due north of Muenster, according to Wiegand.

The bomb run was proceeding on its inexorable course in spite of the steady attrition in the CBW's ranks, and the release of Lt. D Johnson's load from the Lead 95th BG was achieved at 1503 hours, so signifying the beginning of the martyrdom of the German city, although the equal martyrdom of the 13th CBW was far from over. In the case of the 95th BG, the second in a final total of five crews fell out under fire from the same assailant of the Riggs bomber, Fw. Wiegand. Both main fuel tanks were set alight and, as if this were not enough, the tail section on 42-30273/BG: F **Patsy Ann III** snapped off. Lt. W Buckley (P) was one of five fatalities as the bomber curved into a dive that ended at Sinningen, close to the Rally Point of Emsdetten.

Around the same time the crew of Lt. Broman on **Fritz Blitz** (42-30272/OE: U), flying Deputy to Capt. Adams' **Miss Flower III** (42-30817/BG: G), observed how this Low squadron B-17 flying Lead sagged away after it was struck by flak coming off the target towards the Rally Point. The bomber was then stabilized sufficiently for all on board to jump clear. Having initially followed their Leader before realizing the true situation, the now isolated bomber was hastily directed back towards the Group formation, but to no avail, since the straggling B-17 was fastened onto and lethally punished. The bail out order was given, an action that must have been desperately disappointing for Sgt. W Thomas (ROG), who was on his final mission; at least he was one of nine survivors to escape the demise of the bomber at Haaksbergen, just inside Dutch territory. This geographic region was where 42-3497/OE: O also ended its operational career at the hands of Lt. L Correia. Damage to the oxygen system over the target culminated with the bomber being abandoned successfully by all but one of the crew.

Finishing off the 100th BG...

There is a postwar impression that the carnage among the 100th BG's ranks was totally effected before the target was even attained, but this is incorrect, since the punishment was still being handed out after "bombs away"; as it so happened, the loss factor

The solemn and reflective faces of these 96th BG combat personnel confirm that a mission is "on" as they queue up to collect their packs from the Parachute Section. The weather appears to be mild if not unusually warm to judge by the vest-wearing airman handing out the packs!

Any collision between a fuel truck and a B-17 provided no guarantee of survival for either driver or combat crew concerned. It is not clear what precipitated this incident, but although the bomber's nose section is destroyed no major blaze actually occurred.

was half as great after the Group banked for home. The P-47s of the 56th BG were by now frantically closing the gap to pick up their charges, but the current absence of escorts permitted the *Luftwaffe* to indulge itself at its grisly peak of efficiency.

The homeward route swung in a gradual left-hand curve and on to the briefed Rally Point at Emsdetten, northwest of the stricken city, but barely had the bomb run been completed when yet another B-17 was culled from the 100th BG. This was 42-30725/LN: Z **Aw-R-Go**, which absorbed strikes in the radio room, killing T/Sgt Vincenti (ROG) and S/Sgt. C Clark (TG); the bomber finally exploded and descended over Lienen, but Capt. C Cruikshank and the other seven airmen bailed out. While also coming off the target the B-17 flown by Lt. W Beddow had the double cruel luck to be run into by an Bf109, after which **Sexy Suzy – Mother of Ten** (42-30723/EP: D) veered into the path of 42-30047/LN: Q **Sweater Girl**. Lt. M Beddows was one of six fatalities on the former B-17, while a reverse pattern of loss occurred on Lt. B Atchison's aircraft; both aircraft crashed near Ostbevern, some ten miles northeast of the MPI.

The final act in the 100th BG's virtual annihilation affected the bomber flown by Lt. J Justice. His crew in 42-42-3229/XR: A **Pasadena Nena** was flying their 18th mission, but the B-17 had suffered flak damage and became detached from the group remnants over the target. They now sought protection from groups up ahead, but after suffering further flak damage to No. 4 engine their bomber fell into a spin that was recovered almost at ground level, by which time most of the crew had bailed out. Shortly after a fighter closed in and raked the B-17 across its breadth to set it on fire. Sadly, although Justice bailed out safely his co-pilot, Lt. J Shields, was subsequently found in the wreckage with one other airman after the B-17 crashed near Ede, in eastern Holland.

...And Framlingham's Torment Increases

The 390th BG's hammering from the defenders, as with the 95th BG, only arose and expanded after Muenster was attacked. The 571st BS was flying the High squadron slot and had suffered the lowest rate of "aborts" (one from nine) out of the six split between the three squadrons. As the Group turned for home the sub-unit came under extremely severe assault that finally excised six B-17s from its ranks, all but one a squadron assigned aircraft.

The first to be mortally afflicted was probably 42-3302/FC: O **Rick-O-Shay**, which took a heavy shell strike and sagged downwards. The dying bomber then appears to have adopted a northerly course before finally expiring, since the crash site was at Suttrup, nearly 40 miles northwest of Muenster; at least all on Lt. E Weldon's crew ended up on the ground.

Exotic "Frightener"

There was by now a regular use of 21-cm rockets fired from under-wing tubes; these were mainly fitted to the Bf110 and Me410 twin-engine fighters, but were also being mounted on some Bf109s and Fw190s. The *Luftwaffe* pilots had no precision equipment with which to aim this particularly fearsome form of weaponry. Three group crews were to be the direct or indirect victims of rockets, commencing with two from the 571 BS. The Rally Point was falling behind when one of the projectiles made contact with 42-3328/ BI: D **Miss Fortune**, flying Lead in the third Element, and split it cleanly in two. Ahead and to Lt. H Sneed's left flew 42-3415/ FC: Q **Miss Behavin'**, into which the forward section of the stricken aircraft impacted as it zoomed helplessly upwards. The aerial partners in what was truly an incident of "misfortune" rapidly disintegrated, and their remains ended up at Burgsteinfurt. Four gunners from Sneed's crew and one from the Starnes B-17 were the sole and very fortunate survivors out of twenty on board. Sneed, Lt. Breckenbridge (CP), and T/Sgt. Olson (Eng.) had survived their Mediterranean immersion in their dinghy after ditching off the Regensburg mission, but blind Fate had finally dealt them a cruel hand. (A second 568 BS bomber, Lt. J Winant's 42-30262/BI: K, had previously suffered the same form of rocket-based destruction near adbergen, with the pilot and five of his crew surviving.)

Over the same zone of activity, yet another 571 BS crew led by Lt. W Smith met its demise while flying on 42-3426/FC: Y **Spider**. Their bomber was also split in two, this time by a flak shell, and crashed at Isendorf; both pilots along with one gunner were killed during the incident. Completion of the squadron's loss pattern was not long delayed, as the Dutch/German border was looming up. Flak had probably badly affected the airframe on 42-30265/FC: V **Pinky** before a final fighter thrust provided the coup de grace that caused the B-17 to disintegrate and crash near Haaksbergen, just inside Holland. The ever-swelling numbers of *Kriegsgefangenen* was increased by eight, the unlucky exception being S/Sgt Look (Eng.), who broke his neck on landing, while Sgt. Converse (TG) experienced the very reverse in luck since he evaded capture.

Better Fortunes...

The 45th CBW was slotted into the stream as the Division's second such sub-force, with the 388th BG supposed to be in Lead position, and due to suffer a single loss. However, both the Lead and Deputy crews had "aborted," and so the group handed over responsibility to the 96th BG and adopted a Low position in the CBW. No matter how combat experienced a crew might be, there lurked the constant risk of failure either through technical failure or, as in so many numerous instances that day, at the hands of the enemy. Lt. P Williams and most of the crew were on their 18th missions, while Lt. I Rogg (CP) was on his 21st. Their B-17 (42-5898/D **Little Lass**) was struck by flak and drifted out of formation just after "bombs away." The isolated aircraft soon attracted *Luftwaffe* attention but still gamely headed on course for home. The central stretch of the Ijisselmeer was passing below when the B-17 was reluctantly abandoned to crash beneath the water, while its crew floated down to captivity at Enkhuizen, on the western shoreline. The 96th BG also surrendered a single B-17 piloted by Lt. D Williams, Jr. This was 42-3516/ BX: S, which had not even had the chance to shed its bomb load onto the city when it went down, but at least the crew did not share its terminal fate after they took to their parachutes.

The 100% survival rate enjoyed by the MIA crews from the 45th CBW was partially mirrored by the remaining two bombers to go down from the 4th CBW, both from Great Ashfield. Lt. J Pettenger's crew was on its 19th mission, but their regular aircraft 42-30275/D **Vibrant Virgin** had gone down over Bremen. Now, 42-6155/P suffered an engine fire and shot-up controls directly after bombing, and all too soon had to be abandoned northeast of Muenster. The Pettenger team survived, unlike two on board 42-3539/G, with Lt. W Whitlow at the controls. The bomber's extended punishment from the fighters lasted from the target to Holten, in central Holland, where three of the parachuting airmen did not end up in enemy hands. However, one of this trio (Lt. J Burch, CP) was unknowingly on borrowed time. He got as far as the southwest of France, where he drowned attempting to cross a river, surely one of the cruellest fates to be realized by a combat crewman. The pilot was extremely lucky to survive his parachute descent. Due to discomfort from bruised buttocks arising from the prolonged mission 24 hours before, he had previously loosened the harness leg straps and forgotten to fasten them before bailing out. As it was, he managed to literally hold on to the lift-webs with his hands while marginally assisted during his fifteen-minute descent by the chest straps that had now risen up to armpit level!

The 100th's Lucky Exception

The decimation of the 100th BG would have been total but for the spirited performance displayed by Lt. Robert Rosenthal's still-acolyte team flying their third mission in 42-6087/LD: **Royal Flush**. The B-17's title alludes to what is an unbeatable hand in the card game poker, and was to prove very appropriate in the light of what transpired this day. "Rosie's" operational career was to span a further 17 months and encompass more than 50 missions, but he must have held grave doubt as to he and his crew's prospect of even surviving the Muenster run. One engine was disabled on the way in, followed by No. 3 having to be "feathered" and the oxygen system seriously disrupted as fighters zeroed in on the group

An anonymous group of B-17s along with a larger formation ahead and above exude solid condensation trails. This action of Nature was breath-taking to behold from the ground but contained twin risks to the bomber crews – midair collision through immersion in the sight-robbing blanket, and sudden assault by enemy fighters utilizing the screen to mount their assaults.

remnants straggling homeward. Two gunners were seriously wounded during the air battle, but the battered B-17 managed to hold course and eventually got clear of all opposition. The fog swirling around Thorpe Abbotts on its return did not prevent Rosenthal and Lt. Lewis from bringing off a perfect landing, albeit on half power.

Also landing at the 100th BG airfield was the single 390th BG bomber originally assigned to fly with the group. Flown by Lt. K Harris, 42-30783/DI: **Stork Club** had constituted the other half of the High squadron along with **Royal Flush** after all other assigned crews had "aborted." However, during the height of the battle Harris had recalled Col. Wittan's advice to link up with the 390th BG should matters "get out of hand," as it were—prophetic words indeed! So it was that with the 100th BG formation falling apart the now-miniscule High squadron sub-force acted on the advice and climbed steeply into the rear elements of the 390th BG flying the High slot!

Six further B-17s from the other two CBW units also touched down at Thorpe Abbotts. Around the same time rapidly drying fuel tanks and the thick fog added to the problem of heavy battle damage on the other 100th BG survivor that had earlier been detached to operate with the 390th BG. Lt. R Schneider finally landed 42-3234/EP: **Little Mike** at RAF Wattisham. However, he overshot the runway and the resultant impact with the uneven terrain broke the B-17's fuselage; three days later it was "written off."

A mix of 4 x 4 and 6 x 6 trucks are loaded or being loaded up with a large group of women from civilian and Service sources, ready to be transported to an VIII BC airfield for a party. Picture is believed taken at Thetford railroad station, around which was located several American airfields, including Knettishall and Snetterton Heath.

Summary

Muenster had proven to be a disaster for the 13th CBW, with 25 of the total 29 MIA crews coming from within its ranks, so constituting a 70% loss factor in relation to the number of its aircraft that even reached the target (41). The sufferings of the 3rd BD, which had so far sacrificed 49 B-17s during the three missions to date, were almost being paralleled by the 1st BD, which had lost 34 bombers, with a further five surrendered among the B-24s of the 2nd BD. This figure exactly equalled the one incurred during the entire course of *Blitz Week*, but the current campaign, unlike the July series of missions, still had to run its course.

The continuing lure of effectively striking at a "bottleneck" category of industrial output was still very much on the minds of the USAAF planners with ball bearings a top priority—and that particularly placed Schweinfurt directly in the firing line, despite the presence of facilities at Stuttgart and in France, as well as Swedish and Swiss import sources. The Bavarian town was well over 200 miles out of the maximum range capable of being flown by the P-47s; the chances of the bomber formations gaining their target and returning home with an acceptable loss ratio, when given the current height of efficiency being demonstrated by the *Jagdwaffe*, ranged from poor to dismal. (The Muenster debacle had occurred over a period barely exceeding 30 minutes, whereas the bombers could anticipate being on their own for between two and three hours should Schweinfurt be briefed.)

Three days now elapsed before Field Orders were created and transmitted by teleprinter to the bomber bases late on the 13th. Schweinfurt it was—and so was commenced a train of events that would forever be seared into the historic fabric of VIII BC and the nation its personnel represented...

"Black Thursday"

The scene is a Briefing hut at an anonymous B-17 airfield on 14 October 1943. The Briefing Officer quietly studies his hushed audience before simply stating, "Gentlemen, your target for today is Schweinfurt," before busying himself with his papers as the inevitable chorus of howls and groans arises and takes an appreciable time to subside. From among the throng one plaintive voice wails "Son-of-a-bitch, and it's my 25th!," to which another airman piped up, "What the Hell are you crying about – it's my first!" On another base the man on the podium reportedly suggested, "This could be a milk run"; the combat crews' reaction to this fatuous statement must have been extremely terse to the point of obscenity!

The lowering cloud condition over southern England did not bode well for the mission's ultimate completion, but when a reconnaissance Mosquito dispatched over central Europe reported clear overall visibility back to *Pinetree* Gen. Anderson issued the command to go ahead. Whereas the two B-17 divisions had split their effort between Schweinfurt and Regensburg on 17 August, this time round they were to make a combined assault upon Schweinfurt. The total number of bombers sent out was 351, of which sixty belonged to the 2nd BD. The B-17 formations managed to form up in good order despite the cloud tops extended up to around 6,000 ft in place of the briefed 2,000 figure. In contrast, assembly problems with the B-24 sub-force were to result in its abandoning the mission, although two groups carried out a diversionary run over the North Sea towards Emden.

All six P-47 Groups were scheduled to participate, but continuing adverse weather conditions resulted in one unit failing to make rendezvous. Two other groups found their efforts hampered by Mother Nature's weather blanket, while a fourth limited its activity to covering the B-24s. All in all, fighter escort provision on the way over was badly reduced; on the other hand, the *Jagdwaffe* pilots withheld their initial onslaught until their adversaries were primarily at the point of no return anyway...

Initial Fortunes...

Six of the 3rd BD's groups had sent out near or full-strength formations, with the 96th BG dispatching no less than 41 bombers to form separate A and B groups out of 152 in all. However, three of this complement would "abort" the mission during Assembly, along with no less than nine more that entered enemy airspace. The exception was the ill-starred 100th BG, which could muster just eight B-17s following its battering over Bremen and Muenster, but all of whom completed the mission. The two Divisions headed into Europe on roughly parallel courses, with LeMay's force crossing in some 30 miles further south over Belgium territory. Then, instead of maintaining this

Lt. Barnhill's 42-3528/QJ: is pulled out of the Barmsee, a lake in Germany close to the Swiss border. The pilots had decided to divert into Switzerland following heavy damage incurred during the bomb run over Schweinfurt on 14 October 1943.

joint approach pattern, the Division angled southward before resuming its eastward route over Luxembourg. The abrupt route change may well have contributed to the relative lack of aerial opposition encountered on the outward leg, but the Division's good fortune was certainly not matched by its contemporary. Almost as soon as the final P-47s were peeling off for England the 1st BD was assailed by a mass of fighters that all too soon began to bite into its ranks and was destined to inflict fully 75% of the Command's losses by mission's end.

Initial Good Fortune

As on 17 August, the 96th BG was delegated as the Divisional Lead. Flying in **Fertile Myrtle III** (42-30366/BX: A) was most of the same skilled crew that had led at Regensburg, including Capts. Kenny (P) and J Latham (B); Lt. D Abel (N) was here displaced by Capt. Jones, while Maj. Hodson (Group Navigator) was also present. Finally, sitting in the right seat was the Group's former CO, Col. Archie Old, now the 45th CBW's Commanding General.

The Task Force's progress towards Schweinfurt was surprisingly but equally gratifyingly unchallenged to any degree before the formations began their approach to the IP around Wuerzburg, some 20 miles southwest of the Primary. Then, one or more passes by fighters crippled 42-30806/QJ: G V Packet so badly that all ten on Lt. J Scarborough's crew took to their parachutes several miles past the IP. The bloodletting had begun for the 96th BG, as well as one other unit within the Division, although it would be fully withheld until the force was homeward bound.

The second casualty's final demise actually commenced during the bomb run when 42-3528/QJ: was a victim of *Herausschuss*, the German term for damaging a bomber to the degree that it became detached from the formation with the prospect of finishing it off at leisure. However, although the B-17 was culled from the 96th BG's ranks, Lt. M Barnhill managed to take up an uninterrupted southerly heading with a view to landing in Switzerland. The bulk of the roughly 200 to 250-mile flight was completed, but then matters went wrong enough for the pilots to make an emergency ditching in a conveniently available lake (Barmsee) east of Garmisch-Partenkirchen, close to the Austrian border but some 50 miles east of neutral territory. The crew got into the dinghies, but were then fired upon by *Hitlerjugend* personnel, with ultimately fatal results for Lt. V Cook (CP).

The Division's bombing effort was to prove to be on a greater scale compared to the already severely mauled 1st BD, but matters could have been worse for the initial CBW's assault thanks to what happened to the Kenny/Old Lead B-17. A flak burst close to the nose badly wounded Capt. Latham; although thrown back from his stool he dragged himself back into position and fought off the pain sufficiently to make a first-class release comparable to his performance over Regensburg. This time round the ball bearing plants received a far more severe degree of punishment compared to 17 August. This was thanks to two factors: namely the enhanced overall bombing accuracy, coupled with a heavier weight of explosives, and particularly incendiaries, delivered between the two Divisions compared to the largely ineffective single Divisional strike in August.

The Screw Tightens

So far the Division had come through with just two losses among the 128 aircraft completing their bomb runs, but the price for gaining access to Schweinfurt would now begin to increase with particular adverse effect upon the 94th and 96th BGs. In the former instance the 21-strong Group lost two crews in fairly quick succession on either side of the Rally Point. Lt. J Mullinax's 42-30149/XM: A2 **Spare Parts** had its No. 2 engine set ablaze by fighter gunfire and disappeared from eyewitness sight near Wuerzburg. Mercifully, all on board bailed out safely.

The second picture shows the tail unit and truncated left stabilizer. The 96th BG bomber was safely "ditched," but gunfire from the shore fatally wounded Lt. V Cook (CP) as he and his fellow crewmembers huddled in the single functioning dinghy.

Pickle Dropper, the second production B-17G -40–VE, lacked the "cheek" gun windows in the nose compartment. On 30 December 1943 no less than eight of Lt. C Brigman's crew evaded capture after the bomber was "bellied-in" near Wimy, in France.

Seven bombers, but only five crews, would not return to Rougham. Prior to the mission a B-17 from the 94th BG had been detached to Snetterton Heath with Lt. Silas Nettles and crew going over to Rougham to pick it up. The general state of the bomber did not endear itself to the crew, and they reflected ruefully on the contrast with their B-17 for the previous mission **V Packet** that today was assigned to Lt. Scarborough. Their doubts about what they regarded as a "clunker" were to prove sadly justified. First, 42-3453/TS: K lost position after suffering fighter-inflicted damage; this included one engine whose propeller could not be "feathered," a situation that left the bomber wallowing helplessly behind. Nettles nevertheless kept on a heading for the target, but his arrival over Schweinfurt found his bombardier, Lt. E Jones, carrying out a single sighting, all other aircraft having already departed.

The wallowing B-17 was not only given the flak gunners' full attention, but all too soon became the focus for further fighter assaults that knocked out a second engine and left a third smoking. The bail out order was given and successfully carried out by all ten. That figure might have been reduced by one when Lt. Nettles' parachute "spilled out" after the ripcord snagged on an obstruction in the bomb-bay—the intended exit point for both pilots. Lt. LeFors (CP) had hesitated in jumping and shut his eyes during this brief period. On opening them he saw Nettles' plight and assisted him in gathering in the billowing silk folds, after which both airmen departed down towards captivity. (A more dramatic but inaccurate account of this incident appeared in a 1960s book on **Black Thursday**. It asserted that Nettles had been the first to jump, but only succeeded in snagging his harness on the bomb-bay frame; had LeFors not hesitated in jumping he would not have been able to help his pilot out of this extremely parlous situation! The true facts as related by Silas to the author in 1977 were surely dramatic enough without being further embellished.) A further irony for the Nettles crew lies in the fact that their fate had been sealed regardless of whether or not **V Packet** was their assigned B-17, since it had also gone down!

Two further 94th BG crews were deleted from the formation before Mannheim. The first down was probably Lt. G Davidson's team in 42-30453/TS: **Thunderbird**, although the bomber's last sighting at 1525 was five minutes after 42-5901/GL: T **Superstitious Al-o-yious** (Lt. E Reed) was last seen by returning crewmembers. Nineteen of the twenty airmen managed to end up as POWs, the exception being Sgt. R Flener (LWG) on Reed's crew.

Battle damage incurred up to this point was destined to claim at least two bombers during the return leg, but only two further crews were fated to come down over Germany. The single Framlingham loss involved 42-29991/FC: T

Patches flown by Lt. F McEwin. The Group had flown as far as the region around Karlsruhe when parachutes issued from the flak and fighter-stricken B-17, which by then had flames liberally issuing from No. 2 engine and a main fuel tank, but once again all ten airmen exited safely. Then, as the French/German border north of Strasbourg was looming up Lt. C Goodner eased 42-30709/QJ: P into a good crash landing at Ingwiller, after which his crew began the open-ended journey into captivity. The clear weather conditions enjoyed on the way over were by now deteriorating to the extent of hindering the briefed P-47 escort cover from picking up their charges over France. On the other hand, "fighter escort" of the unfriendly sort would continue sniping at the Division's ranks and would reap a small but regular reward as the bombers crossed out of Germany.

No Respite over France...

The Division was still maintaining a due westerly course as Germany gave way to France, but over the ensuing 20 to 30 minutes six more crews would forfeit their hoped-for positive conclusion to their combat tours. The area around Metz was where two B-17s descended. Lt. T Beal's 42-30457/QE: N **Jimmy Boy** was abandoned northwest of the city, with four of the ten airmen ending up in Resistance hands, while further to the south Lt. R Bye slid 42-3348/AW: G **Dottie J III** in for a crash landing; the same number of this crew also managed to evade capture. Yet another 94th BG crew lost out in 42-3338/QE: P when fighters downed Lt. S Dodge's aircraft north of Toul. This time round Fate was unkind to the pilot and four others, as they were killed.

The culling proceeded apace between Rheims and Sedan. This time the victim was a 95th BG aircraft 42-30135/BG: H **Trouble Shooter** (Capt. W McPherson, POW) that had limped back from Schweinfurt despite losing one engine and suffering a descended landing gear. The pilots decided to head for Switzerland, but the retarding effect of the lowered wheels along with progressive engine failure were prime contributory factors in the pilots' decision to finally carry off a successful crash landing that culminated with all going "into the

The P-38 Lightning has tended to be a rather maligned fighter in terms of its presence within the 8th FC. However, until the advent of the P-51 it was the sole USAAF escort capable of providing long range cover for the bombers during the crucial winter of 1943/44.

Gen. Spaatz shakes the hand of Capt. Sumner Reeder following the award of the Distinguished Service Cross (DSC). The medal was the result of Reeder's successful bid to bring his severely shot-up B-17F back from the Stuttgart mission (6 Sept. 1943). Sadly, after completing his combat tour and returning home he was killed in a flying accident.

bag" (An RAF term for being captured). One of this crew not on board today (fortunately for him) had previously been in a position to go home but had decided to continue operations. It was Lt. Wilmot (B), who at the time of his tour completion and when presented with his DFC by Gen. LeMay had been adjured by that Senior figure "Not to tell the folks back home how rough it was in the ETO since the truth would adversely affect civilian morale"—advice that became irrelevant, since Wilmot stayed on in England!

The final casualties among this group of unfortunates affected the 96th BG. St. Revigny, north of Dizier, lies somewhat to the south of the homeward track being flown, and this was where 42-30040/AW: A **Wabbit Twacks III** ended up after fire from cannon shells set the bomb bay and radio room on fire. Lt. C Baer (CP) was killed during the attacks, while Lt. H Harmeson and the other eight on board bailed out successfully. Lt. J Horton had seen his B-17 (42-3430/BX: U **Carolina Boomerang**) absorb heavy strikes as the group was angling towards Rheims. The city was falling behind when the B-17 peeled out with two engines "feathered"; shortly after the bomber was safely abandoned by the entire crew.

Brennan's Circus

Fourteen Division crews had failed to run the flak and fighter gauntlet and crashed on enemy soil, but the final MIA tally was destined to rise to fifteen. Lt. J Brennan had applied the title **Brennan's Circus** to 42-30383/XM: D2, but today's mission had looked like the end of the line for bomber and crew. The loss of one engine thanks to fighter damage west of the IP left the B-17 trailing ever further behind the Group, and an inability to jettison the bomb load convinced the pilots to turn back and drop to minimum altitude for the protracted run home. The diving straggler continued to be assaulted by several fighters, but miraculously came through the hail of gunfire, and eventually shrugged off all their attention. Over the Low Countries it was ground fire from every available large and small-caliber weapon that steadily inflicted more punishment upon **Brennan's** airframe, but she was held on course, despite the gradual decline in overall engine power. The final hurdle as the coastline was crossed resulted in the gunfire barrage encountered leaving just one engine functioning. Incredibly, Brennan revved up power on the single engine to maximum and skimmed the sea surface along with Lt. G White's (CP) aid. The dying B-17 kept her crew in the air for sufficient time and distance clear of the Continent and within sight of England before she had to be ditched. Even then she did not let Brennan's crew down, since the action left all ten alive and waiting in their dinghies to be picked up by the ASR Service.

The Luck Factor

The 96th BG Lead bomber very nearly did not come home after it was again assailed by flak near Rheims. Two engines were set on fire and Maj. Hodson killed, while the pilots, along with Latham and Jones, were wounded in varying degrees. Nearly 10,000 ft of altitude was lost before recovery and extinguishing of the flames was achieved. The inevitable swarm of fighters tackled the bomber but could not bring it down, and it staggered onwards before crossing the English Channel and settling down at RAF Gravesend, a fighter airfield on the southern edge of the Thames Estuary. A second Snetterton-based crew experienced equal if not greater luck when their bomber 42-30602/BX: X **Dry Run IV** was involved in a collision with a Bf109, the result of which was to cut away most of the central fin structure. Having survived the impact the B-17 went into a spin that was sustained for most of the drop from 23,000 ft. Lt. Burdick and his co-pilot finally corrected the bomber's parlous attitude using the automatic pilot and headed northwards, albeit now on half power. Another RAF airfield at Hornchurch, north of the Thames Estuary, was where the B-17 eventually found a temporary home.

Flight Deck Crisis

The 96th BG was to be short of seven MIA crews, a figure that might well have risen to eight after Lt. R Bolick, in charge of 42-30736/MZ: A **Paper Doll**, was fatally injured and Lt. E Downs (CP) seriously wounded by a 20mm shell. The dying pilot slumped over his control column, but recovered sufficiently to arrest the bomber's fall away from the formation before indicating to Downs he should take over. In turn Downs, although sustaining arm and leg injuries, initially managed to respond. Meanwhile Lt. Miles McFann (N) had come up and assisted T/Sgt. J O'Rourke (Eng.) in transferring Bolick into the nose, where he almost immediately expired.

McFann's experience of piloting was limited to light designs and not much at that. Nevertheless, he assumed the vacant right seat (Bolick had previously changed places with Downs in order to hold better visual contact with the rest of the Low squadron) and with Downs help maintained a course for home. Downs' condition was such that he flitted in and out of consciousness during the seemingly endless passage across France and the Channel, but he and McFann finally arrived over England's south coast, only to find an undercast and dusk looming up. Added to this crisis scenario was the total loss of operable radio and navigation equipment. (All the more credit was due Lt. H Edelstein for navigating the aircraft successfully under Dead Reckoning (DR) principles.) It was only by flying short triangular legs under Downs' direction—a procedure indicating an aircraft in distress—that McFann was able to summon up RAF aircraft, whose pilots led the B-17 down through the murk towards RAF Ford. The landing approach was made with McFann handling the throttles, Downs working his control column with his one intact arm, and O'Rourke calling out speed and height. In the circumstances the resultant safe landing could be deemed to have bordered on the miraculous!

Black Thursday's final tally of MIA aircraft was 60, and a further number, largely from the 1st BD, immediately or subsequently declared Category E. Among this latter figure was 42-3347/C Charlene, borrowed from the 385th BG but flown by Lt. E Chesmore and crew; the shot-up condition of the B-17 allied to an imminent total fuel consumption compelled those on board to bail out rather than risk a landing, and their charge came down near Bovingdon, Oxfordshire.

Finis for a Theory

Second Schweinfurt was to be regarded by historians as representing a prime watershed in USAAF bombing policy. Any pretensions to continuing with regular unescorted heavy bomber missions into Europe were surely laid to rest after 14 October 1943. The *Luftwaffe's Jadgwaffe* (Fighter Command) held all the cards in its bid to successfully contest the B-17s' and B-24s' effective progress. Heavy armament and close formation flying was too simplistic a twin-measure with which to successfully stave off the machine gun and cannon batteries possessed by the enemy's single and twin-engine interceptors, as well as the clever attacking tactics evolved over the past year. To their deadly effect was being added hundreds of 88mm, 105mm, and even 120mm heavy flak weapons whose gunners could cast up an almost equally lethal web of shells. Little could be done to remove these ground-based threats, although radio countermeasures and the use of "chaff" would somewhat alleviate the overall situation in the months ahead. (Flak, in effect, was always to be the detested "deterrent," a word often uttered during Briefing sessions....)

The fighter threat could be brought under control, but only if sufficient numbers of long-range fighters with a quality of performance matching or exceeding that of their Axis contemporaries could be placed at the "Big Friends'" disposal. The RAF's graceful Spitfire met all combat requirements, other than the most urgent USAAF need—range. The P-47 was a design that was a little behind the Spitfire in overall combat capability, particularly in turning circle, although its diving ability was incredible. The looming advent of engine boost equipment and an advanced propeller variant would push the Thunderbolt's overall performance significantly upwards, although the very thirsty 2,800 hp Pratt and Whitney would conversely continue to place a degree of range restriction upon Republic's "T-Bolt," even with the extra fuel capacity provided by drop tanks. The P-38 Lightning, whose operational debut was on 15 October, was destined to provide at least a solution to the range issue. On the other hand, the ability of any twin-engine aircraft to outperform single-engine designs was ever a matter for debate, while the vapour trails thrown out by the USAAF fighter's two Allison engines was a clear visual warning to the *Luftwaffe* pilots that such "bogeys" were hostile, whereupon the appropriate countermeasures could be indulged in.

"Waiting in the wings," as it were, was a third fighter now emerging in steady if not yet overwhelming numbers from the North American Company's factories. In time it would be the answer to the aforementioned problem. It was to be all the more ironic that its perceived deployment in the European Theater of Operations (ETO) was not with a view to supporting strategic operations, but rather those involving the tactical function of the embryonic Ninth USAAF's B-26 and A-20 groups! This was an action (or rather a potential mal-action in terms of the strategic Bomber Offensive) whose continued application could have added the finishing touches to the abandonment of daylight operations, with all that it implied for Allied prospects of defeating the European Axis powers in the near future—or even at all.

6

WINTER HIATUS

(NOVEMBER 1943 – JANUARY 1944)

Black Week's Ebb Tide

The particularly "bloody nose" dealt out to VIII BC's crews and bombers during the second week of October led to the latest period of retrenchment for the remainder of the month. Four missions were briefed in this time, of which only one was carried out with any result. On the 17th and 18th the bombers lifted off for Dueren, situated between Aachen and Koeln. The relatively small town was to be literally blasted off the face of the earth one year later, but its industrial facilities were to be spared on both current occasions after "recalls" were issued as the formations were tracking out over the North Sea.

Two days later the same town was briefed, and nearly 300 bombers again headed out but, as on the two previous occasions, they encountered Mother Nature at her most demanding, with cloud layers extending up to 30,000 ft. The other two Divisions registered an almost total failure to bomb (or in the case of the 2nd BD to carry out its briefed diversionary action) apart from the 379th BG, who dropped on Woensdrecht airfield. The 3rd BD enjoyed better fortune, with 86 crews from six of the seven groups releasing nearly 200 tons of explosives on Dueren. The assault was carried out for the first time with the PFF aircraft utilizing the British-designed *Oboe* system, which promised a much more accurate bombing result compared to *H2X*.

The *Luftwaffe* was up in numbers and pecked away at the formations. Nine B-17s would not return, seven of which were from LeMay's force, most taken out on the return route. The 385th BG's 42-5913/Q **Shack Bunny** was observed turning back shortly before reaching the target, but Lt. V Fryer's charge was finally abandoned close to Echt, just inside Dutch territory; all ten airmen descended safely, of which nine were soon in German hands. Two more B-17s from the 4th CBW never returned, with just two survivors among the 20 airmen concerned. Lt. H Sharp III was piloting 42-3130/QE: O **Nip N' Tuck** that was seen to fall out into a spin; it came to earth south of Venray, on the Dutch/German border, along with eight of the crew. Lt.G Lohlein's crew in 42-30303/TS: M **Raider II** gradually lost altitude and distance with the Group and was never seen again, its lonely unidentified grave the bottom of the North Sea along with its occupants.

The 45th CBW surrendered two crews, both from Snetterton Heath. What was described as a furious fighter assault took out 42-3439/MZ: V, flown by Lt. C Gerger Jr., north of Eindhoven. All five airmen up front bailed out, but their B-17 remained aloft and wandered further northwards before skimming the ground on approach to the village of DeBilt. Here one wing struck a tram power line and then a large tree, the effect being to slew the bomber directly into the path of a house. Two adults and a child occupant lost their lives in the tragic incident, along with all five gunners in the rear compartments, although the airmen were probably already dead as a result of the aerial attacks. Further south, near Mons, in northeast Belgium, the final act was played out by 42-30732/BX: P **Shack Rabbit II**. Fighter gunfire almost sawed off the tail section of Lt. R Grimes' aircraft; four crewmembers were either killed during the attacks or, in the case of Lt. Picket (CP), died afterwards. Two out of the remaining crew, including the pilot, were blessed in evading capture.

Single B-17s from the 95th and 390th BGs completed the MIA figure. In the former instance, Lt. R Rongstad managed to get back over the North Sea before ditching action became necessary, but the entire crew on board 42-30114/BG: L were later picked up by an ASR launch. (Sadly, fortune deserted the pilots and seven others on this crew when their bomber crashed shortly after take-off on 19 November.) Left behind at Veghel, close to Eindhoven, were the eight surviving members on Lt. H Schuyler's 42-30719/CC: P **Shazi**.

Three B-17Fs of the 388th BG are lining up for a planned mission to Dueren, Germany, on 20 October. Six days before the Group had been one of three 3rd BD units to remain unscathed off the Black Thursday mission to Schweinfurt. The same luck would attend today's run, but only because the mission was recalled thanks to cloud cover extending up to 30,000 ft.

November Fortunes

The largely deep penetration nature of October's operations, few as the actual missions had been, was not repeated during November. German targets spread between the Ruehr and the cities of Bremen and Wilhelmshaven featured in the briefing sessions on eight occasions, with two northerly diversions up to Norway added in. The first run on the 3rd was to Wilhelmshaven, and involved a further USAAF adaptation to blind-bombing procedure. Whereas the first use of such equipment on 27 September had involved the British *H2S* system, today witnessed the introduction of ***H2X***. This was a more refined version of *H2S* with a functioning wavelength of 3-centimeters compared to 9 centimeters for its British contemporary. Over 560 bombers from all three Divisions participated, of which 221 were from the 3rd BD. An interesting feature of the mission was the dispatch by the 96th BG of 50 B-17s, which formed up into three sub-forces that in turn provided two Groups within the 45th CBW, and a "first" for the VIII BC. Total MIA losses were seven, but two of these were self inflicted by a mid-air collision. A single crew from the 94th BG was included in this statistic when flak in the target area set 42-31101/XM: **Margie** on fire. Only two out of Lt. Brunson's (KIA) team jumped clear before the B-17 exploded and bore the other eight airmen to their deaths, their bodies being later unearthed from among the wreckage.

Two days later, the choice of target unconsciously preceded by many months the Allied air forces' full concentration on a much more vulnerable "bottleneck" industry than ball bearings within the Nazi inventory—oil. Gelsenkirchen, in the north of the Ruehr, possessed a major synthetic oil refinery that was the focus for assault by the 1st and 3rd BDs. Having been awakened at a pleasantly later time than normal, the crews coursed over their target during the early afternoon and several hours later were back home less seven B-17s. Fighter opposition as on the 3rd was generally sporadic but was still brought to bear, as instanced in the case of the 388th BG's 42-30789/T flown by Lt. W Bramwell. As Gelsenkirchen was looming up cannon shells riddled the bomber and knocked out No. 2 engine. The bomb run was nevertheless completed, following which the pilots pulled out of the formation and headed home alone. Lokeren, just west of Antwerp, lies around 150 miles from Gelsenkirchen, and it was here that the by-now abandoned B-17 crashed after the eight surviving crewmembers had bailed out several minutes before. A second group bomber, this time flak-afflicted, had lagged behind the group after bombs were released. Lt. R Walker grimly held a solo course for home and progressed as far as southwest Holland before his ailing charge forced him into carrying off a crash landing in 42-30142/F **Pistol Packin' Mama**. Only two fatalities were suffered, albeit in a sadly unnecessary manner; two gunners bailed out when the B-17's height was too marginal to permit safe deployment of their parachutes.

One of the remaining two MIA losses came from the 13th CBW. Flak damage to 42-37748/LD: V (Lt. T Martin) on the outward route forced the pilots to turn for home, but only two crewmembers emerged alive after the B-17 descended into the sea. The 94th BG's 42-30166/XM: L **You Cawnt Miss It** (Lt. J Killian, KIA) suffered a similar fate on the return leg. Fighter gunfire strikes resulted in the bomber exploding and striking the shoreline waters near Haamstede, with fatal results for all but two on board. Lt. John Pyles and crew, having struggled to bring their bomber back from Wilhelmshaven on what was their first mission, were again engaged in a desperate bid to get home. Flak had badly lacerated the left wing trailing edge's inner section, while fighter strikes had added to the overall damage. In spite of this, the pilots held position and landed back at Rougham. However, Fate was far from finished with this crew...

An unspecified target featured on the Briefing maps (8th), but the mission was "scrubbed" at an early stage—cruelly not soon enough for Lt. P Hargett and crew in 42-3353/QJ: H. The B-17 lifted off the Snetterton Heath runway just after 0600 hours, but instead of banking into its initial turn was seen to fall away and blow up near West Harling, with all ten airmen dying in the process. Muenster, of sinister memory for the 3rd BD, was assigned the Division on the 11th, and eight Group formations that included two from the 96th BG headed out over the North Sea. However, only three groups went over the target; a combination of PFF aircraft failure and Lead pilot error left only the 94th, 385th, and 390th BGs with a combined total of 58 bombers completing the bomb run and releasing 122 tons of explosives and incendiaries upon the already battered city's marshalling yards, compared to the "area bombing" effort on 10 October. The cost was four bombers, all but one from the 94th BG, and all apparently incurred on the way back.

Lt. R Rails, flying 42-39812/XM: N **Casey Jones**, was observed to go out of control and almost certainly came down in Dutch estuarial waters or the North Sea, since no crash site was ever listed. Only Lt. J Thompson (N) escaped alive, while one body was subsequently washed ashore on Schouwen Island. Gunfire ignited the No. 3 engine on 42-39855/QE: N **Ole Bassar**, and seven crewmembers managed to jump clear before Lt. P Kane's (KIA) aircraft exploded, the remnants falling near Willemstad, due south of Rotterdam. The third Group victim was assailed by Fw190s, whose strikes created a fire in one wing; 42-39868/QE: K assumed a banking maneuver that rapidly developed into a spin before it exploded and descended into a stretch of water directly opposite where Lt. Kane's B-17 had ended up. The three survivors from Lt. B O'Hara's (KIA) crew were doubly fortunate in that they were blown out into mid-air and then rescued by Dutch fishermen following their immersion in what must have been extremely chilly water. **The Wild Hare** (42-30795/J) from the 385th BG completed the loss tally. Fire in the No. 3 engine incurred over Muenster inexorably spread to finally induce an explosion, although all on board Lt. J McGowan's aircraft did bail out beforehand. However, S/Sgt. J French (ROG) later died either from wounds received or a bad landing.

Two B-17Gs from the 96th BG cruise across a patchy clouded sky. BX: D **Cookie** in the foreground bears the Division insignia only on the vertical fin, while the fuselage code letters are dulled-down. Bomber was one of eleven MIA on 11 April 1944 when none of Lt. Splan's crew survived the bomber's descent into the Baltic Sea.

Pyles' "Luck"

Lt. Pyles and his crew's misfortunes arising from their first two missions continued on the 11th. Just prior to "bombs away" the oil tank for No.2 engine was punctured, and almost immediately the engine lost its oil pressure and had to be switched off. A fighter swooped in from ahead onto the crippled B-17 as it lost its position within the High squadron's rear Element, and its shells set the fuselage on fire, after which the bomber lost nearly 10,000 ft. altitude before being pulled out. A windmilling propeller on No 3 led to power being switched off on this engine, and as if this was not trouble enough, a gunner then reported that the right main landing gear was fully extended! It was clear that no fighters were immediately in sight, otherwise the fate of both bomber and crew would have been sealed. The situation was still critical, since there was a long way to go before the relative security of the North Sea would be on hand. A convenient cloud layer was eased into just as four fighters loomed up, but these were evaded, as a further descent to ground level was effected. The power from Nos. 1 and 4 engines proved sufficient to keep the aircraft aloft all the way back to Rougham, but the shot-up throttle linkage to No. 4 prevented its closure during the landing. While the pilots were considering whether to face an over-shoot at the runway end or deliberately ground loop their errant bomber the engine ran out of steam; even so, heavy braking was necessary to prevent an over-shoot. It now proved impossible to taxi the machine off the runway due to the lack of power, thus blocking the passage of other returning aircraft.

The crew were granted an immediate 48-hour pass to London. Prior to their return they entered a cinema near the station, and were barely seated when the newsreel showed a crippled B-17—this was none other than their bomber from the Gelsenkirchen mission as confirmed by the "Square A" insignia and extended right main landing gear! The natural urge to yell out the fact did not endear them to the audience or the cinema manager; nor were their efforts to obtain a copy both at this point or in Group Intelligence on return to Rougham appreciated, with the latter source tartly reminding them that they could face censure for divulging sensitive information, however natural their reaction might have been....

Vapour trails dragged by other 385th BG B17s form a dramatic backcloth to **Dragon Lady** (42-30836/V). On 13 February, during a cross-Channel assault on V-1 sites in the Pas de Calais, flak so badly damaged the 385th BG B-17F that 2ndLt. Herron had no alternative but to "ditch"; he and three other crewmembers failed to survive the action.

Bremen's Lure

Bremen, on the northwest German coast, would now feature in four missions before Christmas, with the first dispatched on 13 November. The indifferent to poor weather pattern resulted in partial abandonment during Assembly by the 1st BD element. As for the 3rd BD, the results turned in by the three CBWs varied greatly.

Only 8 out of 60 crews from the 13th CBW struck a target of opportunity, while 20 out of 33 from the 4th CBW hit the Primary; this contrasted with the 45th CBW, where 49 of the 61 sent up struck the target. It seemed all the more frustrating that all recorded Division losses were self inflicted. The sole 96th BG crew failing to return were reported to have collided with another unidentified B-17; the crash site for 42-37830/MZ: V was at Ommen, in Holland, with Lt. H Marks and six crewmembers forfeiting their lives. Great Ashfield possessed two empty dispersals that evening: 42-30717/O **Man O' War** (Lt. W Dawurske, KIA) came in lethal contact with 42-39860/A flown by Lt. B McCall. Dawurske's bomber lost a sizeable section of its left wing and snapped into a vicious spin. However, six crewmembers managed to get clear before the doomed aircraft impacted near Ahlhorn, south of Oldenburg. McCall's B-17, minus its tail gunner's compartment, remained aloft until close to the English coast, where it was ditched, the sole other fatality being the pilot. (Sgt. W Butler's (TG) body was found by the Germans in the severed tail section.)

Ryukan, in southern Norway, possessed sufficient industrial plants to come in for Divisional attention on the 16th. Over 90% of the 160 crews taking off were later granted mission "credit," as over 300 tons of 1,000-lb bombs plastered the Primary at a cost of one 390th BG bomber, although a second group bomber was evacuated after fire took hold during Assembly. **Schiflis Skunk** (42-30455/CC: R) delivered all ten of Lt. R Becker's crew into the dark maw of the North Sea after fire caught hold and the B-17 dropped out of formation. A further three days elapsed before the next mission, with Gelsenkirchen again selected. However, adverse weather encountered over Europe resulted in the city being spared for the time being; some Groups returned with their bomb loads, although targets of opportunity within German territory, as well as in Holland, were also struck. Once again the dangers inherent in taking off with bombers loaded up to and often over their maximum operational weight was demonstrated at Horham. Lt. K Rongstad had barely lifted 42-31123/BG: J into the air when it was seen to stall out and strike the ground very close to a farmhouse; part of the bomb load exploded and blazing fuel ignited the thatched roof of the semi-detached property, inside which cowered two married couples and one child, all of whom were mercifully spared, although not their dwelling. This was in contrast to the ten American airmen who were now added to their nation's blood debt in putting down Nazi Fascism.

Bremen Again...

Today (26th) witnessed the latest planned attack on Bremen's industry by all three Divisions, although there was a marked variation in the numbers of B-17s assembled by the 3rd BD; just 19 were sent out by the 13th CBW, while the 45th CBW dispatched 86 in all. (The 385th and the 94th BGs were assigned a separate French target, while elements of the 100th BG were also present, judging by the losses suffered here.) The city was ever a potential hotbed for the Allied bombers, and lived up to its malign reputation at least for the 1st BD, whose ranks were shorn of nineteen out of the total of 29 MIA bombers. The 45th CBW gave up all three B-17s within this figure, one in unfortunate circumstances. A 401st BG bomber flown by Lt. S Dailey (42-37838/SC: F **Fancy Nancy**) was involved in a mid-air collision with another B-17, believed to be 42-30317/K **Second Chance** flown by W McGown. The ball turret was knocked off Dailey's aircraft, but it remained aloft and landed back at Deenethorpe, although the scale of damage later led to its being scrapped. McGown's B-17 sadly did not live up to its name—hardly surprising, since the rear fuselage was chopped off and the resultant spinning action held the crew in place until the final impact near Ahlhorn. The other Knettishall loss was equally self inflicted, this time by incendiaries from another aircraft thought to be a 96th BG bomber from the High group. Two of these knocked off a stabilizer and severed the tail section on 42-3555/N **Tiger Girl**, giving only two of Lt. G Bramham's crew any chance of bailing out before crashing east of Delmenhorst. Finally, the 96th BG's 42-30854/QJ: E **Black Heart III** found an anonymous grave for itself and Lt. K Phelp's entire crew in the North Sea on the homeward leg.

At Rougham, Lt. Pyles and six of his regular crew were among the 42 teams assembled for briefing with the target being Ivry-sur-Seine, located in the southeast suburbs of Paris. The

The cherubic-featured boy photographed with three ground crew of the 100th BG is Sam Hurry; the picture was taken in December 1943. In recent years Sam has been fully involved with the magnificent aviation Museum created within the refurbished control tower at Thorpe Abbotts.

ability of the P-47s to penetrate the Continent within sight of the French capital did not prevent the *Luftwaffe* fighters from indulging in their favored frontal attacks from the IP and for a goodly period of time on the return route. It was perhaps gratifying as the bombers finally cleared the French coast that only three of their number had been culled, but not so for the 94th BG, from whose ranks that figure had been extracted. The relatively severe combat tests so gallantly surmounted by Lt. Pyles during his and the crew's inaugural trio of missions was now to be exceeded in the worst possible manner. An Fw190 inexorably continued its approach into the left side of 42-30821/GL: **The Sweetest One's** fuselage. The stricken B-17 almost immediately disintegrated under the brutal impact, and only S/Sgt. H Norris (TG) managed to evacuate his position in the severed tail section and float down into the hands of the Resistance and eventually return to England. (Lts. C Hatcher (CP) and A Delzoppo (B) and S/Sgt. E Smith (G), all regular members of Pyles' crew, had been ordered to switch crews prior to this mission; not only did this arbitrary action save their lives today, but all three avoided the Grim Reaper's axe to complete their combat tours.)

Two B-17s from the 333 BS also went down. The combined effects of fighter and flak damage finally did it for 42-37815/TS: **Miss Lace** and half of Lt. W Porter's (KIA) team, the bomber coming down at Plessis-au-Bois, bare kilometres outside Paris' northeast boundary. Lts. M Nienaber (P) and H Mays (CP) held 42-3185/TS: L **Queen Bee** aloft in a steadily descending attitude for most of the passage northwards before a bail out; was ordered. The B-17 went in near Londineres, southeast of Dieppe, but only eight of its crew survived, with the pilot's misfortune being to suffer a failure of his parachute pack. Two from this crew evaded capture, as did the same number from **Miss Lace**. A fourth Divisional MIA casualty was incurred near Paris when 42-31215/XR: H finally succumbed to fighter attacks, with the eight surviving members from Lt. G Ford's crew descending either into captivity or into Resistance hands. What probably made these losses even more unbearable was the fact that the Primary or any alternative target was not attacked.

Bremen – the Lure Continues...

For the third time in November, but not the last during 1943, the crews of both B-17 Divisions were greeted at briefing by the sight of the map's red ribbons ending at this northwestern industrial city on what was the penultimate day of the month. Each Division launched virtually the same total of

The geographically inhospitable stretches of Norway's mountain chain form the backcloth to a 95th BG formation on 18 November 1943. The target this day was molybdenum mines at Knaben. **Heavenly Daze** (42-5918/ET; J) served the Group from 13 June until 11 January 1944, when it was shot down by fighters during the costly mission to Oschersleben; all but one of Lt. Foley's (POW) crew survived the ordeal.

The same frigid Norwegian landscape is being traversed by the 390th BG. CC: G Gung Ho is one of the early B-17G airframes that were bereft of any "cheek gun" window frames; some units did adapt the small windows to accommodate a machine gun, although the visibility factor was much restricted. Recently assigned on 13 October, the bomber lasted until 10 September 1944 when all but three of Lt. McIntosh's crew were killed during a strike against Nuernburg.

bombers from the overall total of 360, but matters were destined to proceed better for the 3rd BD in terms of bombing results. The late autumn weather pattern consisted of clouds extending up to nearly 30,000 ft, and of the 178 crews sent out by the 1st BD only 50 struck either the Primary or targets of opportunity, compared to 104 for the 3rd.

As ever, the defenses handed out a fair measure of punishment, with nine out of the 13 MIA bombers failing to return to their airfields in Suffolk and Norfolk. Four groups were affected in this manner, with the 96th BG leading the ever dismal statistic. The Divisional losses appear to have only commenced as the formations were on their way back judging by the times and crash sites. Syke lies about ten miles south of Bremen, and it was near here that the 96th BG's 42-30359/QJ: D came down in separate sections after being thoroughly battered by fighter gunfire. Lt. L Langley was one of eight fatalities, but amazingly S/Sgt. E Moran (TG) escaped with his life, even though he did not get out of his position before the rear fuselage struck the ground.

A 385th BG companion in misfortune that also succumbed to fighter attacks near Syke was 42-30204/K **Gremlin's Buggy**; it was believed that all four airmen killed in the action were already dead before Lt. R Yoder called for a bail out. Around the same time a second Snetterton Heath crew were "hitting the silk" as their afflicted mount 42-3546/QJ: A **Wildfire**, flown by Lt. T Parke, was giving up the unequal battle; its final resting place was well southeast of Bremen at Eystrup. The fourth bomber to come down on enemy soil did so as the bomber stream was halfway between Bremen and the Dutch/German border. Horham's 42-6039/BG: H was harried to its violent destruction in mid-air south of Friesoythe by the ever-persistent *Luftwaffe*, but not before all but one of Lt. L Palmer's crew had abandoned the B-17.

Natural Hazard

The North Sea would prove almost as formidable an opponent to the bomber crews' chances of survival during the course of WWII as was now to be proven today. The first of five crews facing this natural barrier was probably from the 385th BG. Capt. W Swope called up as he detached his B-17 (4-37874 **Who Dat Ding Bat**) from the Group, his message being that he was attempting to get back to England despite a current fuel level that gave no guarantee of success, and in fact, the bomber's dispersal was empty that evening to confirm that the odds had gone against his crew. It was only the discovery of a crewmember's body in a dinghy washed up on an English beach over two weeks later that provided sad conformation of all ten airmen's fate.

Joining them in anonymous eternity were no less than 37 out of 40 more airmen. The 96th BG's 42-37811/ BX:, flown by Lt. H Meuli, disappeared from sight over the target area with no subsequent trace of bomber or its crew, while 42-37802/BX: bearing Lt. G Hendrickson was confirmed as crashing into the North Sea, as was 42-3352/ GL: V **Virgin's Delight**, flown by Lt. W Chyle. Finally, progressive engine failure on the 388th BG's 42-3505/E forced Lt. R Maupin to carry out ditching procedures when almost within sight of England, but his efforts availed him and six of his crew naught.

The build-up of VIII BC aircraft and crew resources proceeded apace during November with the full arrival of two B-24-equipped groups and two operating the B-17. A rather jarring note regarding the passage of the aircraft on the trans-Atlantic route was the loss of four crews from three of the units concerned, the exception being the 401st BG. The 401st BG was duly assigned to the 1st BD, while the 447th BG increased 3rd BD strength to eight Groups. However, it was to be Christmas Eve before the local population around Rattlesden would hear the burgeoning roar created by that airfield's bombers heading off and upwards to add their weight to the Daylight Offensive for the first time.

Solingen in the southwest of the Ruehr industrial complex, was targeted on the 30th, but was destined to remain partially unscathed thanks to adverse weather patterns that caused the 1st and 2nd BDs to turn back. Around three-quarters of the 3rd BD force of 117 B-17s deposited some 224 tons upon the Primary and left a marginal "calling card" of two crews MIA. The 390th BG surrendered 42-3557/DI: C **Esquire** to fighter assault as Solingen was looming up. Two of Lt. J Leo's crew died, one of whose loss was caused by an unopened parachute pack. **The Spirit of 76** (42-3317/ QW: Y) was a flak victim, and was abandoned by Lt. A Hensler and crew over eastern Holland; Lt. W Lohmann (N) was the sole member to die, and his body was not recovered from the river Maas until the following summer.

There should have been one more B-17 participating in the mission, but its burnt out remains were already lying near Wakes Colne, not too distant from its Great Ashfield base. Fire was an ever-latent threat to any bomber, especially when laden with the bombs, ammunition, and fuel necessary to carry out its function. Capt. R Smith in 42-30096/V **Liberty Belle** (385th BG) was flying Low squadron lead, and after breaking through the cloud layer decided to assemble the several aircraft in his vicinity by firing a flare. Unfortunately this detonated within the fuselage and actually struck Smith in the face as it gyrated around the cockpit to set the whole area ablaze. The decision was taken to abandon the bomber, and the bomber put on autopilot with the intention of heading her out over the North Sea. However, there ensued a physical tussle between Smith and his co-pilot that ate up precious seconds as the latter retarded the throttles. (Smith later opined that his fellow-pilot had a phobia about bailing out and probably preferred to stay with the B-17 with the hope of bringing her down safely.)

On 1 December 1943 **Lady Liz** (550BS) completed her last mission at Great Ashfield; she lies forlornly in a field with the right landing gear ripped off and the left wheel dug into the soft Suffolk soil. The five-month veteran B-17F's state merited immediate "Category E" treatment.

Whatever his reasoning, he ignored Smith's entreaties to head for the forward hatch after the bail out bell had been punched. With a badly swollen face and right hand caused by burns Smith floated down through a snowstorm, but then had the added misfortune to break a leg on landing and suffered the fracture of several vertebrae, apart from which he encountered great difficulty in collapsing his parachute. He would face six months hospitalization, but at least he was alive; not so his co-pilot and three others, who died after the B-17 reportedly had one wing fold up and the main airframe explode, the remains striking the ground at Wakes Chappel.

December 1943: Salvation on Hand...

Maj. Don Blakeslee (4th FG CO) was on temporary detachment from Debden to Boxted, where he was about to pass on his combat experience to the acolyte pilots of the 354th FG led by Lt. /Col. Kenneth Martin and operating the Merlin-powered P-51B, which was equally raw to combat in the "Big League of Sky Fighting" or any other theater. The recently-arrived Group had been assigned to the 9th USAAF, but was then detached to serve under VIII Fighter Command direction, hence the presence of Blakeslee. He duly took off with Martin as his wingman to conduct a sweep that took in the Belgian and northeast French coastlines, a mission that witnessed no involvement with the *Luftwaffe*. Unbeknownst to anyone within USAAF circles was the ultimately realized benefit that the Daylight Offensive was to accrue from the introduction of this superlative fighter design. The skies around the B-17s and B-24s would from now on be more and more controlled, and all efforts of the *Luftwaffe* to continue punishing the "Big Friends" to an unacceptable degree more and more thwarted. The *Jadgwaffe* in effect had to be brought to the point of total ineffectiveness. However, this desirable scenario (one that was even more mandatory in its execution before an Invasion of Western Europe could be deemed to have a chance of success) lay several months ahead...

December opened with a renewed attempt to attack Solingen, as well as enemy resources nearby at Leverkusen. Whereas the 3rd BD was the only Division to make a strike the previous day, now a reverse pattern of success and failure arose. In fact, the Division did not even gain enemy airspace before the crews were recalled. For the next three days the bombers were ground-bound thanks to the weather, this despite the existence of a number of *H2X*- equipped aircraft, but conditions eased sufficiently on the 5th for a split mission to be launched. In the case of the 3rd BD, its crews were again faced with a wearying extended flight to the southwest French coast, one that would be repeated on Old Year's Day.

Bordeaux/Merignac airfield housed the long-range reconnaissance Fw200 "Condors" that ranged out over the Atlantic and liaised with the U-Boats in the interdiction of Allied convoys plying across the North Atlantic. The bombing of targets in Nazi-occupied Europe was still strictly limited to visual sighting and release action; the order was to otherwise bring back or jettison bomb loads. The onset of winter weather on this occasion ensured that the Primary remained intact. To the frustration at making a physically demanding flight for no return was added the pain of losing a number of crews, eight in all.

The 4th CBW absorbed five out of this number, one of which involved German military personnel in an extremely unsavory if not criminal act. Lt. T Kleuser's 42-3397/H **Fighting Cock** was attacked by fighters and turned back towards the French coast with an engine on fire and under constant pursuit. The pilots successfully ditched the bomber near Bordeaux and close enough to the coastline for a shore patrol to open fire on the dinghies. One of these was punctured and its occupants left to drown, while one officer later died of wounds received at the time. What should have been a relatively safe passage to a Stalag had ended in the peremptory "execution" of no less than seven of the ten airmen. A second group crew flying in 42-3294/G **Suzanne** enjoyed far better treatment, but from neutral rather than French-based authorities. Lt. N Maryonovich turned back shortly after the formation turned for home, but seems to have then pursued an extended course over 400 miles, and flown either along the north coast of Spain or across northern Spanish and Portuguese territory, since the ditching location was off the coastline of the latter-stated country! In the event, all ten airmen came through the experience to be interned indefinitely.

The Grim Reaper extracted a bloody harvest among the thirty crewmembers on Rougham's three lost aircraft. None from Lt. Lt. J Perrine's crew survived 42-3349/XM: E **El Mangau**'s fiery explosion in the target area, with nine of the crew ending up as names on a "Wall of the Missing." The same total extinction of life among the ten-man crew of Lt. J Devine flying in 42-37747/XM: A **Bucket of Bolts** occurred over the Brest Peninsula, where the B-17 finally came down. The third ten-man team on 42-30376/QE: **Southern Belle** managed to bring their B-17 back as far as the English Channel, where Lt. J Fant executed a successful ditching and subsequent pick-up by an ASR launch.

Dusk was steadily shrouding the southwest coast of England as Lt. R Moyer, flying 42-30350/Y, which was battle-damaged and running out of fuel, desperately searched for an airfield. Finding none he bailed out the crew, leaving the B-17 to fall harmlessly into the sea. Back in northern France another 388th BG bomber (42-30837/S **Ole Bassar**) lay in pieces after being shot down along with eight of the eleven-man crew headed by Lt. P Todd (POW). Another Channel ditching in the same region involved 42-3297/FC: W **The Bad Penny**. This time round all ten airmen from Lt. N Palmer's 390th BG crew were fished out alive, but one later died from exposure.

Emden's Cost

The staccato pace of operations during the first half of December was emphasized by a five-day spell of inactivity most probably enforced by the perverse British weather. Then, on the 11th the entire VIII BC strength was directed against another seaport, Emden. The assault was delivered in approximately 50 minutes, and the crews of the 1st and 2nd BD

A 708BS "original" B-17G is easing in for a smooth landing at Rattlesden. The enclosed waist-gun Plexiglas frames proved to be a key physical bonus for the gunners in terms of comfort compared to the misery engendered by the open hatches on the F and even initial G-Models of the Boeing design.

Lt. George C "Santa Claus" Parker stands on the right with his 96th BG crew. On December 1943 his B-17G 42-3261/MZ: Q **Short Stride** was struck by flak and exploded; he was killed along with Lts. R Bilodeau (CP) and G Ladd (B).

Sleepytime Gal (42-3388/F) was originally with the 388th BG but transferred-in to Great Ashfield in late 1943. She lasted until 24 April 1944 when six of Lt. Nesen's (KIA) team were consumed in a failed "ditching" attempt. Note the dulled-down Group marking and the original heavy-framed and shallow top turret fitted to the B-17F Model.

must have felt a combined sense of achievement and relief, the latter reaction undoubtedly due to the fact that just two crews out of 305 gaining mission credit had gone down. Not so among their contemporaries from the 3rd BD, who suffered almost a 7% loss rate (14 out of 218 attacking).

The aptly-numbered 13th CBW, operating in the vanguard of the Division, came back light eight crews, five of whom were culled from the 390th BG. This unit was Lead group, and the Lead B-17 was being piloted by Lt. H Skogmo with Maj. V Hansel (Group Operations Officer) as Mission Commander. Fighter attacks from both single and twin-engine fighters were constant as the formations were tracking in from a point on the German coast almost due north of Emden with the IP was passing below. It was then that a 21-cm rocket struck 42-31122/BI: A **Six nights in Telergma**—a reference to the crew's North African sojourn following the Regensburg run. The doomed bomber dropped inexorably into the North Sea close to Norderney, in the Frisian Island chain, leaving two officers and one Enlisted man out of the eleven-man complement to parachute close to the island's shoreline and into captivity. Lt. I Lifson (N) had got out through the nose hatch as fire gained hold and the bomber went out of control; he was circled by a Bf110 that made two passes but did not open fire as he drifted downwards. He subsequently received a severe beating from a civilian mob in the Frankfurt railroad station, and it took the intervention of *Wehrmacht* personnel to rescue him and his two companions from even worse treatment.

Around the same time 42-30411/BI: J **Rose Marie** was falling out after being thoroughly shot up by cannon shells; Lt. J Lashly's call for the crew to evacuate came none too soon, since the tail section soon snapped off with the remains crashing down at Norden. The same location spelled the end for eight of Lt. G Fish's (KIA) crew after 42-37823/CC: D succumbed to a flak and fighter combination. (This ratio of dead to survivor was the exact opposite to the Lashly crew's experience.) The attrition among the group ranks continued relentlessly at this point when 42-30223/DI: S, flown by Lt. G Ryon, had parts of one horizontal stabilizer and the vertical stabilizer blown away by gunfire. The aerodynamic imbalance so created probably threw the bomber out of control, and it exploded shortly after. Westeraccum lies some eight miles northeast of Norden, and it was there that the shattered airframe descended; two crewmembers survived being blown out of their aircraft. The fifth loss, this time to flak, occurred near Groningen, in northern Holland, with 42-30667/CC: V **Wild Children** the victim, although all ten on Lt. F Gerald's crew survived as POWs.

The single 100th BG loss was incurred almost simultaneously to the Skogmo/Hansel B-17, as well as to the same form of weapon, the rocket. A single crewmember escaped alive from 42-37715/EP: G **Sugar Foot** before it descended beneath the waves close to Norderney. The CBW's suffering today was completed by a pair of bombers from Horham. **Blondie II** (42-30182/QW: E) never made it to the

A sizeable number of spent flak shell bursts are being skirted by 42-29943/BG: K **Situation Normal** as she continues on her bomb run. The ball turret is vertically aligned to provide its occupant with a full view of the bomb strike. A few weeks after this January 1944 picture was taken, half of Lt. Mailman's crew were killed during the 6 March mission to Berlin when fighters downed their charge over Barnstorf.

IP and was last seen with an engine on fire. Langeoog, just east of Norderney, was where the stricken B-17 found a watery grave, along with Lt. J Moore and crew. Five gunners in Lt. R Beatty's 42-30218/OE: W were either killed at their posts, or in one case died later in a Dutch hospital at Leeuwarden, in northwestern Holland, after the lagging bomber was picked out and set upon; it came down near Ferwerd to leave the five survivors facing the doubtful experience of "Kriegydom."

There should have been a ninth B-17 from the 13th CBW failing to return, 42-30320/CC: S **Coy Decoy** piloted by Lt. R Parker. His charge was first damaged by flak discharged from one of the Frisian Island chain. Then the bomber was attacked by no less than four Bf110s in the course of which fire erupted in No. 2 engine with the flames extending over the wing surface. The seemingly doomed bomber was headed for the deck and home, but as it was skirting Groningen four of the nine surviving crew, all gunners, elected to bail out. Although they ended up alive in a POW camp, they would probably have cursed their luck had they known that the fire miraculously went out and the aircraft made it all the way back!

4th CBW Fortunes

A lesser scale of attrition (5) affected the 4th CBW. The dreadful efficiency of the 21-cm rocket, at least when it made contact with its victim, was once more demonstrated on 42-30168/L **Slo-Jo**. The impact was believed to have caused Lt. T Jenning's (KIA) aircraft, still with bomb load on board, to explode violently two miles west of Langeoog Island; it was

On some occasions, seriously damaged bombers unable to carry out a wheels-down landing were diverted for repair directly to Honington, home for the 1st Strategic Air Depot (SAD), which served the Division. On 4 January 1944, 42-31989 from Horham was slid in to the Depot. Restored to combat status, **Black Magic** ended up in Switzerland on 27 February along with Lt. K Havlik and crew.

surprising that three crewmembers got out alive to be picked up from the sea by a German crash boat. The second 385th BG loss occurred on the homeward leg. Lt. F Poore appears to have got as far as the Dutch coast, but in a steadily descending flight pattern, before the fighter-inflicted damage on 42-30816/J **Mary Ellen III** that included a burning engine forced him to call for a bail out;. This was successfully executed by at least nine crewmembers, although one landed in a canal and drowned after failing to release his parachute. Their bomber scattered itself liberally near Zuurdijk/ Warfhuizen. The Dutch coast was looming up for Lt. E Pollock's 42-3488 when the flak-damaged Great Ashfield bomber was given the coup de grace by assaults from up to six fighters. With one engine ablaze eight crewmembers abandoned the aircraft, which came down near Sneek; Pollock and two others evaded immediate capture but were put "in the bag" following their detection in Antwerp while being moved down the Resistance chain towards a hoped-for happy conclusion in neutral Spain. Sgt. Harwell (WG) was one crewmember who initially evaded capture to be taken in by a Dutch family; however, the extent of his wounds coupled with the latent threat of deportation or death for his caregivers should the Germans discover his presence in their house led to his being handed over next day.

Rougham had dispatched 41 crews, of which 30 went over the target, but only 28 landed back at their Suffolk "home." The CBW was swinging west from Emden when rockets made fatal contact with 42-39859/XM: P **Sweet Sue** and killed all four gunners in the rear fuselage. Lt. B Capehart and the others hastily made their exit before the bomber crashed into mud-flats close to Delfzijl, across the narrow estuary separating the Dutch port from Emden. Fighters brought about the demise of 42-30415/GL: P **Lucky Lady** near Orvelte where it crashed; all but one of Lt. H Berwaldt's eleven-man crew survived, the unfortunate exception being killed by small arms fire as he floated down. The extra airman was a photographer who got more than he bargained for! Closing off the Divisional losses was a single Knettishall bomber (42-31020/J) downed over Holland. Flak and fighter gunfire had crippled this B-17 so badly that Lt. C Hughes bailed out himself and the five other survivors, leaving his charge to self destruct near Finsterwolde, due east of Groningen.

"Average" in Courage

S/Sgt James Reed (385th BG) had been the ball turret gunner on the Jennings crew and one of the seven fatalities. He had been written up by Andy Rooney and Bud Hutton for inclusion in their book *Aerial Gunner*, with the relative account bearing the heading "Average," the young airman being perceived as the perfect example of just such a USAAF gunner. Today would have seen him complete his 19th mission, but in recent weeks the strain of combat operations, and in particular the regular loss of his fellow veterans, had really begun to emerge. Two missions back the sight of Norway's mountains had caused him on return to reflect on the comparison with his home state's (Pennsylvania) similar geography, after which he sank further into himself for several subsequent days. His transfer to Lt. Jennings' team that signalled a fatal outcome to his hopes of surviving his tour occurred a short time prior to the Emden mission. He was indeed "Mr. Average" in the saddest manner possible, being one of the 26,000 airmen who were never to see the dawn of victory over Europe....

Continuing the Marine Theme...

The second December mission directed against targets in northwest Germany went ahead on the 13th with another assault upon the Naval port of Kiel, where the 13th CBW had bled so freely exactly seven months before. No less than nine sub-units participated, three of which were Composite groups. One of these revealed an interesting variation, in that it appears to have been the first to involve elements from separate CBWs, being formed from the 96th, 388th, and 390th BGs. The first named Group had just flown three loss-free missions to somewhat

Another incident where a Division B-17 was "bellied-in" at Honington occurred on 30 January. This time the group concerned was the 100th BG, with this 349BS aircraft named **Gold Brick** and still featuring open waist windows as the subject. Better fortune attended its return to flying status because it went home in June 1945.

Frenesi (42-39775) displays her thoroughly shot-up state off the Oschersleben mission of 11 January 1944. Six of the eleven-man crew bailed out after it went out of control, but Lts. W Cely (P) and J Churchill brought their charge back under control for a safe return to Rougham.

Cely (right) and Churchill gaze up at the No. 2 engine that is stripped of its cowling; further strikes can be seen around the navigator's compartment. A Silver Star was later bestowed upon Cely for his actions this day.

The sleek and ever-comforting outline of a P-51B holds close formation with a 96th BG B-17. The 357th FG's distinctive red and yellow check pattern on the forward cowling and spinner is discernible. Note the clear and potentially dangerous similarity with the *Luftwaffe's* Bf 109G that caused some bomber gunners to open up on these "Little Friends" during early operations with the fighter!

dispel the negative atmosphere generated by the four crews MIA from Bremen (29 November). Matters were about to take another and even more heartrending downward spiral over the next 48 hours, however. The group had dispatched 54 bombers, of which two were downed. Lt. G Parker was flying with the main group, which was forced to seek a target of opportunity in Hamburg. This major city's flak batteries were rightly feared for their efficiency, and as the formation turned for home one or more shells impacted upon 42-3261/MZ: Q **Short Stride IV**, which blew up; Lt. W Kelly (N) was the sole officer survivor, along with the entire Enlisted man complement. The B-17 came down in the Hamburg suburb of Wansbeck. Also lost from group ranks was 42-30602/BX: X **Dry Run IV** flown by Lt. E Chesmore. As the bombers were skirting the Frisian Island chain a well directed flak barrage crippled the bomber to the extent that the pilots turned back. Unfortunately the "lame duck" was picked up by two Ju88s as it flew over northeastern Holland and dispatched to crash in the region around Groningen. A single crew from the 4th CBW Composite group also joined these two in failure. **Shack Bunny** (42-3551/S), from Great Ashfield, had got through to Kiel, but was fated to be another Ju88 victim. Cannon shells set the bomber on fire as the target was receding out of sight; although all ten of Lt. J Fowles' crew bailed out before their B-17 dived to destruction northwest of Schleswig, only nine survived.

"Friendly Fire" - The Worst Scenario?

To date the 96th BG's experience in combat had not varied greatly from its VIIIBC contemporaries. Some 48 B-17s had been consumed in action over the course of 60 missions commenced seven months before. The extremes of good and bad fortune had been demonstrated by the fact that no crews had been lost out of the 4th BW's total of 24 when the Group led the Regensburg strike on 17 August, whereas seven, nearly half of all Divisional losses, had gone down on the *Black Thursday* mission.

The need to fly compact formations in order to both present a solid defensive stance against the *Luftwaffe*, as well as to ensure a good bombing pattern, contained a potentially lethal factor, that of collision. Holding formation with an aircraft of the dimensions of the B-17, coupled with a current lack of mechanical devices such as "formation sticks" to ease the pressures on the pilots, was a physically and mentally tiring function. The controls were accordingly none too light, and often did not immediately respond to any sudden or exaggerated deviation, for example, when an aircraft became immersed in the invisible but powerful slipstream effect thrown back by preceding Elements.

The risk of a *Luftwaffe* attacker colliding with a bomber had to be accepted as ever liable to occur, whereas the thought of two or more bombers bringing about such a grisly act verged on the unbearable. It was this particularly needless and

The smoke-pot trails laid on by the German defenders of Bremen form a backcloth to 42-3268/MZ: Z and its fellow bomber as the 96th BG head for home on 26 November 1943. This B-17F had arrived at Snetterton Heath in early July, and as **Boots II/Carol Jane** would soldier on for another forty days before succumbing, not to the enemy, but to probable mechanical failure.

cruel scenario that now would be visited upon the Snetterton Heath airmen, not once but three times.

Bremen was again displayed on the Briefing maps, and as before had to be approached either across northern Holland or by threading a passage through the closely-grouped Frisian Island chain. Neither option provided much guarantee of freedom from enemy flak, which was much more effective despite Higher Command's bid to suggest it only had a "deterrent" effect upon operations.

The *Luftwaffe* was up and engaging the groups, of which two were composed of 96th BG crews. The target was attacked between 1309 and 1322 hours, and a course was then set for home across northern Holland and over or (ideally) between the most westerly islands in the Frisian chain, of which Texel and Terschelling were the largest in terms of size and flak defensive capability. At any rate, it was in the area between northwestern Holland and the Frisians that two of the three "strikes" that could be treated as totally self imposed occurred.

The first strike occurred as the North Sea was steadily, if painfully, appearing in sight. Two 337 BS crews led by Lt. M Freemole and E Smith, encased in 42-37739/AW: N **Royal Flush** and 42-31086/AW: O respectively, came together and plunged to their deaths along with all twenty crewmembers southwest of Leeuwarden. The second grisly incident was not long delayed. Gunfire from a fighter was so severe that it totally severed one engine on Capt. H Mott's 42-31113/QJ: **Zilch**. The mass of metal weighing hundreds of pounds hurtled down upon one wing on 42-30872/AW: R **Blonde Bomber** flown by Lt. L Kerrick. Mott's aircraft sagged downwards to tangle wings with Kerrick's machine which, even if it had avoided being run into, was probably already fatally affected through being struck by the detached engine. Both stricken giants tumbled seawards due west of Terschelling, bearing yet another twenty hapless American airmen to their deaths.

In the "A" group, Lts. E LeBlanc and M Schroeder, also from the 337 BS, were reportedly taking evasive action from the constant fighter lunges when the latter pilot in 42-30860/AW: L strayed into the path of LeBlanc's 42-3265/AW: Z **Holy Mackerel** as the coastline was about to be crossed. The Schroeder piloted aircraft dropped away to swiftly crash into the sea, whereas its companion in misfortune descended onto Dutch soil south of Harlingen. Two of the latter team got out alive from a total of twenty airmen. The truly shocking number and nature of all these deaths was further compounded by what happened to the seventh group aircraft to go down. Fighter strikes around this stage of the homeward leg fatally crippled 42-3249 /MZ:, which then became the second Group B-17 to find a grave on the seabed north of Texel, along with all on Lt. C Greer's crew.

Single losses within the 95th and 390th BG formations were also suffered. Lt. C Gill's 42-30348/CC: N **Royal Flush** did not even bomb, being culled by a fighter/flak combination and crashing near Bad Zwischenahn and having been abandoned by its crew. On the homeward stretch between Bremen and Texel the casualty ledger in terms of crews downed over Europe was closed when Horham's 42-30255/QW: V **Lonesome Polecat II** came down in the sea west of Texel; Lt. F Delborn Jr. (P), the co-pilot, and one gunner forfeited their lives, whereas the other seven successfully bailed out either over the mainland or Texel island.

Three airmen within the returning formations had also made the supreme sacrifice. In addition, four bombers regaining friendly soil were "written off" VIIIBC records; this included **Fertile Myrtle III**/42-30366/ BX: A, which had led the 4th BW's assault on Regensburg and the 3rd BD thrust on *Black Thursday*. The controls were too badly shot-up to attempt a landing, so the veteran B-17 was successfully, if reluctantly, abandoned over the Norfolk coast by Capt T Kenney's crew, the same team that had been on board on both these momentous occasions.

The *Luftwaffe's* presence today, although far from slight, did not bring about a great number of "kills," only one of which was suffered by other than the 3rd BD. In the case of the 96th BG, which suffered seven of the overall MIA figure of ten, only two at most of the destroyed B-17s could be attributed wholly or partially to the *Jadgwaffe* pilots, so the pain at losing such a sizeable number of crews was surely increased given the nature of their departure.

Bremen – Not Again!

For the fifth time since the beginning of November the by-now detested name of Bremen cropped up at Briefing, this time on 20 December. The 96th BG had particularly bad recollections, since no less than thirteen crews had gone down during this string of missions. The numbers of escorts almost paralleled the bomber force (491 to 546), but the defenses still managed to cull 27 of the

Two officers stand on the right stabilizer of **Boots II/Carol Jane**, which is now a shattered wreck with all fabric surfaces burnt off. On 5 January 1944 the ex-381st BG B-17F failed to get properly airborne and bore Lt. J Marshall and crew to their deaths in the resulting explosive impact with the ground at Larling.

The same day that **Boots II/Carol Jane** met her end over England also spelled the demise of 42-3541/QJ: N, although the B-17G displays no squadron codes here. Named **Little Girls**, the aircraft was "ditched" on the 5 January 1944 run to Bordeaux by Lt. E Davidson, an action that the pilot and at least four others survived, albeit as POWs.

B-17s and B-24s, nearly half of which were borne by the 1st BD, compared to seven each from the 2nd and 3rd BDs.

Divisional losses were spread between the CBWs with the 13th worst affected—four—with three coming from the 390th BG. Once again, the attrition appears to have largely commenced only after the Division's formations had bombed and were rallying almost due north of the target. Osterholz-Scharmbeck lies quite close to Bremen's northern boundary, and it was near there that 42-37883/CC: D finally succumbed to flak and fighter damage, with Lt. F Hoffman (P) one of two fatalities. Soon after 42-37763/FC: D slipped back from the group and was last seen being latched onto by several Fw190s; it progressed as far as the region around Wilhelmshaven before Lt. W Riley gave the bail out command, and Sillenstede, several miles northwest of that seaport, was where his B-17 crashed. The day's punishment for the Framlingham fliers was completed by the disappearance over the North Sea of the flak-affected 42-30476/BI: L **Rovin' Ramona** along with all of Lt. J Reeve's crew.

The "Unlucky thirteen" accumulation of MIA losses suffered by the 96th BG on the previous four runs to Bremen was further extended by two. Problems with one engine that lost its oil content and prevented propeller "feathering" left Lt. B Fuller (P) in an increasingly parlous position as the group steadily disappeared after "bombs away." Matters continued to deteriorate as fighters pecked at the straggling aircraft 42-30368/BX: R **Gil** until little option was left but to jump into captivity in the vicinity of Aurich, close to Emden. **Green Fury II** (42-3288/BX: B) had also suffered damage just ahead of the target, and Lt. S Budleski (KIA) grittily held position at the rear of the formation, but was coming under almost continual fire as the group was crossing out near Norderney, in the Friesian Islands. Of the largely veteran 13-mission team one was killed and one wounded at this point. An engine was shredded by the latest lunge by two Bf109s; the pilot now gave the order to bail out;, but almost immediately the bomber exploded and its remnants fell on Norderney. The four surviving crew owed their lives to a combination of being blown out into mid-air and then being picked out of the sea by several vessels.

The latest VIIIBC victim to end up encased within the waters of the North Sea came from Knettishall. The flak over Bremen had been very intense, and had landed what were almost certainly mortal blows to 42-31084 in Lt. K Eccleston's hands. The bomber was last reported heading down on fire and with bomb-bay doors jammed. Of the crew, only three bodies were subsequently washed up at locations as far north as Sylt Island, on the Danish/German border. A fourth 13th CBW crew from Horham also failed to return in 42-31305/OE: M flown by Lt. W Kelley Jnr. (KIA). Fighter gunfire had struck home over the target to set two engines on fire, and the region around Osterholz-Scharmbeck quickly collected its second B-17, along with seven bodies and three immediate survivors, two of whom later died of their wounds.

Christmas was impending, but any lingering hopes of "Peace and Good Will" for the festive event seemed dim, as the latest mission was dispatched on the 22nd with Muenster as the selected target for the Division. Almost 200 crews bombed the Primary and came home three light, all single group losses. The 95th BG's 42-37766/BG: F fell out under apparent control and then came under attack by a *Rotte* of Fw190s, whose fire caused their victim to sag and finally fall into a spin. Lt. M Mangis corrected this mal-action and kept his B-17 in level flight long enough for six crewmembers to bail out. Sadly, both pilots and two others were already killed or unable to evacuate the bomber after it exploded and came down at Langeveen, in Holland. Bombing had been completed when Knettishall's 42-37773/T **Full House** lost an engine and drifted back and out of sight. The frigid Ijisselmeer waters swallowed up the B-17, along with all but two of Lt. W Bull's crew, who fortunately landed close to a seawall. Further west 42-31071/LD: U **Dorhelcia** came down in the equally uninviting North Sea and only one of the ten men led by Lt. T Goupill ever found a grave after being cast up on the English shoreline.

The Pas de Calais region in northeastern France was destined to become the epicenter for the V-1 Offensive launched in June 1944. At this time the nature and intended use of the strange "ski sites" structures liberally springing up here was unknown. However, a concerted and regular attempt to disrupt their construction was now begun. On Christmas Eve over 700 B-17s and B-24s went up to make the short easy paced flight and unload nearly 1,700 tons of explosives at no cost in bombers or crew.

Closing Off 1943

The Christmas Eve foray was the last for six days, and every opportunity was taken to celebrate the Christian festival in what were sadly autocratic circumstances. Flight training and other functions was nevertheless indulged in, but with several instances of aerial or ground incidents that "wrote off" six B-17s, along with eighteen fatalities in one instance; in the latter case most of the deaths cruelly involved 95th BG personnel who had completed their 25 missions and were being ferried to Southport on board the ironically titled 52-5791/BG: E **Ruthless**.

Still Striking Out...

The final two days of what was a momentous, if not always positive year for the Daylight Offensive involved missions that were widespread geographically, and in the first instance reached quite deep into the Nazi heartland. Ludwigshafen was far from falling into the "shallow penetration" category since it was located inside enemy territory, and in terms of range was none too short of Schweinfurt, for example; the city possessed large chemical production plants and was accordingly targeted.

Upwards of 600 escorts, the majority of which were P-47s dispatched by nine of the twelve groups involved, did their usual best to protect the even larger 710-strong bomber stream. However, the *Jadgwaffe* managed to exact a reasonable toll of 23 "heavies," with nine each coming from the 2nd and 3rd BD sub-forces. The three B-17 CBWs lost crews in numerically descending order: four (13th), three (4th), and two (45th). The 100th BG's current reputation as a "hard luck" unit was not improved by two further losses. The first was 42-5997/EP: F **Heaven Can Wait**, which was successfully evacuated by Lt. F Smith near Monthois, northeast of Chalons-sur-Marne, where their battered B-17 came down. Furthermore, no less than eight airmen evaded capture, although the two pilots were the unlucky exceptions. By grim contrast, the two evaders from 42-5861/XR: J **Laden Maiden** (Lt. Owen "Cowboy" Roane's original B-17) were even more fortunate, in that they were the sole survivors from Lt. M Leininger's crew. Elsewhere within the 13th CBW, 42-30674/ET: C **Destiny's Tot** just faded out of sight into the clouds to finally crash northeast of Beauvais; at least all of Lt. R Smith's crew survived, with further luck attending him and six crewmembers who evaded capture. The fourth loss involved 42-39759/FC: G **Pickle Dropper**, which had bombed the target and was still on hand as the Group bypassed Charleville-Mezieres. Then a fighter attack disabled an engine and the B-17 was forced out on its own, losing a second engine soon afterwards. Lts. C. Brigman (P) and T. Terrill (CP) held their charge steady in a descending path that culminated in a successful crash landing near Hirson. One crewmember later died of his injuries, but the Resistance added a further six evaders to its already sizeable total (23) from among the CBW's ranks.

The 385th BG was almost within sight of the English Channel when 42-3097/Z **Ground Hog**, having suffered damage from cannon shells, began her final journey to destruction. The crash site was several miles north of Arras, a name synonymous

Stranger in the camp. An RAF Halifax Mk.V (Special) series has found a temporary home at Snetterton Heath, having probably diverted off an operation the previous night. Aircraft belongs to No. 76 Sqdn based in Yorkshire as part of No. 4 Group, RAF Bomber Command.

with the tragic battles of the First World War. Two officers died within the bomber, but the Germans only captured two of the remaining eight from Lt. R Eckhardt's crew. T/Sgt. Steele (Eng.) was killed by a cannon shell, but all other members of Lt. E Frye's team came through unscathed after 42-30249/X **El Sabo** was eased into a crash landing on French soil; Frye and two others were also blessed with evading capture. The third group within the 4th CBW was the 447th BG, whose operational debut had been six days before. The hard facts of combat life were now brought to bear at Rattlesden, as 42-31173/L in Lt. J Schrero's hands, was fatally crippled and fell out of the High group to strike the ground at Marines, some miles outside Paris' northwestern boundary. The pilot, along with three of his crew, forfeited their lives, with a single evader emerging from among the seven survivors.

Twenty airmen were absent from Knettishall that evening with only eight surviving their ordeals. Half were on board 42-31131/O **Satan's Sister**, which became the indirect victim of prop-wash emanating from a formation ahead of the 388th BG. Another group B-17 crossed Lt. A Carlson's path and made contact with his bomber close to the radio room; the impact caused the B-17 to split in two, and it fell away to come down northwest of Ludwigshafen. One officer and three gunners in the rear fuselage somehow managed to bail out. The offending bomber was believed to be 42-31176, which finally surrendered all ten crewmembers to captivity after Lt. Gwin ditched in the sea. The same scale of loss was experienced on board 42-31149/**My Day**. On the way back this B-17 had suffered an engine fire and loss of its propeller, followed by a second engine destroyed by fighter gunfire. The steady loss of altitude left the bomber easy prey for the Channel coast flak gunners who added more damage. Lt. P Comella (KIA) was finally forced to ditch fairly close to the Isle of Wight in the Channel; this was successfully achieved, but sadly the heavy sea then running swept no less than six of the ten crewmembers away from contact with the dinghies and they perished, the others being pulled out by an ASR Launch.

Another Long Run

Any prospect for a relaxed approach to New Year's 1944 celebrations were firmly nailed on the head in the early hours of 31 December. Not only was a mission due, but it involved yet another extended flight down to Bordeaux, as far as the 4th CBW was concerned. The other five groups faced a shorter run to Paris. All sixty-one crews dispatched to the former target got through to unload on Bordeaux/Merignac airfield, while only five of the 125 bombers attacking an industrial plant in Paris failed to gain mission credit. While the 1st BD suffered fifteen MIA crews, the tally for the 4th CBW stood at three. Lt. S Wainwright's 42-6037/QE: suffered a rapid series of hits during the bomb run and shortly after was focused upon by fighters to finally spiral to its destruction near Royan; the pilot was one of only four out of the eleven airmen to survive. Far better luck attended Lt. E Sullivan and crew on 42-31110/QE: M **Pacific's Dream**. Progressive engine failure thanks to flak strikes impelled the pilot to call for a bail out; to a 100% survival rate was added the bonus of six among the ten evading capture and all regaining English shores by the early summer.

The third victim fell near the Secondary target, Cognac/Chateau Bernard airfield, after taking a terminal flak strike in one wing and close to the cockpit. Lt. R Moore's 42-31125/J **No Regrets** relinquished its No. 5 slot in the High squadron

B-17G 42-31519, one of the early additions to the 447th BG's strength in England, flares out over the runway's end. The Medium Green applied to the central fin contrasts with the overall Olive Drab to camouflage. On 29 April the aircraft was successfully "ditched" by Lts. McGuire and K Anderson.

The distinctive "finger four" formations of a P-47 or P-51 Group are seen in this picture. In the foreground is 42-30226/ET: L – **Spook V**, whose wing, stabilizer and fin leading edges have had the rubber de-icing boots removed. Lt. Higgins (P) was one of five fatalities on 29 January 1944 when the B-17F was MIA off a mission to Frankfurt.

and was abandoned by the seven surviving crewmembers. The Paris attack went in simultaneously with the southwestern thrust and was completed with a single MIA crew from the 96th BG that made a severe unit statistic of 57 crews lost on operations inside 66 missions. The 338 BS' 42-31121/ BX: E came down near Abbeville, in the Picardy region of northeastern France, with none of Lt. R Woodward's crew getting out alive.

The VIII BC's blood-letting for 1943 was thus completed, with every indication that the situation was unlikely to improve for the foreseeable future. The German industrial fabric had been hurt to some degree since the Daylight Offensive had been intensified, particularly during the second half of the year. However, all its key industries, a sizeable proportion of which lay inside central and eastern Germany, as well as Poland and Czechoslovakia, remained largely intact. Equally of concern was the current strength and operational expertise of the *Jadgwaffe*, whose suppression if not total annihilation was a vital prerequisite for a successful invasion attempt by the Western Allies.

January 1944

The inaugural 1944 mission to Kiel (4 January) was to be the last flown under the VIII BC nomenclature—not that the participating airmen would have either known of the fact or cared about anything but their chances of completing the current requirement of 25 missions. Gen "Tooey" Spaatz and Gen. Doolittle had been brought back from the Mediterranean as part of Gen. Eisenhower's entourage for *Overlord*. In turn, the latter-named subordinate of the Supreme Commander had taken the place of Gen Eaker, who now transferred rather reluctantly to take command of the Theater of Operations vacated by Spaatz and Doolittle. Spaatz took up command of the recently-created United States Strategic and Tactical Air Forces (USSTAF), an umbrella organization covering all European operations. Doolittle's brief was to head the 8th Air Force, a title displacing VIII BC in terminology but not altering the operational structure or the remit of the B-17 and B-24 units within the "Mighty Eighth."

Both England-based Commanders, along with Eaker, now took note of the instruction issued by Gen "Hap" Arnold just prior to New Year's Day. This reminded them of the current large-scale and ever-burgeoning turnout from German aero factories; on the other hand, he reminded them of the equally fruitful turnout of crews and aircraft back in America. Finally, full emphasis was placed on the need to batter the *Luftwaffe* in general and its *Jagdwaffe* in particular prior to the twin-pronged invasion of Western Europe. Arnold's concluding statement was as follows, "Therefore my message to you – this is a MUST – is to destroy the enemy air forces wherever you find them, in the air, on the ground and in the factories." (In the latter quoted instance the basis was laid for Operation *Argument* launched in late February. This in turn was an outcome from *POINTBLANK*, an Allied plan formulated in June 1943 that pinpointed upwards of 80 special targets whose destruction would seriously, if not terminally cripple Nazi military and economic output.)

Over 1000 tons of explosives and incendiaries rained down upon either the Primary at Kiel or targets of opportunity from the high proportion of the 569 bombers dispatched; this included 166 3rd BD crews, who lost six among this figure. Sadly, two were due to the latest recorded mid-air collision, this time between two Snetterton Heath B-17s, thus further adding to the group's already heavy casualty list of almost one aircraft per mission. The formation was altering course to the IP in the face of strong sunlight, a fact that may have contributed to the incident. At any rate, Lt. J McLean's 42-30815/MZ: **Short Stride IV** became entangled with 42-5953/ BX: **Skin and Bones** (Lt. G Davis). Three gunners on the former-named crew were the lucky exceptions among the twenty airmen involved, while the bombers crashed close to Meppen. The North Sea swallowed up 42-30162 /GL: X **Picadilly Virgin** along with Lt. W Hudgens and all but one of the eleven-man crew, since no further immediate trace was established following their detachment from the formation. Better fortune attended all on board Lt. A Bean's 42-40046, as they abandoned their crippled bomber and drifted down into captivity. Two 390th BG crews completed the MIA figure in terms of crews but not bombers. **Dull Tool** (42-30289/BI: H) finally came down in Denmark, but six crewmembers drifted down into the Baltic from where just two were very fortunate to be picked up alive from the terminally chilled water by Danish fishermen. A Dutch "grave" near Scharwoude, on the enlarged peninsula between the Ijisselmeer and North Sea, accommodated the remains of 42-30320/CC: S Coy de Coy I, thankfully without any of Lt. R Patterson's crew.

The crew of HMS *Verdun*, a Royal Navy destroyer, were part of the escort for a northbound convoy off the East Anglian coast when they were alerted to the fact that a bomber was about to ditch. The 95BG crew concerned was led by Lt. P Millward in 42-6098/OE: R **Superstitious Aloysius**. Considering that the weather conditions featured a Force-6 with cresting wavetops it was a miracle that the B-17 was safely brought down into the water. Only one dinghy promptly inflated, into which no less than eight airmen clambered, while the pilot and S/Sgt. McComber (BT) hauled out the other raft that had stubbornly refused to automatically inflate. After a great struggle the deed was achieved, but Millward insisted in "taking a leak" in the appropriate wind direction before stepping aboard! Within 30 minutes a circling RAF "Walrus" amphibian was joined by *Verdun*, whose crew now had the tricky task of attempting to secure the two rafts that were rapidly drifting away with their thoroughly soaked occupants. The task was finally accomplished with the airmen grateful for a safe delivery into the water by their bomber, whose first and last mission this had been.

Hard Times at Snetterton Heath...

While the other two Divisions dispatched a reduced force back to Kiel on the 5th with a separate force sent to Tours, in France, the 4th and 45th CBWs once again faced the protracted trip to Bordeaux/ Merignac airfield. The mission commenced badly for the 96th BG during take-off from what was a mist and frost-shrouded airfield when 42-3268 /MZ: **Carol Anne** came down barely one mile clear of the airfield to kill all of Lt. J Marshall's crew, although one gunner lingered for 24 hours before expiring. Even worse was in store for the already severely-penalized Group, not only today but over the ensuing six months.

The initial fighter response appears to have occurred around the IP. Not long after, Lt. Stakes, piloting 42-31164AW: T, ordered his crew to take up their crash positions as he headed down towards a successful crash landing; S/Sgt. C Robinson (WG) was already mortally wounded but was made

Shortly after New Year's Day 42-31319 arrived at Deopham Green, and between 5 February and 26 April was on hand for the decisive air battles executed during that time. Her end came on the latter-stated date when problems on take-off led to her crash landing and subsequent removal as salvage. Note the extremely dulled-down group insignia on the fin.

as comfortable as possible before his companions split up in what evolved into a successful evasion act by six of them.

It was the 339 BS that absorbed the bulk of punishment with four B-17s downed. Lt. G Pierce was within the homeward bound formation when 42-39816/QJ: H was picked off and dispatched into the Bay of Biscay's ever-frigid waters; a French fishing boat that was fortunately operating around the crash site picked up S/Sgt. G Norman (WG), but nobody else was so blessed. Around the same time Lt. Reuff in 42-37808/QJ: S lost one engine and suffered serious damage to the oxygen system. The crew was ordered out, and all ten duly survived to be captured north of Bordeaux. Further along the homeward route the latest fighter forays put 42-3541/QJ: N **Little Girls** temporarily out of control, whereupon four gunners bailed out. Lt. E Davidson regained control, but was finally forced into a ditching that saw five survivors out of the six still on board scrambling into a dinghy and eventual pick-up by the Germans. The attrition continued apace among the group ranks, and the fifth and final bomber was culled. Capt. D Cole's B-17 (42-30665/QJ: E **Hunyak**) had already suffered flak damage and lost an engine before the now-straggling aircraft was picked upon and thoroughly shot-up to finally lose one complete stabilizer. The pilot was the sole fatality out of this crew after it finally blew up.

...and Rougham

Matters were little better for the 94th BG, with four losses spread among three squadrons. One of the two 410th BS losses involved **Lil Butch** (42-30112/GL: Z), flown by Lt. A Powell. He was one of seven fatalities during the course of his bomber's downing in the target area. Lt. G Johnson's 42-31212/QE: K suffered some flak damage on the bomb run, but following "bombs away" kept on course for England until the formations were crossing over northwest France. It was then that, shortly after sustaining another pasting from flak, a brutal fighter pass fatally crippled the B-17 as well as killing three gunners. Their seven fellow-airmen all took to their parachutes, and after landing safely joined a growing total of Rougham evaders—21 in all off the mission! Among this positive figure were five from 42-30444/XM: C2 **Black Jack IV**. The scale of damage to this B-17 soon culminated in its crashing north of Bordeaux. Both pilots (Lts. H Lockwood and C Adcock) and three more from the nine survivors gained shelter from the civilian population and eventually returned to England, but for the others their safe parachute descent only led towards the less welcome confines of a POW camp.

Back at Rougham, an Infantry sergeant had enjoyed a reunion with his brother the previous day and now awaited his return from this mission. His grief could be appreciated by the group personnel when he was informed that his brother, Lt. Raymond Born, had failed to bring back 42-30200/GL: R **Slo-Time Sally**. It would be many weeks before a measure of relief for the sergeant, and indeed his entire family, could be realized when the news filtered back via the Red Cross that Lt. Born had survived. All but one of the crew got down safely on French soil, either by parachute or after the B-17 was crash landed; both pilots ended up POWs, while the other seven airmen evaded that fate. Single crews from the 385th and 447th BGs were added to the 4th CBW loss register, as was one Horham crew from the 13h CBW.

"The tail gunner was killed" was the terse if happily inaccurate conclusion to this picture's caption in an earlier publication. In fact, S/Sgt. Roy Urich survived being blasted out into midair from Lt. Valesh's B-17G (100th BG) on 24 January 1944. Presence of an RAF airman on right is explained by the fact that the bomber diverted into RAF Eastchurch, in Kent. It is incredible that anybody could live through the scale of damage wrought upon the airframe.

Ludwigshafen Again

On the 7th the target was Ludwigshafen, relatively deep in western Germany at a distance out of the escort range of all but the P-51s of the 354th FG, and almost sure to stir up strong *Jagdwaffe* opposition. In the event barely 3% of the attacking force failed to return, including two 3rd BD bombers, although the PFF-directed bombing return was similarly marginal thanks to a heavy overcast. Snetterton Heath mourned the loss of 42-30130/AW: J **Klap Trap II**. The group was heading for home when Lt. R Peterson gradually lost position, but seemed to have the B-17 under apparent control when last seen. The bomber's subsequent violent disintegration in mid-air left two survivors, one of which was S/Sgt. A. Weiss (TG), who managed to extricate himself from the severed tail section and pulled his ripcord. The 94th BG's 42-31234/XM: **Johnny Walker III** was close to the Belgian/German border and west of Luxembourg

Black Hawk/Guzzlers was fortunate to return to Snetterton Heath on 29 January 1944, having been shot up by fighter gunfire; five other group B-17s did not, three of them lost to collisions. The B-17F that had been assigned in June 1943 was finally retired from direct combat duties as a conventional bomber, but her operational career was not yet over....

City when it was crash landed at Arlon by Lt. J Barber, his mount having suffered heavy damage from fighter gunfire; the Germans quickly apprehended five of the seven survivors.

Brunswick Beckons

Brunswick, located east of Hannover, was another large industrial city worthy of attention, but equally well out of escort cover range. On the 11th the 2nd and 3rd BDs were dispatched there, while the 1st BD faced a separate potential martyrdom over Oschersleben further to the south. By the day's end the records presented an exact *Black Thursday* scale of MIA loss, 70% of which emanated from the ranks of the 1st BD.

Ever worsening weather patterns as the Divisions were wending their way over Holland and into Germany culminated in a "recall" signal being issued and acted upon by the 2nd BD and all but one CBW from the 3rd BD; the 1st BD was adjudged to have penetrated too far for the "recall" to be issued, and in fact its twin-pronged assault upon aircraft production factories at Oschersleben and Halberstadt was completed by the majority of the 291 crews sent out, albeit at a ferociously expensive cost.

Half of the B-24 force did unload on targets of opportunity at a minimal cost of two bombers, whereas a small proportion (47 out of 234) of the B-17s struck the Primary, with a further 161 attacking targets of opportunity in Osnabrueck, Bielefeld, and Peine. The Brunswick attackers were from the 4th CBW, with the 94th BG in Lead position, and the "recall" was only received as Brunswick was rapidly appearing. Since the signal's veracity could not be confirmed, Lt/Col. Thorup as Commander made the decision to go on and, after circling the area, commenced a bomb run that concluded with a solid bomb pattern descending upon the Waggum factory.

The current absence of escorts meant that the *Jagdwaffe* pilots could give unfettered vent to their vicious energies, which they now proceeded to do against the Rougham raiders in particular. To the single-engine assaults was added the now familiar incursions of Bf110G-2s and/or Me410s approaching from the rear to fire their 21-cm rockets into the formation. Six 94th BG crews had gone down in January so far, and now that figure would be exceeded by two, spread among all four squadrons.

Two 332 BS crews reportedly came down in the target area. One was Lt. Fairchild's team flying in 42-3530/XM: H, the other being led by Lt. J Cota on board 42-39767/XM:.

Fairchild was one of the nine fatal casualties from his B-17, while Cota became a POW along with seven of his crew. Lingen and Rheine, both close to the Dutch border, with the latter town some 15 miles to the south, became the final resting places for another brace of group bombers. The 331 BS' 42-31216/QE: L, piloted by Lt. J Rubin, crashed at the northern location, although he and eight other crewmembers bailed out. Lt. D Sharpa (POW) lost two of his crew in 42-39822/TS: O close to Rheine.

Although the Group was suffering regular losses, at least the majority of crewmembers were getting out alive. Lt. S Butler was the sole fatality on his 42-29961/QE: Y **Southern Queen**, which crashed near Pattensen-Holthesen, while Lt. W Service (POW), in charge of 42-37798/QE: X **Big Stoop**, and seven crewmembers bailed out safely with his aircraft coming down at a location named as Rahden. Even greater, if conditional, fortune awaited nine airmen in Lt. S. Lemley's 42-30425/TS: J **Roger Dodge Her**, which finally descended at Abensen, since they also jumped clear and floated down towards captivity.

Lt. R Randall (410 BS), who was piloting 42-30248/QL: X **Southern Queen,** had seen his charge suffer jammed open bomb-bay doors, and the drag inevitably caused the B-17 to fall behind. The loss of an engine and a rocket strike against a wing root were followed by the bomber falling into a partial spin that initially prevented the nine still-living crewmembers from acting upon the bail out order. Fortunately this lethal motion was corrected sufficiently for all to jump clear.

Luck of the Draw

Two bombers were fortunate to return to Rougham, the first of which was flown by Lt. W Cely. **Frenesi**'s (42-39775/ TS: K) sufferings began just after the bomb run when one engine was disabled. Both wingmen were downed to leave the bomber trailing the Lead element. The constant battering being handed out tore large chunks from the right wing, fuselage, and elevators until a temporary loss of control saw the aircraft entering into a spinning dive. Five of the crew and a supernumerary base photographer not unnaturally assumed

The "Bloody 100th's" ill fortunes aloft during its first few months were sometimes matched on the ground. These foam-smothered wrecks are part of a collision between no less than three B-17s on 27 December 1943 while landing. On the right is the tail section of EP: B **King Bee** with its fin embedded in one wing of 42-37772/LN: S **Flyin' Jennie** and its severed and canted-up forward fuselage laying to the left. No injuries were borne by any of the crews concerned.

The P-47 continued to be the main escort fighter as 1944 was entered. Here a 62FS example adorned with "Lil' Abner" artwork as adopted throughout the squadron is snapped from the waist position on a B-17 from the 96thBG.

it was time to abandon their dying aircraft and bailed out. Cely and Lt. J Churchill grimly held course to the west despite the regular attention from the *Luftwaffe*, the German pilots surely amazed that this isolated victim could take such punishment and still remain airborne. It not only did so, but finally cleared enemy territory and ultimately landed at Rougham. The scale of damage ensured that what was the Cely crew's regular aircraft had initially to be declared surplus to operational requirement and "scrapped." The pilot's later reward for his efforts was the bestowing of a Silver Star.

Lt. C. Hatcher III, a group "original," had already had his fair share of combat problems that included bringing back a seemingly mortally crippled B-17 on 11 November. Now he was on board Lt. G Kascuta's 42-31289/GL: **Belle of Maryland** positioned in the High squadron's second Element as No. 4 or No. 6. All too soon the pilots found themselves moving up as No. 3 to the Lead bomber following the loss of three other squadron aircraft. A head-on attack by a fighter then set the nose compartment on fire and, although the bombardier and navigator kept fighting the conflagration with all available fire extinguishing equipment, the result was only partially successful, in that the flames were confined to the immediate area of the fuselage. Acrid smoke was streaming back into the cockpit, and an inability to "feather" No. 1 engine added to the pilots' problems, while that power plant ominously began to emit smoke and flames on final approach to Rougham. The B-17 was safely put down on the runway before this extra complication arose and the fuselage fire extinguished by the fire trucks, but the "Belle" joined **Frenesi** on the scrapheap.

Spreading the Cost...

The 94th BG's severe punishment was visited to a lesser degree upon one of the other two CBW units, with three crews from Rattlesden joining the MIA list. While bypassing Hannover fighters cut 42-31107 out of the formation, and Lt. H Jarrell (P) became one of eight fatalities before his B-17 crashed at Retburg. Diepholz, west of Hannover, was where 42-31082 became yet another fighter victim, but with diametrically good fortune for all but two on board Lt. C Hickey's crash landed bomber. The third crew regained British soil minus their aircraft, 42-37824 **Miss Boo**. Successive loss of two engines between the target zone and the enemy left the B-17 a straggler, and not long after the Continental coastline faded behind Lt. R Foots' machine the other two engines began to fade. Amazingly, all ten airmen managed to get out onto the wings and launch the life rafts despite their bomber sliding under the waves within 60 seconds; soon after an RAF Hudson appeared overhead, but it was several more hours before the welcome outline of an ASR launch loomed in sight.

Four groups from the 13th and 45th CBWs suffered single losses in three instances. The 388th BG doubled this sad figure, however. Approaching the Dummersee on the way in, 42-30215/J **Slightly Dangerous II** lost an engine. Soon after the "recall" signal was received well inside German territory a second engine had to be switched off and the propeller "feathered" with the inevitable loss of formation position. Just west of Hameln, at Flakenholz, the B-17 was abandoned to its fiery fate after the nine-man crew led by Lt. L Carpenter jumped out. The **Berlin Ambassador** title for 42-378676/E was fated to remain unfulfilled as regards the bomber ever gaining access to the Nazi capital. Having also been forced out of formation thanks to fighter-inflicted damage, the ailing B-17 headed back; on nearing Zwolle, in Holland, some of the crew bailed out, but Lt. G Hoehn held control of his rapidly failing charge long enough to steer it clear of the town. Sadly he was killed in the resultant crash, along with two others, while a fourth airman died later in hospital.

The two 13th CBW crews came down on land. From Horham, 42-5918/ET: J **Heavenly Daze** out on its own received no response to Lt. J Foley's call for fighter cover; close to Oldenburg, all but one crewmember finally abandoned the burning B-17. The single 390th BG casualty was Lt. C Sanders Jr's 42-39879/CC: A, which "gave up the ghost" over Lingen/Ems, where it crashed along with one already-dead gunner. The saddest loss out of this trio was 42-3504/QJ: F. The 96th BG B-17 was seen to ditch, but although the coordinates were radioed in by another circling group bomber no trace of Lt. R Ford's crew was ever found by the ASR service.

"No-Ball" Diversion

The warped but ingenious scientific qualities of the Nazi regime would again be demonstrated in mid-June 1944 with the advent of the V-1 Flying Bomb Offensive. As 1944 opened, the presence of a growing number of unspecified sites within the Pas de Calais region of France was continuing to exercise the minds of the Allied High Command. So it was that the "heavies" were now dispatched in sizeable numbers to inhibit, if not totally nullify this unknown but seemingly sinister build-up. Three days after the Brunswick run, 198 Division crews out of 552 in total joined in on the assault of the sites. Another seven days then elapsed before the bombers again took off in earnest with the same region the focus of assault. The short duration of these missions was surely welcome to the crews, but there was no guarantee of immunity from loss, even if the MIA figure between these twin thrusts was only nine out of a total of 925 crews granted mission "credit." The single Divisional loss involved 42-37818/BI: D **The Pub**, which absorbed a flak strike on one engine during the initial target run-up, followed by a second motor set on fire during the second bomb run attempt. Lt. C Baugher's subsequent homeward course sadly ended in the Channel, ending with his death along with three of the crew, the other six descending by parachute onto French soil.

The frustratingly unpredictable weather patterns undoubtedly contributed to the current limitations in attacking German industry's heartland, and it was only on the 24th that all three Divisions were cleared to head out towards a range of sources at Frankfurt. However, continuing adverse weather over England caused the 2nd BD to "abort" while little better luck attended the efforts of the other two Divisions. Barely 10% of the B-17 crews even struck a target of opportunity; 56 crews from the 3rd BD unloaded upon a power station at Eschweiler, these being the exception to a general "recall" signal that the other sub-forces had already acted upon.

Two crews from the 95th BG was the sole MIA cost for the Division; however, another airman from the 100th BG was also MIA, but survived in the most exceptional circumstances. Lt. F Valesh's **Hang the Expense Again** (42-39867/EP: E) was part of the group formation "aborting" the mission when the bombers over-flew an airfield near Ostend. The flak gunners laid down a sharp barrage, one of whose shells literally blew the tail turret apart, along with much of the lower rudder. Miraculously S/Sgt. R Urich, although severely wounded, not only survived the experience, but managed to deploy his parachute. With all rudder control gone and elevator control only exercised via the automatic pilot it was almost equally miraculous that the crippled B-17 was kept aloft to finally divert into RAF Eastchurch in Kent.

Regaining the Strategic Path...

Frankfurt's immunity from assault on the 24th was delayed by five days when 863 crews were briefed and sent aloft, with 291 out of the 3rd BD's 309 dispatched B-17s getting through to their Primaries. The *Jadgwaffe* pilots, along with the flak batteries, did their best to disrupt proceedings by bringing down 29 of the attackers, although half this figure in turn represented those enemy pilots brought down by the American escorts.

Both views highlight the white cowling and fin bands initially used to distinguish the Republic design from its Fw 190 opponent. The absence of drop tanks and loose bomber formation in background indicate this is the return leg of a mission.

The 45th CBW suffered nearly half the Division's losses (13), with the 96th BG short of five crews and a single loss borne by the 388th. The Snetterton group had been assigned the Low and High positions in the CBW, but the 37-strong joint force somehow became separated from the stream during final target approach and paid the price when it was focused upon by up to sixty Bf109s and Fw190s. The savage close-in nature of the fighter passes brought about two mid-air collisions between bombers and their tormentors. First, an already crippled Bf109 impacted with 42-38001/BX: (Lt. L Anthony), with nobody observed emerging from the stricken bomber. Then, another Bf109 failed to avoid running into Lt. L Kandl's 42-30859/MZ: O **Skylark**, which split in two. The ball turret and one waist gunner were the very fortunate exceptions to escape with their lives as their bomber tumbled to its destruction.

Two of the other losses were self inflicted in what would be a distressingly regular occurrence in future months. Almost immediately following the loss of **Skylark**, a gunner on Lt. H Hammond's 42-31436/MZ: frantically called in to say 42-31151/AW: S, flown by Lt. D Sisler, was veering dangerously towards the former B-17. The aircraft came together before avoiding action could be taken, but remained airborne long enough for 13 personnel out of the 20 involved to bail out. Lt. Sisler was one of the fatalities, while Sgt. Maxey, on Hammond's crew, was already dead from his wounds before the collision occurred. The sole direct loss to the enemy involved **The Flying Ginny** (42-3552/BX: L). Strikes in the nose compartment set it on fire, after which Lt. C Farris successfully bailed out his crew.

The former named group had now lost fifteen crews during January, a severe enough attrition rate. However, unbeknownst to the Snetterton Heath airmen was that the first half of 1944 would see their ranks shorn of a round 100 B-17s, with mid-air collisions featuring prominently within this shocking scale of suffering. (Strangely enough, the Group would never earn the same reputation as a "hard luck" outfit compared to nearby Thorpe Abbotts and its *Bloody Hundredth* residents.)

Great Ashfield contained three dispersals whose distraught ground crew gazed upon the vacant dispersals normally occupied by their assigned B-17s. Two were from the 549th BS. First, 42-30251/T Piccadilly Queen (Lt. R Notestein) was brought down by fighters at Kaiserslautern, Germany, and six of the crew, including the pilot, were killed. Lt. R Palmer had charge of 42-30354 **Hustlin' Hussy** (549th BS), but the crew's isolated progress during the return leg was brought to an end over the town of Anderlues, in southern Belgium. The bomber

Rougham's TS: R has made it back from Bordeaux on 31 December 1943, but a force landing at St. Mary's in Marsh has culminated in a very heavy impact that has broken the B-17G's back. Several records have shown this aircraft as MIA with Lt. Sullivan's crew, but the pilot is recorded as going down in 42-31110/QE: M **Pacific Dream**!

This B-17G was assigned to the 95th BG on 13 December 1943. Its operational career extended over thirteen months until 20 January 1945, when it came down near Eulsheim in intact condition apart from its rudder; seven of Lt. Beard's nine-man crew reportedly evaded capture.

had been straggling since before the bomb run and now the latest fighter pass brought her down. Nine airmen bailed out, leaving one gunner dead at his post, and only two of this number was immediately captured. Lt. Palmer did initially evade capture to gain cover with a Belgian family, but was discovered on the premises by a German search party. He then had the horrendous experience of witnessing the summary execution of his benefactors (a farmer and his wife) before being led off into captivity. All ten in Lt. R Bostick's charge survived the ultimate loss of 42-97506 at Gonnesweiler, north of Saarbruecken, following previous strikes from fighters.

One of the two Horham losses reflected RAF Bomber Command's spirit of "Press on regardless." Lt. J Higgins (42-30336/ET: L **Spook No. V**) maintained course even though one engine had been knocked out over the French coast. A second engine's loss over the IP persuaded the pilots to jettison their load and attempt a solo run towards England and face the prospects of ditching, rather than head south for Switzerland. The gallant bid to get back home finally failed near Bastogne, in Belgium. The B-17 came down at Lutrebois, and five crewmembers, including Higgins, shared her fate. The same percentage of deaths attended the loss of 42-3545/BG: A further on at Oolgem, southwest of Ghent, but this time three of the five survivors evaded capture, although Lt. Roznetinsky (P) was not among them.

The inevitable extreme variations in fortune affected the remaining losses. **Devil's Mate** (42-31108) was brought down near Koblenz with all of Lt. C Allen's Rattlesden crew. Framlingham's 42-30334/DI: E was involved in a collision with a fellow aircraft; the right wing was mangled by the other B-17's propellers and the controls were adversely affected. In spite of this the now straggling aircraft was banked southwards, but the gallant bid by Lt. W Harding and crew to reach Switzerland finally failed near Friederichshafen, with all ten taking to the air. Mixed fortune awaited Lt. F Hennessey's team after 42-3285/Q **Mary Ellen** was blasted by flak over Frankfurt; the B-17's subsequent demise near Cambrai, in Belgium, left six of the 388th BG crew alive, of which two evaded capture.

Germany's aviation industry located in Brunswick was the intended target on the penultimate day of January, but adverse weather conditions again thwarted any attempt by the two B-17 Divisions to deliver a precise blow. Instead, the city center and selected targets of opportunity provided disappointingly vague alternatives for the 599 bombardiers concerned. The sole consolation was the relatively low loss rate (20), with single crews from three 3rd BD units included in this total.

Two of the three suffered damage on the way in that saw both pilots turning back either under, or calling for fighter cover. P-51s picked up 42-31146 (Lt. M Putnam), but a combination of a flak strike and further punishment from a pack of fighters saw the 447th BG machine, which by then was on less than half power, being abandoned near Goch. The other crew did not proceed so far before 42-31209/O's (388th BG) increasingly critical state forced Lt. O Bianchi to press the bail out bell before following his crew out south of Diepholz; one member failed to survive the descent, while three others also lost their lives in the bomber. Finally Lt. R Lojinger, having bombed the target, then became detached from the Great Ashfield formation; the B-17 (42-31181) was observed to fall out of the sky near Bissendorf but without any of its crew.

This mission effectively closed off large scale operations for the month with a small force of B-24s striking V-1 sites in the Pas de Calais on the 31st. Momentous events that were to dictate a slow but irreversible upsurge in Allied fortunes over central Europe unknowingly awaited the American aviators, whether in their cumbersome bombers or immeasurably more fleet fighters, during the ensuing months of February and March 1944.

7

Emerging from the Darkness

The Daylight Offensive was now finely balanced. The B-17s and B-24s were managing to strike key targets at fairly regular intervals and at a reasonable distance into the Nazi hinterland. On the other hand, the *Jadgwaffe* fighters and their flak support were still proving a formidable barrier to expanding bomber operations in a large scale and cost effective manner across the length and breadth of their domain. The key to breaking down that resistance primarily lay in the hands of the 8th Fighter Command, with the P-51 perceived as the "shining sword," and therefore the key element in reaching that goal. However, the North American design was currently available in extremely small numbers, and in the weeks ahead it was to fall upon the P-47 Groups in particular to do their very best to blunt the enemy assaults upon the bomber stream, even if they were unable to totally disrupt and extinguish their adversaries' malign effect...

The 447th BG holds course firmly for its target during the winter of 1943/44. Nearest B-17 is an early G-Model as confirmed by the lack of "cheek" gun Plexiglas mounts. The initial batches of the Bendix chin turret-equipped bombers were rushed into service in order to boost forward firepower against the current *Luftwaffe* tactic of attacking from ahead.

B-17G 42-31876/QW: Q **Fire Ball Red** had a short operational career. Having arrived at Horham in mid-January 1944, the aircraft had "aborted" the mission of 17 February. On landing it over-shot and impacted with a cement mixer to end up in this shattered state, fortunately without injury to its crew.

The month was three days old before the full force of the 8th AF was unleashed against a familiar target—Wilhelmshaven and its port facilities. Next day, Frankfurt was the focus for attack by a similar strength force. On the first occasion a mere four crews had been downed. However, two arose out of a mid-air collision between B-17s from Great Ashfield, one of which was 42-39952/551BS (Lt. R Morse); even if any of the ten airmen had managed to parachute clear, the frigid North Sea waters 20 miles east of Great Yarmouth would quickly have expunged their lives through drowning or exposure; a similar fate awaited Lt. H Heuser's crew on 42-39938.

Five times that figure ended up as MIA on the 4th, with half coming from the 3rd BD, including a second brace from the 385th BG and three from the 100th BG. In contrast to their colleagues the day before, all twenty of the Great Ashfield airmen survived their aircrafts' loss. Lt. W Horstman's 42-31295 succumbed to fighters north of Liege, but while six airmen ended up as POWs the other four evaded capture. Incarceration also awaited all on board 42-31355, flown by Lt. R McAdams, which was straggling on the homeward leg when flak brought it down.

Rosie's Riveters (42-30758/LD: W) had served since August and bore the nickname for one of Thorpe Abbotts' most legendary and ultimately surviving airmen, Robert Rosenthal. This B-17, unlike its original pilot, would never reach friendly shores again. Flak was adjudged to have inflicted fatal damage that saw the bomber tumble to destruction at Wiesbaden, but not before Lt. R McPhee's crew had jumped clear. One of the other two group losses had a diametrically tragic conclusion. Lt W Green's 42-37975/LD: U was last seen over the Dutch coast under apparent control, but with smoke exuding from the airframe as it sank into the undercast. Two bodies subsequently washed ashore to bear sole witness to their bomber's and colleagues' last resting place under the sea. Finally, there was a single fatality on board Lt. J Brown's 42-39799/XR: **M Dodie**, which came down southeast of Kasterlee, in Belgium. Elsewhere, 42-31292/CC: F, which was a flak victim, staggered back as far as Lekkerkerk, in Holland, where Lt. C Strait bellied her in to face imprisonment along with his crew.

By contrast, Fortune deserted all but two on Lt. G DeJean's crew after flak excised part of a wing and stabilizer on 42-31781/A **Cock of the Walk**, leaving the bomber's remnants to impact north of Bonn following a mid-air explosion.

The third daily sortie witnessed a switch to French aviation-orientated targets; however, the Division's specific target, an Air Depot at Romilly-sur-Seine, remained intact, and the Secondary at Villacoublay airfield was struck without loss.

To date in February the loss ratio (26 out of 1337 completed sorties) was gratifyingly minimal, especially when considering that two of the three target choices had been well within the ambit of the German defenses. On the other hand, the Americans' adversary was still largely intact, and therefore ever likely to strike back in punishing form. There would be no viable alternative to the 8th Fighter Command bringing the *Jadgwaffe* into regular battle and breaking the back of its resistance in so doing, even if that entailed exposing the bomber crews to equal punishment in the short term. The bald truth was that the USAAF had now to engage in a battle of attrition that would hopefully realize the truth of Gen. Bedford Forrest's ungrammatical but telling assertion, "to win a War, you have to get there fustest with the mostest." That battle was on the verge of being commenced, but its outcome was naturally unclear...

Brunswick Blues...

A weather affected run to French targets (6th) involving single losses to the 95th, 96th, and 447th BGs was followed by a surprisingly small-scale effort of two CBWs directed against Frankfurt (8th), with Divisional casualties still pleasantly low on both occasions—a total of seven spread between five groups. This was of little consolation at Deopham Green, where the latter mission cost the 452nd BG three of these crews. The first was downed on the way over when 42-37946 lost an engine. Not being able to hold formation, Lt. E Truex turned for home. The bomber got as far as northern France before fighters shot it out of the sky near Le Havre, but not before the crew safely bailed out. Lt. R Lorenzi lost one crewmember during fighter assaults upon 42-31325, but all others evacuated their doomed charge that crashed near Amiens. Another French location near Laon was the last resting place for 42-39940; one crewmember sadly suffered parachute failure, while Lt. L Jamsson (P) was one of seven POWs out of the other nine.

The current run of fortune in this basic respect was soon brutally disrupted, however, next day. Brunswick's aero industry was briefed for nine groups, who sent out a surprisingly low average of 19 crews. On the other hand, the fighter escort strength was three-fold in numbers and involved eleven groups. However, two groups were destined to be grounded by weather while three others failed to make prompt rendezvous with their *Big Friends* during the return flight. The probable result of these manifold failures was the severe punishment handed out to the bomber force, when 29 out of the 169 sent out ended up as MIA, with only the 385th BG returning intact.

All three CBWs shared in the overall loss figure, with eleven coming from the 13th and 45th and seven from the 4th. It was the 95th BG that led this ever-sad statistic with seven crews going down. One of these (42-37971/OE: W) included a navigator who had literally spent several hours at Horham. Lt. M Spencer had arrived late the previous evening and was allotted a bunk in the hut occupied by a Group veteran, Lt. "Ed" Charles. Ed had offered to assist him to unpack, but Spencer said all he wanted to do was go to sleep. Early on the 10th he was awoken out of his deep slumber and peremptorily informed he was on the mission list! Although "enjoying" one of the shortest combat tours on record at Horham or any other bomber base, he was at least destined to survive as one of eight POWs on Lt. Tuberose's crew, and was forever known as "the man who came for breakfast!" (His A2 jacket was "adopted" by Ed and now resides in the 390th BG Tower Museum, Framlingham.)

4th CBW

The 94th BG lost one quarter of its 21-crew strength while participating as Low group in the lead 4th CBW. Returning airmen said that the *Luftwaffe* attacks came in on either side of crossing Holland's Ijisslemeer. The 331st BS absorbed four of the five losses, one of which was 42-39984 (Lt. F Barker, POW), out of which six airmen jumped. Gross Hehlem, adjacent to Celle, was on the final target approach, and was where all ten of the crew successfully evacuated their doomed bomber, 42-38107 (Lt. A Repas). Another loss occurred just after the bomb run; 42-31080/QE: **Hey Moitle** (Lt. P McWilliam) crashed at Lauingen, just east of Brunswick, along with half of its crew. The squadron's misery was completed by 42-30378/QE: A **Good Time Cholley III**, but at least the complete crew, headed by Lt. D Anderson, escaped alive from a crash landing after being shot out of formation prior to the IP and forced to make a solo run for home—their "good" fortune in ending up as POWs was tempered by the fact that today had been their 13th mission! The final Group loss was Lt. W Gingold's 42-31838/TS: **Sack Time Charlie**, on which three crew members were killed, the crash site being at Levern, near Osnabrueck.

The Wing's losses were added to when the 447th BG surrendered a pair of crews. First, 42-31096 **The Squirming Squaw** (Lt. J Jellison) impacted near Evenkamp but with none of its crew on board; Lt. P Beall (P) was one of five survivors from 42-31167's final loss near Barver.

45th CBW

The 452nd BG had only commenced operations five days before and was on its fourth mission with three losses to date. Today's run surely sent a shockwave through the Group ranks after five crews were arbitrarily chalked off its establishment. Two crews suffered the particular trauma of mid-air collision. The German towns of Diepholz and Hemsloh lie close together, and it was

Four B-17s of the 390th BG have broken away into the airfield pattern in preparation for landing. The temporary nature of many WWII constructed British airfields is demonstrated here, with the T2 hangar on the left and the mix of corrugated iron Nissen huts and standard buildings. Building on right appears to be an abandoned or requisitioned farm structure.

Members of the 96th BG are (perhaps reluctantly) being inculcated into the manifold intricacies of cricket by a group of local children. Although a sport normally played in summer, the bare tree branches confirm this "out of season" example.

there that the respective airframes of 42-31318 (Lt. M Turner, POW) and 42-39961 (Lt. Tiska. KIA) came to earth; eight others among the twenty personnel received the gift of (incarcerated) life, among which was a single member from Triska's B-17. A Dutch field at Leeuwarden formed the crash site for one of the remaining three MIA aircraft after fighters dispatched 42-37950 **Dinah Mite**, out of which all on Lt. Sharpless' crew jumped. Lt. H Noell evacuated himself and six of his crew from 42-37960 **Delta Girl** prior to its demise near Meppen, with all three gunners in the fuselage rear having died under the fusillade of gunfire. The same survival/loss ratio occurred within Lt. K Smith's crew flying 42-31338 **Hard to Get**; the formation had just bombed when two engines were disabled and set ablaze by cannon shells, whereupon Smith pressed the bail out bell, leaving his charge to descend east of Hildesheim.

Added to the 45th CBW's woes were three MIA crews each from the 388th and 96th BGs. Lt. J Feeney's 42-31115 **Hells Bells** was one of two Knettishall victims descending on the Continent at Uitgeest, in Holland, the pilot proving to be one of seven killed when the B-17 exploded in mid-air. Prior to this 42-39804/E was torn out of the sky south of Vechta, killing Lt. P Evans and six of the crew. The third loss occurred over the North Sea with no recorded survivors on 42-31336/H, piloted by Lt. R Tolles. Snetterton's 339th BS surrendered two B-17s. There was a measure of comfort for all on Lt. R Scott's 2-31617/QJ:, in that all became POWs. Lt. H Thompson, in charge of 42-31566/QJ:, probably completed the bomb run but paid a terrible price when flak brought the bomber down along with all ten occupants at a location never confirmed. F/O E Magilavy also steered 42-31492/MZ: **Discoveree** over the target, but then flak also struck home to fatally wound a waist gunner and leave the other nine little choice but to jump from the stricken aircraft. (Blind Fate militated against five airmen—one in the worst possible manner—on Lt. Dickert's B-17. This 96th BG crew was flying its 25th mission, but during the air battle four crewmembers bailed out; the fifth returned to England, but only as a corpse, Sgt. C Rayburn (ROG) having paid the ultimate price.)

13th CBW

The punishment inflicted upon the 95th BG seems to have been incurred soon after crossing into Germany and prior to bombing. Three of the seven bombers came down within seven minutes between Nordhorn and Furstenau, two of which displayed a common survival/loss ratio. Lt. C Cole (P) was one of the fatalities on board 42-37826/OE: O, which crashed southeast of Nordhorn, but Lt. J Kelly got himself and six crewmembers safely out of 42-31658/BG: G, which came down north of Furstenau, some 20 miles further east. Brandlecht, near Nordhorn, was the final resting place for 42-97447/BG: E, on which Lt. H Wilson (P) forfeited his life after the bomber went into an uncontrollable spin; the 7/3 factor again applied, but this time in exact reversal compared to the other two crews.

The group's ranks were seemingly being rapidly culled at this point, judging once again by the times and locations of crashes. **Irish Luck** 42-31054/QW: Q ran out of this precious commodity near Hollan, close to Diepholz, along with a single member on Lt. C Huddleston's (POW) team; minutes later at Wietmarschen, near Lingen, 42-30609/OE: N **Pistol Packin' Mama** became a shattered pile of metal, although once again all but one of Lt. S Balman's (POW) crew escaped that grisly fate. (The Tuberose/Spencer B-17 42-37971/OE: W mentioned beforehand crashed at Recke, near Osnabrueck, some 40 miles distant from Nordhorn, so illustrating the swift scale of loss this day.) The final B-17 to go down appears to have progressed the closest to its target, albeit not fulfilling its bombing brief; 42-30173/OE: G **Circe**, flown by Lt. J Pearson (POW), fell in flames south of Nienburg, taking three crewmembers to their deaths.

Four more losses were shared between the other two CBW units. A seven-month veteran at Framlingham, 42-30337/DI: B **8 Ball -Flak Hack**, made her last mission with Lt. G Dover and crew as far as Striepe, where a crash landing was effected, although only three personnel ended up alive, with Dover one of the seven dead. The other MIA bomber staggered home as far as Blokzijl, in Holland, after being comprehensively shot up. Nine of Lt. J Burke's crew bailed out of 42-31218/ FC: E **ETO-It is**, of which six evaded immediate capture, but only two finally won through to England the following autumn. Lt. D Croft was on the bomb run in 42-31265/XR: when his B-17 was reportedly fatally crippled by fighter attack; he did not survive, unlike his crew, who got out prior to the bomber's crash southwest of Hannover. The second 100th BG loss involved 42-30062/LD: O **Bastard's Bungalow**, on which Lt. A Scroggins (P) also became the sole fatality as his aircraft descended near Nienburg/Weser.

Hoisted with His Own Efficiency Petard...

The following account is true; only the individuals' names have been deleted. The group was in the process of taxiing out for the mission when it was discovered that the Lead bomber was still firmly stuck in its dispersal with a mechanical problem. The Air Executive was hastily dispatched in the CO's car to make contact with the first B-17 in the line, which would now have to assume the group Lead function during Assembly until (hopefully) the actual Lead bomber could get airborne.

Having reached the runway's end, the Executive jumped out of the car without switching off the engine or lights and raced to the still static aircraft; barely had he opened the rear door and climbed inside when the pilot cracked open the throttles. By the time the revised situation had been communicated to him it was too late to arrest the headlong rush down the darkened runway and the aircraft lifted off the runway. So far the only problem appeared to be the supernumerary presence of the Executive—only he was wearing normal clothing that was totally unsuitable for prolonged high-altitude flying. Worse still, there was no spare parachute or oxygen mask on board.

The only option seemed to be for the pilot to abort the mission, but now arose a second problem. The group took a dim view of "abortions," and it was the Executive himself who

When 42-37972/XR: F arrived at Thorpe Abbotts in November 1943, prospects for its long-term survival were very bleak, given *Luftwaffe* dominance at this time. However, **Gold Brick** would rack up 100 missions and end up on the scrap heap at Kingman, AZ. Severe damage to its right stabilizer was caused by flak during the Group's mission to Hamburg on 7 April 1945.

was most severe on any crews doing so. Now he was in effect "hoisted with his own petard of efficiency." What to do, since he could not even bail out?

The group continued the monotonous climb to the Assembly point, and it was then that the assigned Lead bomber slid into position; however, this did not resolve the position for the Executive, who was already feeling the cold while breathing off an emergency bottle. Imagine his secret relief when a "recall" signal was issued thanks to adverse weather conditions over the target!

The group had to remain airborne several hours in order to burn off enough fuel to make the landing back at the airfield as safe as possible. Back on the ground, the CO sought out his eternally grateful subordinate and asked him as politely as possible "why the hell did you leave my car with engine running and lights blazing?" The response was, "Sir, you will not believe me if I told you!" (The Executive subsequently assumed command of another bomber group.)

Left: Sgt. Eddie Leighty was an "original" member of the 447th BG. He flew as a waist gunner and is posed by his B-17 in full flight gear. He survived his combat tour and, after going home, returned to the Rattlesden area, where he married and settled down with a local girl, Peggy; this very happy partnership lasted until his death in 2000.

Below: Sgt. Leighty stands fourth from right under the nose of what is believed to be the crew's regular B-17G **Feather Merchant** (42-97572); Lt. Bill Greenwell (P) stands under the other side of the Bendix chin turret, while Lt. D Fokinakes(CP) squats in the center of the four-man ground crew.

Run-up to "Big Week"

Although missions were flown over the next two days, neither involved the 3rd BD, while the 1st BD was perhaps surprisingly unleashed for a solo run to Frankfurt (11th), and *No Ball* sites came under B-24 scrutiny on both dates. The accent on the latter target category was repeated on the 13th when the 1st BD alone was "grounded."

Losses over the Pas de Calais were sparse at four B-17s out of 256, but these all came from the 4th CBW, two of which involved ditchings. Great Ashfield's **Dragon Lady** (42-30836/V) staggered back as far as the Channel coast off Dungeness; Lt. E Herron sacrificed his life in carrying out this emergency act while two further crewmembers also did not survive. The 94th BG's 42-30427/GL: W **Lil' Operator** was badly damaged by fighter gunfire and suffered one crewmember killed in action before Lt. Bradee was forced into gambling on a safe entry into the Channel waters; this happily came off, and the nine living airmen were fished out. Rattlesden bore the other two MIA losses.

The opening mission for Lt. L Bevor's 96th BG crew could have well been their last. One flak shell went right through the right wing (fortunately without exploding), but the second detonated almost inside the open bomb bay. Fuel streamed from a punctured tank as the B-17 was thrown bodily upwards; one of the 2,000-lb bombs fell out while the other remained in place, but with the tail fuse shot away. Incredibly, the weapon did not detonate before Sgt. Miskel (Eng.) managed to work his way along the mangled catwalk to free it from the shackles and literally kick it clear. Back over England, several of the crew bailed out on Bevor's orders since he had been informed by Miskel that a normal landing was out of the question due to the state of the airframe. However, two crewmembers had been critically injured and any plan to bail them out too was abandoned, since there was a strong chance they would not survive the experience. As a result, 42-3556/BX: L. **Dear Mom** was directed very tentatively for what happily transpired as a successful landing approach into West Malling, an RAF airfield. Sadly, by then one of the two serious casualties had died. (Bevor and Miskel were at least two individuals from this crew who completed their combat tours, during which time they probably never had anything approaching a repeat of what happened on 10 February!)

There now arose a six day period in which the sole heavy bomber operations involved a small force of 52 B-24s landing the latest blows upon *No Ball* sites (15th). There was naturally nothing to indicate to the combat crews scattered across winter-shrouded East Anglia that their Command superiors were ready to launch a sustained six-day Campaign against Nazi Germany's aero-industrial resources. All the average airmen knew, or indeed cared, was that the prospects for completion of their combat tour were being compromised by this enforced "ground time." It was accepted, however reluctantly, that the continuing unpredictable winter weather patterns were a major factor in retarding the pace of operations. Nor was there any guarantee that the onset of spring or even summer would bring about improved weather conditions with an attendant upsurge in missions. However, as 19 February dawned the Allied meteorologists confirmed the fact that an eastward-flowing warm front was about to descend upon Western Europe and remain there for several days at least. Here was the opportunity to launch and sustain Operation *Argument* against the enemy's aircraft airframe, engine, and supporting materiel industries.

Courage – What's That?

The American crews lived with fear—or to give this mental state of mind a more acceptable term, "apprehension"—all the time they were on combat operations.

Combat flying involved a range of physical and mental stresses that were a world away from the exciting "Wild blue yonder" image often exercising the public's mind both during the Conflict and even long after it was over. One pilot, when

Members of a 96th BG crew on a visit to an RAF bomber base watch as a 4,000-lb blast bomb known as a "Cookie" is hoisted into a Lancaster's bomb-bay. The simple but pungent message to the enemy chalked on the front reads "Duck, you b-----d!"

Several members of the same 96th BG crew are seen in handshaking pose with their contemporaries from RAF Bomber Command, most of whom appear to be sergeants; RAF aircrew ranks featured a much greater proportion of NCOs to officers than did the USAAF. The B-17G in background is BX: G, named **Goering's Nightmare.**

The ultimate insult? The tinned-meat product "Spam" was, along with mutton and Brussels sprouts, one of the most loathed items of food to adorn the Mess tables of the American forces. This Lieutenant is surely wondering at the naivety of whoever dispatched the can by mail from the States—or was it a practical joke by the individual or individuals concerned?

asked what had been his memories of combat operations, responded "Well, I was tired, cold—and scared!"

A crewmember based at Great Ashfield never forgot the stark verbal reminder backing up a painting in a 588th BS latrine. The anonymous artist had painted a head-on approach by a Bf109 with all guns blazing; beneath was a caption that baldly said "If you can't shit – **look at this**!!" Any pretensions to living out the deceptively romantic existence already mentioned were swiftly crushed within a very short time of commencing missions. It was only the sense of respect for one another, coupled with the mutual need to support his fellow-airmen in any circumstance, however parlous, that instilled and sustained a spirit of "sticking it out" within the individual's mind. Those who could not sustain this stance were largely not looked upon with distain, but rather with sympathy. It was, and ever will be, dangerously simplistic to talk about "courage" and "heroism" in judging personal conduct during a conflict. "Courage" can be regarded as a psychological currency that some people expend faster than others and/or end up bankrupt; "heroism" is a more negative rather than positive mindset, in that the individuals concerned are managing to cloak their natural apprehensions as opposed to adopting a care-free attitude towards the real prospect of suffering injury or death in combat.

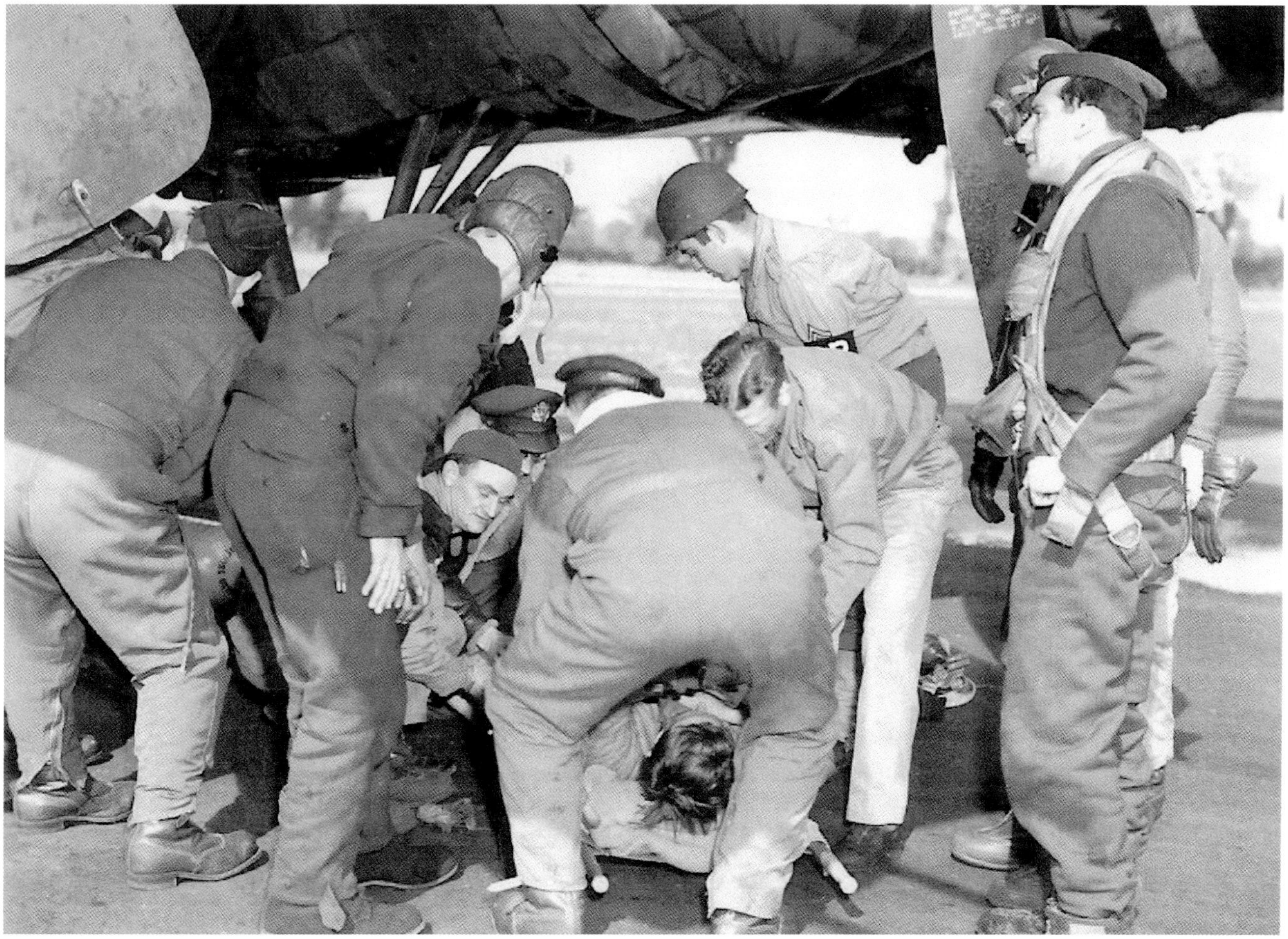

The mission has just been completed, but for one airman the torment goes on. In this instance a radio-operator on board a 96th BG has suffered injury and is being placed on a stretcher as caringly as possible. Note the style of boot worn by the crew members with their backs to the camera.

The official caption states "Gen. Doolittle discusses pre-mission details." It is more likely that the intended flight is non–operational, since Doolittle never flew a mission while CG of the 8th AF. The officer third from left is from the RAF judging by his uniform and flying boots, as well as the British-pattern parachute harness.

"Let Battle Commence!"

A full four months had transpired since the USAAF "Heavies" based in England had carried out a sustained Campaign of assault upon Germany. *Black Week's* four major missions had not only cost the Command 148 B-17s MIA as well as a sizeable number declared "salvage," but the avowed intention to strike a terminal blow upon the ball bearing industry had not come about. In addition, from then onwards the ample provision of effective long-range escorts was a mandatory need if the Bombing Offensive was to be even maintained, let alone flourish.

Now, on 20 February, the early morning Sabbath quiet was to be harshly invaded as the motors on 1,003 assigned B-17s and B-24s coughed and stuttered into life. What was the intended initial strike for Operation *Argument* now signalled the latest sustained assault upon Germany's aero-industry. The promise of clear weather had not yet materialized since low cloud was prevalent over southern England. The overall mission plan was for the three Divisions to strike widely separated targets, with Leipzig, Brunswick/Gotha, and Tutow the briefed zones. The latter source, up on the Baltic coast, was allocated to the 3rd BD, which sent out 314 crews spread between the nine groups. All the targets were deep into enemy territory, thereby inviting strong fighter reaction. Fifteen fighter groups—over 830 *Little Friends*, including the second P-51 unit (357th FG)—were on hand and up aloft to counter the anticipated *Luftwaffe* reaction. However, the extended distance to Tutow meant that escort cover for this element of the mission would be sparse and range-restricted—not a pleasant factor for the 3rd BD crews to ponder, especially if the *Luftwaffe* should intervene in any strength...

Division assembly passed off almost without incident, although a 385th BG crew lost three members after their B-17 developed problems and crashed; Lt. Ruby's 42-40004 was the bomber in question. Passage over the cold North Sea, southern Denmark, and the Baltic Sea culminated in a frustrating result. Failure of the blind bombing equipment on the PFF Leader meant that the cloud-shrouded Primary could not be picked out, so release on this and two other locations was conducted on an ETA basis—in effect, an "area bombing" effort. The other sub-force also abandoned its briefed assault on Posen and Kriesing thanks to the restricted visibility and unloaded upon Rostock and other targets of opportunity.

The overall bombing effort was extremely poor considering the effort expended in aircraft and crews. On the other hand, casualties were surprisingly light: two dispersals

Solid condensation trails from higher-flying bombers act as an outline for a B-17G from the 100th BG. This act of Nature created what were described in a wartime documentary as "magnificent trails of treachery," since they gave away the formations' presence to the enemy.

at Thorpe Abbotts were vacant that evening, along with five more B-17s from four other airfields, although one of the 100th BG bombers diverted into Sweden.

The 100th BG had lifted off as snow flurries were interspersed within the cloud layers.

Lt. A Harris was piloting 42-39792/LN: X as part of the High squadron when he dropped out with an engine on fire; the damage was not terminal, since this was the bomber that then achieved a safe if eventful passage northwards to Sweden. Not so fortunate was Lt. R Smith's crew on 42-37790/LD: Y **Ain't Mis Behavin**. A rocket strike over Stettin subsequently induced the pilot to attempt a similar run into Sweden when the Danish coast was looming up. Shortly after, a group of fighters latched onto the bomber and shot it up so comprehensively that a bail out became compulsory. Several of the crew evaded immediate detention, but only one out of this number succeeded in finally getting through to Sweden with Danish Resistance help.

The overall scale of loss on the 20th was a very gratifying one of just over 2% in place of the anticipated figure of around 20% as estimated by the naturally apprehensive authorities at Pinetree. Nor did the situation deteriorate materially twenty-four hours later when nearly the same figure of crews dispatched (861, of which 762 dropped mainly on targets of opportunity) returned with sixteen crews left behind on the Continent and one ditched. A quarter of the MIA losses were from the 3rd BD, but two further crews were lost after the formations had crossed in over the coast.

The MIA tally on the 21st was shared by crews serving at Horham, Thorpe Abbotts, and Snetterton Heath. Fate was unkind to fourteen of the 20 airmen of the 95th BG. First, fighters downed 42-3462/ET: B **San Antonio Rose** west of Utrecht, along with Lt. M Marks (P) and seven of his crew. The ever-cold North Sea waters off Egmond absorbed the remains of 42-30634/QW: O **Liberty Belle**, in which were entombed six airmen, including Lt. J McGuigan (P), the four survivors having fortunately bailed out and floated down onto Dutch soil just before their B-17 exploded. The single empty 100th BG dispersal normally housed 42-37796/LN: T, but now the bomber lay on her belly in a Dutch field at Halfweg, near Amsterdam, with Lt. W Fletcher and crew "in the bag" (An RAF term for capture). No such luck applied to half of Lt. A Smith's (KIA) crew on board 42-39814/AW:; They died after

a strike on a fuel tank caused the bomber to disintegrate and fall south of Wunstorf.

"Last-hurdle" Tragedy

The cloud layers were fairly solid as the groups were gradually losing altitude in readiness for their final landing approach. The flat, desolate stretches of Reedham Marsh, in Norfolk, were echoing to the roar of Great Ashfield's B-17s, among whom were 42-31370/550BS and 42-37963/549BS, piloted respectively by Capt. Hutchison and Lt. W Pease. The former officer was a veteran from the Regensburg mission, and he and his crew were about to complete their 25th mission; also on board was a photographer to record the event. A few minutes more and the crew would be relieved from the constant stress of combat operations and could plan for a return to their homeland.

The former CO of the 96th BG, Col. Archie Old, now CG of the 45th CBW, shakes hands with the very tall figure of Maj. C Godecke. On 1 May 1945 the major's aircraft tested the German flak gunners' "promise" not to fire on the group that was bearing supplies for the Dutch population—a promise that was thankfully maintained much to the relief of all on board the B-17!

This anonymous bombardier has his basic function limited to "toggling" the bomb load. In place of the bombsight is a twin .5 machine gun mounting in the Plexiglas with a piece of armour plate underneath. This defensive measure was introduced on some B-17Fs that were then positioned in critical formation positions; only the arrival of the Bendix chin turret (faintly seen on the two visible bombers) provided a decent weight of forward firepower.

The persistent cloud patterns were causing problems for the crews even as they loosened up the formation during the descent. What then transpired when the two aforementioned bombers collided was not confirmed at the time. Postwar analysis of the incident suggested that Lt. Pease became a victim of vertigo and in the process pulled sharply upwards in front of Hutchison's aircraft, causing the latter aircraft to chop off its fellow-machine's tail section. Eyewitnesses claimed that following the collision the Pease-controlled machine was seen to be adopting a steady glide action, despite this generally being an aerodynamic impossibility, before it then dipped sharply into the ground and disintegrated, but this technical issue was of academic interest to the hapless crew, who were all killed. Their fate was arguably more cruelly duplicated by Hutchison and his tour-expired team as well as the photographer. The knock-on effect of such "last-hurdle" casualties was to further depress the spirits of their colleagues in the battle to complete the current run of missions (soon to be extended to thirty).

Continuing Good Fortune

So far during *Big Week* the 3rd BD had borne approximately one-third (eleven) of the 37 crews declared MIA, although to this figure was added the total loss of the Hutchison and Pease teams. No further Division losses were incurred on the 22nd, but this was not thanks to the enemy. Instead, the adverse weather conditions forced Gen. LeMay to issue a "recall" before the formations had even crossed over the North Sea on their way to Schweinfurt, since proper Assembly had not been achieved in any effective manner at this stage. (The 1st BD took heavy punishment while assaulting a triangle of targets southwest of Berlin, losing 38 out of a total of 41 shared with the 2nd BD.)

It was a further 48 hours before the Command's crews were called to action on a day that would witness a further 44 crews added to the overall MIA figure. Once again the *Luftwaffe* seemed to direct its major thrusts at other than the LeMay-led fliers, when three-quarters of the 49 losses came from out of the B-24 ranks. Three aircraft plants at Tutow, Posen, and Kreising, up in the Baltic region, were assigned the 3rd BD, but once again adverse weather forced the attackers to seek unidentified targets of opportunity that included the port of Rostock; in addition, 20% of the force dropped their loads prematurely thanks to an accidental release of its markers by the PFF leader. Five crews did not return, of which one from Knettishall escaped into neutral Sweden; this was 42-30661 **Veni Vidi Vici** flown by Lt. A Montgomery.

"Hurry up and wait" summed up the mood of most ground crews after a mission had been dispatched, since they tended to hang around the airfield rather than disperse to their billets. This group of 96th BG personnel are anxiously awaiting the return of their charges and secretly praying that their B-17 will not feature on the MIA list.

Two of the less fortunate crews were from the 385th BG. Lt. J Terrace, Jr. did not survive 42-30662's final demise off Ruegen island, in the Baltic, whereas his crew all bailed out successfully. Aerial rocket damage to 42-31349 saw the B-17 lagging ever further behind on the way back with a final sighting over the Baltic and two fighters attacking; three crewmembers from Capt C McIlveen's group were later washed up on various shorelines. The latest 95th BG casualty involved 42031561/OE: Z flown by Lt. E Costales, with the shot-up bomber finally crash landing on Danish soil.

Big Week's Final Thrust

The final mission of *Big Week* involved all three Divisions heading out and down into central/southern Germany. The 3rd BD

Miss Donna Mae (42-30433/GL: U), a 410BS B-17F, has slewed to an inelegant halt on her collapsed right landing gear. An early Rougham arrival in July 1943, she would be put back in service and end her combat days in Sweden following Lt. Vaughn's decision to head there on 11 April 1944. Her namesake from a fellow squadron would not be so fortunate.

A proportion of an armorer's existence on the flight-line was spent manoeuvering trolleys and other mobile transporters around the aircraft. Three 96th BG airmen are pushing such a unit, laden with incendiary bombs to judge by the weapon just visible on the right; instruction on its nose advises personnel not to insert the fuse until the bomb is secured in position within the bomb-bay.

Sometimes the arrival of an RAF aircraft on a USAAF airfield was unheralded. This 51 Sqdn Halifax Mk. III has over-shot runway and broken its back as well as badly ripping the fuselage underside through contact with the railroad line located on the northern perimeter of Rougham (94th BG). Holes in the flap appear to be due to gunfire, indicating an emergency landing off a Bomber Command operation. Incident occurred in early 1944.

dispatched the greatest number of crews—290 out of 754 overall—but its hitherto surprising immunity from real punishment ended this day with twelve crews lost while assaulting Regensburg's aero-industrial facilities. A third of these came from the ranks of the 45th CBW, which had unfortunately found itself way ahead of the bomber stream thanks to persistently strong tailwinds. However, it was one Group (the 96th BG) that suffered in total as regards bombers, if not crews. The fighter attacks began even as the formation was over France.

Three days previous S/Sgt C Haywood, then flying as tail gunner to Lt. Herring, had survived injury, even though a massive hole had been blown in the B-17's center fin section. Now he was flying with Lt. R Lindstrom in 42-31142/QJ: U, which lost its No. 1 engine thanks to oil pressure failure following a flak hit. The B-17 still held in position up to the target, but as the return leg was being made a second engine had to be shut down. The resultant strain on the other two functioning engines proved too much for No. 3, which burst into flames. Following the inevitable drop-out from the formation, the landing gear was lowered as a "surrender" sign to several approaching Fw190s, and all ten airmen, two of which evaded capture, jumped near St. Martin, in Belgium. (Lt. R Swanson (N) suffered a gun wound in one knee that was not immediately attended to, and this lack of attention then resulted in the leg's amputation due to gangrene having set in.) The other Group crew lost was led by Lt. A Smiley (KIA) in 42-38043/MZ; there was one other fatality on board this bomber. Two further aircraft bearing 452nd BG crews—42-30123/MZ: W **Big Dick** and 42-39841/AW: U—also failed to return to Snetterton Heath. All nineteen airmen on these B-17s flown respectively by Lt D Jarrett and W LuPole ended up as POWs.

13th CBW

Four B-17s went down from 13th CBW ranks, spread between the 100th and 390th BGs. One of Thorpe Abbott's B-17s, 42-30788/LN: R **Mismalovin**, lost an engine just after bombing and inevitably lost height and distance, followed shortly after by the unwelcome but largely ineffectual attention from fighters, whose gunfire nevertheless killed Lt. P Mordowitz (N). The pilots managed to keep on a homeward course, but four further crewmembers were either killed or severely wounded by the persistent combination of fighter and flak-fire. The final misfortune occurred when the ailing bomber over-flew Calais and almost immediately began to enter what became an irreversible downward bank to the left. S/Sgt. W Cook (TG) realized that Lt. S McClain was losing control and was about to assume a crash position when the aircraft impacted with the Channel's surface. Cook was rendered unconscious, but fortunately recovered to be picked up by the Germans, along with one other crewmember; for his pilot and two others, so near to completing their combat tour on what was their 22nd mission today, it had ended fatally.

The normally graceful outline of the B-17 is marginally disfigured by the "bathtub" fairing under the nose, which houses an early version of *H2X* as introduced into service by the 482nd BG in late 1943. Note the large-scale fuselage insignia with red surround and dulled-down white area on **Stinky**, which served at Alconbury between 5 August and 10 November 1943 when it was salvaged following a heavy crash landing.

Both Framlingham B-17s came down on French soil. One loss occurred near Sedan on the way in when Lt. G Rains' 42-37880/DI: T **Liberty Belle**, which developed engine problems that forced the bombs to be jettisoned, was taken down by fighters along with its pilot and three others. One less crewmember lost his life on 42-30434/DI: A, which had been assailed by fighters and flak; Lt. R Bowman (P) was one of the dead with his aircraft crashing near Laon.

Four crews from the 4th CBW also went MIA, again spread between two units. Great Ashfield's sacrifice occurred over the target area. Only three airmen got out of Lt. D Gray's (KIA) 42-30822 when it exploded thanks to flak strikes. The single fatality on board 42-3422 **Winnie the Pooh** also involved the pilot, Lt. N Davis. The bomber had one engine ripped out by flak during the bomb run, and soon after went into a spin that ended with an impact near Kirchdorf, south of Regensburg. Rattlesden's losses, both from the 710th BS, commenced on the way over with 42-31431, which succumbed to flak and finally blew up in mid-air near Saarbruecken; fortunately, by this point all of

Damage incurred during the Frankfurt mission on 4 February 1944 resulted in a very heavy force-landing in Norfolk for 42-30188/MZ: S **Temptation**. The wrenching of the top turret from its base indicates the severe degree of distortion to the forward fuselage, but all ten crewmembers remained unscathed.

A vegetable field near Maldon, in Essex, has been invaded by the bulk of a Great Ashfield B-17G. The 550BS aircraft had transferred-in from the 94th BG in September 1943, but now on 2 February 1944 her combat days were over as she faced salvage action.

Lt. L Chardi's crew were floating down on their parachutes and heading for a Stalag. Lt. E Kautt lost S/Sgt. C Long (TG) when a fighter riddled the tail section on 42-31563. The B-17 dropped away and down, and the nine surviving airmen jumped out near Landau with their bomber reportedly crashing further west near Pirmasens.

Big Week's Ramifications

Most of the crews landing off the missions on 25 February had little thought about the strategic implications of the past six days; their prime reaction as ever was tired relief at surviving another mission on the road to combat tour completion. The *Big Week* operations had struck a firm but not irreversible blow at German aero-production. It is now known that overall production of airframes, engines, and support equipment increased in the months ahead. However, the Germans were forced to disperse a fair degree of their productive capacity to bomb-proof alternative sites, such as underground caves in the Harz Mountains. This effort took time, and time was not on the Nazis' side.

A signal success arising out of the launch of *Argument* lay not in materiel destruction on the ground, but rather in the air. The *Jadgwaffe* was now being brought to battle in defense of its Nation's industrial fabric and was already beginning to suffer from the depredations wrought among its pilots by the 8th FC. American fighters MIA totalled around 35, but a far greater number of Bf109s, Fw190s, and their twin-engine comrades had gone down; this was allowing for the American fighter pilots' exaggerated claims for 217 "kills"—to which was added a further 186 officially credited to the bomber gunners. Of even more significance to future hopes of totally destroying the enemy's Fighter Arm was the fact that an increasing number of their *Experten* (Aces) were being killed. Their loss in turn left the less experienced pilots, whose training periods prior to arriving

A B-17F from the 390th BG is on final approach to Framlingham. A mechanical problem encountered at this critical stage of landing could easily result in a crash that would lead to injury or death for the crew. Several Bell tents are pitched in the right background.

at front-line units were being more and more restricted, basically adrift on their own, and therefore terribly vulnerable to the marauding and thoroughly aggressive USAAF *Little Friends*.

The "Wild Blue Yonder's" Physical Challenge

"There was the awful, enfeebling shroud of total exhaustion... panic gasping, sucking in draughts of dehydrated oxygen.. dried-out lungs and mouth and tongue, and every tooth glued on forever by several sticks of worn-out chewing gum." This was how a 385th BG pilot described one aspect of his experience of combat flying.

The physical challenges posed by prolonged flying at high altitude demanded the maximum of effort by each individual to surmount, and this was the case without the added pressure imposed by the enemy's defensive system. Combat flying was clearly perceived as the province of the young with an emphasis on selecting men in their late teens or early twenties. Even so, to the constant psychological pressures imposed on each airman in the face of extreme danger was added the strains on the body system. Regular operations took an accumulating toll in terms of tiredness with all that this implied on reacting to emergency situations.

For a start, the already weary crews, having attempted to sleep in basically uncomfortable beds housed in Nissen or Quonset huts with inadequate heating facilities, would generally be woken out of their slumber in the middle of the night, don their clothes, and proceed to the Mess halls; there they would attempt with varying degrees of success to digest the food and drink provided. After Briefing they would be transported to their allotted dispersals, where they would board their aircraft. The engine start-up would now impose an increasingly adverse effect upon them. Noise is a tiring factor in itself, and in this instance the sheer volume thrown out by the Wright Cyclones would tend to hammer at the brain. The act of Assembly, which could last up to two hours, strained the already overloaded motors, and with it beat further upon the mind with the monotonous drone cast out into the atmosphere. The eyes would become heavy with what was akin to the after-effect of consuming a handful of barbiturates, and it was regularly the case that crewmembers so affected had to be shaken back into consciousness.

The artificial intake of oxygen demanded the wearing of a mask, but the enclosing of the lower face within its rubber shape could induce a sense of claustrophobia. Some airmen furthermore found that it was necessary to retain a degree of hair stubble in order to cut down on the mask's discomfort upon their skin. Always lurking in the background was the threat of losing consciousness and even expiring due to the mask having iced-up and cut off the oxygen flow.

The joke that the aircraft was filled up to the last drop of fuel and its crew emptied their bladders to the last drop (usually against the landing gear) held little humor in practice. The retention of fluid to any degree was liable to play havoc with one's system up in the stratosphere. Nor was it too easy to relieve one's self via the chosen outlets on the bomber, since it was none too easy to open up the several layers of clothing in order to gain relief. Worse still was the likely effect on the body of an involuntary "wetting." Not only could the resultant chill factor lead to serious erosion of limbs through frostbite, but the act could also "short out" the electric suit to add to an airman's discomfort. The ball turret gunner was arguably in the worst position among any crew, since he was generally sealed in his mobile gun mount between approaching and departing enemy territory, and one that lasted many hours on long missions.

The lack of parachute harnesses and other combat gear, such as boots, indicate that Capt. Wilson is outlining the details of a non-operational flight. Kneeling to his immediate left is Capt Charles Zettek, who was to become a senior bombardier at Knettishall and introduced a system for blind bombing based on a grid scale as used by the RAF.

The case of a 95th BG gunner was by no means an exception. He had suffered a failed bladder and the suit had "shorted out." The temperature was noted by Lt. F Goff (N) as -45 degrees, and by the time the gunner was able to vacate his position his constant shivering bout was only a forerunner of worse. Goff recalled the brave but surely pinched smile on his colleague's face in the truck delivering them to debriefing. He was removed to the hospital, but the surgeons were unable to stabilize his system in time to prevent the onset of gangrene in both affected feet, which were amputated. (Goff further seethed inwardly in recalling the still brave reaction of the young man lying in his hospital bed when the crew paid a post-operation visit.)

Excess bowel wind was certainly discomforting at high altitude. An inability thanks to improperly digested food to

On return from a French target on 5 February 1944 Lt. D Kasch's 96th BG crew abandoned 42-3501/MZ: K **Kasch's Kids** over Dymchurch, on the English Cannel coast. Unfortunately, the B-17G sliced into a bungalow with this devastating result that killed two sleeping British soldiers and left the right-outer wing with group insignia resting amidst the rubble. On 8 April 1944 Kasch and Lt. Schadler (N) were killed during the second full mission to Berlin.

"pass wind" via the rectum, in particular, was no laughing matter on a mission. Only a descent to unassisted breathing altitude could provide the necessary if rather impolite relief! More seriously, the sufferer could find himself doubled-up in pain and in no condition to function properly whether flying, navigating, or defending the bomber, thus bringing an added degree of danger both to himself and his crew.

It was an article of faith that a combat crewmember had to be free of all basic illnesses before flying a mission. A simple condition such as a head cold presented nothing more than a degree of discomfort at ground level, but up at operational altitude the situation could develop into a critical one. Pleurisy, an infection of the Pleura, in medical terms, but inflammation of the lining of the lungs to the layman, was one condition that could have a serious and even fatal outcome. A basic inability to clear one's nose of mucus due to the oxygen mask's presence could result in the wearer attempting to relieve himself by taking the life-sustaining equipment off; should he become involved in a prolonged bout of "clearance" he could pass out and not be in a position to be revived before the *Grim Reaper* struck home in his unrelenting fashion. "Bends," a condition normally affecting deep-sea divers, was another potential danger. Nitrogen bubbles in the bloodstream that plugged arteries at arm or leg joints would render the victim almost helpless with the agony so induced; unconfirmed reports of airmen so disturbed by the onset of "Bends" that they bailed out in order to ease the torment went the rounds.

On into March...

February closed with a pair of missions whose duration was almost at opposite short and extended range. On the other hand, such losses as were suffered were not as might be anticipated on the 29th (Brunswick), when just one B-17 was lost out of 226 taking off. It was the previous day's run to the Pas de Calais that notched up five MIA crews, all from the 4th CBW, out of a meager figure of 41 making bomb runs over *No-Ball* sites. By now the Germans were more than aware of the Allied bombers' intentions towards these targets, and the flak battery provision was accordingly high, with an attendant liability for the bombers to suffer its effect.

8

Berlin - The Crucible

On to Berlin...

Up to now the 8th AF's main thrusts into Germany had been to targets on its western, northern, and southern flanks. Central Germany had received some attention, especially during *Big Week*, when a core of locations principally to the southwest of Berlin had been targeted. RAF Bomber Command was regularly striking deeper into the Nazi homeland, albeit in a nocturnal manner; in addition, the enemy defenses were making what was known as the "Battle of Berlin" an increasingly expensive and finally unsustainable experience in terms of crews lost against the anticipated collapse in German morale arising from the RAF assaults...

Of the three Great Ashfield MIA crews, Lt. H Inglis' team on 42-31203/548BS fared best; a "ditching" off Folkestone ended up with just one fatality. By contrast, Lt. S Clark and seven other crewmembers were consumed in their flak-stricken 42-31751/549BS' crash near Boulogne. The same loss-scale affected Lt. G Kinmann (KIA) and crew on 42-38121/551BS after flak blew off the tail, causing the B-17 to descend into Boulogne. Two Rattlesden-based crews were MIA. Lt. C Harris' 42-31186/709BS was abandoned over the target and only T/Sgt. J Towle (Eng.) evaded capture from among the ten-man crew. The 711BS surrendered 42-31204, which exploded following flak strikes, killing Lt. E Pouts (P) and leaving just three survivors to face imprisonment.

Although the Nazi capital was a prime industrial source for attack, there was no doubt that the B-17s and B-24s would have to extend their depredations across the length and breadth of the Nazi empire before there could be realistic prospects for a successful conclusion to the European Conflict. On the other hand, there was the natural desire on both sides to either attack the city, or conversely make such attacks prohibitively expensive. *Big B*, as Berlin has gone down in military aviation parlance, was to prove a natural magnet for both major combatants. The ball lay firmly in the Americans' court in taking up where the RAF was (ironically) already at the extreme of its effort. (In fact, only one more RAF attempt to assault Berlin would be launched on 24/25 March, which would end in failure along with 72 Lancaster and Halifax crews declared MIA.)

The enemy's capital had been briefed for daylight attack back in November, but had been "scrubbed" thanks to the weather. However, it was the much-hammered city of Frankfurt that appeared on the Briefing maps on the 2nd, but not for the 3rd BD. The Division instead was sent out to France in reduced numbers, in the form of the 13th and 45th CBW. In addition, only five of the six assigned units made it across the Channel and into eastern France, where the airfield at Chartres was bombed at a cost of a single 390th BG crew.

"Gentlemen, your target is"...

> "Don't send my boy to Berlin, the dying mother said;
> Don't send my boy to Berlin – I would rather see him dead...."

There is a savage contradiction inherent in this couplet, since the prospects of the woman's contradictory desire bearing fruit were tragically all too real in 1944. The bomber crews knew that they would have to head out for *Big B* one day, but wished to deny the fact in any manner, and for as long as possible. On the still night-shrouded and chilly atmosphere of 3 March their apprehensions were finally realized when Berlin was briefed. The "Big League of Sky Fighting" was demanding the ultimate in effort and probable sacrifice from its USAAF participants. (The fighter pilots were firmly included in this respect, since they would be equally challenged in terms of physical endurance, given the distance to be flown and the likely opposition to be encountered, if not bested. It is also

The 390th BG's **Cincinnati Queen**, belonging to the 569BS, was already a combat veteran of around six months when the first strikes on *Big B* went in. It was over the German capital that she was fated to make her final mission on 21 June; on board was Lt. M Dunsmore's crew, whose precise fate is not confirmed.

easily forgotten that these airmen were literally on their own—functioning as combined pilot, navigator, and gunner—with nobody else to pull them out of a crisis; it was little wonder that they had to exhibit a natural air of controlled aggression to combat such potentially harrowing circumstances.)

"Here We Go..."

The long-awaited but equally dreaded call for the B-17s and B-24s to head out for *Big B* having again been realized, the overall reaction of the assigned crews to the announcement was probably aptly summarized by the thoughts of a 96th BG airman, who surmised "No, leave it to the RAF – they're doing just fine!" However, it was now the turn of the USAAF to pick up the ball from the RAF, although the *Big City*, as it was known within the latter-named Bomber Command, would still feel the weight of its assaults, to be principally delivered by Mosquitoes of the Light Night Striking Force (LNSF).

Well over 700 bombers were sent aloft, but the Nazi capital was destined to receive a three-day reprieve thanks primarily to ever-worsening weather as the formations traversed the North Sea and began to cross in over the enemy coastline around the river Elbe region. To the natural condition of solid cloud layers extending up to at least 30,000 ft was added the literally blinding intensity of vapour trail patterns. This was a lethal cocktail for self inflicted losses to arise as the formations began to "abort" the mission in response to the official "recall" signal. Some sub-units unknowingly intruded into the flight paths of others, an instance of this being the 1st CBW, which found itself embroiled in the trails exuded by the still-oncoming 4th CBW...

Nine B-17s from both B-17 Divisions did not return, three of which were from the 4th CBW. Eyewitnesses from the 94th BG recalled bombers flashing by close above and below the Group, followed almost immediately by a massive flash that tragically indicated a bomber or bombers blowing up. Eyewitnesses from Bury St. Edmunds stated on return that Lt. Ahlwardt's 42-38075 had indeed been run into by another aircraft, while a separate 385th BG report also talked of a mid-air collision, with debris from the disintegrating B-17s crippling a third. None of Ahlwardt's crew survived, and the shattered remnants of their bomber fell to earth at Itzehoe, near the east bank of the Elbe Estuary.

Two further 4th CBW B-17s from the 447th BG were lost. One of these was 42-31112, flown by Lt. Graham, and this aircraft was also reported to have been involved in a mid-air collision. On the other hand, it was almost certain that this aircraft was not the one involved with the 94th BG bomber, since it was flying within the CBW formation. (Further mystery concerns the Ahlwardt B-17's loss, since ***all*** other MIA losses this day were incurred in the "normal" manner, which was to fighters or flak.)

The circumstances of their loss meant nothing to any of the Rattlesden airmen because none survived the experience.

Eight of their companions on the other MIA bomber also tasted the bitter seeds of combat failure in 42-31148; the aircraft staggered back to a North Sea ditching that killed Lt. D Ralston (P) and seven others in a particularly tragic manner. The bomber had suffered a succession of "runaway" propellers on two engines and was eased properly into the sea, but although it floated for several minutes the bulk of the crew failed to get into the life rafts. One was released from the hatch without being secured and was whipped away by the high-running sea, while the other was badly torn. Several crewmembers were also swept off their precarious perch as Lt. T McKiernan (CP) recollected. He was fortunate to get

The "Square K" of the 447th BG carried by the B-17 at top left has led some sources to state the mortally crippled aircraft angling downwards on fire as coming from this group. In fact, it is the 482nd BG's PFF aircraft assigned to lead the 3rd BD on 6 March 1944. Seconds after this picture it exploded, killing eight of the twelve-man crew, one of whom was B/Gen. Russell Wilson.

into one of six individual dinghies that he and S/Sgt. V Cullen (Eng.) had been attempting to lash together when he in turn was swept into the snow-flecked North Sea. Contact with other crewmembers scattered around was soon lost, and it was an extremely exhausted and lucky airman who, almost three hours later, was hauled on board an ASR Launch that answered the "fixes" radioed in by two P-47s. The sole other survivor was S/Sgt C Horak (BT), who had managed to clamber aboard the first main dinghy after it was swept off the fuselage.

One of the three crews absent from debriefing at Thorpe Abbotts did arrive safely on the ground with their B-17 42-38017/XR: O, which had previously suffered an engine loss as well as one crewmember seriously injured. Lt. L Gossage had headed in what was estimated to be towards Sweden. An airfield was finally sighted, but after the engines were switched off and the crew clambered out they faced no neutral reception; instead, the approaching soldiers bore the distinctive coal-scuttle helmets of the German Armed forces. In fact, the airfield was at Schleswig-Jagel, in Occupied Denmark! Lt. Vollmer lost half his crew to fighter gunfire that shredded 42-39817/ XR: A **Murderer's Row** and sent her into a series of dives and zooms before she broke up violently. The region around Itzehoe was where Capt. R Lohof's 42-31970, flying as group Lead, also came down, fortunately without any of her crew, who were on their 23rd mission, still remaining on board.

Berlin's structural fabric remained unaffected by the USAAF's intended depredations on this occasion; on the other hand, there was no doubt that the formations would strike at the city with its myriad of vital industries. As it was, the first blow would occur within 24 hours, albeit in a manner that was small-scale as well as being against all official Standing Orders...

4 March 1944 "Bending the Rules"...

The basic principle behind the USAAF patterns of formation flying was not only to ensure that every Group maintained the highest degree of integrity in order to successfully combat the *Luftwaffe*; it was also to ensure that the bomber stream was similarly kept closed up. Should a Group find itself in any

Opposite, Top: Briefing for the first completed mission to Berlin is about to be initiated at Rattlesden. S/Sgt Eddie Leighty (sitting second from left in foreground), who was several years older than the average combat crewman, later acidly reflected "The I.O. said 'Men, today we bomb Berlin.' My reaction was 'I don't know about men being there – I do know there were a lot of frightened boys!!'"

Bottom: S/Sgt. Leighty sits on the left side of the truck as he and his 447th BG fellow-airmen prepare to be taken out to their B-17s. Some of them can manage a smile in spite of the undoubted sense of trepidation that must be on their minds at the thought of going to *Big B*. Perhaps the sole fatality borne by the 447th BG this day – Lt. Socolofsky's ROG, who was blown out of his compartment without his parachute by a flak strike – is the unlucky exception among this group.

way isolated it was expected either to turn for home, or more practically to regain contact with the "stream" as expeditiously as possible. Should a "recall" be issued, it was the even stricter duty of all unit leaders to respond unconditionally on pain of courtmartial in the event of disobedience. Just as straggling bombers were left to their own devices for the greater good of the Group concerned, so there was no room for "heroics" in forging on towards a target with what amounted to a "penny packet" formation that invited total annihilation should it be brought to bay.

In the film *Twelve O'clock High* there is a sequence where Gregory Peck ignores the "recall" signal, and on return from what had evolved as a successful strike explains his lapse to Millard Mitchell (playing Gen. Pritchard, Peck's CG) as being due to radio malfunction on his B-17! This scenario in the postwar Hollywood presentation may well have been based on the events surrounding the 95th BG on 4 March 1944.

The weather conditions on 4 March proved to be marginally worse over England, with snow flurries and limited visibility making take-off and assembly very risky—so risky that the 2nd BD abandoned the mission, while several B-17 units got as far as the coastline of Europe before also "aborting." The outward route was initially angled southeastwards towards the region south of the Ruehr, where the bombers were to angle up towards Berlin. Once again, the solid cloud banks extending up to 30,000 ft combined with heavy vapour trail patterns even when the bombers attained clear air space adversely affected the integrity of the "stream" to the extent that some Group elements were hard pressed to maintain visual contact with one another. It was hardly surprising that the recording of a "recall" signal was responded to wholesale by the various units—all but the 95th BG, leading the 13th CBW, that is.

The radio operator on the Col. Mumford/Lt. Al Brown Lead B-17 questioned the legitimacy of the signal, in that it did not accord with the code for that day, nor was it presented in a correct manner according to Standard Operating Procedure. It appeared that Col. Mumford accepted the ROG's assertion that the signal was a German "plant" and decided to keep on his target course. (However, on return he said that no "recall," genuine or otherwise, had been received!)

The recurrent heavy cloud cover probably shielded the compact group of 32 bombers from interception as it took up a northeasterly direction for the IP. Twenty-one of the sub-force was all that was now on hand from the original figure of 38 dispatched by the 95th BG to form Lead and Composite elements within the CBW, with a further eleven 100th BG crews also holding course. Although the formation was registering on enemy radar screens, there was the possibility that its track may well have become confused with the radar "signatures" of any fighter force or forces sent up to intercept. (There was an infamous precedent for this back on 20 October. Despite the recall of the entire VIIIBC attacking force, Hermann Goering had insisted on treating what transpired as *Luftwaffe* fighters dispatched to intercept the now-returning formations as being USAAF formations proceeding ever further eastwards. Only when the solid cloud layers began to break up was the true situation revealed to the sly merriment of *Luftwaffe* personnel in the *Reichsmarshal's* presence, although a belated admission was made by *Der Dicke* that he had misinterpreted the situation!)

Left: The 447th BG's 42-31227, flown by Lt. Socolowsky, has returned from the first full *Big B* strike, albeit in a thoroughly shot-up state. The picture angle, although displaying major damage to the central fuselage and bomb-bay doors, conceals the full and normally mortal extent of the punishment to the actual bomb-bay. *Right:* This is the gutted center section on Lt. Socolovsky's B-17G /42-31227 following its return to Rattlesden off the Berlin strike of 6 March 1944. The rear main wing-spar was severed and the ROG blasted out of the top of the radio-room hatch by the twin flak strikes; the ball turret remained within the bomber, having been detached prior to the photograph being taken.

However, this continuing immunity could not last forever, although it was flak rather than fighters that struck the first blow as the bombers were tracking in between Brunswick and Magdeburg. Lt. M Worthy's 42-31734/QW: H was observed by Lt. M Durr (Navigator on the Mumford/Brown Lead B-17) to absorb a fatal blast and fall away with several parachutes blossoming out; the final crash site was at Etgersleben, south of Magdeburg, but no fatalities were realized among the ten-man crew.

The cloud cover had partially dissipated before the IP northwest of Berlin was reached. By now the bombers were undergoing regular attention from fighters. However, it was flak that actually initiated the demise of 42-31785/OE: N **Slightly Dangerous**, flown by Lt. Dunham, when the loss of an engine struck by a shell caused the B-17 to sag out of formation during the bomb run. The bomb doors had to be cranked down before the bombs could be dropped, but even this lightened condition brought no respite from an encircling group of fighters. Both waist gunners were killed, and all but Sgt. L Pifer (BT) bailed out; he had not heard the bail out bell, and it was only when he glanced downwards as he was firing one of the waist guns that he realized his extreme peril, as the aircraft was within seconds of crashing near Stendal, due west of Berlin! A swift exit resulted in his making an awkward landing and in a broken ankle and several broken ribs, but this was a small cost considering he had survived.

The briefed target had been located at Klein Machnow, in the southwest city zone, but even the presence of two PFF B-17s was no guarantee that the bomb loads did anything more than create a general spread of destruction within *Big B's* overall boundaries. The true damage was arguably to the morale of the German High Command—Goering's 1940 boast that "No enemy aircraft will ever fly over the Reich Territory" had long been thrown back in his face. A subsequent, equally fatuous utterance by *Der Dicke* concerned Berlin itself, "If bombers appear over Berlin you can call me Meier." RAF Bomber Command had also rebutted this, particularly during the 1943/44 *Battle of Berlin* period, but their nocturnal presence was aural rather than visual to the citizens below. Although today's sortie also remained largely out of their vision, the stunning fact of burgeoning Allied airpower ranging over their capital city and ultimately over all of the "Reich territory" was now only to be delayed for 48 hours...

Meanwhile, the USAAF formation was fated to surrender a further three B-17s, two of which were from Horham. Lt. Roehm was No. 5 in the composite sub-formation of nine bombers, but his 42-31565/OE: U was dealt an ultimately fatal blow by flak just after "bombs away." The B-17 dipped steeply down, but this action was corrected and a course for home taken up. French soil was passing below when the end came, with all ten bailing out to leave their aircraft to crash on the WWI battlefield of Mons; sadly, one gunner's parachute failed to deploy while three of the others enjoyed the other extreme in fortune by managing to evade capture.

From the time the bombers banked for home and up to the time when Frankfurt was being bypassed enemy fighter assaults were at least warded off; the presence of a handful of 4th FG P-51s during the run into and out of *Big B* undoubtedly

Schifless' Skunk has taxied to a halt off the first completed Berlin mission (6 March 1944). The ambulance rushed up to the position has just been loaded with an injured crewmember taken from the 390th BG bomber, which is a combat veteran bearing twenty-two bomb symbols under its name.

The close escort apparently provided for the 447th BG by a P-51B from Leiston (357th FG) would be of no benefit, since any *Luftwaffe* marauder could have struck and been away before a viable response could have been made. Picture taken prior to 29 April 1944 when 42-37868/B was downed during a mission to Friederichshafen along with four crewmembers from Lt. Blom's team.

helped to curb the worst of the attacks. B-17G/42-31910/ET: P (Lt. Brownlow) had only arrived at Horham on 2 March, and now she was taken out of the sky to crash at Marienberg, south of Frankfurt, along with three of her crew. The sole Thorpe Abbotts loss was also reportedly incurred over Berlin. Lt. S Seaton was piloting 42-38016/LN: B **Seatons Sad Sack**; all but one of the crew descended by parachute into the relative safety of captivity. A degree of revenge was extracted by T/Sgt. H Stearns in 42-39872/ **Rubber Check** when he sighted upon a Bf109 boring in from directly ahead and sent him down in a fiery spin into the clouds; the gunner was only able to savour his success for a mere two days before ending up in a POW camp, however. The overall 16% loss factor drawn from the bombers' ranks, although noticeable, was still amazingly low, given the potential annihilation of most or all of the participants in the circumstances.

Five more Divisional crews joined the 13th CBW crews on the MIA list, two from the 94th BG. Lt. D Pollock (KIA) lost half his crew when flak brought 42-38169/QE: down, and a single fatality occurred on board 42-39801/XM piloted by Lt. J Blake, which came down near Dixmude, in Belgium.

6 March 1944
"Here We Go Again..."

Big B's lure for the USAAF authorities at least remained in place next day, but this time the bombers stayed on the ground after the intended mission was "scrubbed." On this same evening the Orders were again cut and issued for the mission, but this time round nothing would intrude upon the ability of the crews to not only get airborne, but more importantly to reach Berlin. The specific target for the 3rd BD was once again the Bosch AG plant in Klein Machnow, while the other two Divisions were allocated targets also in or adjoining the southern fringes of *Big B*.

The Division was allocated a central position within the bomber stream, with the 1st BD "up front." This normally meant that the latter named sub-force could expect the initial *Luftwaffe* onslaught, given the enemy's propensity for head-on assault.

The atmosphere among the 100th BG crews was probably no different to any other body of American airmen. The "jinx" reputation of the Group had somewhat receded since the bloody events of Regensburg and Muenster in the previous autumn, with subsequent overall losses, however regretful, no higher than any other bomber unit. The muted pleasure at sharing in the first mission over Berlin would probably still be lingering in the minds of the participants, such as Lt. Granack's crew, with Sgt Stearns (Eng.) notching up one credited "kill" that day. Today would prove to be outstanding too, but in a starkly different manner...

Assembly was completed without incident for other than a single fatal crash for a 392nd BG B-24. Each B-17 Division was configured for the most part in parallel positioned CBWs, with the trailing sub-force echeloned to the left of the Lead sub-force. However, the 3rd BD had dispatched A and B CBWs comprised of just Lead and Low boxes of groups compared to the Lead, Low, and High structures of its fellow B-17 Division. The course this time around did not deviate north or south, but involved a direct easterly aim at Berlin. However, the situation was unknowingly deteriorating for the 13th CBW's A and B elements as the Dutch/German border was being traversed thanks to Mother Nature. The entire 1st BD, along with the 4th CBW at the head of the 3rd BD sub-forces, was being blown ever-further south of the briefed track due to as-yet undetected veering wind patterns—not so the 13th CBW, which was about to pay a tragic price for its navigational precision...

Among the gathering *Luftwaffe* forces was *Stab* and I/JG11 led by Hptm. Rolf Hermichen, II/JG11 headed by Maj. Gunther Specht, and III/JG11 in Maj. Anton Hackl's charge. This formidable trio of battle-experienced pilots assembled their units, along with further support from elements of JG1 and JG54. The overall strength of 107 Bf109s and Fw190s then took up a course towards the oncoming bomber stream as it crossed into Germany.

"No Contest" at Haseluenne...

The natural expectation that the head of the stream would be the focus for *Luftwaffe* assault had in turn led to a good proportion of the large escort strength being accordingly allocated "up front"; by savage contrast, a mere handful of 56th FG P-47s that had ironically missed linking-up with its Group (which was briefed for 1st BD cover) were instead weaving ahead of the 13th CBW formations. The clear weather conditions and current absence of enemy countermeasures gave a false sense of security to some of the less experienced American airmen; the veterans, in contrast, must have sensed that the situation was too good to last, and their natural foreboding was about to be realized.

The *Luftwaffe* fighters at last sighted the massed dots of the oncoming bombers, which in this instance involved the 13th CBW. The swift closing rate meant that the attackers had a bare several seconds to open fire upon their adversaries, after which they risked colliding with their victims. In spite of this lethal limitation almost all of the first as well as the several succeeding waves of fighters managed to avoid this mutually disastrous fate. In turn, the hail of cannon and machine gun weaponry focused upon the B-17s resulted in a wholesale thinning out of the American ranks, with the 100th BG taking the brunt of the punishment.

An exception to this basic rule was provided by an unidentified Fw190 who headed in towards 42-31306/LD: V Nelson King leading the B Low group, whose sixteen-strong ranks would be particularly decimated. Lt. J Swartout's bomber lost a sizeable proportion of its fin and rudder but still kept on course and would return home. This good fortune

The Spartan interior of one of Thorpe Abbott's T2 hangars encloses **She-Hasta**, a 351 BS B-17G. The NMF bomber, having been assigned on 6 March, lasted until 29 July 1944; then, it was "ditched" by Lt. Greiner following fighter-inflicted damage, an action that only one of the nine airmen failed to survive, the others ending up in German hands.

was not enjoyed by fully fifteen other crews, with at least six bombers peeling off in all variations of distress during the initial onslaught.

The High squadron was fated to lose its entire strength. Capt. Miner, piloting 42-38059 in the lead, was probably killed, along with his co-pilot, and their bomber swept into an ever-increasing dive angle that finally fractured the nose Plexiglas and thrust the navigator outwards without his parachute pack. A fourth crewmember was lost during the bomber's terminal dive near Haseluenne. Nobody survived the demise of Lt. Z Kenball's 42-30278/LD: R, while Miner's other wingman, Lt. Barton in 42-31800LN: U, managed to bail all his crew out of the blazing B-17. Only three on Lt. W Terry's crew escaped from the disintegrating mass of 42-97482/ **Terry and the Pirates** flying No. 5 position, while **Ronnie R** (42-97491), with two engines and its bomb bay on fire, was evacuated close to the Dummersee by all but one of Lt. D Radtke's team.

Lt. N Young's 42-6099/AW: E **Winnie C** is sagging relentlessly downward over Berlin on 22 March. The left stabilizer has been struck and partially severed by several M-47 incendiaries from a fellow-group bomber. No parachutes were observed, and all ten airmen were lost as a result of the ever-tragic circumstance.

Lt. Don Kasch (front, left) and crew reached the 96th BG in December 1943, but they were just one of around 100 crews MIA during the first half of 1944. On 8 March 42-30847/MZ: N was one of six culled from the formation; Kasch was killed by fighter gunfire, and Lt. Eugene Schadler (front, second from right) did bail out with the other eight but was found dead on the ground.

The final disappearance of the sub-unit from the sky featured Lt. Barrick's 42-39994, but fortune was to shine upon all on board **Barricks Bag**. With two engines disabled the bomber lost height and distance, and seemed ready for final dispatch either through structural failure or from the guns of a fighter. The pilots took a seemingly hopeless gamble in heading northwards towards Sweden after jettisoning the bomb load. No further attention from the defenders came their way as they headed on a steady but gradually lowering course; their luck was really in when they unknowingly blundered over an airfield at minimum altitude but flew on unscathed. The interminable passage to neutral safety was finally achieved with a landing at Bulltofta, during which one main landing gear collapsed.

The town of Haseluenne proved to be the epicenter for the tangled aerial action as the slaughter proceeded apace with a further four crews being culled from the Low group. Swartout lost his Nos. 4 and 5, Lts. G Brannan and M Rish. Brannan ordered his seven surviving crewmembers out following 42-31735/EP: **Lucky Lee's** terminal battering; sadly, one of them later died in captivity after suffering severe injuries during the action. **Spirit of 44** (42-38044/EP:) finally fell to earth at Quackenbrueck, about 15 miles east of Haseluenne, after breaking in two, with Lt. Rish and three others losing their lives. The diamond formation flown by the reduced Low squadron was cut in half. First, 42-30170/XR: G, an elderly B-17F now bearing its fourth successive title **The Pride of the Century**, was being flown by Lt. C Montgomery, who was the sole fatality; Lt. R Koper, piloting 42-31051/EP: K **Goin' Jessie**, was probably trapped by the intense fire that blossomed throughout the fuselage, in contrast to Lt. G Lien (CP), who fought his way out to become one of three survivors. (Swartout's No. 2, Lt. Handorf in 42-38011/EP: P **Kind A Ruff**, came through the air battle, but on the return route over Diepholz—ironically not far from Haseluenne—a Bf109's gunfire set one wing on fire. Barely had Sgts Willsey (WG) and Lawrence (TG) cleared the B-17 when it exploded to kill all others still on board.)

The Haseluenne action further increased Thorpe Abbotts' losses to fourteen, beginning with Lt. A Amiero's crew flying 42-31731/LD, who suffered the group's second-highest proportion of deaths (nine out of ten), the fortunate exception being a waist gunner. **Bigass Bird II** (42-30799/XR: L) succumbed around the same time, along with three of Lt. W Murray's crew, including the pilot, who was decapitated. Lt. J Lautenschlager was piloting 42-38197 **Half and Half** in a formation shared with the 95th BG. Strikes in the bomb bay set it on fire and S/Sgt. J Stryweski suffered the cruel fate of an unopened parachute to become the sole fatality, his aircraft descending near Visbek, north of Vechta.

Horham's Torment

The 95th BG was destined to pay exactly twice as high an entrance price for reaching the German capital as had been exacted on the 4th. Nineteen crews had been dispatched, of which six of this figure were downed during the initial assault upon the CBW. Five crews survived in total: Lt. Conley's 42-97495/ET: C was one of the first to be lost as it came down near Barnstorf, while 42-29943/BG: K **Situation Normal**, flown by Lt. A Mailman, also crashed near the same town. A third B-17, 42-32002/OE: X **Berlin First**, crashed in this area, but successfully shed all ten airmen in Lt. T Barksdale's charge. The relatively good luck for the Group personnel in terms of survival continued with 42-39793/QW: V's loss near Quakenbrueck, when Lt. R Read pushed the bail out bell, upon which all on board jumped clear. Finally Diepholz, close to Barnstorf, collected the remains of 42-31251/BG: P, which thankfully was emptied of Lt. T Keasby's team at the time. The sixth loss at this point involved Lt. M Russell's 42-38024/ET: Q, on which one crewmember was killed prior to the B-17's final crash at Colnrade.

The most fortunate group within the CBW was the 390th BG, which surrendered just one of its nineteen participating aircraft. Lt. R Starks lost his life along with two of his crew when 42-31935/FC: A was shot out of the formation to crash at Hemmelte, near Cloppenburg. The 13th CBW's martyrdom

FC:A is photographed in the late winter or early spring of 1944. Assigned to the 390th BG on 17 March she has already accumulated over ten missions. Her combat career tragically conclued on 7 July when a midair collision with 42-97983 over Holland cost Lt. L Gregor and seven of the crew their lives. Note the small size of the squadron letters and carry-over of the serial onto the rudder.

Mon Tete Rouge II arrived at Deopham Green on 12 March 1944; she is seen in a mixed NMF/camouflage group of bombers. On 4 December the 731BS bomber was MIA, having crashed at Bitburg with the loss of one-third of the nine-man crew led by Lt. Downy.

was largely completed at this stage of the mission, but three further crews would be added to the MIA list. In addition, no less than eleven further bombers from other Groups, including the Lead PFF, would share in this ever-grim tithe before the day was through...

A Senior Loss

The Lead PFF B-17 for the 3rd BD was carrying B/Gen. Russell Wilson (CG, 4th CBW), as well as Maj. F Rabo and a crew of ten, one of whom was arguably of even more note than his superior officer. He was Lt. John Morgan, who as a co-pilot with the 92nd BG on 26 July 1943 had held the badly damaged B-17 on course for nearly two hours while being physically battered by his dying pilot. This was an action that later saw him awarded the Medal of Honor.

Now **Chopstick G-George**/42-3491 was one of ten 482nd BG bombers operating today, and having reached the IP led the Division into the flak-filled skies over *Big B*. Cloud cover almost at the last minute resulted in the Primary being abandoned in favor of suitable targets of opportunity that in the 4th CBW's case would be in the Steglitz district, several miles northeast of Klein Machnow. Scant seconds from "bombs away" a flak shell impacted with the right-inner fuel tank and ignited the volatile contents. The B-17 was held on course until the load of smoke markers and bombs had gone, after which it steadily banked away and into a glide. A bail out had been called for, but almost immediately the aircraft blew up. Three-quarters of the airmen, including Gen. Wilson, were killed, but Rabo and Morgan survived—the latter falling with his parachute pack unattached until he was almost on the ground, at which point he managed to engage his harness hooks and pull the ripcord.

The Return Leg's "Debit Ledger"

The 13th CBW had lived up to its unlucky number status and taken the whole of the Division's losses so far, apart from the Wilson/Rabo PFF bomber. Although a further three crews would be given up by this sub-force, it was the 45th CBW that would come in for most of the enemy's attention as Berlin faded far too slowly behind the bomber stream. However, the final 100th BG casualty was incurred at this point. The loss of an engine to the Berlin flak had inevitably left Lt. F Granack's 42-39872 **Rubber Check** trailing the group. The navigator suggested heading for Sweden, but all too soon the pilots' attention was taken up with survival, as several fighters closed in for concerted assaults. Two crewmembers were killed in the process, and finally Granack reluctantly called for a bail out, which all eight survivors completed successfully; their dying B-17 was last seen by Granack still flying westwards with smoke streaming from the engines...

The 388th BG had struck industrial facilities on the northern fringes of Berlin, and all twenty-seven aircraft were still on hand within the ranks of the 45th. The CBW, with its two sub-formations, assumed the trailing position within the 3rd BD. The Division in turn was now flanked by the other two Divisions, since the withdrawal pattern of the bomber stream had switched from the original "line astern" format adopted for the inward leg to this "parallel" structure. However, there was no more guarantee for immunity from fighter assault, since the Allied escorts, although sizeable in number, were still too few to guarantee constant cover for more than a proportion of the bomber stream—as the action over Haseluenne had amply demonstrated.

As it was, the Division's crews were none too disturbed by the *Luftwaffe* until the rear elements of the stream were closing upon the German boundary with Holland. By then, a relatively small and fragmented force of Bf109s and Fw190s (forty-four, spread among five *Gruppen*) was simultaneously being directed into position to sweep through the selected formation from the front. In this instance the brunt of what would be the day's last concerted action was borne by the 45th CBW, and the 388th BG in particular.

The series of lunges, mainly coming in from between two and ten o'clock but added to by several rearward approaches, was commenced and concluded in a matter of less than five minutes, but the chilling result was a culling of nearly half of the sixteen-strong Knettishall formation flying as Lead in the B CBW, along with one from its companion group the 452nd BG. The concentrated fighter gunfire ripped into the B-17s, forced as ever to fly in a virtually immobile manner thanks to their closely packed formation.

Lt. Grindley's veteran crew in 42-31194 lost two of its number, with a third bailing out but later dying of his wounds. Lt. M Givens, leading another veteran crew, saw the Nos. 3 and 4 engines on 42-31135 **Suzy Sagtitz** set on fire, whereupon all but one of the crew acted upon the bail out signal. Both these bombers finally came down directly below the bomber's flight path, whereas both 42-31240 (Lt. J McLaughlin) and 42-38177 **Shack Rabbits** (Lt. A Christiani) lingered in a northerly direction before tumbling to destruction on either side of Hamburg; McLaughlin had put his doomed charge on autopilot prior to successfully evacuating his crew, but half of the other crew lost their lives.

Cruel "Finale"

Diametric fates awaited the remaining three MIA crews. Lt. C Wallace also directed his heavily damaged 42-31163 **A Good and Happy Ship** in a northerly direction with the intention of flying into Sweden—a distance of nearly 200 miles in broad daylight with the defences ready to pick off bomber and crew almost at their leisure. As in Lt. Barrick's earlier case, "Fortune favored the brave" on board the 388th BG cripple, since the neutral source claimed its latest aerial visitor between one and two hours later!

Capt. P Doyle (S2) is interrogating the crew of Stingy (42-31053/BX: W), among whose number is S/Sgt. Kenneth Dixon (left). The Sgt at least survived his combat tour, unlike the B-17G, which went down following a midair collision on 9 November 1944 after serving more than thirteen months with the 96th BG.

A third veteran crew from Knettishall was led by Lt. L Watts, flying his 25th mission along with three others, while none of the remaining six had less than 21 completed missions. Prior to departure Watts had promised his crewchief Sgt Allert a proper "buzz job" of the airfield on his return. Now the B-17 (42-37886 **Blitzin Betsy**) was holding position below and behind Capt. P Brown's 42-40054, which was group Lead.

One of the attacker's landed lethal strikes on the Watts bomber that killed Sgt Brassfield (TG), flying his last mission, as well as exploding oxygen bottles up front and firing numerous fuel lines. With his forward vision almost totally impaired by smoke and flames, Watts had no visual indication that his B-17's flight attitude was angling steadily upwards as he endeavoured to hold her steady while the crew bailed out. All too soon the upper nose struck the right wing on Brown's bomber, whereupon both aircraft began a terminal downward path...

The immediate future for Watts seemed bleak, as the bomber developed a spinning motion before easing into a dive that still held him firmly in his seat. The entire cockpit roof had been excised in the collision, a factor that luckily worked to his advantage when he was finally ejected into mid-air to become one of six survivors. On Brown's bomber, six of the eleven airmen emerged alive after their charge exploded just inside Dutch territory, but the pilot was not among this fortunate number.

The corrugated frame of a Nissen hut provides a minimum degree of comfort for the officer complement of a bomber crew. Three are engaged in reading newspapers or books; the fourth in the background appears to be in a reflective frame of mind.

The gradual changeover from camouflage to NMF on American bombers is demonstrated in this view of two 452nd BG B-17Gs. Even so, 42-97256/N bears an element of the original finish with a replacement right-outer wing section. The aircraft served at Deopham Green from 16 March until its destruction on the ground at Poltava on 21/22 June 1944.

Closing the Ledger

The relatively small force of thirteen B-17s from Deopham Green had already lost one of its number between Berlin and Hannover. Flak had administered two strikes, the second handed out over the second location which proved fatal to 42-31337 (Lt. H Sweeny); although all bailed out successfully, one airman later died from his wounds. Now, 42-31373 **Flakstop** was thoroughly sieved in the fuselage and both wings, with power lost on Nos. 3 and 4 engines. Shortly after the left wing burst into flame and Lt. C Wagner held his charge in descending flight long enough for five of the crewmembers to take to their parachutes and land safely; in doing so he forfeited his own life, since he went down when the B-17 crashed in Holland.

Elsewhere, single bombers from the 94th and 95th BGs were lost during progression to the Dutch/German border. Lt C Johnson's 42-38022 had already gone down at Plantluenne along with two crewmembers, while Lt. L Garland bailed out his crew from 42-31299/BG: M **Junior** near Assen during the current air battle. (The 95th BG's eighth MIA crew were already gone near Magdeburg thanks to a combination of flak and fighter damage; Lt. F Frantz and eight others had got clear from 42-3529/ET: T, however.)

Another Technical "Miracle"

The onlookers at Rattlesden watching all 24 dispatched B-17s circling for landing must have been astounded as they gazed upon the undersides of 42-31227/ **Dottie Jane**—or rather, the bare remnants of the section normally supporting the radio room and rear of the bomb bay, since it was otherwise absent. During the bomb run a flak shell had not only removed the fuselage skin, but had also smashed the rear main spar, causing the wings to literally droop, while the right bomb bay door was ripped off and the left shredded. Sgt. A Moore was blown out through the radio room hatch without his parachute, but it was unlikely that he had remained alive from the concussive effect of the explosion. All but one of the bombs had been dislodged from their shackles, but miraculously had remained inert as they tumbled out.

Equally amazing was that Sgt. K Olsen (BT) had survived the blast, although suffering wounds to his lower body that subsequently saw his removal from combat and return Stateside. Having evacuated his turret, he still faced a common and critical problem along with Sgts. R Merz (RW) and L Emrich (TG); the oxygen supply had been so damaged that all three had to take turns breathing from walk-around bottles, a process that extended over one to two hours. The left waist gunner, Sgt. R Benjamin, had also suffered serious injuries to his lower torso that later rendered him also unfit for further combat duties. Apart from the unfortunate ROG, it remained a credit to the Boeing design that it had held up so well structurally to what was normally a lethal degree of punishment, but had brought home the other nine crewmembers on Lt. A Socolowsky's crew. *Category E* treatment was the sole option for the B-17 that had ironically taken the crew on their 13th mission, although Sgt. Moore had flown one more.

Burgeoning Crisis

The Nazis had been "bearded in their Capital den" for the first but far from the last time, although a high price had been exacted from the American ranks without a corresponding sound effect upon the enemy's industrial fabric. On the other hand, the *Jagdwaffe* had also suffered to the tune of 46 pilots killed or wounded. Among the former category was at least one *Experte* (Ace). This was Oblt. Hugo Frey (III/JG11) who, being posthumously credited with four 'kills," was adjudged to have been brought down by return fire from 388th and/or 452nd gunners, his Fw190 crashing at Sleen, in Holland. The loss of such a pilot was one more step on the road to bleeding the *Luftwaffe* ranks dry in terms of combat experience, and therefore easing the path of the Strategic bomber forces in their quest to eliminate Germany's industrial base.

One Down – Seventeen to Go! (8 March 1944)

The second of four major thrusts at *Big B* during March (with a further fourteen destined to follow up to late March 1945) was initiated on the 8th. All nine 3rd BD groups participated, but only 179 crews were sent out compared to 242 two days previous. On this occasion the Erkner ball bearing plant was the single selected target for the entire 8th AF force of over 600 bombers. Unbeknownst to the 3rd BD crews was the fact that they would again absorb the highest proportion of losses among the three Divisions, as well as having the lowest percentage of crews even gaining mission credit...

The advent into combat of what unquestionably developed into the finest all-round fighter of WWII, the P-51, was now gathering pace. Two days previous just 100 out of the 801 escorts sent out were from the North American factories, spread between three groups (4th, 357th, and 354th FGs). Today's operations witnessed somewhat of a quantum leap in numbers, since 174 Mustangs were assembled, with the 355th and 363rd FGs adding their weight to the overall total of almost 900. However, the average of less than 20 per group was still only one-third of that dispatched by the nine groups operating the P-47, which sent out 613 fighters. The air battles during March and April would still see the bulky Republic design in the majority, but that margin would be noticeably reduced by then. Regardless of such statistics, the *Jagdwaffe* would find itself up against increasingly incontestable odds...

On 6 March the 96th BG had emerged unscathed from the punishment otherwise handed out to the 45th CBW; a picture taken at debriefing showing smiling personnel standing by the status board on which was chalked "All Home" aptly summed up their mood that day. But the Grim Reaper was not about to relax his lethal grip upon the Snetterton Heath fliers as yet, while he would wield his scythe with equal ferocity among the 388th and 452nd BGs' ranks.

The 3rd BD formations proceeded in sound order across the North Sea and Holland, but the first indication that their progress would again be challenged arose within scant minutes of penetrating the Nazi hinterland. The 45th CBW flew Divisional Lead with the 96th up front, but following the first head-on thrusts by the *Luftwaffe* the situation began to deteriorate. The Lead B-17 suffered fighter inflicted damage that caused it to lose speed, thereby further retarding the entire CBW's already pedestrian progress before the pilots finally "aborted." What transpired as a 45-minute concerted series of fighter assaults upon the bulk of the CBW was soon in full swing with little apparent intervention by the *Little Friends*.

Lt. G Pond in 42-39988/QJ: A **The Iron Ass** elected to take over the CBW lead, but barely had this been achieved when the latest head-on pass took out three engines, leaving the crew with no option but to bail out. Capt. N Thomas' 42-31912/ AW: L was probably another early casualty to judge by its final demise west of Hannover; this time nine crewmembers reached the ground alive. Lt. D Kasch lost his life in 42-30847/ MZ: N **Pegasus** as did his navigator, Lt E Schadler, although the latter actually died after being bailed out by his fellow airmen; the dying B-17 impacted near Vechta.

The carnage continued apace, with Lt. Lemanski's 42-31576/QJ: G drifting out of formation in between Brunswick and Magdeburg; it was luckily abandoned by all on board to crash near Helmstedt, infamous in postwar years as a major road and rail crossing-point into Eastern Germany. Around the same time Lt. C Ross, piloting 42-31403/MZ: Y in the rearmost corner of the formation—known with feeling as the "Purple Heart" location — eased his damaged charge into a banking turn in a swiftly vain attempt to head back to England. Further gunfire

A very lucky local resident around Snetterton Heath is being treated to a detailed model of a Jeep with full insignia applied. Thousands of East Anglian children were destined to benefit in similar kind from the open-ended generosity of their American benefactors, to whom they were surely poignant reminders of a normal world back across the Atlantic.

This PFF B-17G from the 96th BG appears to be leading its formation perilously close to what are the slopes of the Alps mountain chain that border southern Germany. The H2X pod in the lowered position suggests a proximity to the briefed target.

strikes killed the bombardier and one waist gunner, while Sgt Ewarts (BT) suffered a particularly horrible fate. Having been seriously wounded, he was assisted in bailing out; he pulled his ripcord precipitately, and the canopy momentarily wrapped itself around the stabilizer before being ripped to shreds when it finally disengaged itself. Berlin was just about in sight when the third 413th BS bomber to be lost slipped inexorably backwards into fighter-intensive isolation. With one engine and the bomb bay ablaze, as well as severe vertical stabilizer damage on 42-31716/MZ: P, Lt. J Swendiman adopted the sole course of sensible action in pushing the bail out bell, to which all but two gunners were able to respond. The B-17 finally impacted at Burg, on the northeastern outskirts of Magdeburg.

The Low group slot within the CBW was filled by the 388th BG, and it was the crews' "privilege" to share the carnage with the 96th BG. The waves of anything up to twelve fighters forced the bomber gunners to divide up their return fire as a welter of cannon shells and bullets lanced into the lumbering formation. Having already suffered damage prior to the air battle, it was 42-38138/A's added misfortune to be rammed in the rear fuselage area by one of the attackers; it was amazing that any of Lt. W Lentz's (KIA) crew, let alone half its strength, survived the almost immediate disintegration of the B-17. Even more miraculous was that nine of Lt. M Moran's (POW) team on **Princess Pat** (42-30829) escaped from their spiralling B-17 after the bulk of the left wing snapped off. Both aircraft came down between Celle and the Steinhudermeer. A diametrically opposite loss factor compared to the Moran-led airmen affected the crew on 42-30340/**Screaming Red Ass**, Lt. Amman and eight others being killed in their B-17's crash at Neu-Ummensdorf, west of Magdeburg. Two more B-17s were culled on the stretch between Hannover and Magdeburg. **Return Engagement** (42-31214) took two of Lt. Pou's crew to their death, including the pilot, when crashing near Nienburg. The second aircraft descended near Helmstedt and broke up in separate sections; 42-37819/P deposited itself on an airfield, along with the entire officer complement led by Lt. L Tobias. Twelve crews MIA in two consecutive missions was a hard cross to bear for any unit...

452nd BG Fortunes

In contrast to its companion groups, the post-mission critique at Deopham Green commented on being under attack for only fifteen minutes, apart from which escort cover was described as "very good." In spite of this relative reduction in hostile attention no less than five crews failed to return. One out of this number was not actually within the group ranks, since Lt. Sorensen in 42-31354 had failed to make Assembly over England and attached himself to another unit. Knocked out of formation during target approach, the pilots finally gave up any prospects of reaching Sweden and headed down for a crash landing on an airfield at Zerbst southwest of Berlin; seven crewmembers ended up as POWs, with one of the three dead airmen particularly unlucky. T/Sgt. O Fulmer (ROG) was thrown out and broke his neck. Toeppel lies adjacent to Zerbst, and it was here that Lt. H Wilson's 42-37954 joined in fatal communion with its fellow aircraft from the group. The shot-up B-17 had also been headed in a homeward direction, but the opposition soon landed further terminal damage, upon which the bomb load was salvoed through the inoperable bomb doors, and the eight survivors "took to the air."

The other three losses were also incurred on the inward route, beginning with 42-31331 **Tangerine**, whose bomb load was jettisoned before Lt. Butterworth dived down and back at minimum altitude towards friendly shores. His efforts availed him none, because he had only progressed to a point northwest of Hannover when a Schwarm of fighters caught up with and set the straggler on fire. The pilots elected to "belly-in" the B-17, but the bombardier was killed in the process.

Yet another bomber was "bellied-in" not far from the Butterworth-piloted bomber, but this time with the bomb load still on board. Lt. T McDonald's 42-38211/M **Sleepy Time Gal** caught the full brunt of two successive attacking waves and some crewmembers bailed out. Two of those still on board were killed before the burning aircraft was deposited on the ground by McDonald, who was by then the sole occupant. A second grim "pairing" of MIA aircraft involved the final 452nd BG crew led by Lt. Stephens flying 42-97525 **Invictus**; their successfully abandoned bomber crashed at Rothensee, close to where Lt. Swendiman's 96th BG B-17 had impacted at Burg.

"Less Worse"...

The horrendous loss scale borne by the 13th CBW on the 6th was thankfully not repeated today, but this was scant consolation for three of the crews from the 390th BG, as well as the single losses from Horham and Thorpe Abbotts. The 100th BG was CBW Lead and trailed the 45th CBW, but only fifteen B-17s made up the group thanks to the losses on the 6th. All held position, and were doubtless thankful that the sustained assault pattern on the preceding Wing did not largely extend in their direction. Confusion among the 45th CBW leaders ended with the formation missing the IP and angling off to the right, whereupon Col. Bennett assumed Lead for the Division.

By this stage one 390th BG bomber was no longer on hand, while a second was already in trouble and destined to fail to run the gauntlet could, in retrospect, be regarded as an operational "turncoat." **Heavenly Body** (42-37812/DI: O) absorbed a solid flak strike that disabled one engine and created a "blowtorch" fire within the central fuselage. Lt. Branum banked out of formation pursued by several fighters, whose continued fusillades badly wounded one crewmember who later succumbed in a German hospital. Some others jumped without being ordered to, convinced their bomber was doomed. It was indeed, and ended its days thoroughly smashed up by the grove of trees into which it had erupted after the pilots crash-landed near Bitterfeld, southwest of Berlin.

Lt. E Nicholls (B) had now completed his 25th mission, but not in the positive manner he would have hoped for. On the other hand, it was a miracle that none of the crewmembers still on board had been killed given the disintegrated state of the airframe, with the tail section up in the air, radio room severed and canted off to one side, and fuel tanks cast bodily out of one wing. The outer skin had been peeled away from the nose section, which in turn had buried itself into the ground and left Lt. Sullivan (N) pinned up against the cockpit bulkhead; civilians later levered the nose up sufficiently to get the navigator free. Lt. Branum had been literally scalped, but survived the dreadful experience, while Lt. Stamphill was even more fortunate, since he was hanging upside down in his dislodged seat. As

The original cadre of PFF-functioning B-17s were assigned to the 482nd BG at Alconbury, and farmed out to specific groups for a mission. PC: E/42-97595 got no further than Snetterton Heath, where it cracked up during landing on 18 March 1944.

On 19 March 1944 a flak shell blew this enormous gap in 42-31968/LD: O **Miss Irish** as Lt. J Gibbons guided her in over the French coast. The ROG was killed, but the pilots held their charge aloft to effect an emergency landing at Raydon (353rd FG). The semi-severed frame held together until the bomber's momentum was at an end, but salvage action was the inevitable result.

for Lt. Nicholls, he had no recollection how he came to regain consciousness leaning against the *exterior* of the nose!

The "turncoat" term was arguably applicable to the operational veteran B-17F 42-30713/BI: G **Phyllis Marie**. Having arrived at Framlingham in late August, she had survived the traumatic events of the VIII BC's "autumn crisis" to amass more than 30 missions to date. Now, progressive battle damage left Lt. Quakenbush issuing the bail out order, but he remained at the controls on discovering one crewmember could not jump. The wheels were lowered, and the landing run in a flat stretch at Werben was progressing in order when a shallow ditch intruded to push the left main wheel up into the engine nacelle, leaving both propellers on that side damaged. All ten airmen had finished with combat flying, but not their bomber. (**Phyllis Marie** was subsequently restored to flying condition and assigned to KG200, whose crews flew clandestine operations using captured Allied aircraft. Thirteen months after her last USAAF mission the still-intact B-17 was discovered by U.S. Army units in a hangar near Leipzig, her "turncoat" days finally over!)

The third 390th BG bomber to go down was in Lt. P Quillan's hands. Persistent fighter assaults finally threw the fire-stricken B-17 into a spin, but all on board 42-31717/BI: A **Hells Bells** still managed to bail out. Single losses from the other two groups completed the 13th CBW's casualty figure, with a pair from the 94th BG also failing to return. **My Devotion** (42-5950/GL: P) was an eight month veteran that was crash landed at Wiesta, near the Dutch border, but happily left eight from Lt. Babington's crew alive, along with the two who had bailed out; 42-31141/XM: N brought Lt. F Scott's crew back as far as Wedemark, near Hannover, where its abandonment left nine survivors to be delivered into German hands.

In contrast to the first *Big B* strike, when clouds prevented sighting of the three Primaries, today's clear weather enabled an accurate if limited degree of punishment to be handed out to the ball bearings plant. A recurring basic limitation with bombing, even by daylight, now emerged, one that ironically owed much to the very success of the first attacking formations. Their bomb loads all too soon created a towering and laterally expanding mushroom of smoke that obscured the Primary from succeeding CBWs' sight—so much so that some groups elected to bomb alternative locations. Although the bomb loads adjudged to have landed within the target area reportedly affected production by up to one-third, there was still more than sufficient ball bearing capacity from other internal and external sources to at least keep Germany's industrial output on a par with what had occurred before this attack. (A more subtle but equally vital haemorrhage incurred by the defenders while opposing this latest incursion was cast up again. The 8th FC pilots had continued to bite into the *Jagdwaffe's* ranks while suffering minimal losses themselves.)

"Not Again!" (9 March 1944)

As with preceding periods of operational concentration such as "Blitz" and "Black Week," so the pace of bomber operations against Berlin began to show a downward trend in respect of participating aircraft. When *Big B* was briefed on the 9th, the overall force dispatched was reduced by about 100 compared to the 8th; further displaying the extra pressures placed upon both combat and ground crews in these circumstances was the fact that the figure of 526 was fully 30% below that going out on the 6th.

There was again little subtlety in the briefed route, with the stream heading across the Ijisselmeer, Holland's internal water mass, to a point near Hannover. From here the bombers were to angle in a northeasterly direction prior to banking right at a point almost due north of Berlin; a final turn towards the west would be assumed for approach to the Heinkel plant at Oranienburg, in the city's northwestern zone, and the Arado plant at Brandenburg, also outside Berlin's western limits.

The mission cast up mixed results, since weather conditions were even more adverse than on the 6th, while difficulties with the PFF equipment caused the 2nd BD to bomb locations other than Berlin. The B-17 Divisions also ended up releasing their loads on the city center in the face of heavy flak barrages. On the other hand, the *Luftwaffe's* presence was reduced to a mere handful of fighters, a welcome fact clearly reflected in the total absence of "kill" claims by the escorts.

Three of the eight bombers declared MIA were from Rattlesden and Knettishall. In the later instance the B-17 concerned had made an epic solo flight back from Berlin three days previous. Then, Lt. B Dopko had literally taken the low route home after suffering flak damage over the target that disabled one engine permanently and crippled a second. An extra touch of fortune occurred as the enemy coast was about to be reached. A flak battery directly in the B-17's path precipitately opened up, allowing the pilots time to bank away and utilize a clutch of buildings as a natural shield. The belated arrival of 42-37839/D **Little Willie** back at the airfield was a natural surprise to those eyewitnesses who had reported its demise at debriefing.

The 4th and 45th CBW's effort to attack Frankfurt on 20 March 1944 was totally thwarted by ever-intensive cloud formations. Here the 447th BG is tracking for home while exuding heavy condensation trails. The B-17G in the frame seems to be lagging and inviting possible assault by the *Luftwaffe*; as it was, all crews returned safely to Rattlesden this day.

Lt. Dopko's crew were again on board, but flying as a "spare" with the 96th BG, due to that unit's scale of attrition suffered 24 hours previous. It was therefore ironic that the sole bomber failing to return was **Little Willie**. Flak struck home again, but this time there was no reprieve, as fire blossomed out uncontrollably from No. 2 engine and all on board bailed out. Rattlesden's two vacant dispersals would normally have been occupied by 42-31208 and 42-31210 **Devils Mate I**, but both ended up under the North Sea, although all twenty of Lt. J Jurnecka and Lt. H McGuire's combined personnel came through the ordeal to be picked up by the ASR Service. The B-17 had again proven its relatively good ditching qualities compared to its USAAF and RAF contemporaries, although pilot skill allied to a smooth sea surface were always added factors in bringing off a successful conclusion to this potentially lethal action.

Berlin's inaugural martyrdom would occur once more during March (22nd), but overall USAAF operations proceeded at a steady pace prior to then. Seven missions were launched that ranged from attacks on the Pas de Calais to deep penetration runs. In the former instance, the first assault proved to be totally ineffective when weather conditions intervened—on the 13th! The reduced force sent out jointly by the B-17 Divisions proved successful with no cost to the 3rd BD. The crews participating on this occasion would have reflected on the contrast with the remaining five missions' duration and intensity of action...

A surprisingly small B-17 force had struck at Muenster on the 11th with a single loss borne by the 447th BG. The aircraft concerned was 42-97484, bearing Lt. H Overdorf's crew, of which only one survived. At least six more should have shared Sgt J Schultz's (TG) good fortune after they bailed out to land on a sandbank. Despite being seen by the Germans, no effort was made to rescue them from their precarious location and all were drowned when the tide swallowed up the area. The run to Brunswick four days later proved to be equally inexpensive, apart from a single 100th BG crew led by Lt. R Knight in 42-39934/LN: **My Achin' Back** which succumbed to flak during the bomb run, and only two officers and the Engineer managed to jump before the exploding bomber took their colleagues to their deaths over Watenbuettel. As it was, very few if any of the combat crews were likely to be lulled into a false sense of optimism that this easy run of missions signalled anything other than a break in the *Luftwaffe's* malign intentions towards their adversaries. Sure enough, next day's run to Augsberg brought home that unpalatable fact...

All thirty bomber groups on hand were dispatched to attack facilities at Augsberg and Friederichshafen; these were targets whose extended distance from England elicited an "Oh, my achin' back" reaction from many a combat crewmember.

The former location was allocated to the 3rd BD, and the bulk of the 206 crews gaining mission "credit" bombed the Primary. In exchange the defenses exacted a total of 13 of the Division's bombers out of an overall 8th AF casualty figure of 23. The worst affected group was the 95th BG, which lost four, with the 385th BG adding another three to the MIA list. **The Ohio Air Force** (42-30737) was one of the latter unit's casualties when it was downed by fighters near St. Quentin, France, along with two of Lt. Krause's crew. A duo of aircraft from Framlingham also failed to return, one of which had been on hand for seven months; 42-30783/DI: M **The Stork Club**, a 31-mission veteran, was bearing Lt. DeMayo's crew, only two of whom escaped alive after fighter attacks brought the B-17 down. Another relative veteran group aircraft 42-

A cascade of 500-lb bombs descend from two 452nd BG bombers in rather murky weather conditions. The group suffered rather severe casualties during the inaugural run of missions during the initial months of 1944.

31262/BI: P **Ole Smoke** went down today, although all but one crewmember led by Lt. D Jankins (POW) did bail out, with the fighter-stricken aircraft crashing east of Stuttgart.

Three of the aircraft concerned did divert into the embrace of neutral Switzerland, one of whom force landed. Lt. JV McLaughlin, flying 42-38195, ended up bailing out himself and the other seven still on board (the other two had already jumped over German territory), leaving the B-17 to crash at Wildhaus. **Little Chub** (42-38160/J) had to finally be ditched in Lake Zug by Lt. R Mayer; all but one of his crew survived their parachute descent into internment.

Although four crews did not return to Horham, none of the forty airmen suffered the ultimate sanction. It is likely the first B-17 to go down was 42-31205/ET: E, flown by Lt. P McCallister, which crashed several miles east of Stuttgart. Next down appears to have been Lt. D Norred's 42-38151/ET: L, which fell to earth near Noerdlingen within striking distance of the target. The POW existence facing these crews was paralleled almost one hour later when fighters landed mortal blows to 42-39989/BG: F's airframe and two engines, whereupon Lt. E Herman gave the bail out order north of Freiburg im Breisgau. A better conclusion to their problems awaited Lt J Reed's team after the bomb bay on 42-31329/BG: H was set on fire during the bomb run. A steep dive was made in an attempt to extinguish the flames, an action that was successful. A southerly heading was taken up for Switzerland, and this too proved successful, although the bomber was force landed at Diepoldsau. (Confusion exists as to whether all ten airmen were on board at this point; five of them allegedly bailed out when the B-17 dived; the MACR record lists one airman as a POW—while Swiss records state all ten were interned! Such instances are the bane of any observer or scribe of military history.) Single losses by four other units completed the MIA figure.

On the 18th and 20th they again went deep into southeastern Germany with very variable results in terms of effective bombing, although the MIA figures in the case of the Division were seven and two respectively. The center of Munich, as well as aero-plants at Oberpfaffenhofen and the experimental airfield at Lechfeld all received attention on the former occasion, but matters went badly awry two days later, with the mission having to be largely abandoned thanks to weather conditions. And then it was back to Berlin.

The 13th CBW lost three, with only one crew remaining intact. This was Lt. R Horn's team on 42-3508/LD: P **Bastard's Bungalow II**, which fell behind due to mechanical problems and was ultimately forcelanded north of Ulm/Donau. (The author met Bob in 1977 and found him to be a kindly soul who was quietly vague about his combat tour; a fellow 8th AF colleague later explained that the Conflict had left its mark upon him.) Only two airmen escaped alive from 42-37913/LD: W (Lt. D Stuke) after it collided over northern France with 42-39830/LN: Y **Berlin Playboy** (Lt. P Martin), from which a sole member also got out alive. Rougham had two crews culled from its ranks, starting with 42-31159 flown by Lt. R Croft, which finally came down near Rottweil. The other was 42-37968/GL: X **Little Audrey** (Lt. H O.Neill Jr.), which piled in close to Munich after suffering a mix of enemy and "friendly" fire, the latter caused by a bomb striking one wing. There were three fatalities in both cases. The same proportion of dead/POW crewmembers occurred on 42-30810/BX: Y, which Lt. R Muirhead vainly attempted to steer towards Switzerland before further fighter assaults ended with the B-17 splitting in two and crashing near Ditteshausen. There was an exact reversal of the foregoing 3/7 statistic on board the final Division loss. **Rick-O-Shay III** (42-37925/FC:) was dispatched into a spiral action following a mass fighter attack. The fortunate trio of survivors had managed to respond to Lt. R Biesecker's bail out order before the bomber exploded.

"Not Again!" – Again (22 March 1944)

Weather conditions over Western Europe during WWII continued to be frustratingly variable, and the 22nd's content of 8/10 to 10/10 cloud proved to be a primary factor in shielding the twin aviation plant Primaries at Oranienburg and Basdorf from assault, despite the presence of PFF leaders. The Friederichsstrasse main railroad station in the capital's center was designated as the Secondary and duly focused upon, but the bomb spread from the formations extended out several miles in most directions to affect a mix of military, government, and civilian property. ("Precision Area Bombardment," to quote Gen. Spaatz, was a reported "tongue in cheek" retort when under pressure by the American media to explain such a departure from the declared policy of precision bombardment!)

Once again the *Luftwaffe* was conspicuous by its absence to the undoubted relief of the "Big Friends," but less so for their escorts. Flak became the sole, if ever pernicious barrier to the bombers' progress, culling nine B-17s and B-24s; three more crews went down in self inflicted incidents, one of which belonged to the 96th BG. Lt. N Young's 42-6099/AW: E **Winnie C** drifted under the path of other bombers on the bomb run. The 100-lb incendiary load in another B-17 was apparently released prematurely at this point, and a number of the missiles chopped off the left stabilizer, and probably also impacted with other sections of the hapless machine. The pilot was not among the four airmen who got out of the aerodynamically imbalanced bomber before it crashed at Falkenhoehe, in the northwest of the city. Not only was this the 35th MIA loss for the group since 1 January; four of these losses had involved collisions between two bombers, with a further two caused by fighters running into the B-17 in question. (Snetterton's severe losses up to the summer of 1944 would still not earn it a "jinx" reputation similar to the 100th; in fact, some airmen from Thorpe Abbotts when meeting 96th BG personnel were fond of saying, "Hell, we console ourselves by sympathizing with your situation!") The same fate awaited all ten of Lt. B Carlson's 94th BG crew on 42-31637/TS: after several flak strikes resulted in the bomber splitting in two, with the truncated sections tumbling to earth in Berlin's Gruenewald district. On the way home Rattlesden's 42-107038 took flak punishment that finally impelled Lt. E Stull to begin bailing out his crew. All survived as POWs, but death awaited several Dutch civilians when the abandoned aircraft came down in an Amsterdam street.

Another "Bastard" Strike

Another bad day for the 45th CBW loomed up on the 23rd when Brunswick, as the briefed Secondary, was hit by 905 of the 224 aircraft dispatched. "The Battlin' Bastards of Brunswick" was an appellation applied by the Americans to the *Jagdwaffe* units encountered in this region, although the encounters between the two adversaries often involved units stationed other than here on the direct High Road to *Big B.* Sixteen crews were lost, of which eleven came from the aforementioned CBW.

Snetterton's misfortunes continued, although only to the tune of two aircraft and one crew actually MIA. Furthermore, it was Ruehr-based flak rather than fighters that caused the demise of Lt. H Taylor's 42-31624/BX: X, although the crash site was in Holland; all ten airmen did end up as POWs immediately, or after three months in the case of Lt. Taylor. The other group loss involved 42-38046/MZ: M, but once again all on board Lt. L Seeman's bomber survived the ditching and, unlike their unfortunate contemporaries, returned to their airfield and the relative comfort of a Nissen hut bed compared to a German prison cell.

The other two CBW elements were punished to the tune of five (388th BG) and four (452nd BG) respectively as the Division skirted the Ruehr before approaching Brunswick from the southwest and departing homewards with Hannover on its left. The steady fighter assaults seem to have borne fruit among 388th BG ranks after the target. Walle lies north of Hannover, and was the location where 42-30808/V, flown by Lt. C Filler (KIA), came down, along with half his crew. **Pegesus Too** (42-31103/R) was Lt. L Wilson's mount (KIA), and progressed no further than Speyerburg, also north of Hannover, when it was struck fatally by a fighter and came down to leave just three crewmembers alive. A third Knettishall casualty recorded as crashing at the same time as Lt. Wilson's aircraft—but much further to the northwest—was 42-31745/T **Heaven Can Wait** (Lt. K McFall, POW). It was shot out of the sky over Wildeshausen, around 30 miles east of the Dutch border, but was vacated by the entire crew beforehand.

The remaining two losses were also apparently incurred as the homeward bound group approached the Dutch border; 42-38120/J, in Lt. P Gerstenhaber's (POW) charge, descended at Sythen, southeast of Borken—another victim of flak, although nine crewmembers did succeed in bailing out. Scant miles to the east, near Haltern, Lt. W Davis and seven of his crew were fortunate to safely part company with 42-3548/X when sections of both wings detached almost simultaneously following previously incurred flak strikes.

The "Square L" insignia of the 452nd BG had first appeared in enemy skies on 5 February. Since losing its first four crews three days later—one that crashed on take-off and three that just disappeared during the mission—its ranks had been further thinned by eleven B-17s claimed in combat, including five on 8 March. That figure was now to be further extended.

The distance between Vechta, Diepholz, and the Duemmersee is no more than 30 miles, but three group B-17s fell in this zone. The gunners on 42-31731 (Lt. R Stephens, KIA) were frantically warding off the regular fighter assaults when one or more focused upon and probably brought about the violent demise of a Fw190; unfortunately, the fighter was close enough for the blast effect to wrench off part of the bomber's left wing; the tumbling descent of their charge permitted just four to bail out before final impact east of Vechta. The mid-air explosion of 42-39933/ **Superstitious Aloysius**, flown by Lt. Young, killed him, and all but two of his crew, with the scattered remnants falling at Roedenbeck Barnsdorf, near Diepholz. This fatal trilogy was completed by 42-39954's loss at Oppenwehe, just east of the Duemmersee, although Lt. L Yates (P) got all his crew safely out before the burning bomber went down. The group was leaving the target behind when 42-39985, flown by Lt. R Brennan, was dealt a fatal blow by the fighters; Rengershausen, near Hameln, provided the crash site with one gunner dead at his position and the ROG destined to suffer an unopened parachute. Deopham Green's latest bout of punishment was ended, but even worse days lay ahead.

The 4th CBW took all five remaining Division losses. Lt. F Johnson managed to guide 42-31120/GL: to an apparently safe ditching for at least part of the crew, as observed by circling P-47s, but when a Royal Navy Launch reached the location no trace of anybody was found. Seven other Rougham airmen, including Lt. A Reno (P), suffered a similar fate when 42-97476/TS: blew up during the bomb run and scattered its remnants at Lobmachtersen. The first of the three Great Ashfield crews to go down was led by Lt. E Stubler Jr. in 42-37959; the co-pilot and five gunners were killed after their bomber was set on fire and disintegrated north of the target area. Lt. F Fulton, his three fellow officers, and three gunners also lost their lives when fighter gunfire exploded their bomber 42-39908 in the vicinity of Boxtel, in Holland. The *Grim Reaper* only failed to wield his scythe on board 42-31102, flown by Lt. J Salyards, after it was brought down by flak on the outskirts of Dortmund.

Three days elapsed before the Division again took to the air to bomb suspected V-1 sites, not in the Pas de Calais, but further west on the Cherbourg Peninsula. Another well-visited French target (Bordeaux/Merignac airfield) was struck next day at a cost of two crews from Knettishall and Rattlesden. The latter Station suffered a second loss over England when soon after take-off 42-38085 **Heaven Can Wait** came down near Cockfield; Lt. W Hudson and his crew were killed either upon impact or after most of the bomb load exploded several minutes later. A third successive French target 24 hours later exacted the same grim tally, with both bombers coming from the 452nd BG. One of these had the bulk of its right wing excised by flak, and this huge scale of aerodynamic attrition threw the B-17 into a tight spin; there should have been no survivors when the bomber exploded, but Lt. R Cook (P) and two gunners from among the ten-man crew had their lives miraculously spared. The other group bomber died in an equally violent manner after a flak shell created a bisection of the fuselage in its center section. One of the four survivors S/Sgt. M Anderson (LWG) calmly attached his parachute pack and finally bailed out as the tail section of 42-97200 spiraled down; two other gunners and the ROG descended into captivity.

A 96th BG crew fared better in terms of survival, at least after 42-97166/AW: **Old Gatemouth** endured three swift flak strikes that sent the bomber temporarily out of control with one engine on fire. The bail out order was reacted to by all but the pilot and one other crewmember after the former reconsidered the situation and returned to the controls; the engine fire was seemingly extinguished by cutting off the fuel supply and the B-17 brought all the way back to an airfield in southern England. Fate was cruelly not finished with Lt. W Young, however...

What proved to be the final March mission for the 3rd BD unknowingly presaged at least a partial seed change in operational function for the 8th AF crews over the ensuing five or six months of 1944. The Western Allied Armies were gathering momentum in their planned bid to execute the long hoped for invasion of Europe, and the B-17s and B-24s, along with their RAF Lancaster and Halifax contemporaries, were about to be called upon to soften the way. The "heavies" would in effect become tactical partners to the 9th AF and the RAF's 2nd Tactical Air Force (TAF) as the Allies sought to bar the passage of the *Wehrmacht* and SS forces towards the planned Anglo/American landings on the Normandy coast...

"God protect me from my friends!"

The intensification of the Allied Bombing Offensive over Germany, in particular, now posed a particular threat to those airmen landing in enemy hands. There was never any guarantee that the rain of bombs and incendiaries would automatically exclude POWs should they be in the wrong place at the wrong time. In effect, "friendly fire" (the contradictory figure of speech that is in current military use and is known as an oxymoron) could easily leave its indiscriminately lethal mark upon anybody.

A good example of this risk factor that fortunately remained latent was later related by S/Sgt L Pifer (BT), one member of a 95th BG crew declared MIA on 4 March in 42-31785/OE: N **Slightly Dangerous**. He and one other crew member had received serious enough injuries for their temporary incarceration in a Berlin hospital next day. Within 24 hours the 8th AF delivered its first full strike on the capital to be followed by two more by the 9th. As previously recorded in this chapter, much of the bombing had been relatively scattered or delivered through solid cloud cover, so increasing the chances of the hospital becoming an unintended target. Pifer and his companions' sojourn in hospital lasted until the 12th, when they were doubtless thankful to be transferred by train to a similar establishment near Frankfurt, little knowing that they were again heading into harm's way.

On the 23rd the Sgts were released and joined a group of "*Kriegies*" who now entrained in boxcars at Frankfurt's main railroad station for the short journey to Dulag Luft. The boxcars were locked, but instead of heading for the interrogation center were then shunted into a marshalling yard. The late winter darkness had fallen when the airmen's ears became attuned to a growing drone that presaged the arrival over the city of a large RAF Bomber Command stream—they were snug in their mobile coffins!

Over the ensuing hour, the flash and tremor of hundreds of bombs mingled with the bark of flak battery weapons formed a frightening backcloth to their involuntary entrapment. Thankfully, the raid inflicted no fatalities among their ranks, and they were left to ponder their fate amid the sounds of screams and shouts and crackling fires, to which was added the occasional boom of a delayed-action bomb.

Next morning the cars were unlocked and the dreadful effect of the raid met their sight as they tumbled out; the railroad station had literally been flattened, so it was a simple miracle that their section of the marshalling yard remained almost unscathed. Nor was the nightmare completely at an end, since later in the day the 8th AF made its latest strike against the city, although the overall effect was much dissipated by adverse weather. Even so, it would only have taken one bomb load to have created a large scale "friendly fire" incident. As it was the Germans "persuaded" many of the personnel to assist with clearing up the worst of the damage before the train headed out—not for Dulag Luft, which had seemingly suffered major destruction from a crashing RAF bomber, but for Stalag Luft VI. (Sgt Pifer and his colleagues from this camp would experience further and much more protracted hardships during the following winter when they endured an enforced march across central Germany that lasted many weeks; this included several "friendly fire" incidents involving strafing Allied fighters that sadly did not spare a sizeable number of the Anglo/American "*Kriegies*.")

The exterior surfaces on the B-17 did not long remain pristine as evidenced by a 100th BG bomber during an attack on coastal defenses in the Pas de Calais. A combination of heavy exhaust staining and scuffed and chipped paintwork can be seen. The National insignia's faded condition is highlighted by what is a recent re-application of the Blue outline, while the "Square D" is also in dire need of re-painting. Both wingtips appear to be replacements.

9

D-Day Looms

(April/May 1944)

The Plan

Although the attacks upon Berlin were deemed necessary from both a physical and a psychological standpoint, they were but an element of an overall need to seriously diminish if not totally throttle German industrial output. As it was, this process would be at least marginally affected by the need to prevent *Wehrmacht* and SS units from being swiftly dispatched to reinforce the defense of the Normandy coastal stretch extending 50 miles westward and north of Caen, where the Anglo/American armies intended to commence their liberation of the Continent. With this in mind the Combined Chiefs of Staff at SHAEF proposed that all road, rail, and even canal routes feeding into Normandy should be systematically taken out; also included on this vital "hit list" were airfields and marshalling yards. Furthermore, they demanded that to the units deployed by the Tactical Air Forces (USAAF 9th and the RAF's 2nd Tactical Air Force) should be added the "heavies" of the 8th and RAF Bomber Commands. The argument for and against this latter provision proved to be brisk, if not heated in presentation, but Gen. Eisenhower basically won the day for the several months operation of what was known as the Transportation Plan.

Strategic issues were never to be totally subordinated to the Plan's demands. This was especially the case given the 8th AF's looming focus directed upon a true "bottleneck" industry—oil, or rather the synthetic variation that was being turned out by a large number of plants spread mainly throughout Germany. April opened with a negative sortie to bomb Ludwigshaven, a Divisional "recall" being issued on the way over. A full week then elapsed before the next mission, when airfields at Quakenbrueck, Achmer, and Rheine took a pounding, along with several other target of opportunity bases at a cost of just four bombers. (The 2nd BD's parallel attack on Brunswick seems to have gained the defenders' full attention again, since no less than thirty crews were downed! But this respite from *Luftwaffe* attention lasted less than 24 hours, and once again it was the 45th CBW that ran into trouble...

Targets up on the Baltic coast were chosen (9th) with aero-plants at Posen and Warnemuende allocated to the 3rd BD. The seven participating groups dispatched a surprisingly small overall force of 151 and came home twelve light, all but one of which came out of the luckless 45th CBW. As it was, its fortunes were not helped by the weather conditions that caused the 452nd BG to abandon the mission, while the main A group of the 96th BG was ordered to link up with the 1st BD, which was ranging further east to strike Marienburg and Rahmel, before making its own run to Posen.

The *Luftwaffe* fighters were persistent in pecking away at the solo formation, but the final toll of two crews, tragic as it might be, was surprisingly low (a good percentage of the attackers were twin-engine Me 410s whose primary armament was the 21-cm rocket, a weapon that was none too accurate in spite of its fearsome reputation.) One of the MIA crews led by Lt. O Williamson ended up in Sweden, where they and their flak-afflicted 42-37985/BX: were interned. This was in stark contrast to 42-40051 /QJ: (Lt. J Massey), after the B-17 and its crew was terminally dispatched into the Baltic, off Lolland Island, Denmark. (After being repatriated to England and rejoining the 96th BG in mid-year, Williamson decided to return to combat operations, acting on the (sadly mistaken) principle that "lightning does not strike twice." On 10 Sept his B-17, 43-37603/BX: R **I'll be Around**, was again the victim of flak, only this time he and his crew ended up in the much less hospitable surroundings of Germany!)

A similar extreme contrast affected two of the three crews lost by the 388th. All ten airmen led by Lt. I Abramowitz in 42-31137 joined the Williamson crew in Swedish internment after force landing at Kalmar. No such luck attended Lt. Sundstrom's crew in 42-107076; the flak-damaged bomber staggered as far as Tastrup, just west of the Danish capital Copenhagen, before crashing and killing all ten in the process. (The proximity of this part of Denmark to Sweden, separated as it is by just several miles of water, suggests the pilots were attempting to get through to the neutral country.) Berkel, Holland, was the recorded crash location for 42-38039 (Lt. R Trubis, POW) with only one of the ten lives shed after flak dealt a mortal blow.

The losses suffered by the other two CBW components was marginally surpassed by the 452nd BG with six. Among the casualties were four from the 728 BS. First, 42-97529 **Dinah Mite II** (Lt. Roy) was shot out of formation and suffered two fatalities before piling in near Todendorf, on the Baltic coastline. Only four of Lt. C Boyd's (KIA) crew on 42-39936 got out alive, while three died on board 42-37941 **Lucky Lady** (Lt. N Bodet). The fourth down was 42-31352 **Leading Lady**, which came down in the Baltic with the loss of all Lt. J Mayek's crew. By contrast, the demise of 42-39974/731BS at Vaerlose, Denmark, was not matched by anybody from Lt. Roener's group of airmen. Lt. J Patterson's (POW) 42-32070 almost certainly came down on Danish soil as well, since four of the crew evaded capture.

The 96th BG's travails on 11 April 1944 commenced even before mission-launch. Lt. McGregor was flying a 413BS PFF bomber 42-9756/MZ: B when he had the misfortune to be intercepted and shot down by an "intruder" close to the assigned airfield of Framlingham. At least one airman on board was killed after the bomber descended at Great Glenham.

Mayhem over Rostock

The abortive mission on 1 April had not prevented the 96th BG the same evening from celebrating their 100th mission flown six days before, with a distinguished RAF/AAF group of Senior Officers, including Gens. Spaatz, Doolittle, Anderson, and Sir Arthur Harris, C-in-C of RAF Bomber Command. This salient statistic had been achieved at the cost of (ironically!) 96 B-17s MIA in the course of flying 2103 effective sorties out of 2667 dispatched. A further four crews had gone down in action since the Mesnil centenary mission, but today's run up to the Baltic coast would add the latest severe blow to the group's ranks, and arguably its general state of morale...

Although the *Luftfwaffe* fighter pilots were finding the odds increasingly in their adversaries' favor there was little slackening in their bid to strike home whenever and wherever the opportunity presented itself. Before the last USAAF aircraft had settled down on its airfield today, no less than 64 bomber crews, along with 16 pilots flying *Little Friends*, would have entered the MIA lists. Thirty-three Division bombers were among these statistics (although four diverted into Sweden), and once again the 45th CBW was particularly hard hit, contributing no less than seventeen to the total.

The Primary at Sorau remained inviolate from assault thanks to blanketing weather conditions, and Rostock was selected by two-thirds of the 275 crews getting through to unload as a target of opportunity, while the Secondaries at Poelitz and Arnumswalde, further east around Stettin, were also assaulted by most of the remaining formations. In the case of the 96th BG just one-quarter of the 27 bombers going out actually discharged their bomb loads over Rostock. The price for this marginal effort was horrendous...

On 11 April 1944 Bulltofta airfield, in Southern Sweden, "welcomed" the two B-17Gs seen here. Lt Gillespie flew his 96th BG battle damaged charge (42-97212/QJ: G) into the neutral location. Lt. Johnson (94th BG), piloting 42-97155/TS: C (seen on the left), diverted for the same reason to become the second of nine B-17s taking this course of action on the day. The 96th BG crew's internment proved a far better fate since ten other Group bombers were shot down!

This is a closer view of 42-97155/TS: C **Dog Tired**. Flak damage was severe enough for Lt. G Johnson to divert into Bulltofta. The overall Silver finish on 3rd BD bombers seen here was not displaced by the colourful CBW markings until well into 1944.

Unlucky 13. On this day in April 1944, during a mission to Augsburg, 42-31691/ FC: O – **Lassie** ended up in this undignified position near Oberglatt, put there by Lt. Cooper and his co-pilot. The flak-damaged bomber is surrounded by a mass of naturally curious Swiss citizens.

Lassie's arrival in Switzerland on 13 April was paralleled by no less than nine other 3rd BD bombers during the mission to Augsburg. Rattlesden's 42-107021/L from the 710BS and flown by Lt. Thornbury was one out of this number. Picture was taken some days later since all guns had been removed.

A gently smiling Lt. Bill Johnson (447th BG) stands by the nose hatch of his B-17. On 13 April 1944 he was badly wounded, but managed to guide his bomber back to East Anglia, where he bailed out his crew; tragically he did not get out before the B-17 piled into the ground.

The eleventh 447th BG (42-31519) failing to return to its airfield on 29 April 1944 rides tail-high on the thankfully calm sea surface; the two dinghies with all of the crew led by Lts. McGuire (P) and K Anderson (CP) await the arrival of an ASR Launch. All ten subsequently completed their combat tour.

All four Squadrons on hand took some form of loss in the air battle, which seems to have been largely centered over the Baltic as far east as the Peenemuende Peninsula, and involved wholesale numbers of Me410s among the attacking force. The 337BS surrendered three, beginning with 42-97129/AW: B **Skipper**, which came down on Danish soil albeit safely evacuated by Lt. Van Hixon and crew. Capt. C Firestone managed to crash land 42-31782/AW: E on Germany's western Baltic coastal fringe, but lost four crewmembers in the futile conflict with enemy fighters. The third squadron casualty involved a true veteran B-17, **Kipling's Error III** (42-5885/ AW:), which also struck the sea near Bornholm Island and took all of Lt. H Johnson's crew with her in a fatal embrace.

Rocket strikes on 42-31447/BX: D **Cookie** dealt a fatal blow to both bomber and all of Lt. J Splan's crew, with the aircraft descending into the sea. Fire had taken hold of Lt. H Beckman's 42-37920/BX: N about the same time, and only two gunners survived their aircraft's subsequent demise. The third 338BS casualty appears to have been 42-97089/ BX:, which was last seen during this phase of the battle, and which presumably also crashed in the sea, since there were no recorded survivors from Lt. P Swanlund's team. The particularly high death toll among the squadron's ranks was added to when Lt. Young's 42-29929/BX: X **Duchess** also came down near Bornholm Island to leave a single gunner survivor from among the eleven man crew. (The pilot had brought home his seemingly fatally damaged B-17 on 28 March, but today had dealt out a much more lethal hand.)

An attempted ditching by Lt. R Winslow, flying 42-3322/QJ: **Full House**, was only partially successful, in that four gunners in the rear fuselage were probably rendered unconscious by the impact, which split the bomber in two, and were drowned.

Lt. R Fleming had his 42-31896/QJ: thoroughly shot up by flak and ultimately dropped down on the way home to crash land on an island near Luebeck; Lt. Norderer (N), who had already been badly wounded, was thrown into the nose and killed to become the sole fatality. Nine bombers had gone down, and the litany of destruction was completed by 42-3535/MZ: L, a 413BS aircraft flown by Lt. K Bethe. Not only did the entire crew get safely out of the final crash landing southwest of Copenhagen, but all ten evaded capture!

Lucky Exception

The eleventh crew fated not to return to Snetterton Heath was flying in 42-97212/QJ: G. Sgt. Fletcher (TG) had been severely wounded in one leg, and as the punishment grew the rear entrance door was jettisoned as an emergency measure. Lt. Gillespie was ultimately informed by his navigator that the chances of getting back to England were problematical, whereupon the decision was taken to make a run northward to Sweden. Fortunately fighter attacks had eased off at this time, so the neutral-seeking flight ended up successfully in less than 30 minutes at Bulltofta, where the injured gunner was given prompt medical attention.

Condensation trails from preceding elements in the bomber stream outline a Deopham Green B-17G. The NMF bomber was named **Mugwump/C'est la Guerre** and served the group from 20 April 1944 until its loss the following 17 January when all on Lt. Skogland's crew bailed out into captivity.

Sharing the Torment...

Six more crews split between the two other groups were excised from the CBW ranks. One of the four Knettishall losses fatally affected all ten of Lt. Osterkamp's crew after 42-97255/563BS fell to earth near Rostock. Two more B-17s crashed in or close to the city boundary. One of these was 42-32003/561BS **Shoo Shoo Baby**, whose demise left a single member on Lt. W Knowles' crew (KIA) alive.

The other was 42-97241/563BS, which was cut from the formation by fighter attacks, with only six of Lt. E Ely's crew, including the pilot, ending up as POWs. The final MIA bomber did not join its unlucky companions on enemy soil. Instead, **Bottled in Bond** (42-97192/562BS) diverted into Sweden's Gardsnaga airfield, but sadly one crewmember did not survive to enjoy this otherwise fortunate outcome for those under Lt. A Thomas' tutelage. From Deopham Green, 42-39995/731BS **Cow Town Boogie** managed to run the northward gauntlet of the Baltic to land at Angeltofta, where Lt. R Schimmel and crew were interned. There was also a full survival rate on 42-97083/728BS **Flatbush Floogie**, albeit in less happy circumstances, since Lt. Gardner's crew ended up in enemy hands, with their B-17 crashing at Jadesbuesen.

Personal Tragedy

Eagerly awaiting the group's return to Horham was Jan Janofsky, a USO entertainer whose brother David was co-pilot to Lt. Schiappacasse on 42-37876/QW: S **Miss Raps-O-Dee**. Her anticipation at making this sibling reunion swiftly turned to shock when she discovered on arrival at the airfield that the B-17 was one of the seven declared MIA. In fact it had been dispatched into the Baltic, and it would be several months of hopeful agonizing before the confirmation of Lt. Janofsky's death and burial on Bornholm Island following his body's recovery from the sea was received.

A second Horham crew's ditching experience was by contrast almost perfect, in that only a single fatality occurred among Lt. A Power's crew; sadly this was the pilot, but it is not clear whether he was already dead prior to 42-97223/QW: X being guided into the Baltic. A third 412BS crew flying in 42-31798/J came down at an unconfirmed location within the Mecklenburg region that includes Rostock; this time only G Maddox (P) and two others got out alive.

The target area was where three of the remaining four crew forfeited their lives or freedom. Lt. D Miles evacuated his entire crew before 42-31835/BG: A plummeted into the ground at Warnemuende, a northern extension of Rostock; by

Above: Temporary reprieve. Pilot Jerry Musser (right), along with T/Sgt Leon Sweatt and Lt. John Flanyak (left), examine the damaged stabilizer on their B-17G **the Reluctant Dragon**. Most of the crew bailed out during the 8 May 1944 mission, leaving the trio to bring home their charge to Snetterton Heath. Nineteen days later both Sweatt and Flanyak were killed, and Musser became a POW while flying a mission to Karlsruehe.

Right: A cruel postscript to T/Sgt Sweatt's death lay in the fact that his wife Pearl was initially informed he had survived as a POW. It was six months before the true facts came to light. Here, she and her son Charles are pictured with an officer on the occasion of the extremely unpalatable information being officially relayed to her.

contrast, the same survival rate experienced by the Maddox crew (three out of ten) befell Lt. R Westmeyer's (POW) team on 42-37935/ET: K, which came down at Bad Doberan, close to Rostock's western boundary. Even worse befell Lt. R Bannerman's team on 42-39869/QW: R, none of whom came through alive after fighters shot their aircraft out of the skies near Bandelstorf, southeast of Rostock. The final loss involved 42-32019/ET: R, with just one fatality inflicted by fighters attacks among Lt. L Francis' crew, namely the pilot.

4CBW

Although the 94th BG lost four crews, two won through to Sweden: 42-97155/TS: C **My Ideal**, in Lt. G Johnson's charge, was landed at Bulltofta, while an undisclosed location was where 42-30433/GL: U **Miss Donna Mae**, flown by Lt. Vaughn, ended up with the twenty airmen interned. Flak damage had forced these diversions upon the pilots, and it was flak that brought down 42-97086/XM: K **American Maid** (Lt. Totushek) over Osterby, near Schleswig, along with four of her crew. The final flak-afflicted B-17 was 42-37918/TS: R **Dog Tired**, but this time all of Lt. Churchwell's crew survived their bomber's crash landing.

Joining the 94th BG duo in internment was 42-30197/N **Mission Belle**; Lt. Pangle directed his 549BS aircraft northward to land at Kristianopel. The other two Great Ashfield MIA crews were less fortunate. The nine-month 548BS veteran bomber 42-3337/C, flown by Lt. J Mullins, spared neither itself nor any of its occupants when it was downed over Stettin. Dargen, northeast of Stettin, was where 42-37977/549BS **Blue Champagne** ended its operational career at the hands of flak gunners, but all ten of Lt. R Bailey's crew ended up as POWs. (Internment, death, imprisonment—here once again there was a grim contrast in personal fates as highlighted by these three crews' combat experiences.)

Rattlesden's pair of MIA crews all survived their aircrafts' loss, but with varying degrees of fortune. The first won through to Bulltofta, in Sweden, being 42-107067/709BS in Lt. Jurnecka's charge. The other B-17, 42-31156/708BS **Big Stoop**, flown by Lt. Pauling, staggered on before flak-inflicted damage proved terminal over Bornholm Island, a Danish possession in the Baltic. Once again, all ten survived when the aircraft was crash landed, but six enjoyed the "bonus" of evading capture for indeterminate periods of time.

Comment

The bald truth was that the B-17s and B-24s were still being outmatched in firepower by their *Luftwaffe* adversaries during straight bomber to fighter confrontations, as instanced on this occasion. This was as much the case with the twin-engine Bf110Gs and Me410s as with their single-engine contemporaries. Whenever freed from USAAF escort attention, as appears to have been the case here, they could engage the bombers almost at will and land punishing strikes with their basic machine-gun and cannon armament, while sowing extreme unrest among the bomber crews if not damage on their aircraft with their supplementary 21-cm rockets. As it was, the opportunities for the *Luftwaffe* "twins" to freely indulge themselves were steadily running out...

More Snetterton Woes

The strategic aspect of operations would continue uninterrupted for another week. However, weather once again thwarted all efforts to bomb targets in central Germany next day, but not so on the 13th, when Augsburg appeared on the Division's Briefing maps. Nearly 900 escorts went out, but their best efforts could not prevent a further 38 bomber crews being lost, the bulk of these being from the two B-17 Divisions. Eighteen crews did not return to their 3rd BD airfields (although fully ten out of this overall dismal figure did wend a successful path to Switzerland.)

Five came from the still luckless 96th BG, and the fighter assaults were noted as commencing soon after crossing the Rhine. Lt. O Brandau lost an engine and headed south for Switzerland, but came down near Bitburg, where all crewmembers on 42-37480/AW: B ended up in captivity. Around the same time 42-31774/BX:L **Vera Mae** was cut out of the formation and shed all ten on Lt. L Bever's crew prior to crashing. The first of three 338BS aircraft to go down was 42-37910/QJ:, which spared all of Lt. C Tate's crew from the same terminal fate when it impacted near Eglingen, northwest of the target. Lt. W Potter, flying 42-32073/QJ: D, was sufficiently damaged for the pilots to take up a course for Switzerland; their efforts were successful for all but Sgt. D Cox. Tragedy attended the final loss after Lt. H Daniel found his 42-40016/QJ: **The Character** badly damaged and forced down and out of formation. Assuming that those in the rear had not received the bail out order, the pilot went aft to inform his crewmembers before returning to the controls to hold his charge steady. The B-17 then entered a steep dive, whereupon Daniels and one gunner bailed out; tragically, the pilot's parachute deployed just too late to prevent a fatal impact with the ground, while Sgt. J Curran impacted fatally with a telegraph pole, and only the other three officers and Sgt. J Drozd (Eng.) actually survived the incident. April was proving to be a particularly cruel month for the 96th BG, but May would prove to be even worse...

First Hurdle Failure

The weather conditions on 12 April were a daunting mixture of low cloud, minimum horizontal visibility, and sub-zero temperatures—challenging enough for an experienced crew, let alone the acolyte team of ten led by Lt. P King; his mount

Numerous American film stars carried out visits to the airfields of the 8th AF. In this case James Cagney prepares to "christen" a 390th BG B-17G that bears the name of one of his most famous feature films depicting the life of American stage artist James M Cohan, who penned among other songs "It's a grand old flag" and "Over there."

The 486th BG only flew combat with the B-24 for just over two months but had its share of incidents. Here, 3R: C from the 832BS has slid to an undignified but seemingly intact halt with the left landing gear dangling; however, the top turret frame looks to be dislodged, as often occurred when the fuselage split at this juncture, so the bomber may now be only fit for "Category E" treatment.

was the seeming combat veteran 42-31088/711BS **Heaven can wait**, even though it had flown but a handful of missions since assignment. The throttles were cracked open and a lift-off achieved from Rattlesden's NE/SW main runway, to judge by what soon transpired. In a recent letter to his wife King had written "Flying over here is a piece of cake," words that now rebounded cruelly upon him and six of the crew. Three of the four gunners huddled in the radio room later reported their feeling that the take-off was over-long and upward motion sluggish. Next thing they knew the propellers were chopping into tree foliage, with branches excising one stabilizer and Nos. 1 and 2 engine cowlings. The final crash site was at Thorpe Morieux, where the bomber careened into a ditch and caught fire. The injured survivors painfully managed to crawl out of the radio room that now formed the rear of the fuselage, the tail section having been snapped off, and remove themselves to a ditch. From there they heard several muffled explosions followed by a mighty blast as the bomb load went up, extinguishing any chances for the other crewmembers that might have still been alive to also get clear. Sadly, Sgt. C Reitzel was on borrowed time, since he was killed in a mid-air collision incident the following 2 October, when 43-38245 and 44-6460 came down at Hitcham and Kettlebacton, close to Thorpe Morieux, with seventeen airmen killed. (A further ironic point on the King crash concerned the fact that on 27 March Lt. W Hudson and crew had been killed when their 447th BG bomber came down at almost the exact same location.)

The Price for Straying...

A four-day respite was probably treated by the combat crews with a mixture of relief at being spared the rigours of combat operations and frustration at not being able to advance their chances of completing their tours. Several locations on the northern and western approaches to Berlin appeared on the Briefing maps on the 18th.

As on the last venture to this area, the stream was routed in both directions up to a point near the Danish/German border before turning towards and departing its targets. *Luftwaffe* opposition varied greatly, with the 1st and 2nd BDs getting through with just five losses in all. Not so the 3rd BD—or more exactly the 94th BG—with eight of the fourteen MIA crews coming from this unit's ranks.

The situation did not deteriorate until well into Germany. The 94th's twenty-one bombers and part of the 385th BG became separated from the stream and were furthermore soon bereft of escort cover after the fighters concerned elected to remain with the main Divisional force as it sought out targets of opportunity (reference to the fighters' action is quoted according to records held at Rougham).

The first of three slashing assaults occurred close to Brandenburg, but with surprisingly little effect, other than to badly damage the Lead aircraft, which was a 413 BS PFF machine from the 96th BG and one of three provided by Snetterton Heath to the 4th CBW. On board 42-97545/MZ: D Maj. L Weimer (94th BG) was fatally injured, and all too soon the battered state of his bomber impelled Lt. G Rieder to bail out the crew. The bomb run had been completed when the next wave of fighters struck, but this time with deadly overall effect. Capt. A Hogan was flying as Command Pilot along with Lt. Schommer in 42-107019/TS: **Wabbit - What's Up Doc?** when one of the 20-mm shells that riddled the B-17 killed the latter officer; after pushing the bail out bell, Hogan was fortunate in hauling himself out through the nose hatch against the centrifugal forces accruing from the aircraft's ever-steeper plunge.

The 331BS ended up bereft of three bombers: 42-31401/QE: D **Old Hickory** (Lt. A Gordon) suffered four fatalities and 42-31874/QE:, flown by Lt. W Williams, came down at Neuruppin, although the eleven-man crew survived. The 410BS came off one worse, losing 42-37797/GL: T **Wolverine** (Lt. Brinkmeir), 42-37852/GL: **The Payoff** (Lt. Dillard), 42-31650/GL: Z **Impatient Virgin** (Lt. McMeekin), and 42-38139/GL: N (Lt. I Pomerantz). McMeekin's bomber lost the bulk of its right wing to a mid-air collision and only two crewmembers got out alive after the bomber disintegrated.

Fatalities were eleven out of forty, with all of the latter-listed crew surviving.

Although the fighter attacks appear to have been concentrated over a few minutes at most, the ultimate crash site for at least one B-17 was well distant from the action. Lt. G Craig's 42-31407/QE: V **Chief Chilletacaux** came down at Gnolen, close to Rostock, on the Baltic coast; the pilots may have been on a course for Sweden, but their efforts failed, leaving the full crew at least alive but as POWs.

Ever-expanding Snetterton Martyrdom...

The second Snetterton Heath-based PFF aircraft was lost when 42-97569/MZ: lost two engines to flak and its pilot, Lt. J Abrell, to a cannon shell, with all other crewmembers evacuating the crippled B-17 and leaving it to crash at Bluethen.

The 96th BG's specific travails were completed when a third 413BS bomber, 42-97597/MZ: D, flown by Capt. E Easterline and flying with the 447th BG, was struck by at least one bomb; the pilots managed to control their mortally afflicted charge sufficiently to bring it down for a crash landing that all ten airmen survived to become POWs.

The presence of three PFF B-17s from the 413BS was confirmation of the squadron's specific function on behalf of the 3rd BD. In late March the PFF duties formerly carried out by the 482nd BG were reassigned to specific squadrons, with the 413BS selected for its Division; in time, first each CBW and finally each group would become self sufficient in this function, but it would only occur in the fullness of time.

Bonded Closer than Family

The relationship between the members of a crew was arguably closer than that between the members of a family. The cynics might say that this was because it was based on mutual self preservation, but this is too simplistic. The bald truth is that there is a human bond between individuals, especially under the pressures of a conflict, that draws them together to see the situation through to its end. The members of a team, whether in any of the three Services, generally did their level best to win through to a situation that concluded positively. There was accordingly nothing worse than to lose one of the company at any stage of the bid to win through to corporate salvation.

Lt. L Pote's crew had fought their way through arguably the roughest period of 8th AF operations between November 1943 and April 1944. Now, on 28 April the crew was on its 28th and final mission to Oranienburg, and later in the day the bomber circled Framlingham, but was seen to be firing red flares. The

The strike camera from the "offending" B-17 has caught a tragedy in the making. The first of a string of bombs has destroyed the left stabilizer on Lt. M Reid's 42-31540/ **Miss Donna Mae** over Berlin on 19 May. The 94th BG bomber then dropped in an ever-steeper dive before one wing became detached, with none of the ten-man crew surviving the incident.

On 23 May 1944 a *Luftwaffe* "intruder" made a run over Great Ashfield and struck one of the hangars, inside which was **Powerful Katrinka**. The B-17G caught alight and was totally burnt out, so becoming the sole recorded example of an 8th USAAF heavy bomber to be destroyed by direct enemy action on its own base.

Below: Second shot of Katrinka's remains reveals the huge hole ripped in the T2 hangar roof by the Luftwaffe "intruder's" bombs that almost certainly impacted with the B-17 airframe positioned directly beneath.

ground observers assumed that this was in recognition of their having completed their combat tour. Tragically, the flares bore the standard message of casualties on board, in this case S/Sgt. D Means (ROG), who had been killed, an issue that cruelly shattered the crew's eagerly anticipated release from all tension on surviving their tour of duty.

Deceptive Lull...

Airfields in Germany (19th) and V-1 sites (20th) threw up contradictory casualty results for the Division; no losses were borne over Germany, whereas the theoretical "milk run," at least in mission duration, to the Pas de Calais reduced overall strength by four. A similar loss scale occurred next day during the attack on Hamm's marshalling yard complex. All involved single unit casualties, with the exception of the 385th BG, who surrendered two on the 21st. The latest deep penetration run down to Friederichshafen (24th) chalked off a further nine crews, again mainly in singles, for the groups concerned. However, this figure was barely one-fifth of the overall MIA figure of 40 mainly provided by the 1st BD, although fully one-third of the crews concerned landed in Switzerland. One of two group losses, flak damage to Lt. McWhite's 42-31253/552BS ensured the 388th BG aircraft's MIA fate, and it crashed at Ochsenhausen but minus its crew. The third 45th CBW casualty involved yet another 96th BG PFF bomber (42-

97620/MZ: (Capt. J Meacham)), from which all on board parachuted safely.

Three of the Swiss internees came from the 94th and 95th BGs. Lt. R McCullum in 42-97138/XM: suffered engine problems on the bomb run and pulled out of formation towards the south to cross over and land safely at Dubendorf.

Horham's 42-31632/OE: Z, flown by Lt. Wilson, also diverted into Dubendorf, as did 42-31993 /BG: F **Gen'ril Oop** in Lt. Cunningham's hands.

Overall 8th AF losses over the ensuing three days continued to be gratifyingly light at fifteen B-17s and B-24s. Of specific interest was the "double header" flown on the 27th. V-1 sites were assaulted during the first strike, while airfields and marshalling yards in France and Belgium were targeted the second time around. The 3rd BD actually bombed Le Culot and Middlekerke airfields as targets of opportunity.

The next 24 hours only involved a small scale 1st BD mission to Avord airfield, but the respite granted the 3rd BD in particular was to be followed by the latest heavy rebuff, with the 385th and 447th BG elements of the 4th CBW most in the firing line...

Big B's Latest Grim Haul

The Nazi capital's industry was focused upon again, and 218 Division crews out of 679 in all took off and assembled as the central element of the bomber stream, albeit in a dangerously strung-out manner that precluded any chance for adequate escort cover. The wayward manner in which the 4th CBW proceeded towards the target added to its crucifixion. Loss of PFF functions on the CBW Lead bomber, coupled with equal loss of visual contact with the stream, meant that as Magdeburg loomed up the sub-force was out on its own. Whether or not the several fighter formations that latched onto the Wing had been deliberately directed by Ground Control was to prove immaterial to the American airmen as battle was joined around 1100 hours.

The 447th BG had dispatched an A and B group, and both were regularly harassed in the roughly 40 minutes over which the attacks extended. Brunswick became the epicenter for three and possibly four losses. Parsau, north of the city, was where 42-37868, flown by Lt. Blom, descended. Weferlingen, Abbenrode, and Destedt lie adjacent to one another outside Brunswick's southeastern boundary; Lt. C Dowler's 42-102421, Lt. W Donahue's 42-37866, and 42-31144, flown by Lt. H Hughes, found their respective last resting places there. Whereas only two crewmembers lost their lives on Donahue's B-17, only single survivors emerged from the other two aircraft. (Sgt. Shrimp (RW), on Dowler's crew, passed out as he was donning his parachute pack with the bomber beginning to go out of control and regained consciousness to find himself under close guard in a military vehicle!)

As the frantic action ground on, 42-102479/ **Mississippi Lady** (Lt. E Farrell) and 42-31124/ (Lt. W Davidson) were knocked down to crash near Eickendorf on the approach to Magdeburg, where a further rash of losses occurred, two of these involving a full rate of crew survival. Lt. A Peper brought his B-17G/42-31161down for a successful crash landing close to the city, while similar good luck attended Lt. H Paris and crew, who cleared their burning bomber (42-31217) shortly before it blew up over Eggenstedt. A reverse fate awaited all but one on board 42-97501 **Gum Chum** (Lt. E Johnson). There was the cruel likelihood that a flash-fire within the fuselage almost certainly burned up most if not all the parachute packs according to Sgt. J Kotualk (Eng.), who floated down at Burg-Bei-Magdeburg.

Hey Mabel! (42-97135) had suffered fire in the fuselage and one engine and other assorted damage; five gunners bailed out after the B-17 dived out of formation, but the fires were extinguished following recovery into level flight. A northward course for Sweden was briefly entered upon, but this hope was violently terminated near Oranienburg after flak batteries engaged their lone target as it unfortunately emerged from the cloud cover. The five airmen still on board joined their colleagues in captivity, although Lt. C Marcy (P) suffered a severe injury to one hand as well as facial burns.

Eleven B-17s failed to land back at Rattlesden, but one of these was resting under the North Sea with its crew on board an ASR Launch; 42-31519 had been ditched by Lts. McGuire and Ken Anderson (CP), and not only was the sea surface almost becalmed, but their aircraft floated for a sizeable time

A bomb crater close to two 385th BG aircraft is further mute testimony to the attack on Great Ashfield. Little or no damage appears to have been inflicted on either B-17G.

The 486th BG flew missions with the B-24 between mid-May and mid-July 1944. H8: E has suffered a heavy crash landing that will reduce her to "Category E"; the fuselage split directly behind the cockpit was an unfortunate and regular structural weakness whenever the Consolidated bomber was "bellied-in."

period before finally disappearing, so allowing a properly executed deployment of both life rafts.

Grim Centennial

The 385th BG was not only flying Wing Lead, but was also on its 100th mission.

The occasion's positive significance would be marginalized by the battering the group was to endure, however, because for seven crews there were to be no celebrations back at Great Ashfield; rather, there would be incarceration in a Stalag for those fortunate enough to live through the experience.

As with the 447th BG, so its companion unit found itself assailed by waves of fighters extending to between fifteen and twenty. The weight of *Luftwaffe* weaponry simply swamped the attempted defensive response by the American gunners, apart from which elements within the formation reportedly manoeuvred to either avoid the fire or the chances of a mid-air collision, and in doing so made themselves even more vulnerable.

The punishment began to tell as Brunswick was being bypassed. Ruhen, close to the city, received the wreckage of 42-31133, although Lt. H Garza bailed out everyone on board; around the same time 42-97559 was cut out of the group to ultimately descend near Helmstedt with a single member of Lt. R Barney's crew. The bomb run into Magdeburg took out two more bombers: 42-31174 flown by Lt. F Hart and 42-97226 (Lt. R Huntingdon), with only three fatalities among the twenty airmen. The low fatality rate was maintained by the remaining three MIA crews—three out of thirty. Lt. I Sexton got all his nine colleagues safely out of 42-107045, and Lt. C Johnson suffered one loss in 42-31773, which crashed at Gleidingen, and double this figure died on board 42-97078 (Lt. W Henry).

The 4th CBW's final MIA tally was twenty when the 94th BG came back two light, being Lt. McGluskin's 42-102520/ TS: and Lt. K Chism's 42-31498/QE: X **Passionate Witch**. Elsewhere four other groups lost eight in total, while a further 35 crews were lost by the other two Divisions.

45CBW

42-31393/560BS **Snafu** sadly lived up to its name when it went down over France, having taken terminal flak punishment; Lt. D Walker (P) was the sole fatality among the crew. Also absent from Knettishall thanks to flak strikes was 42-37980 / 562BS (Lt. J Covner), whose demise in Dutch territory was not matched by anybody on board. The 452nd BG suffered three MIA aircraft, all 729BS assignees. Lt. H Nelson (P) became one of five evaders from 42-39920 **Karen B**, but only three of the other five survived as POWs. Lt. G Haakenson's 42-39981 **Section 8** crashed at Lieren, in Holland, with all ten crew also ending up as POWs. The luckiest crew today was on 42-31784, flown by Lt. Suckow, which the pilots successfully ditched for later pick-up by a launch.

13CBW

Two of the three CBW losses affected the 95th. BG. **Flagship** (42-37988/ET: M) delivered all ten, led by Lt. H Vilberg, safely before crashing. The other crew also survived; 42-31320/ QW: **I'll be Around** was another B-17 that disappeared under the North Sea. Flak had inflicted damage that included the loss of half power, and the bomber was held aloft until ditching became necessary. Lt E Leaser's crew took to their dinghies to await their POW fate. *Big B* was still living up to its fearsome reputation as a "graveyard" for the 8th AF!

Final Reinforcements

Up to the beginning of May the Division's complement of groups available for operations stood at nine, but during late March and into April its ranks had been swelled by the arrival of the 34th, 486th, 487th, and 490th BGs. (A fifth group, the 493rd BG, was ready to move to England in early May.) This welcome upsurge held a logistical sting in the tail—all five groups were equipped with B-24s!

To the logistical problems accruing from operating two distinct aircraft designs within the same Division was added the distinct flight characteristics of the B-24 compared to the B-17.

By the early spring of 1944 camoflage was steadily giving way to natural metal finish (NMF) on 8th AF bombers. This 452nd BG B-17G named **Avenger III** demonstrates the revised scheme. Assigned to the group in March, it survived combat operations for some six months; then it was downed at Ludenscheid during a mission to Mannheim, but all nine on Lt. B Latici's crew bailed out.

The expression on the nose of this B-24J-165-CO admirably sums up the feelings of airmen from the 34th BG, if not on all other 8th AF units. The mission tally is applied to the armor plate that was sometimes added after bombers arrived in Britain. This aircraft was later transferred out to the 466th BG at Attlebridge.

The Consolidated bomber held a definite advantage in speed and bomb-carrying capacity compared to its contemporary. On the other hand, the aerodynamic qualities of the slim Davis wing were limited in efficiency when the B-24 was flown in tight formation. Then, too, the power turret added to the nose, as well as other extra equipment applied to the B-24H and J variants assigned to the new units, gave the pilots a measurably more difficult task during a mission. For example, if the aircraft's attitude was other than slightly nose-down it left the controls rather "heavy" to handle, so imposing inordinate physical strain on the pilots. In time the authorities would order a wholesale conversion to the B-17; in the meantime, the new clutch of groups would tend to be dispatched to separate targets, sometimes in concert with the 2nd BD.

May 1944
The "Plan" Gathers Pace

The Transportation Plan aspect of heavy bomber operations started to kick in as May commenced, albeit very slowly,

The black and white checkerboard design on a mobile Runway Control trailer towed behind a Dodge vehicle bypasses two B-17Gs at Lavenham. The discarded nose canopy from a bomber adorns the roof to form an observation platform.

D-Day saw the introduction of the 493rd BG to combat operations, and **Baby Doll** (42-50554/L) was on hand from the early days at Debach. In August the B-24J-1-FO suffered damage thanks to a crash landing.

although the B-26s and A-20s of the 9th USAAF were fully engaged in this vital function. A double mission was flown on the 1st, although the first foray for the 3rd BD involved its units assaulting V-1 sites. The second run saw all three Divisions dispatching reduced numbers that in the Division's case omitted the 4th CBW, with three marshalling yards targeted. Operations during the next 48 hours were restricted to GH-assisted missions by elements of the 2nd BD, which was directed against V-1 sites. However, strategic issues were still the priority to judge by what transpired up to the 8th.

Berlin was again the focus of attention (4th), but only for the 1st and 2nd BDs, apart from which the mission proved abortive thanks to layered cloud patterns. V-1 sites absorbed more punishment from the 2nd BD over the next two days, with the accent on GH-assisted operations and with the 93rd BG continuing to provide this PFF facility. Then it was back to Berlin for both B-17 Divisions. The mission was conducted using PFF equipment, and more positively—for the crews at least—a minimal casualty rate of eight out of over 550 attacking aircraft. A single 96th BG bomber fell into this category, along with one from the 385th BG. The former group had now flown the last ten missions for the loss of

Ice Cold Katie has "mounted" a preceding B-17 on the Rougham perimeter track; the result is the excision of most of the other bomber's left wing structure. **Katie** was later transferred out to the 379th BG, but finally returned home within the ranks of the 457th BG.

Left: The 5,000th B-17 to be constructed at Seattle since Pearl Harbor is apparently anonymous as regards serial number, but is already a distinctive airframe, with employees adding their signatures to the liberally scrawled-upon airframe surface. She was tuned out in late May 1944 and dispatched to the 8th AF.

Below: The same B-17G is seen in March 1945, albeit no longer anonymous. The serial is 43-37716 and code letters BX: H confirms her assignment to the 96th BG with the name **5 Grand**. However, an element of the signatures is obliterated by the 45th CBW color bands on the fin and rudder. (Later removal of the central fin "advertisement" screen had conversely permitted further signatures to be applied thereon.)

only two crews, but if those Snetterton personnel still on hand from the start of 1944 harbored any hopes, however tentative, that Lady Luck was directing herself in their favor, two of the ensuing five missions would pronounce harsh judgment upon such an outcome...

The 45th CBW was allotted the center slot in the Division stream but got ahead of itself, and unfortunately was squeezed out of position by the time the formations had crossed into Germany and were traversing the Duemmersee (Lake Dummer) a prominent navigation point due north of Osnabrueck. The A group consisted of a revised unit limited to fourteen instead of the normal minimum of eighteen, plus two PFF B-17s, and was assuming Lead for the CBW's A force; a further sixteen bombers with one PFF aircraft made up the B group. It was then that the latest martyrdom of the 96th BG commenced its grisly course.

The A Group PFF Lead had previously aborted and Lt. J White's 42-97631/ MZ: took its place. This B-17 was one of the first to be mortally afflicted by having an engine set on fire that resisted all attempts to be extinguished; the pilots eased out of formation and the landing gear was lowered. A further pass by fighters culminated with the bomber exploding, killing White and two other officers, including Maj. Shoemaker, with the other eight airmen surviving. Another initial casualty was the B group leader 42-39998/QJ: N, with Capt. M Shoesmith at the controls. It was seen to peel out of formation, and may well have been attempting a solo run home, since Resthausen, where the aircraft crashed, was some way off to the left of the stream's course. At least all ten airmen were floating down by parachute beforehand.

Lt. Nisworger was piloting 42-97782/AW: E, which had the added misfortune to be run into by an Fw190 reportedly piloted by Ltn. L Muenster, a 95-victory *Experte* with 5/JG3. The pilot did not survive the resultant disintegration of his B-17, but this occurred only after seven crewmembers had either responded to the bail out bell or were fortunate enough to escape the blast when still on board. The bomber's remains came down at Kirchlinteln, close to Verden, where White's aircraft lay. (There is a mystery regarding Muenster's involvement in this incident. He *was* killed on this date, but German records indicate he had rammed a B-24 while his fighter's crash location was at Wollersheim, at least 60 miles to the southwest! The fact that the 96th BG was to join with the 2nd BD in attacking Brunswick would appear to bear out the German-based assumption, since the return route would have almost certainly been over the region where the Fw190 came down.)

The area around Verden collected at least three more B-17s beginning with 42-102444/QJ: **Smilin' Thru**, piloted by F/O L Green, which tumbled to destruction at Retban. Hiddestorf was where 42-97403/AW: U came down, with only two members of Lt. M Faucher's (KIA) bailing out, compared to all on the other crew. Down at Holtorf was 42-102525/BX: R, with Lt. C Birdsey (P) one of eight dead crewmembers.

At this stage the stream was angled northeast with a future right turn for the run-in to Berlin. In contrast, the 2nd BD had been assigned to attack Brunswick, which currently lay to the southeast. It was probably soon after losing its initial clutch of crews that the 96th BG appeared to have maintained contact with the B-24s and diverted towards Brunswick as well. One more crew went down during this leg. Lt. F King's 42-38062/BX: U suffered severe damage to the rear fuselage, including much of the control surfaces being shot away. In spite of this parlous state, the pilots managed to keep control, although in a descending manner that finally ended in a crash landing at Ostenholz, north of Celle; King later suffered a leg amputation, but nobody was killed.

The bomb run was hardly completed when Lt. H Eye's 42-102482/QJ: A was culled from its position and fell into a dive with its left wing ablaze; both pilots brought their charge back into level flight and finally brought off a crash landing at Wolfenbuettel, on the outskirts of Brunswick, albeit at the immediate cost of their lives, while a third crewmember

The fire-blackened right fin and rudder belong to one of two Sudbury B-24s involved in a midair collision during Assembly for the mission of 20 May 1944. Ten of the airmen involved in the incident lost their lives.

died later in hospital. The homeward leg was barely under way near Hildesheim when yet another B-17 succumbed to fighter pressure; this was 42-102451/BX: T, flown by Lt. G Sterler, who ended up with Sgt. E Muszynski (TG) as the sole survivors before his aircraft piled in at Sehlem. The MIA tally reached double figures shortly after with Lt. J Fitzpatrick (P) one of nine killed when 42-38190/QJ: K exploded and fell to earth at Lindhorst, close to Hannover.

Reluctant Dragon (42-38133/AW: O) should have become the third 337BS loss after it was badly shot up, and in fact six of the crew did evacuate their seemingly doomed aircraft during the air battle. Lt. J Musser, along with Lt. Flanyak (B) and T/Sgt. Leon Sweatt (Eng.), held their nerve and their posts while the fourth remaining crewmember lay dead at his waist-gun position; several hours later the B-17 was taxied into its dispersal, there to await removal to a hangar for repair and return to combat. (It would finally be lost on 30 November 1944; nor would Fate be any kinder to two of the three airmen who had brought her back this day.)

A quartet of Framlingham bombers went down along with a single 100th BG aircraft. Lt. O Miller (P) and one other crewmember failed to survive 42-31603/CC: N **Belle of the Brawl's** final descent over France. Half of Lt. T Hammond's crew flying 42-31913/FC: **ETO-Itis/Shy Ann** also lost their lives, although the pilot survived. The nine-month veteran 42-3498/FC: L Red **Head/Hap's Hazard** ended her extended combat career in the worst manner for all of Lt. J Son's team, none of whom came through alive after fighters dispatched the B-17 at Ostenholz, midway between Hannover and Hamburg. **Mary Lou** (42-39911DI: N), flown by Lt. W Simmons (POW), was also culled by the fighters, although eight crewmembers ended up as POWs.

Lt. Valesh (100th BG) earned the dubious reputation of "writing off" at least six B-17s, all perversely named **Hang the Expense**. This is No. IV, a PFF-equipped bomber primarily assigned to the 96th BG but attached to the 100th BG. This incident occurred on 18 May 1944, and the ripped-off right landing gear and flap confirm the bomber's salvage status.

A waist gunner on **Betta' Duck** mans his .5 for the benefit of the cameraman. Although he is seen in full flight gear the picture is taken on the ground as confirmed by what looks like a stack of "Jerry Cans" in the background. The open waist window layout on this B-24 variant was displaced by fixed Plexiglas frames on subsequent production batches.

The sole 4th CBW loss from among the other five Division crews involved a Lead crew from the 385th. Lt. A Drobysh, in charge of BG 42-31786, suffered a runaway propeller on No. 3 engine following "bombs away" and dropped out of formation. The propeller soon became dislodged and sliced into the fuselage, fortunately without injuring anybody, but cutting into the forward compartment's electrical system. The straggling B-17 was temporarily joined by a P-51, but several minutes after his departure in the vicinity of Bremen a *Schwarm* of Fw190s loomed up and launched a head-on attack, which spelled the end of the road for their victim. The pilots held their doomed bomber aloft long enough for all on board to bail out and end safe, but rounded up and incarcerated in Bremen itself.

"Carpet" Cover

Although the *Luftwaffe* could still deal out severe punishment, its efforts were now largely restricted to intercepting bomber formations bereft of escort cover. Flak, on the other hand, was being encountered in ever-growing strength, whereas some form of gunnery and evasive action could be indulged in against the enemy fighter force, there was very little the bomber crews could do other than plough on through the barrages thrown up by the ground gunners. This was especially the case during the run-up to the target. Remarks by some Briefing officers regarding flak as a "deterrent" were largely greeted by amusement bordering on cynicism by the combat crews; they knew full well that even if mortal strikes were avoided by the bombers even a near miss could exact a lethal effect upon the crews thanks to the myriad shards of shattered metal from each burst.

The Germans employed *Wuerzburg* radar ranging sets with which to predict the bombers' altitude and course, thereby providing the flak batteries with the necessary information to cast up an accurate barrage. Conversely, *Carpet* was an electronic transmitter created by the British that radiated "jamming" signals on the same frequency as *Wuerzburg*. The equipment had been in USAAF service since late 1943 after assignment to the 96th and 388th BGs, but up to now appeared not to have been used on operations to any degree—a surprising omission in view of the burgeoning numbers of heavy-caliber flak guns being deployed over the major German cities, as well as the anticipated routes flown by the bomber streams. However, a major delay in its implementation had occurred; this was due to the slow supply pace of the individual Army Radar Transmission sets (APT, the P denoting radar equipment). Only at this time were sufficient sets on hand with which to jam the complete frequency range on which the *Wuerzburg* equipment operated. (*Chaff* was being, and would continue to be, regularly used to create a basic "screen" effect for the formations, but the clouds of aluminium strips ultimately lost their effectiveness as they fluttered downwards.)

The two consecutive runs to Berlin in May had followed the same final approach route to the city, but it was only on the second occasion that *Carpet* was deployed. In spite of the fact that the entire stream took 14 minutes to traverse the target area compared to the 10-minute run the previous day, the USAAF Authorities later established that the scale of flak damage was materially lower.

Two of the three days after the 8th entailed mass assaults upon airfields and marshalling yards across France, Belgium, and Luxembourg, while the third day (10th) had resulted in an abortive effort to head into Germany; Mother Nature had again successfully intervened, regardless of the comprehensive range of technical support available to the 8th AF in assembling and dispatching its strength.

The Nazis' Achilles' Curse

The search for key industrial resources whose destruction would create an incurable haemorrhage in the Nazi war effort had by Spring 1944 been correctly, if belatedly switched from ball bearings to oil. So it was that on 12 May the bomber crews were directed against a clutch of synthetic oil plants at Merseburg, Lutzkendorf, and Zeitz, and in the 3rd BD's case Zwickau and Brux in Czechoslovakia. All of these targets lay deep into southeastern Germany or its occupied Czech neighbor, so any thoughts of a "milk run" were firmly held in abeyance, and with good reason.

Nearly 300 B-17s formed the Division's quota, with the 45th CBW heading for Zwickau—and one of the worst beatings handed out to such a sub-force during the entire Campaign. Fully twenty-seven of the 41 crews lost this day would come from its ranks. In addition, the 447th BG would contribute seven out of a 4th CBW MIA total of eleven.

Snetterton's Nadir of Fortunes

Despite protests, the practice of reduced-size formations was still in force at Snetterton Heath, with 26 B-17s split between A and B groups. Whether or not a standard-sized pair of sub-forces would have fared any better in the light of events is ever open to question. The bald truth was that the *Luftwaffe* held most of the cards when confronted solely by their *Big Friend* adversaries. All initially went well with the mission as the stream headed towards the Rhine. But matters went badly awry for the CBW as it was in the Koblenz/Frankfurt region.

A sizeable group of single and twin-engine fighters (the latter involving Me410s from II/ZG26) launched a series of attacks extending over 20 minutes. The first wave reportedly took out both Lead bombers and the A Deputy as well. Four days before Capt Knupp and Col. Lemley had aborted while flying the same function. Now, 42-97654/MZ: and most of its crew would be handed no similar reprieve; half the right wing was sawn off by cannon shells, and the resultant tight spiral held all but the pilot and one other airman in its centrifugal grip until the impact near Bad Camberg. Capt. J Link's Deputy B-17, 42-97167QJ: N, took all but Lt. F Risckelman (N) with her in her terminal dive. Then, the B group Lead machine 42-97567 /MZ: F absorbed a lethal blast in the nose compartment that killed Lt. T Moore and his co-pilot, and only four of the eleven crewmembers managed to bail out, the bomber crashing close to Wiesbaden.

A further clutch of crash sites in between Wiesbaden and Frankfurt involved five crews. **7th Son** 42-107189/QJ: M (Lt. R Simons, KIA) came down at Dauborn, and 42-31343/BX: (Lt. R Lewis, KIA) was downed at Usingen, along with 42-107123/BX: (Lt. H Tucker, KIA); the death toll between these three aircraft reached 70%. Enemy action was responsible for all losses so far, but the next two occurring in the B group were self inflicted, and involved that bogey of close formation flying, and one that seemed to inflict the 96th BG more than most groups—mid-air collision. The aerial disintegration of 42-31343 was the probable reason why Lt. H Moore (POW), flying 42-102452/AW: R, swung sharply out of its path. Lt. Hon (KIA), flying 42-97382/AW: K, took similar action, and the two B-17s made fatal contact. Eight airmen cleared Moore's doomed machine, but only one gunner was similarly blessed on the other aircraft; both wrecks littered the ground near Wehrheim.

Lt. J Musser had brought his badly damaged B-17 back from the disastrous Berlin mission four days before, but this time round he was destined for a POW camp. His B-17/42-31718/AW: T appeared to have survived the series of attacks, but eventually the scale of damage forced the pilots to carry out a forced landing near Vogelsberg; two crewmembers were already dead, and the injury to Musser's hand, as well as that inflicted upon one of his gunners, merited their later repatriation in March 1945.

Another early casualty was 42-102571/QJ: U, flown by Lt. R Lawrie, and in which Lt. C Jones (N) made an instinctive gesture that would save his life. After the attacks commenced he clipped on his parachute pack. During a subsequent attack the B-17 lurched violently and fell out of control, whereupon Jones headed for the forward hatch and bailed out to become one of only two survivors.

The ghastly toll was completed with a duo of losses. Lt. C Filer was badly wounded, but endeavoured to hold 42-31621/BX: **Stormy Weather** aloft, despite progressive engine failure and loss of a stabilizer. Sadly both pilots perished, along with three gunners when the bomber finally went out of control. Lt. W Kinman held on course for the target, but the damage to 42-31014/AW: A **Smokey Stover Jr.** ultimately proved too great and the entire ten-man crew bailed out. The 96th BG's latest martyrdom was completed, and there was no guarantee that this horrendous scale of punishment would not again be visited upon the luckless personnel; indeed, May operations would involve another notable reversal for the group, although nothing akin to today's scale.

Deopham Green Travails

The sufferings of the 96th BG since the beginning of 1944 were to be roughly paralleled within the 45th CBW by the 452nd BG as experienced on this mission. The group had already taken

The more expansive nose area on the B-24 compared to the B-17 lent itself to more generous artwork; this was particularly the case when applying shark mouth designs as seen here on 42-94953 **Misanthrop**, a 490th BG bomber.

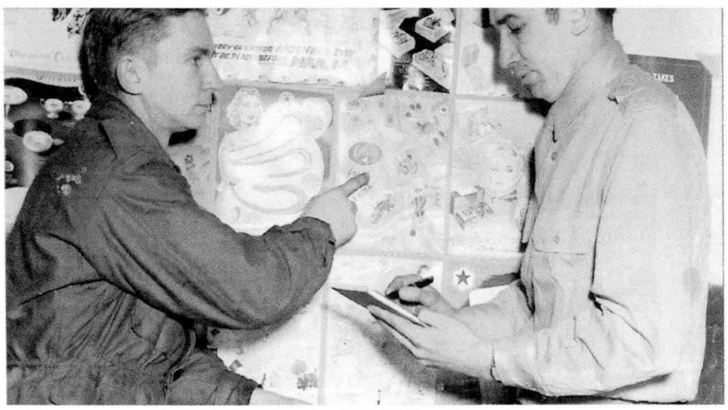

Mother's Day was well attended to by the personnel at Snetterton Heath. In the first picture a large group of airmen are crowded round the table where the two seated individuals are handling each order. In the second the selection of a specific card is being made by the individual on the left.

several severe handlings since commencing operations that had each cost between four and six crews, but today would witness by far the worst scale of unit punishment (14 crews and 16 bombers lost) that even exceeded that borne by its fellow group from Snetterton.

The bulk of the casualties were again incurred in the Koblenz /Wiesbaden / Frankfurt region. The worst affected squadron was the 728th, with five out of a final loss figure of eight B-17s. Lt. Hochstetter's crew safely cleared 42-97209 close to Frankfurt, while 42-97361 **The Punched Fowl** also came down near the city at Ohren to leave six survivors out of Lt. Halbleib's team. Buedingen and Buedesheim formed the final resting places for 42-97371 **Hairless Joe** (Lt. Atkinson) and 42-107089 (Lt.Slanin), but only three crewmembers from the latter B-17 were killed out of the twenty in all. Merzhausen, well north of Frankfurt, proved to be the last resting place for 42-97864, albeit not for Capt Patrick and crew.

Further destruction was impressed upon the group at this point. Half from Lt. Naylor's crew on 42-97235/ 729BS failed to survive the final crash at Taunus, and 42-37947/ 730BS **Princess Pat** (Lt. Davis) came down at Dachsberg, yet another location near Frankfurt, albeit minus the entire crew. Further west at Bad Kreuznach, south of Wiesbaden, lay the wreck of 42-39940/ 731BS flown by Lt. Jameson; 42-97786/ **The Hardway**, the second 729BS B-17 to fall, was down at Koblenz with Lt. Thomas (P) one of six survivors. A third squadron casualty involved 42-97143, which was shot down near Wicher, and from which only two of Lt. Stogsdill's crew emerged alive.

Another 50% survival rate among the ten airmen was realized on 42-39939/ 730BS **Duchess**, flown by Lt. Homer, which crashed at Ruedersdorf to become the second of three squadron losses. The second of the 731BS' share in the MIA figure was incurred at an earlier or later stage, since its crash site was at Liege, in Belgium; 42-39941 **Lucky Lady** had been claimed by flak, but at the cost of a single member on Lt. Noble's crew killed, while two of the other nine evaded capture. Mechanical problems were credited with the third squadron loss when all of Lt. Martin's crew on 42-39976 **My Achin' Back** joined the lengthening tally of USAAF "Kriegies."

Few details of the crew on board, or the precise fate of 42-39937/ was on hand, but it was another 728BS loss. The squadron's penultimate loss involved 42-97094/ **Why Worry** in Lt. Ward's hands, which was sufficiently battle damaged for a successful ditching and subsequent ASR Launch pick-up to be brought off in the North Sea. A near-perfect second ditching involved 42-31345 Lady Stardust II, also 728BS, from which nine of Lt. Eastman's crew emerged alive.

4th CBW Fortunes

The 94th BG had sent up 27 crews, six of whom formed part of the 447th BG formation. The main sub-force went to Brux and came home light two B-17s. Attacks upon the group commenced around Frankfurt, with massed assaults from ahead that included rocket-firing Me410s. Lt. W Williams, flying 42-102584/XM:, began dropping back after one pass, and the last seen of the aircraft was of its heading down on fire with parachutes popping out. Then 42-31704/QE: P also eased out of formation to be finally dispatched at Bad Orb, along with two on Lt. W Walker's crew.

In the twisting melee of lunging fighter manoeuvres lay the constant threat of unavoidable collision with the American formations, forced to fly in virtually rigid lines of flight in order to maintain group integrity. This was to be the grisly fate for 42-31787/548BS, as well as the Bf109 or Fw190 whose pilot failed to clear the oncoming B-17's path; nine of Lt. Worster's team went to their deaths, as probably did their adversary. A second 385th BG bomber made the return flight across the North Sea, but 42-107109/550BS **Stork Club** was apparently ditched in the Thames Estuary by Lt. Seehuff.

The Rattlesden fliers were assigned to Zwickau and paid a high price for entry when seven B-17s failed to return. Two 711BS crews culled by the fighters were 42-97179, flown by Lt. Pettus, and 42-102395 in Lt. Mandrell's hands; the respective crash sites at Friedberg and Giessen happily ended up fatally only for the aircraft, with all twenty airmen bailing out. Capt W Larson reached the ground alive along with his entire crew after 42-38164/709BS fell to earth, but only a single survivor emerged from 42-107020/708BS piloted by Lt. E Wright (KIA) after it descended near Ailingen. The fifth loss involved 42-107072, a 710BS aircraft flown by Capt. K Johnson (POW) and Capt. Van Every's 42-97815, also 710BS, came down without the crew.

Six group aircraft had gone down over Europe, but the seventh team suffered a greatly different range of experiences after Lt. Moses (POW) ditched 42-31794/ 709BS close enough to the enemy coastline for he and two others to be captured. Of the remaining seven two were killed, one evaded, and four were recorded as "Returned," a reference to airmen regaining friendly soil.

13th CBW

The 13th CBW escaped with relatively light casualties (three), including two from Thorpe Abbotts. Lt. A Kinder's 42-31504/ LD: E **Rosie's Riveters** suffered two disabled engines, one of whose propellers was windmilling; the combination of power loss and drag finally impelled the pilot to bail out the crew south of Koblenz and near the Rhine river resort of St. Goarshausen. The other flak-affected bomber was 42-97127/XR: J, flown by Lt. J Moore, and from which he bailed out himself and the eight surviving crew. The third CBW loss involved a six-month veteran Horham aircraft, 42-39884/ ET: N, in which Lt. E Jablonowski lost his life, along with seven of his crew.

Another *Big B* Cull

Oil was back on the target selection menu next day, but not for the 3rd BD, which was dispatched to hammer marshalling yards at Osnabrueck; nine groups comprising 199 bombers in all struck the Primary with a single loss from the 447th BG. The Primaries for the 1st BD remained inviolate thanks to adverse weather conditions, unlike Tutow's aero industrial plants, which were hit by the B-24s. A G-H strike at V-1 sites (15th) was the sole 8th AF mission over the next five days before the formations were directed towards Berlin on the 19th.

The full weight of the B-17 force, twenty-one groups in all, was directed against the capital, with the 2nd BD going in against Brunswick. The current domination of the 8th FC against its adversary did not prevent the *Luftwaffe* rising in strength and culling a proportion of the 28 bombers failing to return to England. This statistic was roughly shared between the Divisions; nine was the 3rd BD's element, with the 100th BG sacrificing one-third.

The 100th's loss was the third in successive days and was incurred in a 1-2-3 order. On the way back a group of fighters intercepted the 13th CBW over the Baltic. Lt. M Rupert, flying 42-38191/ in the group's rear ranks, was taken out near the western edge of Denmark's Lolland Island. The eight still

Elmer Fudd was the inveterate cartoon enemy of Bugs Bunny and his lisping voice usually uttered the main words of the artwork in such manner; the expression along with Bugs astride a bomb is painted onto 2C: J, a Ford-built B-24H assigned to the 487th BG. The undulating camoflage demarcation line was a feature on Liberators produced by the Ford Company.

Four of the seven B-17Gs have just released their bomb loads, unlike the remaining three; the resultant bomb pattern is likely to be somewhat dispersed. Bomber in the center arrived at Deopham Green 24 hours after D-Day and soldiered on with the 728BS until New Years Eve; then it became one of two MIA aircraft, although eight of Lt. Traynelis' crew ended up as POWs.

surviving airmen answered the bail out bell as the burning B-17 threatened to go out of control; this was despite being over the sea. The descent into the water left just one crewmember alive and three bodies that were subsequently picked up at sea or washed ashore. Lt. R Horne's crew on 42-97607/XR: H was last seen heading northwards, but the bomber was then shot up by several Fw190s. The damage was apparently sufficient for the pilots to carry off a ditching out of which the entire crew scrambled into the life rafts and paddled some miles to land on Danish soil; all were in German hands within 24 hours.

A second group ditching not only left the crew alive, but able to return to Thorpe Abbotts; Lt. J Rogers brought his 42-37807/LN: O **Roger's Raiders** safely into the North Sea's ever-uncertain embrace despite having serious engine problems and losing the tail section in so doing. The life rafts were broken out and paddled clear but the proximity of the crash site to the Danish coast, allied to the loss of all emergency equipment, did not promise a return to friendly shores. The daunting odds did not dissuade the crew from taking up a course for home. They plied their solo route until, almost two days later, an ASR aircraft that was responding to the report of another homeward bound B-17 made a successful drop of the motorized lifeboat it was bearing. Then, during the westward journey two Danish fishing boats were met, whose crews took them aboard and (perhaps naturally) indicated an eastwards direction for the Americans. However, what could be described as persuasive "friendly fire" from the 8th FC fighters now circling the scene in turn persuaded the fishermen to sail for England!

"Self-inflicted Wound"

Two crews were lost to causes other than flak or the *Luftwaffe*, one of which belonged to the 94th BG. It was an absolute article of faith that during bombs away all bombers had to hold firmly on course; any deviation was likely to cast up the prospect of being struck by bombs. **Miss Donna Mae II** (42-31540/XM: B), bearing Lt. M Reid and crew and flying in the Lead squadron, was observed to edge underneath a string of 1,000-lb bombs released by one of the aircraft in the High squadron. The first of these hit the left stabilizer to leave the remnants hanging vertically. The aerodynamic imbalance did not throw the stricken B-17 into a spin, but rather sent it into an increasingly steep dive that culminated in one wing tearing off. No parachutes were seen before the aircraft was lost to view, and in fact nobody did escape alive (the grim incident was caught on the offending B-17's strike camera).

The 100th BG nearly added a fourth B-17 to their MIA tally in a similar incident. In this case the extremely close trail of five 1,000-lb bombs from a 94th BG aircraft dropping past 42-38047/EP: O **Fever Beaver** and the almost simultaneous descent of one stricken bomber out of that unit (certainly **Miss Donna Mae II**) towards the 100th BG machine forced violent evasive action upon Lt. J Massol. A flak-damaged engine that caught fire but was happily extinguished, and further terminal damage to a second engine inflicted by fighters on the way back left the straggling bomber to finally regain Thorpe Abbotts alone; however, it then required major repair work that included a replacement wing, two engines, fuel tanks,

Two Elements from the 96th BG are making well-formed and stately progress above a semi-solid cloud layer. The steady transition from camouflage to silver finish aircraft during 1944 is well illustrated. Two of the three B-17s in the latter category also bear the more functional Cheyenne tail turret that displaced the "wedge-shaped" unit seen on the other bombers.

and a rebuild of the radio room. More positively, a return to operations witnessed it attaining by VE-Day the second highest mission tally for a surviving 100th BG aircraft at 125.

For the 452nd BG the mission began negatively during Assembly when a 388th BG aircraft collided with 42-38145/730BS **Rosilie Ann**; the pilots managed to keep her airborne and brought off a crash landing at Old Buckenham but lost two crewmembers. One group crew closed out their combat tour over Europe, but all ten airmen survived the loss to flak of 42-39990 **Junior**, flown by Lt. Gaal. Single losses by the 95th, 388th, and 390th BGs ended with happier outcomes for two crews. Horham's 42-97290/BG: H **Smilin' Sandy Sanchez** won through to Sweden where it was force landed at Akesholm, while the Knettishall team led by Lt. W White flying 42-107160/562BS **Little Joe** survived a ditching. The 95th BG crew were particularly fortunate to gain neutral territory since their B-17 had gone into a flat spin that was only corrected close to the ground. Even then their situation was perilous because only two engines were still operating. All excess equipment, including the ball turret, was jettisoned, but the lone bomber was very fortunate to evade enemy attention; further hostile attention came not from only from German, but also Swedish coastal defenses, and the crippled B-17 was slid into a crash landing by Lt. S Waltham close to its intended destination of Ystad airfield.

Marshalling yards (20th) and the same target source as well as airfields (23rd) claimed the Division's attention, while sandwiched in between was a run to Kiel (22nd). Of interest was the inclusion of the 486th and 487th BGs' aircraft as part of the 2nd BD's strike against airfields on the 23rd. Losses between the three missions totalled a mere three, although single crashes borne by both groups during take-off and Assembly on the 20th proved to be doubly tragic due to the mission being abandoned.

The Lavenham loss on the 20th highlighted the unpredictable fortunes involved in operations that faced every combat crewmember. Lt. F Goethe's 42-52743/4F: M had developed engine problems shortly after take-off, and the resultant bid to regain the airfield failed with the aircraft smashing into the ground at Long Melford. Normally, the result would have been a massive explosion that would leave nobody alive; in this case, although five were killed outright and a sixth died later, the other four airmen were either thrown clear or managed to haul themselves clear of the wrecked fuselage. A proportion of the bomb load that had been fortuitously scattered around did explode but with no effect upon the survivors.

Berlin Bites Back – Again

Over 600 B-17s were assembled to make the latest tilt at *Big B* on the 24th, with airfields around Paris assigned to the 2nd BD.

Heavy contrails further impeded progress already made difficult by heavy cloud formations. The *Luftwaffe* was waiting as the formations crossed in over northwest Germany and angled down towards Berlin. Although less than 100 made contact with the stream, a sizeable proportion did latch onto one group that was still isolated long after experiencing Assembly problems—the *Bloody Hundredth*. What now transpired was the fifth out of eight such disasters to afflict the Thorpe Abbotts aviators during WWII...

The Low group's Low squadron was focused upon from behind, and four bombers were dispatched in relatively quick succession around the Hamburg region. First, 42-102648/XR: L piloted by Lt. R Roeder broke into three sections when it was struck by simultaneous fusillades of fire from behind and to one side. Prior to the disintegration the ball turret gunner's door had broken away, so he climbed out of the turret; in a cruel twist of fate, when the B-17 broke up the radio operator was thrown out without his pack, whereupon the BTG grabbed his unfortunate colleague's pack! He was only one of four to survive his aircraft's loss that ended with a crash at Seulfeld/Itzstedt, due north of Hamburg, and Lt. Roeder dying of his wounds. The same area witnessed the loss of 42-102624/XR: (Lt. C Johnson, KIA) with one fewer survivor out of the ten on board. Berkenthin, near Ratzeburg, some twenty miles NE of Hamburg, took possession of the remains of 42-102528/XR: O **Times A Wastin'** bearing Lt. H Jesperson's crew, who were averaging 16/17 missions—unlike their mount, which was indulging its first mission. Half the crew were killed either prior to or during the bomber's violent disintegration under the hail of gunfire. What was noted as Rothenhain in the MACR but was more likely Rothenhusen, near Ratzeburg, supplied a grave for 42-102635/XR:, along with all ten of Lt. M Hoskinson's novice crew.

Two of the other five losses occurred in a more piecemeal manner, beginning with **Nelson King** (42-31306/LD: V). This B-17 had survived the loss of much of its vertical stabilizer on 6 March. On this mission its airframe was riddled with cannon shells and bullets, and it finally went out of control to crash near Silmersdorf, southwest of the Muritzsee; Lt. Siewert (P) died along with two of his crew. The next aircraft to be culled was almost certainly 42-97095/LN: Y, which came down at Friesack, slightly NW of Berlin, and located under the stream's approach route; Lt. D Pearson lost only one crewmember during the incident.

The B group Lead B-17, 42-97845/LN:, contained Capt. J. Geary on his second tour accompanied by Maj Fitzgerald (350BS CO); also on board was Lt. J Harris, who had been permitted to resume operations after returning as a Swedish internee off the first *Big Week* mission. A close flak strike immediately after bombs away put the first nail in the bomber's coffin when one engine was knocked out. The diminished power level caused the aircraft to straggle, and all too soon come under sustained aerial assault. Finally, when about halfway between Berlin and Hamburg a fuel tank erupted in flames and all on board bailed out over Parchim, a night-fighter airfield. (The subsequent march through a village after being rounded up left the airmen very grateful for the protection of the German military from the clearly enraged civilian throng assembled along the streets.)

The B group Lead had been taken over by Lt. F Malooly, flying his 27th mission with his equally veteran crew in 42-31534/LN: N **Powerhouse**, but his assumption of responsibility proved to be short lived. A burst of 20-mm fire riddled the aircraft and the right wing swelled up on fire. The plane finally exploded as the crew were jumping out, but all miraculously survived, albeit with facial burns in some cases caused by the flames streaming back past the rear hatch. Goerike, SW of Wittstock, was where the B-17's fragments descended. Berlin was barely cleared when the litany of group disaster was completed with the loss of 42-31941/LN: W **Big Stoop**. Lt. L Williamson's charge was flying off Lt. Malooly's wing as No. 3 in the element, but was reported as drifting out and down. Bueckwitz, near Wusterhausen, was the B-17's crash site, but although all ten airmen were reported to have bailed out only eight won through alive to a POW camp. The *Bloody Hundredth's* tithe of nine crews constituted two-thirds of the Division's overall losses.

Overlord Looms

The final week of May was taken up with missions on six of the seven days, the majority of which, as far as the 3rd BD was concerned, tended to favor the Transportation Plan brief. Marshalling yards were the primary feature on the 25th, 27th, 30th, and 31st, with a smaller scale strike launched on the 30th; gun batteries on the French coast involved single CBW-strength forces (25th and 26th), along with V-1 sites (30th). Oil plants were struck on the 28th and 29th, while airfields and aviation industry sources merited CBW-strength attention (27th and 30th). During this period 32 crews were listed as MIA, with the most expensive missions surprisingly not the runs deep into Germany on the 28th and 29th. As it was, the highest individual unit loss was incurred by the 390th BG during the first-listed mission against the oil industry, although the currently luckless 96th BG would be close behind in terms of suffering.

Doomed Endeavor

T/Sgt/ Leon Sweatt was a combat veteran with the 96th BG who had assisted his pilot, Lt. J Musser, to bring home a badly damaged bomber on 8 May. The strain of indulging in regular operations was revealed in his correspondence, as was his willingness to face the ultimate sanction—death. Two excerpts serve to illustrate his frame of mind, and perhaps by extension the thoughts of so many of his contemporaries:

> 13 May – (to his parents, concerning his wife and baby son): "She (Pearl) writes me every day – all about Charles and the things he does. He's getting to be quite the boy….I know he will be spoiled, but who cares?...I've had some experiences during which I was certain my time had come, but I wasn't afraid; I kept praying that I'd live to fight again. There are better men than me giving their lives all around me. It's a job to do and we are doing it….Men here don't stray too far from their God with such death all around. I've made my peace and if it's my time, that's all there is to it."

A happy event in the midst of turmoil. Lt/Col. A Moffat (Ground Executive) addresses the audience on the occasion of the 96th BG's 100 Mission party. The top table includes (L-R) Gens. Fred Anderson, Carl Spaatz, and Jimmy Doolittle, with Col. J Travis (Group CO) on Doolittle's right; and former CO Archie Old is far right. Date was 1 April 1944, and even harder times were ahead for the Snetterton Heath fliers.

> 25 May - (To a friend in Texas): "I've seen an awful lot of things I hope to forget, and I've had some experiences that have aged me about ten years....I'm not afraid of death, I've faced it too often. There's only one thing that can help you at such times, just lots of prayer and faith in the Lord to take care of you wherever you are....There are no hypocrites or atheists in these places. You'll turn these planes into chapels coming home....By being here, doing what I am doing, I feel like I am keeping my boy from this same thing years from now. (A sadly unrealised hope in the light of post-War events such as Korea and Vietnam). You people at home keep buying War Bonds and help all you can. We can do the fighting....hope this thing winds up over here and we'll be home again soon."

Snetterton's Persisting Hoodoo

The travails of the 96th BG during the first five months of 1944 had not only been incurred thanks to enemy action, but to a degree were self inflicted. In that period of time a sizeable number of crews had been involved in separate midair collisions, while one had been bombed out of the sky. On 27 May twenty-one crews were briefed for yards at Karlsruehe, with a further six assigned to attack locations at St. Valery en Caux on the French coast.

The main group sub-force assembled in good order and was holding course as the French coast near Dieppe passed underneath. Lt. J Borkowski's 42-102515/ BX: J was in the Low squadron Lead position, while ahead but close at hand was Lt. J Ziegler piloting 42-97269/ AW: U as No. 1 in the Lead squadron, and having Sgt. Sweatt on board as a "spare." Suddenly both bombers were seen to come together after coastal flak speckled the sky, resulting in BX: J apparently taking evasive action upwards and to the right. The fatal embrace that ensued saw both aircraft catch fire with BX: J whipping into a vicious spin and AW: U breaking apart. Of the twenty airmen involved only two from Borkowski's team survived the event. For Leon Sweatt, today's mission was the tragic culmination to hopes of living out his life. (An arguably worse situation would affect his wife; she was initially informed that her husband had actually ended up a POW and was only cruelly disabused of this positive outcome fully six months later.)

One such self inflicted incident was bad enough, but a second was fated to occur as the group was approaching the target. Both B-17s concerned were flying in the Low squadron, with Lt. W Brean's 42-102475/BX: in No. 2 position and Lt. C Irving flying 42-102561/AW: D as No. 6; among Irving's crew was Lt. J Flanyak (B), who had also flown with Lt. Musser and Sgt. Sweatt during the 8 May mission. Once again no direct enemy action appears to have created the coming together of the two bombers, whose fuselages both split apart to tumble to destruction near Pforzheim. Three from Brean's and four from Irving's aircraft respectively bailed out to face captivity. Lt. Flanyak joined Sgt. Sweatt in making the supreme sacrifice, as did the remaining twelve airmen from these two crews. Four crews wiped out without enemy intervention was a particularly hard blow to an already beleaguered bunch of airmen. As it was, the high tide of severe losses for the Snetterton aviators had unknowingly peaked, although with thirty crews lost by the month end, there was no way in which this favorable situation could be anticipated.

The single biggest unit loss during May's final week occurred at Framlingham, with five of the twelve Division losses on the 28th. Fighters were credited with four B-17s, two each from the 570 and 571BS. Ebendorf, just north of Magdeburg, was where 42-31985/DI: P **Devils Aces** (Lt. Ingram) came down along with seven crewmembers; Lt. Mathias, in charge of 42-32089/DI, by contrast got himself and his crew clear from the B-17 before it went in at a location stated to be Holzhausen. (Which one is unclear, since there are nearly thirty towns bearing the title where the crash occurred.) The other affected sub-unit lost 42-37806/FC: Z **Starks Ark** flown by Lt. H Holmes (POW), which was downed near Walternienburg, albeit with just one fatality, while 42-31651/ FC: G **Decatur Deb** flown by Lt. H Strate (KIA) crashed in Madgeburg, with the same dead/survivor rate as **Devils Aces**.

The majority of Division losses in the same period involved single group crews, but on three occasions a 45th CBW unit surrendered two. For example, on the 28th flak took out Lt. Feljsted's bomber 42-39845 **Hulchers Vultures** over Wiera, north of Frankfurt, but all ten airmen safely evacuated their doomed machine. Flak also downed 42-102485/ R **Bare Essential** over Holland, as well as killing three of Lt. Coddin's crew, so excising two teams from Knettishall's strength. Next day, 42-97549 **Round Tripper** and 42-97808 were removed from the 452nd BG's inventory. Again both were flak victims, with all of Lt. F Brogan's team bailing out over France, as did Lt. Lowell's crew over Belgium; four of the former group of airmen managed to evade capture, but both pilots were among those heading for a Stalag.

MIA statistics – 3BD

Month	Number
April	134
May	128

10

FORCING THE PACE

Third in Line – First among Equals

"The Crusade"

For several months, the key question exercising the vast majority of minds within the Anglo/ American military ranks was "When will the Invasion occur?" The answer to this very necessary action to end the Fascist tyranny scourging Europe was almost on the point of being presented. The bomber crews had played a part in softening up the enemy's communications and thereby hindering their ability to respond swiftly during the initial few days following the planned landings on the Normandy coastline between Caen and the approach to Cherbourg. As June began the 8th AF focused wholly upon the interdiction of road, rail, and airfield links on the approaches to where Operation *Overlord* would commence.

The B-17s and B-24s only began June operations on the 2nd with a relatively small scale assault on railway facilities and airfields in central France, followed next day by attacks on coastal defenses and other military targets in the Pas de Calais. The third successive day's concentration on tactical locations involved a "double header" assault spread between the Pas de Calais and in and around Paris that saw nearly 1,000 individual sorties dispatched. The continued concentration on similar sources on the 5th must have had the combat crews quietly convinced that these assaults were building up to a climax of some sorts, with the invasion as a firm favorite. There was little or no way of knowing that the entire Operation's intended launch date of 5 June had been postponed, as it transpired, for a further 24 hours due to the ever-shifting weather front streaming in from the Atlantic. Even as the bomber formations were returning to their airfields, the first elements of thousands of American, Canadian, and British troops already loaded on to their appointed vessels watched the mooring ropes being cast off and a southwards course for France steadily taken up across the choppy, seasick inducing Channel waters—*D-Day* was finally on!

Support Strike

The 8th AF's part in *D-Day* was to consist of two missions; the first would be intended to provide close support to the invasion forces. This would take the form of a massive saturation of the German defensive positions immediately behind the five beachheads immediately prior to the myriad of landing craft disgorging the first wave of infantry, tanks, and field guns.

All airfields had been sealed off, and the availability of sidearms at some bases was yet another indication that something momentous was pending; in addition, Lead crews were already in the know, having been briefed prior to midnight. Even so, the awakening of the Main Force personnel in the early hours of 6 June was nothing out of the ordinary, since it was the norm rather than the exception in terms of beginning a mission procedure. It was only when the Briefing officers at every heavy bomber airfield pulled aside the map covers that the full import of the day's mission became apparent.

Take-offs began between 0200 and 0300 hours, with the units forming up and following a zigzag series of courses in order to assume the correct position within the stream. The final target run-in by the Divisions was made in a parallel manner so that the defensive positions would be struck simultaneously. However, the hoped-for swamping of the gun batteries did not largely come off since the bulk of bombs landed too far inland; ironically, this was later ascribed to the bombardiers holding up release of their loads in order to ensure no "short bombing" of the landing beaches occurred! (A further diminution in the overall weight of assault happened when nearly 700 crews from the overall force either did not bomb at all, or in a small number of cases sought out targets of opportunity around Argentan, located well inland from the beachhead zone).

As it transpired, the landings proceeded in sound to good order apart from on *Omaha* beach, and even there

A recumbent combat crewmember tucked into his bed forms the artwork for **Sack Happy** (42-97873/Y), assigned to the 563BS at Knettishall on 1 June 1944. This B-17G was finally the victim of a crash after take-off on 24 February 1945, but at least the entire crew were spared their aircraft's terminal fate. The officer appears to be wearing a backpack parachute kit.

the initially parlous situation that almost had Gen. Bradley deciding upon its abandonment had seen a resurrection in Allied fortunes by early afternoon. A second mission dispatched later in the day involved 782 crews compared to the 1800 sent out on the first strike. Once again, there were many crews who did not bomb thanks to the persistent heavy cloud patterns, and the sense of being involved in a momentous historical event was overtaken by disappointment if not a feeling of anticlimax in the minds of many combat crewmembers. The *Luftwaffe* had been conspicuous by its absence, and only six bombers were lost this day. However, two of these involved a midair collision affecting the 493rd BD—a tragic manner in which to commence the group's operational career—while the 34th, 389th, and 490th BGs each lost one B-24 between take-off and crossing out over the English coast. The remaining loss was a 487th BG aircraft to flak.

"Helton's Hellcats," as the Debach-based 493rd BG were to be known, had sent out 36 crews, but experienced difficulty in assembling in the heavy cloud conditions, with one squadron only linking up around the IP. As it was, the continuing solid undercast caused the mission to be aborted. It was all the more tragic that the collision occurred after the group had emerged into clear airspace at their altitude. A wing tip on one B-24 struck the tail-plane on a second bomber and both descended into the undercast, with the latter aircraft beginning to disintegrate. A single member on Capt. G Cooper's crew in 44-40471/863BS somehow scrambled clear, but none of Lt. D Russell's ten-man crew escaped the demise of 42-94789/862BS.

Tactical Concentration

D-Day's advent signalled a concerted bombing assault by the 9th USAAF and 8th AF for ten out of the next eleven days. The overwhelming strength of the Anglo/American Air Forces during these operations was clearly reflected as far as the American "Heavies" were concerned. The overall MIA figure was a mere 39 out of more than 10,000 individual sorties, ten of which belonged to the 3rd BD. Road and rail communications stretching from St. Nazaire, on the French Biscay coast, to locations in Belgium and Holland, along with airfields across the same geographic divide were also regularly hammered. Enemy reinforcements, with armored vehicles in particular, were forced to run the gauntlet of bombers, fighter-bombers—the latter including rocket-bearing RAF Typhoons and USAAF Thunderbolts—and suffered both irreplaceable losses, as well as serious delays even when equipment gained final access to the Normandy battle front.

An extra bonus for the bomber crews related to these missions; not only did they involve relatively short flight

The use of parachutes to arrest the progress of an aircraft suffering brake failure was a regular occurrence. Here B-24/42-94942 **Why Worry? II** has ground to a safe halt at Mendlesham thanks partially to the retarding effect of the parachute canopy that can be seen slowly deflating.

Purty Baby adorns the nose of B-24J-155-CO 44-40299. The bomber arrived as part of the original 493rd BG cadre based at Debach. It was crash landed at Woodbridge Emergency airfield on 25 June 1944 and subsequently transferred out.

times over hostile territory compared to the general pattern when flying into central Europe, but the current pace at which missions were being flown was likely to bring about a swifter end to a crewmember's combat tour compared to past individuals' experience. The previous average of at least six months required to complete the mandatory figure of 25 or 30 missions would be reduced in some future cases to as little as two or three months, at least up to the autumn of 1944.

Comment

The low rate of losses at this or any stage of the offensive tends to detract from the stark fact that a combat crewmember could and did regularly face the prospect of being killed or injured (or in some instances traumatized even when physically unharmed) in other than a direct combat scenario. Aircraft crashed on take-off or landing; some developed fatal mechanical problems during Assembly, forcing their crews to jump for their lives if able to do so; midair collisions during this same stage were a third feature of what came under the generic heading of "operational" incidents, as were aircraft lost on practice or other non-combat sorties. Equally tragic, albeit pitched in a more anonymous manner, were the individual cases of combat crew returning with their bomber who would never see the conflict's conclusion since they had been killed during the mission in question—not only by fighter gunfire or flak, but arguably and more pointlessly by inadvertent misdirected fire from another bomber's gunners.

During the forementioned period in June 1944 an ever-distressing number of aircraft slotted into this loss category, as was instanced on 6 June. Within the 3rd BD's ranks alone, two B-24s came down over English soil with fatal results for thirteen airmen. On the 8th the Division suffered one MIA loss; however, a 486th BG B-24 and 388th BG B-17 tumbled from the sky during Assembly with only several survivors successfully exiting the Sudbury-based bomber. Loss of one's life, limbs, mental health, or freedom was hard enough to absorb in the face of the enemy's counter action—how much harder must it have been when the crisis arose without adversarial intervention.

Fernnachtjager Menace over Mendlesham

There was another threat to the Allied bomber crews in the form of *Fernnachtjager* ("Intruder") attacks, an issue that thankfully remained largely latent during WWII. The use of I/NJG2's Ju88s and Do215s in this role over England during 1940/41 had been halted by Hitler; his reasoning was that the German people would be more heartened by actually witnessing the destruction of RAF bombers rather than relying on reports of distant success, however genuine these might be. (The fact that the successes were actually not large did not detract from the sense of unease among RAF airmen regarding their chances of falling prey to the *Luftwaffe*, especially on return from an operation.) The RAF in turn had not been so reticent, and by 1943/44 was regularly indulging in similar operations, with the Beaufighter, and latterly the superlative Mosquito, as the almost perfect instruments of torture to be visited upon the *Luftwaffe*, particularly in its own National backyard.

On 22 April 1944, in a rare example of creative mayhem, a mere handful (four) of Me410s from V/KG51 had played Hell with the 2nd BD's B-24s as they headed in towards or circled their various airfields in the dark following a late-day mission to Hamm; the number of bombers either directly brought down by the fighters or who crashed during their landing runs ran into double figures.

The 34th BG had participated in the battering of airfields and bridges in between Nantes and Tours. It was the group's 13th mission, and an unknowingly grim portent for what was to befall three crews. The mission had only commenced around 1500 hours, and it was very late in the evening with rather overcast conditions on hand when the crews finally approached Mendlesham. Suddenly, the ROGs began to receive information about "bandits in the area"; the pilots were

This 447th BG B-17G has over-shot the runway of what is believed to be RAF Sutton Bridge in Lincolnshire. Aircraft was declared "Category E" on 10 July 1944.

Two B-24s of the 486th BG are snapped at the point of bomb release, with a smoke marker issuing from the bomb-bay of the bomber on the right. The group converted to the B-17 in late July when the group code letter changed to W.

further advised to disperse and seek landings further west. As it was, a proportion of the B-24s still had their navigation lights on when the *Luftwaffe* struck.

Lt. H Eastman had taken off as a "spare," but had been required to complete the formation. His bomber 42-52738 (391BS) was assailed and brought down to crash into an equipment hut; Sgt E Irwin (WG) alone scrambled out of a waist window and parachuted to safety. Lt. S Brain, flying Element Lead in 41-29572, had witnessed Eastman's fiery demise off his right wing; he switched off his navigation lights and made a bid to clear out of the way by dropping down to minimum altitude. His efforts quickly proved to be fruitless, as another fusillade of fire impacted with his bomber and set it on fire. Despite being at a perilously low bail out altitude all ten airmen did seemingly get out, but two of their number were later found dead near the crash site at Nedging, some 10 miles southwest of the airfield. The third total loss involved 42-94911 **Sweet Sioux**, flown by Lt. W Dreher and located in the group Lead element. T/Sgt. J Blackman (Eng.) recalled that some three passes in quick succession directed from below finally set the bomber on fire. This time seven crewmembers evacuated the aircraft before it slammed into the ground just two miles east of Mendlesham. (The reference to gunfire from underneath could indicate the presence of Me410s rather than later reports of the attackers being Ju88s, although the unit involved has never been confirmed; the former design was equipped with flexible machine gun barbettes on the center fuselage that swiveled up and down.) The night's casualty list culminated with a crash landing at Eye (490th BG) by Lt. O Hanson flying 42-52696 following a culling from the rear of the High squadron that fortunately ended with no fatalities. (Sadly the pilot's lease on life finally ran out the following 30 November along with three of his crew.) Although the 8th AF never flew many missions that culminated with a return in the dark, it did launch numerous missions before the full resumption of daylight—conditions that would have suited "Intruder" operations perfectly.

There was one hitherto conflicting aspect of the incident that has finally been corrected. Heinz Roekker, a former *Luftwaffe* night-fighter *Ace* with the highest number of successes for a surviving *Nachtjagd* airman, has often been credited with being one of the pilots taking part in the attack. He has assured me that this was not the case, and that the sole such sortie he was involved with over British soil occurred against RAF Bomber Command in March 1945!

B-24 Fortunes

The initiation into combat of the 493rd BD was the final one borne by the five Division groups operating the B-24. The first had been the 486th and 487th BGs, whose simultaneous debut was 7 May; then the 34th and 490th BGs went out on the 23rd and 27th May, respectively. MIA losses during May had been low at nine overall, but as ever this statistic was not shared out evenly, with the Lavenham-based group suffering no less than six.

The 487th BG's fourth mission on 11 May saw the formation pounded by accurate flak in the vicinity of the target zone, whose effect soon told on the Lead B-24. Flying in the right seat to Lt. F Vratny was Lt/Col. B Ley Jr. (group CO and CBW Leader), upon whose order all eleven airmen vacated their stricken bomber. The pilots had vastly differing experiences. Col. Lay ended up as one of four evaders, whereas Vratny, after enjoying similar initial good fortune, ended up in Fresnes Prison, Paris; from here he became one of the group of Allied airmen transported to, and very fortunate in all but one instance to survive the horrors of Buchenwald concentration camp. Their mount, 41-29468/2C: B, buried itself in the ground.

Fortune by contrast deserted all but four of the other twenty MIA airmen. The Deputy Lead bomber 42-52763/2C: was crash landed by Lt. E Brodsky, but only he and two others scrambled clear before the bomb load erupted to kill the seven still unable to follow suit. The third flak-torn machine (42-52444/2C: A) was sagging downwards with an engine and forward fuselage on fire when an explosion separated one wing, and only one gunner on Lt. L McCleary's crew survived the aircraft's disintegration by being blown clear. Completing the day's misfortune was the loss over England of 41-29481/4F: C, which crashed near Chicester, but not before all on Lt. J Duncan's team were floating down under their parachutes.

The other three group MIA losses during the month were incurred singly between 28 and 30 May. However, the targets in question—Luetzkendorf and Polelitz's oil refineries and Muenster-Handorf airfield—were much deeper into hostile territory and could be expected to exact a toll; this was particularly the case when attacking Germany's oil production industry, since such key targets were heavily ringed with flak batteries.

Getting Lost – At One's Peril...

The chances of losing visual contact with one's group was all too easily realized, especially when given the often cloud-strewn airspace over Western Europe. This was what happened to Lt. E Sechrist and crew flying in 42-3114/BI: G on 8 June, but with far worse consequences than normal. The solid blanket experienced on take-off from Framlingham persisted right up to 30,000 ft, and then no other bomber from any unit came in view. The navigator was then asked for a "fix" that presumably led the pilots to believe they were still over England or its coastline, and a descent through a convenient break was carried out—only for the single B-17 to become the target for flak gunners located on a French airfield when cloud cover was finally broken at 2,000 ft! This unfortunate miscalculation proved fatal for the bomber, which was quickly reduced to a flying wreck; the bail out order was flashed, but Sgt. Helps (TG) proved to be the sole fatality either before or after the bomber exploded and fell at Maissemy. (Sgt. M Ruta (LWG) not only evaded capture but ended up fighting with the Resistance.)

Tactical Concentration

Tactical support continued apace in the days immediately following D-Day. The solid escort "umbrella" coupled with the *Luftwaffe's* inept reaction ensured bomber losses were minimal. In the Division's case it lost eleven MIA crews in the course of seven missions up to 17 June. On the other hand, this statistic was not evenly shared out, as the 493rd BG well knew, since a further three B-24s, all 561 BS, were added to the three lost between the 6th and 8th. Laon/Athies airfield was struck by 39 aircraft on the 14th. Flak fatally crippled 44-40460 **Won Long Hop** flown by Lt. F Addy as he attempted a third bomb run; the pilot was the sole fatality, with four of the nine others evading capture. A POW camp awaited all of Lt. O Brewer Jr.'s crew after 42-52750 came down at Steene. Finally, 41-29569 crashed near Debach, killing all ten of Lt. C Heintz's crew. This was the sixth aircraft loss in six missions to date, with eleven more B-24s fated to go down before conversion to the B-17 in early September; thus were the sobering "facts of combat life" brought home to the group personnel.

On 20 July 1944 the 94th BG received its latest aircraft that soon bore the name **Dorothy V**. Its five month service with the 333BS came to an end on 3 January 1945 when it over-shot the runway on return from Fulda and was salvaged. Of interest is the replacement Olive Drab rudder with Medium Green blotching that was a feature on interim batches of the B-17F assigned to the 1st Bomb Wing in 1942/43.

Strategic "Interludes"

Although the vast bulk of missions were currently in support of the Allied armies, there were a few exceptions to this activity, with oil the chosen focal point. On the 15th the 3rd BD was briefed to attack oil production facilities at Hannover /Misburg, an action duly (and gratifyingly) carried out without loss by two-thirds of the attacking force of 267 bombers. Strangely enough no Divisional operations other than for its B-24 element (17th) were again flown until the 18th, when three of the five groups on hand formed part of strikes against several airfields centered round Le Mans.

Hamburg, next to Berlin, held a deserved reputation for sustained heavy resistance to the Allied bomber incursions. Therefore, when two-thirds of the 8th AF strength was directed at oil plants in the city and adjacent Harburg on the 18th the crews' expectations of a rough ride must have appeared justified. Nor were the prospects for the 3rd BD apparently much rosier when it was again dispatched against Hannover/ Misburg. Weather conditions intervened positively and negatively; the *Luftwaffe* made little or no intervention, but bombing results even using PFF proved to be disappointing, with only one quarter of the force dropping on the Primary and the rest seeking targets of opportunity. Losses were small at three out of an 8th AF figure of eleven.

The power of the Allied tactical forces to interdict the German's effort to reinforce the Allies' Normandy bridgehead was probably sufficient to justify these deployments of the 8th AF away from their primary duty in assisting the Allies' thrust into Normandy; after all, there were sufficient units within the 9th USAAF and the RAF's 2nd Tactical Air Force (TAF) to maintain the pressure upon their adversaries without the weight of the heavy bombers, whose presence was an added as opposed to a necessary factor in this operational equation.

The 19th saw the continued involvement of the 8th AF in ground support operations, as well as assaults upon V-1 sites, the latter activity being even more urgent now that the V-1 offensive had commenced on the 13th. However, the strategic aspect of operations was ever on the horizon, as the combat crew discovered the next morning. The need to destroy the German oil producing capacity was deemed central to the parallel need to win the conflict against Nazi Germany. So it was that a number of oil-related targets were on the briefing maps, with the 3rd BD heading out towards what was to become the 1944 equivalent of Schweinfurt – Madgeburg/Leuna; in addition, the B-24 groups were separately dispatched to Hannover/Misburg. However, the tactical matter was not ignored, since the 2nd BD sent a proportion of its force to attack the Pas de Calais.

By now the Nazi authorities must have been aware of the mortal threat to their oil industry, but there was nothing to be done other than to defend the locations as best they could. Merseburg

Artist Frank Beresford was busy with his portrayal of a Snetterton Heath B-17G when he received close "backing" from the 96th BG's mascot "Lady Moe." The diminutive North African donkey was brought back at the conclusion of the Regensburg "shuttle" mission in August 1943.

The offensive against Germany's oil industry commenced some weeks before the 486th BG formed part of the force pounding the plant at Lutzkendorf on 28 May 1944. The heavy smoke pall as the Group turns for home would force succeeding units to rely upon *H2X* or similar electronic equipment to achieve a solid strike that might match that achieved through visual sight of the now ironically well-shrouded target.

was a key element in this vital enemy equation and was all too soon ringed by a veritable armada of heavy-caliber flak guns extending to at least 500 in number—a frighteningly formidable barrier for the American crews. If Ploesti had already become regarded as the graveyard of the 15th USAAF, then Magdeburg was destined to enjoy that grim sobriquet in respect of the 8th AF! However, on this occasion the attacking force managed to clear its target with just seven crews failing to regain their dispersals.

Three of this figure came out of the ranks of the so-far luckless 96th BG. Celle was the crash site for 42-97363/AW: N, out of which Lt. W Hunt's nine surviving airmen bailed out. Erxleben was where the other two B-17s descended. The first was probably Lt. H Seefurth's 42-97366/MZ: D, which was taken out by flak to descend in a fiery plume along with its pilot and five of the crew. The other was 42-102612/QJ: U, flown by Lt. R DeBrandis, whose entire crew bailed out; however, the body of Sgt. A Lambrecht was never found, and it was possible that he had become the latest victim of civilian summary justice.

Berlin was briefed for its latest battering on the 21st, with the 3rd BD assigned a combination of an aero-industry plant at Basdorf and locations within the city boundaries as its Primaries. By the day's end over 1100 bombers had dispersed their deadly cargoes within *Big B's* boundaries, but the defenders had culled a still painful tally of 45 crews, ten of which belonged to the 3rd Division, with four of this tally being borne by the 452nd BG. However, two from Deopham Green, as well as Great Ashfield, were among thirteen of the MIA crews gaining neutral territory in Sweden.

Two of the 452nd losses were down to that constant bogey associated with formation flying, collision. Lt. H Lerum's 42-31359 and 42-102662 flown by Lt. E Armm impacted fatally, and out of a total of nineteen airmen only five, including a single example from Armm's crew, ended up as POWs. Flak damage to 42-31810 (Lt. M Anderson) and 42-107036, in Lt. J Sorenson's charge, forced a northern diversion and ultimately successful landings at Sovde and Ringoby respectively for the twenty crewmembers. They were joined by Lts. M Totten and M Lohmeyer's 385th BG crews in 42-3490 and 42-38135, although only seven on the latter team actually arrived alive in Sweden.

Operational Variations

Although the current Divisional strength was split between nine B-17 groups and five operating the B-24, there continued to be occasions where the latter design was assigned to separate targets or alternatively joined forces with the 2nd BD. This was a better operational arrangement, since the flight characteristics

Toll on the High Road to Germany. **Little Warrior** of the 493rd BG has absorbed flak strikes that have caused the fuel tanks to "torch" and envelope the central wing and fuselage sections. Lt. Hanson (P) was one of the initial survivors, but was reportedly shot after landing safely on German soil. Mission was directed against Boehlen's synthetic oil facilities on 29 June 1944.

of the Boeing and Conslidated "twins" were markedly different, with speed and climb rates favoring the B-24—not that the B-17 crews would willingly acknowledge this! On the 22nd the split occurred, with the B-24 units attacking Dreux airfield and a Paris oil dump and the B-17s pounding bridges and marshalling yards around Paris, although the latter constituted targets of opportunity. Next day a succession of airfields east of Paris involved a much-reduced force of three B-24 groups again linked with 2nd BD units, while the 45th CBW struck railway services at Nantueil. The overall cost was four B-17s and two B-24s involving single group crews apart from a pair from the 96th BG.

One of the three survivors from Lt. J Horne's 42-102552/ QJ: J enjoyed several bouts of immediate or ultimate luck. He was Sgt. F Cowan (ROG), who initially found himself totally disoriented when the B-17 went over on its back; somehow, he managed to find his parachute pack and work his way all the way to where the tail section had broken off and bail out. Then he succeeded in drifting clear of the burning target area, although his landing was hard. The third and arguably greatest element of luck occurred after he had gotten into the hands of the Resistance. He was betrayed and found himself incarcerated in Fresnes Gestapo Prison in Paris, from where he became one of the Allied POWs shipped out by train to Buchenwald Concentration Camp—a potentially terminal destination until the party was rescued thanks to *Luftwaffe* intervention.

A strategic/tactical mix (24th) saw the Division dispatching seven B-17 groups to assault Bremen's oil industry, and the 93rd CBW was part of a separate force assaulting French airfields. A third mixed B-17/B-24 force heading for France largely aborted its run thanks to heavy cloud. The current daily run of Division missions was concluded with a "double header" next day. The first involved only B-24 units making a run to two French airfields. This was followed by the available B-17 units heading out for at least six Primaries mainly involving key bridges structures. Over the past four days MIA casualties continued to be marginal at thirteen, with five further crews involved in "operational" incidents on return. Examples in this category included the 34th BG, which wrote two B-24s off its records on the 22nd.

Both pilots were seriously wounded by a flak strike on 42-52759 **Lucille** that killed the bombardier and blew a large hole in the lower nose. T/Sgt. A Gibbons (Eng.) took charge of the controls after helping to get the nose turret gunner out of his now perilous position. Despite having little flying knowledge, and with one engine, both rudders, and most instrumentation disabled on the stricken bomber, he successfully held course for home; even the loss of a second engine that threw the bomber off course by adversely affecting the remaining control surfaces did not foil Gibbons' Herculean work. By the time the English coast loomed up, however, the B-24 was almost stalling out thanks to power diminution in the two still-functioning Pratt

This equestrian event somewhere in East Anglia has an Anglo/American slant; the uniformed rider leading the trio of horses is a member of the 8th AF. American personnel participated alongside their British ally in many sports, even including that peculiarly English pastime - cricket!

Chief Wapello taxies past the Lavenham control tower. The airman emerging from the hatch ahead of the top turret is acting as a guide to the pilots; the lateral vision from the cockpit was seriously restricted thanks to the B-24's high wing position along with the engine mounts.

and Whitneys. F/O F Hayes (P) was assisted to bail out and the others followed suit. Having set the bomber on autopilot Gibbons beat a hasty path to the bomb bay, but had barely jumped clear when his temporary charge lifted its nose and dropped into a spin towards the waiting Channel waters.

The other group aircraft to be declared "Category E" was 42-94782 **Off Limits** in Lt. S Gipson's hands. Loss of one engine over the target was then followed by a second going "out" on the way back. The extra drain on fuel reserves caused by boosting the two remaining powerplants left a dangerously small amount on hand as the B24 was finally approaching the Kent coastline at minimum altitude. The gravel-based soil of Dungeness Point was hardly the best surface on which to attempt a forced landing, but any other option was now waived by the spluttering failure of both remaining engines. The aircraft crunched into the ground and scooped up a quantity of stones via the bomb bay, and undoubtedly suffered major structural damage on the lower fuselage before grinding to a safe halt for all ten airmen at least.

The second mission sent out by the Division on the 25th involved twin aspects of operations. The 189 bombers wended their way to a number of target bridges ranging from south and north of Paris and over towards the area west of Dijon, in eastern France. However, within the ranks was a number of B-17s whose primary function was to drop supplies as well as OSS secret agents to link up with the French Resistance; the code name for this operation was ***Zebra***, and it was not the last time the Division would indulge in this duty variation.

A single day's respite for the 8th AF saw all three Divisions dispatching a joint force of nine groups for what evolved into an abortive strike against supply points for V-1 sites. Better fortune attended the 28th attack on airfields, bridges, and an oil dump stretching eastwards from Paris. The month's final tactical thrust against two French airfields (30th) was limited to an element of the Division's B-24 establishment.

The penultimate day in June involved the 8th AF in a combined mass strike at Germany's oil and aircraft industries. Boehlen's refineries escaped relatively lightly, as only one third of the Divisional force of 179 aircraft reached the Primary. In

Half and Half/42-97940 served at Great Ashfield with the 548BS for just over three months. This photograph confirms her vicious demise near Kentford on 13 Sept. 1944. The forward fuselage was later reputedly joined up with another B-17's rear section, but this seems unlikely in view of the total excision of the radio room.

contrast, two-thirds of the B-24 force that included the 34th, 486th, and 493rd BGs plastered their various locations with Madgeburg as the epicenter. The single loss borne by the 493rd BG over Fallersleben produced a gruesomely dramatic photo of the incident. A gunner snapped 42-94812/862BS Little Warrior as a flak strike ignited the fuel tanks and the stricken bomber lifted its nose abruptly upwards prior to careening out of the formation. None of Lt. J Hansen's crew survived, although the pilot was reputed to have reached the ground alive, his subsequent death presumably occurring at the hands of civilians or military personnel.

Comment

Confirmation that the 8th Fighter Command now largely ruled the skies over Germany was evident in that only fifteen bombers were MIA out of 705 completing the 29 June mission. However, that degree of control related to holding back the *Jagdwaffe's* counter ability to take on the bomber stream at its leisure and over a protracted time period as had been the case up to early 1944. There would always be opportunities for bands of fighters—particularly the dreaded *Sturmgruppen*—to evade detection long enough to visit their terrible firepower upon the unfortunate group in question. To this threat was being added the lurking presence of jet and rocket-propelled interceptors; should these designs become operational in numbers, there was the grim prospect of the Allied escorts who were still conventionally powered and designed at least being taken on effectively and ultimately being thwarted in *their* ability to shield the *Big Friends* from insupportable loss scales. "It's not over until it's over" must have been a phrase on the minds consciously or otherwise of the Combined Chiefs of Staff!

A third of the MIA losses this day (15) came from the Division ranks, with a further B-17 from the 390th BG ditched; this was Lt. R Moody's 42-97830, leading the Low squadron's second Element, which had lost two engines and, having dropped out of formation, was finally put down successfully into the sea at a point just out of sight of the Dutch coastline. An ASR launch arrived on the scene to pick up all ten airmen, and all seemed set for an uneventful return to England. It was then that a twin-engine aircraft reported as a Ju 88 swooped down on the vessel to make a strafing pass that killed two of Moody's crew.

July 1944

The bad old days of minimal operations due to inclement weather conditions were largely long gone by mid-1944 as July's pattern would confirm, with 25 of the 31 days involving some degree of heavy bomber operations. The battle in Normandy was progressing, albeit at a fitful and sometimes painfully slow pace. The natural defensive qualities of the *Bocage* landscape with its small fields and solid banked hedgerows was custom built for resistance operations, and the Germans, as ever, proved masters at the art of inflicting heavy casualties, particularly among the Allied armored units (The "Kill" to loss ratio was later established as 6 to 1 in favor of the Germans as regards tanks alone.) With this factor in mind it was all the more imperative to keep the battle zone sealed off from enemy reinforcement. As at Alamein and similar confrontational battles, Normandy was to prove nothing other than a military "slugging match," where the Allies could afford to lose more equipment and even men than their adaptable and often courageous adversary and still come out ahead in the end. (If Gen Sherman's assertion that "War is Hell" is to be accepted, then the current campaign would prove its crude validity.)

As it was, there was a diversionary aspect to use of the heavy bombers that related to the current V-1 offensive against southeast England. The rain of missiles was by now proving to be arguably more of a threat to civilian morale than a viable means of bringing about any degree of disruption to British industrial output. The mission on 1 July clearly had the threat in mind, but Mother Nature intervened and only one group actually struck its target. Next day featured a larger scale repeat by thirteen groups whose bombardiers went for some thirteen launch sites in the Pas de Calais. These assaults would never do more than marginally

Within less than a month of being assigned to Knettishall's 560BS, 43-37523/J was slid into a field following the 20 June 1944 mission to Madgeburg. Capt. Charles Maring was the pilot, and it is ironic that the following November he was killed over the same target thanks to a midair collision with another B-17.

disrupt the scale of attack; only the advent of structured zones of anti-aircraft guns, fighters, and barrage balloons between the English coast and London would steadily blunt the robot offensive that would finally meet its demise with the physical occupation of the region by British/ Canadian forces in late August.

The interdiction of the ground and air approaches to Normandy largely continued apace from the 4th to the 14th, although the Pas de Calais came in for some treatment in terms of its V-1 locations, and the 8th AF's strategic brief was not totally ignored either. As for the Division, it lost only three crews up to the 8th, a period that included a mission to Boehlen on the 7th, when the 2nd BD had taken 28 losses over Lutzkendorf compared to the Division's loss of two. Nor did matters in this respect deteriorate markedly during the ensuing five days, when Munich was targeted on three occasions. On the other hand, the eight crews downed in assaulting the Bavarian city—of which seven in all from the 94th, 100th, 385th, 390th BG, and 447th BG teams won through to Switzerland—would have vociferously disagreed with this "cosy" situation, happy as these circumstances turned out!

"Pray – in Your Own Time!!"

It was natural for combat crew to utter a silent prayer to the deity, an act which even the most devout religious sceptic would occasionally indulge in. What was not acceptable was to neglect one's duty in doing so. On one occasion the tail gunner did not respond during the routine oxygen check, raising natural concern that he had succumbed to anoxia. However, when another gunner was dispatched from the waist to the tail he found his colleague fully conscious. The reason he gave for not responding was that he had been engaged in praying.

When the mission was concluded the pilot drew the gunner aside and instructed him to go down on his knees and pray; he should only stop when he had accumulated more than a sufficient "clutch" of prayers, so that the need to do so aloft would never recur and he would not endanger himself and his crew in future. The pilot informed his crew that he did believe in prayer, but that the time to indulge one's self was *before* take-off. Anybody caught praying in flight would be removed at once. The moral of the anecdote was "You can knock down a lot more of the enemy by shooting at him as opposed to praying at them!"

Operation *Cadillac*

An interesting operational variation occurred for the second time on the 14th that involved the dropping of weapons, but not upon the enemy. The steady, if sometimes tragically disrupted build-up of the various Resistance networks in France and Belgium had latterly translated into a "secret army" of individuals whose efforts at adding to the disruption of enemy communications in particular was now beginning to bear full fruit. As July progressed urgent requests were submitted for more arms and ammunition to be delivered. Three widely-dispersed drop zones at Limoges, Vercors, and St. Lo had been put forward, and on the chosen date all nine B-17 Divisional units sent out a force of 359 aircraft bearing a total of 3,700 containers. The bombers went in at minimum altitude during final approach to the drop zones and further retarded speed by lowering their landing gear to ensure an accurate drop. All but an estimated 2% of the containers was quickly retrieved and dispersed by the grateful French, who put their contents to good use. This was of particular relevance to the St. Lo assignments, since Operation *Cobra* was less than two weeks away from its

The 447th BG's 42-39886 crash landed on 29 June 1944 and was then brutally pushed off the runway by several Cletracs; the scale of damage either from the crash or the clearance action resulted in the bomber being salvaged. Vehicle in foreground is an RAF transport known as the "Queen Mary," used for moving disassembled aircraft, whether intact or the result of a crash.

inception. Any Resistance activity to back up the U.S. Army's attempted breakout from their positions just north of the town would be more than welcomed, and this upsurge in weaponry would be of great value in supporting such an endeavor.

The next spate of both 8th AF and Divisional daily missions extended between the 16th and 21st, with the emphasis switched largely to missions into Germany. The 3rd BD went to Munich (16th), but had to be content with hitting the Secondary at Stuttgart. A single subsequent tactical mission was followed by two split efforts on the 18th and 19th. On the first occasion the B-24s provided ground support to the Normandy armies, while the B-17s attacked Kiel and an oil refinery at Hemmingstedt. Then next day the B-17 groups went out almost in full force to strike industrial targets that included Schweinfurt; the B-24s were allocated targets in the Saar region, but only a small proportion bombed the Primary at Saarbruecken. Overall Division losses for this duo of missions (eight) were surprisingly light, and even lighter 24 hours later while operating over two targets of dreaded note. The oil complexes at Merseburg and Lutzkendorf were ringed by massive flak batteries, but on this occasion only laid claim to two definite victims, one of whom (41-29561/863BS flown by Lt. Winkenhauser) ditched off East Anglia with all crewmembers saved to return to Debach. Fate would not always be so benevolent towards either the Division or its companion units over-flying these prime targets.

The 34th BG were on the approach to Saarbruecken (19th), and in good order when two aircraft in the Lead squadron inadvertently manoeuvered into each other's path. One wingman eased down to the left while the Lead B-17 rose upwards. It is likely the right wing propellers on the lower bomber 42-51190/18BS **Ann** gouged into 42-94893/391BS **Hells Bells**, whose left wing propellers performed a simultaneous grinding action on its companion in distress. Neither aircraft immediately blew up, but simply began a process of disintegration that extended for some seconds in what one eyewitness described as a "slow motion" scenario. One excised wing was seen to soar upwards with both engines still at full bore before sagging downwards in a falling leaf action. Nineteen airmen had bare seconds or minutes to live as the intermingled wreckage tumbled inexorably towards Schiffsweiler and Friedricksthal.

On board **Hells Bells** Lt. W Hart (CP) and Lt. Blevins, an Intelligence Officer flying as an observer, were extremely fortunate to live through the violent explosion of their bomber. Blevins was badly burned as he was down by the bomb bay about to take photographs, but owed his survival to having his parachute pack in place. Hart was rendered unconscious by the explosion and probably cast out through the fuselage side after it was ripped away by the separating right wing before coming-to halfway towards the ground. Completing the group's misery was 44-40248/391BS **This Above All**, which was brought down by target flak; the undisclosed location over which the surviving six crewmembers jumped must have been in France, with Saarbruecken laying scant miles distant from the Franco/German border, because Lt. E Haggins (P) and four of his crew evaded capture.

A row of parachute-retarded canisters tumble from the bomb-bay of a 94th BG B-17. The date is 14 July 1944, and the occasion is the dropping of weapon supplies to the French Maquis (Operation *Cadillac*) at three widespread locations. The mission involved around 360 bombers.

The fact that the Division was currently enjoying a low loss scale over the six-day July spell (twenty-two crews MIA) concealed the fact that the other two Divisions, particularly the 2nd, were not faring so well. In the same period, no less than thirty-eight B-24s had been culled in the course of two missions, while the 1st BD had absorbed 36 losses in three missions. The first five of the seven remaining July missions for the 8th AF were tactical, and were to witness a continuing overall low loss rate, but the final two would see an upsurge in this statistic for the 3rd BD, with the 100th BG again at the forefront of attention.

Cobra Strike

Two particularly key tactical missions were dispatched on successive days (24th and 25th). The bulk of German armor was still forcibly retained around Caen thanks to the consistent if also wayward British/Canadian Army's pressure applied against the 7th Army; in addition, the steady attrition of that Panzer unit's strength was assisting in the largely unhindered Allied build-up of men and equipment, particularly as regards U.S. resources. After seven long, grinding weeks, the conditions for the U.S. Army units until now stalled-out in front of St Lo to commence an irresistible advance appeared to be on hand. The armor and support infantry and artillery would fan out across the Normandy and Brittany landscape, and in the former instance threaten the 7th Army with encirclement by the elements arcing eastwards to link up with their ally coming down from Caen.

In order to shatter the defenses in front of the U.S. 1st Army it was deemed necessary to assault them with saturation bombing. As regards 8th AF participation, all three Divisions sent out nearly

The 3rd BD provided the force for *Cadillac*, and here the 96th BG is commencing its run for the drop. The bomb-bay doors are open, but the landing gears have not yet been deployed to slow the aircraft over the drop zone.

1600 bombers to soften up the German lines ahead of the launch of Operation *Cobra*. The stream's line of advance was ill-advisedly directed from north to south, instead of a westerly approach that would parallel the American front lines; the resultant degree of "short bombing" that occurred killed some U.S. soldiers, while barely one-third of the B-17s and B-24s released their loads thanks to a persistent ground haze. Bomber casualties at three were spread between the Divisions.

Dugan Wagon (42-94757) was of the seventy-two 34th BG "originals" flying on what was the group's 41st mission. Its regular crew, headed by Lt. R Lindstrom, were not participating, which was a huge stroke of luck, albeit not for Lt. E Harre and his team. A flak strike tore off No. 4 engine and set No. 3 ablaze, casting the lumbering bomber into an incipient spinning motion that was not arrested before it impacted on the ground, killing all ten occupants.

Visibility was better next day, but it proved impossible to maintain clear visibility over such a relatively small target zone, especially with the huge increase in bomb tonnage effectively brought into force—over 3,000 tons compared to just under 1,000 tons. All the planning to ensure a clean strike on the Germans still did not prevent further "short bombing" that added another 110 U.S. soldiers to the death list, including Gen. McNair. Casualties were light, with a 100th BG crew one of the five on the MIA tally.

A minimal Division loss of six occurred on the 21st, two of which came from 96BG ranks as Regensburg's aero-industry was targeted. Fighters put paid to 43-37573/QJ: H, bringing it down at Russenhofen and killing Lt. G Beaudry (P) and two others. Then flak took out 42-32045/QJ: R **Silver Slipper**, which was safely abandoned by Lt. C Quinby's entire team, with the bomber piling-in at Reil, close to Koblenz.

Thorpe Abbotts' Latest Crucifixion

Over the last forty-five missions the 100th BG had seemingly put its "jinx" reputation to bed with just twelve crews declared MIA. But the *Grim Reaper* was not yet ready to relax his specific grip on the group as "Black day" number six now loomed up. Merseburg was targeted two days in succession and proved to be particularly expensive for the group. The first assault (28th) was in its final stages with the stream heading in towards the English coast when 42-32009/LN: X (Lt. A Spear) and 42-97621/XR: P (Lt. Stansbury) came together, with Spear's aircraft, flying in the Low squadron, rising up and striking the other B-17, also positioned in the squadron, with its fin; one waist gunner from the former aircraft somehow bailed out to be picked up from the sea, whereas the other eighteen airmen perished. Nine airmen on a third crew were already down alive, but with two others dead, on German soil. Capt F Mason and Lt. Noble were

The 486th BG holds on for the bomb run through the spent bursts of a flak pattern. H8: G, in lower left, lasted almost six months at Sudbury. On 5 January 1945 it suffered damage that forced a diversion into a continental airfield where it was abandoned for salvage.

piloting the PFF B-17 42-97555/ **Island F for Fox**, which took flak strikes over the target; with fire gaining hold in the fuselage and an engine out the bomber was soon abandoned to its fate.

Merseburg's latest hammering occurred on the 29th with a combined 1st/3rd BD strike by nearly 600 bombers of which fifteen were taken out, all but two from the latter Division. For the 100th BG, post-mission reports indicated that the situation began to deteriorate on the final run-in to Merseburg, with the Low squadron particularly affected by being split up, a situation taken full advantage of by the defenses. However, it is likely that one B-17 was already gone by this stage. Wuelfingerode lies due west of Merseberg, and it was here that 42-31903/LN: T (Lt. Jones) finally descended as a victim of the fighters, with five of the nine-man crew being killed. In contrast, six of the other seven losses were mostly spread in a close-spaced line south of the target. Bad Koesen and Punschrau lay almost side-by-side west of Zeitz. Only one of Lt. J Phelps' crew emerged alive following 42-31723/XR: R **Sparky's** demise at the former location thanks to a flak/fighter combination, while Lt. Clark's 43-37655/XR: fell at the other location along with five of his crew after its despatch by the *Luftwaffe*. A second B-17 taken out by fighter assault and coming down at Punschrau with the same death/survival ratio was 42-31537/LN: S flown by Lt. W Fitzroy (POW), on what would have been the final mission for him and several others. A second duo of B-17s crashed near Mannstedt, west of Punschrau, being 42-107211/ XR: N, whose fate was matched by eight on Lt.Gustafson's crew, and 42-97829/LN: O **Regal Eagle** (Lt.G Steussy); in this case the nine airmen escaped alive.

The final two losses came out of the group's B formation, which had at least struck the target, albeit as part of the 4th CBW, compared to the total failure of A group, whose loads had gone wide. Capt. R Schomp's 42-102667/EP: J/R **Yankee Wahine**, having been mortally wounded by flak, crashed at Kleinebersdorf, near Jena, but all on board were granted the gift of life. The flak gunners had struck home directly or indirectly against at least two of the MIA aircraft, and their malign effect would ultimately bear fruit with 42-107007/EP: B **She-Has Ta** (Lt. W Greiner, POW). The stricken B-17 staggered on for home with a temporary P-38 escort that finally had to break off due to fuel shortage. According to survivors' recollections what was taken for the Channel but turned out to be the enemy coastline skirted by the Frisian Islands became a last resort site for a ditching; all survived the immediate impact, but one badly wounded man was trapped and drowned despite the efforts of fellow crewmembers to get him out of the rapidly sinking aircraft. The potential peril of death from exposure still lurked in the background for the survivors in their dinghies, because it was a full four days before they came in sight of what turned out to be Ameland Island, close to Northern Holland; here they were met by a suitable "reception party" and ultimate transport via Dulag Luft (The *Luftwaffe's* main Interrogation Center north of Frankfurt) to a Stalag.

The one remaining July run (31st) involved another split activity that, in the case of the 3rd BD, saw its B-24 element sent to bomb airfields in France. Meanwhile, ten of its B-17 units prepared to share another "achin' back" thrust into Germany's heartland with the 1st BD, this time striking at industrial resources in and around Munich. The assaults went ahead, with all three Primaries battered at a cost of ten crews MIA, two of whom diverted into Switzerland. The 94th BG came off the worst, with half the Division's loss factor of six, although only one crew fell into German hands. Flak appears to have been the culprit in all three instances. 42-31906/ GL: J, flown by Lt. D N Johnson, took strikes on the bomb run that disabled one engine, and when last observed was descending steadily as the group rallied north of Munich. The final crash at Guenzenhausen, west of Landshut, left six of the nine-man crew alive.

A second flak-stricken bomber, 42-38034/XM: E **Twat's it to You** (Lt. V Lewis), drifted out of position between the target and the Rally Point, but was then headed in a southwesterly direction for what evolved into a successful landing at Dubendorf in Switzerland. The third flak-affected bomber, 42-38007/XM: **Hello Mr. Maier** in Lt. Ellis' hands, held on long enough to get out over the North Sea before being eased into its waters from where all nine airmen were later picked up. (The aircraft's title clearly referred to Hermann Goering and his ill-judged 1940 boast "If a single enemy bomber flies over the Reich then you can call me *Maier*"!)

One of the two 388th BG aircraft "written off" group records was 42-102435, although all of Lt. Crider's crew escaped alive as POWs. A second Knettishall bomber, 44-6090/A **Dangerous Lady**, did not survive the mission, but at least she delivered her crew safely after she was crash landed back at the airfield.

Comment

The diminishing loss scale in bombers and their crews by this point in the offensive must have been heartening to the personnel. On the other hand, the veterans would probably have tempered any sense of a permanent downturn in the future. A good example of the cost to any unit participating in the aerial assaults to date can be gleaned from 94th BG's records. The group entered combat in May 1943 with a force of approximately 40 B-17s that required 400 airmen for their operational function. Up to July 1944 marginally over 1,100 crewmembers had ended up MIA; 122 out of that total had enjoyed internment or made a successful bid at evasion, but the majority had either been killed or taken prisoner. In crude terms the group had been cleaned out of its aircrew establishment up to three times the original figure; to express it another way, in roughly fifteen months of combat it had taken no more than five months to achieve a 100% attrition rate in relation to combat crew strength! It was little wonder that most crewmembers sooner or later developed a fatalistic approach to their combat tours in terms of a successful outcome.

"Aphrodite"

For some time prior to the advent of the German V-1 offensive on 13 June 1944, the American authorities had been investigating the possible use of missile designs using radio control methods. The enemy's robot assaults appear to have accelerated plans on this matter, and on 23 June 1944 Project *Aphrodite* was initiated. However, any comparison with the custom-built missiles in German use—whether the current V-1 basic aerofoil or the even more deadly, if also more indiscriminate V-2 ballistic weapon, as well as the Hs293 and *Fritz X* guided bombs—were pure fantasy. The American response was very basic, in that the "missiles" mooted for use were not new developments, but rather were drawn from the 8th USAAF stocks of redundant bombers.

The Project was handed to the 3rd BD, and the initial order for such aircraft was set at sixty-five, all of which would be "War Weary" B-17F and G Models. All surplus equipment on the first group of ten airframes was stripped out at 1st SAD Honington in order to attain a maximum all-up-weight (AUW) of 32,000 lbs. Then the aircraft were transferred to Burtonwood; here twin *Azon*

The severed tail unit on this B-17G lies some distance apart from the fuselage (left). Cause of the separation was a P-51 that careened out of control and, after cutting through the bomber, burst into flames. The smoking remains can bee seen in the far center. Incident in which the fighter pilot was killed occurred at the 1st Strategic Air Depot (SAD) Honington on 30 July 1944.

The 490th BG heads out on a mission; three of the B-17Gs in this shot are from the 851 BS, whose bombers bore a + sign ahead of the aircraft letter. All bear red bands to the top of the vertical fin as a group insignia.

receivers were installed and attached to the autopilot. Further refinements were the inclusion of antennae and an automatic radio altimeter. The bomb bay was strengthened with cross beams in order to accommodate the planned explosive load of some ten tons of TNT. Four "Mother" aircraft also fitted with *Azon* equipment were on hand to conduct feasibility tests, not from Burtonwood but from Bovingdon, west of London, where the volunteer crews were provided with the necessary flight training, along with target and route navigation instruction. (Almost needless to say, all radio control trials of the "Baby," during which stability problems arose, involved pilots in the cockpit!)

The focus of target attention was fixed firmly upon the various massive bunker constructions within the Pas de Calais that were intended to house the latest of the Germans' *Vergeltungswaffe* (Revenge Weapon), the V-3. On 7 July the "Babies" and their "Mothers" transferred to Woodbridge; TNT was the content on board nine B-17s, with the tenth bearing jellied petroleum. However, Woodbridge's primary function as a Master Diversion airfield on whose surface crippled aircraft normally descended increased the risk of a disaster should one careen out of control and impact with an "Aphrodite" aircraft. Consequently, on 12 July the deserted airfield at Fersfield, further inland, was selected as a base.

The first four sorties were launched on 4 August with a view to striking at four specific sites in the Pas de Calais. Due to the perceived limitations of radio frequency no more than two "Babies" could be dispatched at one time. On board the two selected B-17s were Lts. Fain Pool and Fischer, whose efforts would be the first of seventeen individual sorties, although the fortunes of these officers would be tragically different. Pool experienced no problems in bringing his explosive-laden aircraft into the position where it could be taken over by the "Mother" controller before he thankfully vacated his cockpit seat along with his fellow airman. Fischer, in contrast, faced a serious problem, in that his B-17 developed an unstable flight attitude, the final outcome of which was for the aircraft to go into a spin; although his fellow airman did bail out Fisher was not so lucky, and was killed in his attempt to vacate his charge, which rammed into the English countryside with an enormous impact. Although Pool's bomber had been properly evacuated, its progress towards the intended target failed in the end, because it went out of control and crashed northwest of Gravelines.

Goering's nightmare plagued the Nazis for over nine months following its assignment as BX: G at Snetterton Heath on 17 October 1943. From there it was transferred to the 390th BG and finally the 486th BG; on 21 July 1944 it cracked up on landing as the severe nose damage attests to, and was promptly salvaged.

The nose wheel unit on the B-24 was often unable to withstand the heavy pressures placed upon it, especially if the landing was hard. In this instance a Mendlesham-based aircraft has performed the "handstand" action and come to a safe if undignified halt; several vehicles including a fire truck and an ambulance are in attendance.

LN:W's time at Thorpe Abbotts was relatively brief. Assigned on 16 May 1944, she was written off group records on 13 July 1944, almost certainly as a result of this runway over-shoot.

On 31 July 1944 **Easy Queen** (862BS) made an emergency landing on Brenzett airfield in Kent, following a mission to bomb Creil airfield north of Paris. The Consolidated-built B-24J was brought back into service and later transferred to the 490th and 466th BGs; she ended her days with the latter group in early October.

The mission of 28 July 1944 to Merseburg was not a good one for Thorpe Abbotts. Not only did three crews go MIA—two to a collision—but two further bombers were "written off" in landing crashes. This is 42-102598/EP: F **Super Rabbit**, which was salvaged exactly three calendar months after assignment.

Short Bier disgorges six of her load of eight 1,000-lb bombs; this weight of explosives was normally the maximum carried by B-24s, The Debach aircraft belonging to the 862BS was later transferred-out to the 490th BG at Eye.

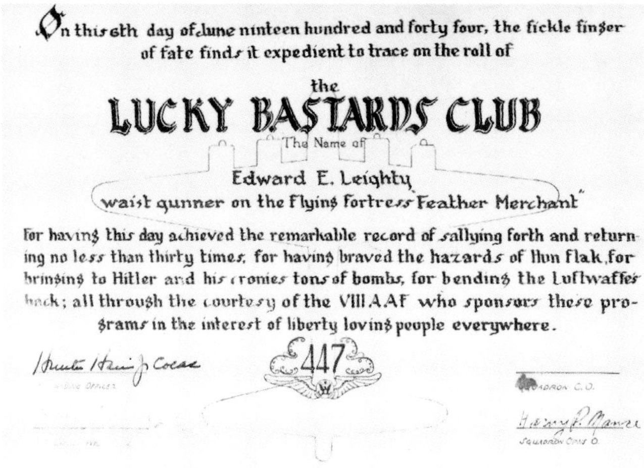

On this 6th day of June nineteen hundred and forty four, the fickle finger of fate finds it expedient to trace on the roll of

the

LUCKY BASTARDS CLUB

The Name of

Edward E. Leighty

waist gunner on the Flying Fortress "Feather Merchant"

For having this day achieved the remarkable record of sallying forth and returning no less than thirty times, for having braved the hazards of Hun flak, for bringing to Hitler and his cronies tons of bombs, for bending the Luftwaffe back; all through the courtesy of the VIII A.A.F who sponsors these programs in the interest of liberty loving people everywhere.

447

Above: The lack of heavy flying gloves and the substitution of a proper helmet by a forage cap over which the headphones are clamped indicate this navigator and his crew are participating in a non-operational flight.

Top Right: What every combat crewmember strove for, but what was denied to so many thousands – the Lucky Bastard Certificate. On 6 June 1944 S/Sgt. Eddie Leighty completed his 25th and final mission and was accordingly granted his document, signed by Col. Hunter Harris (447th BG CO).

Right: **Picadilly Lilly** displays her potentially wayward charms on the 34th BG's 44-40458/4BS. The B-24J has amassed 24 missions whose bomb symbols are mainly applied to the armor screen mounted below the pilot's position.

This "friendly fire" incident at Framlingham on 29 June 1944 actually involved the 100th BG's 42-97090/LD: D. The small brick building in between the control tower and the NW/SE subsidiary runway has been partially demolished; the three-month operational sojourn of the bomber was ended next day, when it was declared "Category E."

Four B-17Gs from the 452nd BG are drawing thin condensation trails as they traverse a pocket of heavy cloud with a P-51 for a companionship. The PFF bomber 44-8429/C-/729BS in the lead was MIA on Xmas Eve 1944; bomber on the right, 44-8518/F, went down on 5 December. 45th CBW yellow-bar markings are absent, a further indication picture is taken prior to their application in January 1945.

No more success was realized with the second duo of B-17s sent out. The first crossed the Channel before visual contact was lost on approach to the target, while the other crashed short of the target due to miscalculations made by its controller aircraft.

There was little doubt that the urgent desire to initiate swift countermeasures to the German threat was being applied with little or no benefit of prior research, such was the almost phobic if natural reaction of the Americans to the perceived threat.

The Authorities' dissatisfaction with *Azon's* general function led to it being superceded by equipment with a perceived greater degree of accuracy under the codename *Castor*. At the same time the operational use of GB-4 weapons within the overall scheme of things was first realized on 13 August with the port of Le Havre as the target. Codenamed *Batty* (ironically, an English slang word for crazy!), the GB-4 was an updated version of the GB-1 glide bomb that was now equipped with radio controlled control surfaces and a TV camera in the nose to enable the controller in the mother ship to direct its path towards the chosen target.

As with the GB-1, the GB-4s were slung in pairs under a B-17 and duly released; sadly, the receiver screen in the "mother" aircraft proved too hazy for any form of accurate aiming and both glider bombs fell short of their objective. Two subsequent missions against submarine pens at La Pallice, France (20th), and naval facilities at Ymuiden, Holland (28th), proved equally fruitless thanks either to technical failure or, in the latter case, to cloud cover that prevented visual sighting for the "mother" aircraft.

Over the ensuing five months eleven *Aphrodite* B-17s were dispatched to targets ranging from the Island of Helgoland to two mainland targets: marshalling yards at Herford and a power station at Oldenburg. Success of any kind still eluded the Americans, and indeed one of the two "Babies"

Up on the Snetterton Heath control tower balcony, "Lady Moe" is probably adding her asinine weight to "sweating out" a mission. The gentle donkey was a feature around every section of the airfield for some two years.

sent to Oldenburg on 1 January crashed, but remained in sufficiently intact state for the Germans to become aware of this exotic form of assault.

Further use of the bombers against targets in Germany were reportedly cancelled due to British reservations about their use inviting retaliatory strikes against the British mainland—a somewhat contradictory stance considering that the V-2 offensive was already in full swing, while the prospect for the *Luftwaffe* to launch standard bombing raids was virtually dead in the water. However, the cancellation only took effect during March, although no missions had been flown in the interim period. (It seems the Americans had wanted to use the bombers against industrial sources inside Germany, although they must have been aware of the very poor future prospects for the system given the abysmal results to date!)

An initial scrutiny of this B-17G suggests it is a standard functioning bomber. However, the twin aerial 'frames under the bomb-bay of 43-37793 confirm this is one of two "mother" ships specially configured to control the progress of *Aphrodite* aircraft.

Lovely Lady's pilots are about to bring off a smooth three-point landing at Snetterton Heath. The B-17G was assigned on 3 May 1944, but is seen here in the 45th CBW color markings applied in 1945. Luck was certainly with the aircraft, because she survived WWII, although ultimate Fortune saw her only delivered for "scrapping" at Kingman.

11

Shuttle Run

So far in the course of the Daylight Offensive the B-17s and B-24s had almost entirely conducted their missions from England, the notable exception being the Regensburg run to North Africa and back commencing on 17 August 1943. Although liaison between the Western Allies and their Soviet partner wove an often tenuous and sometimes almost acrimonious pattern, the plan for USAAF heavy bombers to fly into airfields in Russia was finally approved and initiated in June. Prior to its launch, the selected trio of bases around Kiev (Poltava, Mirgorod, and Piryatin) were stocked up with the necessary logistics of bombs, ammunition, fuel, etc, supplied largely via the road links with the Middle East depots located in Persia (now Iran). However, the first of what were codenamed *Frantic* missions was allotted to the Italian-based 15th AF and flown on the 2nd.

It was upon the 3rd BD that the honor fell to fly the first British-based *Frantic* mission. Two CBWs, the 13th and 45th, were tasked with providing the aircraft; a fighter escort of P-51s was also assigned that would also fly to Russia, focusing upon the full 4th FG and a single squadron from the 352nd FG. An extra provision was the need for ground crew to service the aircraft during their detachment. With this in mind some thirty-three personnel were selected and spread among the groups to serve as "spare" gunners in addition to their normal ground-based duties. S/Sgt Bob Gilbert would have a particularly exciting experience compared to his contemporaries, although it would not be in Russia...

This picture could easily be titled "four USAAF crewmembers looking for a B-17 to fly." Picture was taken in the aftermath of the disaster at Poltava that claimed 47 bombers from the 45th CBW's ranks on 21/22 June 1944. The shattered hulks of several B-17s can be seen in the background.

This is a closer view of one of the 96th BG's losses at Poltava; it is believed to be 43-37781/AW: R, now the late mount of Lt. C Schram and crew. Nothing remains identifiable forward of the waist position other than the mass of the four Cyclone engines.

On 21 June the *Frantic II* mission was sent out as part of a primary thrust at Berlin. Ruhland, lying in between *Big B* and Dresden, possessed a large synthetic oil plant at Schwarzheide, and this was allotted to the 163 Division B-17s. The presence of the main force over Berlin was expected to lure the *Luftwaffe* away from the Russian-bound attackers. The plan appeared to have worked all too well for the Russia-bound formation, since progress to Ruhland and beyond passed off almost routinely; this positive outcome proved to be not so for the Berlin bomber stream, which came home 45 bombers light!

Unbeknownst to Lt. L Hernandez and crew on the 452nd BG's 42-38202 **BTO in the ETO** was that four of their fellow teams were among the MIA tally, a tally that they were about to add to as the bombers headed away from Ruhland and began to cross over Poland. The formation was skirting Warsaw when a sharp fighter attack suddenly developed; only the one pass was made, but it was enough to inflict mortal damage upon the Deopham Green bomber. The burning aircraft was evacuated by its ten occupants, who all drifted safely onto Polish soil. Amazingly seven of the crew, including Sgt Gilbert, were spirited away into hiding by Polish civilians. So began a several-week sojourn for the Debden mechanic that then saw him transferred into Russian hands for eventual return to his airfield in mid-August.

"Der Grosse Schlag" (The Big Blow)

The lengthy flight went off virtually without further enemy involvement, although four 100th BG bombers were forced into premature landings around Kiev, and at last the B-17s began circling for landing at Poltava (45th CBW) and Mirgorod (13th CBW), while the fighters went into Piryatin. (One of the aforementioned 100th BG crews led by Lt. Williams had a momentary scare when 42-31708/EP: R **Skipper II** had to be force landed in a field due to fuel shortage. "Greeting" them was a group of farmers bearing lethal-looking implements who naturally regarded the Americans as Germans, having probably never seen a B-17 before; a potentially fraught situation was rectified by one gunner speaking to the Russians—in Bulgarian, thanks to his forebears having emigrated from the language's country of source! The fact that the bomber's wheels had flattened the field's wheat crop would hardly have endeared the crew to their Allies, either.) Unfortunately, the eastwards progress of the formations had not gone unnoticed by the Germans; an aircraft was quickly dispatched to make contact with and "shadow" the B-17s to wherever they were destined. The *Luftwaffe* crew duly noted the act of landing at Poltava, in particular, and upon return and debriefing, plans were drawn up for a counter-blow. Nemesis was soon to overtake the 8th AF detachment in terms of its aircraft, at least...

Two officers from the 96th BG are observing the female members of a Russian kitchen unit during the first 8USAAF "Shuttle" mission in June 1944. The acidic comment written in the top left corner of the picture is worthy of note!

A lone American airman poses among three of his Russian Allies with a ruined building in the background. Woman on the left with an ample bosom appears to have a very uncomfortable perch—no less than a Jerry can for fuel! The other woman seems to be camera-shy.

Vulture Strike

The 45th CBW personnel had taxied in and lined up their B-17s in a single extended arc on the sparse Poltava surface. Such a close-packed arrangement of some of the aircraft was inviting trouble in the event of a bombing raid similar to the annihilation of aircraft on Clark Field in the Philippines at the onset of the war with Japan. However, this was mid-1944, and the *Luftwaffe* bomber force was becoming ever more impotent, in addition to which the Kiev area was well distant from the German airfields—or was it?

The He 111s of II/ and III/ KG4, and individual *Gruppen* from KG27, KG53, and KG55 were currently based around Warsaw with the two KG4 units well versed in the art of "path finding." A quick briefing was held with Poltava the target for the first two named units and Mirgorod for the third; these sub-forces would have their targets illuminated by II/ KG4 and III/ KG4 respectively. The airfields were some three hours flight time away, and the attacks were planned to go in simultaneously around midnight.

The weather conditions were far from perfect for the *Luftwaffe* crews, with heavy cloud and thunderstorms encountered, and at least four of II/KG4's bombers aborted for various reasons. As it was, errors would occur both in ETA accuracy as well as flare release over the correct target. On the other hand, matters were to proceed in a materially far worse manner for the Americans...

Gen Archie Olds (45th CBW CG and acting as Task Force CO) was present, and naturally attended the banquet laid on for their guests along with two other USAAF Generals and Gen Perminov. A number of U.S. correspondents were present who would soon know the extreme frustration of not being permitted to relay the facts about the rapidly unfolding disaster to their editors thanks to military censorship that furthermore extended beyond WWII.

The banquet only commenced around 2300 hours and was barely into its course when the air raid sirens sounded their

The 100th BG force heading for Russia on 21 June 1944 should have included these two B-17Gs. Although the 418BS bomber (right) seems to be basically intact, it followed its more unfortunate 350BS partner onto the scrap-heap. In addition, the sole Russian-speaking crewmember was on board LN: G and was also left behind!

yowling chorus as an initial warning of approaching enemy aircraft. Out around the airfield the airmen were billeted in tents, and now hastily donned whatever clothing was to hand while rubbing the sleep from their eyes and also cursing the enemy for breaking into their hard-earned sleep pattern! Air raid shelter provision was even more basic, taking the form of slit trenches that barely covered one's body even when adopting a prone position according to some eyewitnesses.

The He 111s assigned to Poltava were soon overhead, but even before the first bomb was released on ETA the airfield had become bathed in stark light for over ten minutes by the "pathfinders'" flares. Unfortunately sufficient PFF aircraft were still on hand when the bombing commenced to keep up the concentration (some of these were probably exploded by III/KG4, since a post-operation report by Maj. Graebner (II/KG4 *Kommandeur*) stated that far too many flares were dropped in relation to the numbers carried by his bombers; in addition, Mirgorod was destined to remain unscathed, so reinforcing the claim that the extra flare concentration was provided by III/KG4 crews misled into thinking they were actually over Mirgorod).

The confusion among the *Luftwaffe's* ranks was of little benefit to their adversaries because all too soon the bombing began to take its deadly toll. The mix of SC50 explosive and SD2 fragmentation bombs, as well as hundreds of incendiaries among the close-packed B-17s quickly began to make their mark. Fire took hold of B-17 after B-17, so adding, at least initially, to a clear sight of their target for the enemy bomb aimers. The anti-aircraft response was extremely poor in numbers and overall firepower, while all the searchlights provided was more illumination of the area. What was not lacking was the often suicidal gallantry of the Russian men and women attempting to extinguish the fires in the midst of what evolved into a two-hour assault. All too often their lives were snuffed out by a bomb exploding at or near where they were functioning, or alternatively when a bomber's fuel tanks erupted. (No firefighting vehicles were on hand; instead, the various parties had to resort to using shovels to throw earth onto incendiary bombs or use sticks to beat at the flames! One 96th BG airman noted that a nearby AA gun position was summarily wiped out, along with the group of women manning it. Further casualties were incurred by the destruction of bomb dump and fuel facilities, while two 96th BG officers lost their lives when a bomb dropped by a wall adjacent to a hospital tent and behind which they were sheltering.

A further layer of official obstruction occurred when the P-51 pilots at Mirgorod asked to be allowed to take off and challenge the *Luftwaffe* force; the reason put forward for refusal was reportedly because Moscow required 24 hours notice before sanctioning any flight! The lack of dedicated night-fighter equipment in the P-51s would have resulted in little or no contact with the bombers, but there was always a chance, however unlikely, of making contact. The scales were rapidly dropping from some American eyes for any prospect of being treated as equals by their so-called "Ally," at least with regard to Russian officialdom.

As daylight broke the scale of carnage was brutally revealed. According to separate report sources, no less than forty-four to forty-seven B-17s out of the seventy-three on hand had been reduced to burned out shells, with each set of four engines squatting forlornly on the ground. Their rear fuselages and outer wing panels had been left virtually unscathed by the fires, although the fabric surfaces on the rudders, stabilizers, and ailerons had naturally not survived in a number of cases. The worst affected group in this respect appears to have been the 96th BG, with just five of its 21 bombers not part of the "Category E" tally. Two C-47s had also been destroyed, while damage from fragmentation bombs and bomb splinters had affected the 26 surviving airframes to some degree, with at least two fit only for cannibalization, 15 capable of return to combat status within two weeks, and a mere nine reparable within 24 hours as stated in Gen. Old's written report to Gen. Partridge (CG, 3rd BD). The CBW had been virtually emasculated, and with it the striking power of the overall Task force.

Poltava's fuel dumps were now short of anything up to ½ million gallons of aviation spirit, and prompt replenishment was mandatory if even the bare minimum of the surviving airworthy aircraft were to execute their next mission. As for the *Luftwaffe*, it had won hands down on this occasion, but the effects on the overall USAAF offensive were less than marginal; the shortfall in bombers could be made up almost at will, either from B-17s now on hand at Air Depots or within a week or so from airframes currently under manufacture in the States. All that had been achieved was a temporary boost in morale within the five participating *Gruppen*.

Having been clearly selected for assault, with no guarantee of there arising a subsequent raid, it became incumbent upon Gen. Old to order a dispersal of his force of bombers, as well as the P-51 escorts to alternative airfields. Sure enough, Mirgorod was sought out to be interdicted by the *Luftwaffe* 24 hours later and suffered sizeable damage to its facilities. The B-17s headed further southeast to three airfields at Zaporozhe, Kharkov, and Kirovograd. However, there was no question of utilizing these as other than transit bases, since all lacked the ability to handle the B-17s at their operational all-up weight; only Poltava and Mirgorod possessed this vital capability. Therefore, if the next leg of the shuttle was to be made, there was no alternative to having the crews take off from their temporary refuge and fly into their original airfields; then loading up, briefing, and mission launch would have to be carried out that same day to avoid being prey to a further nocturnal visit from the *Luftwaffe*.

Comment

There appears to be a divergence of opinion regarding *when* the dispersal order was given and who issued it. Col. Moller claims that the 13th CBW dispersed on the arrival day. What was taken to be a *Luftwaffe* PRU aircraft was seen after arrival and all efforts to gain permission for P-51s to take off and shoot it down were refused on the incredible grounds of national

Big Time Operator from Deopham Green bears a right-outer wing section whose camouflage contrasts with the otherwise NMF finish. On 21/22 June 1944 its combat career ended on a foreign airfield when it was one of the many 45th CBW bombers destroyed at Poltava by the nocturnal *Luftwaffe* strike.

pride; the Russians stated that they would feel demeaned if they could not defend their own airfields should they come under attack—an ironic observation in the light of impending events! Discussing the potential *Luftwaffe* threat with Col. Wittan (13th CBW CO), the decision was taken to disperse the bombers. By this time darkness was upon the countryside, but the full moonlit conditions permitted the crews to use map reading as a navigational means to seek out their temporary refuges; on arrival at what was a grass strip possessing no lighting system near Kharkov Col. Moller landed first and, turning his B-17 along the line of approach, kept his landing light on as a basic guide to the other pilots.

Quite why Gen. Old did not appear to even consider, let alone carry out, the same procedure for the other CBW is unclear, although he would have had his time more than taken up with discussions with his hosts. It raises the issue (however unlikely) of whether or not Col. Moller became confused between dates by sighting the post-attack surveillance aircraft that turned up on the 22nd with the one reportedly seen *prior* to the attack? On the other hand, the fact that the 13th CBW was stated to have taken off after dark appears to back the assumption that the evacuation occurred on the night of the 21/22nd and not the next night. Having become aware of the disaster at the neighboring airfield by the early hours of the 22nd, there would have been little or no reason to delay the emergency action until after dusk, when more than enough time would have been on hand to carry out the transit flight in far more visually secure conditions.

On to Italy

The second leg was to be flown down to Italy, but two targets were proposed by the 15th AF authorities to Olds. He settled for an oil refinery at Drohabycz, in Poland, compared to a communications center in Rumania. The original 25 June date for its inception was finally postponed late in the day due to poor weather conditions. By this time, however, the bombers had been loaded up and were incapable of landing back at their temporary night-allocated airfield. Consequently, the already hard-pressed ground crew had to reduce the bomb and fuel loads to a safe level before the dispersal procedure could take place. Making this effort all the more protracted was the lack of equipment with which to either load or unload the bombs.

Next morning the bomber crews returned to Poltava and Mirgorod, and this time the mission did go ahead, but with the

This B-17G in common with a sizeable number of contemporaries never saw overseas service, but was assigned to training duties for acolyte crews. Note the extension of its serial number to the wing underside; this was done to discourage low-flying activities.

single-figure numbers of 45th CBW bombers still operationally viable ordered to link up with the 95th BG as its High squadron. Once again enemy opposition was almost nonexistent during the mission, other than for a handful of fighters and occasional light concentrations of well-directed flak. A solid strike was made against the Primary, and the force flew southwards with an almost continuing lack of interference to finally land at several 15th AF airfields within the Foggia Plain, north of Italy's geographic "heel." The 100th BG's Capt. F Mason and Lt. M Ehorn flying High squadron Lead did lose an engine to target flak and fell behind, but were covered by the escorting fighters and subsequently joined up with the group at Tortorella.

Extended Sojourn

The return of the *Frantic II* force to England would not occur for another nine days. A good proportion of this time was spent either "in the sack," relaxing on the available stretches of beach or on sightseeing visits that for some senior staff entailed being flown over to Naples, compared to the other personnel, who had to make do with the scenery adjacent to their airfield.

But the extended time period did not mean that the 8th AF crews remained ground-bound. On 3 July the 13th CBW was briefed to participate in a mission to the marshalling yard complex at Arad, in Rumania; as one prominent Thorpe Abbotts airman stated tongue-in-cheek, "To show the 15th AF how things are done in the Big League"—as if the Italian-

Capt. Charles Dunn served as navigator not only for the 96th BG, but latterly as the Lead for the entire 45th CBW. Here he and his Army nurse bride are snapped as they emerge from the church where they have just been wed, one of hundreds of Service couples to join in matrimony.

based crews were having a much easier-paced existence against the German defenses in Europe's southern zones. (It was little wonder the personnel looked scornfully upon their contemporaries and treated them as the "Hollywood Air Force!") In the event, the mission passed off without apparent incident, so there was little chance for the CBW crews to comment positively upon their allegedly superior methods of seeking out and accurately striking a target. However, the 100th BG released upon a locomotive works that had reportedly been missed by the assigned unit; whether the group in question was from the 15th AF or the 13th CBW was not confirmed! A further 48 hours elapsed before the homeward leg was announced. Beziers, in France, possessed a sizeable marshalling yard, and this was selected for attack. As the force was heading towards its Primary and skirting the French coast near Toulon eyewitnesses watched their 15th AF colleagues hammering installations within that important seaport in the face of heavy flak. The few fighters appearing were held at bay by the escorts, and with the bomb loads delivered the bomber force headed on a direct course for Beachy Head, on the English Channel coast; from here it swung up east of London and on to the six Divisional airfields. *Frantic II* was completed, but this was not the last time the B-17s would head out for Russia...

Culture Shocks?

For the American airmen, with their open if rather brash manner of presenting themselves to the world, the initial contacts with the Russians must have been puzzling if not disappointing. After all, both societies were reputedly based on equality, so the insular and suspicious reactions of their Allies to the presence and approach of the New World visitors must have come as a surprise. They could not have known at this time of the far from democratic structures in Soviet Russia that would all too soon lead to the Cold War for the ensuing four decades. Simple things like playing a joke on somebody could literally have fatal consequences for the perpetrator. On the first day, while indulging in a drinking session with the Russians, one airman slyly filled a Colonel's glass with water instead of vodka; the look of extreme anger directed towards the waiter after he drank from the glass could have culminated in punishment ranging from prison or dispatch to the Front, or even death. On another occasion a pilot confronted a soldier whom he had seen slipping away with his watch. When the theft was confirmed the mediating Russian officer shocked the American by stating that the man would be shot—not for stealing the watch, but for "disgracing the Soviet Union!"

A quite innocent response by Col. Moller (95th BG and 13th CBW Deputy Lead) to a question during one of the social occasions laid on by his hosts subsequently became an issue between the USAAF and Russian Commands, and further illustrated the gulf between the two nations' thought processes in the political sphere. A forbiddingly silent man sitting beside the very attractive female interpreter suddenly shot out a question to the Col. "who do you want elected as President in the forthcoming elections?" Moller, undoubtedly responding as a Republican supporter, stated that he felt Roosevelt had been in post too long. He expanded on the matter by pointing out that the U.S. system normally did not permit an incumbent to hold the presidency for more than two terms and Roosevelt was bidding for his fourth. The man, who turned out to be one of Stalin's infamous Commissars, broached the question again, to which Mollar provided the same answer. The matter was not pursued any further, not on this occasion at any rate...

On arrival back in England he presented his Mission Report to B/Gen. Partridge (CG, 3rd BD), who enquired if Moller was a Republican. Having established this, he then explained that there had been a top-level communiqué from the Soviets about his (Moller's) refusal to back his president. In response to the Col.'s jocular reaction that such a trivial issue could have raised even a minor political storm, Partridge pointed out that a similar response from a Russian airman on arrival in England in relation to Stalin would have led to his summary execution on return home! It mattered not that the right to elect one's choice in the political sphere did not exist in Russia. The Col. acknowledged that this confirmed his growing feeling of alienation between the Western Allies and Stalin's nation, and made him realize how easy it was to take his democratically-confirmed rights for granted. (With hindsight, it is clear that autocracy rather than democracy was the current driving force in wartime Russia, as well as for a long time after the Conflict's conclusion.)

Re-run

It was at the beginning of August that the second 8th AF "shuttle run" to Russia was carried out with a force one-third the size of the June sortie; this time only the 95th and 390th BGs were selected and finally lifted off on the 6th. The aviation industrial target for the 78 crews was up on the Baltic coast at Gydnia/Rahmel, and their movements were well cloaked by an overall force of over 1100 B-17s and B-24s striking at several targets located between Hamburg and Berlin. The few fighter thrusts encountered well into the mission did no material damage and the groups continued on to land at Poltava.

"Spot" Promotion!

The social formalities were again indulged in with a concert, but the preliminaries included an incident that could have caused mutual embarrassment to both nations had the true facts emerged at this point. Apparently Lt. P Fiess (95th BG) had previously been pointed out by one of his crew's gunners as the "Commander"; the female interpreter making the enquiry took this to mean he was the Task Force leader, whereas the gunner was assuming they would accept Fiess as the *airplane* commander, this term having been demanded by the Top Brass to be used during the shuttle run. When the interpreter caught sight of Fiess among the throng she grabbed him and led him up to the front of the stage and to an empty chair positioned between the Russian General and Gen. Kissner, the actual Task Force CO—a clear case of spot promotion with a vengeance!

The evening passed off without further event, but next morning while in the food queue Fiess was again spotted by the interpreter and pulled away to a special Mess tent. This time around Kissner or one of his retinue did not stand on ceremony, but came across to firmly remove the special pot of coffee that had been placed in front of Fiess, a privilege not granted to the "Hierarchy's" table! Having made a tart comment to the effect that "we go by rank in this Man's Army, regardless of what our hosts might think," he was walking away when Fiess' colleague was heard to say what a story the incident would make, whereupon he promptly turned back to their table. He now threatened them with instant court-martial if the tale ever got out; his reasoning was that if word of what had transpired ever found its way to the Soviet authorities it could not only cause extreme embarrassment, but could also lead to a further increase in the already underlying tension existing between their Nation and the Western Allies.

The next two days were taken up with flying consecutive missions. The first was a return trip from Poltava with the target an oil refinery at Trzebinia, in Poland, although only fifty-five B-17s out of the original force of seventy-five participated. All returned safely to their Russian airfield. Next morning the overall Force took off and headed southwestwards towards Italy. The Rumanian airfields at Bizau and Zilistea were struck in the course of this "shuttle" run leg and again no losses were suffered. However, it was a further 96 hours before the final run back to England was launched. This time yet another airfield at Toulouse/Fancazal, near the Franco/Spanish border, was plastered by the bulk of the sixty-nine bombers constituting the Force.

On 10 September the 96th and 452nd BGs landed back off an extended run down to Nuremburg, less one crew from Snetterton. Lt. O Williamson had previously diverted into Sweden on 9 April, but had returned to England and further combat duties. This time round he was facing a Stalag following the loss to target flak of his B-17, 43-37603/ BX: R, which crashed near Weissenburg, but by then free of all nine crewmembers. The 96th BG personnel could not have been too pleased to learn later in the

A line of close-packed B-24s progress along the southwestern perimeter at Lavenham; overhead two B-17 Elements are unconsciously posing a challenge to their Consolidated "cousins"; in fact, the 487th BG would soon convert to the Boeing design and commence operations in August.

evening that on the morrow their group, along with the 452nd BG, would be again heading towards the Soviet Union for the latest *Frantic* mission. Nor could their morale have been bolstered by memories of the debacle at Poltava on 21/22 June when their Allies' defensive measures against the major *Luftwaffe* strike had proved utterly useless.

The specific target on the 11th was Chemnitz, which was bombed by all but one of the 75 bombers dispatched under 20th FG cover. Mirgorod airfield was reached without incident. Two days later, in what was destined to be the shortest *Frantic* mission out of the four 8th AF sorties, an iron and steel works north of Hungary's capital, Budapest, was assaulted, with the force flying on to Italy. Here the crews remained grounded by weather until the 16th, when a homeward path was beaten, albeit without any attack on a specific target being recorded.

Shuttle Finale (*Frantic VII*)

By mid-September the Polish Home Army defenders within their capital, Warsaw, were embroiled in an increasing and ultimately fruitless battle against large-scale SS and *Wehrmacht* units; the presence of Soviet columns barely east of the river Vistula but remaining static gave added bitterness to their looming martyrdom. All efforts were being made to support the Poles by the Western Allies, at least through the dropping of supplies into the military cauldron. The latest and what transpired as the final *Frantic* mission (No. VII) was laid on and rescheduled for the 18th. (Three days previous adverse weather conditions had forced the recall of what would have been *Frantic VI* involving 110 crews.)

This time round it was again the 13th CBW that was assigned the duty, with 110 B-17s provided by all three groups dispatched bearing 1248 containers in all, packed with ammunition, medical items, etc. The outward course angled up to the Danish/German border and altered to an easterly heading while skirting the Baltic before assuming a final heading for Warsaw; no other 8th AF formations were over central Europe, so it was deemed even more necessary than usual to side-step the *Luftwaffe* defenses by adopting this evasive course. All but a handful of the crews arrived at a lower than normal level over the stricken city to release their loads, although what proportion fell into the right hands was uncertain; the dropping altitude of around 18,000 ft must have caused considerable drifting of the parachutes and probably landed some containers into German-occupied districts. Despite the presence of many 88mm flak guns, both for aerial defense and for use against the Poles, only one B-17 from the 390th BG was lost during this stage of the mission; a second was sufficiently damaged by flak to cause its "grounding" on arrival at Mirgorod with its crew facing a protracted return journey as passengers via Persia, North Africa, Italy, and southern France.

This visit was the shortest among the three "shuttle" missions flown by the 8th AF since the force was heading back towards Italy within 24 hours. This steady fore-shortening pattern was maybe as symptomatic of the growing atmosphere of unease extending to distrust between the two emerging superpowers as it was of the perceived military value to be gained from the actual missions. The first interim target this time round was a Hungarian marshalling yard at Szolnok, close to the capital Budapest, after which the usual southward course was taken up towards the Foggia Plain airfields of the 15th AF. This part of the flight proved far from routine after the formations flew over Brod, in Yugoslavia, where a hitherto unreported group of flak guns threw up an accurate barrage.

Although no bombers were brought down there was a miraculous escape for 42-31412/EP: G **Mason and Dixon** and her crew. Two flak shells had impacted with the left wing near No. 1 engine but did not explode before exiting, nor did either create what would have been a lethal fireball had either struck a fuel tank; however, one had almost severed the main-spar, and it was a further miracle that the increasingly turbulent air patterns as the bomber descended over Italy's rugged terrain and on towards their designated airfield did not cause the dangerously weakened spar to snap. (The B-17 was declared "Category E" upon inspection by the Base Engineers, but that ruling was cancelled and the B-17 turned up at Thorpe Abbotts some weeks later. It then resumed operations, and in fact ended its days at a Stateside "boneyard" in December 1945.)

During this final Italian stop-over, further disparaging remarks were addressed to some personnel regarding the unfair priority in supplies and even entertainment accorded the 8th AF. On the other hand, there was a reverse sense of expressed envy whose subject was social in nature—namely, American beer! It appeared that the 15th AF was far better provisioned in this respect since the England-based crews rarely if ever saw their choice of this desirable beverage extending beyond the warm and soapy substances on hand, courtesy of their British "pub" hosts!

Comment

Frantic VII's final mission-leg that also closed the ledger upon the entire scheme seems to have culminated in an anti-climax, since no actual target was recorded when the eighty-four B-17s still operational took off for England. The level of cooperation from the Soviet authorities had varied notably; also the size of, and the attendant scale of damage inflicted by, the forces concerned, although painful, did not create a significant upsurge in pressure upon the Nazi industrial or military frame. An additional limitation to continued operations was the lack of support equipment compared to England. For example, the loading arrangements were primitive, as exemplified both by basic stowage operations and the occasions whenever loads had to be changed—in the latter instance the Russian personnel just opened the bomb doors and toggled the weapons onto the ground to the consternation of the Americans. The use of Russian bombs could have created ballistic and associated drop-measurement problems for the bombardiers, had not an advance party that included 95th BG combat officers dispatched in February 1944 not carried out bombsight tests that initially proved the bombs were going badly astray. Bombsight calibration adjustments were then made that resulted in consistent accuracy thereafter. However, the extent of Russian bomb utilization was never clear, most film evidence shown post-war displaying the normal range of USAAF bombs.

12

"They also Served..."

Behind Every Combat Crewmember...

One of the inherent weaknesses of national media, especially in a democracy, is the freedom to focus upon information that will sell its printed products immediately and in the greatest quantity, as opposed to stating a litany of bad facts, however informative the latter might be. The same lack of propriety generally applies to television.

Allowing for the constraints of censorship during a conflict, a similar situation has sadly tended to apply. Tales of activities in the actual field of combat received the vast bulk of correspondents and film makers' attention, especially as regards the Air War. This is a matter that has evoked a lot of embarrassment for the combat crewmembers as well as a quiet undercurrent of frustration mingled with resignation among the many thousands more "backroom boys" who worked anonymously to ensure the maximum degree of safety attended their fellow-airmen's progress into and—equally vitally—back from Europe's embattled skies.

It was hard enough to carry out intricate mechanical work such as on a B-17's engines without the further and uncomfortable encumbrance of a gas mask. At least the three mechanics' faces would be protected from the often bitter cold and damp of the East Anglia region in which they were stationed!

There is a further separation to be considered when discussing the part the ground support airmen played in this military partnership. Regular references to "ground crews" are often, but almost equally mistakenly, taken as applying to the mechanics either out on the airfield dispersals to work on a specified machine, or in the airfield buildings occupied by the Air Depot personnel. As it was, for all the hundreds of men operating in the field of mechanical engineering, there was another pool of personnel upon whom both combat and ground crews were dependent: doctors and medical assistants, cooks, Operations Room staff, store keepers, clerks, drivers, mail men, MPs, etc.

Technical Problems

The constant need to mobilize aircraft production at the fastest possible pace often resulted in problems varying from the minor to the potentially lethal. The experience of the technicians at Framlingham was typical of this constant battle to provide the combat crews with the best possible chance of survival in terms of equipment efficiency. The following instances of technical limitations and how they were overcome highlight the situation.

It appears that a number of B-17Gs were rushed into combat service despite the fact that some key components were not functioning in the intended manner. The 1943/44 winter period witnessed many crewmembers reporting frozen windshields and other Plexiglas units thanks to inadequate heating. Matters deteriorated on some bombers to the extent that the pilots were forced to open the cockpit side windows in order to gain the necessary visual sighting of their fellow aircraft—a potentially lethal situation for all concerned. Frost-

Assigned to the 493rd BG in September 1944, this B-17G (43-38568) named **Little Davey II** never progressed further than the river Deben near Ramsholt following take-off for the mission of 20 February. Only Lt. F Stindt (P) and Sgt Haynie (Eng.) survived the tragic incident.

encrusted windows could be seen even when the bombers in question had landed back off the mission.

Examination of these B-17s revealed that the new heating system—air heated by passing over the exhaust stacks as opposed to the original use of glycol heaters located into the exhaust stacks—lacked the fluted exhaust headers required to generate sufficient heat exchange. (The headers were formed of six-inch diameter straight piping.) An urgent reference to the Boeing technical representative elicited the admission that the proper fluted stacks were still not on hand. However, he also recalled an experiment to provide a practical variation. Holes had been drilled in the exhaust stacks and the surrounding edges formed into "scoops," an action that enabled exhaust gas to seep out and pass directly to the air-to-air heat exchanges mounted in the wings. The one detail he could not remember was the number of holes drilled.

The Group Engineering personnel were apprehensive about taking this course of action because of the probable effect upon the turbo-superchargers. These needed a maximum manifold pressure level to be maintained when brought into operation; the engineers felt that this could not be achieved due to an excessive loss of exhaust pressure that could arise from the drilling procedure. The likely outcome was an increase in bombers being forced to "abort" the mission.

A guess was made as to the diameter of the holes and around twelve combat-ready B-17s were (unofficially) modified overnight, and all involved held their breaths as the mission went ahead with the aircraft concerned participating. By the end of the day all appeared well, since no "aborts" occurred. Indeed, all went well over the succeeding several weeks until the supply of fluted stacks began to arrive.

The engine supercharger units comprised between 250 and 300 "bucket" shapes and revved up to 27,000 per minute. Any damage caused by mechanical stress or gunfire usually entailed a lengthy and tedious detachment and replacement. The need to take this action on a regular basis was alleviated when one airman pointed out that the unit, if otherwise in good condition, could be maintained in a balanced state by breaking off a "bucket" directly opposite the missing "bucket." In this way much time and energy was saved.

Not all intended correctional measures proved to be of benefit to the 390th's operational efficiency. An apparent time-saving measure that tuned out to be counterproductive concerned the "slow-timing" of replacement engines. Once the defective engine had been detached and the new engine was in place the latter had to be taken aloft for several hours testing. This was no problem, provided not too many aircraft were so simultaneously affected. Engine changes were time consuming in themselves, apart from which the reduction in combat ready numbers was a critical matter, especially when the Command was involved in continuous daily operations such as *Big Week*. The suggested alternative action was to fit a single bomber, usually one downgraded from combat to "war weary" status, with four overhauled units, after which these could be held in stock as it were; the action also reduced the number of bombers required for "slow-time" procedure. The down side to the suggestion lay in the fact that the mechanics would have to install and detach the engines concerned—and then still have to carry out a second installation procedure when the need arose! (The time for engine detachment and replacement to be completed was averaged at eight hours.)

A Master Sgt and two other ground personnel are having difficulty in lifting a bulky test apparatus up and through the narrow rear entrance door. Note the enclosed waist window with its distinctive framing.

Control Tower Staff/Weathermen

To the average combat crewmember liaison with the control tower was often a vital physical and aural link. The 24-hour service provided by the airmen in what was a hub feature of any airfield was essential for the prompt and secure flight paths of every aircraft, whether based there or from some other location. A sub-duty connected with this function was the marshalling of fire/rescue, ambulance, and Cletrac vehicles at the relevant airfield sectors.

At mission start the tower personnel were responsible for ensuring that the proper sequence of taxiing prior to take-off was adhered to; careful watch was kept to avoid ground accidents should, for example, an aircraft run off the perimeter track or suffer some failure as it moved along that might cause a collision. This could be a taxing duty in daylight, but consider the following enhanced range of problems. Unlike a modern airport that is brightly lit and marked out in every way possible with visual guides to a taxiing pilot supported by radio supervision, the launching of most missions in the dark meant that lights were kept to a minimum, while radio silence was generally adopted for fear of enemy monitoring of the airwaves.

A driver has charge of a Cletrac; the use of these solid-framed, tracked vehicles on an airfield varied from towing equipment to emergency situations. In the latter instance, vehicles were, for example, used to crudely push bellied-in bombers off the runway or even perimeter track in order to keep the way clear for succeeding aircraft.

The existence of adverse weather over the airfield on mission-return added further pressure to the staff as they endeavoured to bring their charges down in as orderly and swift a manner as possible. Communicating a calm but firm stream of advice to the pilots, some of whom were inexperienced and liable to reach a stage of extreme unrest in these circumstances, required a good degree of practice. On days where no missions were flown or during the hours on either side of a mission, the Control staff had to monitor the movements not only of their own aircraft but other arrivals, such as replacements, or visiting aircraft either making a normal arrival or diverted the airfield's way due to an emergency. The relative lack of comprehensive radar monitoring of aircraft across the length and breadth of the country, coupled to the literally hundreds of aircraft simultaneously aloft, was yet another pressure that the staff in general rose to and conquered.

Also housed in the control tower was the meteorological staff, who were ever a focus for sly or even sometimes blunt remarks regarding their general efficiency. Given that forecasting in the present times can still be a matter of conjecture, it is hardly surprising that in an era bereft of satellites or sophisticated ground-based equipment weather projections could and did go awry. In addition, the location of the British Isles off a continental landmass has tended to cast up unpredictable and perverse weather conditions. (A prime example of how matters could go badly awry in postwar years occurred in 1987. One autumn evening, a well-respected British TV forecaster said he had received a phone call from a listener in which she heard a "hurricane" was imminent; she was reassured this was not the case, but scant hours later just such a phenomenon loomed out of the southwest to devastate the southern counties of England!)

The small body of some eleven officers and men at each airfield were detached from the centrally-based 18th Weather Squadron. Theirs was a two-way exercise in function; while providing information for the proper and safe dispatch and return of the crews, they also fed information on the weather conditions back to their Division HQ. Details included cloud intensity, wind speed and direction, visibility, air pressure, and temperature—every aspect that could contribute to creating an overall weather pattern for the entire region from which the USAAF operated, and which could then be relayed back to the various groups.

Fire and Rescue Service

Another specialist and vital body among the ground personnel was staffed by those who drove the fire and rescue trucks, and for whom danger was never too far away. They manned their vehicles round the clock in readiness for the inevitable incidents among their unit's aircraft complement. Take-off and landing were the stages of a flight that largely witnessed a bomber displaying a faltering progress through the air, progress that often culminated in a heavy or fatal impact with the ground.

It was then the duty of the rescue personnel to extinguish the flames, and wherever possible to extricate the crewmembers from what was sometimes a basically intact airframe, but all too often was one badly or even totally twisted and mangled. To the danger posed by ignited fuel tanks was added the equally volatile belts of ammunition and sometimes all or part of the bomb-load that had somehow survived either the initial take-off crash or that had failed to release in the case of a returning aircraft; in the latter instance the explosives "cooking off" in the heat regularly caused death or serious injury to still alive crewmembers and their intended saviors. The reactions of the rescue personnel to the gruesome task of extricating badly mangled or burned bodies from a crash undoubtedly paralleled those of the medical staff.

Flight Surgeon Duties

A Flight surgeon in the American Air Force had a particularly difficult duty to perform. His clients had all volunteered in the service of their nation, and therefore had no recourse to protest when the full effect of what they were facing arose. This was all very well in theory, but was more questionable in practice. The bald truth was that the average Flight Surgeon ended up bearing so many of what were "pooped out" aviators upon his shoulders. He could appreciate the pressures that such airmen were facing, but he had also to balance this against the need to prosecute the war effort, which could only be carried out by these same individuals.

The battle between logic and military needs reached a crisis point in early 1944 within the 3rd BD at least. Jack McCrittick was a Flight Surgeon serving with the 95th BG who recalled that he, along with a number of his Division contemporaries, addressed the problem of combat pressures in letter form direct to 3rd BD HQ and its CG, Curtis LeMay. The response was immediate, with every Flight Surgeon summoned to LeMay's office. His remarks were brief but terse:

Firefighting in the case of aircraft was a duty with no absolute guarantee of safety for the personnel. This 96th BG B-17G is beyond saving and is probably not bearing a bomb load to judge by the casual dress of the airman and close proximity to the blaze. On the other hand, an explosion of a fuel tank that could place his life in jeopardy could never be ruled out.

"I know you are professionals - but we are too. I don't want you to interfere with the way we are running the war… and we will not appreciate any more correspondence on this matter!"

However autocratic the General's response might seem, it was clear that the conflict was being prosecuted for the greater good of the majority, regardless of the cost to the personnel who hopefully would bring matters to a successful conclusion for all concerned.

Safety was Relative

For the most part a doctor's function on an airfield was conducted well away from physical risk. However, there were always exceptions to this comfortable existence. Perhaps a wounded airman who urgently needed treatment was trapped in a returning aircraft whose bomb-bay held un-discharged loads—was priority to be given to the removal of the bomb load at the possible expense of the man's life, or should medical assistance come first regardless of the risk to the doctors and orderlies in attendance?

An instance of such a dilemma arose at Thorpe Abbotts on 8 May 1944. During that day's mission to bomb an airfield at Laon, in France, 42-107011/LD: piloted by Lt. B Williams was struck in the rear gunner's compartment by a 100-lb bomb that lodged itself tight against Sgt. R Cohen's left side, as well as seriously injuring him. All attempts to manoeuvre the deadly weapon free

Above: A pair of what appear to be 300-lb bombs dangle from the crane jib while the smiling armorer on the right totes an incendiary bomb. The task of loading these weapons was physically demanding as well as dangerous. Often, having installed the bombs, they had to be removed when the type of load was changed or a mission was cancelled. *Top:* Strength was regularly needed in the loading of aircraft with bombs. An armorer at Thorpe Abbotts is toting a metal frame to which is attached 20-lb M41 fragmentation bombs. Six are in position, although up to eight could be accommodated.

The proper handling of parachute canopies and their supporting cords was of paramount importance, given that a man's life would depend on this factor being fully and correctly exercised.The material also had to be carefully handled on grease and dirt-free surfaces to ensure the silk or later man-made fibre shrouds as well as the cords did not deteriorate.

failed, and it must have been a very apprehensive crew that held course for home; they would have had their apprehension level increased had they known that the bomb was fully armed....

Once on the ground, and having established that the gunner was still alive, the Ordnance personnel confirmed the arming vane and stem were missing so that the slightest movement could set it off. Working with quiet but tense precision the men eased the pressure on the nose fuze with a length of wire and then loosened and detached the armed tail fuze. A further measure to ensure nothing untoward happened was to place restraining hawsers around the bomb to hold it in place. Capts. Kinder and Stover were the doctors right on hand and considering ways to extract Cohen even while the de-arming process was going on. It was the more slightly-built Stover who managed to wriggle into the compartment confines and, after seeing how one of the gunner's boots was trapped by the bomb, cut off the offending thong and began to ease the victim forward. After some minutes the airmen was got outside and into a waiting ambulance; sadly, his lease on life expired not long after reaching the base hospital.

The Medics

To the non-discerning individual the duties of a medical assistant were probably regarded as at best mundane and at worst boring. After all, there were Flight Surgeons on hand with generally far greater experience in tending to the human frame as well as acting dispassionately at what was likely to be encountered in the way of gruesome injuries. But the effect on anybody's mind of regularly viewing what a cannon shell or exploding flak shell had done to a body was often numbing, as opposed to being glossed over as a tragic aspect of the cost of war. Even worse was the task of sifting among the shattered and sometimes still smoke-shrouded airframe of an aircraft; the smell of cooked flesh pervading one's nostrils; picking up dismembered limbs; cables, wires, and metal shards having to be cut away or otherwise untangled from a body before it could be wrapped in a blanket for removal to the mortuary. Such scenarios could and did leave long-term if not permanent scars on a medic's mind. Whenever the red flares arced up from a circling bomber indicating wounded aboard, the medics would be ready to act in every way possible to ensure the ultimate survival of the personnel concerned, no matter how serious their injuries might be. The loss of an airman undergoing treatment left behind a sense of hollowness among the medical staff almost akin to that of a crewchief mourning the loss of his bomber.

Cooks

What was a cook in a military sense? The simple answer is that he was a man who had often been co-opted into this function against his will, an assumption that is applicable both in peace time and in war. However true this assumption might be, the

One of the key groups on an airfield was also arguably the most under-rated—namely, the kitchen staff. The work was unexciting to say the least, but if the personnel had not been regularly fed then they in turn could not have functioned properly. (This was despite all the regular cracks regarding the quality of some of the products.)

An MP checks the credentials of a British workman. Security on a WWII airfield was none too easy to maintain, given the casual manner in which most bases sprawled into the countryside as well as possessing often minimal artificial barriers.

bald truth is that the flight, and even the support personnel, were basically dependent upon his and his colleagues' efforts. Combat operations demanded that the crews be properly fed, and this vital issue was totally dependent upon such anonymous personnel who attended to this primary need, without which the combat crews and ground support personnel could not properly function. It was not down to the cooks as to what was available for setting in front of the airmen; they just got on with preparing the ingredients on hand, whatever their quality of taste and nourishment might be.

The Eighth might have been "well nourished" in the words of a leading British aviation author, but this did not automatically grant its personnel regular first-class choices in the range of available dishes. For every occasion when the combat crews were presented with the prized pre-mission egg there were times when, for example, the hated chipped beef that bore a cynically crude description in the fliers' minds was on the menu. Mutton was another "delicacy" to be avoided, with some ground crews resorting to K Rations in their barracks rather than tackle the singularly greasy and unappealing dish. Nor were these custodians of the culinary art always content to remain ground-bound; it is a fact that a sizeable number out of this key support group subsequently volunteered for combat duties and faced up to the risks attendant in flying missions.

Security

Another body of personnel who faced implied or actual hostility from the airmen was the MPs. Policemen are always looked upon askance, and the American custodians of military law were no exceptions to this. However, they had a function to complete, and most of them did so in a fair and impartial manner, even if their methods bordered on the super-efficient at times. It was a fact that the policemen not only had to ensure that their fellow-countrymen obeyed the letter of the American military law; there was also a question of relations between the servicemen and their British military and civilian contemporaries, which did not always run smoothly. Security around and within the confines of each airfield was laid at their door. It mattered naught that the Germans never attempted any form of ground-based assault upon any facility during the entire conflict; constant vigilance was demanded and largely complied with in order to ensure would-be saboteurs would have their efforts thwarted at every turn.

As regards any threat that might emanate from the air, other personnel were assigned the duty of manning and operating the anti-aircraft units, which generally consisted of 20- and 40-mm calibre guns on mobile platforms. To the monotony of having little or nothing to do, since *Luftwaffe* forays directed at the Anglo/American bases within East Anglia were very sparse from 1943 onwards, was the physical discomfort afforded by the unpredictable albeit often unpleasant British climate—these airmen could empathize fully with their colleagues out on the flight-lines!

Chaplains

The spiritual needs of everybody serving on a USAAF airfield, at least all who wished to avail themselves of such emotional support, was the primary duty of the chaplains. Normally all three

An MP motorcyclist bears the armband denoting his function. The MPs were also tasked with maintaining discipline among the personnel in a manner that won them few friends; this was especially the case whenever off-base brawls erupted, whether among the Americans or sometimes with local civilian involvement.

major faiths (Protestant, Catholic, and Jewish) were represented.

As it was, the apparent sedentary function of these "men of the cloth" cloaked an intense desire to help the combat crewmembers in particular to come to terms with the odds against their surviving an operational tour of duty. This was none too easy to communicate to the airmen since chaplains, unlike some of their contemporaries within the ground personnel officer ranks, were expected to conform strictly to their "non-combatant" status. How to convince somebody of putting his trust in the Deity to bring him through when your feet are anchored firmly to the ground and therefore safe from the dangers aloft? How to further convince him that there was no guarantee of ultimate survival even when following the precepts of one's religious tracts, whether the Bible or the Talmud?

In one or two instances chaplains took it upon themselves to seek permission to participate in a mission. The problem with granting clearance primarily lay in the fact that these "applicants" were treated as non-combatants under the Rules of War. Furthermore, their presence inevitably took up a degree of essential facilities such as oxygen, of which there was barely an adequate supply for the regular crewmembers. A third objection was both physical and psychological; the supernumerary's presence meant he might get in the way during a crisis, apart from which there was no guarantee he would react promptly and properly in such a situation. Nevertheless, there is at least one confirmed example of a chaplain making one if not up to five missions.

This officer is seated in what the British called a Link Trainer. With the hood down pilots could perfect the art of "blind" flying. This was a vital aspect of combat flying, given the "clamped" weather conditions of cloud, fog and winter snow patterns regularly existing over the European Theater of Operations.

Unpleasant but Necessary Duty

One of the less pleasant but necessary duties was to sort out the personal effects of combat crewmembers declared MIA. The post of Effects Officer was not an official item in any group's Table of Organization, but somebody was usually delegated along with at least one assistant. The rooms occupied by the airmen concerned were visited as soon as possible, and personal items separated from official issue equipment, such as flight gear, the latter being returned to the Supply Section. The remaining material was then carefully listed before being packed away in containers that would eventually find their transfer to a depot in Kansas; there the containers would remain indefinitely with a view to their contents being claimed by relatives. One of the side issues in checking personal effects was to weed out anything embarrassing or incriminating; for example, correspondence from the "girl friend" of a married man, whose receipt by his wife and/or family would cause anger or unnecessary hurt. (Of course, there were many occasions where the airman in question had hinted or even declared that his squadron colleagues could avail themselves of some or all of his effects should he be shot down; such an activity was part and parcel of the combat scenario, despite disapproval in some higher circles at what was seen as an act akin to vultures picking over a carcase.)

All too infrequently there were occasions where the effects were still on hand when the individual concerned turned up. An example of this occurred at Horham when, just as the gear in question was being packed, news came through that its owner was not only alive, but had already evaded capture and slipped over into neutral Spain—like Douglas MacArthur, "he would return!"

Wireless communications was another feature of airfield life that had to be maintained in regular working order. Here, an airman is scaling a telegraph pole. He has to use strapped-on leg-irons since the pole is not equipped with metal footrests.

This as-yet anonymous B-24 with a neat shark mouth is seen during a test flight from Warton, the USAAF's central Air depot in Britain. She was later assigned to the 490th BG, where the title **Flying Ginny** was conferred upon her. However, on 9 June 1944 she was declared to be salvage for unknown reasons.

Unpublished Bravery

During WWII there was a constant reference in the national newspapers to those combat crewmembers who had won awards for their courageous actions during the course of a mission. The fact that such awards were earned in naturally dramatic circumstances added to the newsworthy content, while reporters were capable of putting a gloss on their dispatches. But what of the hundreds of thousands of anonymous ground personnel when one among their number received an award? Was the Soldiers Medal or even the Bronze Star granted to a "ground pounder" regarded as being on the same status as regards reportable news as the Distinguished Service Cross or even the Distinguished Flying Cross? The answer should have been a loud YES, because the recipient had usually put his life on the line in the same manner as his airborne contemporaries, especially when surrounded by ever-volatile aircraft, whether or not these were bombed and fueled-up or not....

The mission preparation at Mendlesham was well under way on 26 September 1944, with **Sweet Seventeen** under the charge of Sgt. D Jordan in the course of being refueled. Then a failure to inactivate the aircraft's master switch during this particularly dangerous stage apparently caused one or more of the machine guns to be set off. The burst of fire went straight into the fuel truck and set its contents on fire. Immediately, the truck driver Sgt. K Anderson jumped into the vehicle's cab after disconnecting the fuel hoses and drove it away in spite of the imminent risk of its exploding and killing him in the process, as well as causing mayhem among the B-17s in its immediate vicinity should this be the case. Some weeks later the award of a Bronze Star was bestowed upon Anderson.

Glenn Miller's music was once described as "the next best thing to a letter from home." These sacks contain the primary item that sustained the average combat personnel's morale, along with his ground-based colleague. This heavily-laden vehicle is parked outside Snetterton Heath's Post office.

Rest Homes – the Pros and Cons

Behind the direct and generally physical back-up accorded the combat crews by the ground crews and the other elements of the ground Echelons lay a further strand of moral or emotional "support" that was more akin to that normally laid into the hands of a psychologist....

The "Jekyll and Hyde" existence enforced upon combat crew personnel inevitably incurred physical and accompanying psychological pressures upon them. The need for detachment from operations was primarily met by the issue of 48- or 72-hour passes every few weeks. The problem with this procedure was that the crews generally headed for London, where most indulged themselves in the frenetic social life of the national capital; "eat, drink, and be merry" was the catch-phrase in vogue, because such indulgences might soon become a frustrating memory for those airmen subsequently ending up as POWs or, worse, a final act for those thousands whose lives were peremptorily brought to a premature conclusion in Europe's embattled air spaces. As a further indication that military needs were paramount, the airmen were required to wear uniform, as opposed to the use of more anonymous and arguably more relaxing civilian clothing.

The concept of the "Rest Home" was one that soon found favor in senior military circles. A number of large estate properties scattered throughout central and southern England were requisitioned for the use of 8th AF combat crewmembers. Whenever a crew was deemed by the Flight Surgeons to be in a corporate state of mind that demanded the services of a Rest Home (or "Flak Farm," as they were referred to by combat crewmembers) the necessary arrangements were put in motion.

The desire to complete their combat tours as quickly as possible led some personnel to protest at what they saw as an unnecessary delay in achieving this goal, but such responses were firmly brushed aside.

The normal period of time away from combat duties was seven days; long enough to gain a modicum of normal life free of Service functions and attitudes, but not too long to leave a crew on return to their airfield having to spend time regaining a state of mission alertness. One physical and also psychological difference between a Rest Home and proceeding on a 48-hour Pass or any form of absence from the Base lay in the choice of clothing. In the former instance, civilian clothes could be worn on all occasions other than at meal times. Then Class A uniform was mandatory, as in all normal instances of going off-base.

There was no bar placed upon individuals' movements other than having to be back on the premises by 2400 hours, while a range of facilities were on hand, with sports well to the fore. The first Rest Home was created in January 1943 at Stanbridge Earls, on England's Channel coast, but the thirty individuals it could accommodate at any one time were officers. Three further Homes were opened that same year with an overall capacity of 175, but only Southport, in Northwest England, offered facilities for both officers and Enlisted men. By late 1944 a total of fourteen Homes located west and south of London (apart from Southport, which was also destined to be the sole facility to cater for both officers and Enlisted men) were in operation; between them marginally short of 600 airmen could be accommodated.

Airfield defense was yet another key element at any WWII airfield, especially those within East Anglia, when *Luftwaffe* aircraft could strike with relative surprise. The duty proved to be largely boring, since very few assaults were actually made. Here, the three-man crew backed by an observer are manning their gun that appears to be of 40-mm calibre judging by the clip being placed in position.

The sole potential downside to being dispatched to a Rest Home could arguably arise at the end of the seven days. Then, however refreshed an individual might be, he was faced with the recurring threat to life and limb posed by a resumption of combat duties. Whether or not he could gear up mentally to this necessary but unpleasant scenario was ever an open question, but the brief interlude from having his very existence decided by largely uncontrollable influences seemed to have worked in the majority of cases, as has been regularly confirmed by veterans of the aerial conflict.

"A Band of Brothers"

Although this chapter has covered the activities of specific sections of the Ground Echelon, it would be invidious to even suggest that their function was more vital than the sections not mentioned in any detail. There is simply no way in which a single chapter can encompass the overall subject in similar manner. Having said that, the following account will hopefully speak for everyone who provided back-up for the combat crews:

> The CO of a 3rd BD airfield, having found sleep difficult to come about with a mission due in the morning, roused himself, dressed, and got into his car to tour his domain. In particular he circuited the perimeter track, stopping intermittently at dispersals for a conversation with the ground crew in question. As he approached one dispersal that was emptied of its normal resident his eyes picked out a shadowy individual sitting on a toolbox. Having (naturally but wrongly) assumed that the airman was part of one of the functioning teams he began to speak to him. The initial reaction was one of very little to say from the man, but after a few minutes, and having realized who the stranger was, he began to unburden his soul.

He was the crew chief for his charge that had gone MIA, and even though several hours had passed since the sad fact was established he had remained at his deserted post. As he then explained:

> "Colonel, I have mulled over everything we did to that aircraft a thousand times. I can't think of a single thing we did not check and double-check—but I still wonder if I went wrong somewhere."

The CO's response was to say he had led the mission and gone over the details of what transpired at the debriefing; he, too, wondered if he had in effect "called all the right shots." The crew chief expressed his genuine surprise at such a response, after which the CO went further:

> "Sergeant, here is some advice originally given to me by our Commanding General (Curtis LeMay). I led a rough mission when a number of our B-17s did not come home; afterwards I did exactly the same as you have been doing. The General, after discussing the mission with me, finally said 'If you reflect on all you said and did and can honestly say you know beyond doubt you did your best within the given circumstances then there is no further reason to reflect on the issue.'"

Condensation trails from other groups provide a sharp backcloth for a 93rd CBW B-17G that bears the usual heavy exhaust staining to the inboard engines, as well as an unusually camouflaged right wing-tip section. Top of the rudder appears to bear the red band denoting the 490th BG.

The final piece of advice to the crew chief was to take note of the advice and gain the necessary impetus to progress with confidence, and even more importantly, a clear conscience.

How many times was this situation visited upon the ground crews as they gazed upon an empty dispersal and experienced the sense of loss that left them heart-sick, as well as having self doubt cast upon their minds as to whether they had unwittingly contributed to the tragedy through failing in their duty. Conversely, this anecdote surely sums up the overall and continuing dedication of all ground crew—and by extension all ground support personnel —to ensuring that the combat crewmembers received the best possible service that would ensure their survival on operations.

The current term "Band of Brothers" tends to be applied to complete groups of combat personnel, such as paratroopers, but its application in this case is nonetheless relevant despite the large measure of non-involvement in the direct Field of Combat. But every screw or rivet tightened or replaced on an airframe; every gallon of fuel pumped into a tank or bomb load carefully secured in place; every parachute carefully packed; every meal cooked to the best of limited supplies and culinary experience; every careful physical administration by a surgeon or medic, as well as spiritual guidance from a chaplain; and every letter or parcel delivered that maintained an airman's morale—these and other "back-up" services on constant hand form too comprehensive a list for detailed inclusion in this summary.

13

Turning the Screw

(Autumn 1944)

The Strategic Bomber Commands were still basically linked to Gen. Eisenhower's requirements as the Battle of Normandy began to develop an irresistible momentum in the Anglo-Americans' favor following the U.S.' 1st Army's breakout around St. Lo. The degree of support to the Allied forces that might additionally be provided by the French Resistance in particular was highlighted in 1 August when the 3rd BD units were tasked with dropping supplies at four locations deep in the southeastern provinces of the country. Although the geographic remoteness of the drop zones from Normandy might indicate an illogical action on the authorities' part, there could have been forward thinking involved that related to a forthcoming action, namely the invasion of Southern France planned for and finally executed on 15 August. The arms so supplied to the Resistance could accordingly be employed in disrupting German countermeasures directed against this second Allied inroad into Europe's Western sphere.

It was back to tactical business between the 1st and 3rd, with the Division flying a double-header on the third occasion. But then came a three-day mission sequence that largely encompassed assaults upon Germany's oil refinery and aircraft production capacity, coupled with the latest strike against Berlin (6th). On the 4th the Division's B-17 and B-24 elements headed out for Hamburg and Hemmingstedt, respectively. Seven crews, all flying B-17s, did not return, with two 486th BG bombers involved in a mid-air collision. Lt. H Walthall's 43-37909/3R: C and 43-38145/3R:, in Lt. L Harper's care, made the fatal embrace and crashed at Rotenburg and Quelkhorn, east of Bremen, with Harper and three others the sole survivors among eighteen. Elsewhere the 96th BG suffered its latest MIA casualty with Lt. J Wynne's (KIA) 42-97195/AW: Q; flak on the bomb run blew up the B-17, whose

A sizeable chunk has been hacked out of the rudder on this Snetterton Heath resident B-17G. The aircraft's combat career extended over just two months. Assigned on 27 October 1944, it was "written off" following an incident on 27 December. Note the regular 413BS practice of combining the squadron and aircraft letters on the fuselage.

Black Hawk/Guzzlers is photographed at Knettishall following transfer from the 96th BG to the *Aphrodite* Project. On 11 Sept. 1944, packed with nearly 22,000 lbs of Torpex, the aircraft was guided towards Heligoland Island. Sadly the pilot, Lt. R Lindahl, broke his neck on bailing out while the B-17 fell short of the target after a flak strike sent it off course.

remnants fell at Wittstadt, along with all but two of the nine-man crew. Next day saw the B-24s dispatched to bomb the aircraft plant at Halberstadt, southwest of Magdeburg, to which the other Division units were sent. Once again the cost was low at four from among the 271 aircraft granted mission "credit." Two of the MIA crews came from the 100th BG, being Lt. A Scott's team in 43-37839/XR: L and Lt. A Gallagher's in 43-37572/XR: S. Flak claimed both B-17s, and only seven from Scott's crew survived out of eighteen airmen in all.

Berlin was scheduled for its thirteenth battering, this time from both B-17 equipped Divisions. The Division's targets were recorded as diesel and aircraft engineering plants within the city, which were bombed accurately for the most part. An exception to this requirement was the 94th BG, whose bomb run was apparently disrupted by the intense and accurate flak barrage. Worse still was the loss of two B-17s to these gunners. Lt. O Spenst's 42-107185/QE:, although crippled, did hold its approximate position until the North Sea was reached, but then gradually faded behind. It was last observed low over the water with only one engine running, and since no further word of the crew's fate was ever determined the assumption was that they had been lost in a failed ditching attempt. A second squadron crew led by Lt. L Hicks in 42-97974/QE: S was fatally crippled during the bomb run, but reportedly staggered back as far as the North Sea, where eight of the nine crewmembers survived their ditching. Of the three other Division losses one (42-32087/728BS from Deopham Green and flown by Lt. L Graber) was fortunate enough to evade the defenses during its northward diversion into Sweden. The overall figure of 24 crews MIA was again pitched at an acceptable level in terms of 8th AF loss rates; flak had played its lethal part in attaining this statistic, but fighters too played their part when the 351st BG was caught by a mixed Fw-190 and Bf-109 force that took out four of the group's six MIA bombers. Loss of a propeller blown off by target flak was followed by Lt. J Hatfield's 43-37805/4F: A dropping away and finally disappearing from sight. The crew was on what would have been their final mission; all nine parachuted safely, but Lt. E Reichel (B) died from his injuries two days later.

A Fast Diminishing Breed...

The switch back to tactical targets absorbed the attention of the crews for the next nine days. At least the participating personnel were gaining a steady number of mission "credits" while the Division's MIA losses were still minimal at thirteen B-17s overall. By now the B-17F variant that had sustained operations up until late 1943 was conspicuous by its virtual absence within 8th AF ranks, but a number were still soldiering on, including a very famous (or notorious, depending on the reading of the situation) example. On 10 Oct 1943 **Royal Flush** (42-6087/LD: Z) had returned from Muenster with Lt. R Rosenthal and crew, the sole main group survivor of the mission. On 11 August the veteran bomber was making its 75th mission and bearing Lt. A Aske's relatively new crew.

War Correspondent Frank Beresford sits with his easel inside the church at Quidenham, close to Snetterton Heath. In the background is the magnificent stained glass window depicting a 96th BG airman gazing up at Christ that was put in place during November 1944. The scene with an airman praying in front of the altar forms the subject on the canvas.

This Sudbury-based B-17G has suffered a collapsed tail wheel, probably after over-shooting the runway, and is being elevated using the air bag positioned directly below the star-and-bar. **Dream King** was a feature with the 508BS from 14 October until her demise to flak on 10 April, an incident that claimed the lives of four out of Lt. Dolan's nine-man team.

Originally Assigned to the 94th BG, this B-17G was then swiftly transferred to the 447th BG. Four months later it over-shot the runway on 25 August, but was brought back into flying condition to finally return home after VE-Day for delivery to the aircraft "graveyard" at Kingman.

A flak strike around the No. 3 engine shortly after bombing Villacoublay airfield in Paris sent the bomber into a spiral, and the resultant crash left five airmen alive. (One was Sgt. C Nekvasil, who would be captured but still managed to escape and be back in England in less than four weeks!)

A mere seventy-two hours later the 100th BG bade farewell to a second veteran B-17F. This was 42-3413/LN: V bearing the title **Hard Luck!**, the bomber having been assigned on 13 August 1943 and its last two numbers relating to that unlucky figure. In fact, the aircraft had belied this potential "jinx" status by operating perfectly to the extent that she functioned on her original engines for 50 of her 62 missions. The end of a long combat road now occurred as the IP was looming up at Ludwigshafen; flak struck home during the bomb run and Lt. D Cielewich's mount began to lose contact with the formation, even though the bomb load had been salvoed. Ironically, the final crash site at Beerfelden, due east of the target city, added to the German death toll, because the B-17 slammed into a farm, killing several of the occupants, whereas all ten crewmembers escaped by parachute.

Oil production was again listed on the Field Orders for the 16th, with Zeitz and Rositz allotted to the Division's B-17 groups while the B-24s went after Halberstadt's airfield. The latter force came home unscathed, while a mere six B-17 crews went down out of the 206 striking at the Primaries. This loss factor was not evenly split among the groups, since four came from the 95th BG, of which two were lost without enemy intervention. Four of Lt. Williams' crew on 42-37879/BG: U **Wrinkled Belly Baby** failed to survive when their aircraft collided with 42-97797/QW: H **Full House**, with the aircraft falling at Rohmdorf and Rondorf; six of Lt. Hannum's crew also did not come through alive from

Rodney the Rocks/Lil' Butch (43-38142/H8: P) delivers its load of 500-lb bombs as flak bursts lightly speckle the sky. This B-17G's eight-month tenure of operations from Sudbury was violently terminated on 30 March 1945 when flak downed it at Pinneberg along with seven of Lt. Veal's crew. Note the Olive Drab central fin and rudder, indicating replacement sections on the otherwise NMF-finished aircraft.

the incident. Lt. Price's 42-31589/BG: O was culled by flak to crash at Altenburg, along with three of the nine crewmembers.

Next day was the second Anniversary of the first ever 8th AF mission, but weather conditions ensured a total "scrubbing" of intended assaults on Normandy-based enemy ground forces. Not so the following day, when a range of rail, road, and airfield locations across France and the Low Countries were plastered by all three Divisions. It so happened that a further six days would transpire before the "Mighty Eighth's" bombers took to the air to strike deep into Germany, with the 3rd BD heading towards oil industrial sources spread between Ruhland and Brux, while its B-24 element struck further north at Kiel. The defenses took a fair toll of the attackers (26), but only five came from the 3rd BD's ranks, although this was little consolation for the 34th BG, flying its last mission before transferring from the B-24 to "Boeing's Best."

Three crews did not return to Mendlesham, beginning with Lt. G Howard's team in 42-94780/4BS **Smitty**, which came down along with all but one of the eight-man crew. A second 4BS crew led by Lt. W Mackey perished in the North Sea on the way back after they abandoned their stricken bomber. The third missing crew enjoyed immeasurably better fortune after 41-28851/7BS **Near Sighted Robin**, bearing Lt. G Avriell's crew, was sufficiently crippled by flak to merit taking up a course for Sweden, so ending the airmen's 34th mission in an unintentional if still positive manner. A fourth group B-24, 44-40443/4BS **Berk's Beserks**, was safely abandoned over England, where the aircraft crashed into a house. (These losses concluded a nine-day period during which the group had also lost all but three from a crew flying in 44-40267 **Bad Penny**, which had to be ditched in the English Channel (15th).)Three days later a mid-air collision with a 493rd BG B-24 brought down PFF bomber 42-94745 **Bold Sea Rover** along with Lt. J Glaze's Debach-based crew.

A second Debach loss on the Roye/Amy mission emphasized the lifetime torment often suffered by a sole survivor. Lt. G Washington's 860BS crew were flying their nineteenth mission in 41-29473/861BS **Bolicat**. Flak killed the pilot, and Lt. Kehoe (CP) gave the bail out order as Lt. N Grant (N) was assisting the severely wounded nose gunner out of his turret and bringing him to the nose wheel aperture prior to jumping. Grant went out on the clear understanding that the nose gunner, Sgt. Doyle, would follow on, but upon deploying his parachute and scanning the sky he saw nobody else floating down. After capture he was informed, but refused to believe his interrogator's assertion, that all other eight crewmembers were dead, but this turned out to be the case. (His extreme good fortune compared with that of his colleagues, to whom he was closely knit, weighed heavily upon his mind in after-years, as he stated in the 1990s video "Behind the Wire" that dealt with USAAF POW experiences.)

The 24 August mission was the start of a four day sequence that was largely strategic in nature. Next day, the research airfield at Rechlin and Poelitz's synthetic oil plants further to the northeast were assigned the Division and punished with a total of over 800 tons of bombs between them, this time at a slightly higher cost of eight crews out of 18 for the whole 8th

The 339BS B-17G in the foreground was destined to come through WWII unscathed following its assignment to the 96th BG on 17 Sept. 1944. This picture was taken later in its operational career to judge by the red color bands of the 45th CBW applied to the vertical fin and wing surfaces.

AF. The Rechlin sub-force included the 95th BG, four of whose formation were taken out. Lt. Powell's 44-6085/BG: H fell near Schwabach, leaving three of the ten-man crew dead. **Belle in the Keyhole**, 43-37898/QW: A in Lt. Shepherd's control, fell to flak, but without any of its crew. Damage to 42-31992/BG: P **Mirandy** forced Lt. Bussen to head for Sweden, where his crew were interned. Single losses to four groups included the successful "ditching" of 42-97166/AW: by Lt. R Bauman and crew off the Suffolk coast. No such happy conclusion faced Lt. J Duncan's crew on board Lavenham's 43-37980/R5: B; flak encountered between the target and Rally Point sent the B-17 minus its right outer wing section spiralling into the Muritzsee's waters, and only Sgt. M Wolyn (WG) managed to bail out.

A shorter run to Brest and its heavy gun batteries cost no aircraft casualties for the Division (26th), but next day a much rougher operation appeared to be looming up when Berlin was briefed. However, the capital was never reached thanks to increasingly adverse weather conditions. Targets of opportunity in northwest Germany were sought out that in the 3rd BD's case involved a mere handful of the 426 B-17s dispatched unloading on Flensburg's marshalling yards and an airfield. Two bombers were missing, but 42-32059 **Poltergeist** was ditched safely for all nine crewmembers to later get back to Great Ashfield. The continuing V-1 offensive merited the latest assault upon launch sites in the Pas de Calais by elements of the other two Divisions, but the main effort was directed against the ports of Bremen and Kiel; the twin-pronged sorties by over 800 crews amazingly passed off without any losses. Indeed, the 8th AF had surrendered barely 1% of the 4000-plus crews involved in this and the previous three completed missions to the enemy.

September 1944

The largely downward trend in overall 8th AF MIA losses was set to continue its welcome course. On the other hand,

The "bombs away" signal for this 100th BG formation is indicated by the smoke markers released in unison with the Lead B-17's load. Three of the other bombardiers have reacted promptly, but the nearest bomber and one on the right appear to have delayed their release, an action that could lead to an over-shoot of the target zone.

the inability to avoid the heavy flak fields defending many of the remaining key targets, coupled with the ever-constant risk of being set upon by a *Luftwaffe Sturmgruppe* tended to concentrate the minds of experienced combat crews at least.

The Division's first monthly run was to bomb gun batteries at Brest (3rd), followed 48 hours later by an attack on Stuttgart's aero-industry; seventy-two hours then elapsed before more aero industrial facilities at Gustavsburg and an oil depot at Kassel were briefed. From all three mission just seven crews failed to return, including two Sudbury B-17s that collided during the Division's second run to Brest (5th).

One of this unlucky pair was 43-37949H8: **Nobody Getszit**, from which just one of the nine crewmembers led by Lt. A Eacham survived. During the same spell only one crew each from the 100th BG and 390th BG failed to return, with the latter diverting into Switzerland. As it transpired, the crews of both these 13th CBW groups were about to face a mid-month crisis extending over the ensuing three days.

Four for the Price of One...

The nature of close formation flying brought home several potential dangers for the bomber crews, the obvious example being mid-air collision. Another danger lay in the effect an exploding bomber could have on its fellow aircraft caught by the blast. The target at Duesseldorf was throwing up the usual flak barrage as the 390th BG was on its bomb run. In the Low squadron lead was **G I Wonder** (Lt. R Longardner), while directly behind and below was 42-97871/DI: P **Bundles of Trouble**, flown by Lt. M Hobbie. Suddenly, a flak strike directly in the Hobbie B-17's gaping bomb-bay caused the 6,000-lb load to explode violently. None of the nine airmen survived their bomber's total disintegration, with the remnants falling at Hubbelrach, several miles northeast of Duesseldorf.

The knock-on effect of the explosion was to scatter most of the other eleven B-17s in the sub-formation with fatal effect upon four. Longardner's aircraft not only miraculously survived the blast, but held on course with two other bombers; however, the extent of the damage was to result in two weeks off combat status for essential repairs to be made. Lt. R Gallagher and three of his crew in 42-102594/DI: were lost in the explosion of their bomber after it was struck by debris from Hobbie's B-17; the crash site was by the Ennepe Dam (one of the projected targets for assault by No. 617 "Dambuster" Squadron, RAF, on 16/17 May 1943). Also fatally affected by the scattering debris was 43-37804/DI:, although a subsequent flak strike added to Lt. D J Harris' problems by knocking out an engine, as well as causing

A mix of high explosive and incendiary bombs are cascading from two of the three 486th BG B-17Gs and should land squarely on the target, given the perfect visibility. Nearest bomber is 43-37931/3R: H **Pursuit of Happiness**, which nearly survived WWII; after nine months of combat operations it was downed by flak over Dresden on 17 April, with none of Lt. Bartl's nine-man crew surviving.

injury to himself and several of the crew. At least he was able to bail out the entire crew after fire took inexorable hold of a second engine. The fourth squadron loss involved 42-97130/DI: Q **Avenger III**, which finally expired at Luedenscheid, well east of the target, presumably having already been successfully abandoned by Lt. B Latici and his eight-man crew. The flak gunners delivering this devastating blow must have been very happy men, even if remaining unaware of the final tally of five B-17s taken out by their endeavours....

Two further Framlingham crews were excised from the records next day on another deep penetration run to Fuerth and Nuernburg, making seven in three consecutive missions. This was bad enough for any unit to bear, but would arguably be eclipsed by what was about to strike the 100th BG on the 11th. The pilot of the sole other Division loss must have rued his decision to resume combat operations. He was Lt. O Williamson flying 423-37603/BX: R **I'll be Around**. On 9 April he had diverted into Sweden, from where he returned to Snetterton during July. The non-operational assignment to test-fly group aircraft led him to reflect that doing so was not much safer than combat, apart from which he had already flown 23 missions—so why not try for 30? Working on the (sadly false) basis that "lightning does not strike twice," he reasoned that he had experienced his dose of being shot down and a recurrence was most unlikely! At least he did survive as a POW along with his full crew.

Recurring "Jinx"

The "Bloody Hundredth's" grim reputation for bearing particularly heavy losses had seen an average of ten MIA B-17s incurred on six previous missions. The latest on 29 July had cost eight crews, but then the next 24 missions had resulted in only six further MIA bombers. Immunity from recurring heavy losses was never guaranteed for any group, as the Thorpe Abbotts crews now discovered.

The Division was part of a concerted effort against oil-related targets, and in its case directed against Ruhland, Boehlen, Bruex, and Chemnitz; the latter target was allocated to the *Frantic* force comprised of seventy-five 96th and 452nd BG bombers, which managed to evade any serious defensive attention. This was a particular stroke of good luck, because the *Luftwaffe* had amassed and launched one of its largest fighter forces for four months.

Gen. Adolph Galland, the *Luftwaffe's* Inspector of Fighters, had long come to the conclusion that the only chance of even blunting, let alone turning back, the 8th AF's Daylight Offensive was to inflict such a massive scale of loss that the authorities would be forced to reconsider their actions in a manner similar to the Autumn Crisis of 1943. Since the Allied escorts were dominating the skies over central Europe, there was no question of a return to the "Happy Times" of the previous year, when the *Luftwaffe* could dictate when and where to strike the bomber formations at its leisure.

The sole option by this stage of WWII was to meet numbers with equal if not superior numbers in the twin hopes of overwhelming the 8th FC's protective screen, and thereby descending upon the B-17s and B-24s in sufficient strength to punish them severely. With this in mind Galland had been carefully assembling an overall force that would deliver the *Grosse Schlag*, or Big Blow. Although later reports referred to upwards of 500 *Luftwaffe* fighters operating today, this figure, even if accurate, was still well short of the ultimate one regarded as the minimum required if Galland's counter-strike or strikes were to have an even chance of success. (In the event his plan never bore fruit following the advent of the Ardennes Offensive, to which Hitler demanded the *Luftwaffe* commit the bulk of the fighter reserves!)

Although the *Luftwaffe* pilots did bring down 40 bombers shared roughly between the three Divisions, the cost far from justified the effort, since over 100 "kills" were in turn claimed by the escorts. One of the participating units was II/JG4, and that evening its pilots could have had reasonable grounds for a celebration, since they had been responsible for nearly one-third of all 8th AF bomber losses (eleven); back at Thorpe Abbotts the reverse mood swing would have pervaded the airfield's atmosphere, since it was the 100th BG alone that had borne this loss figure.

The Lead section of the group's C formation was provided by the 350BS. It was led by Capt Giles in 43-37863/LN:, with Lt. A Trommer in 42-102657/LN: Y to J Giles' right and Lt. J Raine piloting 43/38047/LN: O on the element's left flank. Directly behind Giles flew Lt. Taylor in 43-38076/LN:. Also in the section was Lt. P Corley's 43-37880/LN: and 43-38043/LN: in Lt. H Schulte's charge. The target at Ruhland was being approached from the northwest when "peace and quiet went to Hell."

II/JG4 had gained an unopposed frontal position to the 100th BG, and now put the *Sturmgruppe* principle into operation, although here it was indulged in the reverse direction compared to standard procedure. Three successive waves loomed up out of the sun and focused upon the currently unescorted group. Within mere minutes all six B-17s led by Giles were either on their way down or turning back for home. His bomber was set

The idyllic leaf-bedecked tree and pond surrounding seems to contrast sharply with the implement of war that is B-17G/43-37861 of the 490th BG based at Eye. The + marking applied ahead of the aircraft letter denotes the 851 BS. This bomber survived from 2 July 1944 until VE-Day.

The target has been thoroughly plastered, and now the 447th BG, having completed the bomb-run, are rallying for the homeward flight. B-17G in foreground is 42-107015 /L **L'il Eightball**; the 709 BS aircraft was another WWII survivor, following assignment on 25 April 1944. Picture was taken before application of CBW color markings from late 1944 onwards.

on fire and started to fall apart, whereupon all nine successfully jumped clear on his command. Lt. Trummer went down with four of his crew in the doomed B-17, as did Lt. Raines and four other crewmembers when their aircraft exploded.

Taylor's bomber burst into flames and initially went out of control; both pilots succeeded in gaining sufficient control to finally attempt a crash landing, but only one gunner survived what sadly evolved into a fatal crash. The salvation from destruction by the remaining two B-17s was only temporary. Lt. Schulte was killed during the assault, and Lt. Kiern (CP) guided the aircraft as far as the Leipzig area before flak fatally bracketed it, leaving the six remaining survivors to jump clear near Machern. As for Lt. Corley, his homeward course was rapidly ended by further fighter attacks, but once again all nine airmen exited safely.

The other two sections suffered albeit to a lesser degree as regards aircraft at least. Two-thirds of the 27 airmen on board 42-97154/LN: A (Lt. W Carlton), 42-102695/LN: F (Lt. Holladay), and 44-6089 (Lt. L Riegel) lost their lives when the trio of B-17s was chopped out of the Low section. The Carlton-commanded bomber's violent demise produced the highest fatality rate at seven, and all three pilots were among the dead.

Lt. C Baker, in the High section Lead, was fighting to hold his blazing B-17 in the air while also unable to instruct the crew to bail out due to the shot-out intercom system. Suddenly the left outer wing on 42-97806/XR: D **Now and Then** was chopped off by the latest fusillade, followed shortly by most of the right wing and the fuselage snapping in two; the truncated airframe stooped into a gyrating dive and finally blew up in mid-air, to leave the pilot and five of the eight-man crew dead. (A tragic aspect to this incident was the fact that this would have been Baker's last mission, albeit not due to his finishing up; orders had been dispatched for his "grounding" due to medical reasons, but these only reached the group 24 hours later!) The other section loss involved Lt. O Everitt's (KIA) 42-97834/XR: T, and once again only three of the nine airmen survived.

Merseberg's Latest Unit Cull

The 493rd BG, known as "Helton's Hellcats," had recently converted from their originally allocated B-24s onto the B-17, and had flown daily cost-free missions with the Boeing design since the 8th. The group was the penultimate one among the five Divisional units to commence B-17 operations, the 486th and 487th having led the way on 1 August and the 493rd BG on the 27th (the 34th BG would launch its inaugural B-17 mission on 17 September).

The second daily assault upon Germany's oil industry was laid on for the 12th, and nearly 350 crews wended their way to Boehlen and Merseberg, where a hot flak reception was always guaranteed. Clear visibility was on hand to provide good sighting for the bombardiers, while the final MIA figure was gratifyingly low at twelve. As on the previous day, the bulk of the crews not returning were from one unit, in this instance the 493rd BG, whose formation shed no less than nine, with the Low "C" squadron the unfortunate focus of attention.

As with the 100th BG, it was fighters rather than the equally feared if also more anticipated flak barrage that inflicted most of the casualties. Fw-190s struck after the bomb run and tore the sub-unit apart. The 863BS lost six bombers, along with at least 23 of the 54 airmen concerned. The worst affected team was Lt. A Tucker's, of which only one survived the demise of 43-38261; four got clear of 43-38098, flown by Lt. J Kittelson and five from Lt. G Owen's 43-38355, while Lt. Cookerham lost one crewmember from 43-38352. Owens was the sole fatality from among the three airplane commanders. Lt. C Spencer's 43-38295 descended at Oschersleben to cost the pilot and three crewmembers their lives, and Lt. J Oates' (KIA) 44-6277 was the sixth casualty with an undetermined fate for his crew.

A clutch of three more B-17s were downed west of Magdeburg. Stapelberg, southwest of Oschersleben, formed the crash site for Lt. A Goodman's 43-38214/ 861BS. Also downed here was 43-38308/860BS in Capt. W Carter's (KIA) charge; half of the ten-man crew forfeited their lives. One of the two remaining total aircraft losses occurred over the suburbs of Magdeburg when 43-38319/860BS succumbed to flak and crashed at Pechau, killing eight of the nine crewmembers, including Lt. E Bisaro (P), one of two brothers on group combat status. Although 43-38227 returned to England, the degree of battle damage suffered was sufficient for salvage action to be taken. Lt. M Durgin's Lead 43-38264 was the sole survivor from its Element and was very fortunate to remain aloft after being thoroughly sieved by the gunfire; the B-17 diverted into Brussels, where Sgt. D Gray (WG), one of three badly wounded crew members, later succumbed in hospital from his injuries.

The ensuing fifteen days involved a staccato spell of operations, with just nine missions flown by the Division, during which only sixteen B-17s were declared MIA. One of these missions was connected with Operation *Market Garden*, the optimistic but ultimately doomed thrust to out-flank the enemy ground defenses by crossing the Rhine river at Arnhem and swinging Allied Army units in behind the Ruehr pocket, whose occupation would destroy the Germans' main industrial base and hopefully lead to a general capitulation before 1944 was over. Otherwise it was targets in the strategic category ranging from oil to marshalling yards that were plastered.

Of the losses inflicted during this spell, two were due to mid-air collision. On the 22nd the 34th BG was on course for Kassel and approaching Buren, north of Paderborn, when two 7BS B-17s came together. All ten of Lt. S Durrett's crew on 43-38399 lost their lives after their bomber's Nos. 3 and 4 engines cut 43-38294 **The Wrangler** in half behind the radio room before banking off to the left with the other fuselage remnant still held in place by its errant motors. The aerodynamic imbalance so created probably threw Durrett's charge further out of control, after which it exploded.

Lt. L Whitehead, piloting the truncated bomber, was also killed, along with three of his crew, and one of the bombers plunged to destruction close to a farmhouse in the village of Hovelriege. The property, belonging to a Herr Henkemeyer, was totally demolished as a result of the B-17's bomb load detonating, while further material damage was inflicted on other village properties. In spite of this, the German civilian's daughter offered a hot drink to one of the American survivors, T/Sgt. W Brauks, after he was intercepted and brought into the village by a teenager to whom the airman (perhaps wisely) handed over his pistol and escape kit. The news of the Henkemeyer family's "traitorous" action was reported to the local SS, who were all for executing the father and confiscating all his possessions (such as might have been still on hand, considering his property's total obliteration!). Fortunately, he persuaded the SS officials that the provisions handed out were necessary to ensure the totally exhausted airman had the energy to get as far as a POW camp. Whatever the truth of this assertion, the fact remains that nothing further happened to Henkemeyer in terms of official action.

Oil was never far from the 8th AF's operational "menu," and on the 28th it was back to Merseberg for both B-17 divisions for September's penultimate sortie. The 3rd BD struck its assigned target at Leuna at a cost of ten bombers MIA, half coming from the 388th BG. However, two of the Knettishall crews were lost in a midair collision after bombing. The C formation Lead B-17, 43-38404/563BS flown by Capt C Maring (KIA), appeared to be taking evasive action; whether

The seemingly pristine condition of this B-17G based at Thorpe Abbotts conceals the fact that she is destined for salvage action on 4 November 1944. Fire damage was responsible for the decision, so ending a short two-month spell of assignment to the 100th BG.

A 100th BG B-17G holds course on the bomb run. The two bombs in view are probably 2,000-lb weapons judging by their size and location on the lower reaches of the central bomb racks.

or not correct, the No.2 aircraft 42-102953/563BS **Shy Ann** (Lt. Lord, also KIA) made a lethal contact with Maring's tail section, which was shorn off. Both machines fell inexorably to their destruction, and only three and two airmen respectively parachuted to safety. Already downed during the bomb run was 42-97219/560BS **Revel's Revenge**, when a flak shell burst between No.1 and 2 engines to send the B-17 into a spin. However, all but one of Lt. Olson's crew bailed out.

Also fatally crippled at this stage was Lt. Frawley's 42-37878 **Millie K** (388th BG), which had both inboard engines disabled and was last seen as the formation headed northwards for home. Although the bomber finally crashed close to Salzwedel, all nine airmen evacuated safely, despite reports that it was earlier observed close to the ground with no parachutes emerging. A further two 388th BG aircraft were crippled by the flak, one mortally. G I Jane (43-37520/560BS), with Lt. Michael in charge, held course for home, but only as far as the Koblenz area; then the bomber's overall condition forced its pilot to order his crew out, whereupon the B-17 plunged to earth at Alken. (Group records state this B-17 had reportedly exploded with no parachutes sighted, which was happily inaccurate.) The other cripple was more fortunate in staggering back to Belgian territory, where it was crash landed. This was 42-102434/561BS **Revel's Revenge**, which had also lost two engines and fallen out of formation; luck was on the crew's side, and all nine were soon returned to Knettishall.

September's last mission witnessed just four Division losses, but two of these were self inflicted. The 493rd BG's 43-38115/860BS **Reluctant Lassie** became the latest casualty to bombs released from above; Lt. D Treece and all but one of the nine-man crew were killed, and their aircraft crashed in the target area. Equally tragic was the other squadron loss, when 43-38480 succumbed to the damage caused by debris from Treece's B-17, bearing Lt. E LaFlame to his death while again just one of the crew survived.

October 1944

The first three October missions passed off with little cost for the 8th AF. Of the 3,062 crews gaining mission credit only sixteen were MIA, with eight coming from the 3rd BD. However, very few of the Division's force got through to the Primary on 3 October, with the bulk attacking targets of opportunity in Nuernberg. On the last mission to attack two airfields at Muenster single losses were borne by six groups. The returning crews would have accepted this as no more than an inevitable aspect of combat life; much worse was lurking in the shadows when Berlin was briefed on the 6th, however.

The Roof Falls in on the 4th CBW....

Berlin's Tegel district contained a key metallurgical plant that was briefed for assault on 6 October. Exactly 1200 crews out of 1271 got through to strike the target at a very tolerable cost of 19 crews. But this costly albeit ever-tragic statistic was far from being shared among either the three Divisions or their respective ranks. All but two came from out of the 3rd BD, but was in turn centered on one group...

It was bad enough when a group suffered severe losses during a mission. What was arguably worse was when that loss factor was reflected within the ranks of one squadron as occurred at Great Ashfield. The 549BS was allotted the High squadron position, which meant it would bomb last in accordance with standard operational procedure. Adding to this aerial exposure was the fact that the 385th BG was the last unit within the entire bomber stream....

The IP at Nauen was looming up ahead of the formation when "bandits" were called in that initially took the form of some fighters at 8 o'clock high. No sooner had the B-17 gunners begun to focus upon this perceived, although still distant, threat when a much larger mass of fighters loomed up from behind out of the sun and swooped into the attack. These aircraft were part of the dreaded JG300, whose primary function was to serve as a *Sturmgruppe*— that is, to seek out and attack any isolated element of the bomber stream. In this case, fighters from JG4 were also on hand. And so it was that the heavy cannon and machine gun barrage unleashed by the Bf-109s and Fw-190s cut an instant swathe through the small B-17 formation.

Lt. Kaplan was flying 43-37548/548BS **Hells Bells** in No. 5 position within the rearmost High element and was latched upon to be thoroughly shot-up with the right wing set ablaze. The bomber lurched into a steep dive that held the crew firmly in place until the action was corrected by the pilots and the bomb load jettisoned, but two gunners were already dead—one being S/Sgt. N Mertz, a replacement who was well into his combat tour—as the other seven prepared to jump. Sadly Lt. Kaplan's name was added to the fatality list after he failed to bail out. The crash site at Liepe was very close to Damme, where the survivors were all incarcerated after being rounded up.

One by one the remaining four B-17s from the High element were dispatched, as was to become the case for the other six in the Lead elements. Lt. R McGhee recalled the events of his last mission on Capt. J Batty's team:

"We took off, assembled and headed east. We were flying Lead for the 549BS, which was the last formation in the bomber stream, but had lost two of the briefed 13 crews thanks to 'aborts'. Shortly after entering Germany radio messages from preceding Groups indicated heavy fighter attacks. (Post-mission reports stated we were flying in an isolated position when attacked but this was not true). After turning at the IP Lt. Jones (N) and I picked up the target as the bomb-run began. We now sighted enemy fighters off to the left some 5 miles distant and our escort engaged them. Almost immediately our formation came under assault from around 35 more fighters coming out of the clouds from above and behind.

"I looked up from my bomb-sight to see an Fw190 to the left and a Bf109 directly ahead, flying as if in formation. I engaged the gun-turret sight and tried to focus on the

A mix of 337BS (AW) and 339BS (QJ) B-17Gs are wending their lumbering way out of the dispersals, with the pair at the left rear easing onto the runway's end. Note the staggered presentation of the squadron code letters compared to the aircraft letter on the two nearside bombers. Picture was taken in the summer or autumn of 1944.

The Deputy PFF B-17G from the 447th BG cants violently to the left, and with flames enveloping its left wing begins to trace a fiery path to destruction. The Lead PFF bomber, although showing the "Square K" for the Rattlesden Group, retains the TS code letters of the 333BS, 94th BG, which was a feature on several PFF transfers-in from Rougham.

> Bf109 but the turret had been damaged and was inoperable. Then our bomber began to develop a second diving action before righting itself at which point I jettisoned the bombs. Jones and I prepared to jump but the hatch was blocked by our Engineer's body. Being off oxygen and at 31,000 ft it was not long before we both passed out. The next thing I knew was that I was falling in mid-air, the B-17 having obviously exploded. I deployed my parachute and drifted down to be immediately apprehended." Jones and Sgt. Fields proved to be the sole other survivors out of the ten-man crew on 44-8143/551BS.

In general, the American bomber crews who ended up MIA were fortunate to have the bulk of their numbers end up alive, whether as POWs or evaders. In this instance the reverse situation arose, with 62 of the 100 airmen concerned losing their lives. The worst affected crew was Lt. Funk's in 42-98016/549BS, where all nine forfeited their lives. A scarcely better survival rate (one from nine) was experienced by Lt. Courcelle's team in 43-38060/549BS **Texas Bluebonnet** and Lt. Taylor's flying 42-98010/551BS. The small town of Liepe, scant miles east of Nennhausen and around 25 miles short of Tegel, became the epicentre for the crash sites of all of these B-17s, as well as the Kaplan-crewed bomber and the final loss from the High section. This involved 43-38217/551BS, whose pilot Lt. Tuley was one of three fatal casualties, with his B-17 falling at Barnewitz, just south of Liepe.

Lt. Jens in 42-102465/549BS **Wee Willie Wilbur** was probably one of the first from the Lead section to feel the fatal effect of the fighters' onslaught. His B-17 also came down near Liepe, and once again just one of the nine airmen on board survived. The No. 4 slot was flown by Lt. Andreas, but his B-17 (43-38430/548BS) was almost immediately dispatched to come down at Koenigshorst, along with its pilot and three others.

Two B-17Gs from Debach have their landing gears lowered, although their position above what seems to be a solid cloud base hardly suggests they are in the landing pattern. The bomber on the left was salvaged following a dispersal fire on 11 March 1945, while 44-8200, a PFF machine, was later transferred out to the 100th BG, where it was assigned to the 350BS.

Lt. Noiseau must have kept 44-6159/549BS **West Virginian** aloft at least until final target approach when it was abandoned by the surviving crew; only the pilot and one other ended up as POWs, with their B-17 piling into the ground in the Brandenburg district of *Big B*. Lt. Issacson's 42-97079/548BS **Dozy Doats** seemingly also held on for the target, but succumbed over the same Berlin district to bear four crewmembers to their deaths. **Roger the Dodger** (42-97275/549BS) bore the lowest fatality figure (one) among the eleven MIA crews; the precise crash site for this bomber is unclear. The lethal effect of the *Sturmgruppe* tactic was clearly illustrated here, with the bulk of the casualties realized within a matter of minutes to judge by the close proximity of the majority of the crash sites.

The *Sturmgruppe* assailants had not finished with the 4th CBW as its sub-forces headed into Berlin, and turned upon the 94th BG's thirteen-strong element flying as the Low group. Two 410BS crews were taken out, beginning with Lt. J Brasher's in 42-31599/GL: O The Filthy Hag, which fell away and down with several fighters crowding in behind. **Our Baby** (43-37630/GL: N) was soon knocked out of formation and lost to view; Lt. N Fausnough lost six of his ten-men team, whereas all nine airmen bailed out from the Brasher B-17. The third bomber declared MIA, although heavily damaged, actually made it back out of formation as far as the North Sea, but here Luck clearly deserted all on board 43-38207/TS:. The rescue aircraft and boats dispatched to the reported ditching site could only find an empty dinghy and two bodies from Lt. C Davies's crew, one of which was Maj. J Blount (333BS CO). The returning crews would have quietly mourned these losses, but they would be in a far more shocked mood a mere 24 hours hence....

Another 4th CBW "Crucifixion"

Germany's synthetic oil facilities came in for its latest crucifixion on the 7th from all three Divisions, who between them dispatched 1422 bombers, all but 21 of which either crossed over their briefed targets or diverted to hit suitable targets of opportunity. If the scale of punishment proved to be severe on the various oil production plants that were struck, then the defenders ensured that a fair measure of punishment would be handed out, amounting to 40 crews, with sixteen coming from the 3rd BD. For the second successive day the loss tally was partially concentrated on one Group at least, with the 94th BG the unfortunate unit concerned. The Rougham ranks had been reduced by four on the two previous days and now that figure was doubled.

Twenty-six B-17s were sent out to Boehlen, of which half flew High with the 385th BG and the other half linked up with the 95th BG. It was the latter formation that was to be embroiled in the air battle that evolved some 30 miles distant from Boehlen. Once again, the mass of between 50 and 60 fighters made swamping assaults upon the B-17s in several waves. The Lead bomber, flown by Lt. G Davies and Maj. Lambert (333BS CO and Command pilot), had its left wing set ablaze; 43-38208/TS: descended near Wiehe less three of her ten-man crew. The same location formed the last resting place for 43-39896/GL: H (Lt. G Williams). The sole survivor S/Sgt. G Perrin recalled that both wings were set on fire and the bail out order was given. No sooner had Perrin jumped clear than the B-17 exploded, killing all remaining eight on board. The savagely swift cull of the Group continued with Wiehe as the epicentre. Lt. P Golden's 42-32020/QE: U **Belle of the Brawl II** crashed at Garnbach; 42-31925/QE: **Goon Girl**, flown by Lt. L Levy, had its tail blown off and fell at Ostramonda; and 42-102616/GL: **Spirit of Valley Forge**, flown by Lt. Wheeler, descended to earth at Langenroda. Only six of the 27 airmen survived their bombers' loss, including one from the Levy-piloted aircraft and two of Lt. Wheeler's crew, with Golden as the sole pilot survivor.

This horrendous casualty rate was almost totally reversed among the three other MIA crews. Lt. J Loesing lost a single crewmember on board 42-97333/GL: **Duchess**, which came down to a crash landing near Sibbersdorf, while all eighteen airmen on 42-97316/QE: **Tommy** (Lt. Warren), which crashed at Furstenburg, and 43-37566/QE: O **Fortress Joker** flown by Lt. H Waldorf floated down into captivity. As on the previous day the crew casualties were reflected among one squadron's ranks, this time with seven coming from the 331BS.

"You Cawnt Miss It?" – Not much!

Sgt. Wilbert Richarz was an ROG based at Framlingham during the latter part of 1944. He recorded various military and social aspects of his and the crew's experiences. One of these was personal in nature and aptly illustrated the risks inherent in finding one's way around wartime Britain, particularly in the dark. Wilbert had a friend who had graduated as a fighter pilot and was assigned to the 357th FG at Leiston. The distance between the two airfields extended just over ten miles, but the road stretches in between were typical of the twisting and winding type found all over the British countryside, apart from which most road signs were still absent following the Nazi invasion threat in 1940.

A mail truck had taken the Sgt over to Leiston, but he had few reference points to aid him for a possible solo return trip, apart from which he was confidently but mistakenly assuming that a vehicle would be on hand. Having spent several hours in his friend's company he prepared to go back to base, but to his dismay found no vehicle on hand. Nothing daunted, he procured a bicycle and set off around 8 PM in anticipation of reaching Framlingham in plenty of time should a mission alert be called for his crew. The first "fly in the ointment" was presented by a combination of heavy mist and pitch darkness. Wickham Market was a major point on the homeward route since it was close to the airfield—the only trouble lay in the lack of road signs, and these could be confusing instead of informative even when in position. After feeling he was seriously losing his way he stopped at a house and asked the woman who answered his knock "Where is the bomber base," but omitting the appropriate name. Since there were several airfields in the area, his security-minded omission ironically got him nowhere.

Approaching midnight, Wilbert was now sweat-soaked and still thoroughly lost. His physical condition was accompanied by a real concern that if not on hand when an alert was called he would be listed as "Absent without Leave (AWOL)" and liable to serious punishment. It was now that a young woman on a bicycle sped past in the opposite direction, upon which he turned round and attempted to catch up with her. His desperate bid to catch up with the understandably worried lady and seek directions to what he almost breathlessly described as "the Base out of Wickham Market" happily succeeded, although he had to take in the

Right: On 11 November 1944 the U.S.Army and U.S. Navy faced each other in an American football game at London's White City stadium. "Lady Moe" was chosen as the Army's mascot. She was escorted to London by Sgt. F Harrington (P R Section), who is seen on the donkey's back. The second picture shows "Moe" along with the Navy mascot, a goat named "Billy Goat Gruff." Snetterton's pride and joy seems to take little interest in her male adversary, however.

Above: A third picture of "Lady Moe" at the White City stadium has Sgt. Harrington seemingly applying physical pressure to the donkey's rear end; the animal's reaction in turn appears to be nil. The species was used to carry very heavy human or material loads back in North Africa.

information as both were cycling along! It was a highly relieved if thoroughly sweat-lathered airman who sped in through the main gate and made contact with his crew as they were heading to the Mess hall, having indeed been called for the mission!

The ill fortune borne by the 94th and 385th BGs was not matched by the Division's units over the ensuing twelve missions up to the month's end, since a mere nine crews were lost in action, although the last one to Merseberg was abandoned thanks to the weather conditions.

November

In contrast to the other two Divisions who were dispatched against oil targets, the 3rd BD opened November with a two-unit assault upon a railroad bridge at Rudesheim. However, these groups were initiating operations with a specialist blind bombing device codenamed *Micro-H*. Next day the latest thrust at Merseburg was made by the full B-17 force, but the defenders demanded and received their usual tithe of bombers, totalling 38. (Two 1st BD groups were caught out of the bomber stream by fighters and lost twenty-two B-17s between them, so illustrating the continuing if spasmodic menace still posed by the *Luftwaffe's Sturmgruppen* in particular.) A dreadfully spectacular casualty involved the 486th BG's 43-37883 **Blue Streak**, belonging to the 834BS, whose ranks had so far remained loss-free for 77 missions. A flak shell blew up a fuel tank, and the entire nose section broke away with the blazing remains photographed for eternity; not surprisingly, none of Lt. D Paris' crew escaped the inferno. A second group bomber was also lost out of the twelve Division casualties, but it was the 447th BG that absorbed most of these losses with five B-17s taken out.

The group's punishment began over Holland on the way in when Lt. P Hayes, flying 44-6511/708BS, found his charge was developing mechanical problems. Whether or not he finally eased out of the formation preparatory to turning back would never be clear, but in so manoeuvering he crossed the path of 44-6571/711BS, flown by Lt. C Moses. The latter B-17's fuselage was severed by the buzz-saw effect of Hayes' propellers, and the truncated sections fell inexorably to earth bearing all but Sgt. R Humphreys (TG) to their deaths. The other bomber was kept aloft long enough to reach and force land on an airfield behind Allied lines. Nordhausen, further east, was where 43-37531/508BS ended up, along with four out of nine crewmembers led by Lt. Wing; he had suffered two runaway propellers approaching the IP and had turned back. Then bombs away had barely occurred when a devastating flak strike on 42-97634/ 711BS' forward fuselage killed Maj. Allen, Capt. Reynolds (P), and the other three occupants, leaving five Enlisted men to bail out. The 710BS' 42-107029 **Tail Wind** lost an engine to target flak, but the straggling B-17 was further crippled on the way back when a second engine went "out." Finally, further flak hits near Osnabrueck forced Lt. R Johnson to order his crew out. Eight ended up as POWs, but Lt. J Esper (CP) was believed to have either been shot in midair or given summary "treatment" after landing according to crew witnesses who were also fired upon; the B-17 buried itself into the ground at Teklenburg, west of Osnabrueck.

The hoar frost clinging to this PFF B-17G from the 96th BG (44-8178/QJ: D) and its surroundings presents a beautiful picture. However, the build-up of ice on flying surfaces that did accrue out of such winter conditions sometimes led to heavily-laden bombers faltering in flight and crashing.

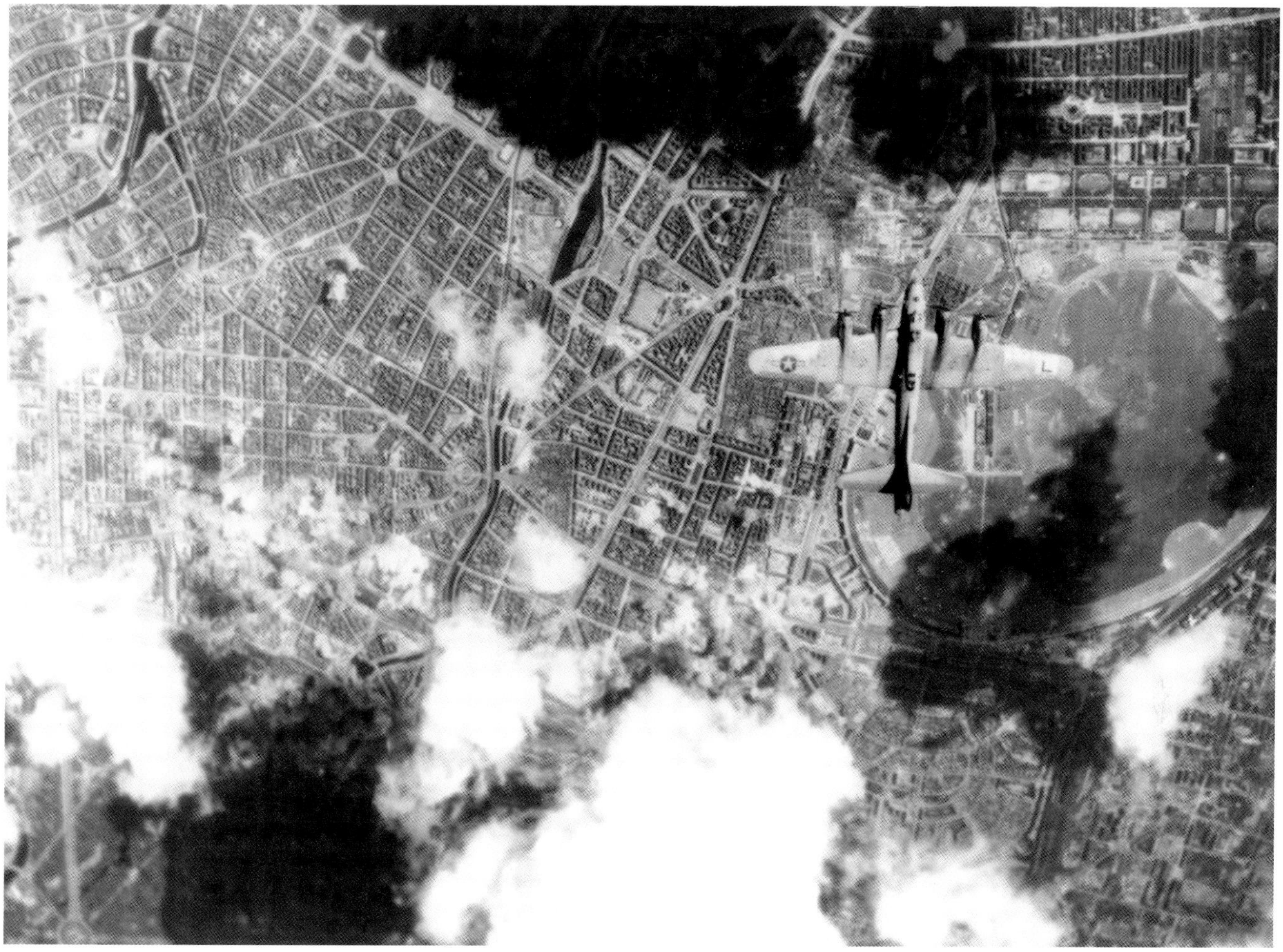

A picture that tends to say it all. Tempelhof airfield in Berlin is being over-flown by the 452nd BG as yet another 8th USAAF mission adds to the destruction of *Big B*'s industrial potential. There is no evidence of flak, and the B-17s and B-24s are likely enjoying almost total immunity from fighter assault in this 1944/45 picture.

Lt. Tetrault suffered a combination of engine failure along with loss of oxygen and electrical facilities, serious problems that culminated in a third engine catching fire around the enemy coastline. He headed out over the North Sea, where a successful "ditching" of 43-37936/711BS left all nine crewmembers alive for subsequent pick-up by ASR Launch. (One other crew also straggling on half power after the bomb run were more fortunate in warding off several fighter passes to land back at Rattlesden; Lt. Rodhe's 42-97803/ was the B-17 in question.)

Since suffering nine losses on 12 September, two appeared to have then become a "bogy" number for the 493rd BG because that figure in MIA crews had occurred on two occasions and now recurred today, as well as on five future missions. Lt. G Whitlock (863BS CO) was leading the group, along with Capt. V Alexander in a 34th BG PFF bomber, 44-8246. As the Rally Point was looming up, a flak shell impacted on the left-inner wing surface and fire took hold along the wing/fuselage area. The B-17 fell off to the left and, after descending slowly for around a minute, then drooped into a steep dive to crash at Sommerda; Alexander was one of four survivors, but Whitlock and six others were killed. Flak was also regarded as the executioner for Lt. R Proudfit Jr's 43-38284/863BS **Straighten up and fly right – the Rock**, although the formation was also under attack by several Me-163 rocket-propelled fighters. The loss of an engine caused the bomber to trail inexorably behind. In spite of this the pilots managed to hold on for home until matters forced an abandonment over Dutch territory near Rijn Saterwoude; one crewmember ended up in German hands, but the other eight not only evaded capture, but were sheltered by the local population until liberation of the region the following May!

Seven missions were flown between 4 and 11 November, all but one of which struck targets inside Germany. The exception occurred on the 9th when support was intended to be provided to Gen. Patton's 3rd Army, but the Division was forced to seek the Secondary at Saarbruecken, despite the other two Divisions reporting at least partially clear conditions for their bomb runs. In addition, the intended Merseburg strike (8th) was cancelled due to weather. Oil plants, airfields, and marshalling yards all took a beating on the other five occasions, and losses were limited to nineteen MIA, although eleven went down on one mission; in addition two bombers were lost over English soil or off the coast, and seven more B-17s were crash landed on the Continent during the same period.

Blind Luck...

On 5 November Lt. R Wright and crew were on their tenth mission to attack Ludwigshaven's marshalling yards, but their 95th BG B-17 was to be one of eleven Division aircraft destroyed. Flak knocked out fuel lines to No. 1 engine, which was switched off; No. 2's propeller "ran away," so making the task of holding course evermore difficult. Further damage to the hydraulics and oxygen system coupled with No. 2's propeller hub catching fire impelled Wright to call for a bail out from the now isolated B-17, an order that was responded to by all but Lts. S Wolfson (CP) and I Levin (B). Both officers were ready to jump from the nose hatch and bomb bay respectively when the offending propeller disintegrated and the fire was extinguished. Wright attempted to signal to his two companions not to jump, but only Levin responded positively. Wolfson, with his back to the cockpit, was not aware of Wright's action and dived out.

Levin clambered back into the co-pilot's seat, and with cover provided by a P-51 held course for Allied lines. The first bid to land on a French airfield failed, and the second approach was made with the ailing B-17 flying just above stalling speed. The crabbing motion caused by the asymmetric power balance ended up with one tire bursting, and with no brakes to arrest

A second view of the crash scene shows how the extreme rear fuselage section with its canted top-fin area has been ripped off and slung round almost in the opposite direction.

The forward section of **Boyd's Boids** (43-37764/AW: B) lies mangled in a railroad cutting bordering Snetterton Heath. The B-17G, flown By Lt. J Boyd, was on final landing approach when it stalled out while the pilots were attempting to go round again...

A third view reveals how the left wing has been excised outboard of the No. 1 engine nacelle, while the remnants of the fuselage center section are sandwiched between the track bed and the inner wing. The railroad tracks are noticeably twisted, and the British "Toonerville Trollies" will not run for a day or so...

The track is now fully restored to its function, as the tail section is removed from the embankment. It is just incredible, given the circumstances, that *all* nine crewmembers survived the incident, with several thrown out of the radio room where they were stationed at the time!

A tight-packed formation of 487th BG aircraft is in the charge of 44-8039/2G: L, whose H2X pod is in the lowered position. This B-17G was later transferred to the 94th BG and ended up salvaged in Germany. By contrast, 4F: J in the foreground returned home in mid-July 1945, but her fate was similarly ordained at Kingman's "boneyard."

the bomber's progress it careered off the PSP metal surface and into the muddy soil. It then pitched high onto its nose before thumping back onto the ground. Of the nine airmen, Wright and Levin were back on friendly territory and six were facing *Kriegydom*—and the ninth was dead in the most brutal fashion, having been granted "summary justice" by civilians. This was Lt. Wolfson, who would otherwise have survived along with his pilot and bombardier had he but been able to respond to the bail out cancellation request. Blind luck had decreed a particularly tragic conclusion to his combat tour.

Three groups lost pairs of crews, including the 493rd BG; Lt. J Kolberg's 43-38264/863BS was plucked out of the sky by flak and crashed at Ludwigshafen, along with five of its crew, while the equally flak-stricken 43-38359/861BS (Capt. E Johnson, KIA) tumbled to destruction at Viernheim, scant miles northeast of the target, taking down six out of eleven airmen.

Tragically-earned Awards

One of the returning B-17s circling Rattlesden on 2 November was firing red flares that indicated wounded on board. The medics attending the bomber after it landed and taxied into its dispersal clambered into the fuselage and carefully brought out the incumbent form of Lt. R Femoyer for removal to the base hospital. The navigator had received serious wounds when the bomber was struck by flak; he not only stuck to his duties after refusing a morphine injection to relieve his sufferings, but insisted on being propped up at his desk in order to continue his duties. Despite accepting the injection after the North Sea had been reached, his lease on life ran out shortly after reaching the hospital. His gallantry was recognized in 1945 by the award of the Congressional Medal of Honor. Seven days later two more Division personnel acted in a similar self-sacrificial manner with the same posthumous outcome....

On 9 November the Division flew its fifth monthly mission, in this case in support of Gen. Patton's badly-stalled assaults upon German defensive positions around Metz, in eastern France. **Lady Janet** (42-97904/R) was in the hands of Lts. D Gotts and W Metzger, but was one of two group B-17s fated not to return to Deopham Green. The bomber was flak-stricken over the Secondary target at Saarbruecken, losing all or partial power on three engines as well as suffering much electrical damage, along with exploding flares that ignited leaking hydraulic fluid. While Gotts directed the ailing and burning B-17 towards nearby Allied-occupied territory, Metzger attended to the severely-wounded ROG. The other crewmembers bailed out, with one using Metzger's pack after discovering his was destroyed. Then Gotts and Metzger settled to the task of bringing their charge in for a crash landing in order to save the ROG, whose wounds rendered him incapable of jumping. Tragically, the chosen crash site was almost at hand when a fuel tank erupted under the influence of the spreading flames; the result was to thrust the bomber out of control, whereupon it disintegrated upon contact with the ground and all three airmen were killed. Both pilots had the Medal of Honor bestowed upon them, to again emphasize the close-knit relationship existing among the majority of bomber crews that arguably was stronger than the blood ties between family members....

A majority of the November missions involved bombing by PFF methods with *H2X*, *G-H*, and now *Micro-H* all being utilized with varying degrees of success. However, bomber operations only recommenced on the 16th, with a truly devastating assault upon Dueren lying square in the path of an intended advance by the U.S. 1st Army. Then came two more non-operational spells for the Division up to the 24th, which was broken only by a mission to Osnabrueck on the 21st before the pace for the remainder of the month picked up with five missions. Over this spell thirty-five crews failed to return with the losses generally spread among the various groups.

Insidious Menace

A fifth of this figure was sustained on the 21st when several marshalling yards became the Secondary or target of opportunity alternative for the Division, instead of the three briefed oil refineries. Seven B-17s were MIA, three from the 96th BG, which included one casualty other than to the defenses. Added to the risk of collision with another bomber in the formation was the invisible but insidious effect of the slipstream emanating from each bomber. The turbulent air patterns could easily throw an aircraft into an uncontrollable attitude....

Lt. H Sullivan's crew were on board 42-102646/AW: A and were in their assigned slot as the "recall" signal was responded to by the various groups. The neat stream pattern became a tangle, and the 96th BG flew through another unit's slipstream. Suddenly Sullivan's B-17 was peremptorily cast onto its back and developed a spinning action. After several turns the spin was corrected, but to the eyewitnesses' horror the B-17 split in two as it was levelling out. None of the nine airmen got out of their flying tomb, which impacted south of Hildesheim. Mother Nature had struck once again, as she had done before and would do in the future. The second MIA crew also all forfeited their lives, although their B-17, 43-37792/MZ: N, was seen to leave the formation under apparent control; Poye, near Osnabrueck, formed the lethal crash site for both bomber and crew. Relative luck attended the crash landing between Appeldoorn and Amersfoort, in Holland, of 42102554/BX: K **Jean O**, from which all of Lt. R Worden's team emerged alive to face imprisonment.

Combat flying carried a large element of Luck, and this factor was more than amply demonstrated by a fourth 96th BG crew today. **Boyds Boids** (43-37764/AW: B) had suffered partial or total failure in two engines, and the crew had jettisoned all available equipment. They made it across the North Sea at minimum altitude and were on final approach to Snetterton Heath when forced to attempt to go around again thanks to another bomber ahead firing red flares indicating wounded aboard. Flying on almost half power, the B-17 failed to respond and dropped one wing that caught the railroad embankment just outside the airfield perimeter. The airframe fractured at the radio room, while the rear section further split in two as the remnants ground to a halt. Amazingly none of the nine from Lt. J Boyd's team was killed, although one sustained a broken leg and several were knocked unconscious by the brutal impact.

There was a second exception to the low loss-rate on the 30th when Merseburg again appeared on the Division's Briefing room maps. The flak barrage thrown up by the target's batteries that greeted the 13th CBW, among others, in the bomber stream soon began to tell, especially among the ranks of the Framlingham sub-force. The bomb run was barely completed when 43-38053/CC, flown by Lt. R Torrance, fell out and down to crash at Grosskayna, mere miles due south of the target, with the pilot one of four fatalities. Scant miles on 43-38456/CC: came down at Zeitz, along with all of Lt. Philip's crew. The destruction proceeded apace with 43-

Unfamiliar territory for the 486th BG's 43-37953/K as it squats next to a B-26 from the 344th BG; the Sudbury-based bomber diverted into this continental airfield for undisclosed reasons. The manner in which the code letters on the B-26 are outlined against the camouflage is a point of interest.

The Merseburg flak gunners landed a fatal strike on Lt. L Kersten's B-17G that ignited the right main fuel tank. The torching flames all too soon initiated an explosion that disintegrated 43-37877/2G: E, but not before Lts. H James (N) and W Ritchhart (B) had scrambled out of the nose hatch. Mission on 30 November 1944 was the last major strike on this key oil refinery complex by the 8th AF.

37519/FC: **Joker** (Lt. Booth, KIA), the latest flak victim impacting near Zwickau. Rommerode lies southeast of Kassel and roughly 100 miles west of Mersburg, so it appears as if the flak damage to 42-107041/DI: M **Ain't Misbehavin'** still permitted Lt. D Meigide to hold course for home before his charge finally gave up; the pilot shared the same sad fate as the other three airplane commanders, as did three of his crew. A companion squadron aircraft, 44-8325/DI: T **Boogie Baby**, ended up south of Mainz at Rittersheim; a flak victim, but by then all nine on Lt. A Harris' crew were safely floating down under their parachutes. Two further group B-17s got back as far as Allied territory on the continent, but were later categorized *Category E*; one was 43-38345/FC: V **Sleepy Time Gal**, which landed at Melsbroek, Antwerp.

Three further 13th CBW bombers were lost, including 43-38211/XR: R from the 100th BG. Flak struck home on the bomb run to send the aircraft into a flaming spin that ended with the still bomb-laden machine erupting amid part of the plant structure; Lt. V Anderson (P) joined five other crewmembers in death. Two B-17s from Horham ended up at Merseburg; Lt. Payne lost two crewmembers from 42-97383/ET: F, while the death toll on Lt. Wicker's 43-38611/BG: X stood at two. A third 95th BG loss involved only the aircraft and the unlucky tail gunner; the pilot—a Lt. Miller—and his co-pilot, nursed their B-17 back until over Belgian territory after target flak had blown away most of the tail compartment, as well as casting its occupant into midair. The crew then abandoned the crippled aircraft to its fate.

Lt. Miller's bombardier had suffered a safe but still unfortunate landing, in that the tree with which his parachute snagged itself cast him into an inverted position, as well as temporarily knocking him out. After recovering his senses, all calls for help as he hung above the ground were seemingly ignored. Then the arrival of two elderly, soberly-clad women promised salvation—but nothing doing! The duo ignored him, and instead of freeing him from his very uncomfortable perch scrambled up the tree limb with amazing agility. Then they drew out pairs of scissors with which they cut the parachute canopy free of the shroud lines before equally agilely regaining the ground, rolling up the canopy, and departing the scene as furtively as they appeared! It was some time later before the

The winter conditions in 1944/45 were particularly severe, making combat operations even more hazardous than normal. Here **Raidin' Maiden**, based at Eye, awaits the delivery of her bomb load—but the trolley will first have to be turned round for the bombs to be hoisted at a forward angle.

stranded airman's calls for help were properly responded to by two men working in a field.

Seven further Division crews also failed to return, including **The Reluctant Dragon**, assigned in mid-January and one of the first B-17Gs to be fitted Stateside with enclosed waist windows and Cheyenne tail turret. The 96th BG aircraft had also been brought back heavily damaged on 8 May by Lt. Musser with only two of his crew still on board. Now, 43-38133/AW: O was crippled on the bomb run by flak and the bombs had to be released manually. A gliding flight attitude was maintained while all excess equipment, including the ball turret, was jettisoned. Sadly, the Allied front lines were looming up when further flak strikes impelled Lt. F Towle to call for the six surviving crew to jump, one of whom did not reach the ground alive.

Summary "Justice" Strikes Again

The 34th BG was one of the contributors to the MIA list on the 30th. Capt. O Hanson had survived the debacle over Mendlesham on 7 June, although he had been forced to crash land near Eye. Now he was piloting 43-38059/391BS with Lt. R Keirn (CP) and T/Sgt P Shull (Eng.) among the crew. Once again it was flak that dealt the death blow to this B-17, but all nine crewmembers reportedly cleared the doomed aircraft before it piled into the ground and floated down to an anticipated POW existence. This proved the case for only five airmen, however.

Sgt. Shull had been apprehended and brought to a building, where his eyes alighted upon a collection of Mae Wests spattered with blood; upon closer inspection he also noted numerous holes pierced in each fabric surface. It was clear that the unfortunate individuals concerned—later confirmed as Shull's pilots, ROG, and ball turret gunner—had been the latest victims of summary "justice" as advocated by Dr. Josef Goebbels. In this case it had been dealt out by pitchfork-wielding farm workers.

(At first sight, it might seem illogical that Germans living in the areas away from the much-bombed cities were so regularly engaged in this nefarious activity since they were generally more divorced from the almost daily assaults faced by their more hard-pressed fellow nationals that in turn engendered technically criminal acts of this nature against Allied airmen. On the other hand, the burgeoning activities of Allied fighters making strafing runs on any moving object, as well as the release of bomb loads, accidentally or otherwise, into open countryside probably aroused the same degree of naked hatred among those either affected by these actions and/or who had lost family or friends in the process.)

The Merseburg mission on 30 November 1944 cost the Division seventeen crews MIA with two further B-17s abandoned abroad. While circling Rougham on return Lt. O Winter and crew were killed when 42-97985 collided with 44-8177; the latter bomber was more fortunate in that it was landed safely.

On 16 December 1944, 42-32066 /QW: D **Silver Slipper**, having suffered serious battle damage, over-shot the Horham runway. The extreme punishment inflicted upon the forward cockpit section suggests the pilots would have been lucky to avoid injury if not death, although their fate is undisclosed.

December 1944

December not only witnessed the full onset of the 1944/45 winter, but must also have ruefully been reflected upon by the Allied High Command as no longer signalling a likely conclusion to hostilities in Europe, thanks to the September failure of Operation *Market-Garden*. Even worse was in store for the Anglo-American ground forces as Hitler's plan code-named *Herbst-reise* (autumn journey) to strike through the Ardennes with a view to capturing the vital port of Antwerp and simultaneously splitting the British/Canadian and U.S. Armies in two was soon to be launched.

It was 3 December before the USAAF "heavies" next took off and assembled for a mission that in the 3rd BD's case was abandoned due to adverse weather. The marshalling yard theme was repeated next day when the 8th AF assaulted these facilities ranging from Koblenz down to Mainz and up to Kassel. Then, a surprisingly reduced force of less than 500 B-17s struck at munitions and tank production in Berlin (5th), followed by the latest foray against Merseburg by both B-17 Divisions. Overall 8th AF losses were surprisingly low at thirty, of which the 3rd BD contributed nine, including all four over Merseburg.

This promising pattern of regular missions was destined to be temporarily interrupted twice up to mid-month, although a further seventeen, involving varying Task force strengths, would go out before the year's end. Only the 1st BD took to the air (9th) to attack airfields and marshalling yards in the Stuttgart area, while the other two Divisions took up the challenge 24 hours later, with marshalling yards again on the list. Yet more of the same facilities were targeted by the B-17s on the 11th, with no less than 1487 bombers from all Divisions going out to comprise the largest-ever attacking force to date—nearly five times that dispatched on *Black Thursday*! The *Mighty Eighth* was living up to this sobriquet, and would even expand upon it numerically during the remaining months of the Offensive....

Comment

The weather conditions had dictated that the vast bulk of bombing be conducted by PFF means. Although accuracy was rarely as good compared to visual sighting of a target, it would appear that sufficient weight of explosives and incendiaries were brought to bear upon the enemy's industrial base to cause a steady if unquantifiable downturn in productive capacity. The synthetic oil and railroad facilities were certainly suffering, but the parallel production of aircraft and support equipment far from declining displayed an upward-directed resilience right up to VE-Day. However, critics of the Bombing Offensive tend to quote the latter aspect of Nazi Germany's output as proof of failure in the Allied aerial assault. What is conveniently overlooked is that the ultimate strangulation of oil production literally grounded the *Luftwaffe* and placed similar unbearable restrictions upon the *Wehrmacht's* overall movements. A brand new airplane, tank, or lorry was of no practical value if fuel was not on regular hand with which to operate the equipment; the *Luftwaffe* was by now also suffering from a

Although reportedly allocated the codes of Horham's 412BS (QW), these are absent from 43-38288's fuselage. Variously named **V for Victory** and **Goin my Way**, this B-17G crash landed off the 19 March 1945 mission, but was restored to flying condition and returned Stateside. Note the absence of the fairing behind the Bendix chin turret.

What are probably red engine cowlings of the 710BS are seen on this Rattlesden B-17G with its collapsed left landing gear. Yellow fuselage bands date the picture to at least December 1944 /January 1945, when they were first applied. Originally assigned to the 94th BG, the aircraft survived combat for ultimate delivery to Kingman, AZ.

growing and finally lethal shortage of properly trained combat personnel. The interdiction of railroad communications in particular proved to be another inhibiter, in this case denying the enemy the means to transport men and equipment when and where these resources were required and without material hindrance.

Operational Frustration

The first winter of WWII in Britain had proved to be the worst for many years, and the same adverse pattern was about to be cast up in what would be the Conflict's final such season. On the 15th both B-17 Divisions headed out for Kassel and Hannover, the latter target being a marshalling yard and assigned to the 3rd BD at a cost of a single MIA crew. As the bombers settled down on their airfields, the heavy fog conditions existing over western Europe were about to provide the perfect "cloak" for the thousands of armoured vehicles and the multitude of support infantry massed opposite the U.S. Army front lines in Luxembourg, and on the brink of initiating their Antwerp-bound assault....

Weather conditions over the bomber bases were critical enough next day for only three groups from the 3rd BD out of both Divisions to assemble and head for Stuttgart's marshalling yards. A better effort was achieved next day when similar facilities in Koeln and Mainz were struck, although a good proportion of the 411 attackers sought targets of opportunity. By the 19th the full scale of the German assault was becoming apparent, and a proportion of the other two Divisions were diverted into attacking a series of what were termed "tactical" targets in the rear zones from where *Herbst-reise* had been launched. Then Mother Nature increased her malign influence upon bomber operations by closing down the bases for the next three days. All this time the German forces were advancing towards their first vital objective—the river Meuse, whose successful crossing would set them on an almost unstoppable course for Antwerp, provided sufficient numbers could attain this primary goal, and more importantly have access to ample fuel supplies from their own or captured sources. As it was, stubborn defensive efforts by some U.S. Army units allied to poor tactical handling of forces on the Germans' behalf was already casting the Operation behind schedule, although there was still no guarantee that the overall advance could be swiftly contained, let alone defeated at this stage.

Mother Nature Relents....

On the 23rd the hitherto badly restricted visibility conditions over Western Europe gave way to relatively clear skies, although the 8th AF dispatched a surprisingly reduced force totalling barely 400 B-17s and B-24s. In spite of this, the seven communications Primaries in the enemy's rear echelons were squarely struck, although the 3rd BD element going to Homburg's marshalling yards had to have recourse to a blind approach using *Micro-H*.

The promise of a high pressure area advancing eastwards that had been previously observed by the Allied meteorologists now broke forth on Xmas Eve, although the sub-zero temperature created local pockets of fog that would lead to several take-off incidents; this was particularly the case for the Midlands area that was home to the 1st BD.

Thirteen days previously, the 8th AF had dispatched its largest ever force of more than 1400 bombers. That figure, massive as it was, would now be eclipsed by the figure of 1884 bombers, one that would never again be equalled. A huge range of communications targets had been selected for assault, with the 4th CBW in the van of the 3rd BD, which in turn was leading the 8th AF.

The Gentle General

Frederick W Castle had originally arrived in England as one of Gen Eaker's small cadre of officers back in early 1942. This quiet but firm-minded and equally firmly expressive

American airman was a world distant from the "rambunctious Yank, here to win the War" image that many Britons held of their Ally's service personnel during (and in some cases for decades after) WWII. He had been appointed to replace the CO of the 94th BG in mid-July 1943 and had carried out this difficult duty in a positive manner that had finally won the hearts of the initially sceptical group personnel.

His subsequent promotion to Brig. General in 1944 had seen appointment to the command of the 4th CBW, which from April that year encompassed the 487th BG operating out of Lavenham. On the evening of 23 December Castle called in his CBW HQ and was informed upon asking that the Wing was on operational alert. He was about to depart when he returned to the Operations Room and raised the supplementary question of who was leading the Division; upon finding out that it was his Wing, he quietly insisted upon displacing the Deputy Chief of Staff Operations, Lt. Col. Macdonald, in the Lead B-17—a particular disappointment to Col. Perkins, Chief of Staff, who had informed his subordinates not to divulge this salient fact to their CG, who had been working himself to the point of exhaustion. Thus, the die was cast for an act of tragic self sacrifice....

Darkness still enfolded the countryside as the vehicle taking Castle to Lavenham wended its way along the winding roads. B-17G/44-8444/2G: N, a PFF equipped aircraft, was squatting on its dispersal with Lt. R Harriman's crew in attendance, with whom Castle was to fly. Take-off was at 0900 hours, but final Wing Assembly was fraught with problems, and the sub-force fell behind schedule. The time lost was steadily being recovered as the force crossed in over Belgium and began to approach the front lines. It was then that some Bf-109s that had evaded the escorts plunged in for an attack.

The Lead B-17 had already suffered power loss in one engine, and Castle finally signalled the Deputy Lead to take over as the now errant B-17 drifted out to one side of the group. It was then subjected to two specific assaults that set two engines ablaze as the pilots attempted to close in again. Castle was heard to calmly give the signal for a bail out as the crippled B-17 staggered unevenly across the sky. The landing gear was lowered as the bomber slowed down to make it easier for the crew to bail out, but both pilots were still aboard when fire caused a wing tank to blow up and sent the B-17 into an irrecoverable dive that ended with a fatal impact near Hods, in Belgium. (The bomb load was still in position, since jettisoning would have placed the lives of Allied servicemen or Belgian civilians in danger.) Six of the other eight crewmembers had been granted the gift of life thanks to what was regarded as the sacrificial actions of Gen. Castle, who was later awarded the Medal of Honor, the final example among the seventeen to be granted an 8th AF member.

The author recalls viewing the fine portrait of the General adorning the hallway in the "Swan" hostelry at Lavenham village way back in 1967; although then having very little knowledge of the airman's history, he was still struck by the quiet authority displayed upon his canvas-based features. Fred Castle was quite simply a true example of a human being who put his life on the line not only for his country, but also for the hard-earned and even harder-retained principles of Democracy enjoyed, and all too often taken for granted by so many Nations living under its guidance.

The 4th CBW lost eleven of the fourteen crews declared MIA from Division strength. The loss-factor was most felt by the 487th BG with seven further B-17s downed. Lt. L Reed was flying Lead for the Low section and came under sustained assault when the fighter attacks developed, as well as probably absorbing a flak strike. With one wing suffering an ever-growing fire the crew began to bail out, an action that all ten carried out. However, the parachute of Maj. L Nash (CP) failed to properly deploy and he plunged to his death in a quarry. The doomed B-17, 44-8121/2G: B, finally crashed at Esneux. Another companion in fate was 44-8192/2C: K piloted by Lt. K Lang, which was flying in the rear of its sub-formation and was soon set on fire to crash near Louveigne; both pilots and three other crewmembers shared their bomber's fate.

Three of the group's squadrons shared in the punishment, the 836BS leading with five crews. Lt. W Waldron's 43-37926/2G: E began to descend with a sheet of flame decorating one wing following the initial pass, after which Lt. R Neu (B) recalled a spinning motion inducing fierce centrifugal forces swiftly followed by a blinding flash, and then he was

On Xmas Eve 1944 descending fog over the Midlands prevented the bulk of the 1st BD from landing back on its airfields located there. In this instance Molesworth's 303rd BG found a temporary refuge with the 96th BG. The extra pressure placed in general upon the staff, and especially Snetterton Heath's cooks, was handled well. The snow has left its specific mark upon the bombers' vertical fins.

The 486th BG's 3R: C was barely clear of the airfield on 31 December on its way to Misburg when the pilots were faced with force-landing the six-month veteran B-17G at Cornard Tye. Fortunately all went well for the crew, as the bomber ground to a halt close to a railroad line, although it was "written off" group records three days later.

out in midair with his parachute deploying. Waldron and one more airman formed the trio of survivors, and the bomber's remnants ended up scattered near Rouvreux. The fourth squadron casualty was 42-102497/2G: A, on which Lt. W Curtiss was one of three fatalities, and which crashed almost simultaneously with Waldron's B-17, in this case at Comblain-au-Pont after all four engines were set on fire.

Barely one minute later 44-8614/2C: J was added to the MIA total when it impacted near Deigne. Lt. H Turnquist (P) suffered a particularly cruel fate. First he was held firmly against the fuselage nose hatch by the airflow before being dragged back into the aircraft; then, having successfully cleared the bomber on the second attempt, his parachute streamed but did not fully deploy and he was killed by the impact. Five of the eight other airmen reached the ground alive. The third 838BS aircraft loss involved 42-98019/2C: L **Mutzie B**, which had aborted the mission and was actually well on the way across the North Sea when matters took a turn for the worse. Lt. R Kraker (839BS) elected to reverse course towards Belgium, although bare minutes away from the English coast, and therefore with further to go to reach continental shores. With fire gaining hold on one wing, the five crewmembers in the rear fuselage assembled by the rear door and decided to bail out despite the sea still being below. Only one (Lt. B Souders, TG) was subsequently fortunate enough to land close enough to the shoreline to be able to swim there despite the frigid water temperature; the others either drowned or died from exposure. Had all remained on board they would have survived the crash landing and return to England.

The fifth 836BS crew loss was in 43-37569/R5: P (Lt. I Ball, KIA), which lost all rudder control during the first fighter pass as well as suffering fires in two engines. Only three crewmembers reached the ground alive, but Lt. C Becker, an Armament officer riding in the separated tail section that struck the ground at Septroux, had a further lease of life for just two days.

Applying the Pressure

The advent of clearer weather conditions permitted the daily launch of the 8th AF with communications still a priority on the target menu. Communications centers and rail bridges west of the Rhine were hammered on Xmas Day, albeit without the 1st BD, much of whose strength had been forced to divert from its fog-shrouded airfields on Xmas Eve. A much-reduced force from the 2nd and 3rd BDs, again assaulting railroad facilities behind the Ardennes battle front (26th), while a wider geographic spread of the same target type (27th) saw bombers from all three Divisions ranging south and east on either side of the Rhine. Nearly 2,000 bombers were dispatched over the ensuing two days to add even greater adverse pressure upon the German ability to feed supplies through to the Ardennes. As it was, the Offensive had largely run out of steam by this point and was under growing counter-attack from Allied forces closing in from north and south of the artificial "bulge" created in the Allied front.

MIA casualties were still proving to be relatively light, with seventeen aircraft and crews so categorized between 25 and 30 December, although several more were involved in fatal take-off and landing incidents, while a further number crash or force-landed. Two losses on the 30th were ascribed to that inherent risk in close formation flying—collision. Two 708BS aircraft (42-97400 **Fuddy Duddy** flown by Lt. Leverett and 43-38473 with Lt. Bates' crew) made fatal contact. Out of the eighteen Rattlesden airmen involved, only two survived from the first aircraft, which crashed near Buchen, in the Odenwald. A tree at the crash site later bore the carved inscription "Flugzeugunglueck, 31.12.1944 USA 10 Tote" ("Aircraft crash (date) ten dead," the latter detail being incorrect by one.)

Costly Year-end Action

A degree of grim reality returned to haunt the Division on 31 December, when the first purely strategic target for just over two weeks was attacked by all its groups. Hamburg possessed several oil refineries that were allotted to the 3rd BD. Germany's second industrial city still held a fearsome defensive reputation that was well earned by the Division, with the 13th CBW the prominent sufferer today.

The *Bloody Hundredth* had sent up 36 B-17s, but on return eight hours later the group was short by exactly one-third. A probable cause in this latest and final group disaster was the decision at Briefing to permit each squadron to bomb separately, thus dangerously loosening group integrity should the *Luftwaffe* intervene—which it duly did! The bomb run had been conducted downwind, but the initial fighter attacks commenced in between the IP and the target. However, the casualty figure was probably initiated by the flak barrage. A strike on 42-31066/EP:H **Fools Rush In** resulted in Lt. F Henderson's charge sagging downwards to collide with Lt. C Williams' 43-38124/EP: S. The latter bomber came down within the city limits, while Henderson's aircraft lingered aloft as far as Radegast, east of Hamburg; both pilots were among the twelve fatalities, with three from each crew surviving. Another early casualty, probably the first, was 43-38535/LN:, which crashed at a location described as Rothenburg in the MACR, but more likely to have been the Hamburg district of Rothenburgsort; fighters dispatched it to its fiery destruction along with Lt. R Whitcomb and four of his crew.

Another factor in the scale of punishment was the strong headwind that met the formations as they turned west at the Rally Point to reduce airspeed to no more than 100 mph. The 100th BG was roughly due south of Hamburg when a clutch of crews was claimed by the fighters. First down could have been Lt. W Blackman's 43-38215/XR: P, which was already in trouble from a previous flak strike, and was by now lagging behind. Two Fw190s closed in from six-o'clock to riddle their prey and set it on fire. Scant seconds later the bomber exploded, miraculously throwing the pilot and one other crewmember out into midair, where their parachutes deployed; three others and bailed out prior to the blast.

Osenhorst and Bartelsdorf lay close to where Blackman's B-17 impacted at Wesseloh, and formed the crash sites for 43-38436/LN: (Lt. C Webster) and 43-38408/LN: **Faithful Forever** (Lt. L Ross). The first B17 was set on fire, and only four of the nine-man crew bailed out safely, both pilots being among the dead. Ross' aircraft was observed to fall into a tight spin, but all on board managed to fight free of the normally lethal centrifugal forces and jump clear.

Lt. J Morin's crew finally came down at Westerhusen, on the western fringe of Emden, having also lagged behind during the initial fighter attacks. He had indicated he was dangerously short of fuel and that two crewmembers had been wounded, one of whom subsequently died, but he and the other eight airmen walked away from 43-38459/LD: V after it was "bellied in." The same coastal zone witnessed the demise of several more B-17s, beginning with 43-38381/LD: Z. Lt. W Mayo had radioed in that he had already lost two engines with a third faltering, and had taken further flak punishment from Bremerhaven's defenses. The final sighting was low down near Spikeroog, in the Frisian Island chain, and since no further trace of bomber or crew was ever established it was clear that the North Sea had swallowed both up. Four more crews were destined to go down, two of which were participants in one of the most astounding incidents within USAAF combat operations. The final "conventional" losses concerned 42-107233/EP: N flown by Lt. W Wilson, with all nine airmen ending up as POWs, while a similar relatively kind fate awaited Lt. P Carroll's crew on 43-31895/LD: Y, which came down at Wesermuende.

The landing run of a bomber provided no guarantee of success until the bomber was in its dispersal. Here, the 490th BG's 44-8098, piloted by Lt. T Edgerton, has been raised following collapse of its landing gear after it touched down. Note the punctured left wheel and absence of a ball turret; the wing section of another B-17 lies in the left background.

An Eight-engine B-17?

Following the Webster's bomber loss, a fatal confusion arose between which crew should fill in the vacant slot. The coastline was barely receding behind the group when Lt. G Rojohn in 42-31987/LN: **The Little Skipper** and Lt. W McNabb piloting 43-38457/LN: simultaneously made for the space. The latter bomber rose inexorably into the path of its fellow aircraft despite a warning of impending collision issued by another pilot. The amazing aspect of the collision was that the B-17s not only locked together without exploding, but that the crude "bi-plane" configuration remained aloft. A further amazing twist came when Rojohn and Lt. W Leek (CP) discovered their bomber's ailerons and elevators still functioned. With three of the other bomber's engines still functioning, the decision was swiftly made to switch off their aircraft's power and commence a tentative banking manoeuvre back to land using their aerial "companion's" power! Not only did the endeavour succeed, but the subsequent steady crash landing approach was equally successful, to the extent that the Rojohn/Leek B-17 actually slid clear of the other upon impact with the ground. The pilots walked clear of their aircraft, having previously bailed out their crew; sadly, only four of this number survived, one of whom was very lucky to escape death by being pulled to the shoreline by his billowing parachute after landing in the sea. McNabb, Lt. N Vaughn (CP), and three other crewmembers joined the fatality figure. (German eyewitnesses seeing the "pick-a-back" duo in flight must have wondered if this was not the latest in an ever-growing list of Allied secret weapons!)

Pairs of crews from the 95th and 390th BGs completed the dismal MIA total for the Wing. Maschen, on the southern outskirts of Hamburg, had been where one Framlingham B-17, 43-38247/CC:, had scattered itself after flak had struck home, killing Lt. W Monit (P) and four others in the process. The general atmosphere at Thorpe Abbotts, dampened enough by the day's loss of over 100 airmen, was lowered a further notch when the strike photos revealed a poor bombing pattern. As it was, the *Grim Reaper* had at last relented in his specific and eight-fold costly pursuit of the 8th AF's alleged "jinx" unit. From this point on the group would complete a further 64 missions up to the Offensive's conclusion and surrender seventeen crews in so doing.

45th CBW

Eleven more Division bombers went down, with the 45th CBW providing seven. Deopham Green had absorbed its share of costly missions since commencing operations in early 1944, and five more crews were taken down today. On 7 June 43-37644 **Feather Merchant** and 43-37673 had been assigned to the 728BS; now both were completing their final mission, as fighters culled them from the formation to crash in Hamburg and Tauenbruecke; Lts V Segers and K Traynelis lost one and two crewmembers respectively. A third squadron loss to the fighters involved 42-97666 flown by F/O J. Kostuck, who proved to be the crew's sole fatality. **Swing Shift Baby** (42-31348/T), with Lt. D Ferguson at the controls, also went down to fighter attack, the crash site being at Rahde, northwest of Hamburg, with the pilot and three of his crew losing their lives.

Flak batteries on the coast at Delfyzl put paid to one of the two Knettishall losses, Lt. E Senter (P) being one of five crewmembers on 43-38845/561BS who failed to survive the incident. Maj. W Harrell and crew were more fortunate in that all ten came through a ditching action off Borkum Island in 44-8207/563BS to end up in enemy hands.

Brief Existence

Single losses were recorded by four other groups, including the 487th BG.

Lt. C Gatlin's 836BS crew had been assigned to fly its third mission out of Lavenham and was among the last to lift off the partially night-shrouded runway some 24 minutes after the group commenced taking off. The subsequent movements of 42-97398/2C remained a mystery according to group records, and since no evidence of a crash site or discovery of any body ever came to light it seemed clear that the North Sea had claimed its latest technical and human victims. Having only arrived on 26 November, the nine young, keen, but vulnerable airmen had risen briefly, only to fall phoenix-like along the tragically expensive Road to Victory, with their names adorning a *Wall of the Missing* forming a stark and sad epitaph.

Victory Assured – But When?

New Year celebrations as midnight on 31 December loomed were generally in natural but muted order; as the evening faded into 1945 the grimly accurate truism "It's not over until it's over" would be quietly but insistently ringing in the ears of every combat crewmember within the 8th AF, and indeed in the minds of millions of Allied service personnel anywhere else where the conflict was raging. Would the individual be alive or in a physical state to celebrate Xmas 1945—only time and Fortune would tell. The German ability to resist against the burgeoning might of the Allies seemed to be fading, but even now there was no guarantee as to when that resistance would be finally crushed....

As regards the combat crewmen's specific situation, there was little comfort in the diminishing ability of the *Luftwaffe* to inflict regular casualties, since its striking power was almost equally matched by thousands of "post-graduate" flak gunners manning the numerous batteries. Then again, the *Sturmgruppen* concept was still alive and well and ready to catch out errant formations. There was little comfort in even hoping for a chance of getting to the ground alive, given the danger to life and limb posed by the civilian population, not to say the often autocratic mal-actions of the SS. Combat life would continue to be unpredictable and cheap until the last shot was fired....

14

Run-down to Victory

Nomenclature Change

As 1945 commenced the "Bomb Division" titles formerly applied to the 8th AF's bomber sub-forces now gave way to "Air Division" (AD). Although the elimination of the *Wehrmacht*/SS "Bulge" within the Anglo-American front lines still had to be addressed, the Allied "Heavies" were nevertheless pursuing their strategic brief. The year's first mission reflected this twin function, with the 2nd AD carrying out the interdiction of communications west of the Rhine and the B-17 Divisions striking at Germany's oil industry. Dollbergen and Ehmen's facilities bore the brunt of the 3rd AD's efforts, although the overall force was limited to the 4th CBW. The Division's full strength was dispatched next day against tactical targets at a cost of four crews MIA. A fifth was lost over England when 42-32112/AW:, a 96th BG veteran B-17 bearing Lt. J Miller's 337BS crew, was seen to adopt a steep and irrecoverable banking attitude that culminated in a fatal impact near a Norfolk town for all nine airmen. (This incident was the first of seven January losses ending with fatal consequences for most group members involved, with two B-17s adding to Snetterton's already unenviable reputation for collisions.)

In what is a virtual "white-out" condition created by a snowstorm, a B17G taxies past several vehicles, including a "blood wagon" with its distinctive Red Cross emblem. The picture was taken at Snetterton, but the aircraft's identification as a 96th BG machine cannot be confirmed.

Cologne's several key marshalling yards were attacked by the Division (10th) with a loss of five out of over 400 crews. Single crews were lost by each affected unit, including Lt. R Rand's twenty-mission veteran team from Horham in 42-97858/QW: Y **Carmen's Folly**. The B-17 was positioned No. 2 alongside the group Lead, but received serious flak damage in one wing and fuselage during the bomb run. Fire broke out on the inner-left wing, and the pilots dropped out and down to around 13,000 ft while attempting to arrest an incipient flat-spin motion. The intercom had been shot out so no bail out order could be issued, but this proved academic when the bomber suddenly exploded, ejecting the pilot and two others into midair, where they deployed their parachutes and drifted down near Grevenbroich, northwest of Cologne.

The weather conditions continued to largely dictate the use of PFF methods for bombing, but the drop-off in guaranteed strike accuracy was balanced by the very low overall MIA figures enjoyed by the 8th AF during January. In the case of the 3rd AD this figure stood at a mere 39 for the sixteen missions flown up to the 23rd, after which a four-day spell saw the bombers anchored firmly to their dispersal when Mother Nature displayed her latest perverse mood.

The losses were largely incurred as single examples by the units concerned, but a notable exception involved the 390th and 487th BGs on the 14th; that day the *Luftwaffe* was reported as being present in strength for the first time since the costly (to the enemy) Operation *Bodenplatte* on 1 January when

The NMF surface on this PFF B-17G from the 95th BG tends to highlight the red CBW markings of a diagonal stripe on the right wing and a second on the rudder. The 412BS-assigned bomber does not carry the QW squadron codes.

a large-scale assault was launched against Allied airfields in Holland and Belgium. Today's strikes would do nothing material to turn the offensive in the Germans' favor, but this was of little consolation for the American airmen concerned. Sixteen Division crews were entered on the MIA list, all but three of which came from Framlingham or Lavenham....

Framlingham Blues

For the 390th BG today was the 243rd mission out of a final total of 300, and was not expected to be easier or rougher than any that had gone before. The clear weather conditions promised a sound bombing result as the CBW was west of Berlin and approaching the IP, but it was then that "peace and quiet" was brutally thrust into the background as a mass of fighters descended upon the 390th and commenced culling the C formation, comprised of just eight B-17s and lagging behind the other group elements, out of the sky.

One of the first crews to go down was led by Lt. E Hanneke Jr. in 43-38665/ CC: M **The Great McGinty**: The solid spray of cannon shells sent the B-17 into a spinning motion, and the pilot yelled out that he could not correct it. Lt. M Johnson (N) had the initial bad luck to spill his parachute pack by grasping it via the ripcord; having managed to hastily gather it up and hook up the pack to his harness, he then had no conscious memory of actually bailing out; instead he regained consciousness on the ground some distance away from a pile of wreckage near Barnschendorf that was almost certainly the B-17 and the funeral pyre for his nine fellow airmen.

Four further group bombers met their end in the same area. Dreetz, Friesack, and Goerne form a close-knit triangle round where Lt. Hanneke's aircraft crashed. Lt. R Richter's 43-38337/BI: N ***Cloud Hopper***, 43-38526/BI: Z **Star Duster** in Lt. Niebergall's hands, and Lt. J Lewis' 42-102673/FC: L/B came to earth at these respective sites. Fifteen of the twenty-eight airmen were killed, with Niebergall the sole pilot survivor. 42-102677/BI: R **Bob Tail Battler** barely progressed several miles south of the other downed bombers before succumbing at Garlitz to leave half the ten-man crew alive, one of whom was not Lt. G Johnson (P).

The attrition continued apace as the bombers were on the point of angling west from the IP onto the Primary, an oil refinery at Derben, north of Magdeburg. Ketzin lies very close to the western boundary of Berlin and was listed in the MACR as where 44-6480/BI: finally fell to earth; Lt. D Thumlert was yet another pilot who sacrificed his life along with six of his eight crewmembers. Yet another 568BS bomber (42-102956/BI: **Doc's Flying Circus**) was downed at a location listed as Vietnitz, but probably Vieritz, some ten miles short of the target; the pilot fatality figure was further added to since Lt. P Goodrich was one of the two airmen killed during what was the crew's penultimate mission of their combat tour. The squadron's fourth casualty was reportedly 44-8426/BI: flown by a Lt. Norman, out of which four emerged alive. One further squadron crew commanded by Lt. W Wiegand in 42-31744/BI: **Little Butch II** was lost, with the pilot and three others killed. So was rounded off a miserable day for the group, one that had seen it sustain the highest MIA casualties for a single mission during its time in England.

Unrewarded "Gallantry Above and Beyond"

Sgt. G Zadora was Goodrich's ROG, and later recalled how the first intimation of trouble arose just as he vacated his post to take up position at one of the waist guns. Suddenly he heard calls over the intercom as gunners called in the first onrush of *Luftwaffe* fighters, among whose ranks were several P-51s and P-47s. Large rents were torn in the bomber's fuselage, and then Zadora was hit with the effect akin to that of "a dozen bee stings." He moved towards the radio room to pick up his parachute, but the compartment was by now smoke and flame shrouded, and he spent precious time on his knees fishing the pack out from under his desk. Then, despite his injured leg, he revived the unconscious waist gunner and assisted him out of the doomed B-17 before going back to the ball turret and rendering the same vital service to the badly injured occupant! (Zadora's actions won him no medal, but he was more than worthy of an award according to Sgt. R Spence, the waist gunner in question; not only was his companion wounded, but the smoke-filled fuselage had forced him onto his knees while making his rescue bid. Furthermore, he was not in possession of his parachute pack at this time, so his actions could so easily have ended up in his failing to get out. Zadora's subsequent POW experiences included the infamous forced march from Stalag Luft IV that extended to between two and three months.)

Squadron Blues

The 487th BG lost a quartet of crews, all from the 838BS, with two whose ultimate demise reportedly commenced as a result of a midair collision. Lt. O Stemple's 44-8563/2C: K, flying as High squadron Lead, had suffered seemingly marginal flak damage while penetrating the enemy coastline. It was only when the pilots attempted to turn at the IP that the aircraft lost the ability to climb or dive, or even to hold course thanks to the control cables finally giving way. The enemy fighters soon latched onto the now isolated B-17 and one wing was set on fire, while Lt. F Nyhagen, flying as tail gunner/observer, was killed at his post. The remaining ten airmen, whose number included Capt. D Reed acting as group Leader, all bailed out, leaving their aircraft to crash at Gutenpaaren, northeast of Brandenburg. (A second fatality was Lt. R Reid (B), who was found dead through unconfirmed circumstances.)

There is a degree of confusion regarding the B-17s supposed to have collided. Certainly one of these was reported as leaving the formation with its rudder missing. This was 42-98013/2G: M piloted by Lt. C Kochczynski, who was now on his second combat tour with the group; sadly, what was his fourth mission was fated to be his last as well as for three of the crew after the bomber entered a spin and then exploded to descend near Luneburg. The other alleged "participant" was 43-37933/4F: C **Yankee Maid** piloted by Lt. H Nyland, who was another group veteran, along with his crew, having arrived at Lavenham on 24 July. A misunderstanding with his co-pilot, who was flying the bomber at the time, saw the latter follow Lt. Stemple's errant B-17 when the latter fell out of position. Problems developed with one engine to an extent that a heading for home was taken up and the bomb load jettisoned. Several minutes later the aircraft was thoroughly shot up during two passes by a group of fighters and Nyland called for a bail out that was adhered to by six crewmembers. The navigator had been badly wounded and was apparently in no state to jump. Both pilots remained on board and headed

Red chord-wise bands around the central wing and stabilizer/elevator areas on this pair of B-17Gs indicate assignment to the 93rd CBW. The Group involved here is the 490th BG; bomber in foreground is 44-8492/848BS, transferred-in from the 100th BG on 11 November 1944 and destined to survive WWII.

down for what turned out to be a successful crash landing west of Ludwigslust; unfortunately, Lt. F Abbote (N) was cast out of the aircraft by the impact and did not survive.

Lt. J Moser's crew was a comparatively novice team, having arrived on 13 December, and their month-long sojourn at Lavenham now came to an abrupt end, although all nine airmen bailed out safely east of Brunswick from their badly damaged B-17, 43-38002/R5: C.

"Cruising" to Victory again?

Six more Division missions went out over the next eight days with an ever-welcome return to minimal MIA losses (thirteen), although the winter weather conditions and mechanical problems played their part in crashes, mainly incurred by the other two ADs, over friendly territory. Transportation was the primary target selection, with marshalling yards high on the agenda, although the 16th and 17th involved assaults upon the oil industry at Magdeburg and Hamburg. The majority of losses were incurred in single measure for the unit concerned, but the 452nd BG proved an exception on the Hamburg mission when its four losses comprised the entire Divisional figure, although the human cost at least was alleviated when two of the B-17s diverted into Sweden. **C'est la Guerre** (42-102397/730BS) lived up to her rather fatalistic title, although all in Lt. Skogland's charge bailed out. Lt. Smith guided 44-8602/731BS into Bulltofta, an act duplicated by Lt. Betts, who set his 43-37745/ 730BS **Lacka Sacky** down at Kalamar.

Other than for a 1st AD thrust against oil targets on the first-listed date, the B-17s and B-24s remained frustratingly ground-bound between 22 and 27 January in the face of the dreadful winter weather conditions. As ever, the combat personnel's feelings at this enforced inactivity must have swung between relief and frustration, the latter sentiment relating to the delay in progressing towards the end of their tours of duty. Then the final four January days proved good enough to dispatch the bombers on three missions, of which only two were completed. On the 31st a "recall" was issued for all three Divisions that were not due to target weather conditions, but rather to the anticipated deteriorating conditions over 8th AF airfields.

The two late January missions were completed with no crews listed as MIA. However, that consistent danger connected with formation flying, collision, struck home

A B-17G of the 100th BG is pictured heavily coated with snow sometime during the winter of 1944/45. Such weather conditions did not prevent the 8th AF from launching missions, although there was a heightened risk to the crews, particularly in attempting to assemble and disperse at either end of a sortie.

On Xmas Eve 1944 43-38760/OE: X failed to return to Horham. Instead, Lt. Purdy crash landed just inside France's border with Germany at Sarralbe, due south of Saarbruecken. The impact was clearly heavy, judging by the state of the engines, but all on board reportedly survived and later returned to their airfield. Color band on nose is dark blue.

B-17Gs of the 34th BG with their distinctive red tail banding applied forward from just ahead of the rudder/fin junction are taxiing out for take-off sometime during the winter of 1944/45. Light colored bands on noses of the left hand and center B-17Gs suggest this could be either the white or yellow variations applied to the 4 BS and 7 BS respectively; band on right hand bomber could be green (391 BS) or red (18 BS).

The six-month sojourn that 44-8178/QJ: D enjoyed at Snetterton Heath came to an end on 6 January 1945, when it was force-landed on the continent. Loss of the tail turret section along with a shot-up left wing and fabric stripped from the rudder and elevators ensured the B-17G's reduction to "salvage" status sixteen days later.

These two pictures depict the ever-tragic aftermath of a midair collision. In this case Lt. A Philiprovitch's 43-38745 impacted with Lt. G Perritt's 44-6137 (both 96th BG). The wreckage fell around the villages of North and South Lopham, and none of the eighteen airmen emerged alive.

among the 96th BG's ranks. Just 24 hours before (28th) Lt. A Philiprovich had landed back with two injured crewmembers, one of whom was declared fit to participate in today's mission, which was bad luck for him. Forming up in the snow-laden undercast, the aircraft were up around 11,000 ft over North and South Lopham when tragedy struck. Lt. G Peretti was holding a straight course in 44-6137/ AW: J when the B-17 flown by Philiprovich (43-38746/BX: G) was seen to manoeuvre across the other bomber's path, and make lethal contact with its port wing, which split the other B-17 in two. Within seconds Philiprovich's aircraft exploded, while Peretti's truncated front section traced a flame-shrouded and spinning course to the ground. The rain of metal as well as the two bomb loads thankfully did not leave their mark on the population, but none of the eighteen airmen was granted immunity from death. (A third group crew had been lost on the 28th. A flak strike on 44-6589/BX: P had sent it into a spin that was corrected by Lt. E Dasso and his co-pilot. Shortly after a second spin developed that was never corrected and ended fatally for all but one crewmember just inside Allied lines.)

Safety was Relative...

An airfield presented a constant safety hazard for all who ventured within its confines. This was a fact that extended from the military personnel who manned the place to individuals from the civilian population. The latter consisted of members of businesses tasked with a range of activities, including construction and even the delivery of items such as bombs.

This B-17G was the third to take off from Rougham in dreadful conditions of snow and limited visibility. The two preceding bombers barely made it into the air, with one smashing a fence at the runway's end. QE: S had just cleared the airfield when it stalled and descended into the ground to burst into flames, Lt. W Weiss and six of the crew were consumed in the blaze. Date was 28 January 1945.

Caution was a mandatory requirement, particularly when out on the airfield perimeter, since aircraft could be taking off or landing at any time of the day. Any laxity in keeping a constant eye open for aerial traffic could be fatal...

On 15 January 1945 an instrument check flight was being undertaken by Lt. H McGregor in 43-38597. The check completed, the 385th BG B-17 headed in for a landing. As it was rapidly approaching the runway's end, the pilots were horrified to see a truck crossing their path; despite frantically pulling up the nose, one landing gear wheel impacted with the vehicle, resulting in the deaths of both British occupants. The bomber suffered no material damage and was landed safely. It appears that the driver had ignored both a "stop and look" sign at the runway/perimeter track junction and, worse still, a signal from the Air Traffic Caravan, and paid a terminal price for he and his companion in the process.

Comment - Secondary Effects of Flak

The ever-growing provision of heavy flak batteries by the enemy, and especially their disposal around the still sizeable numbers of key targets, was primarily viewed as a threat to the chances of bomber crews bringing themselves and their charges back home. However, there was a secondary if more technical menace presented by the gunners, which related to the subsequent airworthiness of the aircraft and therefore their operational availability.

An Intelligence evaluation of one group's experience over one infamous location highlights this issue affecting all B-17 and B-24 units to a greater or lesser degree. The section dealing with flak states "Merseburg /Leuna; intense barrage and tracking, very accurate. Some damage received on bomb run just before 'bombs away', but 90% damage received as formation turned off target." Of the 33 B-17s sent out two were MIA, but the more insidious punishment handed out to the returning aircraft is reported thus:

Battle Damage

Minor	Major
ten	twelve

Those machines placed in the second category would have had to have been deleted from the operational list for as long as the necessary repair work took to bring them back into use. Although by 1944/1945, thanks to the massive productive output back in the States the aircraft establishment of the average group was roughly double that enjoyed by the first generation of American "heavy" units, the reduction in available numbers as outlined here was at least an irritating restriction in the bid to bring maximum pressure to bear on Germany's war effort. In addition, the personnel of the Sub-Depots usually charged with handling the "major" cases would experience a further twist in their already heavy workload.

Civilian Morale – on a Knife-edge?

The onset of the V-1 offensive on 13 June, followed by the V-2's involvement around September, were not so much physical interruptions to Britain's war effort as psychologically damaging to the nation's morale, particularly its civilian element. The conflict had already extended over nearly five years and was proving to be ever more of a drain upon the individual's commitment to seeing matters through to the end, an end that was still hardly in sight.

Sgt. W Sturdivan was on a Pass to London along with two other 34th BG personnel. They were about to check out of their

On 25 February 1945, almost one year after its assignment to the 95th BG, 42-31989 /ET: B staggered into Switzerland, where Lt. Havlik brought off a heavy crash landing in a heavily wooded area. Despite the severe splitting of the fuselage all ten airmen survived to end up interned. There is evidence of the red color band around the nose that was applied to 412BS aircraft after July 1944.

The tendency for the Wright Cyclone engines to exude oil is clearly exemplified by this under-view of 43-38798/XM: M, with heavy staining of the nacelles and central wing area. Only three of the 94th BG bombers display visible evidence of the red chevron wing marking that was part of the Group's specific color coding within the 4th CBW.

hotel, whose structure bore witness to the current battle in that a number of windows were boarded over. Suddenly their ears were battered by a tremendous explosion whose blast shredded most of the remaining glass panes and sucked the debris out onto the street. As the airmen were getting to their feet again they heard the weird after-effect of what turned out to be a V-2 strike that sounded just like the passage of a second bomb which then abruptly cut out. On collecting their gear and vacating the premises their eyes alighted upon heaps of brick and glass remnants, while the air was filled with cries and screams from numerous individuals. Nearby a horse that had been drawing a milk wagon lay on its side in a state that merited its immediate putting down.

It was then that a woman approached Sturdivan, and with tears streaming down her face, pleaded with him; "Why cannot you do something to stop all this destruction? Can't you do something?" He responded as positively as possible by saying "We're trying, lady – We'll see what we can do to stop it," but his words must have left him and his colleagues with a natural sense of inadequacy. In fact, there was little or nothing that could be done by the Air Forces to halt the V-2 assaults, since the massive rockets were not fired from fixed launching sites as with the V-1; instead, the weapons were borne on mobile launchers that could be set up anywhere and at short notice. Only the advance of the Allied armies far enough eastward for the rockets to be placed out of range of eastern England would bring an end to the torment currently posed by this ballistic menace.

February 1945

The staccato mission pattern caused primarily by the weather resurrected itself in the first week of February when only three successful large-scale missions were launched. On the 1st 616 B-17s made a loss-free attack on railroad communications in Western Germany, while the escorts recorded no "kills," which was equally surprising despite an undercast that required bomb loads to be guided onto their targets by *H2X* or *Micro-H* equipment. Two days elapsed before both B-17 Divisions headed out with 1,003 aircraft for *Big B*. Weather conditions were marginal on the way over, but proved to be largely clear over Berlin for what was the fifteenth full-scale assault upon the city, and the fourth successive one involving the 1st and 3rd ADs.

Although the Primaries selected were marshalling yards in the Tempelhof district, the crews had been informed that one of the *Wehrmacht's* Panzer Armees was currently transferring through the city and on to the Russian Front. Opposition to the formations' bomb runs came wholly from the flak batteries, whose gunners inevitably left their malign traces among most of the 27 MIA bombers. The bomb loads tumbled down not only onto the Primary, but also into the city center, with the sorely-battered Friederichsstrasse railroad station one of the facilities struck.

The 3rd AD bomb runs had been partially conducted by PFF means, since visual reference had been blanketed out by the preceding 1st AD's assault. The 13th CBW in the van absorbed the bulk of the Division's punishment with six out of the ten MIA aircraft. Lt. J Taylor's 43-38899/ET: N came down at Werneuchen, several miles outside Berlin's northern boundary, and 42-102951/BG: Q was the second Horham casualty. Taylor's crew all bailed out safely, but there was just a single survivor from Lt.R Morris' complement after the bomber finally crashed at Den Berg, on Texel Island in the Frisian chain.

Double this casualty figure was realized by the 100th BG. The Lead bomber was 44-8379 flown by Capt J Ernst, with Maj R Rosenthal acting as Division CO. "Rosie" had already flown just over 50 missions since his combat debut during the "Black Week" of 8-14 October 1943, but today was very nearly his last. One fuel tank was ignited by a strike bare seconds prior to "bombs away," but its load was released before the Deputy crew was directed to take over as the now smoke-filled cripple eased out of formation and headed east. Bare minutes later the crew were ordered out and ten out of the eleven jumped clear to land on either side of the Soviet Front some 35 miles away from Berlin. Rosenthal was one of the fortunate element who landed in "friendly" territory; even so, he had to yell out his American status to his "liberators" in order to ensure they did not treat him as a *Luftwaffe* flier.

Also fatally crippled at the same time was 44-6500, but none of Lt. O Cottner's crew survived the violent gyrations of their B-17 when it flipped onto its back after a fuel tank exploded and the wing folded up. The third group casualty was 42-102958/ LN: Z, which was heading for the Rally Point when flak again struck home. Fire caught hold in one engine and Lt. Beck's bid to extinguish the blaze by diving came to naught; when last seen the fuselage was wrapped in flame and a spin had developed, from which the two airmen in the nose were the sole members to escape the otherwise fatally-embracing centrifugal force. The carnage was completed at this stage by 44-6092/LD: F, which had discharged its load before veering off to the right with Lt. W Oldham and the eight-man crew successfully abandoning the burning bomber. Two crews each from the 45th and 93rd CBW completed the MIA total, but one aircraft managed to get to Sweden. It was Deopham Green's 43-38358/730BS **Slightly Dangerous** (Lt.

On 20 January 1945 Lt. Greenstreet's 44-8151/CC: O was damaged by flak and finally crash landed near Steinbourg, in eastern France. The bomber's slithering progress up onto a slope is easily traced thanks to the snow-bedecked landscape.

The red squares applied to the center fin sections on at least three of these B-17Gs—with two in the far background displaying the squares on their rudders as well—identify the group as the 385th BG based at Great Ashfield. Aircraft letter on bomber in center appears to have been displaced from the upper fin to the rudder.

Sweet Chariot (44-6888/AW: R) has come to the end of the road following a very heavy crash landing. The rear fuselage is canted at a distinct angle to the forward section, while No. 3 engine and nacelle have been torn completely out of the wing. Bomber was originally assigned to the 96th BG on 4 January 1945. Parallel red bands on the fin are the Group's specific identification within the 45th CBW.

All 'Er Nothin' has completed a successful crash landing on 23 February 1945 following the loss of the left main landing gear. The 490th BG bomber (42-98017/N) flew with the 849BS from 3 August 1944 and was brought back to combat status, finally returning Stateside in late May.

W Fry), whose damaged airframe held out until the airfield at Ringoby was reached. The single 490th BG crew within the MIA total enjoyed a similar slice of luck when 43-38150 (Lt. S Spiege) reportedly made an eastward run as far as Soviet-occupied territory where the bomber was force landed.

"Final" in Both Senses...

There was an eleventh and arguably even more tragic loss over England. Lt. L Kloud's crew in 43-38031 **Blue Grass Girl** had not only survived the run to Berlin, but were easing in over the coast within the 486th BG formation and heading towards a landing at Sudbury that would see them complete their combat tour. The crew were all apparently gathered up front when flames were observed breaking out around the waist windows. As the bomber dropped out and down no more than four parachutes blossomed out, while a fifth crewmember apparently jumped too late for his chute to deploy. The remaining four airmen, including the pilots, were still on board when the B-17 slammed into the ground close to Reydon. The nature of such a loss was particularly demoralizing to the unfortunate airmen's colleagues, even though everybody recognized there was never any guarantee of salvation whether one was flying his first, interim, or (in this case) final mission—the word "final" in this context proved cruelly relevant.

(Dr. Goebbels made subsequent great propaganda play arising out of this latest **Big B** strike, regarding the alleged "terror" aspect of the Americans' bombing effort on 3 February, especially since the civilian casualty figure was the highest recorded in any of the missions against Berlin. On the other hand, the 2,541 deaths, even if representing sizeable figures, were still far short of the 25,000 reported by neutral sources. A great swathe of destruction had been torn out of the central area, but whether this had a material effect upon the onward advance of the Panzer Armee was never really established.)

The relatively close-parked nature of aircraft on 8th USAAF airfields, as seen at Framlingham, indicates how free from aerial assault its bases were deemed to be by 1944/45. B-17G in foreground, named **Reluctant**, was assigned to the 570BS on 4 September but did not survive the conflict; it was downed on the Berlin mission of 18 March 1945.

"Operational" Losses

The mission on 6 February again highlighted the risk inherent in combat flying, even when not in direct contact with the enemy. First, a midair collision between 43-38167 and 43-37894 (490th BG) during Assembly caused both to crash, although only one crewmember was killed along with two English civilians. Then a third Eye-based crew bailed out also during Assembly. On return, all ten crew on the 486th BG's 43-37992/3R: P lost their lives in a crash. Further ill luck attended a fourth 490th BG team of twelve who also suffered a fatal crash while attempting to land their battle-damaged B-17 in France, while 43-38054/851BS (490th BG) ended up "Category E" following a crash landing at Darsham on return, as did three more: two from the 100th BG and one from the 487th BG. Nine Division aircraft were thus written off records in addition to the three declared MIA.

The Bendix chin-turret cover from **American Beauty** is detached and sits on the dispersal surface. The 708BS B-17G enjoyed a better fate than many of her contemporaries, since she survived combat operations up to VE-Day, having originally arrived at Rattlesden the previous 16 June. Note how the area around the serial is still in NMF finish, and a virtually obscured Group insignia appears on the upper fin.

This view of an 838BS B-17G from the 487th BG is taken bare weeks before the final 8th AF mission occurred on 25 April 1945. The bomber was only assigned to the Lavenham-based unit on 3 March. Here it is delivering its load of 100-lb incendiary bombs onto what is probably a "socked-in" target to judge by the cloud conditions.

Two of the Lavenham losses fell into the MIA category. The 837BS' 43-38044/4F: D **Piccadilly Lilley** took off very late and was not recorded as joining up with the group, although it did head for its target. Flak struck home and Lt. C Parker called for a bail out close to Gera, due west of Chemnitz, into which some of the eight survivors floated down; their bomber expired some twenty miles southwest of the town. The second B-17 made it back to England's Channel coastline, but 44-6299/2G: Q was then deemed so short of fuel that Lt. T Bamberg's crew "took to the silk," leaving the bomber to fall harmlessly into the sea. (Lt. R Portsch over-shot the runway and smashed into a heavy piece of machinery; 44-8606/2G: C was "written off," but its nine occupants remained unhurt.)

Adjusted Assembly Procedure

Up to the beginning of 1945 bomber formation assembly had taken place over southern England. Not only did this entail a series of elaborate manoeuvers over a somewhat restricted geographic region, but the need to reach operational altitude prior to departing friendly shores consumed a fair proportion of fuel content, leaving a dangerously small overall margin both in the case of long-range strikes or in the event of a diversion being necessary due to weather conditions over the bases. Now, with the vast bulk of French territory in Allied hands, there was full scope for Assembly to take place in equally secure conditions over this massively-expanded continental airspace. Snetterton records quote an example where the group crews flew individually to a point south of Paris where they duly formed up, while the easier rate of climb to altitude would also have left a greater reserve of fuel. (Whether the French population in the selected zones would have appreciated this transfer away from British shores is questionable, but the British certainly would have hailed the respite from the attendant dangers of midair collisions that were a constant feature of Assembly, especially when conducted in the face of the Island's notoriously fickle weather patterns!)

Ever Onwards to Victory...

The 8th AF spread its massive tentacles across the rapidly expiring but still resisting Nazi hinterland for most of the month, although the second planned sortie (8th) ended in frustration when a "recall" was issued during Assembly over East Anglia. MIA losses overall totalled fifty-five during seventeen missions, so demonstrating the paucity of the enemy defenses; the 3rd AD's contribution was eighteen while participating in fifteen of the missions. The numbers of bomber crews dispatched when all three Divisions were operating rarely fell below 900, while the average figure worked out at around 1,100.

Several Primary targets avoided punishment thanks to the often wayward weather. On the 9th the Division had to be content with attacking two Secondaries, although one of these at Duelmen was as oil-related as the briefed Primary. St. Valentine's Day proved to be the next mission launched when Chemnitz's marshalling yards were hammered by all fourteen groups, and marred only by one crew MIA and a further two B-17s from the 490th BG lost in a midair collision. Contrasting fortunes attended the next two missions. The intended assault on Magdeburg remained a thwarted ambition other than by the 2nd AD; next day (16th) only the 3rd AD attained its Primary of Frankfurt's marshalling yards, with the other two Divisions recalled before crossing the North Sea.

PFF-assisted bombing was indulged in by separately dispatched forces 48 hours later. Five groups went for marshalling yards at Osnabrueck, while four others bombed similar facilities at Rheine and two a railroad bridge at Wesel, a town that would be the main focal point for the major Allied crossing of the

A 413BS B-17G is surrounded by a low-lying smoke trail discharged from the large truck lurking behind the bomber's vertical fin. The CBW color bands confirm the picture was taken during or after January 1945 when the markings were applied to the 96th BG.

Rhine launched in late March. From now until the month's end both the Division and the remainder of the 8th AF would be aloft in continuing four-figure strength on all but one day. This was particularly the case on the 22nd/23rd when Operation *Clarion* was launched. The USAAF authorities' intention was to deliver huge and hopefully terminal blows upon Germany's transportation system ranging from marshalling yards to road junctions. An overall figure of 3583 crews were granted mission "credit," although a good proportion were limited to bombing targets of opportunity. For example, on the first mission less than 10% of the 3rd AD force struck their briefed marshalling yard Primaries, although the same target type featured in the debriefing reports by several sub-forces. A regular feature of both days was the briefed altitude that was half that normally proposed in order to achieve maximum bombing accuracy.

Incident at Rattlesden

Despite a heavy repair list of three seriously damaged B-17s and sixteen others bearing varying degrees of punishment off the 20th mission, the order for a maximum effort next day was wearily but positively responded to by the ground personnel. Final loading preparations were complete and engine run-up tests proceeding around 0400 hours when a critical situation arose within the 710BS' dispersals. B-17G/42-97819 was on full power on No. 1 engine, the thrust factor being enough for the left landing gear wheel to jump its restraining chock. The errant bomber lunged forward in an arc towards a fuel truck and the whirling propeller blades sliced into its innards, exposing the volatile fluid, which sprayed in all directions. Almost immediately a massive explosion rocked the area as the truck exploded and set the bomber ablaze; the driver and the ground crew on board the bomber managed to scramble clear and run for their lives. All too soon the bomb load "cooked off" and blew the B-17 apart, as well as creating a 50-foot crater.

The fire fighting Section were soon on the scene, but their attempts to stem the flames that had taken hold of 42-97826 **Big Shorty** on the adjoining dispersal soon became vain. The decision to abandon the bomber to its fate had scarcely been taken when it also blew up. They and their colleagues were blown in all directions by the concussion, but amazingly survived this potentially lethal pressure wave as well as the various scattered pieces of debris that included an entire engine mount. Other squadron bombers had been affected by the rain of red-hot metal that undoubtedly created fires within their airframes. The decision was now taken to hold back the fire trucks in order not to risk the men's lives and to clear all personnel to a safe distance—a very wise decision, since no less than four more B-17s were "written off" as they were terminally damaged by the concussive effect and debris. Not surprisingly the entire mission was "scrubbed," but next day a full complement of 37 crews took off for Operation *Clarion's* opening strike. A happy postscript lay in the fact that nobody lost his life, although six airmen were injured.

Tragic Prophesy

The 25 February mission was deep into southeastern Germany to attack Muenich, and with solid flak concentrations being anticipated a number of *Chaff*-loaded B-17s were briefed to fly ahead of the Division stream in order to disrupt the gunners' calculations. T/Sgt. R Shepherd (ROG), who was making a second combat tour, expressed deep apprehension regarding his chances of surviving today's run to what he said was "a bad one." This was an attitude his colleagues from Lt. D Proctor's crew found disturbing, coming as it did from a normally taciturn and self-possessed airman...

The clear conditions—as opposed to the briefed heavy cloud cover—experienced over the target did not bode well for the small *Chaff* formation who were positioned well ahead of

B-17G at bottom left of the picture below is seen close-up. The fuselage is split in two and the forward section is canted up in the air.

Below: This scene of devastation is the aftermath of a serious incident at Rattlesden on 21 February. During mission preparation a B-17 jumped one wheel chock and impacted with a fuel truck. The remains of both units lie intermingled towards the center-top of the picture. Aircraft parts from this and several other B-17s are scattered far and wide. The two bombers at top right appear to be intact.

the stream with 43-39018/AW: P **Dinah Mite** leading. Well into the bomb run several flak bursts bracketed the 96th BG bomber, the last one impacted with and destroying the radio room as well as inflicting a fatal head wound on the sadly prescient Shepherd. A second crewmember, Sgt. M Council (BT), also received a ghastly head wound that ultimately cost him the sight of one eye.

The sorely wounded B-17 was banked in the direction of Switzerland and had the good fortune to gain that neutral sanctuary, but matters might have been very different, as the crash landing attempt was made close to Diepoldsau. The chosen site was very narrow, and the bomber was swung round in a half circle through contact with one of several large rocks before slamming into an embankment. Had the aircraft's direction not been so altered its momentum almost certainly would not have been arrested before it had crossed the Swiss boundary with Austria! Council received medical attention and removal to an eye clinic, unlike poor Shepherd, whose coffin was borne by his crew prior to burial with full military honors several days later. (Switzerland proved to be the haven for two other 8th AF crews, one of whom came from the 95th BG.)

Berlin received attention from the 8th AF (26th) with minimal bomber casualties at three out of 1135, the largest force to date, dropping their loads into the Nazi capital, which had by now become the city receiving the greatest individual punishment of all the nation's major locations. The cumulative loss of oil fuel resources to the enemy was now clearly reflected in the total absence of the *Jadgwaffe* over what was arguably its prime protective source.

This is the B-17G at the extreme top-right of the first picture. The PFF aircraft appears to have suffered little damage other than to the nose Plexiglas and lower rudder; nevertheless, it was declared "Category E" and removed from the 447th BG's establishment.

Directly across from the PFF aircraft is 42-107177. The explosive blasts have rippled the rear fuselage skin and stripped the fabric off the rudder. The entire airframe is still intact, but salvage action will be taken. Ground crew are sweeping the dispersal clear of all loose debris.

A near view of the fuel truck whose contents precipitated the violent incident. The twisted remains of one propeller are wedged in against one bare wheel hub. In the background is one of the two PFF bombers that in its case did not result in salvage action.

The date is 7 March 1945, and 44-6152/729BS, with a large mission "log," has completed an exact nine-month operational spell at Deopham Green. The landing accident has resulted in a crushed ball turret. Small tractor unit under the forward fuselage will be attached to a tow vehicle and the B-17G hauled away for "Category E" action.

On 20 January 1945 this PFF B-17G arrived at Lavenham. Barely one month later (28 February), and although appearing to be in prefect order as seen here, she was salvaged following a fire incurred during a training flight 48 hours previous. The bomber on the right is minus its tail turret section.

Berlin's specific martyrdom at the hands of the American bombers was not yet over, but the remaining sorties could well be placed in the category of "picking over the bones." February concluded with two equally massive strikes at marshalling yards, railroad viaducts, and communications centers that incurred a continuing marginal cost in crews, none of which was borne by the Division. (An interesting aspect of attacking viaducts concerns the one at Bielefeld. Up to March 1945 this important structure had remained intact despite hundreds of tons of bombs being deposited in its vicinity. Then on 14 March came the Lancasters of 617 (Dambuster) squadron bearing 10-ton *Grand Slam* aerodynamic bombs. One of these arced into the ground adjacent to the viaduct, and its subterranean detonation created an act similar to the "Hangman's drop" by literally blowing the ground from under at least eight arches, thereby rendering the bridge permanently out of commission.)

War is Hell – for the Other Guy!

A 390th BG crew were on their way to a Rest Home when one of its number got into conversation with a Canadian infantryman in the same compartment. The soldier evinced a great deal of admiration for his continental "cousins" and added, "You chaps are the real heroes of the war; my heart goes out to you when I see your planes going down in flames."

Subsequent to this statement the airman elicited the fact that his Allied travelling companion had been wounded no less than four times and was on his way back into action! It was pointed out that on return from a mission the airmen were faced with nothing rougher than a cooked meal and rest in their barracks bed—infinitely better terms than C Rations usually eaten in the extreme discomfort of a foxhole. Then there were the regular Passes dished out, compared to the likelihood of an indefinite and often very un-restful spell on the Front line with no such comfort. The USAAF personnel might well have to live up to their slogan "Live in Fame, go down in flame," but the life of a "footslogger" was in no way preferred, even in such potentially fraught circumstances. In effect "War is Hell" no matter how, where, and for how long it is experienced.

March 1945
Miracles Happen - Occasionally

Mister Lucky (42-38035/550BS) had so far lived up to its title since assignment to the 385th BG in December 1943, having survived the ferocious air battles of the first half of 1944. On 1 March the veteran B-17 was in Lt. C Armbruster's hands with S/Sgt. J Jones riding in the tail. The formations encountered heavy clouds over the Belgium coast on the way to Ulm, and it was then that 43-38273, another 550BS aircraft flown by Lt. Rusecky, slammed into Armbruster's bomber to sever its rear section and send it and most of the crew to their doom; nobody on the offending B-17 survived either.

In the severed tail section Jones, having sensed his aircraft was descending, and gaining no response from his pilot over the intercom, decided to bail out. This proved impossible due to his escape hatch failing to budge and any forward exit being blocked off by the tangle of metal around the point of severance. Having finally become fatalistic at his survival chances he lit a cigarette and then passed out—for the ensuing three days.

On the ground, Belgian eyewitnesses watched the tumbling B-17 remnant descending in what was probably a "falling leaf" manoeuvre that was reasonably slow-paced thanks to the controlling action of the elevators (otherwise the rate of fall in a vertical configuration would have an almost fatal outcome for any airmen on board.) When the mass of metal finally struck the ground several of the civilians rushed over and were amazed when the inert figure in the tail was extricated and found to be alive. Jones subsequently recovered in an Ostend hospital to become the sole and most unlikely survivor of the tragic incident.

Great Ashfield's self-induced suffering as March opened was doubled next day at the enemy's hands. The group was in the van for the entire 8th AF, but according to Lt. R Krahn, flying 43-37871 in the High squadron, diverted from the Primary to the Secondary target (Dresden). The sub-units were in the middle of deploying in squadron order for the bomb run when a bunch of Fw 190s descended upon the High squadron. Krahn's B-17 was thoroughly shot up and set on fire; although he completed the bomb run and swung away east towards the Soviet lines it soon became apparent that the bomber was doomed, as the fire that had gained hold on No. 3 engine threatened to penetrate the firewall and create an even greater conflagration within the main fuel tanks. As it was, the bail out order resulted in all the crew getting out alive. Lt. E Vaadi's 42-97979/550BS **Leading Lady** came down near Ruhland with the entire crew also ending up as POWs. Of the two remaining losses, one involving 43-38148 /549BS (Lt. L Tripp KIA) was more costly, since it resulted in only two crewmembers out of the nine escaping alive.

The bad days of heavy losses were well behind the 96th BG, but the *Grim Reaper* still sought out its crews to exact a blood debt of three this day. Two of these were incurred in a distressingly familiar scenario for the group, midair collision. The crews were assembled and ready to depart the English coast. Leading the Low section was Lt. B Gatch in 43-37767/QJ: **My Ideal**, while

A notation on the back of this picture states that 42-97328 of the 388th BG flew 106 missions—one more than the "bomb" tally on the nose! Aircraft was assigned to the 561BS in late March 1944.

the following Element leader was Lt. H Stillwell flying 44-8697/MZ:. Suddenly Stillwell's B-17 rose up and impacted with the Lead bomber, resulting in the latter breaking in two. The nose of the other bomber was shattered and it drooped sharply into a dive that caused both wings to become detached. It was not surprising that the ASR Launches called to the watery location found nobody alive among the scattered wreckage. Better if not pleasant fortune as POWs met the crew of Lt. W Hemphill on board 43-38828/MZ:; after the aircraft was hit by flak over Minden it described a descending course for several minutes before finally coming down at Besterode, near Kassel.

The continuing run of almost daily missions was being realized with very few or sometimes no MIA losses within any or all of the three Divisions. Even when such casualties were incurred they rarely reached double figures overall, while this negative aspect was spread among the various groups so affected. It was 15 March before an individual unit suffered to any degree when Rattlesden surrendered four crews out of seven from the Division. Oranienburg's marshalling yards were pulverized by nearly 500 bomb loads, but the flak gunners on the target approaches left their mark on the Rattlesden formation. Salzwedel was where Lt. H Jessen and seven of his crew met their deaths after 43-38731/708BS was knocked out of the sky. Then at Schoenhausen, further southeast, fatal strikes on 43-38849/711BS left Lt.L Karst with no option but to bail out himself with six of the eight surviving crewmembers. A third flak victim ended up at Osted, in Denmark; this time round all nine on Lt. Putnam's crew bailed out of 42-97836/710BS **Bugs Bunny**.

The same MIA figure was registered over Berlin three days later, with five coming from the 13th CBW. The lurking presence of the jet-propelled Me 262, whose overall performance was alarmingly superior even to the P-51, and a technical world ahead of the lumbering USAAF bombers, was again realized. However, the badly strung-out 100th BG's Low squadron made the resultant interception even easier for the *Luftwaffe* sextet of jets from 9/JG7 led by *Oblt* Wegmann that zoomed into the attack near Salzwedel, ready to deploy the R4M rocket for the first time; these weapons were carried in two wing racks each containing twelve. **Skyway**

The figure of a Hitler-headed, skulking rat adorns the nose of 42-39930/730BS. The veteran Deopham Green B-17G's mission tally and well-worn exterior are testimony to her part in putting down the Third Reich's plans for European domination. The drop tanks being loaded are filled with Naplam.

Chariot (43-37521/EP: K) had its left stabilizer sawn off by an initial burst of 20-mm cannon fire and then was cast into a spin following a third pass, after which six of Lt. R King's crew bailed out just before the B-17 exploded. Minutes later, Lt. E Gwin's 43-38861/EP: **Sweet Nancy II** had two engines set on fire and lost its tail section following a dive and pull-out manoeuvre; the pilot was one of four fatalities.

Better fortune attended Lt. P DeWeerdt and all but one of his crew on board 44-8717/LD: T, a Lead PFF B-17, reported as absorbing a rocket strike on the left wing root that set it on fire. The pilots held it steady for the crew to jump; the tragic exception had apparently refused to bail out and almost certainly went in with the bomber. (A separate account indicates that the explosion blowing the pilot clear of his bomber also killed the airman in question.) A measure of direct and indirect revenge was exacted; Wegmann's fighter was fatally crippled by return fire from the B-17s and he bailed out after sustaining severe injuries resulting in a leg amputation, while three more Me 262s were lost either to the escorts or to a midair collision.

A fourth crew did not return to Thorpe Abbotts but did escape incarceration. Lt. M Jensen suffered wing and engine damage on 44-6295 to an extent that forced him to head eastwards to an eventual forced landing near a town in Poland. This was an action that signalled the start of a protracted return to England via Poltava and Italy, using every means of transport from a horse and cart to C-47 and B-17, and only ending on 25 April. No less than six Division aircraft among nine other B-17s made similar emergency diversions into Soviet-occupied territory this day—hardly surprising in view of their Ally's ever-closer proximity to Berlin. One came from Mendlesham, being 43-38912/18BS, which had lost half its power; Lt. R Myers elected to head east and finally crash landed in a Polish field. By the time the crew arrived back in Britain the war was over, and so their mission tally of fifteen at the time of the Berlin run became a final one.

Two dispersals were left empty at Framlingham, but one crew at least ended up alive, albeit as POWs, after **Little Moron** (43-37564/FC:, piloted by Lt. E Freeman, was downed by flak at Dreilingen. Lt. S Mroz was in charge of 44-8265/DI: **Reluctant**, but the exact fate of he and his crew as well as the B-17 is unclear. A pair of B-17s also remained absent from Great Ashfield, although only one went down in enemy territory; this was Lt. H Bloom's 44-6944/551BS. **Kentucky Winner** (42-

102481/ 550BS) was also flak-afflicted, but was then directed east towards Russian lines and crash landed by Lt. W Cocke Jr.; he and all but one crewmember survived the experience.

Another Unequal Contest

Yet another 100th BG crew was culled by the Me 262 on the 21st; this was Lt. B Painter's team on 44-8613, which was taken out just after bombing the Secondary at Plauen to leave only the pilot alive; a second bomber (44-8503/LD: A) suffered heavy damage from another jet assault but returned to Thorpe Abbotts, albeit only in a salvageable state. Over at Eye the 490th BG mourned the loss of three crews that had also felt the especially lethal effect of the Me 262 during the first of two such encounters within 30 days. A single crewmember came safely through the loss at Elsterwerda of 43-38575/850BS, flown by Lt. H Ballard (KIA), while Lt. W Audette joined five of his team in death on board 43-39130/848BS, which came down at Strehla, due west of Dresden. The third crew, led by Lt. Schultz (KIA) in 43-38072/ 848BS, suffered in equal measure with Ballard's team when only one ended up in captivity, while the B-17 crashed at Falkenberg, scant miles beyond the target. (The bulk of the Primaries for the 8th AF had been airfields suspected of housing Me 262 units.)

The projected main ground assault across the Rhine north of the Ruehr that involved the British 21st Army Group and Gen Simpson's 9th U.S. Army was duly initiated on the evening of 23 March. Next day the brief for the 8th AF's Divisions consisted of interdicting enemy airfields, while the 2nd AD additionally allotted groups to drop supplies to the Allied Parachute units, a duty that cost the groups so involved most of the nineteen MIA aircraft. The successful breaching of Germany's western natural defense signalled the end to Hitler's ever-waning ambitions of European conquest as the Anglo/American forces surged south to encircle the Ruehr and northwards towards Bremen, Hamburg, and the Danish border.

The "Operational" hoodoo struck twice within 24 hours at Mendlesham. On the 25th Lt. Bennett lifted the 18BS' 44-8605 off the runway, but he and his crew were dead fifteen minutes later. It was later surmised that in an effort to avoid a collision the pilots had inadvertently stalled out, and the bomber was observed to enter into a spin; the resultant attempt to correct this mal-action with too little altitude on hand snapped the aircraft in two and it plummeted to earth just inside the airfield boundary, where its bomb load erupted. Next day extremely poor weather conditions were encountered on return from Plauen and instructions were issued for each B-17 to peel off and execute an instrument let-down utilizing Buncher 19. Minutes later, Control tower staff suddenly became aware of two closely-spaced explosions to the southwest. A 452nd BG aircraft (43-38876) and 43-38402/391BS, flown by Lt. H McCutchan, had blindly run into each other, and all eighteen crewmembers forfeited their lives—three B-17s and twenty-seven airmen lost without hostile intervention.

Following two cost-free missions, at least in terms of MIA casualties, the Division joined in on the penultimate March strike to Germany's second industrial city, Hamburg, over which three of the five crews lost came from its ranks. Four days previous the reduced force of 152 bombers had included the 34th and 452nd BGs, two of whose crews had collided and thumped into the ground at Framsden and Cressingham. This had been Deopham's second such tragedy inside nine days; on the 18th 43-38879/728BS, flown by Lt. Bishop, had come down off the Dutch coast after impacting with 43-30982/728BS, whose crew did not share their fellow-airmen's ghastly fate and even managed to land safely.

March was also proving to be a bad month for the 34th BG in terms of collisions, with Lt. F Predo and crew's incident on the 26th the third such event. On 4 March Lt. J Mueller's 43-38338/18BS had crashed over French soil following impact with an unidentified bomber and eight of the nine-man crew forfeited their lives. Then, on the 23rd 43-38971/18BS, flown by Lt. M Bolsar, had fallen out and down thanks to flak strikes before crossing the path of a Rattlesden B-17 and exploding, leaving none of the nine crewmembers alive.

The same Divisional casualty scale occurred on the mission to Zeitz's oil production facilities that closed off March operations. The 96th BG's penultimate sacrifice involved two crews. Target flak downed 43-38935/MZ: A along with all on Lt. E Murphy's crew. Then two airmen died after 43-39105/AW: Q (Lt. W Seidenburg) crashed near Fulda. The clock was rapidly running down for the bomber offensive, but all too many American airmen would never live to savor the fruits of victory in the few weeks remaining before the last call to action was sounded....

The 96th BG is taxiing out for a flight sometime in the late spring of 1945 to judge by the tree foliage. AW: M/44-8788 on the right is a PFF aircraft with the Bendix chin turret removed. Serial on fin appears to have a dark background compared to the overall NMF finish on the airframe.

April 1945

April commenced with an abortive strike against Danish airfields, followed two days later with a second northern-directed sortie against U-boat yards at Kiel. The latest crew to seek sanctuary in Sweden became a victim of the persistent tracking flak barrage, whose weaponry included batteries based on water-borne barges. Lt. C McFarland's 43-38871/QJ: **Ractup** was so flak-afflicted that he decided to head northward; his successful bid for internment also signalled the final loss for the Snetterton-based group.

The disappointing bombing result achieved by the 100th BG was further exacerbated by the loss of one B-17 and most of its crew. On the way home, while still close to the enemy coastline, Lt. W Baldwin was seen to lower the landing gear on 43-38992/EP: S after stating he was low on fuel, before banking away into the undercast. One of the two survivors reported that the pilots had taken up a revised course for Belgium, but were skirting the lower end of the Frisian Island chain when flak struck home. The two airmen concerned managed to bail out of the burning B-17 prior to its falling away and exploding; a third crewmember had also bailed out but was subsequently killed, probably through resisting arrest, since he had previously told one of the survivors he would never be taken alive.

Kamikazi, German Style

A mix of targets was appearing on the Briefing maps that extended from airfields and marshalling yards to equipment depots and railroad stations. It was a run primarily conducted against the first target category that cost the Division its highest MIA rate for some time (fourteen) when a full-strength force went out against Kaltenkirchen and Parchim, as well as two depots north of Berlin on 7 April. Today, unbeknownst to the American bomber crews, their progress was to be contested by a very autocratic variation in *Luftwaffe* tactics, namely ramming. A specialist unit known as *Sonderkommando Elbe* had recently been formed with its pilots briefed to carry out this specific action that paralleled Japanese *Kamikazi* operations. It would be the 2nd and particularly the 3rd AD's ranks that would be the focus for the enemy unit's assaults.

The 100th BG was bypassing Hannover when the *Luftwaffe* intervened. Lt. A Calder's 42-97071/LD: P **Candy's Dandy** was rammed, and both the B-17 and its Bf 109 assailant were observed to spin downwards in flames; all of Calder's crew were killed, with their bomber crashing near the Steinhudermeer (Lake). The loss also to fighters of 44-8334/XR: M in Lt. W Howard's hands occurred around the same time, but two-thirds of the crew, including both pilots, bailed out. The Bf 109 or Fw 190 responsible almost immediately became an accidental or deliberate casualty when it closed in behind 43-38514/XR: J **E-Z Goin'** and struck its rear fuselage. The amazing aerodynamic qualities of "Boeing's Best" now manifested themselves. The top fin and rudder section and half the left stabilizer were sheered off by the impact, but far from falling out of the sky the pilots held position and course for home and finally put their bomber down at Thorpe Abbotts. Nor was the aircraft's flying career over, because the rear fuselage was replaced, and it finally ended up at Kingman, AZ's "bone yard" in late 1945!

The 452nd BG came back short of four aircraft, of which two were ramming victims. First, 43-38868/728BS was taken out in this manner by a Bf 109 and only two of Lt. W Richardson's ten-man team escaped alive. The second reported loss in this manner involved 42-31366/731BS **Old Outhouse**, which came down at Stadthagen, with Lt. D Owens and all other eight crewmembers losing their lives in the process. **Ida Wanna's** (44-8634/728BS) loss was also ascribed to fighters, but whether ramming was involved is unclear; what is clear is that Lt D Sharp and six of his crew failed to survive the final crash at Heide, northwest of Hamburg.

The Steinhudermeer area provided the grave for one of two Knettishall losses, credited either to a ramming act or by debris discharged from another B-17; whatever the cause, none of Lt. Bars' crew was left alive to confirm the exact reason for 43-38869/ 563BS **Paula Sue's** demise. Luneberg, southeast of Hamburg, was where 42-97105/561BS came to ground, along with four of Lt. L Hickman Jr's crew, including the pilot, with the bomber's loss recorded as due to ramming.

Two dispersals remained empty following the 486th BG's return to Sudbury, with one of the bombers falling tragically victim to a recurrent hazard arising from close-formation flying. As the bomb loads were being discharged upon Parchim airfield one or more of the missiles made a fatal union with the airframe of 43-39163/H8: S **Happy Warrior**. Although terminally crippled, the B-17's lethal impact with the ground was matched by just four of Lt. W Center's (POW) ten-man crew. 44-8528/2S: L **Flak Sack**, in Lt. Krenz's hands, was another flak victim on which one crewmember forfeited his life; one of the other nine avoided capture with the 486th BG bomber piling in at Seehausen. (There are eight German towns bearing this name, but five are too far east or south of Parchim, while two of the remaining three are adjacent to Bremen, so the location south of Cuxhaven on the Elbe is the most likely one forming the crash site.)

Single losses were suffered by four other groups including the 490th BG, but the Eye-based group should have suffered a second in another ramming incident. The Bf 109 concerned lunged at its intended target from an 8 o'clock angle and landed its right wing tip against the B-17's waist gun location. Amazingly the effect was lethal only for the fighter, whose wing disintegrated, after which it carved an erratic course underneath the bomber. Serious damage to the waist, ball turret, and right wing with two engines disabled still did not lead the latter aircraft to a similar terminal fate. In fact, 43-38058/850BS bore Lt. C Cagle and crew back to a Continental airfield; the sole crew injury was borne by Sgt. C LeNeve (BT), whose broken arm was a small price to pay for surviving the wrecking of his turret. The *Rammkommando* pilots had struck home on what was destined to be their sole recorded assault, but the results were not very good for the effort expended, apart from which the Bombing Offensive's conclusion in another eighteen days would render their services basically null and void.

Winding Down the Clock....

There now occurred over the next three days a persistent if overall small loss scale for the Division and the 8th AF, when MIA figures of twenty and thirty-five were respectively recorded. The desperate defensive measure cast up by the ramming unit demonstrated how the *Luftwaffe's* strength, if not the quality of its personnel and aircraft, was largely spent. On the other hand, the existence of jet-propelled designs, principally the Me 262, was something to be rightly regarded with trepidation by the bomber crews; the 487th and 490th BGs would be the latest units in the Division to suffer at their hands....

Marshalling yards at Plauen and Hof among others were hit with five crews lost, all from the 4th CBW, and three from the 486th BG. Flak took out all three of the bombers: 43-37942/3R: J **Blue Fairy** (Lt. W Wood) and 43-38020/2S: T **Anthracite** (Lt. A Sauler) came down at Rehau, adjacent to Hof, with both pilots and one other out of the sixteen airmen killed. Also lost over the same location was 44-8712/4N: S **Lonesome Polecat** along with two-thirds of Lt. Hohmann's (POW) crew. Next day the Division toll was six over four Primaries in and around Münich. The casualty rate crept up to nine (10th) when a similar group of targets between Magdeburg and Neuruppin were assigned. Brandenburg/Briest's airfield, a reported Me 262 haven, was the focus of attack for the 486th and 487th BGs, and two more crews never returned to Sudbury, making seven lost in four days; one was led by Lt. M Thaler, who bailed all his crew out of 43-37820/ 3R: T, leaving the flak-stricken bomber to impact at Ziesar. Simultaneously sharing this fate at the flak gunners' hands was 44-6580/ 2S: P **Dream King**, on which Lt. K Dolan (POW) lost four of his crew.

The target was rapidly approaching with Lavenham's High squadron dangerously spread out and therefore presenting a weaker defensive posture to would-be attackers. It was now that the Me 262 menace struck, with one lunging down upon 44-6913/4F: C **Queen of Hearts** in a single surgical strike that set No. 3 engine and fuel tank on fire. Lt. E Sell salvoed the bomb load and banked round in a desperate bid to regain Allied lines. All too soon the blowtorch effect of the fire seemed about to collapse the wing, so the bail out order was passed on by two crewmembers moving in either direction due to the intercom being inoperative. The pilot was the last out of the ten-man crew to successfully abandon the B-17 and he was barely out in midair when it exploded to spread itself over Zobbenitz, northwest of Magdeburg. The group was already one short at this stage. Lt. R Althouse's 43-37987/R5: J **Mean Widdle Kid** took a flak strike and began a circling manoeuvre that developed into a temporary loss of altitude before levelling off. Shortly after one wing broke off, but nine crewmembers had already evacuated the aircraft; sadly S/Sgt W Peake (TG), who had to be assisted out, was later found with an unopened parachute.

The bomb loads had been accurately delivered and the group was on its way home when the Me 262s again struck to cull two more B-17s from the High squadron, the first of which appeared to be 44-8702/2G: S **Forever Amber**. A slashing attack from in front stitched a row of incendiary shells into the inner-right wing and fuselage, and smoke and flames immediately trailed out of the wing. Formation was briefly held before Lt. M Hauenstein's mount began to slew inexorably out of control with S/Sgt. E DeLachia (TG) slumped over his guns and the sole crewmember failing to survive.

The Lead B-17 was almost simultaneously assailed from behind with a fierce fire taking hold around the cockpit area and almost certainly contributing to the death of Lt. L McGinnis (P). As the doomed bomber eased off to the left still in level flight Maj. G Richmond (squadron Command pilot) yelled "Get out" over the intercom, an order to which he and seven of the eight other airmen responded positively as 44-8808/2C: T commenced a descending turn that ended fatally near Tangermuende.

...Too Damn Slow for Some

A total of nine more Division missions was destined to be flown before 21 April, and in that period a total of eight crew were MIA out of an 8th AF figure of nine; a miniscule loss-scale considering the 7,000 individual bomber sorties dispatched. However, this extremely positive statistical situation could only be viewed in retrospect, since every last airman currently had no control over whether or not he would fall into this grim category. The last vestiges of enemy resistance might be plain to see from a strategic viewpoint in London or Washington, but the bombs, shells, and bullets cast up by the Nazi defenders were still a mortal threat to their numerical and technologically-superior adversaries in the field of combat. A further twist to the bomber crews' ultimate survival lay in the constant risk of their aircraft failing at any point before entering or after departing enemy airspace. Only a permanent separation from military flying of any kind could grant them the chance of living out their lives....

It was the fourth mission after the 10th before the initial two MIA crews forming the final clutch of Division losses was recorded, both adding to Sudbury's recent run of ill fortune. One was 43-38001/H8: B **Old Miss Agnes** flown by Lt. Allbright, which was downed by flak at Dresden and added nine more, albeit rather temporary *Kriegsgefangen* into the enemy's grasp. Two days later eleven groups of the Division headed out to bomb rail targets in southeastern Germany. The mission promised yet another "achin' back" run lasting many hours, but little else in the way of opposition—a vain hope for some groups, however...

The 490th BG was one of the last generation of units to join the 8th AF in mid-1944. Since then the crews had flown 156 missions at a relatively small cost of eighteen B-24s or B-17s claimed in combat, although almost double that number of aircraft had been written off in operational crashes. In the light of what transpired it would seem that the group were part of the force briefed to assault facilities at Pirna, south of Dresden. As the formations homed in upon their targets the *Luftwaffe* in the form of the Me 262 was already airborne and ready to react.

The jet-propelled fighters homed in upon their very pedestrian B-17 opponents, and it was the Eye-based group that unfortunately bore the brunt of their assaults for the second time inside a month. Four crews in all were culled from the Eye formation with the crash sites of three in between

Zwickau and Dresden. Schoenau, east of the former-named city, was where 43-38078/849BS impacted to leave a third of Lt. Norvell's (POW) nine-man crew alive. Lt. W McCallister's (KIA) 43-38135 came down at Marienburg, southwest of Dresden, with just two out of nine crewmembers surviving. A second 849BS bomber flown by Lt. Stowall crashed in or close to Dresden, but this time nine of the ten on board lived through the experience. (Details on the final loss, 43-38048/ **Ole Timer**, are sparse.) The Me 262 haul of victims extended to the 447th BG; 42-31188/709BS **Dead Man's Hand**, flown by Lt. R Glazener (POW), was knocked out of the skies over Dresden, albeit with a single fatality among the ten on board.

E-Z Goin's bomb-bearing turtle is admired by an officer at Thorpe Abbotts. The B-17G-90-BO airframe was seven months into its combat career when it went out on 7 April 1945 to Hamburg. Awaiting the formations were fighters from a specialist unit of volunteers titled *Rammkommando Elbe*...

Closing the Combat Ledger

The penultimate Division mission (20th) saw three CBWs, with the 490th BG one of the units, heading back to Brandenburg, where it had bled just twenty-four hours previous; this time round all progressed well as the city's marshalling yards were plastered at no cost in aircraft. Next day only the 4th and 45th CBWs were dispatched further south to take out airfields linked to the Me 262. The un-stated Primary or Primaries were left untouched thanks to heavy cloud cover, and in fact debriefing queries were raised at some bases as to why the mission had been allowed to go ahead, since formation flying proved very difficult to maintain in the conditions. As it was nearly every group unloaded using *H2X* on the town of Ingolstadt, north of Münich, an ironic manner in which to conclude the 8th AF's avowed policy of precision bombing and perhaps indicative of how the "Total War" aspect had overtaken purely military matters during the final months of the conflict.

No opposition from fighters or flak had been encountered, and so it was particularly tragic that the last Division loss over enemy territory proved to be self-inflicted. Lt. J Kirk was piloting 42-97342/XM: H **Struggle Bunny** in the right-rear of the 94th BG's Low squadron, and was therefore subject to the build-up of "propeller wash" from the preceding elements. Just after the bomb run his B-17 was observed to suddenly roll over and fall vertically into the clouds, a victim of the treacherously unpredictable airflow effect; only one of the eight-man team got out before the B-17 went in near Halle. And so the Division's blood debt was concluded in this cruelly pointless manner. Nor was the day's casualty list yet completed; the 452nd BG's 43-38356/863BS **Quivering Queenie** ended up being crash landed on a continental airfield, an act that killed eight crewmembers.

As far as the 3rd AD personnel were concerned 21 April 1945 proved to be a case of "It's Over, Over there" in respect of combat operations. Four days later their 1st and 2nd AD contemporaries returned from bombing Pilsen and Salzburg, equally unaware that never again would they be faced with the early morning CQ calls of "Up and at 'em" that signalled the start of another wearying and fraught-with-danger assault upon Hitler's *Festung Europa* (Fortress Europe). Also never to be repeated (other than in the Pacific Theater up to August 1945) was the current concept of massed bomber formations; the looming advent of the Nuclear Age would put an end to its need in future Conflicts.

E-Z Goin' is seen back in her dispersal after the Hamburg mission. Most of the left stabilizer and the top section of the fin and rudder have been excised after one of the *Rammkommando Elbe* fighters attempted to bring the bomber down by a pre-meditated act of collision. Despite the fearsome scale of damage, the aircraft was repaired and returned home with the 482nd BG two months later.

15

"Deliverance"

To the British it was "Manna"...
To the Americans it was "Chowhound"...
But to the Dutch population it was "Deliverance!"

Three B-17s from the 34th BG are holding an echelon right flight path and have the landing gears extended to slow down their progress. The open bomb-bay doors will soon disgorge their valuable loads of supplies for the Dutch. Note the extensive flooding due to the Germans opening the dyke water-control gates.

"Withering on the Vine"

The failure of Operation *Market/Garden* in September 1944 had serious consequences not only for the overall progress of the Anglo/American ground forces, but also for that element of the Dutch population still firmly under Nazi occupation. The German Commander in this zone, Gen. Blaskowitz, along with Hitler's representative for Holland, Artur Syess-Inquart, maintained a harsh grip upon the subjected people to the extent that food supplies in particular, along with other essentials, such as heating materials, fell to dangerous levels. This was bad enough at any time, but the severe winter of 1944/45 only added to civilian woes.

By March 1945 the situation had deteriorated to the point where thousands had succumbed, and many more were on the point of expiring, from lack of nourishment and warmth. Desperate measures to combat this terminal fate included the eating of flower bulbs and sugar beets, and the burning of any combustible matter. As early as the previous October Queen Wilhelmina had appealed to Roosevelt for help, but his response was to promise all possible assistance only *after* Liberation. During early 1945 three cargo ships under Red Cross auspices had been permitted to deliver several thousand tons of supplies, but the quantity involved could not sustain the population for more than a short time period (the daily caloric content available was arguably less than that "enjoyed" by concentration camp inmates, so it was little wonder that the eventual death toll of around 15,000 was reached.)

Around February/March further correspondence on the subject of Holland and its people's plight flowed between Roosevelt and Churchill. The President's letter referred to the greater need, both literal and diplomatic, to get supplies through regardless of having to negotiate with the enemy to do so; in the long term more damage might be inflicted to the cause of international solidarity that a current refusal to have any truck with the adherents of National Socialism might benefit the advance towards Victory. Churchill, for his part, was in full agreement,

This snapshot of the Dutch village with neat houses surrounded by freshly-budding trees gives no indication of the desperate plight of its starving occupants. The strips of material may well have been laid out with a view to attracting the attention of the low-flying bombers, although the actual drop would have to be in an adjacent open area.

The 96th BG is seen in the process of releasing its load of supplies for the Dutch. The packages are cascading from the nearest B-17's bomb-bay and overall delivery is accurate, to judge by the large white cross acting as a target "marker."

adding that if the Allies were to wait until the entire country was liberated before the Dutch could gain access to the supplies many more that had already died would be the grim result.

The crossing of the Rhine by Gen. Montgomery's Anglo/American forces on 24 March was followed by a general advance northwards towards Bremen and Hamburg. Within three weeks the British and Canadian units had effectively sealed off Blaskowitz's soldiers in western Holland from all physical contact with Germany by occupying the country's eastern region. However, the Allies were still reluctant to fight their way through the much more heavily built-up and populated occupied zone, since the resultant destruction would bring about civilian casualties—an ironic twist considering the current physical travails borne by the same civilians! The presence of nearly 120,000 German soldiers, however constrained by hunger, would nevertheless have surely guaranteed a pitched and bloody battle with their Allied adversaries before Liberation had been brought about.

True to the code of the German High Command, Blaskowitz refused to consider a unilateral general surrender despite the hopelessness of the situation. Moreover, the drying up of his own supplies as the military noose was tied around communications with the Homeland was soon arousing mass hunger pangs among the *Wehrmacht* personnel in addition to the deprivations long borne by their reluctant "charges." (On the other hand, his contemporaries elsewhere were still active despite their parlous position, so he was within his rights to fight on in the hope of a miraculous restitution in Nazi fortunes being brought about.)

Syess-Inquart, on the other hand, did enter into discussions regarding a relief programme, which were initiated in late March. As regards possible RAF participation, the original Plan involved the Halifaxes and Stirlings of No. 38 (Transport) Group; a logical choice at the time, but one which was felt could not deliver the projected daily quantities of supplies (estimated at 1,000 tons) with the available numbers of aircraft likely to be on hand. In addition, as late as 24/25 April the German military at least expressed extreme reluctance to permit the unfettered movement of Allied aircraft on the rather spurious grounds that their defensive system would be prey to surveillance and subsequent assault! However, the counter-threat to treat any hostile act against the supply drop aircraft as a war crime seemed to have worked, because Syess-Inquart dispatched a letter next day agreeing to the Operation!

"Swords to Ploughshares" – The Aerial Version

Even as the combat crews of the 3rd AD were indulging in the final sequence of missions, planning for a massive food relief programme to bring succour to the Dutch was reaching its practical stage. The Allied Chiefs settled upon those heavy bomber forces concentrated in East Anglia as being tasked with the duty. In the case of the RAF the Lancasters of Nos. 1 and 3 Group were the chosen means of delivery, while for the 8th AF this meant the 3rd

This picture is taken looking down through the gaping bomb-bay. Several packages are just falling clear of the racks, while the pin-points of dozens of other packages from this and accompanying B-17s are outlined against the drop zone.

AD. Twenty-five RAF squadrons would be involved in the actual food drops, while a further six Lancaster and two Mosquito units from No. 8 (Pathfinder) Group would mark out the designated drop zones. Ten B-17 groups from the 4th, 45th, and 93rd CBWs would comprise the force to be dispatched by the USAAF.

The codenames selected for the operation were *Manna* and *Chowhound* respectively. The British example referred to the Biblical "Bread from Heaven" that sustained Moses and those he led through the Wilderness; the Americans went for a more practical if prosaic term in relation to satisfying one's need for food. More significantly and regardless of the differing official terminology, the common objective of the exercise on behalf of the Dutch population was one of deliverance from the hands of the *Grim Reaper*.

Preparation

There was no need to adapt the bomb-bay of the Lancaster for the operation. The 33-foot single-cell and horizontally-aligned layout of the bay lent itself equally well to the carriage of the implements of War and in this instance those of Peace and Liberty. This was not the case for the B-17, since its racks were configured vertically, and therefore not so suited to the stacking and release of the sacks and boxes of supplies. Instead plywood floors hinged on their outer edges were installed on either side of the central bomb rack frame. The inner edges were suspended from the bomb release mechanism in the middle. A salvo switch was specially fitted, which upon activation caused the platform halves to swing down. Retraction was then to be carried out via four heavy rubber shock cords attached to the platforms' inner corners.

Terms of Engagement

After a protracted period of discussion between the Allied and German authorities an agreement was established. The B-17s and Lancasters were to enter and depart Dutch territory at specified points on the North Sea coastline. Blaskowitz's flak gunners in turn were to hold their fire. In the run-up to the action, the latter aspect of the operation naturally left the airmen rather concerned

Hostilities are finally over, and the public around Snetterton Heath have been invited onto the airfield. They are studying the outlines of a PFF-equipped B-17G nose-to-nose with a P-51D believed to be from the 339th FG flying out of Fowlmere, in Cambridgeshire. The budding trees seem to symbolize the regeneration of normal life in Europe, however painful and long-term the process would prove to be.

ET: F from the 95th BG is seen in its operational function prior to VE-Day. A smoke marker has been released as a "bombs away" indicator to the group formation. The PFF B-17G had transferred-in from the 100th BG on 23 January 1945 and was to return Stateside and thence to Walnut Ridge as a "graveyard" candidate in February 1946.

about relying on the gunners' integrity. Having survived the worst of Germany's defensive system, the airmen were extremely reluctant to risk their lives, given the vulnerability of their low and slow-flying progress, since they would be "sitting ducks" in the event of an "incident" occurring, accidentally or otherwise.

The operation was originally meant to commence on 25 April, but Mother Nature put the latest spoke in the 8th AF's wheel with conditions that totally grounded the aircraft. This was all the more cruelly disappointing for the Dutch who had been alerted by radio to the supplies' imminent delivery, and who had to endure their parlous existence for three more days before the initial RAF sortie occurred. In fact, it was adverse weather conditions over the assigned drop zones that led to the extended delay for the 8th AF. Nor was weather over East Anglia much improved on 1 May when the decision was nevertheless taken to initiate operations in the face of clear conditions across the North Sea.

"Let's Go!"...

Low cloud and intermittent rain showers provided unpleasant partners working against safe Assembly, in this case intended to be made around 1,500 ft., since the food drops would be carried out at a lower altitude. All went well with the overall force, as seen in the case of the 45th CBW B formation. Flying in one of the 41-strong formation dispatched from Snetterton Heath was a bomber bearing Maj. C Godecke and leading an Element with a specific and potentially lethal duty.

The Major recalled that the mission was being flown despite no official clearance from the Germans to make unmolested flights over the Occupied zone yet confirmed. A full ammunition load was therefore carried on all aircraft. As a further precaution, on approach to the Dutch coast the three B-17s would detach themselves from the formation, the other 38 B-17s being left to orbit over the sea. The Godecke trio would then act as a "sacrificial goat" to test the flak gunners' sincerity by flying in over the land! (Godecke later reported that as the crews watched the 88-mm guns tracked the bombers as they crossed-in and flew at minimum altitude past the gun sites; he said he had never been as afraid on any other mission as here.) With no hostile response thankfully made, he radioed the formation to make its approach and attached his Element to the rear as it passed by and headed for its allotted drop zone, an airfield close to Holland's capital, The Hague.

"Manna Cometh Forth"

As the bombers tracked majestically over the airfield the thousands of 10-in-1 Ration pack boxes—the numerical term relating to a complete day's meal for ten individuals, and containing items ranging from ham omelettes and candy to cigarettes and even toilet paper—were cast out into midair as the platforms were released. Down on the ground the upturned faces of thousands of Dutch men, women, and children were observed along with a display of their reactions. Many were running, others waving their hands in which were clutched flags, sheets, or similar items; a goodly number were demonstrating a more pertinent if not also poignant response to this first evidence

Jerry Boy's prospects of surviving combat could not have been rated high, since she joined the 385th BG in late January 1944. In fact, the 549BS B-17G came through the conflict, only to be "written off" following a fire on 6 June 1945. The vertical fin carries the red checkerboard design applied to group aircraft from February 1945. NMF "Cheyenne" tail turret is a field modification, as it contrasts with the overall camouflage finish.

There is a supreme irony in the wording on this placard photographed on 11 May 1945, which literally stands in the presence of 44-6888/ AW: R **Sweet Chariot**. The 96th BG bomber over-shot the runway, but fortunately came to rest on the far side of the road without incident for the local residents!

of "Manna from Heaven" by going down on their knees and praying while tears flowed in plentiful quantity.

Here, after five long years of either watching the spider-trails of the Americans by day or hearing the muted roar of the unseen legions of RAF bombers that promised ultimate if open-ended salvation from repression and soiling fear at the hands of the Nazi regime was evidence of an imminent return to the world of Freedom. The "broad sunlit uplands of Life" as foreseen by Winston Churchill in his rousing speech just after assuming Prime Ministerial Office in Britain's (and by extension the Free World's) darkest hour in mid-1940 were looming large in April/May 1945, and the Curse of Hitler was finally being lifted from the brows of Mankind.

Equally, among the airmen's ranks there were many who felt a lump in their throat or even starker emotions at these responses to this very necessary if belated mission of mercy. One pilot among

This line of 385th BG B-17Gs displays an interesting variation in CBW markings. The first and third aircraft bear the red checkerboard design, although the aircraft in foreground only carries this on its central fin. Second B-17 in the line has no such marking on either fin or rudder, while the checkerboard on the fourth visible tail structure is restricted to the rudder with the central fin in Olive Drab!

The flamboyant artwork on **Ruby's Raiders** was only applied to the right side of this B-17G's nose. The partially-applied yellow chevron denoting service with the 4th CBW was introduced in December 1944; it was deleted, as was the "square G" on the fin, when the 385th BG was re-assigned to the 93rd CBW two months later.

their number recalled an image that arose out of his youthful visits to the cinema and was now transposed to the current time:

> "A typical situation in the silent Westerns was a wagon train under siege by circling Indians. Down to their last bullets and fearing the worst, they would scan the horizon in the hope of relief. Then, in the nick of time, charging into sight would be a troop of U.S. Cavalry, banners flying and sabres flashing. Every kid would leap to his feet at the sight, whooping and hollering. That's now what I felt like—the Cavalry riding to the rescue, with the people down below in the same albeit modern position akin to the wagon train. We flew on, with my reaction split between elation and tears as the magnitude of what we were doing began to sink in—we were attempting to snatch an entire Nation back from the brink of starvation...."

Grim "Comedy"

The virtual cascade of packaged and boxed material tumbling out of the sky could have easily led to injury or even death to any individual unfortunate enough to be in the way. This risk did not prevent some individuals from taking chances in securing some of the items, however, with sometimes comical effect, at least as far as the airmen were concerned. One individual riding his bicycle along a canal tow-path was seen to jump off his mount and dive into the water after a package while the bicycle pursued its own wayward course. A similar scenario involved two people in a boat who took the same direct action in order to retrieve a sack that had temporarily hung-up before falling clear into the water. Such actions would seem precipitate to the casual observer. When one is facing a life or death situation as these people were, simply nothing could be ruled out in order to increase the odds of surviving, even at risk to life and limb as might have been the case here. As it was there were injuries and even several deaths as a result of people ignoring the risk posed by running after items even as the airspace within the drop zones was still saturated with the cherished products. (One man was reportedly killed by a single tin of powdered egg—not surprising, considering that it would have assumed the characteristics of, as well as descended not far short of the pace of a missile!)

"Killing with Kindness?"

Although a test-run with a Lancaster had confirmed the basic feasibility of dropping the goods unassisted by parachute, there were numerous occasions where packets and similar containers burst open on impact, scattering the precious commodities across the drop zones in often inedible form. Even then, hundreds of individuals attempted to scoop or spoon-up the remnants and eat them on the spot. This was a natural but very risky process for them, given that the rich nature of much of the food could easily react seriously if not fatally with their internal organs, which had shrunk under the influence of long-term malnutrition. This danger in turn was why the Dutch authorities made strenuous attempts to collect and concentrate the supplies at specific locations and categorize them into various necessary types of sustenance before issuing them in controlled amounts—otherwise the expression "killing with kindness" could literally be realized! A further problem was to exist between the Dutch and the Germans; the latter naturally provided much of the vehicular transport, but were accused of skimming off a large element for their troops. The Germans in turn accused the Dutch of siphoning off supplies by simple theft!

"Blind" Luck

The weather conditions on the second day of the operation were none improved, with snow squalls adding to the difficulty of assembling through low cloud. One 96th BG crew led by Lt. Patchen was extremely lucky to come through the mission even before crossing out over the English coast. The group's course took it directly towards a group of Early Warning radar masts, one of which made contact with and sliced off one wing-tip on the B-17. The bomber was kept aloft and successfully brought in for a landing at its airfield. Lt. T Austin was No. 3 to Lt. W Schramm, and noted how his Leader swung clear of the formation after cutting through a brief snow flurry. However, in doing so the two B-17s lost contact, and it was decided to head out and over Holland alone. Then, just after making the drop the windshield wipers on Austin's bomber failed in the face of a persistent light rain. He had little option but to maintain formation via the cockpit side window, confident in the straight course being maintained by Schramm. It was only on return to the airfield that he discovered the other B-17 had also lost its wiper operation and was equally "blind!"

Logistical Tally

The delay in 8th AF participation lasted 48 hours beyond the first RAF sortie on 29 April. During this 48-hour period just over 700 Lancasters had released around 1,500 tons over six specific zones. Over the ensuing eight days a further 5,500 tons cascaded from the RAF bomber force's bomb bays. The seven-day spell of 8th AF operations resulted in no less than 415 tons being delivered to its five assigned zones. The fact that the individual RAF load supplied was an estimated 2.28 tons against 1.86 tons for its contemporary was no reflection upon the USAAF effort, although the use of B-24 units might have increased the latter Air Force's share.

The fact that the Germans had stuck to the exact letter of the agreement by desisting from firing upon the formations persuaded the Allied authorities that the original provision of full armament on the B-17s was now unnecessary. This basic relaxation in turn meant that the gunners could now be displaced by ground personnel who wished to participate in the operation. For the next seven days ending 8 May the Anglo/American "heavies" trundled their way across the North Sea to deliver the daily dose of *Manna*. Each day's end witnessed a safe return of all participating bombers and their crews to their airfields. However, there was a small but tragic sting in the tail to the overall operation that would occur right at the point of its conclusion....

It's Not Over Until it's All Over...

On 7th May 1945 the 95th BG based at Horham prepared to fly the last of six missions to Western Holland that had "Manna/Chowhound's" now peaceful intent behind its execution. One of the participating crews going out on their second *Manna/Chowhound* sortie and headed by Lt. Lionel Sceurman was attached to the 334th BS. The group's final combat mission had occurred more than two weeks previous with all that this entailed in bringing the airmen back to a sense of normal living. Today's flight would be somewhat of a joy ride not only for the seven-man crew, but also for the six ground crew personnel that included the aircraft's crew chief. The only marginal pressure that could not be totally dispelled even at this stage of the conflict was the fact that the German flak batteries were still fully manned and presumably ready to engage any bomber straying off the designated route....

Prior to take-off Sceurman had approached Lt. Tony Braidic, who had been the original bombardier on the crew; after six missions the latter had been taken off the crew with a view to being trained for operations on B-29s in the Pacific and his place taken by Sgt. Dave Condon. Sceurman asked Tony if he wanted to fly with what had been his original crew but he declined—a decision that was not based on logic, since

The mangled state of this Horham-based B-17G would indicate that she is fit only for salvage; the damage was inflicted on 16 December 1944 when she over-shot the runway. However, full restoration to flying condition was made, with an ultimate return home for the 412BS aircraft the following June.

he was scheduled to participate with another crew, but one that almost certainly was destined to save his life.

The take-off, assembly, and crossing of the North Sea went off in good order, as did the dropping of the supplies from around 1,500 ft over the city of Utrecht, due south of Amsterdam and the cross-out on the way back. B-17G/44-8640 was holding formation as the formation traversed the sea from which a slight haze was rising to a height not far short of the bombers' altitude. The English coast was fast approaching when the crisis broke.

On board, Lt. Sceurman was up in the nose with Lt. Cook (N), leaving Lt. Jim Schwarz in control, when Sgt. Kuper (Armourer/gunner), standing behind the co-pilot, reported that No. 2 engine was running "rough." Schwarz agreed that there was something amiss since he could smell smoke, while a developing trail of oil pouring out of the cowling and a loss of oil pressure was further visual confirmation. The pilot came back into his seat and ordered the engine be switched off and the propeller "feathered" while the crew-chief for the aircraft recommended the landing gear be lowered as a further aid to combating the flames that had now taken hold of the engine. Altitude was steadily lost until at around 500 ft. the pilot alerted the personnel to stand by for a bale out, since he did not think there was sufficient time for "ditching" stations to be assumed prior to the impact with the sea and all attempts to put out the fire with the fire-extinguishers having failed. At 1527 hours, and with the English coast less than ten miles distant, the B-17 ploughed into the North Sea. The 8th AF's blood debt in flying missions over Europe had finally been sated....

Lt. Schwartz clambered out of his seat and down to the nose hatch, by which time Lt. Cook and two others had already jumped. The last had been Sgt. Condon, and he alone was destined to survive from out of this element of the crew. Worse still was the fact that Lt. Schwarz alone out of the remaining personnel was to be granted the gift of life. Even then they were fortunate, because both were in the water for between 30 minutes and one hour.

A Lancaster of No. 550 squadron had witnessed the B-17's precipitate entry into the sea and began circling the area and sending out the map coordinates before diverting to attract the attention of a nearby vessel and bring it to the crash location.

The pilot was ordered to continue overhead; in the meantime, the vessel's crew began a search. One of the airmen then sighted a figure, who responded by getting to the Mae West thrown out of the bomber. An RAF Walrus amphibian appeared along with a PBY flying boat of the Halesworth-based 5th Emergency Rescue Squadron, and between them fished out three still-live survivors, of which one died on the way back. The expression that heads this section had come home in all its tragic portent.

What had been a mission of mercy for a beleaguered people had brought death to their saviours. Instead of a return to their homeland, five would find a premature last resting place in a military cemetery on either side of the Atlantic, while the bodies of the other six would find eternal repose under the trackless wastes of the North Sea.

This is a monochrome version of one of the pictures in the book's color section, albeit with the crew posed by the shattered left stabilizer. **Bit O' Lace** (42-97976), serving with the 447th BG, suffered the damage over Kiel on 4 April 1945, the latest in a series of similar, though not always so severe, incidents.

Equally tragic was the fact that today's effort signalled the closure of the entire *Manna/Chowhound* project, so a safe return to Horham would have almost certainly guaranteed a full future life span for all eleven airmen.

The following rendition is a poignant valediction to their sacrifice....

"Swarms of swallows bringing food
Visions of Victory
Thoughts of Freedom
For the starving
For the powerless
For the discouraged ones
They all laugh and cry....

"They waved from bridges
From canals
From squares and viaducts
They climbed on roof-tops
Once bent down, they straightened
Their backs again
And shook hands

And cheered at every plane
For this was a miracle
Salvation from above
'Manna' rain
Bringing relief, true blessing
Mighty moment
We waited for months to see it."

(This simple, striking poem was written by Elizabeth van Maasdijk to commemorate the events of the massive food-dropping operation.)

The RAF's participation in *Manna/Chowhound* was supplied by the Lancasters of Nos. I and 3 Groups, Bomber Command with No. 8 (Pathfinder Force) Group marking out the drop zones. Two of the bombers are crossing over an anonymous Dutch town with its citizens gazing up in wonder and anticipation.

16

High Road to Freedom

Combat operations over Nazi-occupied Europe carried constant risk to life and limb for all concerned. In addition, anyone succeeding in bailing out could normally expect to land up in a POW camp unless the crew in question was fortunate enough to divert into Sweden or Switzerland. However, the fact that the Germans had used force of arms to occupy continental Europe's western and central strands conversely provided RAF or USAAF personnel with the chance of (1) evading capture by gaining the assistance of the civilian populations and (2) completing a bid to get back to Britain via the various clandestine "lines" of communications laboriously created by the Resistance and leading down towards Spain, or in some instances across to Switzerland.

The Americans who were presented with such a chance held a major natural advantage over their RAF contemporaries—daylight. An observer on the ground could tell that the parachute floating down supported an Allied flier, whereas RAF operations primarily being conducted by night meant that the great majority of its unfortunate personnel landed without being similarly visually tracked. Consequently it was much more difficult for the latter to confirm their genuine status to those from whom they sought assistance; in turn, there was inevitable doubt in the

Although this B-17G was recorded as received by the 8th AF on 5 July 1944, she was probably held at a Depot until the 490th BG began to convert from the B-24 to the B-17. The black rectangle behind the C indicates assignment to the 848BS at Eye. The No. 4 engine cowling seems to bear a colored cowling.

This B-17G arrived at Framlingham on the eve of *Black Week* (7 October 1943). Reportedly bearing the names **Dinah Mite** and **Pub Pete**, it went out on a "milk run" mission to the Pas de Calais on 21 January; the anticipated short-haul run ended in disaster when flak claimed the B-17G along with its pilot, Lt. C Baughar.

minds of such potential "supporters" that confronting them was an Allied airman as opposed to a German "plant" intended to infiltrate Resistance cells.

"Home Runs" (1)

Once in friendly hands there ensued several variations in terms of whether or not the airman or airmen in question could commence their onward path towards a return to Britain; furthermore, the ultimate location from which the bid for Freedom would be completed, as well as the pace at which the overall endeavour could be carried out, threw up notable variations.

The most regular route along which evaders were channelled was the one that was directed towards neutral Spain. The journey to be made extended up to several hundred miles depending upon where the airman had parachuted to earth in the far reaches of Holland, down through Belgium and Luxembourg, or into the massive hinterland of France. It followed from this that in numerous cases lay the need to cross one or more national boundaries. Then, the mode of transport could involve a combination of choices involving public transport (rail or bus), car, and bicycle, or even walking. Over everything lay the heavy hand of doubt and apprehension; was every civilian encountered a true friend of the Allies or an enemy collaborator?; were the fake documents issued to an evader capable of standing up to security checks by the Germans or their Fascist-based supporting organisations in the Occupied countries, such as the French Milice, or even the National police forces?; might an individual betray his non-Continental origin through committing some verbal or social *faux pax*?

Evasion Over Land

On 20 October 1943, during a mission to Dueren 42-30719/ CC: P **Shatzi**, having fallen behind its group, was intercepted by fighters and dispatched near Beghek, north of Eindhoven, in central Holland. Lt. J Hurst (N) not only bailed out but was the single example among the eight survivors to evade capture, although he could have received severe injuries from a bovine source when he was forced to out-pace a bull in the field into which he had descended!

His precipitate "arrival" in Europe was the start of a three-month odyssey that began when he encountered a Dutchman who relieved him of his sodden clothing, caused by his diving into a drainage ditch away from the bull, before both cycled away from the scene. Two weeks concealment in a house—during which time he was interrogated in order to prove his genuine status—should have ended with his transfer north for reputed pick-up by a submarine. After another two weeks, however, this plan was cancelled, and he began the much more protracted journey southwest towards Spain.

By then he was given the role of playing a deaf mute painter, but the attempt to cross from Belgium into France nearly failed at the border post; fortunately the financial bribe offered the officials was taken, and Hurst, along with his guide, boarded an express to Paris, where a short stay was followed by another rail journey down to Lyon. From there the party's progress was much more deliberate and slow in reaching Perpignan, in the shadow of the Pyrenean mountain chain. The true physical test now awaited the evading party assembled there.

In mid-December the snow was piled high on the mountains to provide a parlous passage even for anybody who was properly nourished and clothed; factors that did not apply to most on hand for the evasion bid. Not only was food at a premium in Occupied Europe, but clothing items, particularly shoe leather, was of an indifferent to poor standard and dangerously unequal to facing up to and surviving the deep-seated snow drifts and freezing stream waters to be encountered in the Pyrenees. In addition, many of the "guides" were not only hardy mountain-experienced people, but were also not of a mind to grant much leeway to anybody who could not keep up with each party's progress, regardless of the conditions. (Hurst recalled one individual who was literally kicked off a ledge to his death because he was adjudged to be holding up progress.)

All but one on Lt. D Proctor's 96th BG crew was very fortunate to evade capture on 25 February 1945. **Dinah Mite** (43-39018/AW: P) lies in Switzerland under both close and more distant examination by the neutral population.The figures in the right background are standing on Austrian soil, and any further forward movement by the skidding B-17G might well have precipitated it and its crew across the border and into enemy hands.

As if this was not bad enough, the constant threat of interception by a German patrol materialized one morning; Hurst was one of the very few to retain enough energy to escape its clutches by wading through a stream and thereby also throwing the search dogs off his scent. The surviving trio of evaders from out of the original party of thirteen, along with two of the guides, then crossed into Spain, where the Spaniards seemingly deserted their charges for several days before returning to bring them an exotic food mix (bananas, a leg of lamb, and wine) before finally delivering them to a "safe" house. It should be remembered that "neutral" Spain owed much to its current Fascist regime being in place thanks to the Axis powers' support between 1936 and 1939, so there was no absolute guarantee of safe conduct to an Allied embassy for Allied aviators even at this point. However, all went well and the British Consulate in Barcelona was reached, from where the final journey to Gibraltar via Madrid was completed; soon after, in early January Hurst was back in Britain.

S/Sgt. M Council's (BT) lower legs are all that can be seen as fellow crew members and several Swiss citizens attend to the severely wounded airman. He had suffered head injuries inside his flak-devastated turret, and in fact did lose one eye, although the prompt medical attention saved his life. His companion, T/Sgt R Shepherd (ROG), who had expressed a premonition he would not survive the day, was the sole fatality following the destruction of his compartment.

"Home Runs" (2) – Return Passage by Sea

The foregoing example of evasion routes was not always to prove the norm. By the winter of 1943/44 the Germans, under the energetic and intelligent influence of Gen. Rommel, were beginning to dramatically increase the defensive facilities of the hitherto so-called "Atlantic Wall" stretching down from Denmark to the Franco/ Spanish border. However, these activities were primarily negative, in that they entailed the development of anti-shipping and personnel measures positioned on the beaches as well as heavy gun batteries in support. Regular patrolling of the coast by the *Kriegsmarine*, on the other hand, was not comprehensively maintained, which in turn permitted Royal Navy patrol boats to make trips to and from the French coast in particular. Not only did these warships deliver material to the Resistance, but they were also on hand to pick up escaping personnel...

The penultimate day in 1943 proved to be the "unlucky 13" mission for Lt. R Smith's 95th BG crew, but although all ten airmen survived the loss of their B-17, Smith and six others managed to get clear of capture by the Germans. In the pilot's case this was the start of an exact calendar month's journey to freedom. The already straggling B-17, 42-30674 /**Destiny's Tot**, had finally succumbed to persistent fighter assault near Beauvais, in between Paris and the Channel coast. Smith was fortunate to land right by a farmer, who buried Smith's parachute before pointing the direction for "friends." As it was, the pilot had to hide in a nearby wood from a German search party; having evaded their attentions he decided to proceed into the darkening gloom, but was then intercepted by three armed Frenchmen who had apparently been tracking his movements ever since his arrival. One of them held a sack which contained civilian clothing for the airman, after which the group walked several miles to Wavenieu and the village police station. Following a protracted conversation between the Frenchmen Smith was taken by car to a house where he met up with his co-pilot and ROG, the latter being the sole crewmember able to speak a smattering of French.

During this initial period of concealment Sgt J Eshius (BT) was brought to the house. By mid-January, having been transferred to a second house in St. Just, the four airmen were informed that they were on their way to St. Brieuc, on the northern coastline of the Brest Peninsula; the polite but firm demand that all surrender their ID tags was greeted with quiet dismay, but nevertheless adhered to. The transport laid on was a large limousine, and the driver's requirement for each to use the revolver issued for the journey should the vehicle be held up at any checkpoint must have further sharpened their minds—if captured alive they would surely be immediately stood against a wall and executed!

All went well with the journey to Paris, and while there a full set of ID cards, ration books, and documents purporting to show a profession were granted each man. St. Brieuc lies over 200 miles due west of the capital, but this time the transit stage was achieved in quicker time by train. By now the four individuals were aware that they would be making a sea journey to Britain courtesy of the Royal Navy provided the necessary weather, sea, and moonless conditions permitted the vessel to gain access to the rendezvous point and sneak away on achieving the pick-up. The final move to the intended embarkation point was a few miles further on, but it was several days spent in a cramped room with the blinds drawn before the Resistance was informed of an impending run from Plymouth's naval base.

On the night in question a total of 25 evaders were guided from their various hide-outs down onto the selected beach and into a cave with the admonition that if the pick-up did not succeed they would be faced with a much more protracted and fraught journey down to the Spanish border. This option never arose, but a potential stumbling black occurred when the first rowing boat loomed up with supplies but not the required money sums to be handed over for each evader—in effect "No money, no embarkation!" However, the situation was happily corrected when the second boat made the financial delivery, but it was a nerve-wracking period before all 25 were all embarked on the warship. The resultant trip back to Plymouth was very uncomfortable for those prone to seasickness, but the malady was a small price to pay for one's freedom. (Two of the remaining crew evaders followed the same route a month later, but the seventh, Sgt. Morrison (Eng.), was forced to remain in his separate concealment at St. Just until late summer and the Allied Armies' arrival in the region due to his "host" having no contact with the Resistance.)

Break-out

Once in enemy hands the chances of regaining one's freedom was largely minimal, but there were exceptions to this rule; in particular, the hospitalization of injured personnel provided a more casual set of surroundings to plan an escape compared to a prison compound. Sgt. C Nekvasil (ROG) had been one of the survivors from the loss of the 100th BG's veteran B-17F **Royal Flush**, which came down near Villacoublay airfield, Paris, on 11 August. He and Lt. C Barber (CP) met up in the same ambulance that transported them to a *Luftwaffe* hospital in a northern suburb of Paris. Not long after arrival both were informed that a move to Germany was imminent within 24 hours. With the assistance of a French-speaking RAF officer Nekvasil managed to get the facts out to the local Resistance body. As a consequence, an attack was launched the next evening; immediately upon its initiation, one among the large group of POWs in the ward slit their single guard's throat, whereupon all made a rush out onto the second floor landing. Unfortunately, several soldiers were on hand and fired upon the would-be escapers, killing a number. However, the situation was saved for those not electing to seek alternative means of escape; one anonymous individual sought out and gained access to a sub-machine gun with which he charged and killed or dispersed the Germans. The personnel then cleared out of the building and headed south for several miles, no doubt guided by the French to a new concealment, a hospital that later turned out to be a stronghold of the Resistance.

When the city rose up against the Germans on the 26th the escapers were asked to assist in rooting out hostile elements. However, on the 31st the consensus of opinion turned towards making a westward run for the approaching Allied armies, and within a few miles of doing so all were in on the initial stage of a return to England that was carried out by air on

4 September. (The commando-like action of the airman in slitting the guard's throat begs the question as to whether this was within the Geneva Convention's rules on legal conduct; Hitler had decreed that any member of an Allied Commando or Ranger force was liable to immediate execution on capture, so this might have been the fate of any re-captured POWs in this case had the manner of the guard's death been established and regardless of who had actually perpetrated the deed.)

"Staying Put"

The British as a national body are arguably still not truly European in attitude, but rather can be viewed as inhabitants of an island mass anchored off that continent. It followed from this especially during WWII that a British serviceman attempting to evade capture would be hard put to conceal his non-European social credentials if left to his own devices. In the case of the Americans a similar disability tended to display itself despite the fact that many of their forebearers had emigrated from Europe. One of the associated basic problems affecting both nations' personnel was that their linguistic roots stemmed from the English language, a fact that conversely left many with little or no knowledge of other languages and their specific mannerisms. In other words, many of them "stood out like a sore thumb" as regards this aspect of human conduct.

Sgt. P. Reynolds (WG) had bailed out of Lt. C Duncan's 42-30050/ **Judy D** after it was dispatched by fighters while coming back from Le Bourget on 10 July 1943. He had been shot in one foot and had sustained injuries to parts of his body. After several months in captivity he managed to gain local support; where he was held and how he escaped has never been divulged, although he could have still been hospitalized from his injuries, with what was possibly a civilian facility proving an easier source for escape compared to a POW camp. A young woman discovered him lying in a field near Fountain-le-Dun the day after he had regained his freedom. An overnight stay in a barn and a change of clothing was followed by a move to the aforementioned village and a house owned by a Monsieur and Madam Violet, the latter of whom spoke English.

However, he was unknowingly destined to continue remaining in "captivity"—albeit in a positive sense—for nearly one year in Fontaine-le-Dun and the adjoining village of Lonqueville, to where he was again transferred on 14 October. With all the ebullience demonstrated by a young American he had eagerly anticipated his early return to Britain. When no further action on this issue occurred for a further month a natural growing frustration at being physically confined over this prolonged period while surrounded by people with whom he could not communicate culminated in a violent mood swing that almost compelled him to clear out and surrender rather than continue in physical and verbal isolation! Fortunately he first decided to head back to the Violet household, where the wife responded by saying "You are going to stay – we are expecting the Allies at any moment." Although premature by eleven months in its final application, the assertion calmed him down.

Over this prolonged period Reynolds was confined to the first floor of a combined food and liquor store located in the town square. The physically restricted nature of this existence often left him feeling angry and depressed. Also he had to be careful not to create any disturbance, since the ground floor had been requisitioned by the *Wehrmacht* for sleeping quarters. Matters nearly took a turn for the worse when a demand was initiated for the upstairs floor to be similarly requisitioned, but this was thankfully soon cancelled. Some evenings were passed playing cards with the owners, with the wife's ability to speak English surely bringing a degree of relaxation for the otherwise mentally cramped American airman.

In September 1944 British Army units were sweeping up along the Channel coast towards the port of Dieppe, which lay a short distance northeast from Fountain-le-Dun. The arrival of a tank unit in the village was the occasion for the Violets to introduce their long-term "guest" not only to the soldiers, but also to the now astonished villagers; the latter—other than a daughter-in-law, the Violet's maid, and the pharmacist, who had twice been summoned when the airmen suffered

Two pictures of the funeral of T/Sgt Shepherd, Lt. Proctor's ROG (96th BG). The first shows the minister walking ahead of the burial party as they bear the coffin to the grave. The second reveals the Swiss Guard of Honor with the burial party on either side of the flag-draped coffin.

conditions requiring attention—naturally had no knowledge of his presence, so tight had the five people concerned retained the fact to themselves!

Striking Back – at a Cost (Fighting with the Resistance)

An element among the hundreds of American evaders decided to adopt a more active stance in challenging the Nazis. This took the form of remaining with the Resistance and participating in sabotage operations. Doubtless the airmen concerned felt that their involvement, however marginal, was keeping faith with the overall bid of the Allies to batter down the Third Reich's monstrous hold on Europe as quickly and comprehensively as possible. The unsavoury but perfectly legal corollary to indulging in such operations was that the Rules of the Geneva Convention no longer applied. If ever captured the person or persons could expect extremely harsh "handling" from the interrogators of the *Gestapo* or the equally odious *Sicherheitsdienst* (SD), with torture and/or execution the inevitable conclusion.

Sgt. M Ruta's crew, headed by Lt. E Sechrist, failed to return to Framlingham on 8 June 1944. The Sgt. landed in a field but then managed to evade the attentions of a German party scouring the area. For the ensuing four days he stayed in his concealment, although becoming ever weaker in body and spirit to the extent that he considered turning himself in. It was then that he moved out of his wooded hiding place to make himself known to a group of woodcutters, who turned out to be involved with the Resistance; however, they naturally were suspicious of the genuine nature of the lone "airman." Fortunately, the arrival of another man who satisfactorily interrogated Ruta cleared up the issue. His several injuries were attended to and he received the first and very sumptuous cooked meal since departing Framlingham.

It was now that Ruta, instead of being fed along the Resistance lines of communications, elected to assist the local body whenever the RAF had arranged a supply drop of arms. At the selected drop-site the canisters were gathered together and transferred to a central storage point. This basically "passive" activity was supplemented by more "active" sorties intended to, in the Sgt's words, "foul up the enemy's communications," which surely involved setting off explosive charges on railway, road, or canal facilities. (Ruta's fate, had he been captured, would have been clear, since what he had participated in was classified as "sabotage" in the enemy's eyes and worthy of summary action as previously outlined in this account.)

Protracted "Home-Run"

It was the second day of *Big Week*, and on board 42-30280/MI: L, a PFF aircraft from the 482nd BG, was Capt. G Binks acting as Mission Commander; also present was Lt. J Punches (N), a member of Lt. R Taylor's crew but detached on this occasion while flying his 23rd mission. On the way home the B-17 was in deep trouble with two engines "out" and steadily losing altitude. By the time Dutch territory was below it was clear the end was in sight, at which point a bail out order was issued.

This picture of a close-knit 100th BG formation was taken after VE-Day. Confirmation of this lays in the huge squadron code letters under the wings; these were applied in order to dissuade pilots from indulging in low-flying since the details could be reported to the authorities by eyewitnesses.

Lt. Punches landed safely, and after burying his parachute began walking westward with his electric suit exposed for all to see; this was perhaps why a Dutch cyclist he encountered took him in hand and led him to a house that became his initial refuge for upwards of a week. Fitted out with civilian clothes and suitable ID papers, he then began a protracted journey for Spain extending over the ensuing six months but destined never to be completed. The procedure adopted for travel by train was for Punches to sit several seats behind his "escort" and follow them off the train and into the chosen house, something that occurred several times within Holland. His sojourn in Holland ended abruptly at the Belgian border one night when he was firmly informed that he "was now on his own."

Nothing daunted, the airman walked on and hid up in a haystack for several days. His presence was seemingly noted by the farmer concerned, who took charge of him and took him to a property in Liege, where he remained for a further two months.

A potential trap awaited Punches when he was being moved again. The new hideout was reached by a sentry-guarded bridge, whose current guardian was noted by the Lieutenant to interrogate passing individuals at random intervals, with upwards of 20 people in between these actions. Next time a civilian was so "collared" Punches ensured that he was within the first handful of people to be directly behind the one so picked out! Having escaped this net he reached the chosen house, where he remained for a further two months, at which point the town was liberated by the U.S. Army.

Betrayed

On 12 August 1943 the 95th BG lost two crews during the mission to attack targets in the Ruehr. One was piloted by Capt C Hamilton with Maj. C Cole (CP), who was destined to evade capture and regain friendly shores in two months. **We Ain't Scared** (42-30194/OE: O) had eased out of formation during target approach and dropped to minimum altitude for the run home; fighters soon finished off the B-17 over Holland and it crashed near Kattenbos, in Belgium, along with five crewmembers. Lt. L Lawson (N) had managed to bail out, but drifted down into Dutch territory close to the Belgium border. By that evening he had been brought to a nearby doctor's house, where his wounds were treated and civilian clothing provided. However, he was also subject to a polite but firm "grilling" carried out to establish his identity; having learned German at high school, he had responded as best he could to the doctor's conversation in that language, but by doing so had cast grave doubts upon his "friendly" status, hence the "grilling!"

He was then temporarily incarcerated in a civilian police station by the policeman in charge before the first stage in going "down the line" towards Spain was commenced. During the ensuing sixteen days Lawson moved by bicycle to Bree, where he and other evaders were introduced to "the Chief," an English-speaking Belgian who transported them to Brussels, where they received forged documents. Then, a week later it was on to Paris by train and arrival at a small hotel where the journey came to an abruptly shocking end. Lawson had barely settled into his surroundings when the room door burst open to reveal several Security Police, one of whom addressed him by his name after uttering the usual German phrase "Fuer Sie ist der Krieg fertig" (For you the War is over).

He was arbitrarily removed to the city's notorious Fresnes Prison, where he came into contact with two other airmen. If he had harboured any suspicions regarding possible betrayal, these were reinforced when his fellow-internees said they had passed through the same house, at which "the chief" had been encountered. The Germans had thousands of collaborators on hand, apart from which large rewards were offered in collecting information on the Resistance Movement, a measure that led all too many citizens in the Nazi-occupied countries to succumb to the financial temptation. The usual threat of handing him over to the *Gestapo* should he not divulge the required information on Resistance people did not shake his resolve, although he did make mention of "the Chief," whose name, as with all others within the Movement, was unknown to him. A week or so later Lawson departed Fresnes on his way to Dulag Luft and then the comparative luxury of a POW camp.

Another long-term combat survivor was **Rum Dum**, which arrived at Great Ashfield on 1 December 1943. This picture shows at least 41 mission "bombs," with others obscured by the No. 3 propeller blade, and eleven swastika "kill" marks. Having survived the worst the enemy could throw in its direction, it was salvaged following a crash landing on 30 May 1945.

17

Low Road to a Stalag

The postwar public's perception of the average POW experience during WWII has owed much to both written and visual presentation. In the latter instance, there have been several major films such as "The Wooden Horse," produced in 1951. This dealt with the successful bid for freedom by three British officers from Stalag Luft 3, Sagan. The title reference is to a vaulting horse made from Red Cross boards, placed in the same position within the

Stalag Luft 3, as seen from a position every *Kriegie* longed for—from the outside. Two *Luftwaffe* personnel, the right-hand one being a gun-bearing Corporal, are walking by one of the towers. The Germans were referred to as "Goons" with the stilt-supported structures known as "Goon towers" by the POWs.

A somewhat over-exposed view of part of Stalag Luft I at Barth still provides details of the accommodation buildings.The wooden structures are raised up on supports in order to minimize attempts to conceal either the existence of escape tunnels or the soil excavated from the tunnelling effort.

compound and under which tunnelling was conducted; the breakout was achieved after several months of toil and all three airmen (or rather two airmen and a British Army officer) were re-united in Sweden within a matter of weeks.

By contrast, "The Great Escape" (1963), although a thoroughly absorbing and fast-paced production, mingled fact with a degree of fiction; for example, none of the three successful exceptions out of the 76 escapees making the break were either American or even British, while the Steve McQueen character in particular would have been top of the final list of 50 re-captured personnel regarded as having caused maximum disruption to their captors in the past and now selected for *Stufe drei* treatment, a *Gestapo* euphemism for execution.

Within these parameters could be placed the 1953 Hollywood film "Stalag 17," but even here there was a degree of license. In most cases the permanent retention of fur-lined flying suits and boots by their owners as depicted in the film would not have lasted more than a few hours before these were expropriated for the use of German servicemen, particularly on the Eastern Front. On the other hand, the mud-strewn camp surroundings and minimal quality of the officially-provided daily "soup" were aspects of "*Kriegie*" existence that the survivors could surely relate to.

"Playing Away" for Keeps

The prospect of ending up alive in enemy hands was arguably an option that did not exercise an American airman's mind so much as whether or not he would complete his combat tour—death or survival were the twin options that concentrated his mind. Crewmembers

Souvenirs in the possession of three 95th BG airmen include a helmet and *Luftwaffe* NCO's peak cap. The *Kriegies* from Barrack 34-B in Stalag XVIIB Krems are (L-R) Tom Kelly, Jake Black, and Al Bergeron. Picture reportedly taken on 26 April 1945 during the forced march across Austria following the camp's evacuation.

were briefed on what was expected of them should they be captured, with "name, rank, and serial number" the only response demanded of them should they be interrogated. This was all very well in theory but, just as with "ditching" or bailing out, there was little or no way of practicing against the eventuality, and therefore no guarantee of how one would react when placed in such a starkly daunting situation. For a start, the individual concerned, who in many cases was barely out of his teens, had managed to escape with his life in often shocking, nerve-shattering circumstances. In turn, this meant that should he swiftly land up in captivity he could easily become prey to any blandishment or threat directed his way. In effect, his "security blanket" had been withdrawn psychologically as well as physically, and he was on his own to face whatever the autocratic Nazi system might launch in his direction.

The first and potentially lethal barrier to be scaled when captured depended on whether the airman was confronted by the military or civilian elements of the population. Although rough handling was sometimes dealt out by the *Wehrmacht* or *Luftwaffe* personnel concerned, in general the captive was then treated according to the Geneva Convention. With civilians, whose ire was by 1943 raised to an almost hysterical level thanks in turn to Josef Goebbels' inflammatory outbursts regarding the terror bombing of the nation's cities, there was no guarantee that within minutes their prisoner would not be subject to summary execution; sometimes the unfortunate airmen was hung, or alternately was beaten to death or even thrown into a burning building after having his hands bound behind his back.

The second barrier to be surmounted usually arose following transport to the main *Luftwaffe* Interrogation Center, Dulag Luft, outside Frankfurt. Here the challenge was purely psychological, but was arguably none too easy to counter by applying the "name, rank, and serial number" limitation drilled into the mind during training. The cells were small with a single window located high up, and the POW could be left to his own devices for as long or as short a period as the authorities deemed necessary before his spirit was sufficiently eroded and he was therefore regarded as ready for interrogation. Turning up and lowering the heating and denial of the use of the toilet, especially when in desperate need, were just two of the measures of mental torture employed. The meagre food and drink provided was also a stark contrast to what the individual had been used to in terms of quantity (if not quality) mere hours or days previous.

A mere week or so prior to the vivid pyrotechnic display at Snetterton Heath such a sight would have greeted Allied airmen over nocturnal enemy skies; then, the myriad of arcing lights would have come from searchlights and lethal flak shells. Instead, the 96th BG airmen are now enjoying a fireworks show to celebrate the end of the conflict.

A B-17G from the 388th BG is taxiing past two companion aircraft from the group. Picture was taken at Linz, Austria, in May 1945, where the group was involved in evacuating recently released French POWs for repatriation back home.

When finally brought out for interrogation, a severe jolt to one's confidence could be delivered when the interrogator produced a detailed file on the captive's unit and began to read out excerpts that left his subject wondering how lax American security must be for the Germans to attain this level of information. (The availability of much printed and even film material gained via neutral sources was a prime source for interrogators on both the Allied and Axis sides.) On occasions, mention of the individual's uncertain military status with an attendant threat that if this was not confirmed he could be handed over to the *Gestapo* was another opening gambit. This move usually applied where evaders had been taken and were in civilian clothing and/or were not in possession of their ID tags; however, the same tactic of a transfer threat in the event of non-cooperation was also regularly applied to personnel coming directly into enemy hands.

The "KLB Club" Set

There was never any guarantee of proper treatment under the Geneva Convention being applied when downed in enemy territory. Once an airman gained access to the Resistance Movement he might still expect to be granted all POW rights in the event of either being picked up by the German military while in transit or even in the event of being betrayed. The problem in such circumstances depended on whether or not he was still in possession of his identification disc; even then, much further depended on whether the soldiers were *Luftwaffe*, —or the infamous SS. Members of the latter force were regularly inclined to make no differentiation between evaders and their civilian helpers, and a number of instances occurred where summary execution was ordained for all concerned.

In the case of 181 Allied airmen, they would be faced with enduring some of the horrors of the *Konzentrationslager* (concentration camp) at Buchenwald. The ever-latent threat of an individual within a Resistance cell turning traitor materialized in the case of the Organization's Paris zone during mid-1944. The large group of airmen that included T/Sgt. Frank Cowan (96th BG), having been "unearthed" thanks to such an event, then found themselves retained in SS or *Gestapo* hands as opposed to achieving the normal course of transit to a POW camp via Dulag Luft. One of their number who protested about the peremptory manner of his handling had his ID disc yanked off his neck, after which the Nazi official yelled "Now, who are you?" by way of confirming that he held no military status and could be disposed of as seen fit—in modern terms, a "non-person!"

Cowan had survived the downing of 42-102552/MZ: S by flak on 22 June when only three in all of Lt. J Horne's crew remained alive after the B-17 slammed into the ground outside Paris. This was ordeal enough for him, but a far greater and prolonged physical and mental test lay ahead. His initial good fortune in being granted protection by the local population turned to bitterness following betrayal to the Germans by what he (rightly) believed to be a Nazi or even a French "stool-pigeon" plant.

The notorious Fresnes Prison in Paris, where the airmen were incarcerated among thousands of political prisoners, became their temporary home until August. Then the imminent liberation of the French capital witnessed their transport eastward crammed into unsanitary rail trucks as far as Buchenwald, where they were unloaded on 19 August. Here they were issued with the standard striped suits for inmates after losing all their clothing, which included their footwear; the single extra issue-item, which would almost certainly sound an individual's death knell should it be lost, was a bowl into which their daily meagre food ration would literally be slopped.

There, although not subjected to work details, the airmen might have languished until slow starvation or execution came their way. Their physical state of comfort was further diminished by being forced to live in the open for a proportion of the period of incarceration. However, their presence in the camp fortuitously came to the attention of a *Luftwaffe* officer, and his enquiries on their behalf ultimately brought about their transfer to Stalag Luft 3, minus just one among their number who had tragically not lasted the draconian course of SS "treatment." (Later evaluation of the SS' attitude towards the airmen indicated that an order for their extermination was on the verge of being issued as the *Luftwaffe* intervention was completed.) After WWII the group created an association with the title "KLB Club," the initials standing for **K**onzentrations**l**ager **B**uchenwald.

An Existence of Sorts?

On arrival at his assigned POW camp the newcomer was usually filled with a mixture of uncertainty and bewilderment. The latter reaction would arise when catching one's first sight of the camp occupants, especially in relation to their "clothing." The bulk of flying clothing had remained in *Luftwaffe* hands, and each individual was dependent upon what he had otherwise dressed himself in; this ranged from full uniform (even dress uniform in some instances where the unlucky holder had anticipated attending some social event on return from the mission and a swift debriefing!) to the basics of trousers, shirt, and maybe pullover. Shoes were generally not worn inside the clumsy U.S. flying boots, but tied onto the parachute harness. However, these vital items sometimes became detached after bailing out. Where a camp such as Barth (Stalag Luft I) or Sagan (Stalag Luft 3) was Anglo-American in nature, the clothing and shoe variation sported by many of the RAF *Kriegies* who had been incarcerated prior to Pearl Harbor was part military and part civilian in its composition.

Any lingering notions of following an individual lifestyle vanished almost as soon as one was assigned a bed in a hut. The hut contents were not only sparse but

The three B-17Gs in the background are (L-R) from the 486th, 94th, and 447th BGs. All are involved in the postwar repatriation of foreign military and civilian personnel—mainly French—from Horching airfield at Linz, Austria.

Another picture taken at Horching depicts seven Sudbury B-17Gs. Many of the civilians due for return to France had been forced laborers, commandeered under the Nazi regime. Group insignia on the nearside bomber is reversed in its square and letter colors, the serial is more unevenly applied, and the aircraft letter is outlined.

relatively cramped, while the beds were arranged in two or even more vertically aligned frames, leaving the lower or middle placed airmen the meat in a human "sandwich." Bedding was often basic in the form of straw-filled covers and bed-boards tended to disappear at an alarming rate since they were needed for shoring-up an escape tunnel!

Food supplies delivered from German sources was often at a bare premium, and it was only the reasonably regular arrival of Red Cross or similar charity organization parcels such as those supplied by the Salvation Army or the YMCA (whose part in this vital activity has sadly been cast into the background of History) that assisted in staving off the onset of critical physical debility. The POWs may have become leaner, but certainly did not attain a parallel and upward state of fitness, given these stark conditions.

The next step was to settle down to the basically drab and open-ended existence of camp life. Boredom was a common state of mind borne by any *Kriegie*. Roll-Call at least twice; walking the circuit either for exercise or just to pass the time away; and window shutters put in place and lights out by a specific time were daily features. The more studious, using available material from the camp Library, either read or began studying a chosen subject that regularly led to the commencement of a postwar career. Also available in most camps was sports equipment as well as musical instruments that were of prime benefit when laying on concerts; the Theatre facility was also the venue for plays. One of the legacies arising from the provision of bound notebooks was the truly wonderful range of superbly detailed pencil drawings created by some POWs within these journals, many of which survived the conflict.

Intermingled with boredom was the mounting frustration of having to share the hut with the same few companions, regardless of whether or not all saw eye to eye on matters, important or trivial. It is arguable that tempers became frayed to breaking point over issues falling into the latter category as much as if not more than the former. However, what might be construed as trivial in normal circumstances often assumed a degree of importance, given the much more constrained atmosphere existing in the world of *Kriegydom*. The bald truth was that almost all social initiative had been removed at a stroke. What to do and where and when to indulge one's wishes were limited to within the camp perimeter as well as being further constrained by the staff's application of *Luftwaffe* rules and regulations.

The need to hear from one's family at regular intervals was of paramount importance to the average *Kriegie*. Letters and packages did get through until the final months of incarceration. However, the contents of letters in particular were often heart-breaking if not ironically pitched in some cases. "Dear John" letters from wives and girlfriends who had finally succumbed to the temptations of enforced isolation from their men-folk were common.

Then there was the correspondence that fell into the savagely ironic category. One airman was (hopefully) bought off from the fact of his wife's infidelity in producing a baby by another man with the news that she had bought him a motor bicycle! (In the film *Stalag 17* a POW receives a letter from his wife who says among other news items "Now, you won't believe it, but I found a baby on our doorstep." At subsequent intervals in the film he is seen scanning the letter and muttering "I believe it." This scenario was probably an exaggeration intended to inject more drama into the film script; on the other hand, it contained elements of the real-life reactions of POWs facing a similar situation.) A more regular but very wounding scenario would be where a POW had received clothing supplied by individuals responding to a Red Cross initiative, and the provider then found out his status. He would then receive a letter indicating disappointment or even disdain that the gift had not gone to the fighting man it had been intended for, the inference being that the *Kriegie* in question had wilfully deserted his Nation's Cause—as if getting shot down could possibly be construed as a premeditated act!

There was a pervading current of apprehension felt by the majority of POWs right up to the conflict's conclusion. There had been more than enough eyewitnesses to the summary treatment handed out, especially by the civilian population, to more unfortunate airmen. The nature of the Nazi regime also left little doubt that the POWs could easily be treated as pawns should the conflict begin to turn permanently in the Allies' favour and the Nazi leaders

Disaster still stalked the ranks of the 8th AF even after VE-Day. On 11 May 1945 Lt. Pratt took off on a training flight. The worsening weather on return to Thorpe Abbotts caused the bomber to crash and overturn near Diss, killing one of the six airmen on board.

seek a more palatable variation to the "Unconditional Surrender" terms demanded at Casablanca in January 1943. Even more unsettling was the parallel prospect of the SS taking over administration of the camps from the much more tolerant if firm *Luftwaffe* administration, with all that this implied in terms of handling, or rather mishandling, outside the requirements of the Geneva Convention.

"Wire Happy" Degeneration

The open-ended nature of captivity was a basic fact of life that most POWs bore with a varying degree of equanimity throughout their period of incarceration. There were a number of exceptions who either suddenly or gradually found it impossible to maintain this necessary attitude of mind in order not to break down. Marital problems were a key matter that could easily lead to a breakdown, especially since there was no way in which the airman concerned could respond in a physical manner. Bad news from home was another catalyst for this primarily psychological degeneration to be set on its course. A third factor was the mere fact of confinement, with the urge to walk, talk, and generally act in an unrestricted manner now a total pipe-dream for the unforeseeable future.

The first signs of this pernicious condition were not discernable, since they often took the normal course of growing irritation extending to obtuse reaction to the words and actions of one's companions. Then a pattern of introverted and eccentric conduct accompanied by prolonged periods of silence was likely to evolve. This was the danger point for the affected airman because there was no guarantee of how he might react, especially in relation to his captors. This was when the expressions "wire-happy" or "going round the bend" were employed by his more balance-minded follow prisoners.

Tragically, on more than one occasion, the trip-wire placed several yards within the outer camp perimeter that denoted the point beyond which the guards had the right to fire if their challenge was not responded to was crossed by the airman who was finally broken in spirit; the inevitable result was at least wounding, although most cases ended fatally. In more fortunate instances medical or psychological treatment was granted, usually at the request or insistence of the Red Cross, with repatriation the very rare result. (On the other hand, several individuals made a deliberate effort to assume the characteristics of "wire happiness," including one notorious incident where the subject, a RAF officer, played the role so well and for so long that he actually became permanently depressed following his repatriation.)

The Final Months

The experiences of the Allied *Kriegies* from July 1944 onwards varied noticeably, with the Enlisted Men's treatment arguably even worse than that borne by their officer contemporaries. This was particularly the case for the personnel incarcerated in Stalag Luft VI—Heydekrug, in Lithuania. Their ordeal began in the midst of a July heatwave when the camp was evacuated in the face of the Soviet advance. A coal boat *Intersburg* was the chosen method of shipment from the port of Memel to Swinemuende further west. For up to three days the airmen remained crammed and battened down into the ship's holds with little or no provision for food or water and suffering the constant terminal threat of the vessel being torpedoed. Their arrival at the latter port and transfer in box cars was only a signal for further brutal treatment handed out to the USAAF contingent. Men were shackled in pairs and forced to run up to what was Stalag Luft IV; all the time they were harassed by dogs and bayonet-wielding Naval cadets while the road was flanked by machine gun nests. It was a miracle that no fatalities were incurred among the extremely concerned POWs, although many suffered bayonet wounds and other injuries. Their immediate concerns were over, but in early 1945 a second and much more protracted ordeal would be faced by the personnel.

Stalag Luft 3

The harsh experience of the airmen now at Stalag IV was about to be visited upon their officer contemporaries located at Stalag Luft 3 (Sagan) in late January 1945. Once again it was the impending arrival of the Soviet Army that impelled the *Luftwaffe* authorities to order an evacuation of the camp—within a matter of hours and in the face of deep snowdrifts

This Vega-production B-17G was originally assigned to the 482nd BG, but then progressed via a 1st AD group to the 96th BG on 28 May 1945; although hostilities were by now over, the 45th CBW red bands were still applied. This aircraft ended its days being salvaged in Germany.

A line-up of B-17Gs at Marrakesh, in Morocco, features aircraft from the 95th, 390th, and 493rd BGs, although the majority appear to be from Thorpe Abbotts. The two nearest aircraft have the ball turrets detached. The third in line is recorded as being transferred to the 100th BG on 20 May 1945 despite still bearing its original unit markings. Aircraft lined up on the left are B-24s, and all are ready to depart for home.

and accompanying high winds! So began an ordeal for the already undernourished *Kriegies* that lasted several days as they trekked westwards, with dysentery and frostbite among the least of their concerns. Just how many failed to survive the trek has never been determined, but the majority thankfully got through this initial ordeal, having slogged their way for nearly 50 miles inside two days. Then, having arrived at Spremburg, shelter and hot food was provided, after which the Germans decided to transport the airmen by train down to Moosberg, north of Münich; there they would reside for upwards of three months before being liberated by Gen. Patton's troops.

Stalag Luft IV

However harsh the treatment of the Sagan POWs might have appeared, it was measured in days, and was arguably a minor variation of similar treatment handed out to the other ranks incarcerated in Stalag Luft IV (Gross Tyschow). Many of these airmen had already suffered the tribulations of the ship-borne transfer from Stalag Luft VI (Heydekrug in Lithuania) the previous July. Now they were forced to embark upon a trek that extended over nearly three months and entailed an epic march of several hundreds of miles across central Germany in the middle of harsh winter conditions.

The initial movement of the columns was westwards, which was natural, given the Germans' understandable desire to get clear away from the rapidly advancing Soviet forces. The POWs, who were already bearing physically weakened frames, could not have conceived the extent of the ordeal that awaited them. Day after endless day they slogged on through the short winter days and rested up in whatever form of rudimentary accommodation was at hand. The vital need to have regular supplies of food brought to them was more honoured in the breach than fulfilled. Worse still was the fact that the columns sometimes became intermingled with mobile *Wehrmacht* elements.

This was a recipe for disaster in the face of the ever-present threat posed by Allied fighters and fighter-bomber pilots, to whom a column presented a tempting target. The few seconds that it took to identity and swoop upon what purported to be an enemy column left little or no margin for error. Sure enough, this tragic scenario resulted in groups of POWs suffering and in at least one instance succumbing to the effects of "friendly fire" as the bombs and streams of bullets lanced into the helpless ranks.

Sgt. Pifer (95th BG) had already come through the risk of being killed by Allied bombs twice within a short time of becoming a POW. Now, during the latter stages of the forced march, the column received a very welcome "gift" in the form of a few Red Cross parcels. His small group of airmen had just sat down to open their allotted parcel in a light mood "akin to children at a Xmas Party," as he described it. Just then a single Allied fighter swooped down upon the churchyard location to deliver a hail of bullets along with rockets, the pilot undoubtedly assuming the column was German in complexion. In his wake he unknowingly left seven dead

The 490th BG and what seems like a dangerously dispersed fellow-93rd CBW group in the upper left background are probably clearing the target, while two squadrons from yet another group crossing over at right angles appear to be going in trail for the bomb run. The grim visual beauty of such a scenario that was a regular feature of 8th AF operations would never be repeated after 1945, with mass bomber formations relegated to the pages of history.

contemporaries along with a number of wounded. (On another occasion, a night "intruder"—almost certainly a Mosquito—inflicted similar lethal punishment upon several airmen from among an RAF contingent resting in a barn.)

It was 2 May before the column, having marched over 800 miles to and fro in an aimless fashion across north-central Germany, finally made contact with a British unit from the 2nd Army. The process of de-lousing and transport by C-47 to Camp "Lucky Strike," near Le Havre, France, were necessary steps on the preparation for return home. (Pifer noted that his body weight was just below half the 165 lbs he possessed on 3 March 1944 when he was captured.)

Stalag XVIIB

The 8th AF occupants of the other major camp (Stalag XVIIB Krems, up on the Danube river in Austria) were destined to share a similar, although not so protracted, experience with their Enlisted brethren from Stalag Luft IV. The order to evacuate the camp was issued and executed on 7/8 April in the middle of a blizzard that taxed the men's already weakened frames. On each of the succeeding twenty days, with the weather still reflecting a discouraging late winter pattern of snow and ice, the airmen trudged an average of twenty kilometres according to Sgt. W Thomas, also 95th BG, who had been captured off the infamous Muenster mission of 10 October 1943. The rumble of Russian artillery could be heard and acted as a spur to their guards. Two recollections stuck in many minds. The first was the hostility displayed by the citizens of Linz; the second, in the vicinity of Mauthausen concentration camp, was the shocking sight of SS personnel clubbing and shooting exhausted members falling out from a column of political POWs with their distinctive pajama-striped clothing. Finally, at the end of April the arrival of a number of food-bearing lorries driven by British soldiers came none too soon, since slow starvation was facing the *Kriegies* after having little or nothing to eat for several days past. (Another diarist from the 388th BG kept a daily journal that referred to first running into U.S. Army units only on 2 May, which suggests the POWs were progressing in separate segments.)

Stalag Luft 1

By far the least physical torment placed upon USAAF inhabitants of the four major *Luftwaffe* camps—in terms of marching around the Third Reich—was experienced at Stalag Luft I, Barth, outside Rostock on the Baltic coast. The onrush of the Soviet Armies that cut off all routes to the west reportedly led to the cancelling of plans for a march. The arrival of their Russian liberators during April did not lead to a speedy transfer back into Anglo/American hands, however. The need to storm the nearby island of Ruegen, which was reported to be strongly defended, led to several requests for assistance; one addressed to Col. "Hub" Zemke (56FG, and acting as Camp CO) suggested the POWs join in the assault as support infantry! It was early May before the nearby airfield was sufficiently tidied up for numbers of B-17s and Lancasters to fly in and begin to repatriate their respective elements of airmen from among the 9,000 on hand. (In the interim period between the Russians' arrival and final evacuation foraging parties had been organized to go out into the surrounding towns and villages and garner sufficient food for the POWs to at least exist upon; other groups had been assigned to guard the camp.)

Bit O' Lace's fine artwork is topped by a reference to the Petty/Varga artist Milton Caniff, the original creator of the female in question. Eighty-three bomb symbols attest to the veteran B-17G's combat career. She now stands with engines detached in the aerial "boneyard" at Kingman, Arizona, ready for the ultimate insult of being broken up and melted down.

18

A Gradual Exodus

The involvement of the 3rd AD in operation *Manna/Chowhound* was just part of a wholesale use of the B-17s prior to and immediately after VE-Day. Arrangements for the repatriation of both Allied POWs and European nationals utilized by the Nazis for forced labour involved both B-17 Divisions from locations as far divorced from one another as Barth and Linz in Austria. Another more relaxed use of the bombers was to fly ground crews around central Europe to see for themselves the part they had played in bringing ruin to the Third Reich, the flights being christened "Trolley runs."

The wholesale re-deployment of the 8th AF to the States (with the current likelihood that much of its strength would then head west to the Pacific for the climactic assault upon the Japanese mainland) commenced during the third week in May. Nine bomber groups were to remain behind, either to serve as part of the U.S. Occupation Forces on the continent or to be used as transports for the initial repatriation of U.S. troops primarily stationed in the Mediterranean Theater of Operations (MTO).

The three retained Division groups were the 94th, 96th, and 100th BGs, with the former two among the original cadre of units forming the then 4th BW back in 1943. The Rougham-based group's assignment to Germany was never fulfilled with final cancellation announced in September. Duties during this interim period were centered on a leaflet dropping operation across Germany and Western Europe (Project *Nickle*). The 96th BG was to have been assigned to Giebelsdadt, near Wuerzburg, but as with the 94th BG the move never took place, being finally cancelled during September. In the meantime, most of its B-17s were transferred out, while most of the long-term personnel were replaced and dispatched home. Flight duties varied from "Trolley runs" during May and participation in the MTO repatriation operation. Unlike the other two "retained" groups, the 100th BG did effect a form of re-deploy to Germany—in this case Holzkirchen, near Munich—but only in terms of the bulk of its aircraft, whose number was added to the several hundreds already concentrated there, and whose future use was unclear. By late June, the only B-17s on hand at Thorpe Abbotts were PFF-equipped machines. A steady winding down of personnel numbers was made during the summer and autumn.

A Proud Legacy

During November/December 1945 the final dispersal of personnel from all three airfields was completed. The 8th AF's absence in East Anglia literally left a silent void; no more roaring engines and squealing brakes in the early hours of the day; never again the burgeoning thunder of massed formations ascending into the stratosphere or laying an ever-lowering blanket of noise as the bombers returned to their military "roosts"; roads bereft of the heavy USAAF traffic; and public houses restored to their rather dour Anglo-Saxon clientele, and similarly bereft of the noise and chatter bearing all these Trans-Atlantic accents. No more parties to be eagerly anticipated by either USAAF Service women or their British military and civilian companions; no more Xmas parties for the local children.

On the airfields, most of whom were deemed to be temporary wartime structures carved out of the countryside, the steady signs of decay were already showing: weeds sprouting along the runways perimeter track and support roadways and path seams and verges; peeling paintwork; rust on metal frameworks, such as hangars and water tanks; and water staining on building exteriors and interiors. To this was sometimes added casual vandalism as individuals made visits, maybe hoping to come across uncollected items that might prove of use, or just smashing glass in the window frames or even the structures for "fun."

The physical presence of the 8th AF would be largely gone by the seventies, with Nature and the needs of roadway construction (Extracted runway hardcore forming the source for the latter) major twin partners in its demise. That which was and indeed never will be expunged were and are the physical and spiritual links between the airmen and their British "hosts." Madingley's sad majesty provides a corporate indication of the scale of human sacrifice laid down upon the Altar of Freedom. Numerous memorials exist on or close to many of the airfields, while the veterans are still making individual or corporate pilgrimages across the *Big Pond*, in the course of which personal contacts are maintained with friends "Over There." What has now rightly gone down in historical annuls as the *Mighty Eighth* will live on in the hearts and minds of the Anglo/American nations and their WWII Allies as a force that made a crucial contribution to the ultimate defeat of the Axis powers and all that their warped philosophies had held in store for the Free World.

Finally, the following salient line from the WWI poem *Flanders Field*, by John McCrae, serves as a simple but poignant valediction for those many thousands of airmen who did not live to savor the Fruits of Victory:

"To you from failing hands we throw the Torch – be yours to hold it high"

COLOR GALLERY

The fin and rudder on 42-97976/D **Bit O' Lace** have absorbed an element of the force of a flak shell. Great rents are made in the rudder's fabric surface, while the fin area is punctured and pitted by numerous shell fragments. The 447th BG letter K is formed from the NMF skin as opposed to being painted, and the area around the serial is also left in NMF.

The same flak burst resulted in an even more devastating impact upon **Bit O' Lace's** left stabilizer; this restricted view shows how the bulk of the elevator has been excised, leaving a tangled web of metal shards. Incident occurred on 4 April 1945.

A 447th BG PFF bomber (44-8393/Y) has its *H2X* radar pod lowered in spite of the sparse cloud cover. The Group color markings are twin parallel green strips on the rear fuselage and a bluish purple chevron on the right-upper and left-lower wing surfaces. B-17G in center is one of the few camouflaged examples still operating out of Rattlesden by early 1945 when this photograph was taken.

The PFF bomber has just released its mixed load of explosives and incendiaries, as well as the smoke marker indicator for the other bombardiers to take toggling action. This shot reveals a swift thickening of the cloud cover, which justifies the probable use of the *H2X* equipment. Yellow fin/rudder, stabilizers, and wing tips indicates assignment to the 4th CBW.

Prior to arrival at Snetterton Heath on 6 July 1943, this B-17F had served at Grafton Underwood as **Piccadilly Commando**. Three months later 42-30040/AW: A was one of seven 96th BG losses on *Black Thursday*, although four of Lt. Harmeson's (POW) team did evade capture following their bomber's final descent near Avincourt, France.

Ole Puss (42-30073/MZ: U) was another Grafton Underwood transfer the same day as **Piccadilly Commando**. She was also written off on 17 April 1944 following a heavy crash-landing at East Wretham (359th FG). Both these B-17Fs possessed the flat "cheek gun" window frames that greatly inhibited forward deployment of the weapons mounted therein.

Stingy (42-31053/BX: W) was reportedly the nickname Maj/Gen. Fred Anderson (CG, VIII BC) bestowed upon his son. One from among the initial batch of Boeing B-17Gs to be produced, this aircraft was assigned to the 96th BG on 26 September 1943. The 19 mission "bomb" tally was surely added to before the midair collision on 9 November 1944 that took out **Stingy** along with seven crewmembers.

Sgt A Goodall confidently smiles from his left waist hatch on the B-17F. Several names and expressions are applied around the hatch edges, while the red surround to the national insignia also stands out. The Sgt tragically became one of the many thousands of 8th AF airmen killed in action. On 11 December 1943, 42-30816/ **Mary Ellen III**, in Lt. F Poore's hands, went down over Holland, with Goodall one of two fatalities.

The mission is on, and a 490th BG crew keep their fingers crossed as their B-17G lifts off the runway after attaining minimum airspeed in spite of its overloaded condition. The photographer is probably the driver for the un-occupied Jeep in the foreground.

Above: Tom Paine was an English radical from several centuries past whose well-pitched and relevant statement adorns the nose of the 388th BG's B-17F/42-30793. Paine was born in Thetford, a town very close to the Knettishall airfield on which the Group was based. This bomber was assigned to the 562BS on 3 September 1943 and was finally salvaged the following 11 April.

Left: T/Sgt. Leon Sweatt is seen with his wife Pearl and their baby son, Charles. The boy would never get to know his father, who was killed during the 96th BG's mission to Karlsruehe on 27 May 1944. He would, however, keep a form of faith with his father's devotion to national duty by joining the USAF and rising to the rank of full Colonel.

Several or many hours later the 490th BG has completed its mission, and another B-17G with its distinctive red bands on the top of the fin/rudder section and outer wings is about to flare out over the runway's end. Take-off and landing were arguably the stages of any mission most fraught with danger.

Shady Lady displays her ample and somewhat risqué charms on B-24J-160-CO/44-40439. This bomber served successively with the 493rd, 34th, and 389th BGs before being MIA on 31 March 1945. None of Lt. G Crock's crew survived after one wing was shot away.

Libra (42-52508) was one of the members of the "Zodiac" Sqdn serving with the 486th BG at Sudbury. In this case the artwork was beautifully applied in a less risqué manner compared to its contemporaries. Note the armor plate positioned by the cockpit and the red fire extinguisher panel.

Flyin' Jenny (42-37772/LN: S) eases her way along the Thorpe Abbotts perimeter track. This B-17 was one of the initial G-Models to be assigned to the 100th BG. Exactly three calendar months later (27 December 1943) she was "written off" following involvement in a pile-up with two other bombers during landing.

The 9th USAAF Tactical force made very good use of its A-20 and B-26 medium bombers in interdicting the Nazi road and rail structure as a means of hindering movement of personnel and equipment. This B-26 from the 391st BG, then based at Matching Green, in Essex, has amassed an impressive number of mission symbols during the winter of 1943/44.

The purposeful bulk of a 56th FG P-47 makes its way along the perimeter track at Boxted. The contents of the two 150-gall drop tanks went some way to satisfying the great thirst of the 2,800 hp Pratt and Whitney motor. Removal of D-Day stripes from upper wing surfaces indicate picture was taken several weeks after the invasion.

The P-38 Lightning was the second of the three major USAAF escorts to operate from English bases; the 55th FG flew its initial combat sortie on 15 October 1943. This picture shows a J-Model bearing red surrounds to the National insignia and was probably taken before assignment to a group.

The elephantine shapes of B-24s from the 493rd BG proceed along the perimeter at Debach. This group was one of five units operating the Consolidated design that were assigned to the 3rd BD but subsequently converted to the B-17; in Debach's case the last mission with the B-24 was flown on 24 August 1944.

Humpty Dumpty's artwork reveals a somewhat sensually-posed woman. The Thorpe Abbotts-based B-17G (43-37815/EP: L) has already put in 21 missions following her arrival on 28 June 1944. Transfer to the 482nd BG in May 1945 and arrival for scrapping at Kingman, AZ, would be the sad conclusion to her combat career.

This pastoral scene of tranquillity with the gathered stacks of cereal is harshly disrupted by the presence of Snetterton Heath's B-17s. Aircraft on the left has its squadron codes applied in white, but the individual letter and serial on the fin is sprayed yellow. Picture was taken during the summer of 1944.

Only the shadow of several 3rd BD bombers is caught in this picture, along with a range of colored parachutes draped on the ground. The occasion was the dropping of weapons and other supplies to the French Resistance; Operation *Cadillac* on 14 July 1944 was the first of several such missions when three widely-separated zones were selected.

The P-38 also proved to be an ideal design for a secondary but equally important function—photo reconnaissance. The 7th Photo Reconnaissance Group (PRG) flew out of Mount Farm, west of London; the aircraft were sprayed in a distinctive blue tone (synthetic Haze), although this gave way to an NMF finish in the final months of WWII.

Top: **Rum Runner** is lined up on the runway at Debach and "ready to roll." Note how the 3R (863BS) code letters borne when the Ford-built B-24H was originally with the 486th BG are dulled down almost to the point of obliteration. The aircraft reportedly saw service with two further groups and returned home after VE-Day.

Middle: A pair of 364th FG P-51Ds is lined up for take-off from Honington. The group insignia consisted of a white spinner and blue and white horizontal stripes on the nose, although both aircraft appear to have yellow in place of the white on the forward cowling Circle on the fin and rudders related to the 383FS.

Left: The need to keep firm control on the brakes while taxiing is well illustrated here; the photographer's B-24 is scant feet away from the preceding bomber. In the background, a third 493rd BG is lined up for take-off. When transfer from the B-24 to B-17 occurred in August 1944, the "X in a square" unit designator was superseded by red color bands on the lower fin and rudder, stabilizers and outer wing surfaces.

This shot of the airfield from which a B-17 is lifting off the runway was erroneously quoted in one of the author's previous books as being within the 1st AD's charge. In fact, it is Honington that served as the 1st Strategic Air Depot (1SAD) and also housed the 364th FG from February 1944 until after VE-Day. The Type C hangars in the background confirm this was originally built as a permanent airfield for the RAF.

A mission has been called and the 96th BG are taxiing out to take part. AW: T/43-37794 was assigned on 12 June 1944, but went MIA over Wiesbaden on 19 Sept., although all nine members on Lt. Bauman's crew ended up as POWs.

The value of color markings to at least identify a B-17 as belonging to a specific CBW, if not a group within its ranks, is seen here. Even at a distance the yellow stabilizers and vertical fin and rudder confirm this unit is a component of the 4th CBW, while the red/yellow wing chevrons relate to the 487th BG.

An ambulance is bypassing the tree-lined 349BS dispersals at Thorpe Abbots sometime in mid-1944. All three B-17Gs are in NMF finish, as were the great majority of USAAF B-17s and B-24s by this stage of the conflict.

The more slab-sided B-24 fuselage with fewer window obstructions up front than the B-17 lent itself better to large examples of artwork. **Tondelayo** is the title for an amply-built South Sea maiden.

Our Gal Sal's camouflage is already beginning to show the fading process brought about by constant exposure to the elements. Lt. Schoen's aircraft sports seventeen mission "bombs," a figure that would grow to over 100 before VE-Day.

Two anonymous officers—the right-hand one wearing a light Gabardine coat, while his companion sports the heavier woollen version—pose by the nose hatch of a B-17F. It is possible that they are the pilots whose nicknames are applied to the hatch surface.

Left: The artwork on this 100th BG B-17G is explicitly rude, with the pig excreting a bomb upon the Third Reich. No less than 35 mission symbols decorate the upper nose area.

Middle: The yellow nose band identifies **Flying Dutchman** as belonging to Mendlesham's 7BS, although the serial is unknown. The large mission-log on the nose and the tree foliage suggest the picture was taken in the early spring of 1945. One ground crew member under No. 2 engine is taking advantage of the weather by stripping down to his vest!

Bottom: The bulk of aircraft maintenance was conducted outdoors regardless of weather conditions. A remarkably clear day provides the backcloth to the detaching of No. 2 engine on a 34th BG bomber; the engine mass hangs from the mobile platform while another unit is supported by a low frame.

A pair of bombs are casually positioned by the dispersal edge for a 490th BG B-24H produced by Ford, to judge by the Emerson nose turret and deep wavy camouflage demarcation line. The group was the penultimate example among the five Division units equipped with the B-24 to enter combat service, in its case on 31 May.

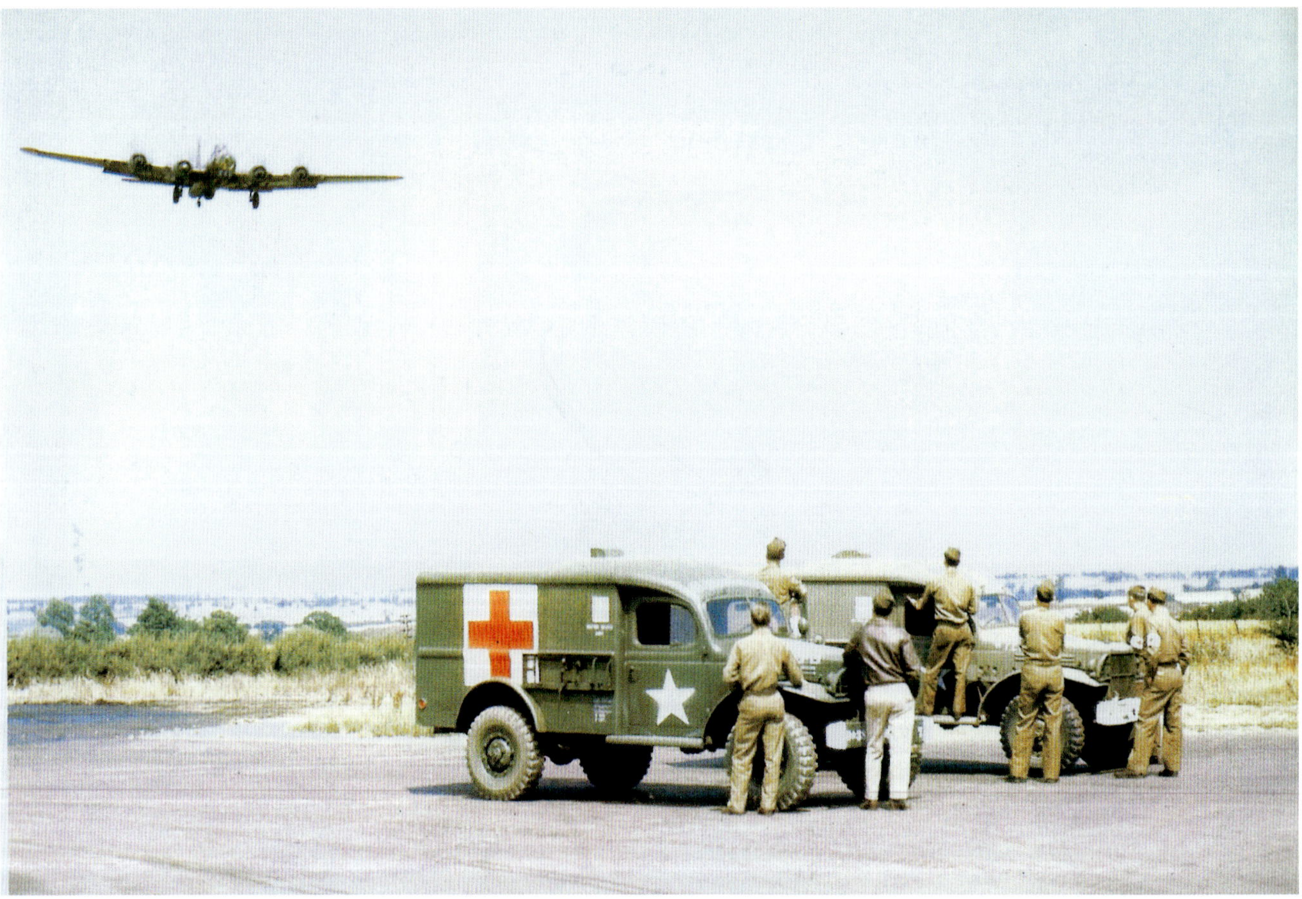

The sight of a red flare from a circling bomber always quickened the pulses of the Medical staff, since it indicated serious or, sadly, often fatal injury to one or more crewmembers. The Medics here are waiting to attend to this B-17G as it hovers over the runway's end.

A 96th BG bomber bearing 337BS codes is seen in the background as several officers watch proceedings from the control tower balcony. The bomber is probably commencing its take-off run, since the Runway Control trailer is located at the runway's end. What appears to be a white rudder is probably a trick of the light.

The level crossing gates with their red warning diamond frames at an East Anglia railroad have caught several vehicles that includes a typical saloon car in the foreground. Petrol for private use was in very short legal availability, so the driver is either in the "essential worker" category or has accessed "Black Market" sources!

Top: **Lil' Edie** (43-38054/851BS) tucks in fairly tight to the photographer's B-17. The aircraft was among the first batch to arrive at Eye in late July as the 490th BG prepared to convert from the B-24. On 6 February 1945 she was abandoned by her crew during Assembly for a mission to Chemnitz and came down near Darsham.

Middle: On 6 March 1944 Lt. Bob Schoen's **My Gal Sal** (42-31767/EP: E) survived the group's crucifixion on the mission to Berlin when fifteen crews were lost. Over one year later the now-veteran B-17G sports an impressive row of mission "bombs." She returned home after VE-Day, having been preceded in 1944 by Lt. Schoen's full crew.

Left: Although this anonymous navigator appears to be fully kitted up for a mission with oxygen mask applied, it is unlikely the photographer would have been permitted such latitude in these circumstances. The likelihood that it is a posed picture in a non-operational environment, which is given some credence by the static propeller on No. 2 engine.

Lt. Howard Leech, navigator on Lt. Gerry Steussy's 100th BG crew, is seen with a Russian officer during the group's participation in the first *Frantic* mission. Note the more basic cut and quality in the latter's uniform compared to his American ally.

On 7 April 1945 the 100th BG lost one B-17 to the *Rammkonmmando Elbe* Bf109s. A second B-17G (43-38514/XR; J) should also have gone down after suffering the partial loss of its fin and rudder as well as most of the left stabilizer in a similar ramming incident. However, she was held aloft and landed back at Thorpe Abbotts; full repairs were effected and the bomber returned home after VE-Day.

This radio-equipped Control Jeep based at Mendlesham is about to provide guidance to the man at the controls of the B-24. The red spinner may denote a squadron marking, but there is no confirmation that such a pattern was adopted by the 34th BG.

Ruby's Raiders (44-6483/G) was "christened" by her namesake, Pfc. Ruby Newell; the WAC had come first in a beauty contest featuring British-based personnel and duly arrived at Great Ashfield for the ceremony. She brought luck to the B-17G since it survived the conflict.

Two officers in the Soviet Army are snapped during a social event laid on for the 3rd BD airmen. The rather formal stance adopted by the dancers is a world away from the "jitterbugging" actions beloved by many of their contemporaries from across the Atlantic.

"The sun is rising out of the Red of Battle," as it is on the point of emerging, its beams casting an channel of light on the deceptively still North Sea. Picture is taken from a 100th BG B-17, and the sharp contrast of the light reflecting against the cloud-strewn sky is a grim portent of the looming battle with the *Luftwaffe*.

Cpl. Ruby Newell was the prize winner in a beauty competition involving the English-based Women's Army Corps (WAC). Her portrait, along with the sobriquet **Ruby's Raiders**, adorns the fuselage of 44-6483/G assigned to the 385th BG. Picture was taken following the introduction in February 1945 of the unit's checkerboard design on fin and rudder seen in the right background.

The smoke trail from this B-17 could be nothing more than the beginning of a condensation pattern, or could indicate a more serious problem. B-17 on the left appears to have its wheels lowered, which was usually a signal for "aborting" the mission.

A hoar frost has descended upon the 100th BG's airfield and liberally decked the frozen, rutted ground and trees in the process. Close-up of the Cheyenne turret mount shows the greater elevation and azimuth function for the guns compared to the more restricted aperture on the B-17F and early B-17G airframes. The gunner was also provided with a better view from the less heavily-framed and expanded Plexiglas cover.

Two officers crouch by the wing-root of this 350BS B-17G ready to be snapped by their colleague, as other officers engage in conversation. The bomber's fate was linked with that of the Steussy crew, because all nine were forced to evacuate its interior on 29 July after it absorbed terminal flak strikes during the mission to Merseburg.

Lt. Steussey's crew are gathered in front of their B-17G, along with two Soviet officers. Their aircraft bears a sizeable mission log that belies the "unlucky 13" applied underneath. However, the crew's luck would not hold...

This tastefully-applied beauty and title **Lotta Stern** graces the nose of 43-37926's NMF surface at Thorpe Abbotts. The 75-BO airframe joined the 100th BG on 7 July 1944, but was later transferred to the 490th BG; she survived the conflict.

Lotta Stern bears an impressive mission tally as she rolls to taxiing speed on the runway at Eye. Although now carrying the red 93rd CBW markings, there is evidence of her former ownership by the 100th BG; the black paint remnants on her rudder denote service with the 13th CBW, within which Thorpe Abbotts operated.

Two B-17Gs from Mendlesham cruise over an almost solid undercast. The ball turret on the lead bomber is vertically aligned, indicating the gunner is either entering his position or monitoring the sky.

What appears to be the usual dull and in this case hazy skyline forms the backcloth to a 493rd BG B-17G. The group's distinctive CBW marking, a red band on the lower fin and rudder length, stands out against the overall silver finish.

A 385th BG formation, as identified by the two B-17Gs bearing the unit's red/white chequered vertical fin marking, is banking around for the run over the allocated *Manna/Chowhound* drop zone. A film double-exposure has given the photographer's bomber a seeming biplane configuration.

With all guns detached, the days of Glory are over for this 100th BG veteran bomber 42-97667/LD:A, which sports at least 47 visible mission symbols. Records indicate the aircraft served first with the 482nd BG, the specialist H2X unit, but the presence of a ball turret in place of the radar pod confirms a transfer back to a standard function.

The war in Europe is over, and **Belligerent Beauty** (43-38942/OE:Y) is photographed during a stop-over in Greenland as the 95th BG heads for home in company with the majority of the 8th AF's strength.

A mixed foursome of officers and Enlisted men are photographed following the liberation of Stalag Luft I at Barth, on the Baltic coast. All evidence of flying gear, especially fur jackets and boots, which were doubtlessly confiscated primarily for the use of German personnel on the Russian Front, is gone. Airman on the left wears a lighter form of footwear compared to the other three.

A Curtiss C-46 Commando taking off (left) and a line-up of other C-46s on the perimeter track of an Austrian airfield (right) bypass two parked B-17Gs. The checkerboard pattern on the nearside bomber denotes its ownership by the 385th BG, while the other belongs to the 34th BG. Both are part of the 3rd AD force tasked with repatriating forced laborers.

Like a ghost from the past, a B-17 sweeps majestically over the U.S. Military Cemetery at Madingley, outside Cambridge in England, on the occasion of a mid-1980s Memorial Day ceremony. Named **Sally B** and based at nearby Duxford Museum, it is one of only two airworthy Fortresses in Europe. The color scheme is that applied to 447th BG aircraft in 1945.

Lines of redundant B-17s are seen at one of the several "graveyards" in the States. The left hand column contains examples from the 486th and 452nd BGs, while the anonymous bomber on the right had amassed an impressive tally of at least 100 missions.

At least four B-17Gs from the 4th CBW groups and one from the 13th CBW can be seen in a second view of the "boneyard." Bomber in foreground bears full 447th BG markings despite records indicating service with the 379th BG. Next in line is an ex-452nd BG aircraft that is nevertheless bereft of the parallel yellow bars on fin and rudder allocated as the unit identity within the 45th CBW.

BIBLIOGRAPHY

S D Bishop/J Hey	Losses of 8th and 9th USAAF Vol. 1	(Bishop Bks. Prod. 2004)
	Losses of 8th and 9th USAAF Vol. 2	(Bishop Bks. Prod. 2007)
R Bowden	Tails to Noses over Berlin	(Design Oracle Partnership 1996)
M W Bowman/T L Woodall	Helton's Hellcats	(Turner Publishing Co. 1998)
D Caldwell	The JG26 War Dairy Vol. 2	(Grub Street 1998)
J Ethell/A Price	Target Berlin (Mission 250)	(Book Club Associates 1981)
R A Freeman	The B-17 Flying Fortress Story	(Arms and Armour 1998)
	The Mighty Eighth	(McDonald and Janes 1970)
	The Mighty Eighth War Diary	(McDonald and Janes 1981)
	The Mighty Eighth War Manual	(McDonald and Janes 1985)
I DeJong	487th BG History	(Turner Publishing Co. 2004)
I L Hawkins	B-17s over Berlin	(Brasseys 1990)
	Muenster – the way it was	(Robinson Typo graphics 1984)
R Le Strange	Century Bombers	(Penfold Works 1989)
M Middlebrook	The Battle of Hamburg	(Penguin Books 1980)
	Schweinfurt/Regensburg Mission	(Penguin Books 1983)
H E Slater	Lingering Contrails of big Square A	(Garrett Graphics Inc.1980)
G Ward/R Doherty	Snetterton Falcons	(Taylor Publishing Co.1989)

INDEX

Abbreviation List

P	Pilot
CP	Co-pilot
N	Navigator
B	Bombardier
Eng.	Engineer
ROG	Radio Operator
RWG	Right-waist gunner
LWG	Left-waist gunner
BT	Ball turret gunner
TG	Tail gunner
BC	Bomber Command
C-in-C	Commander in Chief
CC	Crew Chief
CG	Commanding General
CMH	Congressional Medal of Honor
Col.	Colonel
C. o S.	Chief of Staff
Capt.	Captain
B/Gen.	Brigadier General
FC	Fighter Command
F/O	Flight Officer
G	Gunner (position not known)
GC	Ground crew
Lt.	Lieutenant
L/Col.	Lieutenant Colonel
L/Gen.	Lieutenant General
Maj.	Major
M/Gen.	Major General
NG	Nose gunner
Obs.	Observer
(Post.)	Posthumous
USSTAF	U S Strategic and Tactical Air Forces

Abbreviations (Luftwaffe)

Ranks

Fw.	Feldwebel
Hptm.	Hauptmann
Ltn.	Leutnant
Maj.	Major
Oblt.	Oberleutnant
Obstlt.	Oberstleutnant
Ofw.	Oberfeldwebel

Units

JG	Jagdgeschwader
NJG	Nachtjagdgeschwader
ZG	Zerstoerergeschwader